Real Estate Law

Real Estate Law

EIGHTH EDITION

ROBERT KRATOVIL

John Marshall Law School

RAYMOND J. WERNER

Chicago Title Insurance Co.

PRENTICE-HALL, INC., *Englewood Cliffs, NJ 07632*

Library of Congress Cataloging in Publication Data

Kratovil, Robert   (date)
  Real estate law.

  Includes index.
  1. Real property—United States.   I. Werner,
Raymond J.   II. Title.
KF570.K7 1983   346.7304'3   82-21575
ISBN 0-13-763292-4   347.30643

PRENTICE-HALL SERIES IN REAL ESTATE

Editorial/production supervision and
interior design: Maureen Wilson
Manufacturing buyer: Ed O'Dougherty

Printed in the United States of America

10 9 8 7 6 5

ISBN 0-13-763292-4

PRENTICE-HALL INTERNATIONAL, INC., *London*
PRENTICE-HALL OF AUSTRALIA PTY. LIMITED, *Sydney*
EDITORA PRENTICE-HALL DO BRASIL, LTDA., *Rio de Janeiro*
PRENTICE-HALL CANADA INC., *Toronto*
PRENTICE-HALL OF INDIA PRIVATE LIMITED, *New Delhi*
PRENTICE-HALL OF JAPAN, INC., *Tokyo*
PRENTICE-HALL OF SOUTHEAST ASIA PTE. LTD., *Singapore*
WHITEHALL BOOKS LIMITED, *Wellington, New Zealand*

To
RUTH, TONY, and MELANIE
and
LENORE and BETH

CONTENTS

PREFACE *xi*

1 SOURCES OF REAL ESTATE LAW *1*

2 LAND AND INTERESTS IN LAND *6*

3 FIXTURES *18*

4 EASEMENTS *26*

5 LAND DESCRIPTIONS *51*

6 DEEDS AND ACKNOWLEDGMENTS *60*

7 RECORDING AND
CONSTRUCTIVE NOTICE *83*

8 REAL ESTATE BROKERS *90*

9 CONTRACTS FOR THE SALE OF LAND *121*

10 CLOSING REAL ESTATE TRANSACTIONS:
LOAN CLOSINGS: ESCROWS *175*

11   EVIDENCE OF TITLE:
       TITLE INSURANCE: ABSTRACTS   *200*

12   INSURANCE   *212*

13   LAND ACQUISITION AND ASSEMBLY   *228*

14   CO-OWNERSHIP   *233*

15   REAL ESTATE FINANCE—
       MORTGAGES   *264*

16   REAL ESTATE FINANCE—
       NEW FORMS OF MORTGAGES   *314*

17   REAL ESTATE FINANCE—
       DUE-ON-SALE CLAUSE   *340*

18   REAL ESTATE FINANCE—
       SALE SUBJECT TO EXISTING MORTGAGE   *347*

19   REAL ESTATE FINANCE—
       PURCHASE MONEY MORTGAGES   *351*

20   REAL ESTATE FINANCE—
       WRAPAROUND MORTGAGES   *358*

21   REAL ESTATE FINANCE—
       JUNIOR MORTGAGES   *362*

22   REAL ESTATE FINANCE—
       INSTALLMENT CONTRACTS   *368*

23   REAL ESTATE FINANCE—
       MISCELLANEOUS DEVICES—GROUND LEASES   *379*

24   REAL ESTATE FINANCE—
       FORECLOSURE AND REDEMPTION   *385*

25   LAND USE CONTROLS—
      BUILDING RESTRICTIONS   *391*

26   LAND USE CONTROLS—
      ZONING AND BUILDING ORDINANCES   *411*

27   LAND USE CONTROLS—
      LAND DEVELOPMENT, REGULATION,
      SUBDIVISIONS, AND DEDICATION   *452*

28   LAND USE CONTROLS—
      WETLANDS, THE PUBLIC TRUST,
      BEACHES, AND NAVIGABLE WATERS   *474*

29   LAND USE CONTROLS—
      HISTORIC AREAS AND LANDMARKS   *481*

30   HOMEOWNERS' ASSOCIATION   *484*

31   THE DECLARATION OF RESTRICTIONS,
      EASEMENTS, LIENS, AND COVENANTS   *489*

32   CONDOMINIUMS AND CO-OPS   *497*

33   PLANNED UNIT DEVELOPMENTS   *535*

34   BUILDING CONSTRUCTION
      AND BUILDING WARRANTIES   *543*

35   REHAB   *566*

36   MOBILE HOMES   *571*

37   LANDLORD AND TENANT   *576*

38 RACIAL DISCRIMINATION
IN REAL ESTATE   *611*

39 TAXES, SPECIAL ASSESSMENTS,
AND FEDERAL INCOME TAX   *624*

INDEX   *639*

PREFACE

In the preface to the seventh edition of this treatise we stated that the law continues to change at a rapid rate. This trend is even more noticeably present today, as events continue to shape the law.

Traditionally, home sales were cash sales and the purchaser borrowed from a savings and loan association. Today, thrift institutions are locked into low-interest, long-term loans and are borrowing short-term at high rates. The stubborn refusal of interest rates to move downward, a product of federal monetary policy, has pushed countless thrift institutions to the wall. Those that survive are making home loans sparingly, and when such loans are made, a bewildering diversity of alternative mortgage plans are offered. All those concerned, including real estate salesmen, are forced to learn the potential financial pitfalls involved in each of the many plans. Many home sales involve the assumption or attempted assumption of an existing low-interest mortgage. As a result, the due-on-sale clause has become the most controversial clause in mortgage history. "Seller-financing available" appears in many ads of homes for sale. So we are all expected to acquire expertise in the pitfalls of installment contracts (land contract) and junior mortgages. All this is reflected in the numerous chapters on real estate finance.

Usury, once the great problem area, has virtually disappeared from the area of litigation. The federal preemption has greatly diminished the importance of this topic.

Some analysts claim that by the year 2000 A.D. more than half the population of this country will live in condominiums, and the condominium chapter has increased in size to reflect this trend. Detached homes continue their downward trend, while planned developments containing attached homes trend upward. The home association, in consequence, is riding the wave of the future.

As the demand for housing continues to outstrip the supply, pressure in the suburbs to admit manufactured homes increases, and the suburbs continue to resist. Still the manufactured home cannot be stopped, since it represents, for many, the only affordable home available. Reflecting this trend, we have included a chapter on mobile homes.

The exclusionary zoning cases continue to exert pressure on the suburbs to admit multi-family dwellings, and racial discrimination legislation, federal and state, adds to this pressure. Racial discrimination decisions have contributed expressions like "steering" and "blockbusting" to the real estate vocabulary. This is a growing concern in the law.

Consumer protection has produced a cleavage both in mortgage law and landlord and tenant law. Home mortgage lenders must display a tender concern for the defaulting homeowner and landlords who find themselves burdened with concepts of the warranty of habitability and retaliatory eviction. Home builders also are confronted with implied warranties and many have elected to provide express warranties to deal with the problem.

Increasingly brokers are held to higher standards, for example, in the expansion of their duties to purchasers.

In short, the period since the last edition appeared has been one of upheaval and change. Our practice of highlighting new developments in previous editions has been proven sound by the times. Indeed no text on real estate law is worth reading unless it stresses new developments and the rapid changes in the law.

One thing is certain, namely: only true professionals can survive in the new environment.

OTHER BOOKS BY THESE AUTHORS:

KRATOVIL AND WERNER, *Modern Mortgage Law and Practice* (1981), Prentice-Hall, Inc.

KRATOVIL, *Modern Real Estate Documentation* (1975), Prentice-Hall, Inc.

KRATOVIL AND KRATOVIL, *Buying, Owning, and Selling a Home in the 80s* (1981), Prentice-Hall, Inc.

KRATOVIL AND KRATOVIL, *Buying, Owning, and Selling a Condominium in the 80s* (1982), Prentice-Hall, Inc.

WERNER, *Real Estate Closings* (1979), Practicing Law Institute

Real Estate Law

1 SOURCES OF REAL ESTATE LAW

1.01 Lack of uniformity in laws governing real estate

In each of the United States, two separate systems of law are in force: federal law and state law. With a few exceptions, federal laws operate uniformly throughout the country. Each state, however, has its own constitution, laws, and court decisions. Because of differences in local conditions, laws relating to real estate vary from state to state, and this variation is a factor that must be kept constantly in mind. However, the basic legal principles governing real estate transactions are much the same throughout the country, and our approach, in consequence, will be to describe these basic principles, mentioning, as space permits, the more important instances wherein the states do not agree.

1.02 Sources of and trends in real estate law

The sources of real estate law include the Constitution of the United States, laws passed by Congress, regulations adopted by various federal boards and commissions, the state constitutions, laws passed by state legislatures, regulations adopted by various state and municipal boards, ordinances passed by cities and villages, and court decisions. The last is the most important source of real estate law.

Important decisions by lower courts are often appealed to higher courts. Those courts, in announcing a decision, usually state the reasons for their decision and discuss the legal principles governing the particular case. Such a decision, with its accompanying discussion, is called an *opinion*. The opinions are bound into books called *reports* and serve as guides in the decision of similar cases in the future.

EXAMPLE: Roots from your adjoining poplar trees penetrate into my land and fill up my sewer and drain pipes. I cut off these roots, taking care to make the cut on my land. Your trees die and you sue me. The lower court holds I acted rightful-

1

ly, and on appeal the supreme court of the state holds likewise, stating that a landowner may in this fashion protect himself against roots of adjoining trees. This is now the law of that state for all such cases that arise in the future. Lawyers will advise their clients accordingly, citing the case, *Michalson* v. *Nutting,* 275 Mass. 232, 175 NE 490 (1931). This case may be found in Volume 275 of the Massachusetts Supreme Court Reports, p. 232, and Volume 175 of the Northeastern Reporter, p. 490. The case was decided in 1931.

Since our American real estate law stems in large part from the real estate law of England, it is not uncommon for courts today to base their decisions on similar cases that arose several hundred years ago in England. However, in dealing with present-day problems, the courts must often evolve new rules of law without much help from the past.

Since law is manufactured from day to day by the judges, it follows that there will be variations from state to state, and from time to time in the same state, depending on the political, social, and economic views that dominate the court at the time a decision is made.

In textbooks, a statement of a rule of law is often followed by a reference to the case in which that particular point was decided. A well-reasoned case decided in any state often commands respect in other states. For example, the decision in *Michalson* v. *Nutting* would be considered a correct statement of the law almost everywhere. This text endeavors to select such cases.

In recent times federal laws have assumed increasing importance in the field of real estate.

EXAMPLE: Federal Open Housing Law.

Also of greatly increasing importance in modern times is the "private law" that lawyers create in the preparation of real estate documents. Those who are new to real estate may fail to understand that the "battle of the forms" is an everyday reality. Landlords' lawyers battle tenants' lawyers over the language of a lease. Mortgage commitments are endlessly redrafted in large deals. In virtually every major transaction, the automatic typewriters are kept busy with constant reworking of the transaction documents that set the law of that particular transaction for its parties.

EXAMPLE: Shopping center leases. In these documents the rights and duties of the parties in various existing and anticipated situations are set forth in some detail. One limitation on the rights of the parties to thus declare the "law" applicable to their situation is found in the tendency of courts today to refuse to enforce contract terms they regard as "unconscionable," meaning grossly unfair.

NEW DIRECTIONS: Seldom in history has the law moved so rapidly in new directions as at present. The Uniform Commercial Code, adopted in nearly all states, permits courts to strike down unconscionable contracts or unconscionable portions of a contract. An unconscionable contract is one that is grossly unfair to one of the parties. Although the code applies mainly to personal property, modern courts choose to regard it as an expression of public policy applicable to all types of transactions. *Morse* v. *Consolidated Fisheries Co.,* 190 F2d 817, 822. Hence they feel free to apply the unconscionability test to transactions in real estate.

EXAMPLE: Landlord leased a filling station to Tenant. The lease gave Tenant an option to purchase. Tenant exercised the option. Due to awkward phrasing of the option, it appeared that it would take more than fifty years for full payment of the purchase price. The court said that Tenant would have to accept reasonable terms of payment or pay all cash. *Rego* v. *Decker,* 482 P2d 834 (Alaska 1971).

NEW DIRECTIONS: We have moved into the age of *consumerism.* Even the largest corporations can be compelled to respect the needs of the consumer. This has launched a wave of tremendous force. The federal Truth-in-Lending Act compels disclosure of interest rates in terms that the ordinary consumer can understand. Similar state laws have been passed. The Interstate Land Sales Act compels disclosures that enable the unwary prospective purchaser of vacant lots to avoid buying a pig in a poke. State laws of this type have also been enacted.

NEW DIRECTIONS: Where there is inequality of bargaining power and where the sophisticated party is pitted against an unsophisticated party the courts are intervening to protect the weaker party.

EXAMPLE: The trend toward reading implied warranties into sales of new homes and into apartment leases furnishes an example of this trend, as does the line of cases limiting the mortgagee's right to declare an acceleration.

NEW DIRECTIONS: Consistent with all of the foregoing is the strong trend in modern decisions toward rewriting *contracts of adhesion.* Wherever a relatively weak consumer is confronted with a contract full of fine print (lease, mortgage, sell-and-build contract, for example) modern courts will pull the teeth of any clause that bears oppressively on the weaker party.

NEW DIRECTIONS: Another development is the recent creation in many states of *home rule municipalities.* The theory is that with respect to its local affairs a municipality should be able to legislate without interference by the state legislature.

EXAMPLE: In earlier times each state adopted a zoning law and each municipality was required to tailor its zoning ordinances to the requirements of the state statute. Today home rule municipalities are free to adopt their own zoning ordinances without regard to the requirements of the state statute.

NEW DIRECTIONS: In the past much of real estate law consisted of rules created by court decisions. Today's trend toward protecting the consumer has resulted in the enactment of much state legislation giving the consumer protection greater than that afforded by the court decisions.

EXAMPLE: In many states laws have been enacted giving the mortgagor additional protection, for example, the right to cure defaults, set aside an acceleration of the mortgage debt, and causing a foreclosure suit to be dismissed. Matters of this character are found under the heading NEW LAWS.

NEW DIRECTIONS: The federal government is intervening in real estate transactions to a greater extent than in the past.

EXAMPLE: The Federal Trade Commission has greatly limited the use of exclusives in shopping center leases.

NEW DIRECTIONS: Quite a trend has developed in recent times for courts to look outside of their own state for guidance in evolving new rules of law.

EXAMPLE: In 1963 the Colorado Supreme Court decided that in every sale of a house erected by a merchant builder there was an implied warranty of habitability and freedom from defects. To arrive at this result, the Colorado court discarded numerous earlier Colorado decisions that held to the contrary. Over half of the states have since followed Colorado's lead and probably all will do so. In brief, state courts do not hesitate today to create new law if that seems to produce a fair result.

Perhaps the most interesting aspect of all of this is that it does not qualify as a NEW DIRECTION. As far back as the year 1600, English courts decided that it was unconscionable to permit a mortgagor's default to end his rights in mortgaged land. Toward this end they invented the equitable right of redemption. And when mortgagees began to insert waiver of this right in the mortgage contract, the courts struck this down as unconscionable. Today the swing of the pendulum is away from enforcing contracts as written and toward resolving disputes in terms of what is fair.

1.03 Economic and social impact upon the law

The law has always been shaped by economic and social forces. Recently, as the age of consumerism swept the late 1960s and early 1970s, many time-honored rules of law were changed. The law recognized the economic power and social force of consumerism. The late 1970s and the early 1980s are being shaped by a force more powerful than the consumerist movement. Inflation has so altered so many economic relationships that the law surrounding those relationships is also in the process of change.

Nowhere is the legal impact of inflation felt more than in the area of real estate law. The changes that inflation has brought to mortgage law alone during the last few years are dramatic. Inflationary pressures on interest rates have caused the advent of variable rate, rollover, and shared appreciation mortgages. Prior law largely did not allow these transactions, yet now they are common. Federal law has preempted state usury laws covering many forms of mortgage transactions. Inflationary pressures on home prices have necessitated new forms of mortgages to facilitate home ownership.

The changes are not limited to consumer transactions. Notably, life insurers and other large investors are shifting emphasis from mortgage financing of large projects to the acquisition of ownership interests in those projects.

The changes yet to come may alter existing relationships even more. For example, will the source of mortgage funds shift from the thrift institutions fed by depositors to the bond market where mortgagors will have to compete for funds on an equal footing with other borrowers?

All of these changes brought about by economic factors will cause a reshaping of the law. The law has always been responsive to these changes and will continue to adjust the relationship of the parties.

Particularly for the student who uses this book as an introduction to the American legal system, it is important to grasp the notion that courts are constantly shaping the law. Events also help shape the law. For example, after World War II, America embarked upon the biggest homebuilding boom in world history. Unfortunately, many of these homes were poorly constructed and the returning veterans who bought the houses were bilked. Storms of protest shook the courts out of their complacent acceptance of the old rules that gave a homebuyer no protection.

2 LAND AND INTERESTS IN LAND

2.01 Land defined
Land includes not only the ground, or soil, but everything that is attached to the earth, whether by course of nature, as are trees and herbage, or by the hand of man, as are houses and other buildings. It includes not only the surface of the earth, but everything under it and over it. Thus, in legal theory, a tract of land consists not only of the portion on the surface of the earth, but is an inverted pyramid having its tip, or apex, at the center of the earth, extending outward through the surface of the earth at the boundary lines of the tract, and continuing on upward to the heavens.

2.02 Minerals
Since land extends to the center of the earth, it is clear that the owner of the land also ordinarily owns the minerals, which are a part of the land, and when the land is sold, the buyer ordinarily acquires such minerals, even though they are not expressly mentioned in his deed. However, a landowner may sell part or all of his land, as he chooses. Consequently, he may sell the minerals only, retaining title to the rest of the land; or he may sell the rest of the land and retain or reserve the minerals to himself.

> **EXAMPLE:** Landowner signs a deed conveying to Mineral Buyer all the coal underlying Landowner's land. Now we have two layers of ownership. Landowner continues to own the surface and may farm it or erect buildings on it. Mineral Buyer owns the coal. Landowner can sell or mortgage his layer of land, and Mineral Buyer can do the same with his. Mineral Buyer automatically has the right to sink shafts from the surface and build roads and tracks over the surface for the purpose of mining and transporting the coal. But he must not remove the coal in such a manner that the surface of the land will collapse.
> Suppose that Farmer sells and grants the coal under his farm to *B* Coal Co. The company tunnels beneath the farm and as it mines the coal uses the tunnels

for transporting coal mined from adjoining areas. May the coal company do this? All courts agree that it may, although the explanations vary from state to state. In some states the interesting theory is advanced that a sale of coal and minerals includes not only the coal and minerals, but also the space they occupy, so that when the coal is mined out the coal company remains the owner of the space the coal formerly occupied. *Middleton* v. *Harlan–Wallins Coal Corp.,* 66 SW2d 30 (Ky. 1933); 83 ALR2d 665.

2.03 Oil and gas

Contrary to popular opinion, oil does not occur in underground pools or reservoirs, but is tightly held in the tiny pores or openings of porous rocks. Natural gas is held in solution in this oil under great pressure. When a well is drilled into the rock that contains oil and gas, pressure is thereby released, and oil and gas gush forth just as a carbonated drink gushes from a warm pop bottle when the cap is removed. The oil will then flow to the low pressure area, namely, the well bore. Some states (Arkansas, Kansas, Mississippi, Ohio, Pennsylvania, Texas, and West Virginia), impressed with the fact that oil in its natural state and before drilling occurs is immovably trapped in the rocks in which it is found, say that the landowner owns the oil beneath his land in much the same way that he owns coal or other minerals. These states are called *ownership states.* Other states (California, Louisiana, and Oklahoma), impressed with the fact that oil does move from one underground location to another when wells are drilled, hold that the landowner does not own the oil until he has pumped it and thereby taken possession of it. This is called the *law of capture. Frost* v. *Ponca City,* 541 P2d 1321 (Okla. 1975). In all states, if the owner of the oil well pumps the oil and brings it to the surface, it then becomes personal property.

In ownership states, a landowner may grant ownership of the oil beneath his land to another person. As a result, there will be two vertical layers of ownership, just as when a landowner sells and conveys to another all the coal and minerals beneath his land. Oddly enough, however, all oil states, including the ownership states, follow the rule of *capture,* which holds that if a man drills on his land, he will own all of the oil and gas produced, even though some of the oil or gas has migrated to his well from his neighbor's land. His neighbor, of course, can prevent such a result by drilling his own wells, *offset* wells, on his own land and pumping the oil that would otherwise move away from his land. All oil-producing states now have laws regulating and controlling the drilling of wells and the production of oil.

Landowners lack the skill, experience, capital, and gambling instinct necessary to drill for oil. Therefore, when the presence of oil is suspected, a landowner gives some oil company an oil lease.

The basic structure of an oil and gas lease was developed by 1895. There are four elements: (1) A cash bonus is paid the lessor for granting the lease. (2) A royalty is paid to the lessor if oil or gas is discovered. (3) The lease stated a fixed term. (4) But the term can be extended if the lessee drills a well or pays *delay rentals* to compensate the lessor for lessee's failure to drill.

As to royalties, the original Producer's 88 lease set out three rules: (1) On oil, one-eighth of the oil delivered to tanks or pipeline for lessor's credit. (2) On gas produced from an oil well, one-eighth of the value at the well payable quarterly. (3) On gas produced from a well producing only gas, one-eighth of the value at the well payable monthly.

Much of the litigation has resulted from controversies as to whether the lessee paid the rental required to keep the lease alive. Hence the lease may have a clause protecting the lease from termination if the lessee has made a good faith effort to make the payment.

The lease usually requires the lessee: (1) To bury pipelines below plow depth. (2) Not to drill nearer than 200 feet to a house or barn. (3) To pay for damages to crops caused by lessee's operations. These clauses appear to be for the lessor's benefit. Actually, they are inserted by the lessee to negate any contention that he has other obligations or liabilities.

Domestic oil has become such a part of our economy, that one can expect much more detail and variety in newer oil and gas leases.

Reference: Cage, *The Modern Oil and Gas Lease—A Facelift for Old 88,* 31st Annual Institution Oil and Gas Law 177 (1980).

The lease then provides that if no well is drilled on or before a certain date, the lease shall automatically terminate, *unless* the lessee pays to the landowner a certain sum of money, called a *delay rental.* Such delay rental is a price the oil company pays for the privilege of keeping the lease in force without drilling. Delay rentals will continue to fall due as long as the oil company delays drilling. The lease will come to an end if no drilling takes place *unless* delay rentals are paid; this is known as an *unless lease.* Once wells are drilled and production begins, the usual lease gives the landowner as his compensation one-eighth of all the oil produced, payable either in oil or in cash, at the current market price, whichever the oil company chooses.

The lease provides that once oil production begins, the lease will continue as long as oil is produced in paying quantities.

In contrast to the *unless lease* is the *drill or pay* type. A drill or pay provision requires the lessee to produce oil, or, as an alternative, to pay rent. In an *unless* lease, the lessee's rights are terminated *unless* production is begun. A *drill or pay* lease allows the lessee to pay rent as a means of keeping the lease in effect though the primary period has expired. 2 W. Summers, *Oil and Gas,* §§ 331–351 (1959), H. Williams, *Oil and Gas,* §§ 601.5, 605 (1977). Any rental paid to keep the lease in force without drilling is called a *delay rental.*

WARNING: Oil leases vary considerably in their provisions. There is no such thing as the "usual" form. Many years ago a lease was printed in Oklahoma and the printers christened it the "Producers 88." It was copied extensively, but so many changes have been made in it that there are now many varying forms bearing that designation. Everett, *Wyoming Decisions Relative to the Law of Oil and Gas and Comments with Respect to Form "88" Leases,* 6 Wyo. L. J. 223 (1952).

Nomenclature. The word *royalty* originated in England, when it was used to designate the share in production reserved by the king from those to whom the right to work mines and quarries was granted. In oil and gas law it is the term used to designate the rent due for the right or privilege to take oil or gas out of a designated tract of land. It is the compensation provided in the lease to the landowner for the lessee's privilege of drilling and producing oil and gas and consists of a share in the oil and gas produced. It does not include either delay rentals or a bonus.

The working interest is the lessee's share of oil, as distinguished from the landowner's interest, or royalty interest.

An *overriding royalty* is an interest carved out of the working interest, often by means of an assignment of the working interest that reserves to the assignor a part of the oil and gas produced by the assignee.

In today's time of energy crisis, the use and ownership of energy producing resources is extremely valuable. Perhaps no resource is more valuable than oil and oil-related minerals. New technology and the increased value of this resource makes the pursuit of energy from sources that were once impracticable or too expensive a realistic alternative. Energy from these sources is now *economically recoverable.*

Oil shale is a good example of this type of resource. Rock that contains some amount of oil is processed through a factory-type operation to free the oil from the rock. Questions relating to the use and ownership of these former discards that are now valuable will be litigated bitterly.

2.04   Air rights

Just as a landowner may sell the minerals lying beneath the surface of the earth, so he may sell the space above the surface of the earth. A railroad company may own a tract of land, needing only enough of the space above the surface of the earth as will provide ample clearance for the tops of its trains. It does not need the space above a height of twenty-three or twenty-four feet from the surface. Yet this space is valuable for building purposes and may be sold or leased to a building corporation. *Indiana Toll Road Comm.* v. *Jankovich,* 193 NE2d 237 (Ind. 1963); 1960 Law Forum 303; Michelson, *Space Law and Air Rights from the Ground Up,* 49 Ill. B. J. 812 (1961).

In the case of the Merchandise Mart in Chicago, which was erected over the tracks of the Chicago and Northwestern Railroad, a plat or map was made and recorded, showing a subdivision in three dimensions:

1. An *air lot.* This consists of the space lying above a plane twenty-three feet above the earth's surface.

2. Quadrangular prism or *column lots* (for steel colums to support the building). These

extend from the surface of the earth up to the air lot and occupy portions of the surface not occupied by railroad tracks.

3. Cylindrical or *caisson lots.* These extend from the surface of the earth down to the center of the earth. The bottom of each column lot rests within a caisson lot.

The column lots, which share the level through which the trains move, were made narrower than the caisson lots to eliminate interference with the movement of trains. The railroad thereupon sold the air lot, the column lots, and the caisson lots to the Merchandise Mart, but retained ownership of the remainder of the tract. Bell, *Air Rights,* 23 Ill. L. Rev. 250 (1928).

Another conspicuous instance of such utilization of space above the earth's surface is the Park Avenue development in New York, where fabulous sums have been invested in buildings over the New York Central and New Haven tracks.

2.05   Trespass

If without my permission you enter upon my land, this is a *trespass.* I have a legal right to sue you even though you have caused no damage, and the judge will award me *nominal damages* of $1.00.

> **EXAMPLE:**   I have no right to go upon the land of my neighbor for the purpose of putting up screens, or painting, or of effecting repairs on my house. *Taliaferro* v. *Salyer,* 328 P2d 799 (Cal. 1958).

If instead of trespassing at the surface you do so beneath the surface, this is known as *subsurface trespass* and also gives rise to an action for damages.

> **EXAMPLE:**   *A* and *B* own adjoining lands. *B* sinks an oil well near the boundary line. This well is angled so that it crosses the boundary beneath the surface and *B* is therefore pumping oil from *A*'s land. This is called crooked-hole drilling. *A* can sue *B* for damages.

Trespass can also take place above the surface in the air space that forms part of the land. The old theory that one's land extends to the sky was adequate when courts were dealing with simple questions.

> **EXAMPLE:**   Thrusting one's arm across a boundary fence is a trespass. *Hannabalson* v. *Sessions,* 90 NW 93 (Ia. 1902). A building owner cannot maintain shutters that swing across adjoining land. *Homewood Realty Corp.* v. *Safe Deposit & Trust Co.,* 154 Atl. 58 (Md. 1931).

However, common sense revolts at the notion that the mere flight of aircraft over one's land is a trespass. Hence, it has been held that the flight of aircraft at high altitudes, causing no inconvenience to the landowner, is not a violation of the landowner's rights. It is only when the flight is low, as when a plane is taking off or landing and causing damage to the landowner, that his rights have been invaded. *U.S.* v. *Causby,* 328 U.S. 256 (1946): flights at level of eighty-three feet forced landowner to give up chicken farm.

2.06   Real and personal property

The distinction between *real* and *personal property* is an important one. An article of personal property, such as an automobile, is called a *chattel*. It is sold by *bill of sale*. In fact, sales of chattels need not even be in writing when the sale price is under a figure fixed by law, usually $500. Ownership of real estate, on the other hand, is transferred by means of a *deed*.

It is a historical fact that rules of law come into existence when and as human beings feel a need for them. In early times when men were nomadic, driving their cattle north for the summer and south for the winter, there was no need for a law relating to real estate. Men did not aspire to the ownership of land. But there was need for a law of personal property to help men decide how cattle could be sold or who would succeed to ownership at the owner's death. And so the first crude rules of property law evolved, relating to cattle. The word *chattel* derives from cattle, the earliest subject of legal ownership. Later, when men learned to cultivate the soil, real estate law evolved to deal with questions regarding the ownership of land. Now lawyers are working through their associations to establish more uniformity, but differences still persist, as between the law relating to personal property and the law relating to real estate.

2.07   Trees and crops

All trees, plants, and other things that grow are divided into classes:

1. Trees, perennial bushes, grasses, etc., which do not require annual cultivation, are called *fructus naturales* and are considered real estate or real property.
2. Annual crops produced by labor, such as wheat, corn, and potatoes are called *fructus industriales* and are considered personal property.

Since growing crops are personal property, they may be sold orally if the sale price is under the figure fixed by law for oral sales of personal property, *Stein* v. *Crawford,* 105 Atl. 780 (Md. 1919), or by bill of sale, as are other chattels.

2.08   Estates in land

Just as land may be divided into layers by a sale of "air rights" thereover or minerals thereunder, so the ownership of land may be divided into various types of interests. The highest type of interest, of course, is complete ownership.

EXAMPLE: *A* owns a tract of land. No one else has any interest whatever in the land. He is said to be the owner in *fee simple*. This is merely a technical phrase connoting ownership of the land. When one hears it said that "*A* has title" to a particular tract of land, it is understood that *A* is the *fee owner,* he owns the land *in fee* or *in fee simple,* or has an estate *in fee simple absolute.* All these are different ways of expressing the idea that *A* owns the land, that his ownership is of unlimited duration, and that so long as he obeys the law, he may do as he chooses with the land, and, on his death, it will go to his heirs, or, if he leaves a will, to the persons named in his will. Lawyers speak of interests in land as *estates.*

Suppose, however, that *A,* being the owner in fee simple of a tract of land, executes a ten-year lease thereof to *B.* Now *A* has parted with a portion of his rights. He has given up for ten years his right to occupy the land and, in return, has received *B*'s promise to pay rent for those ten years. *B* has acquired the right to occupy the land in accordance with the provisions of his lease, but has not, of course, become the owner in fee simple. He has merely acquired a *leasehold estate* or *term for years* in the land. A leasehold estate, even where the lease is for many years, is, for most purposes, legally considered to be personal property. *Chicago* v. *University of Chicago,* 134 NE 723 (Ill. 1922) (lease for 1,000 years).

> **EXAMPLE:**   Landlord makes a lease to Tenant. Tenant assigns the lease to Assignee. Tenant's wife need not join in the assignment because dower rights do not exist in personal property.

But for some purposes a lease is said to be a *chattel real.* That is, it has some of the attributes of real property. Thus, a lease is entitled to be recorded in the real estate records, like a deed or mortgage of land. *Lincoln National Bank & Tr. Co.* v. *Nathan,* 19 NE2d 243 (Ind. 1939). The same would be true of a mortgage of the leasehold estate. A leasehold estate can be partitioned in the same manner as real estate. *Pierce* v. *Pierce,* 123 NE2d 511 (Ill. 1954).

The word *estate* is used to express the degree, quantity, nature, duration, or extent of an interest in land. Complete ownership is an *estate in fee simple,* but there are many other estates, such as *life estates* and *leasehold estates.* Each differs from the others with respect to the rights and duties of the owner of the estate in question.

2.08(a)   Divisions of land ownership

As can be seen from this and other chapters, ownership of land can be divided according to time.

> **EXAMPLE:**   Landlord gives Tenant a lease for ten years. Tenant enjoys the beneficial use of the building (part of the ownership bundle of rights) for ten years.

Or divided vertically.

> **EXAMPLE:**   *X,* a railroad, makes a deed of several air space levels to a developer to permit construction of a commercial development over its tracks.

Or divided according to the substance in the land.

> **EXAMPLE:** A farmer makes a deed to a coal company of the coal beneath his land.

Or divided among co-owners.

> **EXAMPLE:** A husband and wife buy a home and ask that the deed run to them as joint tenants. Each is a one-half owner.

2.08(b) Life estates

The owner of the life estate can use and enjoy the land only during his lifetime.

> **EXAMPLE:** Landowner dies leaving a will giving land to Widow for her life, and, at her death, to their children, C and D. Widow thus acquires a *life estate* in the land and becomes a *life tenant*. She is entitled to the reasonable and necessary use of the land for her lifetime, but she must not do anything that will in any way injure the permanent value of the property. She may collect and use the rents of the land, but must keep the property in repair and must pay the real estate taxes and the interest on the mortgage. She must not drill any new oil wells or open new mines, but may take oil or minerals from existing wells and mines. On her death, all her rights in the land will cease.

Life estates may be created by will or deed. Often, to save the expense of probating his will after his death, a father while still living will give a deed of his land to his son or daughter, and in the deed will reserve to himself a life estate.

Certain special kinds of life estates are created by law, rather than by will or deed, such as dower, curtesy, and homestead.

2.09 Trusts

A *trust* is an equitable obligation, binding a person (who is called a *trustee*) to deal with property over which he has control (which is called the *trust property* or *trust estate*) for the benefit of persons (who are called the *beneficiaries*), any of whom may enforce the obligation. Trusts are of various kinds.

> **EXAMPLE:** Landowner dies leaving a will by which he gives all his property to Trustee, in trust, with power to sell the property and make investments, the income of the trust to be payable to Widow during her lifetime, and on her death the trust property to be distributed among Landowner's children then living. Since this trust was created by Landowner's last will and testament, it is known as a *testamentary trust*.

> **EXAMPLE:** Landowner signs a deed conveying his land to Trustee, in trust, with power to sell the property and make investments, the income of the trust to be payable to Landowner during his lifetime, and after Landowner's death to Widow during her lifetime, and on her death the property to be distributed among Landowner's children then living. Since this trust becomes effective during Landowner's lifetime, it is known as a *living trust*.

EXAMPLE: Buyer plans to acquire a tract of land. However, he wishes to conceal his ownership of the property. He also wishes to prevent his wife and his judgment creditors from acquiring any interest in the land. On purchasing the land, Buyer directs Seller to convey the land to Trustee. The deed gives Trustee full power to sell and mortgage the land, but does not mention Buyer's name. The deed is filed for record. The deed to Trustee and also a separate unrecorded agreement signed by Buyer and Trustee recites that all title to the land is vested in Trustee and that the beneficiary's (that is, Buyer's) interest is only personal property. However, in the unrecorded agreement Trustee agrees that he will deal with the land only when directed so to do by Buyer. Buyer has accomplished his purpose. The public records do not disclose his ownership of the land. Since the trust specifically provides that Buyer's interest is only personal property, no dower rights attach, and judgments against Buyer are not liens on the land. *C. T. & T. Co.* v. *Mercantile Tr. and Sav. Bank,* 20 NE2d 992 (Ill. 1939). This is called a land trust.

The land trust is recognized as valid in Florida, Illinois, Indiana, North Dakota, and Virginia. Kenoe, *Land Trust Practice* (1974); Garret, *Land Trusts,* 1955 Law Forum 655; 18 U. Miami L. Rev., 699 (1964); 14 Kans. L. Rev. 97 (1965): 45 N.D.L. Rev. 77 (1968).

2.10 Cemetery lots

When a cemetery corporation sells a lot, or burial site, the purchaser does not become the absolute owner of the lot. The deed gives him merely an easement right of burial. *Steele* v. *Rosehill Cemetery Co.,* 19 NE2d 189 (Ill. 1939); 109 U. of Pa. L. Rev. 378 (1961). He also has the right to enter the cemetery to care for the graves, subject to the reasonable regulations adopted by the cemetery company as to visiting hours, monuments, grave decorations, and so on. Like any other easement, the easement of the burial may be lost by abandonment. *Trustees of First Presbyterian Church* v. *Alling,* 54 N.J.S. 141, 148 A2d 510 (N. J. 1959).

2.11 Modes of acquiring ownership of land

While title to or ownership of land is most often acquired by deed, by will, or by descent, there are other modes of acquiring title to land, among them, condemnation and adverse possession.

2.11(a) Condemnation

When land is needed for some public use, it can be acquired by the exercise of the power of eminent domain. The power of eminent domain is exercised: (1) by the United States, the state in which the land lies, cities, villages, school boards, and other public bodies; (2) by quasi-public corporations, such as railroads and public utility corporations; (3) in some states, private individuals have the right of eminent domain in limited instances as, for example, when they are landlocked. The power is subject to two conditions: The use to which the property is to be devoted must be a public one, and just compensation must be paid.

Exercise of the power of eminent domain involves a condemnation proceeding, which is usually a court proceeding initiated by the city or other public body desiring to acquire title. The just compensation to which the landowner is entitled is the fair, market value of the land at the time of the taking of the land. This value is often determined by a jury.

By condemnation, the condemnor acquires either an easement or fee simple title, although federal legislation now permits the United States to acquire by condemnation the right to occupy the land for a term of years only if that is what is desired. If an easement will serve the purpose for which the land is to be acquired, the condemnor, under many laws, acquires only an easement.

> **EXAMPLE**   As a rule, an easement only is acquired by a railroad condemning for a right of way, a city condemning for a street, a telephone company condemning for a telephone line, or a drainage district condemning for a drainage ditch. In such cases, even though the landowner receives the full market value of the land condemned, he retains the ownership of the land so condemned. The point is of importance, since if an easement for street or right of way purposes acquired by condemnation is later abandoned, the original landowner still retains his ownership free and clear of the easement. *Bell* v. *Mattoon Waterworks & Res. Co.,* 92 NE 352 (Ill. 1910).

In many cases, however, it is necessary that fee simple title be acquired, as when land is condemned for a courthouse site. Many states, therefore—Illinois, Kansas, Kentucky, Massachusetts, Michigan, Minnesota, Ohio, Pennsylvania, Texas, Virginia, and Wyoming, for example—permit the condemnor to acquire fee simple title by condemnation.

2.11(b)   **Adverse possession**   Often the public records will show a complete and perfect succession of perfect deeds from the government down to John Smith. This is known as the *record title* or *paper title.* Yet the true ownership of the land may be outstanding in someone who holds possession of the land without a single document to show his ownership. The ownership here referred to is that acquired by taking possession of the land and staying in possession for a certain number of years fixed by the law. At the end of that period, which varies from state to state, the party in possession has ownership to the land. He need not have any deed to the land. He may have entered on the land without any right whatever to do so. He need not place any instrument on the public records showing his title. Yet he owns the land.

The law providing for the acquiring of title to land by going into possession was passed for two reasons: (1) It encourages the use of the land. If persons living in other states or other parts of the state own land in our vicinity and make no attempt to use the land for very long periods of time, it is better for the community to have the title placed in someone who is more interested in using it. (2) Ownership of real estate often depends on transactions that occurred so long ago that the witnesses who were familiar with the transaction are dead or have forgotten the facts.

Not every possession of land will ripen into ownership. For this to occur the possession must be legally *adverse;* that is, the possession must be *actual, hostile, notorious, exclusive, continuous,* and *under claim of right.*

For possession to adverse, it must be actual. As the judges put it, the occupant must unfurl his flag on the land and keep it flying so that the owner may see, if he wishes, that an enemy has invaded his domain and planted the standard of conquest. In other words, the occupant must do something that will make the owner notice that a stranger has occupied his land. This does not mean, however, that the occupant must live or reside on the land.

> **EXAMPLE:** *A* fences and farms some vacant land adjoining his farm in Illinois. This continues for twenty years. He now owns this adjoining land by reason of his adverse possession.

This rule is of importance in boundary disputes, since if a landowner erects a fence on what he claims is the boundary of his land and claims all the land to the fence, his possession will eventually ripen into ownership even though the fence is actually over on his neighbor's land. The same is true when a building encroaches over and upon adjoining land.

Usually possession is not *hostile* when the person in possession occupies a relation of trust and confidence toward the holder of the paper title.

> **EXAMPLE:** A father's possession is not hostile to the child, the possession of a husband is not hostile to the wife, and the possession of an agent is not hostile to his employer.

The requirement that possession be *notorious* merely means that the possession of the occupant must be such that the real owner would be likely to notice it.

Adverse possession, in order to ripen into title, must be *continuous.* However, seasonal possession is often sufficient, for the possession need only be such as is usual with respect to land of similar character. For example, it is sufficient if farmland is farmed in the farming season, timberland logged in the logging season, and so on.

> **EXAMPLE:** *A* occupied *B*'s hunting shack each year during the hunting season. Ultimately, *A* acquired good title by adverse possession. *Kraus* v. *Mueller,* 12 Wis.2d 430, 107 NW2d 467.

For a person to acquire title by adverse possession he must claim that he is the owner of the land, but it is enough if his acts and conduct indicate that he claims to be the owner of the land.

EXAMPLE: *A* and *B* owned adjoining lots, *A* owning Lot 9 and *B* owning Lot 8. *A* built a frame cottage on Lot 9, but the same extended two feet over on Lot 8. He thought the house was entirely on his own lot and never made any oral claim to this two-foot strip. He paid taxes on Lot 9 and *B* the taxes on Lot 8. After twenty years, a survey was made which disclosed the encroachment. Although *A* had made no oral claim to the two-foot strip, his acts namely, erecting a building on this strip, showed that he claimed title to the strip. He therefore had acquired title by adverse possession. *Cassidy* v. *Lenahan,* 128 NE 544 (Ill. 1920).

As is evident, adverse possession resembles prescription in the law of easements. However, it is often said that adverse occupancy often, at the *surface* of the ground, ripens into ownership by adverse possession. Adverse *use* ripens into a prescriptive easement. The utility of this distinction is reasonably obvious.

EXAMPLE: *A* and *B* own adjoining lots 7 and 8. Both lots have a home on them. *A*'s home is so constructed that the eaves extend over *B*'s lot. When *A*'s home is demolished, it would be absurd to hold that *A*'s prescriptive easement runs in favor of any new home. How in the world would the air space formerly occupied by the eaves be located? A simple solution is to hold that when a prescriptive easement is created, it runs in favor of the house. When the house is gone, the easement is gone.

3 FIXTURES

3.01 In general   A *fixture* is an article that was once personal property, but that has been installed in or attached to land or a building in some more or less permanent manner, so that such article is regarded in law as a part of the real estate.

> **EXAMPLE:**   A kitchen sink is personal property, a chattel, in a plumber's shop. It becomes a fixture and part of the real estate after it is installed in a house.

The distinction of whether an item is classified as a fixture is important for three reasons. First, does a contract and deed for the sale of realty pass ownership to these items even though they are not specifically listed in the contract? Ownership will pass to the buyer if the items are fixtures—part of the real estate. Ownership will not pass to the buyer (unless the items are expressly conveyed) if the items are chattels—personal property.

> **EXAMPLE:**   Seller contracts to sell his house to Buyer. All that is described in the contract is the land. Buyer is entitled to receive the house as well as the land, because the house is a fixture and is legally part of the land. Buyer is also entitled to receive the kitchen sink, furnace, toilets, and all other articles installed in the building with a view to remaining there permanently. However, Buyer is not entitled to Seller's furniture. Articles of furniture are chattels. They do not pass with a sale of land unless specifically mentioned in the contract. Seller can take his furniture with him when he moves. He cannot remove the sink, furnace, or toilets.

Second, if a tenant installs these items in leased premises, do they become so much a part of the real estate that they cannot be removed when the tenant moves out? See § 3.04. Third, the special rules that lenders must follow to obtain a security interest or mortgage lien upon these items are in part dependent upon the item's classification as realty or personalty. See Kratovil & Werner, *Modern Mortgage Law and Practice* Ch. 9 (2d ed. 1981) and § 3.05, following herein.

3.02 Tests to determine whether an article is a fixture

It often becomes important to determine whether or not a particular article is a fixture.

In determining whether or not an article is a fixture, courts apply the following tests:

1. The manner in which the article is attached to the real estate.

EXPLANATION: If an article is attached to a building in such a permanent fashion that it could not be removed without substantial injury to the building, it is usually held to be a fixture. This test, in early times the only test of a fixture, has lost its preeminence in modern times. *Finley* v. *Ford,* 304 Ky. 136, 200 SW2d 138 (1947). However conservative courts continue to attach importance to the test.

EXAMPLES: Water pipes, linoleum cemented to the floor.

2. The character of the article and its adaptation to the real estate.

EXPLANATION: If an article was specially constructed or fitted with a view to its location and use in a particular building, or if the article was installed in the building in order to carry out the purpose for which the building was erected, this tends to show that it was intended that the article should become a permanent part of the building. It is usually considered a fixture.

EXAMPLES: Pews in a church; a theater sign constructed for a particular theater; screens and storm windows specially fitted to the house; electronic computing equipment installed on a floor specially constructed for it. 5 ALR3d 497.

3. The intention of the parties.

EXPLANATION: There is a pronounced tendency today to emphasize the factor of intention. *Am. Tel. & Telegraph Co.* v. *Muller,* 299 F.Supp. 157 (D. S. C. 1968). Was the article attached, the courts ask, with the intention of making it a permanent part of the building? Tests 1 and 2 are helpful in determining the intention of the parties, but once that intention is determined, it must govern. It is not the secret intention of the person installing the articles that governs. The test is an objective one, and intention is determined from the nature of the article, relation of the parties, adaptation, mode of annexation, and all the surrounding circumstances. Thus, the question boils down to this: Would the average person consider this article a permanent fixture?

EXAMPLES: Gas stoves are often installed in apartment buildings for the use of tenants. They are intended to remain there permanently, since they increase the rental value of the apartments. Therefore they are considered fixtures, even though they can be removed from the building with comparative ease. *Leisle* v. *Welfare B. and L. Assn.,* 232 Wis. 440, 287 NW 739 (1939). The same is true of electric refrigerators installed in apartment buildings. *Guardian Life Ins. Co.* v. *Swanson,* 286 Ill. App. 278, 3 NE2d 324 (1936); 7 ALR 1578. Air conditioners are necessities, not luxuries, in a modern apartment and are treated as fixtures when installed by the owner in a more or less permanent fashion. *State Mutual* v. *Trautwein* 414 SW2d 587 (Ky. 1967); 43 ALR2d 1378. Again, it is important to remember that conservative courts are accustomed to stress Rule 1 above and would not consider a gas stove, electric range, or refrigerator installed in an apartment building a fixture. *Elliott* v. *Talmadge,* 207 Ore. 428, 297 P2d 310 (1956); 52 ALR2d 1103. There is substantial agreement on the point that a gas stove or refrigerator installed in a private house is not a fixture, since the owner usually intends to take it with him when he moves. The law of fixtures, however, is constantly developing, expanding, and changing. As customs have changed, articles once considered personal property have become fixtures. *Strain* v. *Green,* 25 Wash.2d 692, 172 P2d 216 (1946). The luxuries of one generation become the necessities of the next. Since intention is the factor that determines whether or not an article is a fixture, the same type of article may be a fixture in one kind of building and a chattel in another. For example, an old-fashioned gas stove (one not built into the wall) is a chattel in a private home and would not go automatically to the buyer with a sale of the land. In an apartment building, exactly the same kind of stove would, in many states, be considered a fixture, passing automatically with a sale of the land. Articles of furniture (tables, chairs, and so forth), whether in a home, hotel, or furnished apartment, are universally considered chattels. *State* v. *Feves,* 228 Ore. 273, 365 P2d 97 (1961). The decisions on carpeting are in hopeless confusion. 55 ALR2d 1044. Obviously, the better rule is that wall-to-wall carpeting installed by the owner is a fixture, especially where installed on a concrete slab or rough plywood.

The test for determining whether an article is a fixture is the objective intention test. This requires an analysis of the nature of the article, mode of annexation, and all the surrounding circumstances. This, of course, means that you cannot determine whether a given article is or is not a fixture by sitting in a law library. You must get out there and look at it.

EXAMPLE: The question is whether an air conditioner in an apartment is a fixture. As stated, the question is absurd. Who put it there? The tenant or the landlord? Tenants mean to take their property with them. Permanent annexation is not in the tenant's mind. The opposite is true of the landlord. Is it an easily removable window unit? Or is it one of 100 identical air conditioners built into apertures in the masonry wall of the building? If the latter, it is almost certainly a fixture.

In real estate law, in general, it is important to get out there and look at the problem.

It will help you understand these fixture tests if you understand a little about the history of fixture law. Hundreds of years ago in agricultural England, where we find the beginnings of this law, buildings tended to be rather simple, and the annexation test worked well enough. In America some problems developed even in early times. A Virginia rail fence rests on the ground but is not attached to it. But the courts thought that, for obvious practical reasons, it ought to go with a sale of land, and they so decided. Later, when factories began to appear, it became evident that the annexation test was obsolete. If I buy a factory, obviously I am buying a going concern; yet under the old annexation test the seller would be allowed to remove the machinery, because this could be done without *injury to the building.* Thus, in response to this need, the courts invented the intention test, which enabled the buyer to claim the machinery. *Hopewell Mills* v. *Taunton Sav. Bank,* 150 Mass. 519, 23 NE 327 (1890); 109 ALR 1427. Still, later, when landlords began to put gas stoves and electric refrigerators in apartments, the courts faced the same problem, and some of them decided in favor of the intention test, but some did not. Those that did not were bothered by the flimsy connection between the appliance and the building, simply plugging a refrigerator in a wall socket, for example. The current problem takes this development one step further. A professional builder equips his homes with a variety of appliances that are attractive to the housewife, who, many builders will tell you, casts the deciding vote in the purchase of a home. The problem of this "package kitchen" has not, as yet, been fully litigated. It is best to ask the builder for a bill of sale as well as a deed, the bill of sale being used to transfer ownership of the appliances. In time, quite possibly, the courts will hold that the appliances pass with the deed as fixtures without the necessity of a bill of sale.

Probably most courts will treat package kitchen items as fixtures:

EXAMPLE: Standard size dishwasher installed in well under formica counter top next to sink and attached to electric wiring of house by flexible metal conduit through junction box; standard model garbage disposal attached to underside of sink; and standard model range hood located over drop-in counter top range were permanent fixtures although removable without damage to the building. *Builders Appliance Supply Co.* v. *A. R. John Const. Co.,* 455 P2d 615 (Ore. 1969); *State Dept.* v. *Town & Country Inc.,* 256 Md. 584, 261 A2d 168 (1970).

As you can see, in determining the intention of the party installing the fixture, the courts consider the nature of his interest in the property. It is unlikely that a tenant would wish to make permanent additions to the landlord's property. Hence the rules concerning tenant's fixtures were evolved, under which most of the tenant's installations are treated as removable chattels. But when the installations are made by the landlord, they are more likely to be thought of as true fixtures, which ought to go to a buyer landlord even though not mentioned in the deed.

3.03 Constructive annexation

Certain objects, though in no way attached to the building, are regarded as so strongly connected with the building that they are fixtures under the doctrine of *constructive annexation.*

> **EXAMPLE:** Ownership of the keys to a building passes when the deed is delivered to the buyer. *U.S.* v. *967.905 Acres of Land,* 305 F.Supp. 83 (D. Minn. 1969).

> **EXAMPLE:** In the sale of a factory, spare or duplicate parts go with the land as fixtures because of their logical connection with the machinery. 109 ALR 1430.

> **EXAMPLE:** A lathe in a factory is a fixture even though it simply rests on the floor and is not bolted thereto. 109 ALR 1431.

> **EXAMPLE:** Car unit for an electric garage door opener.

3.04 Articles removable by tenants

Special rules are applicable in the landlord and tenant situation. Articles that a tenant is allowed to remove are classified into the following three classes:

1. Trade fixtures.

> **EXPLANATION:** In order to encourage a tenant to equip himself with the tools and implements of his trade, articles installed by a tenant for the purpose of his trade or business are classed as *trade fixtures* and may be removed by the tenant at the expiration of his lease. Intention is significant here also, for it is obvious that the tenant intends to take such articles with him when he moves.

> **EXAMPLES:** Airplane hangars; bowling alleys; greenhouses; booths, bars, and other restaurant equipment; gasoline pumps and tanks in a filling station; barber chairs; soda fountains; oil derricks.

2. Agricultural fixtures.

> **EXPLANATION:** Articles installed by a tenant farmer for the purpose of enabling him to farm the land are called *agricultural fixtures* and may be removed by the tenant when he quits the land.

> **EXAMPLES:** Hen houses; tool sheds; maple-sugar houses.

3. Domestic fixtures.

> **EXPLANATION:** Articles installed in a dwelling by a tenant in order to render it more comfortable and attractive are removable by the tenant.

EXAMPLES: Bookshelves; venetian blinds.

The three classes of articles that a tenant is allowed to remove are often referred to collectively as *tenant's fixtures. Fixtures,* as described in preceding sections, are real estate. *Tenant's fixtures* are personal property. Observe, also, that *the trade fixtures rule applies only to articles installed by tenants,* not to articles installed by *the landowner. Young Elec. Sign Co.* v. *Erwin Elec Co.,* 477 P2d 864 (Nev. 1970).

EXAMPLE: Gas pumps installed by a tenant in a rented service station are clearly trade fixtures. Pumps installed by a landowner would be true fixtures and would automatically go with a sale of the land. Machinery in a factory is a fixture if installed by the landowner. *Foote* v. *Gooch,* 96 N.C. 265, 1 SE 525 (1887).

It is important to remember that lease forms, invariably drafted for the landlord's benefit, often contain clauses forbidding removal of the tenant's installations. 30 ALR3d 998.

EXAMPLE: A lease of a filling station provided that at the termination of the lease all improvements on the premises would be the property of the landlord. The tenant was not permitted to remove gas pumps and tanks he had installed. 30 ALR3d 1034.

It is important also to remember that if the tenant moves out leaving his trade fixtures behind, they become the property of the landlord. 6 ALR2d 322. In the process they change from chattels to real estate, and ownership passes from tenant to landlord.

3.05   Secured financing and fixtures

When only the landowner and the real estate mortgagee are involved, the rule is that fixtures bought, paid for, and installed by the landowner *after* the execution of a mortgage on the land become subject to the lien of the mortgage and cannot thereafter be removed by the landowner. In this situation, in other words, the mortgage lien attaches to *all* fixtures, even trade fixtures, thereafter installed by the mortgagor on the mortgaged premises. Such fixtures must not be removed without the mortgagee's consent. *Bowen* v. *Wood,* 35 Ind. 268. However, trade fixtures installed by a *tenant,* whether installed before or after the mortgage, are removable by the tenant. *Standard Oil Co.* v. *La Crosse Super Auto Service,* 217 Wis. 237, 258 NW 791 99 ALR 60 (1935).

The Uniform Commercial Code has been adopted in nearly all fifty states. Under the code, a security interest in a chattel, including a chattel that has been or will be installed as a fixture, is created by means of a *security agreement,* which replaces the old *chattel mortgage* and *conditional sale contract.* This document, however, is not recorded. Instead, a brief notice of the existence of the security agreement is filed. This notice is called a *financing statement.* Where an article has become or is to become a fixture, the financing statement must be filed in the recorder's office where mortgages on real estate are filed. When thus filed, it gives notice to all that there exists a security interest in the article. Subsequent purchasers of the real estate and subsequent mortgagees of the land are bound by this filing, and if a default occurs under the security agreement, the articles can be repossessed and removed by the security holder without liability for any incidental damage to the building occasioned by the removal. If the financing statement is not filed as required by law, a subsequent purchaser or mortgagee of the land is protected against removal of the articles and need not pay the unpaid balance due on the articles. Where the article is purchased and installed on the land *after* the recording of a mortgage on real estate, the holder of the chattel security lien may remove the article from the real estate in case of default regardless of the incidental damage to the building. However, he must reimburse the real estate mortgagee for the cost of repairing any immediate physical injury in the building. Kratovil & Werner, *Modern Mortgage Law and Practice* Ch. 9 (2d ed. 1981).

3.06 Agreement of the parties

All of the rules are statements of law that the courts have framed. These legal rules should not be interpreted to mean that the parties cannot alter the impact of the rule by their agreement, which may make personal property out of what the law would consider real property and vice versa. *Lilenquist* v. *Pitchford's, Inc.* 525 P2d 93 (Ore. 1974).

> **EXAMPLE:** Landowner and Tenant agree that, notwithstanding the fact that the law would cause items installed in the leased premises to be tenant fixtures and removable by the tenant at the conclusion of his term, the items shall become part of the realty. This agreement will be enforced by the courts.

This agreement would not, however, be binding upon third parties unless they took with notice of its terms. 35 AM.JUR.2d *Fixtures* § 18.

3.07 Severance

If the landowner actually removes an article from the land or from the building to which it has been attached, with the intention that the removal shall be *permanent,* such article becomes personal property again and does not pass by a deed of the real estate. Thus, if a landowner tears down a fence and piles the material on the land, such material does not pass by a deed of the land. The fixture has again become personal property by *severance.* If the removal is for a *temporary purpose,* as the removal of a piece of machinery for repairs, the article remains a fixture, notwithstanding its removal from the soil, and passes by a deed of the real estate.

3.08 Building erected on wrong lot

A perpetual source of legal controversy concerns the rights of one who through innocent mistake erects a building on the wrong lot, usually a lot adjoining the one he actually owns. Some states allow compensation to the builder in such cases. *Voss* v. *Forgue* 84 So2d 563 (Fla. 1956); *Olin* v. *Reinecke,* 336 Ill. 530, 168 NE 676 (1929); *Hardy* v. *Burroughs,* 251 Mich. 578, 232 NW 200 (1930); but other states deny any compensation on the ground that if a man builds, it is his duty to see that he builds on the right lot. 5 De Paul L. Rev. 321 (1956); 104 ALR 577; 76 ALR 304.

The basis for the court decisions awarding compensation to the party making the innocent mistake is the law of *restitution,* which is designed to accomplish precisely that. The newer cases go strongly in this direction.

EXAMPLE: Landowner hired Builder to erect a house on Landowner's lot. Builder hired Surveyor to place the survey stakes. Surveyor, by mistake, placed the stakes on the lot next door. Landowner was entitled to a lien on this lot (which was owned by a third party) for the value his building contributed to the lot. *Duncan* v. *Akers,* 262 NE2d 402 (Ind. 1970).

NEW DIRECTIONS: The courts are taking the view that the innocent improver is entitled to compensation unless he acquires *actual* knowledge of his mistake before he begins construction. *Johnson* v. *Stull,* 303 SW2d 110 (Mo. 1957). If the true owner, without protest, watches a stranger building on his land, he is sure to be subjected to a lien for the value of the building. It is grossly unfair not to warn the stranger of his mistake. *Benedict* v. *Little,* 264 So2d 491 (Ala. 1972).

4 EASEMENTS

4.01 Easement defined

An *easement* is a right acquired by a landowner to use the land of another for a special purpose.

> **EXAMPLE:** Servient and Dominant own adjoining tracts of land. By a written instrument, signed, sealed, and recorded in the proper office, Servient grants to Dominant the right to cross Servient's tract at a particular place for the purpose of ingress to Dominant's tract from a certain highway. The right thus created is called an *easement*. Servient remains the owner of the land over which Dominant travels. Dominant has only a special and particular right in that land.

4.02 Easement appurtenant runs with the land

The easement described in the preceding section is an *easement appurtenant.* An easement appurtenant is created for the benefit of a tract of land. Consequently, for such an easement to exist, there must always be two tracts of land owned by different persons, one tract, called the *dominant tenement,* having the benefit of the easement, and another tract, called the *servient tenement,* over which the easement runs. In the example given in the preceding section, Dominant's tract was the one enjoying the benefit of the easement. It was therefore the dominant tenement. Servient's tract was the servient tenement since it was the tract subject to the easement.

The dominant tenement need not adjoin the servient tenement. *Allendorf* v. *Dally,* 6 Ill.2d 577, 129 NE2d 673 (1955). However, it usually does.

An easement appurtenant is regarded as being so closely connected to the dominant tenement that, upon a sale and deed of such tenement, the easement will pass to the grantee in the deed, even though the deed does not mention it. Such an easement is therefore said to *run with the land.* In the example, if Dominant should sell his land to Purchaser, Purchaser would automatically acquire the right to cross Servient's land. Whoever owns the dominant tenement owns the easement. A separate sale of the easement is not permitted.

Usually an easement is created by a landowner over his land and is in favor of another landowner. However, an easement can run in favor of any interest in land.

EXAMPLE: Landlord leases a store to Tenant and in the lease grants Tenant an easement of ingress and egress over Landlord's adjoining land. This is valid. Easements in favor of tenants are common.

4.03   Easement and license distinguished

It is often difficult to distinguish an easement from a *license*. Ordinarily an unauthorized entry on the land of another is called a trespass and makes the trespasser liable to pay damages to the landowner. The owner may, however, grant permission to enter for a particular purpose. This permission is called a license. An example is a theater ticket which authorizes the purchaser thereof to enter the theater for the purpose of viewing the performance.

An easement is usually created by a written instrument; a license is often created verbally. An easement is a more or less permanent right; a license is of temporary character. A license is a purely personal right and cannot be sold; the ownership of an easement changes with the ownership of the land to which it belongs. An easement cannot be revoked; a license is revocable.

EXAMPLE: *A* and *B* owned adjoining lots. They entered into a verbal agreement to establish a party driveway on the common boundary line between the lots. *B* thereafter built concrete walks and steps to the driveway. After this driveway had been in use for two years, *A* notified *B* that he intended to construct a driveway entirely upon his own lot and expected *B* likewise to provide for himself. When *A* sought to erect a fence along the common boundary, *B* filed a suit to prevent him from doing so. The court held that *A* was within his rights. Since the agreement was merely verbal, a license, not an easement, was created, and a license is revocable. *Baird* v. *Westberg,* 341 Ill. 616, 173 NE 820 (1930). With the present aversion to the unconscionable, it is doubtful the court would so hold today. *Monroe Bowling Lanes* v. *Woodfield Livestock Sales,* 244 NE2d 762 (Ohio 1969).

Also, courts today are likely to treat a license as an agreement for an easement where large sums of money are spent in reliance on it.

EXAMPLE: Landowner owned Blackacre. Buyer wished to purchase the north half to erect a motel and restaurant. Contract of sale was entered into. Buyer explained that he would need to install drains over six inches of Landowner's land. Landowner orally agreed that he could do so. The deal was closed. Landowner later demanded that Buyer remove the drain. The court held that this was an oral agreement for an easement that became irrevocable by *part performance* when

Buyer erected his buildings. *Anastoplo* v. *Radford,* 14 Ill.2d 526, 152 NE2d 879 (1959); *Moe* v. *Cagle,* 385 P2d 56 (Wash. 1963); 11 Columb. L. Rev. 76 (1911).

> **EXPLANATION:** In reading the *Anastoplo* case a lawyer would remind him-self that the phrase *part performance* has different meanings. For example, if Sell-er orally agrees to sell vacant land to Buyer, and Buyer takes possession and builds a home, Buyer can compel Seller to give him a deed. Here part perfor-mance is proof that an oral contract of sale was made. 73 Am.Jur.2d *Statute of Frauds* § 427. But in the *Anastoplo* case the acts of Buyer placed him in a position where refusal to give him the right to maintain the drain would cause *Buyer unjust impoverishment.* 73Am.Jur.2d *Statute of Frauds* § 408.

And in instances where formerly the courts might have treated a document as a revocable license, today the courts tend to regard it as creating an irrevoca-ble easement.

> **EXAMPLE:** Landowner owned a two-story store and office building. Land-owner gave ABC Advertising Co. the right to use his roof for five years for a large advertising display. The court treated this as creating an easement in gross. This achieved the fair result of preventing a revocation of the instrument. *Baseball Pub. Co.* v. *Bruton,* 302 Mass. 54, 18 NE2d 362 (1938).

> **EXAMPLE:** In accordance with a verbal agreement, *A* and *B,* adjoining own-ers, erected buildings with a party wall and party stairway on the common bound-ary between their lots. The agreement was held irrevocable. *Binder* v. *Weinberg,* 94 Miss. 817, 48 So 1013 (1909).

Parenthetically, mortgage lenders are constantly working to clear up prob-lems created by oral agreements between neighbors. Should a neighbor apply for a mortgage, a party driveway existing under oral agreement would instantly be detected and reported by the mortgage appraiser. The loan process would be stopped and the neighbors would be required to sign and record a written agreement.

4.04   Easement in gross

An *easement in gross* resembles an easement appur-tenant but there is no dominant tenement.

> **EXAMPLES:** Right granted to a telephone and telegraph company to maintain poles and wires over grantor's land; right granted to a city to construct, maintain, and operate a canal through grantor's land; easements for railroads, street rail-ways, pipelines, and power lines.

Right-of-way easements acquired *by corporations* such as railroads and pub-lic utilities (*commercial easements in gross*) may be mortgaged and sold. *Northern Ill. Gas Co.* v. *Weincrank,* 66 Ill. App.2d 60, 214 NE2d 15 (1965), 12 U. of C. L. Rev.

276. Like an easement appurtenant, an easement in gross is irrevocable. The owner of an easement in gross need not, and usually does not, own any land adjoining that over which the easement exists.

4.04(a)   Easements in gross—apportionment—Cabletelevision

The question of the apportionability of an easement in gross has assumed new and special significance since the advent of CATV. Typically a utility company acquires from the landowner, by grant or condemnation, a broad easement in gross to install electric and telephone lines. Currently, a CATV corporation approaches the utility and obtains a license or easement to attach its coaxial cables to the existing utility poles. Theoretically, this adds a burden to the landowner's land and raises a further question as to whether an easement in gross can be conveyed to a third person or its use divided with a third person. There appear to be few decisions on the subject. Some hold that the easement in gross is legally apportionable. *Hoffman* v. *Capital Cablevision Systems, Inc.,* 383 N.Y.S.2d 674 (1976). Many states will so hold if the original easement grant refers to "assigns" or contains other language permitting assignment. 5 Restatement Property, 3053 § 493b. But some courts hold that such an easement cannot be apportioned. *Jolliff* v. *Hardin Cable TV Co.,* 22 Ohio App.2d 49, 258 NE2d 244 (1970). This is poor law and creates problems.

> **EXAMPLE:** Developer grants ABC Utility Co. an easement to install electric and telephone poles and wires in the development. CATV Co. seeks an easement to install cables. It must go to Developer for this easement but cannot use the ABC poles.

4.05   Creation of easement

Easements may be created by *express grant, agreement, express reservation, implied grant, implied reservation, prescription, condemnation, sale of land by reference to a plat,* and by *estoppel.*

4.05(a)   Express grant

A landowner may create an easement over his land by express grant.

Since an easement is an interest in land, a grant of an easement should contain all the formal requisites of a deed. It should be in writing, should sufficiently describe the easement, the land subject thereto, the character of the easement (easement for ingress and egress, and so forth), and should be signed, sealed, witnessed, acknowledged, delivered to the grantee, and recorded in accordance with local rules governing deeds. But no particular words are necessary, and omission of the seal is not a fatal defect.

> **EXAMPLE:** The first example given in this chapter is an illustration of the creation of an easement by grant.

Although an instrument granting an easement is technically known as a *grant*, this is no guarantee that an instrument granting an easement will be so labeled. Very often an instrument in the form of a deed will operate as a grant of an easement by reason of the insertion of language limiting the use of the land to a particular purpose.

> **EXAMPLE:** Landowner signed a warranty deed conveying to Buyer, an adjoining landowner, a strip of land "to be used for road purposes." The quoted phrase appeared immediately following the property description in the deed. It was held that this deed did not make Buyer the owner of the strip, but only gave him an easement thereover for road purposes. *Magnolia Petroleum Co.* v. *West,* 374 Ill. 516, 30 NE2d 24 (1940).

A grant of an easement may be incorporated in a deed that conveys land.

> **EXAMPLE:** Landowner owns Lots 1 and 2. He sells and conveys Lot 1 to Buyer. After the property description in this deed, the following clause is inserted: "For the consideration aforesaid, the grantor grants to the grantee, his heirs and assigns, as an easement appurtenant to the premises hereby conveyed a perpetual easement for ingress and egress over and across the south ten feet of Lot 2 in the subdivision aforesaid." The deed accomplishes two objects: (1) It transfers ownership of Lot 1 to Buyer. (2) It gives Buyer an easement over the south ten feet of Lot 2.

The authors have enjoyed much success by suggesting the use of Professor Kratovil's Model Easement Grant that appears on pp. 32-33.

4.05(b)   **Express reservation**   A landowner may, in selling and conveying part of his land, reserve in the deed an easement in favor of the tract retained by such landowner.

> **EXAMPLE:** Landowner owns Lots 1 and 2. He sells and conveys Lot 2 to Buyer and, after the property description in the deed, inserts the following clause: "The grantor reserves to himself, his heirs and assigns, as an easement appurtenant to Lot 1 in the subdivision aforesaid, a perpetual easement for ingress and egress over and across the south ten feet of the premises hereby conveyed."

As in the case of grants of easements, reservations of easements, not labeled as such, are of frequent occurrence.

> **EXAMPLE:** Landowner sold and conveyed certain land to Buyer by a deed containing the following clause: "Saving and excepting therefrom a strip of land forty feet wide along the bank of the east fork of Austin Creek all the way across said land, for a road to be built at some future time." The court held that, although the deed purported to except from its operation the forty-foot strip in

question, nevertheless ownership of the forty-foot strip passed to the grantee in the deed, but the grantor had an easement thereover for road purposes. *Coon* v. *Sonoma Magnesite Co.,* 182 Cal. 597, 189 Pac. 271 (1920).

4.05(c)   Creation of easement by agreement

Easements may be created by contract or agreement, such contract or agreement being, in effect, a grant of an easement. A familiar illustration is the party wall agreement.

Indeed, the law requires no technical formula of words to create an easement. The only essential is that the parties make clear their intention to establish an easement. *Scanlan* v. *Hopkins,* 270 A2d 352 (Vt. 1970).

4.05(c)(1)   Party walls

Suppose you own Lot 1 and I own adjoining Lot 2. You plan to erect a building on your lot, and I propose to erect an identical building on mine. If we can get together, we can effect an economy by means of a *party wall.* We will erect our buildings in such a way that on the common boundary line where our lots meet only one wall will be built, straddling the line, half on each side of it. Each of us will use that wall as a wall of his house. It will support my floors and roof and yours also. The economies of such an arrangement are obvious. The cost of the wall is shared. Land is conserved. Windows are eliminated, as is the expense of maintenance of one outside wall.

Legally I own the half of the wall that rests on my lot, and you own the half that rests on your lot. I have an easement of support in your half of the wall, and you have an easement of support in my half. Owners planning such an arrangement enter into a party wall agreement. Naturally a written agreement should be used, for an easement is an interest in land, and the law requires that interests in land be created in writing.

Suppose I plan to build at a time when you are not yet ready to go ahead. Here the party wall agreement gives me the right to put half of the wall on your lot and further provides that when you decide to build you will pay me half the cost of the wall.

The duty to repair a party wall falls equally on both owners. If either owner repairs the wall, he is entitled to collect from the other owner half the expenses thus incurred.

Unless the party wall agreement provides otherwise, either owner may increase the height of the wall without the consent of the other owner. However, the entire expense must be borne by the party who heightens the wall, unless the other owner decides to use the added wall.

Additional points on party walls. (1) Each owner has the right to extend the beams of his building into the party wall, but not beyond the centerline of the wall. (2) Use of the wall for flues and fireplaces is legal. (3) If an owner chooses not to erect a building on his side of the party wall, he may use that side of the

MODEL EASEMENT GRANT*

This EASEMENT GRANT is made between_____ _____(hereinafter referred to as "the grantor") and_____ (hereinafter referred to as "the grantee").

The following recitals of fact are a material part of this instrument:

A. The grantor is the owner of a tract of land described as follows and hereafter referred to as "Parcel 1":

(Here insert legal description)

B. The grantee is the owner of a tract of land described as follows and hereafter referred to as "Parcel 2":[1]

(Here insert legal description)

C. The grantor wishes to grant and the grantee wishes to receive an easement over, under and across that part of Parcel 1 described as follows and hereafter referred to as "The easement premises:"[2]

(Here describe the land to be subject to easement)

D. Parcel 1 is presently improved with a building used for_____and Parcel 2 is improved with a building used for_____.

Now, therefore, in consideration of_____ and other valuable consideration, the receipt and sufficiency of which are hereby acknowledged,[3] the following grants, agreements, and covenants and restrictions are made:

1. GRANT OF EASEMENT. The grantor hereby grants[4] to the grantee, his heirs and assigns,[5] as an easement appurtenant to Parcel 2,[6] a perpetual[7] easement for ingress and egress[8] over, under and across the easement premises.

2. USE OF EASEMENT PREMISES. Use of the easement premises is not confined to present uses of Parcel 2, the present buildings thereon, or present means of transportation.[9] The installation or maintenance by the grantee of pipes, conduits, or wires, under, upon or over the easement premises is forbidden.[10] Exclusive use of the easement premises is not hereby granted.[11] The right to use the easement premises, likewise for ingress or egress, is expressly reserved by the grantor. In addition, the grantor reserves the right to make the following uses of the easement premises:

a. The right to erect a building over the easement premises, provided all of such structure shall be located at a height of not less than_____feet above the surface of the easement premises, but construction of the improvement shall be so conducted as not to unreasonably interfere with grantee's use of the easement premises during construction.[12]

b. Any subsurface use that does not unreasonably interfere with grantee's use of the easement premises.[13]

3. USE OF PARCELS 1 AND 2. As long as this easement grant remains in effect Parcel 2 shall not be used for other than commercial or residential purposes and no building other than one suited only for commercial or residence purposes shall be constructed thereon.[14]

4. ADDITIONS TO DOMINANT TENEMENT. Said easement is also appurtenant to any land that may hereafter come into common ownership with Parcel 2 aforesaid and that is contiguous to Parcel 2.[15] An area physically separated from Parcel 2 but having access thereto by means of public ways or private easements, rights or licenses is deemed to be contiguous to Parcel 2.

5. DIVISION OF DOMINANT TENEMENT. If Parcel 2 is hereafter divided into two parts by separation of ownership or by lease, both parts shall enjoy the benefit of the easement hereby created.[16] Division of the dominant tenement into more than two parts shall be deemed an unlawful increase of burden and use of the easement may be enjoined.

6. PARKING. Both parties covenant that vehicles shall not be parked on the easement premises except so long as may be reasonably necessary to load and unload.[17]

7. PAVING OF EASEMENT. Grantee covenants to promptly improve the easement premises with a concrete surface at least_____feet in width suitable for use by delivery trucks and[18] will at all times maintain same in good repair.[19]

8. WARRANTIES OF TITLE. Grantor warrants that he has good and indefeasible fee simple title to the easement premises, subject only to the following permitted title objections:[20]

(here list encumbrances)

9. TITLE INSURANCE AND ESCROW. Should grantee so desire, he may apply forthwith for a title insurance policy insuring the easement hereby granted and grantor will make available for inspection by the title company any evidence of title in his possession.[21]

10. RELOCATION OF EASEMENT. Grantor reserves the right to relocate the easement premises as follows.[22]

1. He shall first notify the grantee of the proposed relocation by mailing notice to the grantee at his last address furnished pursuant hereto showing the proposed relocation, probable commencement and completion dates, all by mailing same, postage prepaid, at least 30 days prior to commencement of relocation.

2. The easement premises shall be moved not more than_____feet from their present location.

3. Grantor shall improve the new easement premises with a concrete driveway similar to the one replaced, to be suitable for use by delivery trucks, with connections at the termini of the driveway to be replaced, and reasonably convenient for the uses then existing on Parcel 2.

4. At the completion of the work, grantor shall record an easement grant in recordable form granting the new easement to the grantee, shall cause the same to be delivered to the grantee, and shall furnish the grantee evidence of title satisfactory to the grantee showing an unencumbered easement in such grantee, whereupon the change in location of the easement

premises shall become effective, and appropriate releases of the prior location shall be executed in recordable form and exchanged between the parties hereto, their successors or assigns.

11. RUNNING OF BENEFITS AND BURDENS. All provisions of this instrument, including the benefits and burdens, run with the land and are binding upon and enure to the heirs, assigns, successors, tenants and personal representatives of the parties hereto.[23]

12. TERMINATION OF COVENANT LIABILITY. Whenever a transfer of ownership of either parcel takes place, liability of the transferor for breach of covenant occurring thereafter automatically terminates, except that the grantor herein remains liable for breaches of covenants of title set forth in Paragraph 8.[24]

13. ATTORNEY'S FEES. Either party may enforce this instrument by appropriate action and should he prevail in such litigation, he shall recover as part of his costs a reasonable attorney's fee.[25]

14. CONSTRUCTION. The rule of strict construction does not apply to this grant. This grant shall be given a reasonable construction so that the intention of the parties to confer a commercially usable right of enjoyment on the grantee is carried out.

15. NOTICE. Grantor's address is_____ _____and grantee's address is _____ _____. Either party may lodge written notice of change of address with the other. All notices shall be sent by U.S. mail to the addresses provided for in this paragraph and shall be deemed given when placed in the mail. The affidavit of the person depositing the notice in the U. S. Post Office receptable shall be evidence of such mailing.

16. RELEASE OF EASEMENT. The grantee herein may terminate this instrument by recording a release in recordable form with directions for delivery of same or to grantor at his last address given pursuant hereto whereupon all rights duties, and liabilities hereby created shall terminate. For convenience such instrument may run to "the owner or owners and parties interested" in Parcel 1.[26]

17. JOINDER OF SPOUSE. _____ spouse of grantor joins herein for the purpose of releasing dower, homestead and all other marital rights, all of which are waived with respect to this easement.[27]

In witness whereof the grantor, his spouse and the grantee[28] have hereunto set their hands and seals this _____day of_____A.D. 19_____.

_____(Seal)
_____(Seal)
_____(Seal)

FOOTNOTES

1. It is not necessary to describe the dominant tenement in the easement grant. The area intended to be served can be gathered from the attendant circumstances. However, as appears from the General Observations, questions often arise. Hence it is good draftsmanship to describe the dominant tenement.

2. Often enough R owning Blackacre, grants to E an easement of ingress and egress over "Blackacre." Obviously it was never the intention of the parties that E would roam over all of Blackacre. The courts have devised a means of pinning down the easement area. 110 ALR 174. But to fail to pinpoint the easement premises is wretched draftsmanship.

3. Since easements existed long before the doctrine of consideration was invented, no recital of consideration is necessary. Occasional decisions nevertheless mention the presence of consideration. It seems best to recite consideration.

4. Words of grant are necessary according to a few decisions. This corresponds to the requirement of words of conveyance in a deed. The numerous decisions holding that easements can be created by contract are obvious proof that the requirement is less formal in easement drafting.

5. There are many statutes to the effect that words of heirship are not necessary to create a fee simple by deed. Easements are rarely mentioned, but by analogy the word "heirs" is not needed to create a permanent easement. But there are some court decisions saying that an easement endures only for the life of the grantor unless words of heirship are included. *Elwell v. Miner*, 174 NE2d 43.

6. An easement appurtenant need not be so characterized. Normally the courts will strain to find the easement is appurtenant rather than in gross. Good draftsmanship requires that the proper label be affixed.

7. The same estates exist in easements as exist in corporeal hereditaments. Thus, you can have an easement in fee simple, for life, for years, etc. *Texas Co. v. O. Meara*, 377 Ill. 144, 36 NE2nd 256, 154 ALR5. It is not the practice to use the estates terminology. Instead of talking of an easement *in fee simple*, we talk of a *perpetual easement*.

8. There is no such thing as a plain "easement." It must be for ingress and egress, for light and air, or for some other specific purpose.

9. The opening sentence of paragraph 2 is a statement of existing law. 3 ALR3d 1287. However, it forces the parties to think about changes that will take place in the future. If the dominant owner tears down his store and erects an industrial plant, will the servient owner be unhappy with this turn of events? If he will be, he must provide against this.

10. This is also a statement of existing law. 3 ALR3d 1278. Again the existence of litigation indicates the need for covering this point.

11. An easement that excludes the servient owner from use of the easement premises is extremely rare. *Etz v. Morrow*, 72 Ariz. 228, 233 P2d 442. An exception is the railroad easement, which is exclusive by its very nature. But dominant owners always seem surprised when they hear the rule stated. Hence it belongs in the grant.

12. This is also a statement of existing law. *Sakansky v. Wein*, 86 N.H. 337, 169A 1. *Minneapolis Athletic Club v. Cohler*, 177 NW2d 786 (Minn. 1970). The presence of litigation indicates it is not generally understood. Of course, there are easements one cannot build over, such as a pipeline easement. *Tide Water Pipe Co. v. Blair Holding Co.*, 42 N.J. 591; 202 A2d 405, 28 ALR2d 626. This would block the dominant owner's efforts to repair a break. For similar reasons the servient owner cannot put a lake over a pipeline easement. *Sumrall v. United Gas Pipeline Co.*, 97 So2d 914.

13. Also a statement of existing law. *E.M. & S.W. R.R. v. Sims*, 228 Ill. 9, 81 NE 782.

14. The dominant owner can change the nature of the use unless the easement grant restricts this right.

15. The dominant tenement is determined at the time the easement is created. Land acquired by the dominant owner thereafter is non-dominant land. It cannot use the easement. *Weathers v. Icoa Life Ins. Co.*, 460 P2d 361 (Ore. 1969). This is the most common error in easement drafting and the most costly. Of course, one can easily draft around the problem. You can make the additions to the *dominant tenement clause* much broader, if you wish. For example:

"Said easement is appurtenant to any land in the Northwest quarter of Section 34 that may subsequently come into common ownership with said dominant tenement."

In passing, attention is drawn to the fact that by the modern rule contiguity of the dominant tenement to the easement premises is not required. *Allendorf v. Daly*, 6 Ill. 2d 577, 129 NE2d 673.

16. The easement runs in favor of all parts, where the dominant tenement is later divided. 10 ALR3d 960. There are some limits, however, which the courts have not clearly defined. 10 ALR3d 968. This grant sharply limits the right to divide.

17. This again is a statement of existing law. 37 ALR2d 944. Litigation over parking suggests the need to spell this out.

18. In the absence of such a clause there is no duty on the dominant owner to pave the way.

19. The dominant owner has the right, though not the duty, to repair. Kratovil, *Real Estate Law* (5th ed 1969) §37. *But see Lynch v. Keck*, 263 NE2d 176 (Ind. 1970).

20. Warranties of title exist only as expressly included in the grant.

21. Where beneficial use of his land by the dominant owner depends on dependable access via the easement, he needs title insurance on the easement as much as he needs title insurance on the land.

22. The servient owner has no right to relocate the easement unless the easement grant confers this right. An awkwardly located easement can virtually destroy the value of industrial or commercial property.

23. Covenants running with the land can be included in the easement grant. An easement grant creates the requisite privity of estate.

24. The original covenantor remains liable even after he has disposed of his land. This clause reverses the rule.

25. A litigant pays his own attorney unless the contract provides otherwise.

26. The dominant owner may wish to get rid of his covenant liability by terminating the easement when other means of ingress have been acquired. This form of clause eliminates the need for a title search of the servient tenement to get the names of the parties to whom the release is to run.

27. The authorities are divided as to the need for a spouse to join. *See, e. g.* Arkansas *State Highway Comm. v. Marlar*, 447 SW2d 329 (Ark. 1969).

28. Since covenants by the grantee are included it is appropriate for all parties to sign and acknowledge this document. Of course, it should also be recorded.

wall for advertising signs. 2 ALR2d 1138, 69 CJS *Party Walls* § 15(e). (4) As a rule, if I wish to demolish my building on my side of the party wall, I may do so, but I must leave the wall intact for the support of your building. *Ceno Theater Co.* v. *B/G Sandwich Shops,* 24 F2d 31 (6th Cir. 1928).

4.05(d) Mortgages

When *R* owns Lots 1 and 2 and mortgages Lot 1 to *E,* he may, at *E*'s insistence, include in the mortgage a grant of easement over part of Lot 2. Such a clause may run somewhat as follows:

> And as further security for payment of the debt above described, the mortgagor mortgages and grants to the mortgagee, his heirs and assigns, as an easement appurtenant to Lot 1 aforesaid, a perpetual easement for ingress and egress over and across the south ten feet of Lot 2 in the subdivision aforesaid.

Where *R* owns Lots 1 and 2 and is mortgaging Lot 1 to *E, R* may wish to reserve, for the benefit of Lot 2, an easement over part of Lot 1. In such case, an appropriate clause of reservation may be included in the mortgage.

The foregoing illustrations show how a *mortgage can create an easement.* When such a mortgage is foreclosed, ownership of the dominant and servient tenements passes into separate hands, and the real existence of the easement begins. Suppose, however, that *R* owns a lot that enjoys the benefit of a *previously created* easement. He mortgages the lot, and in the mortgage nothing is said concerning the easement. The mortgage is foreclosed. The purchaser at the foreclosure sale enjoys the benefit of the easement, for *an appurtenant easement runs with the land even though it is not mentioned in the mortgage or in the foreclosure proceedings.* 38 Cal. L. Rev. 426.

Also, an easement acquired by a mortgagor subsequent to the giving of a mortgage automatically comes under the lien of the mortgage and passes to the purchaser at any mortgage foreclosure sale. *First Nat. Bank* v. *Smith,* 284 Mich. 579, 280 NW 57, 116 ALR 1074 (1938).

The effect of a mortgage on an easement and vice versa depends on which is *prior in time. Prior in time is prior in right.*

> **EXAMPLE:** Owner mortgages Lot 1 to Lender in 1971. The mortgage is recorded and the mortgage funds are paid to Owner, thus creating a valid mortgage. In 1972, Owner gives his neighbor an easement of access over Lot 1. In 1973, Lender forecloses his mortgage. The mortgage being *prior in time* to the easement was *prior in right.* The foreclosure destroys the easement. *Kling* v. *Ghilarducci,* 3 Ill.2d 455, 121 NE2d 752 (1954).

> **EXAMPLE:** Owner gives Neighbor an easement of access over Owner's Lot 1 in 1971. It is recorded. In 1972, Owner mortgages the lot to Lender. Later, the mortgage is foreclosed. The easement being *prior in time* is *prior in right* and is not affected by foreclosure of the mortgage. 46 ALR2d 1197.

Lay persons are at times disturbed by the notion that foreclosure of a mortgage can destroy an easement that was bought and paid for. It must be remembered that the law assumes that every sensible person has the title searched before he spends a penny. The title search would reveal the mortgage. One who buys an easement in the face of a prior recorded mortgage does so with his eyes wide open and deserves no sympathy. He should have received the mortgagee's subordination to the easement.

4.05(e)   Implied grant or reservation

Often when the owner of two tracts of land sells or mortgages one of them, there is no mention at all of easements, and yet as a result of the transaction an easement is created. In such cases, the situation of the land is such that the courts feel the parties intended to create an easement even though they did not actually say so. Such easements are called *implied easements.* They are created by *implied grant* and *implied reservation.* When a landowner uses one part of his land for the benefit of another part, and this use is such that, if the parts were owned by different persons, the right to make such a use would constitute an easement, then upon a sale of either of such parts an implied easement is created. *Cheney* v. *Miller,* 485 P2d 1218 (Ore. 1971).

> **EXAMPLE:** Owner owned two adjoining lots, on each of which there was a two-story building. The buildings were separated by a partition wall. The stairway to the second floor was located entirely on one lot, and there were doors through the partition wall by which occupants of the second floor on the other lot reached their apartments. Owner sold and conveyed the lot on which the stairway was located to Buyer. There was an implied reservation of an easement for the use of the stairway, and Owner could continue to use such stairway even though the deed made no mention whatever of any easement. If Owner had instead sold Buyer the lot that had no stairway and had retained the lot on which the stairway was located, there would have been an implied grant of an easement to Buyer to use such stairway. *Powers* v. *Heffernan,* 233 Ill. 597, 84 NE 661 (1908).

4.05(e)(1)   Requirements for creation of implied easement

The following are the requirements for the creation of an implied easement:

> 1. The prior use of one part of the land for the benefit of the other part must have been apparent and obvious. That is, the use must have been such that it would have been disclosed on a reasonable inspection of the premises. The theory is that the parties intended to continue the obvious arrangements existing when the sale took place. *Burns Mfg. Co.* v. *Boehm,* 356 A2d 763 (Pa. 1975).

> **EXAMPLE:** Suppose a man owns Lots 1 and 2, and sewage from his house on Lot 1 drains through an underground pipe running across Lot 2. There is a catch basin on Lot 2. If *A* buys Lot 2, the presence of the catch basin with a visible cov-

er on the surface of the ground will give *A* notice and thereby create an implied easement for drainage over Lot 2. 58 ALR 824.

Note that we start with a situation where one person owns two or more adjoining tracts of land. He uses one tract for the benefit of the other. This use would be considered an easement if the lands were owned separately. For this reason, the arrangement is often said to create "quasi-easements" or "almost easements"—things that resemble easements. Remember that, at this point, *true* easements do not exist because an easement connotes rights of one person in the land of another person.

2. The prior use must have been continuous.

EXAMPLE: A visible and necessary drain is thought to be continuous in its operation. Usually a permanent and clearly defined way is thought of as continuous. Thus, where *A* owned two adjoining lots and constructed a driveway on the common boundary line between the lots and thereafter sold one of the lots to *B,* an implied easement was created for use of the driveway as a common or party driveway. *Walters* v. *Gadde,* 390 Ill. 518, 62 NE2d 439 (1945); *Gorman* v. *Overmyer,* 199 Okla. 451, 190 P2d 477 (1947). Another example would be a party wall, and still another would be a well on the boundary line serving two adjoining properties. *Frantz* v. *Collins,* 21 Ill.2d 446, 173 NE2d 437 (1961).

3. The easement must be necessary. That is, the easement must be highly convenient and beneficial to the property. The test of whether or not an easement is necessary is this: Can a substitute for this easement be obtained without unreasonable expense and trouble? If it cannot, the easement is necessary.

4. The ownership of the two tracts of land must be in one person when the use commences and become separated thereafter, so that one person owns the benefited tract and someone else owns the burdened tract. 94 ALR3d 502. This is obvious, for as long as one man owns both tracts there can be no easement. By definition, an easement is a right in another's property. The manner in which the separation of ownership takes place is immaterial. Usually it takes place when the original owner sells either the benefited or the burdened tract to another person, but any other manner of separating the ownership will do. For example, if the owner of two such tracts places a mortgage on one of them, and such mortgage is later foreclosed, the ownership of the two tracts passes into different hands and an implied easement is created. *Liberty Bank* v. *Lux,* 378 Ill. 329, 38 NE2d 6 (1941). Or if the owner of two such tracts dies, leaving a will by which he gives one tract to *A* and the other to *B,* an implied easement will be created. *Hoepker* v. *Hoepker,* 309 Ill. 407, 141 NE 159 (1923). Or if a tract of land is divided up by a partition suit, an implied easement may be created. *Deisenroth* v. *Dabe,* 7 Ill.2d 340, 131 NE2d 17 (1955).

Suppose Landlord rents Tenant an apartment, office, or store. Naturally Tenant will have implied easements to use the stairways, elevators, fire escapes, porches, bathrooms, etc., that are used in common by the tenants. 24 ALR2d 123. It is true that the lease does not create a separation of ownership, but it puts lawful possession into two or more different persons, and that answers the purpose of the rule.

As is evident, all implied easements are appurtenant easements.

4.05(e)(2)   An easement can be implied from the circumstances

> **EXAMPLE:**   Owner owns a lot having lake frontage and a lot landward of the beach lot. He sells the landward lot to Buyer with an easement for use of the beach. An easement will be implied to cross the beach lot to reach the beach. *Ames* v. *Prodon,* 60 Cal. Reptr 183 (1967).

4.05(e)(3)   Implied easements—common scheme or plan

It has been pointed out that where two adjoining owners erect buildings with a party wall straddling the boundary line an easement is created even though no written document exists. This idea can be carried a step further. Where two adjoining landowners engage in a scheme of common development that cannot exist without easements, easements exit.

> **EXAMPLE:**   Owner #1 owns Lot 1 and Owner #2 owns Lot 2 adjoining. By verbal agreement they erect buildings with an arcade of shops straddling the boundary line between the lots. Easements for the arcade now exist even though there is no written document. *Blakeney* v. *State,* 163 NE2d 69 (N.C. 1968).

> **EXAMPLE:**   Owner owns a large lot on which he erects row houses or town houses at right angles to the street. He sells off the town houses. Implied easements come into being for ingress, egress, sewer, water, electricity, etc. *Gilbert* v. *CT&T Co.,* 7 Ill.2d 492, 131 NE2d 1 (1956).

4.05(f)   Easement of necessity

When the owner of land sells a part thereof that has no outlet to a highway except over his remaining land or over the land of strangers, a right of way by necessity is created by implied grant over the remaining land of the seller.

Students seem fascinated by the easement of necessity. They tend to confuse it with the implied easement. The easement by necessity rests on the philosophy that land is a valuable community asset and none of it should be rendered landlocked and useless. To allow a tract of land to go to waste because it lacks access is an intolerable waste of a valuable resource. The implied easement, on the other hand, rests on the assumption that the obvious and beneficial use was intended to continue after ownership of the parcels was severed. For this reason, the courts require only that the use be highly beneficial for this also tends to establish that it was intended to continue.

In the case of an easement by necessity, a totally *new factual situation* is created. A tract of land, previously part of a larger parcel that had access to the outside world, is suddenly converted into an island with no means of access. The courts create a *new* means of access so that the island can remain useful. Easements by necessity are rare; implied easements are common.

4.05(g)   Prescription   *Prescription* is the acquiring of a right by lapse of time. An easement may be acquired by prescription. Usually, the period of time required for the acquisition of an easement by prescription is the same period as that required for the acquisition of ownership of land by adverse possession. This period, called the *prescriptive period,* varies from state to state. Periods of ten, fifteen, and twenty years are common.

> **EXAMPLE:** Owner owned a private alley and an apartment building adjoining thereto. Neighbor owned a neighboring apartment building. Without any permission from Owner, Neighbor's tenants constantly used Owner's private alley in order to enter their apartments from the rear. Whenever Owner's tenants parked their cars in the alley, Neighbor would call the police and have them put out. This continued for more than twenty years. Then Owner attempted to stop this use of the alley by Neighbor's tenants. It was held that he could not do so, since Neighbor had acquired an easement by prescription. *Rush* v. *Collins,* 366 Ill. 307, 8 NE2d 659 (1937).

> **EXAMPLE:** Owner owned a house and lot. He constructed a garage in the rear of the lot. Because the space adjoining his house was inadequate for a driveway, he constructed one that ran partly across Neighbor's adjoining land. This was done without seeking Neighbor's permission. Owner used this driveway for over twenty years. He has a prescriptive easement to continue to use it. *Nocera* v. *De Feo,* 340 Mass. 783, 164 NE2d 136 (1959).

The following are the requirements for the creation of an easement by prescription:

> 1. The use must be *adverse.* If it is under permission or consent of the owner, the use is not adverse. There must be such an invasion of the landowner's rights as would entitle him to maintain a suit against the intruder. If the use by me of my neighbor's land is, on its face, permitted by my neighbor as a matter of neighborly accommodation, the use is not adverse or hostile.

> **EXAMPLE:** Owner had a driveway running to his garage in the rear of his house, Neighbor often used this driveway to get his car into his backyard. He never sought Owner's permission, although they were good friends. This use will not ripen into a prescriptive easement. It is, on its face, a matter of neighborly accommodation. *Stevenson* v. *Williams,* 188 Pa. Super. 49, 145 A2d 734 (1958).

> 2. The use must be *under claim of right,* in that there must be no recognition of the right of the landowner to stop the use.

3. The use must be *visible, open,* and *notorious,* so that the landowner is bound to learn of it if he keeps himself well informed about his property.

EXAMPLE: The secret placing of a drainpipe in a wooded gully would not be considered notorious.

4. The use *must not be merely as a member of the public.* The use by the claimant of the easement must be sufficiently exclusive to give notice of his *individual* claim of right.

5. The use must be *continuous* and *uninterrupted* for the required period of time. That is, the easement must be exercised whenever there is any necessity therefore, and the use must be of such frequency as to apprise the landowner of the right being claimed against him.

EXAMPLE: Occasional entries upon a neighbor's land, for example, to put up screens or storm windows, to paint a wall, to trim a hedge, or to clean gutters, are not such continuous use as will ever ripen into a prescriptive easement. *Romans* v. *Nadler,* 217 Minn. 174, 14 NW2d 482 (1944).

It is not necessary that the adverse use be that of one person only.

EXAMPLE: In Illinois the prescriptive period is twenty years. Suppose that *A* and *B* are neighbors. *A* builds a driveway over *B*'s land without *B*'s permission. He uses it for five years. *A* sells his land to *C,* who also uses the driveway for five years. *C* sells to *D,* who uses the driveway for ten years. Now *D* has a prescriptive easement. The prescriptive uses that *A, C,* and *D* made can be *tacked,* that is, added together to make up the required twenty years. 171 ALR 1278. Also, since the easement was used for the benefit of a tract of land, it is an easement appurtenant and will thereafter run with the land so benefited. 171 ALR 1278.

Nearly all prescriptive easements are appurtenant easements.

Where an easement is acquired by prescription or any other means, the easement owner automatically acquires as rights incidental to the easement all rights needed for the useful enjoyment of the easement.

EXAMPLE: *A* and *B* owned adjoining lots 7 and 8. *A* erected a three-story building on Lot 7. He attached a fire escape to his building on Lot 7. It extended over the space above Lot 8. As is customary, the lowest member of the fire escape extended in a horizontal direction, hinged in such a fashion that it could be lowered to the ground level of Lot 8 in case of fire. After twenty years, *B* threatened to build under this horizontal member. The court held that *A*'s prescriptive easement included, as a right incidental to his right to maintain the fire escape, a right to lower this horizontal member into an unimproved area beneath. *Poulos* v. *Hill,* 401 Ill. 204, 81 NE2d854 (1948).

4.05(g)(1) Party driveways

Suppose you and I own adjoining lots, each with a house on it, and pursuant to a verbal agreement we build a party driveway, straddling the boundary line between our lots and serving our garages in the rear of our lots. Each of us uses this driveway continuously for the required period of time. Most courts hold that a party driveway easement has been created by prescription. 98 ALR 1096. This is quite a legal oddity, for obviously such common use is permissive, not adverse. Yet to prevent injustice courts allow prescriptive easements to be created by such use. *Peterson* v. *Corrubia,* 21 Ill.2d 525, 173 NE2d 499 (1975); 27 ALR2d 332.

4.05(g)(2) State laws

State laws have been enacted, as in Illinois, that prevent the creation of an easement by prescription if the landowner posts signs forbidding use of his land. This relieves the landowner of making periodic inspections of his vacant land to see if strangers are using it.

4.05(g)(3) Public highways

When the public has used a privately owned strip of land for the purpose of passage for the required period of time, courts often hold that an easement for a public highway has been created by prescription.

4.05(h) Creation of easement by condemnation

Although in some states laws provide that complete ownership of the land may be acquired by condemnation, the general rule is that where land is taken by condemnation for a street, highway, railroad right of way, or telephone or electric power line the taker acquires only an easement. All such easements are easements in gross.

> **EXAMPLE:** City wishes to open a street across Owner's land, but Owner is unwilling to sell. City files a condemnation suit against Owner, and a judgment is entered fixing the full market value of the strip to be taken for the opening of the street. City pays this amount into court. Although City pays the full market value of the strip, it acquires only an easement thereover, and Owner remains the owner subject to the easement. Thus Owner may construct subvaults beneath the street without any liability to City for payment of rent.

4.05(i) Sale by reference to plat

Where a landowner subdivides his land into lots, blocks, streets, and alleys and thereafter sells lots in the subdivision, each purchaser of a lot automatically acquires an easement of passage over the streets and alleys shown on the plat or map of the subdivision, even though the deed to the lot makes no mention whatever of such right. Such a private easement becomes important where the subdivider attempts to close up a street or alley before the public has acquired the right to insist that such street or alley remain open. The lot owners are in a position to keep the street open by virtue of their easement rights, even though the street never becomes a public street. 7ALR2d 607.

The plat also gives the city rights in the dedicated streets and public rights. In some instances the city acquires full ownership of the dedicated streets. In other cases it acquires only an easement. 11 ALR2d 549.

4.05(j) Easement by estoppel

There are other instances of the creation of an easement by *estoppel.*

EXAMPLE: Owner owns sewer and water pipe in a street running past his house and other vacant land he owns. Owner makes a deed of a vacant lot to Buyer but nothing is said about the sewer and water pipes. Buyer builds a house and Owner without objection watches Buyer tie into the sewer and water pipes. An easement to use the sewer and water service has been created by estoppel. *Monroe Bowling Lanes* v. *Woodfield Livestock Sales,* 244 NE2d 762 (Ohio 1969).

EXAMPLE: Corporation leased a co-op apartment in its apartment building to Tenant. Corporation had a plat in its office, showing a recreation area with swimming pool adjoining the building, and its agent always referred to this recreation area when making his sales pitch on apartments. An easement by *estoppel* has been created. Tenant can use the recreation area. *Hirlinger* v. *Stelzer,* 222 So2d 237 (Fla. 1969).

4.05(k) Declaration of easements

Easements are used so extensively in the town house, condominium, and planned unit development that they are physically separated from the deeds and mortgages and incorporated in a separate document. As a matter of convenience, this document also includes building restrictions, liens, and covenants and is called a Declaration of Restrictions, Easements, Liens, and Covenants.

4.06 Unlocated easements and relocation

If R owns a large tract of land and grants to E an easement thereover, manifestly it is not R's entire tract that comprises the servient tenement, for it is not intended that E shall wander aimlessly over the premises. It is, rather, the intention of the parties that some small part of the tract shall become the easement tract. The parties have simply failed to specify the precise location of the easement. In such cases, the owner of the servient tenement has, in the first instance, the right to designate the location of the easement, provided he exercises such right in a reasonable manner, having regard to the suitability and convenience of the way to the rights and interests of the owner of the dominant tenement. If the owner of the servient tenement fails or refuses to locate the way, the owner of the dominant tenement acquires the right to make his own selection of a location, having due regard to the interests, rights, and conveniences of the other party. 110 ALR 174. Court action may be necessary if the parties cannot agree. Disputes and litigation can be avoided through the simple device of employing a surveyor to locate and monument the easement tract on the ground, whereupon a legal description can be prepared and included in the easement grant.

4.06(a)   Pipeline easements   Most unlocated easements are pipeline easements. Pipelines extend over many miles of ground. The pipeline companies send out *right-of-way* crews to acquire the easements. Once a member of such a crew has determined the ownership of a farm, he whips out a simple form which the farmer and *spouse* sign. It gives the pipeline company an easement over the entire farm. This is perfectly valid. *Collins* v. *Slocum,* 284 So2d 98 (La. 1973).

A land developer who buys a farm for development cannot live with an unlocated easement.

> **SUGGESTION:**   The developer should contact the pipeline company and purchase a release of the easement over all of the farm except the land through which the pipeline runs. Homebuyers cannot have pipelines running under homes. Record the release of the easement. Usually no problem is presented. The pipeline company keeps the pipeline near the highway to facilitate repair. If there is a mortgage on the pipeline, that is also released except as to the line of the pipe.

Once a pipeline has been installed in a pipeline easement, some courts hold that additional pipes or a larger pipe cannot be installed. *Winslow* v. *City of Vallejo,* 148 Cal. 723, 84 P 191 (1906). The far better rule is precisely to the contrary. *Standard Oil Co.* v. *Buchi,* 72 N.J.Eq. 492, 66 A 427 (1907), 17 Yale L. J. 200, *Weaver* v. *Natural Gas Pipeline Co.,* 27 Ill.2d 48, 188 NE2d 18 (1963). This problem should be covered in the grant.

Once an easement has been placed in location or its location fixed by the easement grant, its location cannot be changed without the consent of the easement owner.

> **EXAMPLE:**   Owner owns two lots. Lot 1 abuts on a highway. He sells Lot 2 to Buyer, simultaneously granting an easement of ingress and egress to the highway. The easement runs through the middle of Lot 1, rendering it unusable. Owner has no right to change the location of the easement. *Sedillo Title Cty. Inc.* v. *Wagner,* 457 P2d 361 (N.M. 1969).

But the easement can be relocated if both parties acquiesce, even without a written document.

> **EXAMPLE:**   In the last example, suppose Owner and Buyer verbally agree on relocation. Owner blacktops a new driveway along the edge of Lot 1 and the old drive is torn up. The easement has been relocated by acquiescence. 80 ALR2d 743.

Pipeline easements will grow in importance as America seeks self-sufficiency in the production of oil and gas. Land men for the pipeline companies seek out the farmers whose land will be crossed by new pipelines. Often they induce a farmer to sign a brief document giving the pipeline company the right to build a line across his farm. This, of course, is an easement in gross. When a land developer later seeks to acquire the farm for development purposes, he will find this easement crossing "the farm." The developer's lawyer will induce the pipeline company to release the easement except as to the narrow strip actually occupied by the pipe. Pipeline companies are cooperative in this regard. Often the pipeline company has a blanket mortgage covering the entire pipeline. This mortgage must be released except as to the narrow strip where the pipe is located. The big banks that hold these mortgages are likewise cooperative. The portion of the farm that is to be developed is cleared of the pipeline easement by appropriate releases.

4.07 Complex easements

Today complex easements are employed in a number of situations.

NEW DIRECTIONS: It is almost commonplace today to find a single multi-story building divided into two ownerships. The lower portion, devoted, let us say, to office building use is owned by *A*. The upper portion, devoted to apartment purposes, is owned by *B*. *B* may even choose to divide his apartment area into condominium ownership so that each apartment is separately owned. Such, indeed, is the situation in the case of the John Hancock Building in Chicago. The structural members of the bottom building support the upper building. Elevator shafts serving the upper building travel through the lower building. Heating, ventilating, and air-conditioning ducts, as well as water and utilities, travel through both buildings. A very lengthy Easement and Operating Agreement is prepared. There are problems, to be sure, but they are all capable of solution.

4.08 Structure easement— easement through structure

Where an easement is created in a *structure* without creating any interest in the land, ordinarily destruction of the structure destroys the easement.

EXAMPLE: Owner owned Lot 1 on which he erected a two-flat residence. When the city passed an ordinance requiring second-story apartments to have two exits, Owner acquired from Neighbor the right to make an opening into Neighbor's building, which was flush against Owner's building, and to use Neighbor's stairway as the second exit. Neighbor's building was destroyed by fire. The easement is extinguished. 154 ALR 82.

4.08(a) Easement in favor of structure

If an easement is created *in favor of* a structure only, destruction of the structure terminates the easement.

EXAMPLE: *X* and *Y* were neighbors. Intending to build a stable for his riding horse, *X* purchased from *Y driveway rights* over *Y*'s land to and from the *stable* to be erected on the rear of *X*'s land. Ultimately the stable was destroyed by fire. The easement is gone. 2 Thompson, *Real Property* 764, 766 (perm. ed.).

4.09   Right to profits of the soil

An easement does not confer on the owner thereof any right to the profits of the soil, such as oil, hay, coal, or minerals.

EXAMPLE: County acquired a highway over Owner's land by condemnation. County has no right to drill oil wells on the land thus acquired, for it has only an easement for road purposes.

It is the landowner whose land is subject to the easement who has the right to oil, minerals, and other profits of the soil.

EXAMPLE: Landowner whose land is subject to an easement for railroad right-of-way purposes may tunnel under the railroad right of way and mine the coal thereunder.

4.10   Use of easement premises—dominant and servient tenements

An easement appurtenant can be used only for the benefit of the dominant tenement. It may not be used for the benefit of any other tract of land. The dominant tenement is the land intended to be benefited *at the time the easement was created.* Land acquired by the owner of the dominant tenement after the creation of the easement has no right to the use of easement. It is nondominant land.

EXAMPLE: Owner owned Lot 1. There was an easement appurtenant in favor of Lot 1 to use a spur or switch track over land adjoining Lot 1 to the west. Owner thereafter bought Lot 2, which adjoined Lot 1 to the east, and erected a power-house on Lot 2. It was held that the switch track could not be used to service the powerhouse since the switch track easement was appurtenant only to Lot 1. *Goodwillie Co.* v. *Commonwealth Co.,* 241 Ill. 42, 89 NE 272 (1909); *Ogle* v. *Trotter,* 495 SW2d 558 (Tenn. 1973). *College Inns.* v. *Cully,* 460 P2d 360 (Ore. 1969).

Particularly in the case of industrial easements, it is well to keep in mind at the time easement is created that the dominant owner may later wish to acquire other neighboring land for plant expansion. The easement grant should provide that such subsequently acquired property shall enjoy the benefit of the easement. For example, suppose that the dominant tenement happens to fall in Government Section 34, then let the easement grant provide as follows:

SUGGESTED FORM: Said easement is also appurtenant to any land in said Section 34 that may subsequently come into common ownership with said dominant tenement.

If the dominant tenement is divided, the easement runs in favor of each part into which it is divided. 10 ALR3d 960.

EXAMPLE: Owner, owning the bed of a lake and the land surrounding the lake, sells Buyer a lot that does not have lake frontage. The deed includes an easement of access to the lake and a right to use the lake for recreation. Buyer sells half his lot to his brother, both parts abutting on the easement of access. Both Buyer and his brother can use the easements. There is some limit, not very clearly defined, on how far you can go with this. 10 ALR 3d 968. Suppose Buyer were to divide his lot into fifty lots. The courts might not permit use of the easements. This is an excessive *increase of burden. Crocker* v. *Advanced Science,* 268 A2d 844 (N.H. 1970).

Where an easement of ingress and egress is created by grant, it may be used by the easement owner for all reasonable purposes, and use is not restricted to such purposes as were reasonable at the date of the grant.

EXAMPLE: Use of the easement by automobiles will be permitted even though an easement was created when horse-drawn vehicles were in use. 3 ALR3d 1287.

With changing conditions more intensive use may be made of the easement than was contemplated at the time the easement was created.

EXAMPLE: At the time an easement of ingress and egress was created, the dominant tenement was occupied by a private dwelling. Later this dwelling was replaced by a hotel. It was held that the hotel could continue to use the easement. *White* v. *Grand Hotel* (1913) 1 Ch. 113.

However, where an easement is acquired by *prescription,* use of the easement after the prescriptive period has expired must remain pretty much the same as the use that took place during the prescriptive period.

If the width of an easement is fixed at the time of its creation, it will not grow wider even though conditions change.

EXAMPLE: In 1918 Owner granted Neighbor a ten-foot easement for ingress and egress. The fact that today's big trucks cannot use so narrow a way does not increase the size of the easement. *Feldstein* v. *Segall,* 198 Md. 285, 81 A2d 610 (1951).

On the other hand, if I grant you a ten-foot passage easement, I have no right to diminish it by placing pillars on other structures in the passageway. You have the right to use the full ten feet for passage. *Wurlitzer Co.* v. *State Bank,* 290 Ill. 72, 124 NE844 (1919).

If you have a driveway easement over my land, you can park to load and unload but cannot park overnight. 37 ALR2d 944. This does not mean, however, that the owner of an easement for ingress and egress has the *exclusive* right to use the surface of the land for that purpose. The landowner, since he remains the owner of the easement premises subject only to the prescribed rights of the easement owner, has the right to make any use of the easement tract that does not interfere with the easement. 52 ALR3d 9.

> **EXAMPLE:** In the case of an easement of ingress and egress, the landowner may travel over the easement tract as long as he does not interfere with the easement owner's right of travel. The landowner, indeed, may even erect structures or run power lines above the easement, so long as he leaves space at the surface adequate for travel by the easement owner. *Sakansky* v. *Wein,* 86 N.H. 337, 169 Atl. 1 (1933); *Cleveland Railway Co.* v. *Public Service Co.,* 380 Ill. 130, 43 NE2d 993 (1942). Or a landowner may tunnel and mine minerals beneath an easement for ingress and egress or build over a water pipe easement.

Since an easement is a right to use another's land for a special purpose only, the easement owner must use the easement premises only for that purpose for which the easement exists.

> **EXAMPLE:** Owner grants Neighbor an easement for ingress and egress over a part of Owner's land. Neighbor has no right to lay gas pipes in the easement premises. 3 ALR3d 1278.

4.11 Maintenance and repair of easement facilities

The fact that Owner gives Neighbor an easement over Owner's property imposes no duty on Owner to pave the easement tract, keep it in repair, or do anything at all for Neighbor's benefit. 169 ALR 1152.

> **EXAMPLE:** Owner gave Neighbor an easement to take water from a well on Owner's land. It was held that Owner was not obliged to operate the pump to furnish Neighbor's water even though that was the physical situation at the time the easement was created. *Gowing* v. *Lehmann,* 98 N.H. 414, 101 A2d 463 (1953).

Therefore if the parties agree that the owner of the burdened land is to have some affirmative duties, they must be spelled out in the easement grant.

Of course, the easement owner has the right to take all steps necessary to make this easement usable. For example, in an easement of ingress and egress the easement owner would have the right to repair or improve an existing road, to lay down a new road, to build bridges across streams, to trim encroaching trees and shrubs, to blast rocks, and otherwise to remove impediments, and so forth. 169 ALR 1147; 20 ALR3d 1026.

Also, where a private road is used by *both the* landowner and the easement owner, they must divide the cost of repairs in proportion to their use of the road, even though the easement agreement is silent on this score. *Stevens* v. *Bird-Jex Co.*, 81 Utah 355, 18 P2d 292 (1933).

If the easement tract is used only by the easement owner and falls into disrepair as a result of his neglect, he has no right to deviate from the prescribed way and travel over other land belonging to the landowner. *Dudgeon* v. *Bronson*, 159 Ind. 562, 64 NE 910 (1902). On the other hand, if the landowner obstructs the easement, the easement owner has the right to travel around the obstruction over other land belonging to the landowner.

4.12   Termination of easement

Easements may be terminated in the following ways:

1. When an easement has been created for a particular purpose, it ceases when the purpose ceases.

EXAMPLE: A party wall agreement ceases when both buildings are destroyed by fire, unless the party wall agreement provides otherwise. An easement for railroad purposes ends when the railroad tears up its tracks and discontinues service. 95 ALR2d 482.

2. When the owner of an easement becomes the owner of the land that is subject to the easement, the easement is extinguished by *merger.*

3. The owner of an easement may release his right to the owner of the land that is subject to the easement.

4. The owner of an easement may terminate it by abandonment. There must be an intention to abandon the easement and acts manifesting such intention.

4.12(a)   Tax sale

In some states a tax sale of the servient tenement extinguishes the easement. In others, it does not. 26 ALR2d 873. In many states, as in Illinois, the matter is governed by statutes that preserve the easement. See also *Arizona R.C.I.A. Lands Inc.*, v. *Arnsworth*, 515 P2d 335 (Ariz. App. 1973); *Fields* v. *District of Columbia*, 443 F2d 740 (D.C. Cir. 1971), citing Restatement of Property § 509 (2); 5 *Powell on Real Property* 225; Kratovil, *Tax Sales: Extinguishment of Easements, Building Restrictions and Covenants*, 19 Houst. L. Rev. 55 (1982).

4.13   Special types of easements

4.13(a)   Streets

Easements vary, of course, as to their scope.

EXAMPLE: Owner grants Neighbor an easement for ingress and egress. This easement cannot be used for installation of water pipes or electric conduits.

However, whenever a city has an easement for street purposes, the courts give this a very broad interpretation. The adjoining owners own the land constituting the street. But the city's easement permits the use of the street for transportation of all kinds, including transportation of electricity (electric poles) or transportation of messages (telegraph poles). Kratovil, *Easement Draftsmanship and Conveyancing*, 38 Cal. L. Rev. 426. The city usually grants to utility companies the right to install these poles. This right is called a *franchise*. So far as cable television is concerned, the CATV company would have to obtain a franchise from the city. But if it intends to fasten its cable to existing telegraph poles, it must also obtain a written agreement from the telegraph company.

In most, but not all, states, if a deed of land refers to an adjoining street or other way, it automatically creates an easement of access over the street or way if the grantor owns the land comprising the street or way. 46 ALR2d 461.

EXAMPLE: Owner owns Lot 1 in Block 1 in Chicago Heights and a strip of land east and adjoining known in the neighborhood as Holden Court. Holden Court is not a public street. He makes a deed to Buyer of part of Lot 1 described as "bounded on the east by Holden Court." This gives Buyer an easement right in Holden Court. This is sometimes called an *easement by estoppel*. 25 Am.Jur.2d 431. Obviously, this is a poor substitute for a properly planned easement grant.

4.13(b)   Scenic easements

As the population continues to explode, concern grows for the preservation of open spaces, especially for scenic treasures that remain in private ownership and offer tempting sites to land developers. Under recent legislation and court decisions the state may condemn or purchase a scenic easement that, in effect, forbids the landowner to build upon his land. The Federal Highway Beautification Act offers incentives to the state to create such easements. *Markham Advertising Co.* v. *State*, 439 P2d 248 (Wash. 1968).

EXAMPLE: Owner owns a stretch of rolling farm land through which a lovely river winds, abutting a highway that commands an excellent view of the scene. The state condemns Owner's right to build upon his farm and pays him compensation for depriving him of this right. He may continue to occupy and farm the land, but it will never be built upon. This right acquired by the state is called a *scenic easement. Kamrowski* v. *State,* 31 Wis.2d 256, 142 NW2d 793 (1966). The state has acquired the farmer's *"development rights."*

4.13(b)(1)   Scenic easements—income tax consequences

The grant of a scenic easement may generate federal income tax and real property tax benefits. A charitable contribution may be recognized for a gratuitous donation of open space or scenic easements in perpetuity without the acceptance of economic benefit to the donor. Rev. Rul. 73-339, 1973-2 C.B. 68. Of course, the recipient of the easement must be an entity, the contribution to which qualifies for charitable tax deductions.

The deduction will equal the difference in value between the value of the land prior to the grant and the value of the land after the grant. Since the land with the scenic easement imposed upon it is obviously worth less than the land without this restriction on development, the real property taxes may also be decreased.

4.13(c) Solar easements   England has a doctrine called *ancient lights*.

> **EXAMPLE:** Owner owns Lot 1 on which he has a house, which has been there for many years. Neighbor owns a vacant lot next door. In England, Neighbor would not be permitted to erect a high building on his lot that would cut off Owner's light.

In America, the situation is treated quite differently:

> **EXAMPLE:** Take the facts of the previous case. In America, Neighbor can build any building that is permitted by local law even if it cuts off Owner's sunlight.

> **EXAMPLE:** The Fountainbleu Hotel in Miami Beach added fourteen stories to its structure. This cast a shadow on the swimming pool of the nearby Eden Roc Hotel. The court held that the Eden Roc was without any legal remedy. *Fountainbleu Hotel Corp.* v. *Forty-Five Twenty-Five, Inc.,* 114 So2d 357 (Fla. 1959). See also *Blumberg,* v. *Weiss,* 17 A2d 823 (N.J. 1941); 1 Am.Jur.2d *Adjoining Landowners* 753.

Of course, if an action is prompted by pure spite, the law will provide a remedy.

> **EXAMPLE:** Owner owns a house, and Neighbor owns an adjoining vacant lot. They quarrel. Neighbor attempts to erect a wall for the sole purpose of blocking light and air from Owner's windows. The courts will stop this.

It goes without saying that the neighboring landowners are able to agree to the creation of such solar easements. See Kraemer, *Solar Law* (1978).

> **EXAMPLE:** Owner owns a lot on which he proposes to build a solar home. He approaches Neighbor. For a money consideration Neighbor grants Owner an easement that limits the height of any building Neighbor may build so that Owner's solar energy will not be obstructed. The easement is recorded. It is binding on Neighbor and all subsequent owners of his lot.

The energy crisis and resultant attention that solar energy has attracted has caused a legislative reaction toward the regulation of the creation of solar easements. While these laws vary from state to state, they frequently require that the description of the easement include the vertical and horizontal angles at which the solar easement extends over the servient tenement. See, e.g., Cal. Civ. Code § 801.5; McKinney's N.Y. Real Prop. L. § 335.b.

Also height restrictions ordinances are valid in proper cases.

EXAMPLE: *Village* zones an area for single-family dwellings and imposes reasonable height, side-line, and front-line restrictions, such that any lot owner can safely build a house utilizing solar energy. The ordinance is valid

---

REFERENCE: Myers, *The Common Law of Solar Access: An Insufficient Protection for Users of Solar Energy,* 6 Real Est. L. J. 320 (1978).

Also among the new laws being enacted are solar zoning ordinances. These ordinances create a zoning envelope. This is a cube of space in which a building may be erected on a lot in such a manner that the land adjoining to the south cannot be improved by a building that obstructs sunlight to the southern exposure of the building roof, where solar panels will be erected. 2 Solar Law Rep. 263 (1980).

4.13(d) Conservation easements

A number of state laws provide for the grant and donation by a landowner to some public body of a conservation easement over his land. Ill. Rev. Stat. Ch. 30, § 401. These conservation easements maintain the undeveloped state of the land to protect wildlife and natural resources. 12 Willamette L. J. 124. The landowners, after granting the easement, can continue to farm. *Ibid.* At times the statute, as in Illinois, contains a laundry list of uses that can be prohibited, e.g., dumping, removal of trees, erection of signs, etc. Or it may limit use of the land solely for nature trails or farming.

Such a donation is a charitable gift that qualifies for an income tax deduction. 16 Santa Clara L. Rev. 559; 12 Willamette L. J. 125. Also, the grant may reduce the local tax assessment, reducing the real estate taxes.

It is evident that the conservation easement closely resembles the scenic easement. The scenic easement seems to have more frequently been acquired by purchase or condemnation. The conservation easement has often been donated, with the tax advantages in mind.

At times the two concepts are lumped together and termed "Acquisition of Development Rights," 75 Harv. L. Rev. 1635; 23 U. of Miami L. Rev. 351. Or it may be called an "Open Space Easement." 16 Santa Clara L. Rev. 359.

All these devices are means of preserving open space for public benefit.

As is also evident, the preservation of open space has become an important goal of our time. Other methods are available, for example, coastal zoning, zoning land for agricultural purposes, and large-lot zoning. (See Ch. 26.) Use of the planned unit development is another method. (See Ch. 33.) Control of wetland development is still another method. (See Ch. 28.)

5 LAND DESCRIPTIONS

5.01 Legal descriptions Every deed, mortgage, or lease contains a description of the land involved. The purpose of such a description, obviously, is to fix the boundaries of the land intended to be sold, mortgaged, or leased. The description delineates a specific piece of land and cannot apply to any other. A street address is adequate for the purpose of guiding guests to your home or for mail delivery, but greater precision is needed to fix the exact point where your land ends and where your neighbor's begins. Hence, we have the legal description. Whenever you read a legal description, keep in mind that before the description had been written, some person, probably a land surveyor, went out and located on the land the boundaries of the tract of land involved. He then put into words directions for locating the lines he had traced on the land. These written directions are called a legal description of the land. Various methods have been devised for describing tracts of land.

5.01(a) Surveys In connection with any purchaser or mortgage of land it is a common practice to have the land surveyed. The survey serves a variety of purposes. It identifies on the ground the boundaries of the tract of land involved. This tells us, for example, whether the land has access to a street. Owners frequently build on a lot adjoining the land they own. Another disaster. It is important to determine if our building encroaches on a neighbor's land or if neighboring buildings encroach on our land. We must know if our buildings encroach on adjoining streets or alleys. Basement stores and parking space often intrude into adjoining streets. This requires examination of the city permit given for this purpose. Our building may violate setback lines established by city ordinances or private building restrictions. If the building is not plumb, it may extend into neighboring air space, which is disastrous. There may be subsurface problems, electric cables, drainage pipes, etc., unlawfully crossing our property. Neighboring doors or gates may open over our land. A telephone line may cross our land, necessitating relocation before building can begin.

Lawyers, title companies, FNMA, FHA, FHLMC, and others may have requirements concerning the survey. The surveyor should be one acceptable to these institutions.

5.02 Metes and bounds descriptions

Metes are measures of length, such as inches, feet, yards, and rods. *Bounds* are boundaries, both natural and artificial, such as streams or streets. In a *metes and bounds description,* the surveyor takes you by the hand, as it were, and leads you over the land. He starts at a well-marked point of beginning and follows the boundaries of the land until he returns once more to the starting point. Landmarks called *monuments* often mark the several corners of the tract. A monument may be a natural monument, such as tree or river, or an artificial monument, such as a fence, stake, wall, road, or railroad.

> **EXAMPLE:** A tract of land in Chicago, Cook County, Illinois, is described as follows, to wit: Beginning at a point in the east line of Mason Street one hundred feet north of the north line of Washington Street; running thence east on a line parallel to the north line of Washington Street 125 feet to the west line of an alley; thence north along the west line of said alley, twenty-five feet; thence west on a line parallel to the north line of Washington Street, 125 feet to the east line of Mason Street; thence south along the east line of Mason Street, twenty-five feet to the place of beginning.

The earliest descriptions in history were metes and bounds descriptions. All property in the thirteen original colonies of the United States was originally described by metes and bounds, the descriptions usually running from the mouth of a stream, or from a tree or a stump.

5.03 The Government Survey

By the treaty with England at the end of the Revolutionary War, the United States became the owner of the vast Northwest Territory, consisting of the present states of Illinois, Indiana, Ohio, Michigan, and Wisconsin. The end of the war found the United States heavily burdened with debts incurred during the war. It was decided that the new land should be sold and the proceeds used to retire the national debt. However, in selling the land to settlers, metes and bounds descriptions could not be used, for the new land was an untrodden wilderness. Hence some new system of describing land was needed. The system so devised was the rectangular system of land surveys, known as the Government Survey. Under this system, whenever a district, such as part of a state, was ready for private ownership, the government arranged for a survey of the land to be made. To begin a survey of this character, it is necessary to have some substantial landmark from which a start may be made. A place that can readily be referred to, such as the mouth of a river, is usually selected. From such a point, a line is run due north to the margin of the district to be surveyed. This first north and south line is called a *prime meridian,* or *principal meridian.* Some principal meridians have been numbered, such as the First Principal Meridian, which runs north from the mouth of the Great Miami River on the boundary between Ohio and Indiana and which governs the surveys of public lands in Ohio. Others have been named, as the Tallahassee Meridian, the Mount Diablo Meridian, the Humboldt Meridian, and the San Bernardino Meridian.

An east and west line is run intersecting the principal meridians at some prominent point. This line is called the *base line.* Both north and south of the base line, additional east and west lines are run at intervals of twenty-four miles.

Since it is the object of the survey to create a huge checkerboard of identical squares covering the entire tract to be surveyed, it is plain that many north and south lines are needed. Owing to the curvature of the earth's surface, however, all true north and south lines converge as they approach the North Pole. This is obvious, since no matter how far apart two north and south lines are at the equator, they must meet at the North Pole. Hence if continuous north and south lines were to be used in the survey, it is clear that because of the convergence of the north and south lines the squares thus formed would grow narrower and narrower as the surveyors worked north. Now this is an imperfection that cannot be altogether eliminated. However, it can be minimized in the following manner: Along the base line, both east and west of the principal meridian, and at intervals of twenty-four miles, lines running due north are run. These are called *guide meridians.* But they are run only as far north as the next *correction line,* i.e., a distance of twenty-four miles. Then new intervals of twenty-four miles are measured off along this correction line, and a new series of guide meridians based on these new intervals is run for another twenty-four miles. This process is repeated until the boundaries of the tract are reached. Similar guide meridians are run based on the correction lines lying south of the base line.

Thus the district surveyed is divided into tracts approximately twenty-four miles square. These tracts are further divided into parts six miles on each side. These smaller parts are called *townships.*

Each row, or tier, of townships running north and south is called a *range.* The first row east of the principal meridian is referred to as *Range 1 East* of that meridian. Thus, the first row of townships east of the Third Principal Meridian is referred to as *Range 1 East of the Third Principal Meridian.* The row of townships next adjoining to the east is called *Range 2 East of the Third Principal Meridian,* and so on. Each row or tier of townships running east and west is identified by the number of townships intervening between it and the base line. Thus, a township in the first row north of the base line is called *Township 1 North.* The township next adjoining to the north is called *Township 2 North,* and so on. To identify a township completely, both the range number and the township number must be given, as *Township 40 North, Range 13, East of the Third Principal Meridian.* The township thus identified is in the fortieth row north of the base line and in the thirteenth row east of the Third Principal Meridian. Such a description is often abbreviated, and becomes *T. 40 N., R. 13 E. of the 3d P.M.*

Each township is divided into thirty-six tracts, each approximately one mile square. These tracts are called *sections.* The sections in a township are numbered from one to thirty-six, always commencing with the section in the northeast corner of the township. Sections are often divided into quarters, and these quarters are also often divided into quarters.

The government system of rectangular surveys has been employed in surveying the lands of the states of Alabama, Florida, Mississippi, and all of the states north of the Ohio River and west of the Mississippi River, except Texas.

Local surveys, which in some respects resemble the Government Survey, will occasionally be encountered in the other states.

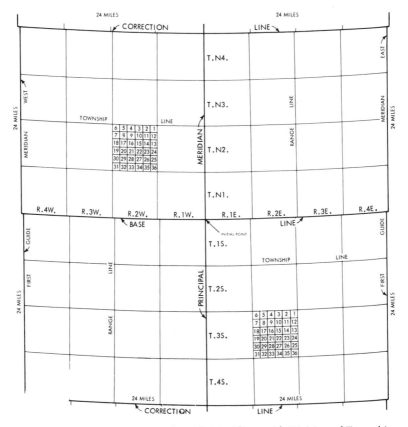

FIGURE 1. Correction Lines and Guide Meridians with Division of Townships into Sections

FIGURE 2. Section of Land Divided into Quarters and Showing Acreage and Distances

- 1 link—7.92 inches
- 1 rod—16½ feet
- 1 chain—4 rods or 66 feet or 100 links
- 1 furlong—660 feet or 40 rods
- 1 mile—8 furlongs or 320 rods or 80 chains or 5,280 feet
- 1 sq. rod—272¼ sq. feet or 30¼ sq. yards
- 1 acre—43,560 sq. feet or 160 sq. rods
- 1 acre is about 208¾ feet square
- 1 acre is 8 rods x 20 rods (or any two numbers of rods whose product is 160)
- 1 section—1 square mile or 640 acres

55

5.04   Plats

Large tracts of land are often subdivided into building lots. Thereafter each building lot is conveyed by its lot number.

> **EXAMPLE:**   Developer believing that the tract is ripe for subdivision, buys the Northeast Quarter of the Northeast Quarter of Section 7, Township 40 North, Range 13 East of the Third Principal Meridian, in Cook County, Illinois. He hires a surveyor, who divides the tract into *blocks,* separated by streets. Each block is divided into *lots.* The lots and blocks are numbered, and the streets and the subdivision are named. For this particular subdivision, Developer selects the name "Highwood." The surveyor prepares a map, called a *plat,* showing the lots and blocks, their dimensions and numbers, the width and names of the streets, the location of the quarter-section lines, and other similar information. After receiving the approval of local officials, the plat is filed or recorded in the office where deeds and mortgages are recorded. A description of a lot in this subdivision will read somewhat as follows: Lot 2 in Block 5 in Highwood, a subdivision of the Northeast Quarter of the Northeast Quarter of Section 7, Township 40 North, Range 13 East of the Third Principal Meridian in Cook County, Illinois.

5.05   Description by popular name

Descriptions by the popular name of the tract have been held sufficient, as where a deed conveys "The Old Merchant Farm." *Hayes* v. *O'Brien,* 37 NE 73 (Ill. 1894).

5.06   General description

A deed sometimes contains no definite description, but merely purports to convey all land owned by the grantor in a certain district, as "all the land owned by the grantor in Cook County, Illinois." Such descriptions, sometimes called *"Mother Hubbard"* clauses, are sufficient to pass title from the grantor to the grantee, but they may not be sufficient to impact constructive notice to third parties who do not have actual notice of the deed. *Luther* v. *Evans,* 576 P2d 1064 (Kans. 1978). To overcome this potential problem, the grantee may record an affidavit that specifically describes the property intended to be conveyed.

5.07   Street address

A description by street address alone should never be used in a deed or mortgage. Since the proper legal description is not always available when a contract for the sale of land is being drafted, descriptions by street address will be found in contracts.

A danger sometimes present in street address descriptions is revealed by the following illustration.

> **EXAMPLE:**   Landlord leased to Tenant "certain premises known as 10 East Chicago Avenue, Chicago, Illinois." The building in question bore this address. It was a restaurant. Landlord owned a vacant lot adjoining, which patrons of the restaurant sometimes used as a parking area, although it was not a regular parking

lot. It was held that a lease by street number includes only the lot on which the building is situated. *Killian* v. *Welfare Engineering Co.,* 66 NE2d 305 (Ill. 1946).

5.08   Area

Land may be described by its area, as the "North one acre of the Southeast Quarter of Section 1, Township 44 North, Range 2 East of the Third Principal Meridian, Lake County, Illinois."

5.09   Adjoining owners

Lands are also described by reference to adjoining lands.

> **EXAMPLE:**   A deed described the land as follows: "Bounded on the east by a fifty-acre tract of land owned by G. B. Turner purchased by him from N. W. Rodden; bounded on the north by the right of way of the Texas and Pacific R. R.; and on the west by a fifty-acre tract owned by the said G. B. Turner and known as the J. F. Neal tract of land; bounded on the south by the Katie Moore Boham tract of land." *Cox* v. *Campbell,* 143 SW2d 361 (Tex. 1940).

5.10   Foreign grant

Portions of this country were once owned by France, Holland, Mexico, and Spain. In fact, the titles to some of the most valuable lands on Manhattan Island are based upon Dutch grants. Hence descriptions employing foreign units of land measure, such as the *vara* and the *arpent,* are often encountered.

5.11   Indefinite description

A deed, mortgage, or other document must describe the land conveyed. The land must be so described that it can be located and identified.

> **EXAMPLE:**   A deed was made of the "southeast half" of a certain section. This deed was held void for uncertainty in the description. *Pry* v. *Pry,* 109 Ill. 466 (1884).

It is often difficult to determine whether a description is good or bad.

> **EXAMPLE:**   A deed was made to "one acre of land in the northwest corner of Block 20" in a certain subdivision. This deed was held good, because a surveyor could go to the northwest corner of the block and measure out a sufficient distance west and south to include one acre of land. *Richey* v. *Sinclair,* 47 NE 364 (Ill. 1897).

A deed of "my house and lot" is not considered indefinite. Oral evidence can be introduced in court to show what tract of land was intended. *Brenneman* v. *Dillon,* 129 NE 564 (Ill. 1920).

When a deed description is too indefinite to identify the land, but the grantee, by consent of the grantor, takes possession of premises that are within the general terms of the description and erects permanent improvements on them, the defect in the description is thereby cured.

> **EXAMPLE:** Owner made a deed to a railroad of "a strip of land one hundred feet in width over the Northeast Quarter of Section 12, Township 14 North, Range 2 East of the Third Principal Meridian." The railroad, with Owner's consent, actually occupied a strip of land one hundred feet in width and erected railroad tracks thereon. The description, though originally too indefinite, became sufficient by occupation.

The rule that possession cures an indefinite description is also applicable to leases and to contracts of sale.

5.12 Description containing omissions

A deed, mortgage, or other document is valid, even though part of the description is omitted, if enough remains to identify the land conveyed.

> **EXAMPLE:** A deed to land described as being in Santa Cruz County, California, failed to name the meridian from which the township and range were numbered. This did not invalidate the deed, since all descriptions of land in that county are numbered from the Mt. Diablo Meridian. *Harrington* v. *Goldsmith,* 68 Pac. 594 (Cal. 1902).

5.13 Correction of deed description by court order

When an error occurs in the land description in a deed and the seller refuses to give a new deed to correct the error, a court order can usually be obtained correcting the erroneous description. This is known as *reformation* of an instrument. And if in the meantime the grantee has been in possession of the land, probably no great harm will result from the error. If, however, the grantee has not gone into possession, as where the land is vacant, third persons, such as judgment creditors of the grantor, may acquire rights in the land superior to those of the grantee. See 4 *American Law of Property* § 1723.

5.14 Streets or highways as boundaries

As previously pointed out, a city often does not own the land comprising its roads, streets, or alleys, but only has an easement thereover for street purposes. When a deed or mortgage is made of land abutting on such a road, street, or alley the land sold or mortgaged generally runs to the center of such road, street, or alley. 49 ALR2d 982.

> **EXAMPLE:** Seller gives Buyer a deed selling and conveying that part of a certain section of land "lying south of Dundee Road." By this deed, Buyer acquires all land in that particular section lying south of the *center* of Dundee Road.

The reason for this rule is obvious. The seller, having parted with ownership of his land, would have no use for the strip of road adjoining thereto.

Hence it is presumed that he intended half of the adjoining road to pass to the buyer with the land sold.

When a street is used as a boundary, keep in mind that legally the street usually includes much more than the paved roadway over which cars travel. It often includes the sidewalk, the planted area known as the *parkway,* and may even include a narrow strip of land on the house side of the sidewalk. Check the recorded subdivision plat to locate the true street line.

5.15   Waters as boundaries

If Seller owns land through which a stream flows and his ownership includes the stream bed, a deed, mortgage, or lease of land "lying south of Plum Creek" will, under a rule analogous to the highway rule, include the south half of the creek. 78 ALR3d 604.

5.16   Parts of lots

Care should be exercised in drafting descriptions of parts of lots.

> **EXAMPLE:** A subdivision plat indicates that Lot 2 in Block 3 is eighty feet wide. Owner gives Buyer a deed to the "east forty feet of Lot 2." When Owner sells the remainder of the lot, his description thereof should be "Lot 2, except the east forty feet thereof," and not "the west forty feet of Lot 2." The reason is obvious. Suppose Lot 2 is actually slightly more than eighty feet in width, as it well may be, for land measurements are not perfectly accurate. Deeds of the east forty feet and the west forty feet of the lot would leave a small strip of land in the middle of the lot still owned by Owner.

When the lot is not a perfect square or rectangle, use of descriptions such as the "east half" or "north half" of the lot should be avoided, since the word "half" usually is considered to mean half by area, and the boundary line will be located with an equal number of square feet on either side thereof. This may result in an unequal division of the frontage of the lot.

A deed of a part of a lot that abuts on a diagonal street should use descriptions like the "northwesterly thirty feet" rather than the "north thirty feet," since, if the diagonal street runs in a true northwesterly or northeasterly direction, it is difficult to determine which side of the lot is the "north" side. Cases will be found where two of the boundary lines may lay equal claim to being the "north" line of the lot.

5.17   Buildings

Since buildings are usually fixtures and, as such, are part of the land, a deed of the land will automatically give the buyer the buildings thereon. They need not be mentioned in the deed.

5.18   Tax bills

Tax bills contain abbreviated, vague, and unsatisfactory descriptions of the land. They should never be used in drafting a deed, contract, or lease.

6 DEEDS AND ACKNOWLEDGMENTS

6.01 Defined

A deed is a written instrument by which a landowner transfers the ownership of his land.

6.02 Types of deeds

The deeds commonly used in the United States are typically referred to as *quitclaim deeds, warranty deeds,* and *deeds of bargain and sale.*

6.02(a) Quitclaim deed

A quitclaim deed purports to convey only the grantor's *present interest in the land,* if any, rather than the land itself. Since such a deed purports to convey whatever interest the grantor has at the time, its use excludes any implication that he has good title, or any title at all. Such a deed in no way obligates the grantor. If he has no interest, none will be conveyed. If he acquires an interest after executing the deed, he retains such interest. If, however, the grantor in such deed has complete ownership at the time of executing the deed, the deed is sufficient to pass such ownership.

A seller who knows that his title is bad or who does not know whether his title is good or bad usually uses a quitclaim deed in conveying.

6.02(b) Warranty deed

A warranty deed (sometimes called a *general warranty deed*) contains certain assurances or guarantees by the grantor that the deed conveys a good and unencumbered title. Such guarantees are called *covenants of title.* These covenants differ somewhat in their scope, depending on the local practice, but those usually encountered warrant or guarantee in substance:

1. That the grantor has good title to the land conveyed. This is called the *covenant of seizin.*

60

2. That there are no encumbrances on the land except as stated in the deed. This is called the *covenant against encumbrances.*

3. That the grantee, or his grantees, will not be evicted or disturbed by a person having a better title or lien. This is called the *covenant for quiet enjoyment.*

If the grantee suffers a loss because the title is not good as covenanted, he may sue the grantor for damages.

If any encumbrances exist that are not mentioned in the deed, the covenant against encumbrances is violated. An encumbrance, within the meaning of this covenant, includes any lien, such as a mortgage, tax lien, or judgment lien, also an easement, a restriction on the use of the land, or an outstanding dower right. The grantor's liability on this covenant is not affected by the fact that the grantee knew of the encumbrance. 64 ALR 1479. If the grantor wishes to escape liability on this covenant, he must insert some qualifying language in the deed, such as *subject to a certain mortgage* (describing the mortgage), or *subject to restrictions of record.* This is called the *subject clause.*

It is still customary in many localities to set out in full in the warranty deed the various covenants of title. However, in many states, laws exist under which the usual covenants of title are implied from the use of certain specified words. When these particular words are used, the deed must be read as though the usual covenants of title were set out in full therein. In Alaska, Illinois, Kansas, Michigan, Minnesota, and Wisconsin, the words *convey* and *warrant* make a deed a general warranty deed. The same result is achieved in Pennsylvania, Vermont, Virginia, and West Virginia by use of the words *warrant generally,* and in Arkansas, Florida, Idaho, Missouri, and Nevada by the words *grant, bargain,* and *sell.*

The fact that the seller is willing to give a general warranty deed is little or no assurance that he has good, clear title to the land. Suppose that I were to sit down this instant and write out a warranty deed conveying the Empire State Building to you. Clearly this warranty deed would give you no title to that valuable property for the simple reason that I don't own it. 26 CJS *Deeds* § 117. You would, of course, have the right to sue me for breach of my covenants of warranty.

6.02(b)(1) Special warranty deed

A *special warranty deed* is one in which the grantor covenants only against the lawful claims of all persons claiming by, through, or under the grantor. This type of deed is called a *grant deed* in some states. The grantor is liable in such case if his grantee is disturbed by some claim arising through an act of the grantor himself. For example, if, prior to the execution of the deed, the grantor has himself placed a mortgage on the land that the deed fails to mention, and thereafter the grantee is compelled to pay off the mortgage, the grantor is liable for damages thus sustained by the grantee. But if the grantor has in no way encumbered the title, but later an outstanding title is asserted by some third person, the grantor is not liable. In some states, Mississippi, Pennsylvania, Vermont, Virginia, and West Virginia, for example, use of the words *warrant specially* is sufficient to create a covenant of special warranty. In California, Idaho, and North Dakota, use of the word *grant* achieves the same purpose.

6.02(c) Deed of bargain and sale

There are deeds that convey the land, and not merely the grantor's *interest* therein. Therefore they are not quitclaim deeds. They do not include warranties of title. Therefore they are not warranty deeds. Such a deed is a deed of *bargain and sale,* or *deed without covenants.*

6.03 Requirements of a valid deed

The essential elements of a deed are a competent grantor, a grantee, recital of consideration, words of conveyance, adequate description of the land, signature of grantor and his spouse, and delivery of the completed instrument to the grantee. In addition, a deed may (though it need not) contain warranties of title, recitals showing mortgages and other encumbrances, a date, witnesses, an acknowledgment, and documentary stamps. Delivery is followed by filing or recording of the deed in the proper public office.

6.03(a) Grantor

Every deed must have a grantor. The grantor is who conveys the property. The fact that the name used by the grantor differs from his true name does not invalidate the deed. The name of the grantor must appear in the body of the deed.

> **EXAMPLE:** *A, B,* and *C* own certain land. A deed is made, and the names of *A* and *B* appear in the body thereof, but all three owners sign the deed. *C's* interest does not pass under the deed. *Harrison* v. *Simons,* 55 Ala. 510 (1896).

However, a deed beginning "In consideration of ten dollars, I do hereby convey" is sufficient if signed by the landowner, even though his name does not appear in the body of the deed. *Bowles* v. *Lowery,* 62 So 107 (Ala. 1913). The same is true where the deed begins with the phrase "The undersigned." *Frederick* v. *Wilcox,* 24 So 582 (Ala. 1898).

A mistake in the spelling of the grantor's name or a variance between the spelling of the name in the body of the deed and the spelling in the signature will not invalidate the deed where the identity of the person intended to be designated is obvious.

> **EXAMPLE:** A deed is good though it names "Emmonds" as grantor, but is signed "Emmens." And a deed is good though it names "Abraham B. Kain" as grantor but is signed "A. Boudoin Kain." *Lyon* v. *Kain,* 36 Ill. 362 (1865).

6.03(a)(1) Grantor competency

The grantor and his spouse must be of legal age and of sound mind. In many states, a deed by a person who has been declared insane by a court is void. Even if the grantor has not been declared insane, his deed may later be set aside if, as a matter of fact, he lacked the mental capacity to understand in a reasonable manner the nature of the transaction in which he was engaged and its consequences and effects on his rights and interest.

> **EXAMPLE:** Widower has three children, Alice, Beth, and Charles. When Widower becomes too feeble to take care of himself, Alice, a married but childless daughter, moves into Widower's home with her husband. As time passes Widower becomes senile and requires constant care. Alice, feeling she should be rewarded for her care of her father, prepares a deed of the home running to herself as grantee and has Widower sign it. After Widower's death Beth and Charles learn of the deed. They file a suit to set it aside. If they can show that Widower was too senile to understand that he was parting with ownership of his home when he signed the deed, the court will set it aside. Cases of this sort occur by the thousands.

6.03(a)(1)(i) Fraud, coercion, and mistake

A deed obtained by fraud, misrepresentation, or coercion may be set aside by proper court proceedings. This is particularly true when through old age, mental weakness, ignorance, illness, or some other cause, the grantor was incapable of coping with the grantee, and due to such incapacity of the grantor the grantee has obtained the property for substantially less than its value.

Mutual mistake occurs where both parties are under some misapprehension.

> **EXAMPLE:** Seller owns tracts one and two. Believing he is buying one, Buyer receives and pays for a deed conveying Tract 2, while Seller believes Buyer wishes to buy Tract 2. The deed will be set aside and the money refunded to Buyer.

6.03(a)(2) Grantor— infancy

In most states, an individual achieves majority, comes of age, at the age of eighteen. Ages of majority, however, vary from state to state. A person who is not of age is an *infant* and, after achieving majority, may sue to set aside any deed executed by him while an infant. If it is necessary that the land of an infant or an insane person be sold for his support or for some other proper purpose, court proceedings may be instituted for that purpose.

6.03(a)(3) Grantor—corporations

A favorable vote of the directors or trustees of a corporation is usually necessary to authorize the sale of corporate real estate. Laws will often be encountered requiring a vote of the holders of two-thirds of the corporate stock to authorize any sale of substantially *all* the corporate assets. A vote of the majority of the members of a church corporation or a nonprofit corporation may be necessary for a sale of the property.

Where the property is owned by a close corporation (a corporation with few shareholders), it should have a meeting of all of its shareholders and all of its directors to adopt the resolution authorizing the sale. The secretary's certificate to the resolution should state that it was unanimously adopted at a meeting of *all* shareholders and *all* directors.

6.03(a)(4) Grantor's spouse

Whether or not the grantor's spouse must join in the deed depends, of course, upon the local law. Generally speaking, however, it is necessary for the grantor's spouse to join in the deed for one or more of the following reasons:

1. In most states, land occupied by a husband and wife as their home is known as their homestead. Any deed or mortgage of the homestead must be signed by both husband and wife, the theory being that the home should not be disposed of unless a new home satisfactory to both parties has been furnished.

2. In most states, a wife has certain rights in her husband's land, and her rights in any particular parcel of land are not defeated by any deed made by her husband unless she has joined in making the deed.

3. Depending on the local law, a husband may have *curtesy, dower,* or other rights in the land owned by his wife, and his signature on his wife's deed is required in order to relinquish these rights.

4. Some of the western states have the community property system, and in most of these states it is required that deeds of community property be signed by both husband and wife.

5. In some states (Illinois, for example) laws have been passed that seem to give some property interest in the land that is awarded to the other spouse in a divorce. This appears to make it prudent to have both spouses join in any deed of the real estate that is owned by either spouse.

It is obvious from the foregoing that the marital status of the grantor should be clearly stated in the deed, as *bachelor, widow, spinster,* or *divorced and not remarried.*

6.03(b) Grantee

Every deed must have a grantee. If it does not, it is void.

EXAMPLE: *A* makes out a deed to *B,* who, unknown to *A,* is dead at the time. The deed is void. A dead grantee is no grantee at all. 148 ALR 252.

The grantee need not be named in the deed if he is sufficiently described.

> **EXAMPLE:** A deed to "John Smith and wife" transfers ownership to John Smith and his wife. *Ballard* v. *Farley,* 226 SW 544 (Tenn. 1920).

A deed running directly to an unincorporated association is void for want of a grantee.

> **EXAMPLE:** A number of persons attended a particular church that was known as the "First Avenue Baptist Church." The church, however, was not incorporated. One of the members of the congregation made a deed of gift of his real estate to "First Avenue Baptist Church." The deed was void. *Heiligenstein* v. *Schlotterbeck,* 133 NE 188 (Ill. 1921).

The fact that the name inserted in the deed is not the grantee's true name does not invalidate the deed. In other words, for the purpose of any particular real estate transaction I may assume any name I wish.

> **EXAMPLE:** If I should buy land and direct the seller to insert the name "Robert Cook" as grantee in the deed, intending to hold ownership of the land by that name, the deed is perfectly valid. *Chapman* v. *Tyson,* 81 Pac. 1066 (Wash. 1905).

This situation frequently occurs with respect to persons who pass as husband and wife although they are not legally married.

> **EXAMPLE:** A deed designated as grantees Fabrio Casini and Lucy Casini, his wife. Actually, Lucy was not the wife of Fabrio, although they passed as husband and wife. The deed was a valid deed, and the grantees became co-owners of the property. *Casini* v. *Lupone,* 72 A2d 907 (N.J. 1950); *Michael* v. *Lucas,* 137 Atl. 287 (Md. 1927).

A misspelling of the grantee's name will not invalidate the deed where the identity of the person intended to be designated is obvious. This is also true of deeds to corporations.

> **EXAMPLE:** I attend a church whose proper corporate name is First Avenue Methodist Church, and, intending to convey land to this church, I make out a deed to The Methodist Church of First Avenue. The deed is valid. *Church of Christ* v. *Christian Church,* 61 NE 1119 (Ill. 1901). This defect is technically termed a *misnomer.* Misnomer does not invalidate a deed.

In a few states, a husband cannot convey directly to his wife, or vice versa, since according to the ancient view, the husband and wife together are but one person, and it takes two persons to make a deed. However, both husband and wife may join in a deed to a third person, who may thereupon convey to the wife.

A deed to a minor or an insane person is valid.

In many states it is required that the deed show the address of the grantee, and a deed will not be accepted for recording unless this appears in the deed. However, failure to show the address does not invalidate the deed.

In the use of a deed involving a corporation, there are a number of matters to check.

1. Does the corporation exist?

EXAMPLE: A deed to *ABC Corp.* is dated December 8, 1980. The corporate charter issued by the state is dated December 15, 1980. The deed runs to a grantee that did not exist on December 8. There is a problem.

EXAMPLE: *ABC Corp.* was created by a charter dated November 1, 1975. On July 1, 1978, it was dissolved by the state for failure to pay its corporation tax. A deed to this corporation is dated December 8, 1980. A dissolution is like the death of an individual. A problem exists.

2. Is any foreign corporation in the deal duly licensed in the state?

EXAMPLE: *ABC Corp.* is formed in Delaware in 1975. It buys an office building in Illinois in 1980. But it has no license to do business in Illinois. A tenant in the building fails to pay his rent. *ABC Corp.* cannot file an eviction suit. Most states will not allow unlicensed foreign corporations to sue in their courts.

3. If a partnership is involved, how should the deed read?

EXAMPLE: *A, B,* and *C* are partners doing business as *Unity Associates.* In most states the deed to the partnership may go either way, to *A, B,* and *C* or to *Unity Associates.*

4. How should a deed to a trust run?

EXAMPLE: A business trust has ten beneficiaries. The trust document names *A,* as trustee, and the trust is known as *Prudence Trust.* The deed should run to *A* as trustee of *Prudence Trust.*

REFERENCES: Partnership deeds, see Kratovil & Werner, *Fixing up the Old Jalopy—The Modern Limited Partnership Under the ULPA,* 50 St. John's L. Rev. 51 (1975). Business trusts, see 88 ALR3d 704.

6.03(b)(1)   Deeds in blank

The problem of whether a deed is void for want of a grantee often arises in connection with deeds where the name of the grantee is left blank at the time the deed is signed by the grantor. Of course if the blank space for the grantee's name is never filled in, the deed cannot be a good deed, for a deed must convey the land to someone.

Where the name of the grantee is inserted by an agent of the grantor after the grantor has signed the deed, the deed is usually valid.

> **EXAMPLE:** Landowner signs a deed complete in all respects, except that the name of the grantee is left blank. He delivers this deed to Agent, with directions to sell the property for not less than a certain sum. Agent interests Buyer in the purchase of the property. Buyer is willing to pay the stipulated price. Agent fills in Buyer's name as grantee and delivers the deed to Buyer. Buyer pays the purchase price, not knowing that his name was filled in after the deed was signed. Such a deed is generally held valid, even though Agent's authority was merely verbal. *West* v. *Witschner,* 428 SW2d 538 (Mo. 1968); 75 ALR 1294. But a deed delivered with the land description left blank is held void in many states. *West* v. *Witschner,* 428 SW2d 538 (Mo. 1968).

6.03(c)   Consideration   *Consideration* is the value given for a conveyance of land. This doctrine, as much of the law of real property, has some rather ancient roots.

In the days of King Henry VIII land was still transferred by *livery of seizin.*

> **EXAMPLE:** Owner wishes to sell Blackacre to Buyer. Both of them were required to be physically present on the land. Owner would press a clod of earth or twig into Buyer's hands and declare that ownership of the land thereby passed to Buyer. This was called a *feoffment.* A written record was made of the transaction. It was called a *charter of feoffment.* Land could not be transferred by deed.

All will remember King Henry's struggle with the Catholic church over his divorce problem. Many nobles opposed Henry. If they were found guilty of treason (and Henry could easily see to that) they would lose their heads (as did Anne Boleyn). They would also forfeit their lands. For this and other reasons many landowners put ownership of their lands in the names of men who were above reproach, to hold "for the use of" the real owners. To put an end to this evasion of his rights, Henry had has rubber stamp parliament pass a law that all such land held by third parties for the benefit ("for the use of") these nobles automatically passed back into the ownership of the nobles, where Henry could easily reach it.

The language of the law was broad. In effect, it stated that where land is held "for the use of *A*," ownership must be considered to be vested in *A*. The clever lawyers of those days saw that the law could be used for a purpose never foreseen by Henry.

> **EXAMPLE:** Owner (of London) wishes to sell his land in Manchester to Buyer. Owner signed a document stating that Buyer had paid $10,000 for the land, that Owner therefore held the land "for the use of Buyer." By virtue of the new law, ownership of the land passed to Buyer. It was no longer necessary for the parties to go on the land. Land ownership could not be transferred by deed. The first modern real estate transaction had been created.

For many years, payment of a "consideration" or price was thought to be necessary, in order to create the "use" in the purchaser. Today consideration is usually recited in the deed, but actual presence of consideration is not necessary.

The deed usually recites that it was given for "$10.00 and other good and valuable consideration."

Deeds are usually drafted with a general statement of nominal consideration to keep the private business dealings of the parties from becoming part of the public record. These efforts are not entirely successful. People who want to know the selling price of land can usually compute that price from the transfer stamps placed on the deed.

> **EXAMPLE:** If the transfer tax is $1.00 per thousand dollars of selling price, a deed with $10 of transfer tax affixed was given for $10,000, notwithstanding the fact that the consideration clause read "$10.00 and other valuable consideration."

If the deed recites a consideration, the fact that the deed represents a gift of the land and that actually no money changed hands will not invalidate the deed. An individual may give away his land if he wishes. However, a man must be just before he is generous. If the grantor is indebted at the time of the making of the gift, his creditors may thereafter have the deed set aside as in fraud of their rights. The payment of a nominal consideration, such as $10, will not suffice to sustain the deed in such a case. A valuable consideration is needed to sustain a deed against existing creditors of the grantor.

6.03(c)(1) Consideration—support deeds

Parents often convey their land to a son or daughter on the understanding that such son or daughter will support the parents for the rest of their lives. Or an elderly person without close relatives may convey his land to a stranger or to a rest home in return for a promise of support. While ordinarily a deed cannot be set aside for *failure of consideration,* that is, for the reason that the grantee failed to receive what he bargained for, support deeds form an exception to the rule. *Bruno* v. *Bruno,* 172 A2d 863 (Pa. 1961). Where the grantee fails to keep his promise to support, the deed can usually be set aside.

> **EXAMPLE:** A father and mother conveyed land to their son. The mother had owned the land, and it had been the home of the parents. The deed recited a consideration of $2,500. The actual consideration, however, was the son's agreement to support the parents and give them a home for the rest of their lives. Several years later, the son stopped supporting them and became so abusive that they moved out and went to live with another son. The deed was set aside. *Worrell* v. *West,* 296 P2d 1092 (Kans. 1956). The grantee is not living up to his promise unless he furnishes kindness and attention, as well as physical *necessaries. Zarembski* v. *Zarembski,* 48 NE2d 394 (Ill. 1943).

6.03(d) Words of conveyance

Every deed must contain words of conveyance. These differ from state to state. In warranty deeds, *convey and warrant* or *grant, bargain, and sell* are often used. In quitclaim deeds the words usually are *convey and quitclaim* or *remise, release, and forever quitclaim.*

6.03(e) Description of land

A deed must describe the land conveyed. See Ch. 5.

6.03(f) Waiver of dower and homestead

In some states, a deed must contain a clause releasing and relinquishing all homestead, dower, and curtesy rights in the premises.

6.03(g) Date

A date is not essential to the validity of a deed, though it is the universal custom to date all deeds.

6.03(h) Signature

The signature of the grantor is essential to the validity of the deed. A *forgery* (a deed to which some unauthorized third person has affixed the grantor's signature) is a nullity and conveys no title whatever.

The fact that the grantor's signature is misspelled will not invalidate the deed.

If the grantor is unable to write, he may sign by mark, in which case the signature line appears as follows:

His
"John X Smith (Seal)"
Mark

Everything but the "X" may be typed. The "X" must be affixed by the grantor.

Occasionally a deed is signed not by the grantor himself, but by an *attorney in fact.* An attorney in fact is simply an agent authorized by the landowner to sell and convey his real estate. In order for such deed to be valid, the following requirements exist:

1. The land owner must first sign and deliver to his attorney in fact a written instrument, called a *power of attorney,* authorizing such attorney to sell and convey the land in question. Such an instrument must be as formal as the deed itself. In states that require a deed to be sealed, the power of attorney must be sealed. In states that require a deed to be witnessed, the power of attorney must be witnessed. All the other requirements relating to deeds should be observed, including acknowledgment and recording.

2. The deed must name the landowner, not the attorney in fact, as the grantor.

3. The name signed to the deed should be that of the landowner. Under the usual meth-

od, the attorney signs the grantor's name and then places his name beneath that of the grantor, as follows:

"John Smith (Seal)"
"By Henry Brown, his Attorney in Fact"

4. The grantor must be alive on the date of the delivery of the deed, since death of the grantor automatically terminates the power of attorney. Insanity of the grantor may have the same result.

5. Since the landowner ordinarily has the power to terminate the agency at any time and thus take away the attorney's power to execute deeds on his behalf, it should be established that the agency actually had not been terminated or revoked at the date of the delivery of the deed.

NEW DIRECTIONS: Some states have enacted so-called "durable power of attorney" laws. These statutes provide that the power continues notwithstanding the incompetency of the grantors. Mich. Stat. Ann. §§ 26.1225(1).

The technical mode of executing the deed of a corporation is for the proper office to sign the corporate name, adding his own signature and official title beneath the name of the corporation. Usually, the corporate bylaws provide that deeds shall be signed by a president or vice president and attested to by a secretary or assistant secretary.

The mere fact that the grantor's name on the deed is signed by someone other than the grantor does not invalidate the deed. The execution of the deed may be ratified or otherwise authorized by the true grantor. If this is the case, the deed is as effective as though the actual grantor signed the deed.

6.03(i)   Seal

In some states, principally eastern states, a seal is essential to the validity of a deed. In most states, however, a seal is unnecessary, though the custom of using a seal persists. But even in those states where a deed by an individual need not bear a seal, a deed executed by a corporation should have the official corporate seal affixed.

6.03(j)   Witnesses

In many states a deed must be witnessed, two witnesses being the number commonly required. Most states require witnessing where the deed is signed by mark.

6.03(k)   Taxes

Many states, counties, and municipalities have enacted laws that impose a tax upon the transfer of property. Under some of these laws, the recorder must refuse to accept a deed for recording unless proper tax stamps are affixed. See Ill. Rev. Stat. Ch. 115, § 9.2a. These taxes vary from state to state and municipality to municipality. Local law and practice must be reviewed.

6.03(l)   Delivery of deeds

Delivery is essential to the validity of a deed. The word *delivery* is somewhat misleading, since it would lead one to believe that it is necessary that the deed be actually handed by the grantor to the grantee. This is not the case. Delivery is simply the final act by which the grantor, who has previously signed the deed, signifies his intention that the deed shall take effect. Whether or not a deed has been delivered depends primarily on the *intention* of the grantor. The test is: Did the grantor *do* or *say* anything to show his intention to pass ownership of the land to the grantee? A deed may be delivered by acts without words or by words without acts, though ordinarily there are both words and acts in the making of a delivery.

> **EXAMPLE:** At the closing of a deal, Buyer hands Seller a check. Seller signs the deed and, without saying a word, hands it to Buyer. There is a delivery.

> **EXAMPLE:** At the closing of a deal all the papers, including Seller's signed deed, are on the closing table. Having received his check, Seller tells Buyer (the grantee) to take his deed. There is a delivery.

> **EXAMPLE:** Seller signs a deed conveying real estate to Buyer and hands it to Buyer, not with the intention of passing title, but with the understanding that Buyer will check the legal description to see if it is sufficient. There is no delivery.

> **EXAMPLE:** Seller signs a deed conveying real estate to Buyer but leaves it in his office while he is still thinking over the deal. Buyer steals the deed from Seller's office and shows it to Third Person, who purchases from Buyer, relying on Buyer's possession of the deed. Third Person acquires no title. There is no delivery of the deed.

6.03(l)(1)   Delivery— several grantors

Suppose *A* and *B* own certain land, and both of them sign a deed running to *C* as grantee. *A* hands the deed to *B* for the sole purpose of having the deed checked by their lawyer. Without *A*'s permission, *B* hands the deed to *C* and collects the sale price from him. This is not a good deed so far as *A* is concerned. He still owns his half interest. One joint grantor, who is not authorized by his co-tenant, cannot make a valid delivery of the deed that will be binding on the latter. 162 ALR 892.

When land is owned by several persons, all of them named as grantors in one deed, and one of the grantors signs the deed and hands it to the grantee with the statement that his consent to the sale of the land is conditioned on the other grantors also signing the deed, such deed is inoperative unless all grantors sign. *Logue* v. *Von Almen*, 40 NE2d 73 (Ill. 1941); Note, 14 Columb. L. Rev. 389 (1914).

6.03(l)(2) Delivery— lifetime of the grantor

Delivery of a deed must be made in the lifetime of the grantor.

> **EXAMPLE:** On Seller's death, an envelope with Seller's name on it is found in Seller's safe-deposit box. The envelope is opened and found to contain a deed from Seller to Buyer. The deed is void for want of delivery.

A deed is the proper instrument for transferring ownership of land from one living person to another, and, in general, this means that the deed, to be effective, must operate while both parties are alive.

However, I may legally deliver a deed to you here and now with a clause therein stating that the deed is to take effect only at my death. The deed gives you the right *now* to enjoy the property at my death. 31 ALR2d 532.

6.03(l)(3) Delivery—third persons

Where the grantor hands the deed not to the grantee, but to some third person, a wholly new set of rules comes into play. A number of different situations present themselves.

> **EXAMPLE:** Seller signs a deed running to Buyer as grantee and hands the deed to Buyer's lawyer, with the intention of giving Buyer ownership of the land here and now. This is delivery to an *agent of the grantee* and is good delivery.

> **EXAMPLE:** Seller signs a deed running to Buyer as grantee and hands the deed to his own lawyer to check its form. There is no intention to transfer ownership and no delivery. Here the deed has been handed to the *agent of the grantor.*

> **EXAMPLE:** Seller enters into a contract to sell land to Buyer and pursuant thereto signs a deed to Buyer. However, he hands the deed to XYZ Bank with directions to deliver the deed to Buyer when certain moneys are paid by Buyer to the bank. This is an *escrow.*

> **EXAMPLE:** Seller signs a deed running to Son, as grantee, hands the deed to Custodian and directs Custodian to hand the deed to Son after Seller's death. This brings up the subject of *death escrows.* This is a good delivery as long as it is clear that Seller intended to part with all control over the land once he handed the deed to Custodian. Oddly enough, the courts allow Seller, in such cases, to use the land during his lifetime. They do not regard this as inconsistent with the passing of ownership to Son. It is as though Seller had conveyed outright to Son, but had reserved a life estate in the property. *Bury* v. *Young,* 33 Pac. 338 (Cal. 1893).

6.03(l)(4) Delivery—family transactions

If a father executes a deed to a minor child, which deed is beneficial to the child, and the father indicates by his words and conduct that he intends the deed to operate at once, actual delivery is unnecessary. Indeed, the courts are most reluctant to upset a deed that is made as a gift by a parent to a child.

6.03(m)   **Acceptance**

For a deed to transfer ownership of land, it is necessary that the grantor intend to transfer ownership to the grantee and that the grantee intend to accept ownership of the land. *Blankenship* v. *Meyers,* 544 P2d 314 (Idaho 1975). That is to say, delivery by the grantor must be accompanied by acceptance of the deed by the grantee. 74 ALR2d 992. Only rarely will disputes arise regarding acceptance, and the courts are not disposed to be technical about it. Indeed, the courts have gone so far as to hold that if the grantor makes and records a deed without the knowledge of the grantee, ownership will nevertheless pass if the grantee, on being informed of the deed, assents to it, even though this takes place after the death of the grantor. *Mann* v. *Jummel,* 56 NE 161 (Ill. 1891). Also, if the grantee dies before learning of the deed, his acceptance will be presumed and the deed held good. *Lessee of Mitchell* v. *Ryan,* 3 Ohio St. 377 (1854). A parent may accept for an infant. *Whitworth* v. *Whitworth,* 210 SE2d 9 (Ga. 1974).

6.03(n)   **Acknowledgment— defined**

An acknowledgment is a formal declaration made before some public officer, usually a notary public, by a person who has signed a deed, mortgage, or other instrument, that the instrument is his voluntary act and deed. *In re McCauley's Adoption,* 131 NW2d 174 (Neb. 1964). This ceremony is the act of acknowledgment.

6.03(n)(1)   **Acknowledgment—certificate**

The officer before whom this declaration is made attaches his certificate to the instrument or fills in the printed form of certificate that appears on virtually all deed and mortgage forms. This is known as the certificate of acknowledgment. It usually recites that the grantor appeared before the officer and acknowledged that he executed the instrument as his free and voluntary act and deed. However, the form of the certificate of acknowledgment varies considerably from state to state, and from situation to situation, i.e., an acknowledgment taken from an individual differs from an acknowledgment taken from a corporate officer. It is important that the proper form be followed. *In re Viking Co., Inc.,* 389 F.Supp. 1230 (1974).

An acknowledgment must not be confused with an affidavit. An affidavit is a statement made under oath and put in writing. At the conclusion of the affidavit the officer, usually a notary, recites that it was subscribed and sworn to. An affidavit is not acceptable as a substitute for an acknowledgment. The two serve different purposes. *Hatcher* v. *Hall,* 292 SW2d 619 (Mo. 1956). The acknowledgment merely makes the *prima facie* showing that the instrument was duly executed. The affidavit or verification goes to the truth of the matters therein set forth. *D. J. Fair Lumber Co.,* v. *Karlin,* 430 P.2d 222 (Kan. 1967).

6.03(n)(2) Acknowledgment—waiver of dower and homestead rights

In some states the certificate of acknowledgment must specifically state that dower and homestead rights were understandingly relinquished.

6.03(n)(3) Acknowledgment—necessity

In a few states, Arizona and Ohio, for example, an unacknowledged deed is not valid. In a number of states, certain types of instruments, such as deeds of married women or deeds or mortgages of homestead land, must be acknowledged. Other deeds, however, are legally valid though not acknowledged. This statement is without significance, since, as a practical matter, every deed or mortgage should be acknowledged. In the great majority of the states an unacknowledged instrument is not entitled to be recorded (59 ALR2d 1302), and an unrecorded title is a precarious one indeed. Lack of an acknowledgment on a deed may render title unmarketable. Other technical reasons make an acknowledgment a practical necessity.

6.03(n)(4) Acknowledgment—who may take an acknowledgment

A deed or mortgage may be acknowledged before a notary public or some other officer designated by the local law. Such a person, it is said, *takes* the acknowledgment of the grantor. Generally, a notary who is an attorney is competent to take the acknowledgment of his client. 21 ALR3d 523. However, if the officer his any financial interest in the transaction, he is disqualified. For example, a grantee in a deed would be clearly disqualified from taking the grantor's acknowledgment. Other disqualified parties include the grantor in a deed, mortgagor and mortgagee in a mortgage, and the trustee in a trust deed. In some states, a stockholder of a corporation that is a party to the instrument is disqualified from taking the acknowledgment of the corporation. In other states the rule is the reverse.

6.03(n)(5) Acknowledgment—venue

The venue of the certificate of acknowledgment is the caption, which is usually shown as follows:

STATE OF ILLINOIS $\Big\}$ (SS)
COUNTY OF COOK

The venue shows the place where the acknowledgment took place, that is, the place where the grantor appeared before the notary and made his formal declaration that the deed was his voluntary act.

6.03(n)(6) Acknowledgment—effect of invalidity

It is important to keep in mind the fact that invalidity of the *acknowledgment* does not make the *deed* void. However, in most states, a valid acknowledgment is essential for proper recording; that is, if the acknowledgment is void, the deed, though recorded, is treated as an unrecorded deed. If that is the result, subsequent owners of the property are not on constructive notice of the rights of the grantee of the defectively acknowledged instrument.

6.03(n)(7) Acknowledgment—foreign

One who owns land located in a state other than that in which he resides, may sign and acknowledge a deed in the state of his residence. The acknowledgment will be valid if it conforms either to the law of the state of his residence or to the law of the state where the land lies. An acknowledgment taken outside of the state where the land lies is known as a *foreign acknowledgment.* In some states, it is required, either by custom or by law, that every acknowledgment taken outside of the state have attached thereto a certificate by a court clerk to the effect that the officer taking the acknowledgment was authorized by law to do so. This is known as a *certificate of authenticity,* or a *certificate of magistracy.* If the certificate goes on to recite that the acknowledgment is in due form, it is known as a *certificate of authenticity and conformity,* or *certificate of magistracy and conformity.*

6.03(n)(8) Acknowledgment—date

The date of the certificate of acknowledgment is unimportant. Hence omission of the date of the certificate or insertion of an incorrect date will not invalidate the acknowledgment.

6.03(n)(9) Acknowledgment—signature of officer taking acknowledgment

The certificate of acknowledgment must be signed by the officer taking the acknowledgment. Otherwise it is not valid. The certificate should also show the official character of the person taking the acknowledgment, as notary public, justice of the peace, and so forth.

6.03(n)(10) Acknowledgment—seal

An acknowledgment taken by a notary public is usually invalid unless his official seal is placed on the certificate. The requirements as to seals of officers other than notaries vary from state to state.

6.03(n)(11) Acknowledgment—date of expiration of commission

Failure of the notary public to show the date his commission expires does not invalidate the certificate.

6.03(n)(12) Acknowledgment—liability of notary—false acknowledgment

Both the notary public and the surety on his official bond will be liable for damages caused by the notary's willful misconduct, as where the notary falsely certifies to a forged mortgage and the mortgage is sold to an innocent purchaser. 44 ALR3d 1243. The notary and his surety will also be liable when the notary's negligence causes damage, as when the notary acknowledges the signatures on a forged mortgage without knowing the parties who appear before him and without procuring any evidence or information as to their identity. 44 ALR3d 555. See also 13 ALR3d 1039 (measure of damages).

6.04   Recording

Virtually all deeds are filed for record in some public office

6.05   Official conveyances

Deeds by executors, administrators, guardians of minors, conservators or guardians of insane persons, sheriffs, masters in chancery, receivers, trustees in bankruptcy, and other similar conveyances usually depend for their validity on prior court proceedings. In addition, numerous technical requirements exist that frequently expose such deeds to attack. A discussion of such requirements is not within the scope of this book.

6.06   After-acquired title

If the grantor in a warranty deed does not have title, or does not have complete title, at the time of executing the deed, but thereafter acquires title, such title will automatically pass to his grantee without any additional conveyance. 44 ALR 1276; 162 ALR 566.

6.07   Title conveyed

If the grantor owns the land in fee simple, and the deed contains no qualifying language, the deed gives the grantee good fee simple title to the land. However, deeds often contain qualifying language, which results in the grantee's acquiring something less than the fee simple title.

> **EXAMPLE:** Seller makes a deed conveying land to Buyer "and the heirs of his body." In some states, Buyer acquires only a life estate by such deed, and his children acquire the remainder. In other states, such a deed will give Buyer the full fee simple title to the land.

> **EXAMPLE:** Seller conveys land to Buyer by a deed that contains the following clause: "to have and to hold for and during the grantee's life." Buyer acquires only a life estate by this deed.

The law on this subject is so complex and contains so many refinements of reasoning that no one but an experienced attorney should attempt to interpret a deed containing any qualifying language whatever. In particular, words such as *heirs, heirs of the body, issue,* and *death without issue* are danger signals. Indiscriminate use of such language is an invitation to a lawsuit.

6.07(a)   Title conveyed by deed—fee or easement

If language is added to the deed indicating the purpose for which the land is to be used, this may result in giving the grantee something less than full ownership of the land. Lawyers talk about the nature of the *estate* conveyed by the deed.

> **EXAMPLE:**   By warranty deed Seller deeded to Buyer "a right of way one rod wide" over certain land. This deed gave Buyer only an easement of travel. A deed that conveys a right, especially a right of way, rather than land, gives the grantee only an easement. 136 ALR 390. As can be seen, the word "easement" is not necessary for an easement to be created. 6 ALR3d 973.

But if the deed conveys the land, with the words of purpose following the property description, the courts are not in agreement.

> **EXAMPLE:**   Seller made a deed to Buyer of a strip of land "to be used for road purposes." The court held that Buyer acquired only an easement for road purposes. *Magnolia Petroleum Co.* v. *West,* 40 NE2d 24 (Ill. 1940). The reason for this is that courts apply rules of interpretation. One of these is that courts cannot ignore any language in a written instrument. If any meaning is to be given the phrase "to be used for road purposes" it is that the land must be used *only* for road purposes. This makes the deed a grant of right to use the land for a specific purpose. That is what an easement is. The *estate* conveyed is not an *estate in fee simple.* Here again the court understands the language used but in a sense or meaning that would surprise a lay person. But in other states exactly the same kind of deed will be held to give Buyer full ownership of the strip. *Biggs* v. *Wolfe,* 178 A2d 482 (1962).

> **EXAMPLE:**   Where a deed runs to a charitable corporation, frequently some reference is made in the deed to the use of the land for the charitable purposes of the corporation. Normally, this nevertheless leaves the corporation with a salable ownership title to the land. Bogert, *The Laws of Trusts and Trustees* § 324 (2d ed. 1964); 4 Scott, *The Law of Trusts* § 348.1 (3d ed. 1967).

> **EXAMPLE:**   Seller deeds his vacant land to Hospital "for hospital purposes." The hospital finds the land not well adapted to hospital purposes. It sells the land to Third Person. This is a valid transaction. Third Person gets good title to the land.

Where a deed runs to a city, village, park district, or other public body and contains language descriptive of the use to which the land is to be put, questions may arise as to the nature of the ownership thus acquired, particularly when such use is abandoned, though in most cases the courts struggle to find that the public body acquired a good, salable title to the land. 28 Am. Jur. 2d *Estates* § 149; 10 McQuillin, *Municipal Corporations* § 28.19 (3d ed. 1966).

EXAMPLE: Seller sold and deeded his land to City "to be used for the use and benefit of the citizens of City," this language appearing in the deed. City found the land unusable for city purposes and sold it to Third Person. This can be done. Third Person acquires good ownership of the land. *City* v. *Jones,* 122 NW2d 503 (Neb. 1963).

The fact that the deed was made because of the threat of condemnation by the public body does not alter this rule. *Mattion* v. *Trustees,* 279 NE 2d 66 (Ill. 1971). *Contra: Kendrick* v. *City of St. Paul,* 6 NW2d 449 (Minn. 1942).

There is an exception to this rule in some states:

EXAMPLE: Seller deeded his land to the city of Milwaukee "for highway purposes." By this deed the city acquired only an easement to use the land for highway purposes and could not sell the land. 136 ALR 399. This exception is confined to deeds for street, alley, and highway purposes, and even then, in some states the city gets good, salable ownership of the land. 136 ALR 394.

Where a deed runs to some public body "for park purposes" there is no agreement whatever as to what such a deed conveys. 15 ALR2d 975.

6.08 Exceptions and reservations

In conveying land, the grantor often wishes to retain some part of the land described or to reserve some right therein. This is accomplished by inserting in the deed the proper clauses of *exception* and *reservation.* An exception withholds from the operation of the deed title to a part of the land described in the deed. Thus, a deed of Lot 1 *excepting the north twenty feet thereof* does not pass ownership of the north twenty feet of the lot. That portion was *excepted* from the conveyance. A *reservation* is the creation by the deed of a new right in favor of the grantor, usually an easement or life estate. Thus, in a deed of Lot 1 *reserving to the grantor an easement for ingress and egress over and across the north twenty feet of Lot 1,* ownership of the north twenty feet passes to the grantee, but an easement is reserved in favor of the grantor. Sometimes the terms *excepting* and *reserving* are used inaccurately, and the courts will hold that a true reservation was created by the use of the word *excepting* or that a true exception was created by the use of the word *reserving.*

EXAMPLE: Seller conveys certain land to Buyer "except the north ten feet for a right of way." Ownership of the entire tract, including the north ten feet, passes to Buyer, but the quoted clause reserves an easement for Seller over the north ten feet. 139 ALR 1348.

It is possible for the grantor in a deed to reserve a life estate in the property conveyed. Often to save the expense of probating a will after his death, a father, while still living, will give a deed of his land to his son or daughter, and in the deed will reserve to himself a life estate. The grantee becomes the owner of the land, and the grantor retains the use thereof for his lifetime.

> **WARNING:** Once such a deed is signed, the grantor cannot recall it. The psychological effect of this change in circumstances often brings about friction between the parent and child. Hence such transactions should be avoided, if possible.

6.09 Hazardous waste sites

Since the use of property as a hazardous waste disposal site may forever poison the land, making it unfit for human or livestock occupancy, the public record should memorialize this fact. The U.S. Environmental Protection Agency has promulgated regulations which require that the landowner record a deed or other document that will, in perpetuity, notify any potential purchaser that the land has been used to manage hazardous waste and the land's future use is restricted. 40 CFR § 265.120. 31 Cath. U. L. Rev. 273 (1982); 1982 J. of Products Liab. 23; 57 Notre D. Law. 260; 84 W. Va. L. Rev. 347 (1982); 1979 Wisc. L. Rev. 709; 70 Ill. B. J. 434.

6.10 Suggestions

1. *Form of deed.* If there is a contract for the sale of land, find out if the contract specifies the form of deed to be given. If the contract specifies that the seller is to give a warranty deed, then, of course, a warranty deed form must be used. If the contract does not specify the form of the deed, in most states a quitclaim deed will suffice. The seller will prefer to use this form, since it subjects him to no personal liability for defects in title. If there is no written contract for the sale of the land, the sellers will again prefer to give a quitclaim deed.

2. *Grantor.* Check the deed by which the grantor acquired ownership and see that his name is spelled the same way in the deed by which he is conveying the land. Any difference in spelling may lead to an objection when the title is examined. If a woman acquires title by her maiden name and subsequently marries, the deed should show both names: *Mary Jones, formerly Mary Smith.* Any examiner of the title will thus find a connected chain of title to the land. The grantor's marital status should be given: *bachelor, spinster, widow, widower, divorced and not remarried.* If the grantor is married, his spouse should also be named as grantor, and their marital status given: *John Smith and Mary Smith, his wife.* A married woman or widow should never be described as "Mrs. John Jones." Her legal name is "Mary Jones." Don't describe yourself as "R. John Smith." Legally your middle name or middle initial is no part of your name. Hence you should at least describe yourself as "Robert John Smith," for it is poor practice to use initials only in legal documents. If the state law requires, give the street address of the grantor and grantee. Special forms of deeds are used where the grantor is a corporation, trustee, executor, and so on. Of course all the landowners must convey if the buyer is to get good title, but different landowners may use different deeds. As a rule, it is best for a husband and wife to join in the same deed.

3. *Grantee.* Have the proposed grantee write out his name on a slip of paper—first name, middle initial, if any, and last name—and copy the name in this identical form in the proper place in the deed form. His or her marital status may, but need not, be given. State grantee's place of residence. If two or more persons are acquiring title, the names

of all must be shown in the deed. If they are taking title as joint tenants, use a joint tenancy form deed. Legal stationers usually print a special form for joint tenancy transactions. Following the names of the grantees in this form is a phrase reading somewhat like this: *as joint tenants with the right of survivorship and not as tenants in common nor as tenants by the entireties.* When husband and wife are taking title, their marital relation should be shown, as *John Smith and Mary Smith, his wife.* If a corporation is taking title, its charter should be checked and the name copied exactly and without the slightest deviation. For example, if the charter describes a corporation as The Elite Hat Shop, Inc., do not omit the *The* and do not spell out the *Inc.* A deed to a trustee should clearly identify the trust. Never draft a deed running simply to *John Smith, as trustee.* Have the deed run to *John Smith, as trustee under Trust Agreement dated June 15, 1946, and known as the Pinecrest Liquidation Trust,* or other proper designation. Have before you the trust instrument creating the trust and describe it accurately in the deed. If the deed to the trustee also creates the trust, it is serving a double purpose. (1) It is operating as a deed of the land and must contain all the necessary elements of a deed. (2) It is creating a trust and must contain all the requisite elements for the creation of a trust. Such a document should be drafted only by one thoroughly conversant with the law of trusts.

The deed should conform to the contract of sale with respect to the grantees. For example, if Seller contracts to sell to Buyer #1 and Buyer #2, Seller should not, even though Buyer #1 request it, make a deed running to Buyer #1 only. That would violate Buyer #2's rights and make Seller liable for damages if Buyer #2 suffers a loss.

If you are creating a corporation that is to acquire real estate, be sure that the corporation's charter has been issued and that all other formalties for corporate existence are complied with *before* the deed to the corporation is made out. In other words, be sure you have an existing, legal grantee to whom to convey.

4. *Consideration.* Let the deed recite a monetary consideration, as *in consideration of the sum of $10 and other good and valuable consideration.* In a few states, it is customary or necessary to recite the true sale price of the land. In deeds by corporations, trustees, executors, and so forth, the deed should recite the true sale price.

5. *Words of grant.* Every printed form of deed contains words of grant. It is not necessary to tamper with these, since the warranty deed form will have words appropriate for a warranty deed and the quitclaim deed form will also have appropriate words.

6. *Description.* Do not attempt to draft a description unless you are sure you know what you are doing. If a title policy, abstract, or Torrens certificate has been previously issued on the land that is being sold, and the land sold is identical with the tract mentioned in the title policy, abstract, or Torrens certificate (that is, there have been no subsequent conveyances of portions of the tract, and so forth), then the description may be copied from title policy, abstract caption, or Torrens certificate, since such documents usually contain accurate descriptions. After the description has been copied into the deed form, have someone read it aloud to you while you follow the description in the title policy, abstract, or Torrens certificate, since even a microscopic error in typing may throw the whole description off.

7. *Subject clause.* If the grantor in a warranty deed wishes to avoid personal liability, he should include in the subject clause all defects in title, such as mortgages, unpaid taxes, existing leases, restrictions, and so forth. However, the contract of sale usually specifies to what objections the title will be subject when conveyed to the buyer; the seller, in preparing the deed, has no right to add items to this list. For example, if the seller agrees, by his contract, to convey the land to the buyer subject only to a certain mortgage, he cannot include in the deed *subject to mortgage recorded as document No. 10356789 and also to restrictions of record.* The buyer has the right to object to the inclusion of the portion relating to the restrictions, since restrictions were not mentioned in the contract. In a quitclaim deed, a subject clause is unnecessary and inappropriate.

8. *Mortgages.* If the land is being sold subject to a mortgage that the grantee is to assume and agree to pay, let the deed so state.

SUGGESTED FORM: "Subject to a mortgage recorded in Book 100, Page 101, as Document No. 999, which the grantee herein assumes and agrees to pay."

Where the buyer is paying part cash and giving back to the seller either a mortgage or mortgage trust deed for part of the purchase money, it is better that the deed contain a recital somewhat as follows: "As part of the consideration for this transaction, the grantee herein has this day executed to _____, as trustee, a trust deed, of even date herewith, securing a promissory note in the sum of $_____, which represents part of the purchase price for said premises." This is particularly desirable where a mortgage deed of trust is involved, since if Seller sells and conveys land to Buyer and Buyer simultaneously executes a mortgage trust deed to Trustee, the public records do not clearly show that the trust deed was given as part of the purchase price unless the deed contains the suggested recital. Of course the trust deed or mortgage should also contain a recital that "this trust deed is given to secure payment of part of the purchase price of said premises."

9. *Statement of purpose of deed.* Inexperienced conveyancers tend to put in deeds various legal-sounding phrases without having any clear idea of what purpose such phrases were intended to serve. This is a very dangerous practice. Do not insert a single syllable in a deed unless you are certain what the legal effect of that insertion will be. Remember that if you add in your deed phrases like "to be used for road purposes," the result may be to create a grant of an easement out of what started to be a deed of the land. It is neither necessary nor desirable to state in the deed the purpose for which the land is to be used.

10. *Restrictions and conditions.* Restrictions and conditions must be drafted with care. Because of the drastic consequences attendant upon the enforcement of a reverter clause, the grantee should view with suspicion any attempt to insert a reverter clause in the deed. If there is a written contract for the sale of the land, the grantor has no right to insert in the deed any restrictions or conditions not provided for in the contract. If the contract provides for a building restriction, but says nothing about a condition or reverter clause, the grantor has no right to provide in the deed for a reverter of title in the event of a breach of condition. Be sure you understand the words you use in drafting restrictions, as, for example, residence purposes, dwellings purposes, business purposes. Certain words have a well-known technical meaning, and if you use such words in a deed, courts will give them their usual meaning, regardless of what special, individual meaning they may have in your own mind. You will not even be allowed to testify that such a word has a special meaning for you. On the other hand, inexperienced draftsmen often use words that have no meaning at all, such as the provision that "only houses of standard construction shall be erected on said premises." It would be difficult to get two people to agree on the definition of "standard construction." Such a phrase is so devoid of meaning that courts cannot enforce it.

11. *Easements.* A deed may contain a grant to the grantee of an easement over other lands of the seller. If there is a written contract of sale, and it makes no mention of such an easement, the seller is under no obligation to include it in the deed. A deed may reserve to the grantor an easement over the land conveyed. If there is a written contract of sale, and it makes no mention of such an easement, the grantor has no right to insert such a clause in the deed.

12. *Waiver of dower and homestead.* Almost without exception, deed forms prepared by your local stationers include the necessary waivers of dower and homestead rights. For this and other reasons, it is dangerous to use a deed form printed in your state in conveying land lying in some other state. Obtain a form printed in the state where the land lies.

13. *Date.* It is the custom to date all deeds.

14. *Signature.* Before permitting the grantor to sign, have him write his name on a piece of paper. Check the spelling with the spelling of his name in the body of the deed. Be sure that the two correspond, since even trivial variations are frequently objected to by title examiners. Type the name of the grantor beneath the signature line and direct him to sign exactly as his name is typed.

15. *Seal.* If a seal is needed on deeds of land in your state, deed forms printed in your state will show a seal on the signature line. If there are more signatures on the deed than there are printed signature lines, be sure the word *Seal* appears after each signature. The corporate seal is always necessary on deeds made by corporations.

16. *Tax stamps.* The necessary tax stamps should be attached where the state law requires.

17. *Witnesses.* Always have two or more witnesses sign the deed if any grantor has signed by mark. If all grantors are able to write, their signatures need not be witnessed unless the state law requires witnesses. Some states required that all deeds be witnessed.

18. *Acknowledgment.*

19. *Recording.* File your deed in the proper public office immediately after it has been acknowledged. Delay may prove disastrous.

20. *Statutory requirements.* Make sure to comply with all applicable state laws relating to various recitations that are required to appear on the face of the deed, i.e., compliance with local subdivision ordinances and plat acts, mailing address of the grantee, name and address of the person preparing the deed. Readiness avoids recording problems and delay.

21. *Take care in preparing the deed.* Erasures and alterations raise danger signals which proper draftsmanship and transcription should avoid. 1 *Merrill on Notice* 106.

7 RECORDING AND CONSTRUCTIVE NOTICE

7.01 Necessity of recording

Every state has a recording law. These laws provide, in substance, that, until recorded, a deed, mortgage, or other instrument is ineffective and void so far as subsequent purchasers or mortgagees of the same land are concerned. The policy behind these laws is that the ownership of real estate should be disclosed by the public records, and that purchasers of land should be able to rely on these records and should be protected against secret, unrecorded deeds and mortgages. Under these laws, although an unrecorded deed or mortgage is good and valid *as between the parties to the instrument,* the grantee or mortgagee is in great danger of losing his rights, because persons who deal with the real estate in ignorance of the unrecorded deed or mortgage will be protected against such unrecorded deed or mortgage.

> **EXAMPLE:** Seller, the owner of certain vacant land, sells the same to Buyer #1 and gives Buyer #1 a deed, which Buyer #1 fails to record. Later Seller dies, and his heirs, not knowing that he had previously sold the land, deed the land to Buyer #2, who records his deed. Buyer #2 purchases in ignorance of the earlier deed to Buyer #1. Buyer #2 gets good title to the real estate. He is an *innocent purchaser* or *bona fide purchaser.*

> **EXAMPLE:** Seller owns certain land. Seller mortgages it to Lender in 1975. The mortgage, through error, is not recorded. Seller sells the land to Buyer in 1976, concealing the existence of the mortgage. Buyer owns the land free and clear of the mortgage. An innocent purchaser is protected against an unrecorded mortgage.

7.02 Constructive notice from the records

The recording laws have a double operation or effect. First, they protect a purchaser or mortgagee who acts in ignorance of an earlier unrecorded deed or mortgage. Second, they also provide that if a deed or mortgage is recorded, all persons who thereafter deal with the property will be deemed to have full knowledge of the recorded document. The courts will not permit a man to say that he acted in ignorance of a recorded document. Every purchaser or mortgagee of the land is said to be *charged with notice* of prior recorded documents. The courts say that the public records impart *constructive notice* of all prior recorded deeds and mortgages.

> **EXAMPLE:** Seller conveys land to Buyer #1, who records his deed. Thereafter Seller persuades Buyer #2 to buy the same land, telling Buyer #2 that he still owns the land. Buyer #2 fails to examine the public records relating to this tract of land. Buyer #2 acquires nothing. He has constructive notice of the deed to Buyer #1.

7.02(a) Office where deeds are recorded

The name of the officer charged with the duty of keeping the public records of deeds and mortgages varies from state to state. He is known variously as a recorder of deeds, county recorder, register of deeds, and registrar of deeds. For convenience, the officer in charge is hereinafter referred to as the *recorder,* and the public office where deeds are filed or recorded is referred to as the *recorder's office.*

7.03 What constitutes recording

A person wishing to record a deed or mortgage simply deposits it with the recorder. Such a deed or mortgage is said to be filed for record. It is thereupon deemed to be recorded, and all the world must take notice of its existence. The recorder copies the document in his record books, indexes it, and returns the original to the person who left it for recording. He does not pass on the validity of the document.

7.04 Persons protected by recording laws

The recording laws are designed primarily to protect subsequent *bona fide purchasers* of the land. A bona fide purchaser is one who has paid the purchase price in good faith and without knowledge of the prior unrecorded deed or mortgage. A mortgagee who loans money in reliance on the public records is also considered a bona fide purchaser and is entitled to the protection of the recording laws.

> **EXAMPLE:** Owner mortgages his land to Lender #1, which mortgage is not recorded. Thereafter, Owner puts a mortgage on the same land to Lender #2, and Lender #2 records his mortgage. Lender #2 does not know of the earlier mortgage to Lender #1. Lender #2 has a first mortgage on the land.

A number of states add the requirement that to be entitled to protection the subsequent purchaser or mortgagee must file his deed or mortgage for record before the recording of the earlier deed or mortgage. Under this rule, for example, it will not suffice that Purchaser has purchased a tract of land in good faith and in ignorance of an earlier unrecorded mortgage. He must also record his deed before the prior mortgage is recorded. But if he records his deed in apt time, Purchaser is protected even if the mortgagee later discovers his oversight and proceeds to record his mortgage.

In some states, a judgment creditor is also protected against prior unrecorded deeds and mortgages.

EXAMPLE: Owner makes a mortgage to Lender on November 15. The mortgage is recorded on November 20. On November 17, Creditor obtains a judgment against Owner. The judgment enjoys priority of lien over the mortgage, since it was rendered prior to the recording of the mortgage.

A substantial number of states, however, do not extend such protection to judgment creditors.

A person who has acquired land by gift is not protected by the recording laws.

EXAMPLE: Owner mortgages his land to Lender. Lender fails to record the mortgage. Owner thereafter gives Daughter a deed to the land as a gift, and Daughter records her deed. Lender can nevertheless enforce the mortgage against her. But if, prior to the recording of the mortgage, Daughter should sell the land to Buyer, Buyer, being a purchaser, would get good title free and clear of the prior, unrecorded mortgage.

If at any time before he purchases or loans money, a party obtains knowledge of the unrecorded document he gets no protection against it. He is not a "bona fide purchaser."

A person who acquires title by will or as an heir of the landowner is not protected.

EXAMPLE: Owner makes a mortgage to Lender, which Lender fails to record. Thereafter Owner dies leaving a will whereby he gives this land to Son. Lender may enforce this mortgage against Son.

7.05   Effect of actual knowledge

Of course one who actually knows of a prior unrecorded deed or mortgage is not protected against it.

EXAMPLE: Owner makes a mortgage to Lender #1 which Lender #1 fails to record. Thereafter, Owner mortgages the land to Lender #2, who knows of the existence of the earlier mortgage. Lender #2 takes subject to the earlier unrecorded mortgage. 45 Am.Jur.2d *Records & Recording Laws* § 172.

EXAMPLE: Owner owns certain land and mortgages it to Lender in 1975. Through error, the mortgage is not recorded. Owner enters into a contract to sell the land to Buyer in 1980. The contract of sale describes the mortgage. Buyer must pay off the mortgage or take the land burdened with the mortgage. He is not protected. He is not an innocent purchaser.

Similarly, where a subsequent purchaser takes with *actual knowledge* of an instrument which was recorded, but because of some defect, does not impart *constructive notice,* no bona fide purchaser protection attaches. 3 ALR2d 589.

EXAMPLE: Purchaser obtained a title report which raised a defectively recorded deed to Stranger. This deed, though taken by the recorder, did not legally give constructive notice because it bore no acknowledgment. Purchaser will not be a bona fide purchaser and will take subject to X's right. 59 ALR2d 1318.

7.05(a) Possession as notice

The law requires every prospective purchaser or mortgagee to examine into the possession of the real estate and to ascertain what rights are claimed by the parties in possession. Whether or not he actually does make this inspection, such purchaser or mortgagee is deemed to know the facts that such an investigation would have disclosed. In other words, possession imparts constructive notice in much the same way as the recording of a deed.

EXAMPLE: Owner sells and conveys his home to Buyer #1. Buyer #1 fails to record the deed but moves into the house. Owner offers to sell the land to Buyer #2. Buyer #2 examines the records in the recorder's office and finds title in Owner, but he fails to examine into the possession of the premises. He takes a deed from Owner. This deed passes no title. Buyer #1's possession gave Buyer #2 constructive notice of this deed.

It is obvious that failure to record or a defective recording of a deed is usually less dangerous than the failure to record or the defective recording of a mortgage. This follows, since the purchaser usually goes into possession of the land after receiving his deed, and this possession gives all the world notice of his rights, whereas a mortgagee rarely goes into possession before a default has been made and is therefore entirely dependent on the public records to give other persons notice of his rights.

In a few states, South Carolina and Virginia, for example, possession does not impart constructive notice.

7.06(a) Prerequisites to valid recording— instruments entitled to be recorded

Deeds, mortgages, release deeds, satisfactions of mortgages, assignments of mortgages, and other instruments affecting the title to land should be recorded. However, it is only the original instrument that is entitled to be recorded. The recording of an usigned carbon copy of an instrument is without legal effect. *Herzer* v. *Dembosz,* 167 NE2d 21O (Ill. 1960).

7.06(b)   Prerequisites to valid recording— defective instruments

In a great majority of the states, an instrument must be properly acknowledged by the grantor or mortgagor in order to be entitled to recording. In a number of states, proper witnessing is accepted as a substitute for an acknowledgment. But, if the instrument is neither witnessed nor acknowledged, or the witnessing or acknowledgment is fatally defective, the instrument is not considered as a recorded instrument even though the recorder accepts it and copies it on the public records. 59 ALR2d 1299.

7.06(b)(1)   Prerequisites to valid recording— defective instruments— legal descriptions

Since a purchaser or mortgagee is under no obligation to examine the records affecting lands other than those that he is buying or upon which he is loaning money, the record of an instrument that was intended to convey or affect the same but which has such an erroneous description that it does not appear to affect the land in question does not bind any subsequent purchaser, mortgagee, or judgment creditor.

> **EXAMPLE:** Owner owns the West Half of the Northwest Quarter of Section 14, Township 38 North, Range 13 East, of the Third Principal Meridian. Owner executes a mortgage to Lender that is intended as a mortgage on this same land but which, through inadvertence, describes the land as falling in Section 24 instead of Section 14. The mortgage is recorded. A person searching the records as to Owner's title has no way of knowing that this mortgage was intended for the particular land in question. Therefore this mortgage does not impart constructive notice, and subsequent purchasers, mortgagees, and judgment creditors will be protected against this mortgage. *Landis* v. *Miles Homes, Inc.,* 273 NE2d 153 (Ill. 1971).

7.07   Chain of title

Except in a few states a title searcher tracing title by means of the public records employs an official index of names, called the Grantor–Grantee Index. Suppose, for example, that the United States Government records show that the United States sold a particular tract of land to John Jones on March 15, 1840. The title searcher will turn to the Grantor Index, which is arranged alphabetically, and, beginning with the date March 15, 1840, he will look under the letter "J" for any deeds or mortgages made since March 15, 1840, by John Jones. Naturally he would not expect to find any deeds or mortgages of that land made by Jones prior to March 15, 1840, because Jones did not become the owner until that date. Therefore the law does not require him to look for any such deeds or mortgages prior to that date. *Glen Ellyn Savings & Loan Assn.* v. *State Bank of Geneva,* 382 NE2d 1267 (Ill. App. 1978).

Suppose he finds that John Jones conveyed the land to Joseph Smith by deed dated September 10, 1860, and recorded November 1, 1860. He will now look under the letter "S" for any deeds or mortgages made by Smith on or after September 10, 1860, the date when Smith acquired title. This process is repeated until he has brought the title down to the present. This process is called *running the chain of title.*

To be considered properly recorded, a deed or mortgage must be in the *chain of title,* that is, it must be dated in the proper chronological order.

> **EXAMPLE:** At a time when his negotiations for the purchase were virtually concluded, Joseph Smith made a mortgage on the land dated September 5, 1860, and recorded September 6, 1860. Both of these dates were prior to the date of the deed by which Smith later acquired ownership, namely, September 10, 1860. A title searcher would not find this mortgage, since he would not look under the name "Smith" for any deed or mortgage prior to September 10, 1860. Such a mortgage is not in the line of title. It is also said that the mortgage is not in the *chain of title. The legal result is the same as though the mortgage had not been recorded at all.* A person buying the land not knowing of the existence of this mortgage would get good title free and clear of the mortgage.

In other words, the records show the ownership of land passing from one person to another, and the name of each successive owner as that name appears on the public records must be searched only during the period of his ownership as such period is revealed by the public records to see what recorded deeds and mortgages he has signed.

Because of the *chain of title theory,* it is important that names be spelled correctly in deeds and mortgages.

> **EXAMPLE:** A deed runs to John O. Malley and a mortgage is thereafter made by John O'Malley. The mortgage is not in the chain of title and is treated as an unrecorded mortgage. The deed is indexed under M, the mortgage under O.

The chain of title theory is a two-edged sword. One, constructive notice is given of those instruments that are in the chain of title. Two, instruments outside of the chain of title do not impart constructive notice. *Pease* v. *Frank,* 105 NE 299 (Ill. 1914).

7.08 Tract indexes In a few states (Iowa, Louisiana, Nebraska, North Dakota, Oklahoma, South Dakota, Utah, Wisconsin, and Wyoming, for example), the name index (Grantor–Grantee Index) has been supplemented by a Tract Index. This index allocates a separate page in the index to each piece of property in the county, and if you are interested in a particular piece of property, you simply locate the proper page in the index, where you will find listed all recorded deeds and other documents relating to this piece of property.

7.09   Record as notice of contents of deed or mortgage

An instrument duly recorded is notice to subsequent purchasers and mortgagees not only of the instrument itself, but also of all of its contents.

> **EXAMPLE:**   A warranty deed contained a covenant that the premises were free and clear of all encumbrances "except a certain mortgage for $900." This mortgage had not been recorded. This was notice to the grantee and to all other persons of the existence of the mortgage.

7.10   Foreign language

A deed or mortgage written in a foreign language, though valid as between the parties thereto, does not impart constructive notice and must be treated as an unrecorded document. *Moroz* v. *Ransom,* 285 N.Y.S. 846 (1936).

7.11   Liens that need not be recorded

There are certain liens, such as real estate tax liens, inheritance tax liens, and franchise tax liens, that are binding on all persons though not recorded.

7.12   Short leases

In a number of states leases that exceed one year in duration (other states, three years) must be recorded. Possession under a longer lease does not impart constructive notice. In consequence, a purchaser or mortgagee of an apartment building, for example, may assume that occupants are there under short leases where no leases have been recorded. This is a practical approach to the problem of large buildings where checking possession is a burdensome task. In point of fact, purchasers and mortgagees never do check all the tenants in a large building. They accept a written statement by the building manager describing the leases and the terms of the leases.

8 REAL ESTATE BROKERS

8.01 Defined   A broker is an agent employed in negotiating the sale, purchase, or exchange of land. Compensation is usually in the form of a commission payable only if a deal is successfully signed up.

8.02 License   In many states, a person is not authorized to act as a real estate broker unless he first produces a broker's license. Real estate brokerage is a profession requiring knowledge, experience, and honesty, and in order to obtain a license, a candidate must have the qualifications that are specified by the local law. In order for a real estate broker to recover commissions, he must have his license at the time he is hired to perform the services for which he claims a commission. *Schoene* v. *Hickham,* 397 SW2d 596 (1966). New York led all the states by requiring a written test for license applicants in 1924. Today license officials belong to a national organization, the National Association of Real Estate License Officials. The brokers' exam is standardized, to some extent. Educational and ethical standards continue to climb steadily. Many states require brokers to take continuing education courses. Other states are certain to follow. A similar trend is evident in the legal profession.

NEW DIRECTIONS: In recent times Real Estate Commissions have shown a strong tendency to hold brokers to high standards of conduct. State laws list many causes for revoking a license. Racial discrimination (steering or blockbusting) is one of them, of course. Acting in a dual capacity is another.

EXAMPLE: A broker advertised to buy real estate. The ad did not disclose he was a broker. He lost his license. *Land* v. *Georgia Comm.,* 237 SE2d 243, 142 Ga. App. 860 (1977).

90

EXAMPLE: Commingling client's funds with personal funds is grounds for revocation of a license.

EXAMPLE: Acting dishonestly in transactions involving the broker individually is grounds for revoking the license. For example, in a deal where the broker was the seller he was guilty of a fraudulent misrepresentation. He was not brokering the deal. He lost his license.

The system of licensing real estate brokers paralleled the growth of professionalism in the real estate business generally. The first university courses in real estate were offered in 1905. By 1913, YMCA courses were offered throughout the country. Today, the real estate business is run by professionals.

The first treatise on real estate was Fisher's *Principles of Real Estate Practice,* published by 1923. Within three years Babcock had published a treatise on appraisals and Mac Chesney a treatise on real estate law.

8.03 Splitting commission with buyer

It has been held that the seller's broker may split his commission with the buyer where this concession is necessary to obtain the buyer's signature on the contract. This is simply a sacrifice on his part. It does not harm the seller. *Lageschult* v. *Steinbrecher,* 35 Ill. App. 3d 909, 344 NE2d 750 (1976); 63 ALR3d 1219.

But other than as above stated, the broker must not split his commission with "finders" or other persons lacking a broker's license. This will defeat a broker's claim for a commission. *Thorpe* v. *Garte,* 250 A2d 618 (Md. 1969).

8.04 Brokers' functions in today's market

The old idea that the broker's task is simply one of finding a buyer has totally disappeared. Today's broker is a highly skilled professional with a great breadth of knowledge of real estate law. Among the matters he must be familiar with are:

1. Zoning, including the ability to point out that a basement apartment in a home is illegal, that occupancy by unmarried persons who are not related may be unlawful, that an area that has numerous apartments scattered among the homes may be unable to keep out additional apartments.

2. Building codes, especially those that require replacement of plumbing and old electrical wiring where extensive rehab is contemplated.

3. Private building restriction problems, for example, those that prohibit building near lot lines and would thus bar an addition to the home.

4. Methods of financing where financing by an institution is unavailable. For example, the take-back (purchase money) mortgage, the installment contract, the wraparound mortgage, the second mortgage, the assumable mortgage, and all the problems, drawbacks, and advantages of each method, including income tax advantage's, retention of old low-interest mortgages, high return on wraparounds, dangers of all provisions, bal-

loon notes, and acceleration clauses, prepayment privileges, benefits to the private lender, and the deed of trust in states having no redemption laws.

5. Benefits and drawbacks of joint tenancies and tenancies by the entireties, for this arises even in preparing the contract of sale.

6. The pitfalls involved where unmarried cohabitants plan to buy a home together.

7. The dangers involved in creating lodging units in homes. There are over 500,000 illegal units of this character in this country. A lodger whose rent has been raised unreasonably, as he contends, may be tempted to complain to the authorities.

8. The pitfalls in buying a landmark home must be explained to a buyer.

9. Buyers who are timid about entering into installment purchases must be informed about escrows and other protective devices.

10. Where informal party driveways are revealed, buyers must be advised to obtain counsel for the preparation of formal agreements.

11. In a condo, the broker must know about restrictions on pets and renting, recreational leases, etc.

12. Brokers must know about the penalties for blockbusting and steering. Racial problems are growing more serious year by year.

13. A broker must be able to explain about assessments and special assessments in condo and planned unit development situations; also the role of the home association.

14. Especially in industrial and commercial properties the broker must know whether the building is a nonconforming use, and if so, that it cannot be expanded.

This list is suggestive only. Other suggestions will be found in Chapter 9. Of course, the broker must not usurp the lawyer's role. But the mere mention to a buyer of an older industrial plant that it is a nonconforming use may enable the buyer to make a quick decision.

8.05   Salesmen

Virtually every brokerage office maintains a staff of salesmen, who do the actual leg work of showing houses and filling in sales contract forms. A salesman is required to have a state license and pass a state exam, but the exam is less comprehensive than the broker's exam. In recent times the broker makes a determined effort to establish the relation between himself and a salesman as that of *independent contractor*. There is a distinction between an *employee,* who must take orders from his employer, and an independent contractor, who is hired to do a job, but does it pretty much his own way. The objective is to avoid the employer–employee relationship, so that the broker need not withhold income taxes, and so forth. There seem to be no decided cases on this new idea. Problems may arise. Salesmen often go to the "boss" on complex deals, and as soon as he starts giving directions he may become an *employer.* But the whole idea is untested. 41 Am.J.2d 735. No doubt many real estate offices prefer the employer–employee relationship. This, of course, gets the employer involved in income tax withholdings, and so forth. In any event, whatever the legal relationship is, courts are bound to hold the broker liable for fraudulent representations made by his salesmen.

8.06   Employment— necessity of contract of employment

A real estate broker acts as an *agent*. The person who hires him is known as the *principal*. Usually, the broker is hired by the landowner for the purpose of procuring a buyer. In return for finding a buyer willing to buy on the landowner's terms, the broker receives a commission from the landowner. Occasionally the broker is hired by a person wishing to buy real estate. In either case, in order to recover a commission, the broker must be able to show that he was hired by the person from whom he claims a commission. If he claims a commission from the seller, he must show that the seller hired him. And if he was hired by the buyer only, he cannot claim a commission from the seller. Otherwise stated, a broker must show that the person from whom he claims a commission employed him to make the sale. However, an employment contract of agency may be *implied* from the conduct of the parties.

> **EXAMPLE:**   Landowner gave Broker a description of his property and requested that Broker sell it at a designated price. This is a contract of employment as agent, and Broker is entitled to a commission if he finds a buyer. The fact that compensation was not discussed is immaterial. Landowner must have understood that Broker would expect to be paid if he produced a buyer. *Long* v. *Herr,* 10 Colo. 380, 15 Pac. 802 (1887).

> **EXAMPLE:**   Broker, without any prior request from Landowner, submitted to Landowner an offer of $3,000 for the purchase of the land. Landowner declined, stating that his price for the land was $4,000. Broker thereupon procured a buyer who was willing to buy for $4,000. Landowner refused to sell. Landowner is not liable for a commission. The mere statement by a landowner that he will take a certain sum for his land is not sufficient to authorize the person to whom the statement is made to act as agent for its sale. Landowner is entitled to assume that Broker is acting for the buyer and will look to the buyer for his compensation. *O'Donnell* v. *Carr,* 189 N.C. 77, 126 SE 112 (1925).

As is evident from the foregoing illustrations, a broker usually tries to collect from the seller. This is due to the obvious fact that it is financially easier to collect money from the seller, who after all is being paid the purchase price of the property, than from the buyer, who may be stretching his finances in order to buy the property. Legally, the fact remains that the broker cannot collect from the seller unless he can show that the seller hired him. If there is no formal listing contract, at the very least the seller must say or do things that make the broker believe he has been hired by the seller. *Reeve* v. *Shoemaker,* 200 Ia. 938, 205 NW 742 (1925). Or the broker must so conduct himself that it is clear to the seller that he expects to be paid a commission. *Korzendorfer Realty Inc.* v. *Hawkes,* 178 SE2d 524 (Va. 1971).

EXAMPLE: Suppose in the EXAMPLE last given, the broker had asked, "When will my commission be paid?" Suppose the owner had replied, "At closing." This is enough to show a contract of employment.

Ordinarily a broker hired by the seller has no claim against the buyer.

EXAMPLE: Seller hired Broker, who found Purchaser. Seller and Purchaser entered into a contract of sale. However, difficulties arose and Purchaser refused to perform. Broker cannot collect anything from Purchaser. His contract of employment is with Seller only. 30 ALR3d 1399.

8.06(a)   Employment— persons who may employ a broker

A person other than the property owner may list the property for sale and become liable for a commission. 12 Am. Jur.2d *Brokers* § 163, p. 902. Any adult can hire an agent.

EXAMPLE: Wife owned certain real estate. Husband listed the property for sale with Broker, who knew that Wife owned the property. Broker found a buyer for the property, but Wife refused to sell. Husband was held liable to Broker for a full commission. Broker was entitled to assume that at the proper time Husband would procure Wife's consent to the sale. *Aler* v. *Plowman,* 190 Md. 631, 59 A2d 196 (1948); *Rose* v. *Knoblock* 194 SW2d 943 (Mo. 1946).

EXAMPLE: The land was held in community property but the husband alone signed the listing. He is liable for the full commission. *C. Forsman Real Estate Co.* v. *Hatch,* 547 P2d 1116 (Idaho).

EXAMPLE: Property was owned by Husband and Wife, in joint tenancy. Husband alone, without Wife's permission, listed the property for sale with Broker, who found a buyer for the property, but Wife refused to sign the contract of sale and the deal fell through. Husband was held liable to Broker for a full commission. 10 ALR3d 665.

8.06(b)   Employment— necessity for written contract

Because of the endless litigation that has arisen concerning the existence of an employment contract, in many states the contract of employment must be in writing in order for the broker to be entitled to a commission and must state the amount of commission agreed on. 9 ALR2d 747.

8.06(c)   Employment— form of contract

Often the hiring of a broker is an informal, oral affair. However, written contracts, called *listing contracts,* are also used. These are usually brief documents, often in the form of printed cards. When such a form is filled in, it contains the following: (1) names of seller and broker; (2) description of property, usually by street address. 30 ALR3d 935; (3) terms of sale, including sale price, whether sale is for cash or on terms, and so forth; (4) duration of broker's employment; (5) commission to be paid; (6) special agreements, such as the provision for an exclusive agency.

8.06(d) Employment—unconscionability

The new law requires the broker to use a listing form that is fair to the party employing him. *Unconscionability and the Real Estate Broker's Employment Contract,* 5 Memphis S.U.L.Rev. 59.

8.06(e) Real Estate board forms

Each of the countless real estate boards is likely to have its own listing form.

8.06(f) Flat fee sales

A new type of brokerage contract has made its appearance.

> **NEW DIRECTIONS:** The flat-fee broker competes with the regular commission broker. He charges a flat fee to the seller, which is much smaller than the regular broker's commission. He gives the seller an appraisal of his house and a FOR SALE sign, and displays a photo of the house and a fact sheet in his office. The homeowner must show and sell the house himself. There is no multiple listing service. The disadvantages are that homeowners do not know how to sell their homes or get financing for the buyer. It is workable when there is a great scarcity of houses. If a sharp speculator shows up as a buyer, the seller is likely to lose.

8.06(g) Contract provisions

Quite commonly a *contract of sale* will contain a provision that a commission will be paid by the seller to the broker at closing. Even if there is no proof of a *contract of employment,* this contract clause suffices to make the seller liable to the broker. *Moran* v. *Audette,* 217 A2d 663 (D.C. 1966); *B. Woodworth* v. *Vranizen,* 539 P2d 1055 (Ore. 1975). The broker is what the lawyers call a "third-party beneficiary." Of course, the broker's rights rest on the terms of the contract.

> **EXAMPLE:** The contract of sale provided that the seller would pay the broker a commission at closing. This contract, however, was contingent on the buyer's ability to obtain financing. The buyer was unable to obtain financing. The broker collects no commission. *Shumaker* v. *Lear,* 235 Pa. Super. 509.

8.07 Code of Ethics

Many controversies involving brokers, especially those involving conflicts between two brokers, are settled by resort to the Code of Ethics established by the National Association of Realtors or by some local real estate board. Punishments are given according to the nature of the offense—the most severe being explusion from the board. This cuts the broker from the multiple listing service maintained by the board, and is an effective punishment indeed.

> **EXAMPLE:** A broker was punished for failure to observe a sign indicating that a rezoning of the land was imminent. As a result, the lot was sold for one-eighth of its market value.

8.08 Open listing

There are several different types of listing contracts. The *open listing* contains no provision forbidding the landowner to sell the land himself or to hire other brokers, and ordinarily an owner may hire two or more brokers unless he specifically agrees not to do so. *Kelly* v. *Beaudoin*, 298 A2d 831 (Vt. 1972). Virtually all informal, verbal listing arrangements are open listings. The disadvantage of this type of contract is that it is likely to produce quarrels over the commission where several brokers produce buyers.

> **EXAMPLE:** Landowner employed Broker to obtain a purchaser. Broker obtained a purchaser on the specified terms, but Landowner refused to pay a commission on the ground that he had already concluded an agreement to sell to a purchaser obtained by another broker. Broker sued Landowner. The court held for Landowner. The primary object to be attained in the employment of agents to sell real estate, the court said, is the production of a single purchaser for such real estate, and that object is attained where one of several agents produces to the owner a purchaser who is ready, able, and willing to buy the real estate on the owner's terms. Where several agents are employed, the sale of the property either by the owner in person, or by any of the brokers, operates at once to terminate the authority of all the brokers, although they had no actual notice of the sale. This is a provision the court "reads into" every open listing.

To put this in a legal perspective, one might say that in every open listing there is an unspoken, implied precondition that to receive his compensation the broker must find a willing buyer before such a buyer is procured by the owner or some other broker.

When different brokers have the property for sale, and no one of them has the exclusive right to make the sale, the broker who first finds a buyer ready, able, and willing to buy is the procuring cause of the sale and is the one entitled to the commission.

8.09 Exclusive agency

Unless there is an agreement to the contrary, the landowner may hire two or more brokers to sell the same property and will be liable only to the broker who first finds a buyer. Fear that time and money spent in locating a buyer may be wasted if another broker is working on the deal has led brokers to favor a listing contract which assures the broker that as long as his employment continues no other broker will be hired. Such a listing is called an *exclusive agency.* The giving of an exclusive agency does not bar the landowner from selling the property through his own efforts, without the assistance of other brokers. If the property owner sells the property through his own efforts, the exclusive agency automatically comes to an end, without any liability on the landowner's part for a commission and regardless of the employment period specified in the listing contract. *Martin Realty Co.* v. *Fletcher,* 103 N.J.L. 294, 136 Atl. 498 (1927); *Des Rivieres* v. *Sullivan,* 247 Mass. 443, 142 NE 111, 88 ALR2d 936. This is a provision the court "reads into" the listing.

The mere fact that the listing contract refers to the broker as an *exclusive agent* is enough to create an exclusive agency. *Harris and White* v. *Stone,* 137 Ark. 23, 207 SW 443 (1918).

Again, to put this situation in a legal perspective, one might say that in every exclusive agency there is an unspoken, implied precondition that the broker must find a willing buyer before such a buyer is procured by the owner.

8.10 Exclusive right to sell

The *exclusive right to sell* goes one step further than the exclusive agency. It not only makes the broker the sole agent of the landowner for the sale of the property, but also provides that the named broker will receive a commission in the event the property is sold by the named broker, by the owner, *or by anyone else.* Thus, even if the owner makes a sale through his own efforts, he must pay the broker. *Bourgoin* v. *Fortier,* 310 A2d 618 (Me. 1973); *Flynn* v. *La Salle Nat. Bank,* 9 Ill.2d 129, 137 NE2d 71; 88 ALR2d 941.

A broker who desires an exclusive right to sell should draft his listing contract with great care. Thus it has been held that a listing contract giving the broker the *exclusive sale* of a parcel of land creates an exclusive agency, not an exclusive right to sell. *Roberts* v. *Harrington,* 168 Wis. 217, 169 NW 603 (1918). Other courts have held that such language creates an exclusive right to sell. *Harris* v. *McPherson,* 97 Conn. 164, 115 Atl. 723 (1922). Again, it has even been held that a contract that gives the broker the *exclusive right to sell* merely creates an exclusive agency. *Sunnyside Land & Inv. Co.* v. *Bermier,* 119 Wash. 386, 205 Pac. 1041 (1922); *Hedges Co.* v. *Shanahan,* 195 Ia. 1302, 190 NW 957 (1922). These courts feel that, to create a true exclusive right to sell, the contract must in unequivocal terms negate the right of the landowner to sell the property himself. 88 ALR2d 948. However, other courts feel that a contract granting the broker an exclusive right to sell means just what it says. *Torrey & Dean, Inc.* v. *Coyle,* 138 Ore. 509, 7 P2d 561 (1932); *Piatt & Heath Co.* v. *Wilmer,* 87 Mont. 382, 288 Pac. 1021 (1930). The better reasoning appears to lie with the courts that require unequivocal language. Mere use of the phrase *exclusive right to sell* does not convey to the average person's mind the notion that it involves a surrender by the landowner of the right to make a sale through his own efforts.

SUGGESTION TO BROKER: Let the listing read that commission is payable to broker if the land is sold during the life of the listing by the broker, the landowner, or any other person whatever.

Occasionally the landowner cannot resist the temptation to negotiate secretly with his own property during the existence of the listing, often with the broker's prospect. He then signs the contract of sale the day after the listing expires. The broker collects no commission. *Simank Realty Inc.* v. *De Marco,* 6 Cal. App.3d 610, 46 L. A. Bar Bull. 67.

SUGGESTION TO BROKER: Let the listing read that the broker is entitled to a commission on a sale to any person with whom negotiations took place during the term of the listing.

Of course, if the broker has an exclusive right to sell that has become irrevocable by part performance as outlined in § 8.14, the seller cannot deprive his broker of compensation by selling through his own efforts, for this is precisely what the exclusive right to sell forbids.

The open listing was the first listing historically to appear on the American scene. The real estate brokerage business began with the growth of the urban population that began in 1850. In its early days the real estate business operated exclusively with open listings.

As is evident, both of the exclusive listings made the old, informal oral open listing obsolete. Written listings became the rule, and remain the rule today, even in states where a writing is not required by law.

8.11   Multiple listing

Multiple listing is simply a means by which brokers in a given area pool their efforts to sell properties listed with any member of the pool. 45 ALR3d 190. The original, or *listing broker,* obtains from the property owner an exclusive right to sell. He then furnishes a copy thereof to all members of this pool, or this is done through a central office. If any member other than the original broker sells the property, the commission is divided between the original broker and the *selling broker* who effects the sale. In some systems the central registration office shares in the commission also. Only the original broker has the right to sue the property owner for a commission. The property owner has no contract of employment with members of the pool other than the original broker. Therefore he can never be sued by them, *Goodwin* v. *Gleck,* 139 Cal. App.2d 936, 294 P2d 192 (1956). However, the members of the pool working on the sale owe the landowner the usual duties of a broker such as loyalty. *Frisell* v. *Newman,* 429 P2d 64 (Wash. 1967).

8.11(a)   Antitrust

Since multiple listing systems may either fix a commission rate or specify a recommended rate, they have come under fire as violations of the antitrust laws. Court decrees have been entered prohibiting fixing of commission rates.

A real estate board that has operated a multiple listing system, limiting the persons who could be admitted to membership, has been held to violate the antitrust laws. *Grillo* v. *Board of Realtors,* 219 A2d 635 (1966).

Other decisions also hold that exclusion of licensed brokers from a multiple listing service is illegal. *Marin County Board of Realtors* v. *Palsson,* 16 Cal.3d 920, 549 P2d 833, 130 Cal. Reptr. 1 (1976).

> **NEW DIRECTIONS:** The United States Supreme Court has held that federal antitrust laws are applicable to brokers' groups that bring about a fixed rate of commission in a given area. *McLain* v. *Real Estate Board,* 100 S.Ct. 502 (1980). All states have laws that forbid price fixing or restraint of trade. Under the combined pressure of federal and state laws, brokers' groups will probably liberalize their membership rules, fearing that excluded brokers may sue for damages. Persons who allege that brokers engaged in price fixing may sue for triple damages. 9 R.E.L.J. 151.

> *REFERENCES:* 14 Cal W. L. Rev. 298 (1978); 70 Columb. L. Rev. 1324; 60 Ill. B.J. 856; 24 U. Fla L. Rev. 266 (1974); 24 Wash. & Lee L. Rev. 67 (1967).

8.12 Performance required of broker

Suppose that *A* contracts with *B* to perform some act for *A,* such as building a house. *A* will pay *B* a stated sum for such performance of the contract. *B* has earned the contract price when he has completed performance of the contract. The same is true of a broker. He has earned his commission only when he has completed performance of a task he has undertaken. Thus, generally a broker has earned his commission when he produces a buyer who is ready, able, and willing to buy on either the terms specified by the seller in the listing contract, or on other terms acceptable to the seller. *Bonanza Real Estate Inc.* v. *Crouch,* 517 P2d 1371 (Wash. 1974).

> **EXAMPLE:** Landowner hires Broker to find a buyer. Broker finds Prospect who signs a contract at less than the price asked by the seller. Landowner and Prospect negotiate until they agree on a price. Broker helps in the negotiations, and therefore earns his commission.

At times, the broker may submit a contract signed by the buyer for the full contract price requested by the seller. Such a contract is a mere *offer to buy.* Until the seller signs it also, he is not bound to the contract. The broker has performed what he was hired to do, and therefore has earned a commission even if the seller changes his mind and refuses to sign the contract.

Likewise, if the seller and buyer reconsider after a contract of sale has been signed, causing the deal to be canceled, the seller remains liable to the broker. 74 ALR2d 459. Also, if the buyer has signed a contract which the seller has also signed, and thereafter refuses to complete the deal, the broker has nevertheless earned his commission. 74 ALR2d 443.

The word *able* in the phrase "ready, able, and willing to buy" refers to financial ability. The buyer must be able to command the necessary funds to close the deal within the time required. *Pellaton* v. *Brunski,* 69 Cal. App. 301, 231 Pac. 583 (1924). He must have the sum of money necessary to meet any cash payment required, and be financially able to meet any further payments. *Raynor* v. *Mackrill,* 196 Ia. 1298, 164 NW 335 (1917). Otherwise stated, he must have the present ability to pay. *Boutelle* v. *Chrislaw,* 35 Wis. 2d 665, 150 NW2d 486 (1967). Thus, a newly organized corporation having limited funds might be considered not *able* to buy. However, it is not necessary to show that the buyer is standing outside the office door with all cash in hand. It is sufficient if the buyer is *able* to command the necessary funds on reasonable notice. *Perper* v. *Edell,* 160 Fla. 447, 35 So2d 387 (1948). Thus, a buyer is *able* to buy if he has already arranged with some mortgage house to loan him the funds necessary to pay for the property. *Schaaf* v. *Iba,* 73 Ohio L.Abs. 46, 136 NE2d 727 (1955). To *produce* a willing buyer requires that the broker must reveal his identity to the seller. 2 ALR3d 1128.

A *willing* buyer is one who is willing to enter into an unconditional cash sale contract enforceable against the buyer at the time it is signed by the parties. Or, if the contract is *conditional* the buyer becomes a *willing* buyer (willing to be personally liable to the seller) only when the condition is performed.

This point is of great importance because most residential contracts contain the condition that the contract is contingent on the buyer's ability to obtain financing. It is normal and expected that the broker will tender a contract signed by the buyer that differs from the contract called for by the listing contract. Once this takes place, the broker's rights rest on the terms of the contract he tendered, and was accepted by the seller. If the contingency inserted by the buyer is his ability to obtain financing, the broker's right to a commission depends on the buyer's ability to obtain financing. *Schumaker* v. *Lear,* 235 Pa. Super. 509.

EXAMPLE: Owner hires Broker to sell his home for $100,000. Broker finds Purchaser, who is willing to pay the price, but needs a loan of $80,000. Owner and Purchaser sign a contract contingent on Purchaser's ability to get the loan of $80,000. Owner was not obliged to accept this condition. Legally, Purchaser was not a buyer ready, able, and willing to buy. Hence Broker has not yet earned his commission. If Purchaser fails to get his loan, Broker earns no commission. *Woodland Realty Inc.* v. *Winzenried,* 82 Wis. 2d 218, 262 NW2d 106 (1978); *Cooper* v. *Liberty Nat. Bank,* 75 NE2d 769 (Ill. 1947); *Slonim Ltd.* v. *Bankers Mortgage and Realty Co.,* 42 A2d 396 (N.J. 1945).

However, since every contract by implication requires a good faith effort on each party to perform, the buyer must make a good faith effort to obtain financing. If he fails to do so, this condition drops out of the contract and the buyer is unconditionally liable to the seller. Hence the broker has earned his commission.

There are numerous other examples that illuminate the matter of the performance required of the broker.

EXAMPLE: No commission is payable if the buyer is willing to sign only an installment contract. 8 ALR2d 382. But, if the *seller* also is willing to sign the installment contract with the buyer, the broker earns his commission when the first installment is paid unless the contract provides otherwise. 8 ALR2d 382. The seller must act in good faith.

EXAMPLE: Seller's broker procured a buyer who signed a contract contingent on buyer's ability to procure financing within a set time. Before the time expired, the seller sold the land to third party. The broker recovers his commission because the seller acted in bad faith. *Wuadrant Corp.* v. *Spake,* 504 P2d 1162 (Wash. 1973).

EXAMPLE: Where the contract of sale is contingent on the buyer's ability to procure lender's consent to an assumption of the existing mortgage, the broker earns no commission until such consent has been obtained. *Kopf* v. *Milam,* 60 Cal.2d 600, 387 P2d 390 (1963).

EXAMPLE: Listing calls for sale on "cash or contract." Broker's buyer signs an installment contract but terms are unacceptable to seller. *White* v. *Turner,* 164 Kans. 659, 192 P2d 200 (1948). No commission.

EXAMPLE: When the broker tenders a buyer who insists on a condition in the contract making his liability contingent on some official action, the broker has not earned his commission unless and until that action has taken place. An illustration would be the requirement of city approval of buyer's plat. *Larkins* v. *Richardson,* 502 P2d 1156 (Oreg. 1972). Another illustration would be a contract of sale of a hospital or convalescent home requiring issuance to buyer of a state license to operate the facility. *Urbanski* v. *Halperin,* 30 Conn. Super. 575. Also an illustration would occur when the buyer fails to obtain a state liquor license. *Blaine* v. *Stinger,* 79 Ariz. 376, 290 P2d 732 (1955).

The broker is entitled to no compensation or reimbursement whatever for unsuccessful efforts to sell unless the listing contract expressly so provides.

Often after a seller has listed property with a broker, and after the broker has found a buyer who is ready, able, and willing to buy at the listed price, the seller changes his mind and looks for some way to turn down the buyer without being liable to the broker for a commission. Such a seller seeks to take refuge behind the rule that if the terms offered by the broker's prospect differ from the terms specified by the seller, the broker is not entitled to a commission. 18 ALR2d 376. Keep in mind that if the broker's listing contract is silent on other terms of the transaction, the law will read various implications into it. And if the terms of sale as set forth in the contract of sale do not harmonize with the terms of sale set forth or *implied* in the listing contract, the seller may reject the broker's prospect without incurring any liability for commission.

> **EXAMPLE:** If the broker's listing is silent, the seller is required to convey only the land, building, and articles that are technically fixtures. If the contract of sale tendered by the broker requires the seller to convey furniture or other personal property, the seller may reject the contract without any liability for commission. *Sharkey* v. *Snow,* 13 Ill. App.3d 448, 300 NE2d 279 (Ill. 1973).

However, customary contract provisions, like those requiring a seller to have good title, are unobjectionable. *Adelman* v. *Caputi,* 181 SE2d 608 (Va. 1971).

But when the broker procures a purchaser ready, willing, and able to purchase on the authorized terms, and through the fault of the *owner* the sale is not consummated, the broker is entitled to a commission. Thus, the broker is entitled to a commission:

> 1. When the deal falls through because the owner changes his mind and refuses to sign the deed to the purchaser or a contract to sell. The rule is the same where the land has increased in value and the owner rejects the broker's buyer for this reason. If the seller refuses to sign, giving as his only reason the fact that he has changed his mind, he cannot thereafter shift his ground and claim that the buyer's offer was not in compliance with the listing. *Russell* v. *Ramm,* 200 Cal. 348, 254 Pac. 532 (1927).
>
> 2. When the deal falls through because the owner's wife refuses to sign the contract or deed. 10 ALR3d 665. This assumes state law requires her signature.
>
> 3. When the deal falls through because of defects in the owner's title. *Triplett* v. *Feasal,* 105 Kans. 179, 182 Pac. 551 (1919).
>
> 4. When the deal falls through because of the owner's fraud. *Hathaway* v. *Smith,* 187 Ill. App. 128.
>
> 5. When the deal falls through because the owner is unable to deliver possession within a reasonable time.
>
> 6. When the deal falls through because the seller insists on terms and provisions not mentioned in the listing contract, as where the seller insists on the right to remain in possession after the deal has been closed. *Brown* v. *Ogle,* 75 Ind. App. 90, 130 NE 147 (1927).
>
> 7. When after the contract of sale has been signed the seller and buyer get together and cancel the contract. *Steward* v. *Brock,* 60 N.M. 216, 290 P2d 682 (1955).
>
> 8. When the deal falls through because the buyer cannot procure financing and the contract is not contingent on ability to procure financing. But see § 8.12(d).
>
> 9. When both parties sign a contract of sale, but the buyer later defaults. 74 ALR2d 454.

> **EXAMPLE:** Seller and buyer sign an installment contract and buyer later defaults. *Engelking* v. *Boyce,* 278 Ore. 237, 563 P2d 703 (1977).

8.12(a) Statutes

A broker must comply with laws governing brokers. If he fails to furnish the seller a copy of the listing agreement (as the local law requires) he cannot recover a commission. *Carnell* v. *Watson,* 578 P2d 308 (Mont. 1978).

8.12(b) Performance after expiration of listing period—withdrawal from sale

Most listing contracts today fix an expiration date. Indeed, some state laws require this. Several rules exist:

1. If the period expires, and the seller thereafter refuses to consider prospects brought in by the broker, he is within his rights. Performance must take place within the time specified.

2. Some listings specify that the broker has earned his commission if within the listing period he "introduces" a buyer to the seller, and within ____ days after expiration of the listing a contract of sale is signed with that buyer. This clause is valid. The broker has performed within the listing period by introducing a prospect to the seller before the listing has expired. 27 ALR2d 1346, 1408. Sometimes the listing speaks of a buyer "submitted by the broker" or a buyer with whom the seller has "negotiated" within the listing period. Again, the broker is entitled to a commission if such negotiations take place. 51 ALR3d 1149. Or the listing may award the broker a commission if the seller withdraws the property from sale before the listing expires. *Blank* v. *Borden,* 115 Cal. Reptr. 31, 324 P2d 127 (1974), 63 Calif. L. Rev. 102. In these cases the seller has agreed to a special kind of performance or event under which the broker need not be the procuring cause of sale. Obviously, such provisions are introduced because sellers often engage in sharp practices in order to deprive the broker of a commission.

8.12(c) Performance on price or terms differing from listing

In the ordinary situation in which the principal promises a broker a commission for finding a purchaser and the asking terms are stated to the broker, the usual interpretation is that the asking terms are intended merely to guide the broker in starting negotiations, and the broker will have his commission if he produces a customer ready and willing to purchase at such price or on such modified terms as the principal may accept. *Bonanza Real Estate Inc.* v. *Crouch,* 517 P2d 1371 (Wash. App.).

8.12(d) Ellsworth Dobbs

There is some recent thinking that since the broker is so much better informed as to the buyer's financial ability to consummate the deal involving a home sale and if the deal falls through because the buyer cannot command the necessary financial resources, the seller should not be liable for a commission. *Ellsworth Dobbs Inc.* v. *Johnson,* 50 N.J. 528, 236 A2d 843 (1967).

REFERENCES: On *Ellsworth Dobbs Inc.* v. *Johnson:* 9 Ariz. L. Rev. 519; Catholic U. L. Rev. 487; 72 Dick. L. Rev. 522; 19 Mercer L. Rev. 460; 30 Ohio St. L. J. 600; 23 Rutgers L. Rev. 83; 13 Vill. L. Rev. 681; 10 W. & M. L. Rev. 240.

NEW CASES: Cases following *Ellsworth Dobbs* are *Tristram's Landing Inc.* v. *Wait,* 327 NE2d 727 (Mass. 1975) and *Shumaker* v. *Lear,* 345 A2d 249 (Pa. 1975). Predictably, this case will become law throughout the country because it squares with the normal expectation of the parties.

In addition to the cases that directly follow *Ellsworth Dobbs,* one can count Rhode Island (*Gartner* v. *Higgins,* 100 R.I. 284, 288, 214 A2d 849, 851 [1965], the District of Columbia (*Moore* v. *Burke,* 45 A2d 285 [1946], and Aabama (*Taylor Real Estate & Ins. Co.* v. *Greene,* 274 Ala. 694, 151 So2d 397 [1963] as basically following *Ellsworth Dobbs* thinking.

Ellsworth Dobbs comes to the rescue of the parties who have neglected to insert in the contract of a sale a clause making it contingent on the buyer's procuring financing. As stated, if the broker's purchaser insists on such a clause, as he normally should do, the broker has not procured a willing and able buyer unless and until financing is procured. But if such a clause is not inserted, technically the seller has accepted the broker's buyer as a willing and able buyer. *Ellsworth Dobbs,* as stated, comes to the rescue and bars the broker from recovering a commission if the deal falls through for lack of financing. This rescue operation affects only the broker's commission.

As between seller and buyer, the mortgage contingency clause is essential. If the contract lacks this clause and the deal blows because financing cannot be obtained, the buyer forfeits his earnest money.

NEW DIRECTIONS: *Ellsworth Dobbs* is followed in Alabama, Colorado, Connecticut, District of Columbia, Idaho, Iowa, Kansas, Maryland, Massachusetts, Nebraska, Oregon, Pennsylvania, New York, North Dakota, Rhode Island, and Vermont. Predictably, this will become the law throughout the country because it squares with the normal expectation of the parties. 5 Memphis St. U. L. Rev. 59, 71.

8.12(e)   "No deal, no commission" provision

While ordinarily the broker has earned his commission as soon as he has found a buyer who is ready, able, and willing to buy, the parties may validly contract, by means of the so-called *no deal, no commission clause* inserted in the listing contract, that payment of the commission is contingent upon the closing of the deal and full payment of the purchase price to the seller. Thus, if the seller cannot clear his title, or if the buyer refuses to go through with the deal, the seller need not pay a commission. 74 ALR2d 437. However, if the seller's refusal to complete the sale is arbitrary and without reasonable cause or in bad faith, the broker is entitled to his commission. *Huntley* v. *Smith,* 153 Minn. 297, 190 NW 341 (1922); *Goldstein* v. *Rosenberg,* 331 Ill. App. 374, 73 NE2d 171 (1947).

In effect, the *Ellsworth Dobbs* case makes every broker's listing contingent on the procuring of financing by the buyer. Also, it is a rule of some real estate boards that no commission is to be collected unless the deal closes.

8.12(f)   Recapitulation

It seems wise at this point to recapitulate some of the rules discussed in these pages. (1) It is really not expected by either the seller or his broker that the broker will instantly produce a buyer ready, able, and willing to meet the seller's terms. Rather, it is expected that the broker will bring in a buyer's contract that offers less (in price or terms) than the seller has asked for in the listing contract. Often, the contract signed by the buyer is contingent on his obtaining financing. This is routine. If that clause is omitted, the buyer will lose his down payment if he cannot procure financing. This is disastrous for the buyer. So all three parties (seller, buyer, broker) do business on the basis of the contract produced by the broker, which is contingent on the buyer's getting financing. This means that the seller and broker have implicitly agreed that the broker's commission is contingent on the buyer's obtaining the financing. When and if this occurs, the financing condition drops out of the contract and the broker has earned his commission. The buyer is ready, willing, and able. (2) In an *Ellsworth Dobbs* case the buyer has been careless. He has omitted the provision making his liability contingent on getting financing. This case really decides nothing concerning the rights of the seller and buyer against each other. Basically, it holds that the broker cannot collect a commission from his seller if the financing cannot be obtained. Always remember that there are two contracts involved, the listing contract between the seller and broker, and the contract of sale between seller and buyer. Do not confuse these two contracts. (3) The "no deal, no commission" clause protects the seller against any liability to his broker if the deal fails to close for any reason, including the buyer's inability to procure financing.

8.13   Procuring cause of sale

A broker who has been hired by the landowner has earned his commission when his efforts were the primary and procuring cause of the sale. When the owner or several brokers have been active and a sale is concluded, a broker, to justify his claim to a commission, must show that he was the efficient cause of the sale. The following are typical situations in which the problem arises:

> 1. The broker finds a prospect and introduces him to the owner. Thereupon the owner and the prospect, without the broker's intervention, negotiate and conclude a sale. The broker is the procuring cause of the sale and is entitled to a commission. *Ranney* v. *Rock,* 135 Conn. 479, 66 A2d 111 (1949).
>
> 2. When several brokers are involved, the rule appears to be substantially this: If the first broker's efforts result in a disagreement or if negotiations are abandoned, and thereafter a second broker steps in and brings the parties together, the second broker is the procuring cause of the sale. 46 ALR2d 865. But if the first broker brings about a substantial agreement, and the second broker merely works out details of the transaction, the first broker is the procuring cause of the sale. In other words, the broker whose efforts predominate in bringing about the sale gets the commission.

There are cases where the broker is entitled to damages or compensation even though he has not been the procuring cause of the sale: (1) For example, in the case of an exclusive agency, the broker will be entitled to compensation from his employer if the employer hires another broker, who succeeds in selling the property, because the employer breached his contract, which obligated him to refrain from hiring other brokers. This exposes the seller to payment of two commissions. 29 ALR3d 1229. (2) Also, in the case of an exclusive right to sell, the broker may be entitled to compensation even if his employer sells the building through his own efforts. Here the employer has breached his contract not to try to sell the building through his own efforts. *Bell* v. *Demmerling,* 149 Ohio St. 165, 78 NE2d 49 (1948). (3) Or the listing contract may provide that the broker will be entitled to compensation if the property is sold to a person with whom the broker *has negotiated,* or *whose name has been furnished the seller* by the broker. Here a broker who engages in negotiations with a prospect collects even though a deal is ultimately clinched by the landowner himself or another broker. *Delbon* v. *Brazil,* 134 Cal. App.2d 461, 285 P2d 710 (1955).

> **SUGGESTION TO BROKER:** Let the listing contract provide that broker will be entitled to a commission if within the specified time the property is sold to a person with whom the broker negotiated. 51 ALR3d 1149.

8.13(a)   Effect of seller's ignorance that buyer was procured by broker

When a seller hires a broker to sell his property, and thereafter sells the property to a buyer procured by the broker, in most states the broker is entitled to a commission despite the fact that the seller is ignorant that the buyer was procured through the broker. *Ranney* v. *Rock,* 135 Conn. 479, 66 A2d 111 (1949); 142 ALR 275. Having hired a broker, the seller should know that the appearance of a buyer may have been caused by the broker. The seller should check with his *broker* whenever a prospective buyer comes in. Inquiring of the *buyer* is rather pointless, for obviously many buyers, hoping to get a reduced price, will conceal the fact that a broker interested them in the property. Suppose, however, that *A*, a landowner, hires *B*, a broker, and *B* interests *C* in the purchase of the property. *C* procures a dummy or strawman, *D*, to make an offer for the property. *A* inquires of *B* if *B* had interested *D* in the purchase of the property. Not knowing that *D* is only a nominee for *C*, *B* says no, and *A* cuts his price by the amount of the commission he would have paid to *B*. *B* gets no commission. *A* has done all he could to protect his broker. *Zetlin* v. *Scher,* 217 A2d 266 (Md. 1966).

If the seller reduces his price to a prospect in ignorance of the fact that the prospect was procured by the seller's broker, some states, as stated above, allow the broker to collect his commission. The seller is at fault because he failed to check with the broker. Other states refuse the broker a commission. 46 ALR2d 872, 877. These latter states feel that the broker should notify the seller of each prospect he procures.

> **SUGGESTION TO BROKER:** As soon as you find a prospect, send a postcard to the seller notifying him of the name and address of the prospect you have found.

The broker can collect damages from a buyer who attempts to cheat him out of a commission.

> **EXAMPLE:** Owner hired Broker, and Broker interested Buyer in the purchase of the property. Buyer then contacted Owner directly and got Owner to cut his price. He did this by representing to Owner that no broker was involved. Owner, feeling he would not be paying a commission, cut his price. Broker discovers this. He can sue Buyer for damages. 29 ALR3d 1251. Buyer was guilty of a wrongful interference with a business relationship.

Quite often in cases like the example last given, the buyer is aware of the broker's rights. He meets with the seller. They arrange with another broker to pretend to procure a dummy buyer, at a higher price, of course. This deprives the first broker of his commission. If the first broker learns of this conspiracy, as he will when he sees his prospect take possession, he can sue the buyer for interfering with his contractual relations with his seller. 29 ALR3d 1246. For similar reasons, he can sue the seller and the second broker. 97 ALR 1275, 146 ALR 1419. Such liability is called *tort liability*. A *"tort"* is a wrongful act.

> **EXAMPLE:** The seller's broker found a buyer, and a contract of sale was signed. The seller and buyer contrived a phony termination of the contract in order to swindle the broker. Both are liable to the broker. *Seno* v. *Franke,* 16 Ill. App.2d 39, 147 NE2d 469 (1957); *Allen* v. *Powell,* 248 Cal. App.2d 502, 29 ALR3d 1218 (1967).

8.14   Duration and termination of employment

Many controversies arise as to the duration and termination of the broker's employment.

8.14(a)   When no time limit is specified

If the listing contract specifies no duration, the broker's authority automatically lapses after expiration of a reasonable time. 27 ALR2d 1346, 1390. If after a reasonable time has expired the broker continues to work on the deal without encouragement from the landowner and succeeds in finding a willing buyer, the seller may, without any liability to the broker, refuse to sell. But even before a reasonable time has expired, if no duration is specified, the landowner has the right to revoke the listing at any time before the broker has found a buyer ready, able, and willing to buy—and even while the broker is negotiating with a prospect, so long as the negotiations are not virtually completed. 49 LRANS 985. Such revocation must be in good faith, of course; for example, the landowner has decided in good faith to withdraw the property from sale. The fact that the broker has expended time and money on the deal does not prevent revocation, for the ordinary broker's listing contemplates that such expenditures will be made and that the landowner will nevertheless enjoy freedom of action. 49 LRANS 994. A special rule applies, however, where the listing contemplates extraordinary expenditures by the broker.

EXAMPLE: A landowner listed a large tract of land with a broker under an agreement that the broker was to grade, survey, and subdivide the land, put in streets, etc., at his own expense. His compensation was to come from commission on lot sales. No duration was fixed. After the broker had completed the subdivision, the owner revoked the broker's employment. The owner must pay damages to the broker. *McMillan* v. *Quincey,* 137 Ga. 63, 72 SE 506 (1911); 49 LRANS 999. The owner cannot revoke until a reasonable time has elapsed.

What is a reasonable time for a broker to sell the property depends on the circumstances. Some properties are harder to sell than others; for example, a one-purpose building, such as a church. A longer period will be allowed in such case than would be true in the case of a quick-selling item, such as a modern single-family dwelling.

814(b) Where the listing contract fixes the period of employment

Listing contracts, often provide that they are to continue for a specified time. In such case, the broker is not entitled to a commission unless within the time limit he procures a customer who is ready, able, and willing to buy.

But, in the following cases the broker will recover a commission even if he fails to find a purchaser within the period of the listing.

1. When the expiration of the listing time is attributable to the bad faith of the owner, as when the owner deliberately postpones agreement with the broker's buyer, hoping thereby to defeat the broker's claim for compensation. 27 ALR2d 1346, 1357.

2. If negotiations are begun within the time specified in the listing contract, continue without interruption, and are completed after the time has expired, the broker is entitled to his commission, particularly where the delay is due to the fault of the owner, as where it is occasioned by a defect in title. The seller is considered to have waived or extended the time limit.

3. When the listing contract contains some clause protecting the broker. For example, some listing forms, in large type, purport to run for a fixed period of time, such as thirty days, but following this will be a fine-print provision continuing the listing until a termination notice has been served on the broker. Other listing forms provide that the owner will protect the broker on sales made within ninety days of the expiration of the listing to prospects with whom the broker had *negotiated* or who had been *introduced* to the seller by the broker before expiration of the listing period. 27 ALR2d 1346, 1408.

CAUTION: Courts are unfriendly to these provisions for automatic extension of the listing period. Even if the listing contract is an exclusive agency or exclusive right to sell, it will be considered an *open listing during the extended period* if it is at all ambiguous. When a listing stated it was to be "sole and exclusive for three months and thereafter until sixty days written notice had been given," it was exclusive only for the initial three-month period. Thereafter it was only an open listing. *Boggess Realty Co.* v. *Miller,* 227 Ky. 813, 14 SW2d 140, 27 ALR2d 1420 (1929); *Wilson* v. *Franklin,* 282 Pa. 189, 127 Atl. 609 (1925); *Central Realty Co.* v. *Cutter,* 406 NE2d 515 (Ohio 1980).

8.14(c)   Revocation where listing fixes a specified time and broker has begun performance

Where the listing contract fixes a period of employment, such as thirty days, the owner may terminate the employment before the agent has expended money or effort, but not afterward. The technical reason for this rule is that the typical listing contract is a *unilateral contract* in which the landowner makes a promise to pay commission when the broker has performed an act, that is, found a buyer ready, able, and willing to buy, and such a contract is revocable by the promisor only up to the time the other party begins performance. *McMenamin* v. *Bishop,* 493 P2d 1016; *Stort* v. *Reinhard,* 183 SE2d 601 (1971); *Hutchison* v. *Dobson-Bainbridge Realty Co.,* 31 Tenn. App. 490, 217 SW2d 6 (1946); *Patton* v. *Wilson,* 220 SW2d 184 (Tex. Civil App. 1949); 1 Corbin, *Contracts* 154; 37 Iowa L. Rev. 370; 12 Am.Jur.2d 796; 64 ALR 404.

In these cases, any revocation after the broker has begun performance is wrongful and makes the owner liable to the broker for damages.

> **EXPLANATION:**   There are many classes and classifications of contracts. One classification divides contracts into unilateral and bilateral.

> **EXAMPLE:**   Owner hires Broker to sell Owner's house for $30,000. Note that Broker does not promise to do anything. He simply does an act, i.e., he finds Buyer, who is willing to buy the house for $30,000. Most broker's listings are of this character. Older decisions allowed Owner to revoke Broker's authority any time before he *completed* his performance. Starting work did not prevent revocation. Some courts still follow this rule. *Bartlett* v. *Keith,* 325 Mass. 265, 90 NE2d 308 (1950).

On the other hand, one or two states hold that an exclusive listing is irrevocable from the date it is signed, even though the broker has not begun performance. This is on the theory that by accepting employment the broker *impliedly agrees* to use reasonable efforts to find a buyer, and this makes the contract *bilateral* and irrevocable until the specified time has expired. *Hayes* v. *Clark,* 95 Conn. 510, 111 Atl. 781 (1920). This implied agreement makes the contract *bilateral.*

In a bilateral contract Owner makes a promise to Broker, and Broker in return makes a promise to Owner. The contract is enforceable when made. Either party may sue the other if that other fails to keep his promise.

In fairness, it should be pointed out that the law concerning unilateral contracts has been a battleground. The decisions are conflicting and unsatisfactory, partly because relatively small amounts are involved and the courts tend to take broker's cases rather lightly. Those who claim expertise in this area have produced no miracles. *See, for example,* 61 W. Va. L. Rev. 274; Murray, *Contracts,* §6.

We are beginning to see listing contracts that are technically *bilateral contracts.* This means that in return for the owner's promise to pay a specified commission for a buyer, the broker promises to perform certain specified acts, such as advertising the property in a specified paper at least once a week. Here the broker has a legal obligation to do as he has promised. Any revocation by the owner before the listing period has expired will be wrongful, so long as the broker is keeping his part of the bargain.

> **SUGGESTION TO BROKER:** Let the listing contract call for some acts by the broker, for example, provide that "broker agrees to publish an advertisement of the property at least once in a newspaper of general circulation in the county." The listing should be signed by the broker. This listing is irrevocable from the date it is signed, assuming, of course, that the broker advertises the property as agreed.

8.14(d) Revocation after broker has performed

Of course, the landowner has no right to revoke the broker's employment after the broker has brought in a buyer ready, able, and willing to buy.

8.14(e) Revocation in bad faith

In all types of listings the owner will be liable to the broker for damages if he acts in bad faith in revoking the broker's employment. 27 ALR2d 1346, 1395. Even when no time of employment is specified, when the broker is concluding negotiations with a prospective purchaser the owner cannot revoke the agency *in bad faith for the purpose of avoiding payment of commission.* In other words, when the broker has found a prospect and is concluding negotiations with him, so that the commission is virtually earned and the broker is approaching success, the owner cannot discharge the broker and thereupon step in and consummate the transaction, thus defeating the broker's right to his compensation. Restatement, Agency § 446.

> **EXAMPLE:** Landowner hired Broker to sell his land. While Broker was negotiating with a prospect, Landowner sold the land to his wife and discharged Broker. Thereupon Landowner and his wife sold to Broker's prospect. They were liable for Broker's commission. *Alexander* v. *Smith,* 180 Ala. 541, 61 So 68 (1912); 36 Boston U. L. Rev. 302.

8.14(f) Revocation by sale

A wrongful revocation of the broker's exclusive right to sell takes place if the owner contracts to sell the land to a purchaser not procured by the broker or even if he gives the purchaser only an option to purchase. The option removes the property from the market. *Hunt* v. *Smallidge,* 321 N.Y.S.2d 825; *Coleman* v. *Mora,* 263 Cal. App.2d 137, 69 Cal. Reptr. 166.

8.14(g) Notice of revocation of employment

When a landowner decides to withdraw his land from sale, he must give the broker notice of the revocation of his employment before the broker has finished the job. If the broker brings in a buyer ready, able, and willing to buy, obviously no judge will allow the owner to say, "I fired you mentally five days ago." 12 CJS 152; 12 Am.Jur.2d 817.

8.14(h) Revocation by sale by a person other than broker

A different situation is presented when the revocation of employment takes place by virtue of the fact that the land has been sold by someone else. As previously explained, in an open listing the employment of all brokers hired by the owner *automatically ends when a ready, able, and willing buyer is found either by the owner or by one of the brokers;* and in an exclusive agency the broker's employment automatically ends if the owner, through his own efforts, finds a willing buyer. No duty to notify brokers rests on the owner in most states, because all brokers understand that in these situations their employment is subject to such automatic termination. *Des Rivieres* v. *Sullivan,* 247 Mass. 443, 142 NE 111; 12 Am.Jur.2d 817. These termination provisions are "read into" the listing contract by the courts. A few cases hold, however, that after the land has been sold the owner ought, within a reasonable time, to notify all his brokers of the sale. If he fails to do so, and if one of his brokers also finds a willing buyer, the owner may be compelled to pay him a commission. *Lane* v. *Albright,* 49 Ind. 275; 49 LRANS 1003.

> **SUGGESTION TO OWNER:** Notify all your brokers promptly as soon as the land is sold.

Suppose that in an open listing a broker finds a willing buyer. However, he fails to notify the owner of this fact, and thereafter the owner signs a contract with some other buyer, procured, let us say, through another broker, the owner being still ignorant of the first broker's successful efforts. The first broker loses his commission. It is his duty to notify the owner promptly on finding a buyer. *Wilson* v. *Franklin,* 282 Pa. 189, 127 Atl. 609.

> **SUGGESTION TO BROKER:** Notify the owner as soon as you have found a willing buyer.

8.14(i) Damages for wrongful revocation of employment

Suppose that under one of the rules discussed in this section the owner's revocation of the broker's employment is legally wrongful. How much should the courts award the broker? Some courts give the broker only the expenses incurred by him for advertising and so forth and a sum that will compensate him for the reasonable value of his services. These are restitutionary damages. *Ferguson* v. *Bovee,* 239 Iowa 775, 32 NW2d 924 (1948); *Nicholson* v. *Alderson,* 347 Ill. App. 496, 107 NE2d 39 (1952); 12 Am.Jur.2d 819. Most courts, however, on one theory or another award the broker a full commission. 37 Iowa L. Rev. 367; 69 ALR3d 1269.

The broker will have a better chance of collecting a full commission if the listing contract has a clause covering the possibility of the sellers' withdrawing the property from sale.

> **SUGGESTED FORM:**   Let the listing provide that the broker will receive a full commission "if, within the time above specified, the premises are sold by the broker, owner, or anyone else, or if, within said period, the owner withdraws the property from sale or terminates the broker's employment." *Baumgartner* v. *Meek,* 126 Cal. App.2d 505, 272 P2d 552 (1954).

8.14(j)   Statutes or regulations requiring stated expiration date

Many states, either by law or regulation, require that the broker's listing state a specific expiration date. This is true, for example, in Illinois, Michigan, and Oklahoma.

8.15   Amount of compensation

In a case where the broker has found a buyer, he is entitled to the commission agreed upon, and if no commission has been fixed by the parties, he is entitled to the usual and customary commission for such services. He is usually not entitled to extra compensation for incidental services.

The compensation is computed on the gross sale price.

> **EXAMPLE:**   Owner owns land on which there is a $12,000 mortgage. He lists the building with a broker at $15,000, and the broker finds a buyer. Although Owner will obtain a net of only $3,000 ($15,000 less the $12,000 required to pay the mortgage) he must pay a commission based on a price of $15,000.

8.15(a)   Lien for commission

A broker hired by the seller has no lien on the seller's land for the payment of his commission unless the listing contract so provides. 125 ALR 921. In other words, even though the broker has earned his commission, his only remedy, if the seller fails to pay, is to sue the seller and obtain a judgment against him. The broker cannot do anything to block sale of the land by the seller to the broker's customer or anyone else.

8.16   Earnest money

The seller's broker ordinarily has no authority to accept an earnest money deposit. 30 ALR2d 805, 810. Quite commonly, however, the broker is permitted to hold the earnest money with no written agreement regarding disposition of such money. If the sale is completed, the money must be returned to the seller. *Mader* v. *James,* 546 P2d 190 (Wyo. 1976). If the sale is not completed, and the buyer is not at fault, the broker must return the money to the buyer. *Mader* v. *James,* 546 P2d 190 (Wyo. 1976); 12 Am.Jur.2d 852; 38 ALR2d 1382. But if the seller is not at fault, the broker is liable to the seller if he returns the earnest money to the buyer. *Lake Co.* v. *Molan,* 131 NW2d 734 (Minn. 1965). A seller's broker, who returns the earnest money to a defaulting purchaser, also loses his commission. 69 ALR2d 1244. Most cases hold that where the seller's title proves defective, or the deal falls through for some other fault of the seller, the broker must return the earnest money to the buyer. 38 ALR2d 1382. But the better rule it seems, is that when a deal falls through, the broker should return the earnest money to his seller–employer, leaving it to the buyer to collect from the seller. *Schultz* v. *Clements,* 7 Ill. App.2d 510, 130 NE2d 1 (1955); 12 Am.Jur.2d 852. The broker should not be asked to assume the role of judge and thus determine, as between seller and buyer, who is entitled to return of the deposit. Of course, either the listing contract or the contract of sale can give the broker specific directions on this score, and he should follow them.

Many states require the broker to keep earnest money deposits in a neutral bank account.

8.16(a) Risk of loss caused by broker's embezzlement

Where the earnest money is in the hands of the seller's broker, the rule is a simple one. If the broker is not authorized *by the seller* to accept a deposit, the money is the buyer's money entrusted to the broker, and he must bear the loss resulting from the embezzlement. 30 ALR2d 808. If the listing contract authorizes the broker to accept a deposit, risk of loss is on the seller.

Even when a seller accepts a *down payment* taken by the broker from the buyer, it does not constitute authority by the seller to the broker to accept the balance of the purchase price. The seller is entitled to assume that the broker was acting as the *buyer's agent* in transmitting the down payment. Suppose that the listing contract authorizes the broker to sign a contract of sale on behalf of the seller. Here the broker necessarily has implied authority to accept the down payment, for a down payment is made when the contract is signed. 30 ALR2d 816. The broker holds the money as agent of the seller, and if the broker embezzles the money, the loss falls on the seller. If the listing contract authorizes the broker to *sell and convey* the property, or if the seller entrusts the deed to the broker for delivery to the buyer, then the broker has implied authority to receive all of the purchase price. This must be so, for the seller's agent, not the seller, will be present at the closing of the deal, and the buyer must pay someone.

A number of states have adopted statutes under which brokers are required to contribute to a fund that is used to compensate victims of a broker's defalcations. *Ariz. R.E. Dept.* v. *Arizona Land Title Co.,* 9 Ariz. App. 9, 449 P2d 71 (1968).

8.17 Splitting commission— two-broker deals

Agreements to divide commissions are frequent and are usually enforced.

EXAMPLE: Broker *A* (who has no office) uses the office of Broker *B*. *A* stated to *B*, "If I ever get a deal in your office, I'm going to split my commission with you." This event in fact occurred. *B* was entitled to half the commission. 71 ALR3d 601.

In general, the participating broker will collect his share of the commission if and when the commission is collected.

EXAMPLE: Broker *A* was hired to sell some parcels of land. He contacted Broker *B* offering to split his commission in any parcel *B* sold. Held, *B* is entitled to his share as and when *A* collects the commission on sales engineered by *B*. 71 ALR3d 606.

A broker may become liable to another broker for wrongful deprival of a commission.

EXAMPLE: Owner listed land for sale with Broker #1. Broker #2 contacted Owner and was told to obtain Owner's terms from Broker #1, which Broker #2 did. Broker #1 found Buyer #1, ready, able, and willing to buy, and Owner accepted him. Broker #1 and Broker #2 agreed that they would share the commission equally. Then Broker #1 persuaded Owner to sell the land to Buyer #2 in a deal with Broker #1 obtaining all of the commission. Broker #1 is liable to Broker #2 for the commission of which Broker #2 was deprived by Broker #1's wrongful conduct. It is wrongful to interfere with a contract right. 34 ALR 3d 730.

And if the broker hired by the seller asks a second broker to help him sell it and the second broker finds a buyer and collects a commission, he must divide the commission with the first broker. *Wheeler* v. *Waller,* 197 NW2d 585 (Iowa 1972). The brokers have engaged in a joint venture, and each party in a joint venture owes a duty of good faith to the other.

If Seller hires broker Broker #1 and Buyer hires Broker #2, an agreement between the two brokers to split the commission is a breach of broker's duty unless both Seller and Buyer agree. Neither broker can claim a commission. 63 ALR3d 1219.

However, if Seller hires Broker and Broker finds Buyer, but Buyer offers less than Seller is willing to accept, Broker may legally share his commission with Buyer. This is often done. 63 ALR3d 1219.

8.18 Duties of the broker: loyalty and double agency

In general, the duties of a broker are the same as those of any other agent. They arise because the broker is an agent. They need not be spelled out in the listing contract. An agent must be loyal to his principal. If, without the knowledge and consent of his principal, he is also acting for the other party to the transaction, the principal may, when he discovers this fact, declare the contract void. This is true even though the transaction is a good one for the principal and the other party acts in good faith and was unaware of the double agency. *Gordon* v. *Beck*, 196 Cal. 768, 239 Pac. 309 (1925). It is to the interest of the seller to obtain the highest possible price and of the buyer to pay the least. Clearly, no one agent can serve both these interests. *Duffy* v. *Setchell*, 38 Ill. App.3d 146, 347 NE2d 218 (1976). Such a broker also loses his commission.

> **EXAMPLE:** Owner hired Broker #1 to sell his land, and Buyer hired Broker #2 to find land of this character for Buyer to purchase. Broker #1 and Broker #2 conferred and agreed to split their commissions down the middle. Neither broker can collect any commission. 63 ALR3d 1211, 1219.

Suppose a broker is hired by the buyer to find land or a building in a certain area, the buyer to pay a commission. Suppose that thereafter a property owner lists land of this description for sale with this broker. The broker reveals this fact *to the buyer only,* and a deal is closed between the seller and buyer, without, however, any knowledge on the seller's part that the broker was originally hired by the buyer. The broker collects his commission from the seller and now sues the buyer. To the brokers' surprise, the buyer claims that the broker cannot collect any commission whatever in a double agency situation. This is correct. The fact that the buyer knew of the double agency makes no difference. A fraud was perpetrated on the *seller,* and the law will not help a party to the fraud, the broker, to collect from the other party to the fraud, the buyer. *McConnell* v. *Cowan*, 44 Cal.2d 805, 285 P2d 261 (1955); 80 ALR 1077, 1087. The fact that the broker felt he was acting for the best interests of both parties is immaterial.

A *middleman*, who merely brings the parties together, leaving them to negotiate, may serve both parties. Here the double agency rule does not apply. 14 ALR 472; 58 ALR2d 42, 58. But if the broker assists either party or in some degree influences the parties, he is not a middleman. It is obvious that very few agencies fall in the middleman category.

The rule against double agency is often applied with great strictness.

> **EXAMPLE:** Buyer requested that Broker find him a home. Broker contacted Homeowner, and a contract of sale was signed. Both Buyer and Broker expected that Broker would receive his commission from Homeowner. Buyer did not expect to pay a commission to Broker. This was also Broker's understanding. Nevertheless, Broker was working for both parties and should have revealed this to Homeowner. *Duffy* v. *Setchell*, 347 NE2d 218 (Ill. App. 1976).

REFERENCES ON DOUBLE AGENCY: Timmerman v. *Ankron,* 487 SW2d 567 (cites authorities); 34 Columb. L. Rev. 552; 20 Marq. L. Rev. 163; 35 Yale L. J. 503; 63 ALR3d 1211.

8.19   Duties of the broker: conflict of interest problems

An agent must not have any individual interest in the transaction without the knowledge and consent of his principal.

> **EXAMPLE:** Owner placed his property with Broker. Negotiations resulted in a sale by Owner to Buyer for $3,200, the brokers receiving a commission of $160. After the deed was given, Owner discovered that Buyer was one of Broker's employees. Owner was entitled to have the conveyance set aside. *Johnson* v. *Bernard,* 323 Ill. 527, 154 NE 444 (1926). Owner also gets the commission back.

The rule even precludes a sale by the broker to his wife unless the seller is informed of the relation. If, however, the broker fully discloses the facts to the landowner, he may buy for himself, for a relative, or for himself and others.

8.20 Duties of the broker: disclosure and nondisclosure

An agent must make full disclosure to his principal of all matters that may come to his knowledge pertaining to the subject of the agency. 2 ALR3d 1123.

> **EXAMPLE:** Owner placed his property with Broker. Broker wrote Owner, stating that he and several other parties would buy the land at $400 per acre. The contract was signed, and Broker received a commission. Later Owner discovered that, prior to making this offer, Broker had received an offer for this property of $600 per acre. Owner was entitled to have the contract canceled. *Rieger* v. *Brandt*, 329 Ill. 21, 160 NE 130 (1928); 7 ALR3d 693.

> **EXAMPLE:** The broker is liable if he transmits an offer to the principal but conceals a more favorable offer. 7 ALR3d 696.

> **EXAMPLE:** While the property is listed with the broker, it increases in value. The owner is ignorant of this fact, but the broker knows of it. He fails to disclose this circumstance to the owner. He has violated his duty of full disclosure. *Eastburn* v. *Jos. Espalla, Jr. & Co.,* 112 So 232 (Ala. 1927); 53 ALR 134.

> **EXAMPLE:** The buyer procured by the broker has a poor financial status. The broker knows this, but fails to reveal it to the seller. A contract is signed, but the deal fails to go through because the buyer cannot raise the necessary funds. The broker has violated his duty of full disclosure. *McGarry* v. *McCrone,* 97 Ohio App. 543, 118 NE2d 195 (1954); *Nugent* v. *Scharff,* 476 SW2d 414 (1972); *Mason* v. *Bulleri,* 543 P2d 478 (Ariz. 1975).

> **EXAMPLE:** The buyer procured by the broker is a distant relative of the broker. He must reveal this fact to the seller. 26 ALR2d 1308. The broker must disclose the true identity of the purchaser. 2 ALR3d 1119.

In other words, the broker's duty is not discharged simply by his handing a contract to the seller for signing. He must notify the seller of all facts that might influence the seller in accepting or rejecting the offer. He must give his opinion as to the price that can be obtained, the likelihood of a higher price being offered in the future, the possibility of making a favorable trade or other use of the property, etc. *Moehling* v. *O'Neil Construction Co.,* 20 Ill.2d 255, 170 NE2d 100 (1960).

The converse of the broker's duty of disclosure is his duty not to reveal secret information to prospective buyers. Thus the seller's broker violates his duties if he reveals to a prospective buyer that the seller will take less than the listed price for the property, for obviously no buyer will pay the listed price if he knows that the seller will take less. *Haynes* v. *Rogers,* 70 Ariz. 257, 219 P2d 339 (1950).

8.21   Duties of the broker: misrepresentations

A broker hired by the seller will be held liable to the buyer in damages if the broker, acting on his own, makes a willful misrepresentation that induces the buyer to enter into the contract of sale. 58 ALR2d 10, 27; 8 ALR3d 553.

> **EXAMPLE:**   The broker falsely represented that the house was stucco-covered brick, whereas it was not brick. *Perkins* v. *Green,* 26 Ariz. 219, 224 P 620 (1924). He was liable to the buyer.

The broker can also become liable to the seller for making fraudulent misrepresentations.

> **EXAMPLE:**   Seller hired Broker, and Broker found Purchaser. Broker made fradulent misrepresentations to Purchaser that induced Purchaser to enter into and consummate the transaction. When Purchaser learned of the fraud, he sued Seller for damages, and Seller paid Purchaser. He was obliged to do so because he was liable for the fraudulent acts of his agent, Broker. Seller can now sue Broker. 61 ALR2d 1237.

Of course, if the buyer chooses to rescind (cancel the deal and obtain return of his down payment) because of a misrepresentation made by the broker, the broker loses all rights to a commission from the seller. 9 ALR2d 504.

8.22   Duties of the broker: skill and care

Like other agents, a broker must exercise skill and care in the service of his employer.

> **EXAMPLE:**   A broker hired to sell land found a buyer and drew a contract of sale which the parties signed. Thereafter the buyer refused to go through with the deal. The court held that the contract was so poorly drawn that the buyer was not legally bound. The broker thereby forfeited his commission. *Dingman* v. *Boyle,* 285 Ill. 144, 120 NE 487 (1918). Moreover, he is liable to the seller for any damages the seller has suffered. *Mattieliegh* v. *Poe,* 356 P2d 328 (Wash. 1960).

> **EXAMPLE:**   A broker hired to buy or trade has a duty to determine the value of the real estate he acquires for his employer. If he fails in this respect and the prop-

erty turns out to be a poor buy, he is liable and forfeits his commission. *Smith* v. *Carroll Realty Co.,* 8 Utah2d 356, 335 P2d 67 (1959).

EXAMPLE: A broker employed to find a property for a buyer must exercise skill and care if he undertakes to close the deal for the buyer without an attorney. Thus if the broker fails to procure a clear title for the buyer, he is liable to buyer for damages. *Lester* v. *Marshall,* 143 Colo. 189, 352 P2d 786 (1960).

EXAMPLE: A broker held liable for loss caused by his ignorance of zoning. *Burien Motors Inc.* v. *Balch,* 513 P2d 582 (Wash. 1973).

EXAMPLE: A broker held liable for careless title search. *Mayflower Mtg. Co.* v. *Brown,* 530 P2d 1298 (Colo. 1975).

8.23 Duties of the broker: liabilities and penalties for breach of duty

Where the broker breaches his duties toward his employer, one or more of several penalties may follow.

1. In almost every case the broker will lose his commission. If he has already been paid, he must refund it. 2 ALR3d 1126.

2. If he has made a profit, as where the broker has bought the property from his employer through a nominee and resold it at a profit, he must pay such profit over to his employer.

3. If his employer has suffered any damages as a consequence of the broker's breach of duty, the broker will be liable for such damages.

4. Where the broker's misconduct is deliberate, as where he secretly buys the property from his employer, the court may see fit to punish the broker by compelling him to pay exemplary damages, that is, damages greater than the damage the employer has actually suffered. *Ward* v. *Taggart,* 51 Cal.2d 736, 336 P2d 534 (1959).

5. For a serious offense, such as secretly buying his employer's property, failing to disclose material facts to his employer, embezzling his employer's funds, etc., the broker may have his license suspended or revoked altogether. 56 ALR2d 573. Fraud in his own land transactions will also result in the loss of his license. *Holland Realty Inv. Co.* v. *State,* 436 P2d 422 (Nev. 1968).

As is true with respect to lawyers, doctors, architects, and others, the courts are holding brokers to higher and higher standards of professional ethics and competence. This is a desirable trend and is likely to continue.

8.24 Duties to purchaser

It will be remembered that a broker is normally hired by the seller. One would think that he therefore has no duties to the purchaser. This is not so.

NEW DIRECTIONS: The newer decisions take the position that the broker is a special type of agent. He is licensed by the state after passing a comprehensive examination. He enjoys a monopoly in that unlicensed persons are barred from the profession. In effect, the state holds the broker out as being a responsible and capable person. He therefore has duties to the purchaser as well as to the seller. *Ward* v. *Taggart,* 325 P2d 502 (Cal. 1958); *Ocala Mfg. Co.* v. *Canal Authy,* 301 So2d 495 (Fla. 1974); *Sawyer Realty Group* v. *Jarvis,* 89 Ill. 2d 379, 432 NE2d 849 (1982).

EXAMPLE: Contract of sale was signed. Seller's broker told buyer contract was invalid. Buyer raised his price and new contract was signed. Buyer found out broker was wrong and sued broker, who was held liable. *Peterson* v. *Auvel,* 552 P2d 538 (Ore. 1976).

EXAMPLE: Seller's broker stated to buyer that heating system was not defective, which was untrue, though broker did not know this. Broker held liable. *Neff* v. *Bud Lewis Co.,* 89 N.M. 145, 548 P2d 107 (1976).

EXAMPLE: Seller's broker misrepresented zoning to buyer. Broker held liable. *Barnes* v. *Lopez,* 544 P2d 694 (Ariz. 1976).

EXAMPLE: If the listing broker furnishes false information to his listing service, and a member of the service transmits this false information to a buyer, the listing broker is liable to the buyer, just as if he himself had made the misrepresentation directly to the buyer. *Grandberg* v. *Turnham,* 333 P2d 423 (Cal. 1959), *First Church* v. *Cline S. Dunton Realty Inc.,* 19 Wash. App. 275, 574 P2d 1211 (1978).

EXAMPLE: Seller hired Broker to sell his real estate. Broker found Purchaser. Broker represented to Purchaser that the existing mortgage bore a rate of 7 percent interest. Broker believed this to be true. Actually the rate was 11 percent. The court held that Broker was liable to Purchaser under the Consumer Fraud Act. Note that Broker was working for Seller and that the representation was made in good faith. *Beard* v. *Gress,* 90 Ill. App.2d 622, 413 NE2d 445 (1981).

EXAMPLE: A seller's broker failed to communicate to seller an offer made by a prospective buyer. As a result, the latter lost the deal. The broker is liable to this prospective buyer. *Amato* v. *Lattor & Blum,* 79 So2d 873 (La. 1955).

EXAMPLE: A seller's broker undertook to procure a mortgage for a buyer, and by lack of care, procured a short-term mortgage which buyer signed. He is liable to buyer.

EXAMPLE: A seller's broker will be liable to the buyer if he misrepresents the age of the building, identity of the school servicing the area, and so forth. 8 ALR3d 550.

EXAMPLE: A broker was suspended for misrepresenting the condition of the heating plant.

8.25 Unauthorized practice of law

The law appears to differ from state to state with respect to the propriety of a broker's filling in a form contract of sale where this is merely incidental to the earning of his commission for procuring a buyer. 53 ALR2d 796. However, if the broker makes a separate charge for filling in a form, he is guilty of unauthorized practice of law. 53 ALR2d 804. Likewise, if a broker prepares a will or deeds to put land in joint tenancy, he is guilty of the unauthorized practice of law. 53 ALR2d 807.

8.26 Authority of broker to sign contract

Ordinarily a broker does not have authority to sign a contract on behalf of his employer. 43 ALR2d 1014.

8.27 Racial discrimination

The law places a heavy burden on the broker and salesman with respect to racial discrimination.

8.28 Franchising

A new development in brokerage law is the advent of franchising. The real estate broker retains his independent status. However, the franchiser furnishes advertising, procedure manuals, forms, and so forth. Each franchiser is furnished a list of other franchisees, which enables each franchiser to furnish a national referral service, for example, in employee-transfer situations. This is a promising new development, but the courts have not yet tested it. If the franchising agreement gives the franchiser the right to allocate territory, that portion of the agreement is likely to draw fire from the federal government. The laws against monopolies forbid territory allocation. Dowling & Hines, *Here Comes the Real Estate Franchise,* 7 Real Estate Rev. 48 (Summer 1977).

9 CONTRACTS FOR THE SALE OF LAND

9.01 Why a contract for sale of land is needed

Where *A,* a landowner, agrees to sell his land to *B* for $10,000 in cash, one may ask why it is necessary that a contract be signed. Why does not *A* then and there give a deed to *B* and *B* pay *A* the agreed price? The chief reason is that at the time the agreement is reached, *B* has no assurance, other than *A*'s statement, that *A* is in fact the owner of the land and that there are no defects in his title. Ordinarily, therefore, *B* will insist that a contract be signed and that it provide for an examination of *A*'s title, such examination to show that *A* has good title, before *B* pays the purchase price. In other words, the prudent purchaser is unwilling to buy a pig in a poke. The cash sale contract defines the type of title the seller will deliver, how, when, and where proof is to be made that title is good, and what is to be done if defects in title are revealed. In the meantime, the parties are bound to their bargain by the contract. The seller cannot sell to someone else who offers a higher price, and the buyer is bound to go through with the deal on the agreed terms set forth in the contract. There are other matters that must be attended to. Insurance policies bought, canceled, or transferred, leases assigned, financing arranged, inspections conducted. These take time. Some device must hold the buyer and seller together while this is done. The contract does just that.

The cash sale contract contemplates that the deal will be closed as soon as the seller's title is examined and found to be good. There is also a type of contract called the *installment contract, contract for deed,* or *land contract.* An installment contract provides for a down payment, with balance of purchase price payable in monthly installments. The buyer receives his deed when all the installments have been paid or when the unpaid balance of the purchase price has been reduced to a certain agreed figure, whereupon the buyer is to receive a deed and give the seller a purchase money mortgage for the balance of the purchase price. See Ch. 19.

9.01(a) Necessity for written contract

It is necessary that the fundamentals of a contract for the sale of land be in writing. Oral contracts cannot be enforced. The law that so provides is known as the *Statute of Frauds*. To satisfy the Statute of Frauds the *memorandum* of the contract must contain the names of seller and buyer, a sufficient description of the land, the contract price, the terms of sale if other than cash, and the signature of "the party to be charged," that is, the signature of the party against whom suit is brought on the contract. A few states require both parties to sign the contract, and there appears to be a trend in this direction. As a rule, oral testimony cannot be introduced in court for the purpose of supplying omissions in the written document. *Kris* v. *Patterson,* 159 Minn. 219, 198 NW 541 (1924). The fact that a sale is intended should also appear in the writing.

The Statute of Frauds may leave the parties in an uncertain situation.

Suppose that I enter an oral contract with you to buy your land, and I give you a down payment. Thereafter, I change my mind. Although you cannot sue me for the balance of the contract price, neither can I get my down payment back from you as long as you are willing to go through with the deal. 169 ALR 187.

Where the only memorandum is one that contains only the bare bones of the contract, the courts will read into the contract some of the missing terms.

> **EXAMPLE:** If the contract is silent on these matters, the courts will assume a *cash sale* was intended with closing to take place in a *reasonable time;* that the sale price and deed will change hands *simultaneously;* that the deed will be a *quitclaim deed;* that the *buyer* will be entitled to *marketable title free from all encumbrances;* that any defects in marketability must be raised *before the deal is closed;* that the buyer will determine marketability *at his own expense,* and so on.

No particular form is required, so that a binding contract may be in the form of one or more letters, escrow instructions, receipt, a check, a promissory note, and so on.

> **EXAMPLE:** Buyer gave Seller his check payable to Seller. On the face of this check was written the following: "Deposit for land on Galvin Road, Watertown, price thirty-two cents a foot." This was the only land that Seller owned. It was held that this was a sufficient contract. 153 ALR 1108.

> **EXAMPLE:** A contract was as follows:
>
> Chicago, January 8, 1904
> Received of Anton Ullsperger $100 on said purchase of property No. 1031 Milwaukee Avenue, Chicago, Illinois at a price of $14,000.
> > C. Meyer
>
> Meyer refused to perform, and Ullsperger sued him. The court compelled Meyer to give Ullsperger a deed. *Ullsperger* v. *Meyer,* 217 Ill. 262, 75 NE 482 (1905).

It will be observed in the last example that Ullsperger, who had *not* signed the contract, was allowed to enforce the contract against Meyer, who *had* signed it. However, Meyer could not have enforced the contract against Ullsperger. This is in accord with the general rule that in a land contract a seller may legally compel performance if he can produce a contract signed by the buyer, and the buyer can demand performance if he can produce a contract signed by the seller. Signature by both parties is not necessary.

Such a contract, although it meets the minimum requirements of the law, is altogether unsatisfactory, as will become apparent from the subsequent discussion. Obviously, it is best to have both seller and buyer sign the contract, and this is the usual practice.

Many documents that are legally sufficient as contracts for the sale of land are quite short, as the foregoing discussion reveals. Moreover, such documents are often given misleading names, such as *sales deposit receipt* or *offer to purchase.* People sign such documents without realizing that they have obligated themselves to buy or sell real estate. Sometimes such brief documents state that the parties will later sign a "regular" real estate contract. The court decisions are conflicting as to the effect of the inclusion of this phrase. As long as the main terms of the sale are stated in the document, most courts hold that the failure to sign a formal, detailed contract is unimportant, especially where the parties proceed with the details of the transaction as though a binding contract existed. *Phillips* v. *Johnson,* 514 P2d 1337 (Ore. 1973); *Sewel* v. *Dalby,* 171 Kans. 640, 237 P2d 366 (1951); 122 ALR 1217; 165 ALR 765. Other states feel that the parties did not intend to be bound until a formal, detailed contract was executed, as called for in the short form, and therefore hold that the short document is not binding. *Scott* v. *Fowler,* 227 Ill. 104, 81 NE 34 (1907); *Brunette* v. *Vulcan Materials Co.,* 119 Ill. App.2d 390, 256 NE2d 44 (1970); *Lippman* v. *Featherston,* 247 Mich. 153, 225 NW 489 (1929).

9.02   Questions the parties intending to enter into a contract should ask

Before *listing* the property with a broker for sale, the *seller* should ask himself:

1. Do I really want to sell?

COMMENT: If I list my property and the broker finds a buyer ready, able, and willing to buy at my price, I must pay a commission even if I then decide that I really don't want to sell.

2. Does my spouse want to sell?

COMMENT: If the broker finds a buyer and I am willing to sign the contract of sale, but my wife refuses to do so, in most states the buyer will refuse to go through with the deal because, unless she signs the contract, she is not legally obligated to sign the deed, and this will leave her dower or other legal rights outstanding. The deal fails, but the broker gets his commission.

3. Am I really in a position to sell?

COMMENT: Suppose my broker finds a willing buyer, but it develops that my title is defective, or I cannot pay off the existing mortgage, or my new house will not be ready for occupancy for a long time. Again the deal falls through, but I must nevertheless pay a commission.

Before *signing a contract of sale,* the *buyer* should ask himself these questions and attend to the following matters:

1. If I am buying vacant land, are there any zoning or environmental ordinances that forbid or hamper the use I wish to make of the land?

COMMENT: Suppose I sign a contract to buy a vacant lot and intend to erect a filling station thereon, and thereafter I discover that the lot is zoned for residences only. I must nevertheless go through with the deal. Suppose my *building* complies with the ordinance. Do my plans provide adequate off-street parking to comply with the ordinance? Or does an environmental ordinance forbid any building on wetlands?

2. Under local ordinances, how far from the front, side, and rear lines must buildings be erected? Does this leave room for the type of building that I have in mind?

3. If I plan to use septic tank construction, is the lot big enough to qualify for septic tank construction under local ordinances?

4. If there is an airport in the vicinity, are there any regulations prohibiting the erection of electric poles or other structures that might prove a hazard to aircraft?

5. If there is a building on the land but I expect to remodel it, are there any ordinances that prohibit such remodeling?

6. Does the building on the property violate existing zoning or building ordinances?

COMMENT: If it does, I may be compelled to remodel the building to conform to the ordinances, or even to tear it down.

7. Is the building a nonconforming use?

COMMENT: If it is, I cannot enlarge or alter it or rebuild it if it is substantially damaged by fire. If it was legally abandoned, the city can forbid its use.

8. Especially if the building is new, has a certificate of occupancy been issued?

9. Does the seller have a permit for any structure that requires a city permit, such as a swimming pool, a water tank on a roof, or a sign that extends over a sidewalk? Where a cocktail lounge is involved, am I, as the buyer, certain that I can procure an assignment of the liquor license?

10. If the contract of sale states that title will be subject to building restrictions, easements, mineral rights, and so on, how will these affect my building plans?

11. Are there sewers and water pipes in adjoining streets, and if there are, will I have the legal right to connect my proposed building to them?

12. Are there any utility lines, including underground lines, drainage ditches, draintiles, and so on, that will interfere with my building program?

13. Are existing streets, walks, sewers, or water pipes fully paid for and if not, will they be paid for by the seller, buyer, or by future special assessments? What does the contract say regarding this matter?

14. Will my building program interfere with my neighbor's drainage?

15. Keeping in mind that the law often says, "let the buyer beware," are there any defects in the building, for example, termites, defective heating plant, basement that floods, inadequate well, or septic tank?

16. Is the soil adequate for my building program, and should soil tests be made?

17. Is the building I'm buying so close to adjoining vacant land that, if my neighbor excavates, there is danger that my building will fall into the excavation?

18. Is my neighbor's building so close to the boundary line that, if I build on the vacant land I'm buying, my excavation will involve possible collapse of his building and possible litigation?

19. Keeping in mind that I will become personally liable for personal injuries as soon as the deal is closed, are the elevators, boilers, gas, water, and sewer in the building in safe condition?

20. Since risk of loss in many states falls on the buyer as soon as the contract is signed, is the existing insurance policy for an adequate amount? Suppose, for example, that the building burns to the ground before the deal is closed.

21. Is the property being used for a purpose that invalidates existing insurance policies?

SUGGESTION: Have the insurance policies checked by a reliable insurance broker. Have a rider (*contract-of-sale clause*) attached immediately to the policies so that you, as well as the seller, are covered. Only the seller is covered until this is done.

22. Are any public projects scheduled for this area that may result in the taking of this property by the public? It is discouraging for a businessman to build up neighborhood goodwill over a period of time and then find his property taken for a superhighway.

23. Are any zoning or building code changes likely to take place that will interfere with my building program?

24. Are there any judgments against me? Once I sign a contract to buy land, the seller will be obligated to deed the land to me, and then my creditors may take it away from me.

25. Where the contract calls for the buyer to accept the property subject to "existing leases," what do the leases provide? If the leases contain clauses that are very burdensome to the landlord, the buyer may wish to reconsider the desirability of entering into the deal.

26. If the contract requires the buyer to accept the property subject to the existing mortgage, the contract should require the seller to furnish, at closing, a statement signed by the mortgagee showing the balance due on the mortgage. The buyer should check the mortgage to make sure it does not give the mortgagee the right to declare the mortgage debt due in case the mortgagor sells the property without the mortgagee's permission.

27. Has the building been designated as a landmark or historical site? Is it in a flood plain?

28. Inquire about proposed new construction in the area which might make the neighborhood undesirable.

29. Confirm operating costs and taxes and determine whether special property assessments are planned. They could impose a financial burden on the buyer.

30. Various certificates are required to show that the building complies with energy laws, ordinances, and regulations.

31. Parking should be checked. Is street parking permitted? Is parking of boat trailers forbidden?

32. The area should be checked for mud slides, floods, earthquakes. Flood insurance is usually available under a federal program. If earthquake insurance is available, probably an additional premium is required.

33. Questions should be asked about need for new school construction. This would result in tax increases.

34. There are many sites where toxic chemicals have been stored. Inquiry must be made to determine if the land in question contains such chemicals. If it does, avoid the property like the plague. Fines as much as $1,000 a day have been levied. Suits by employees who become ill can total astronomic sums.

35. In addition, inspect the neighborhood carefully to determine if a zoning change is imminent.

EXAMPLE: The neighborhood includes both homes and apartments. This suggests that the owners of vacant lots may press for zoning changes that will enable them to build condo apartments.

36. If you plan to rehab an older building, check with an architect before you sign the contract. The city may have a "grandfather clause" that insulates older buildings from enforcement of the building code. But when major rehab occurs, the ordinance may require that you bring the entire building "up to code." This means new wiring, new plumbing, the works. The expense may be great.

In any case, you should get an architect's estimate of the probable cost of rehab before you sign. Also check with a lender to see if you can obtain a loan that covers your refinancing needs on the purchase, and also the cost of rehab.

Before signing the contract, the seller should ask:

1. Is my title to the property a good, clear title? If not, I may be liable for damages if I cannot clear the title.

2. What problems will I have with my existing mortgage in the property? If I, as seller, must get my existing mortgage released, I should check to see that it has a prepayment clause, and, if not, determine that the mortgagee is willing to accept prepayment. I should also get the mortgagee to agree either to accept payment at the closing of the deal or to deposit his mortgage papers and release or satisfaction thereof in escrow since I will have no funds to pay the mortgage debt before then.

3. Can I accept the buyer's word that I will not have to pay my broker a commission? The buyer may be seeking a reduction in the seller's asking price on the ground that no broker's commission is involved. Check with the broker as to the truth of the buyer's claim that the broker was not instrumental in interesting this buyer in the property.

4. Can I comply with all ordinances applicable to my property? A number of laws and ordinances have been enacted recently that require the seller to have his home inspect-

ed immediately prior to sale. The inspector is sent by the Building Department. If he finds there are no violations of the building code he issues a current certificate of occupancy. If he finds violations of the building code, these must be corrected before the deal is closed.

Other matters to be considered before contract is signed. In these days of tight money, the broker is inevitably going to bring in buyers who are unable to pay cash and who will ask the seller to agree to an installment contract, a purchase money second mortgage, a sale subject to existing mortgage, and so on. One way of handling this is to insert in the broker's listing a clause that "terms of financing must be personally acceptable to sellers." This means that, for whatever reason, the sellers can reject the buyer unless he agrees to the seller's terms. Then the seller's lawyer will examine the contract the buyer has signed and make such changes as he sees fit. The buyer's lawyer, in turn, will suggest further changes that will protect his client. Many possible variations are possible, among them:

1. Seller may be willing to take back a purchase money second mortgage if it is done in the form of wrap-around.

2. The seller may insist that the deal take the form of a tax-free exchange, so as to defer seller's income tax problems.

3. The seller may insist on an installment sale in order to obtain the income tax benefits.

4. In any installment sale the buyer may want the seller's deed to be placed in escrow or the title to be placed in trust for the seller and buyer.

5. If the buyer is able to obtain a mortgage from an outside lender, the buyer's lawyer will check the loan commitment carefully. If it is for a loan with a fluctuating interest rate, the lawyer may want to argue that the lender should put a "cap" (maximum) on the rise in interest. This suggests that the financing contingency clause in the contract of sale should state that the terms of the financing are subject to approval of the buyer's lawyer.

6. If the contract calls for sale subject to the existing mortgage, some clause is needed making the deal subject to the lender's approval where a due-on-sale clause is present. Here the lender may consent only if the buyer agrees to an increase in the interest rate; the buyer should make this aspect of the deal subject to his approval.

7. If the buyer wishes to sign the contract before it has been checked by his lawyer, he should insist that the contract be subject to personal approval of his lawyer (except as to price) within a certain number of days. *Indoe* v. *Dwyer,* 424 A2d 456 (1981).

8. If the buyer wants the home inspected before his purchase becomes final, he will want the contract contingent upon approval of the building to the satisfaction of buyer's building inspector within a specific number of days.

9. If the buyer insists that he will buy only if he obtains outside financing satisfactory to buyer, which many buyers insist on today because the forms of financing show wide variations, the seller may wish to reserve the right to sell the building for cash if such a deal can be firmed before he is notified that the buyer has his financing.

9.03 Informal contracts

On occasion a contract of sale is entered into informally.

> **EXAMPLE:** Buyer sends Seller a letter offering to purchase certain land for $100,000. Seller writes back accepting the offer. A contract exists.

One problem here relates to the fact that the "acceptance" may seek to add terms to the offer or change it in some way. Any such change, if material, is treated as a "counteroffer." It is tantamount to a rejection of the offer.

> **EXAMPLE:** Seller sends Buyer a letter offering to sell Buyer certain land for $100,000. Nothing is said concerning the type of deed to be given. Buyer writes back stating, "I accept your offer but will insist on a warranty deed." In almost all states the deal is dead. Buyer rejected the offer. 16 ALR3d 1430. Ordinarily, the purchaser is not entitled to a warranty deed unless the contract calls for it. However, the rigor of the older decisions is likely to be tempered in modern times. Uniform Commercial Code § 2-207 states that additional terms in the acceptance do not prevent formation of a contract unless the acceptance is expressly made conditional on assent to the additional or different terms. This provision was intended to get rid of the technical "ribbon matching" or "mirror" rules of the decisions requiring the acceptance to conform literally and in every respect with the offer. *Dorton* v. *Collins Aikman Corp.,* 435 F2d 1161. The UCC thinking is finding its way into the area of real estate law.

9.04 Unconscionable contracts or terms

Section 2-302 of the Uniform Commercial Code provides that the court may refuse to enforce an unconscionable contract, or strike an unconscionable clause, or so tailor enforcement as to prevent an unconscionable result. This section crystallizes a trend that was already present in the progressive court decisions. 18 ALR3d 1309. But it will serve to push the courts faster and harder in this direction. The literature on the subject is extensive.

> **EXAMPLE:** Seller gave Buyer an option to purchase the land. Buyer exercised option. If the literal terms of the option were enforced, Buyer would have more than fifty years to pay the purchase price and would have no security meanwhile. The court ordered that Buyer must either pay cash or accept reasonable terms. *Rego* v. *Decker,* 482 P2d 834 (Alaska, 1971). This tendency has been accelerated as a result of the Uniform Commercial Code § 2-302.

9.04(a) Unconscionability and good faith

It has been said that the twin requirements of conscionability and good faith unite to subject the contract to a sort of push–pull effect. The courts *pull* an unconscionable provision out of the contract.

> **EXAMPLE:** A provision in the contract whereby one party waives all defenses to the enforcement of the contract is unconscionable and void. *W.J. Seufert Land Co.* v. *Greenfield,* 496 P2d 197 (Oreg. 1972).

Under the requirement of good faith, the courts *push* into the contract a provision needed in the interests of justice and fair play.

EXAMPLE: Even if the contract is silent, the courts push into the contract a requirement that the title must be marketable. See as to unconscionability, 67 Cornell L. Rev. (1982) (citing many authorities).

9.05   The seller

Just as a deed must have a grantor, a contract must have a seller.

EXAMPLE: A hotel known as the Glen House, together with its furniture, was sold at auction to Joseph Grafton for $90,000. He refused to go through with the deal. The only document signed by Grafton was the following:

I, the subscriber, do hereby acknowledge myself to be the purchaser of the estate known as the Glen House, with furniture belonging to it, in Green's Grant, New Hampshire, and sold at auction, Tuesday, May 16, 1871, at 11 o'clock a.m., and for the sum of $90,000, the said property being more particularly described in the advertisement hereunto affixed; and I hereby bind myself, my heirs, and assigns to comply with the terms and conditions of the sale, as declared by the auctioneer at the time and place of sale.   Joseph Grafton

The court held that this was not an enforceable contract of sale, since the seller was not named therein. *Grafton* v. *Cummings,* 99 U.S. 100 (1878).

The following are the chief requirements as to the seller: (1) If the title is held by co-owners, all should be named as seller. (2) The seller should be an adult of sound mind. (3) If the seller is a corporation, the sale must be authorized by its directors and sometimes by its stockholders. (4) Where the seller is a trustee or executor, a check should be made to determine that he had the power to sell the land, since neither an executor nor trustee has power to sell land unless the will or trust instrument expressly gives him that power.

A contract by a shareholder in a corporation to cause the corporation to sell and convey corporate land is valid. *Borg* v. *Warner,* 16 Ill.2d 234, 156 NE2d 513 (1958).

Subpurchase.   Not uncommonly a seller in a contract is himself merely the buyer under another contract relating to the same land. This is unobjectionable.

EXAMPLE: Seller contracts to sell to Buyer #1 and Buyer #1 contracts to sell to Buyer #2. They can hold a double closing, preferably in escrow, and Seller and Buyer #1 will get their money, and Buyer #2 will get ownership of the land. *Waggoner* v. *Saether,* 207 Ill. 32, 107 NE 859 (1915).

9.05(a)   Signature of seller's spouse

In some states, the spouse of a landowner has certain rights, dower, and curtesy in the land and these rights cannot be extinguished without the spouse's signature. When the seller's spouse, in such a state, has not signed the contract of sale and refuses to sign a deed to the property, courts differ as to the courses open to the buyer. In general, the buyer may decline to go through with the deal and may obtain return of his down payment on the ground that the seller is unable to deliver clear title.

In those community property states that require the wife's consent to a disposition of the community property, the wife's consent is needed for a valid contract to convey community real estate.

Where land is occupied by a family as their home, then regardless of whether the land is owned by the husband or the wife, both must join in any deed of the land. Laws relating to homestead require the double signature. Both must join in the contract to sell.

In states that have abolished dower and curtesy, and that also permit either spouse to convey his or her own land without the signature of the other spouse, the spouse's signature is not necessary either on the contract of sale or on the deed, unless, of course, the land to be sold is a homestead.

In states that have abolished dower, but have substituted some statutory interest that the wife retains if she fails to sign the husband's deed, the courts show the same conflict of opinion as prevails in the states that still have dower. Some allow a deduction from the purchase price to compensate the buyer when the seller's spouse refuses to sign the deed and some do not. *Free* v. *Little,* 31 Utah 449, 88 Pac. 407 (1907).

The failure of the spouse to join in the contract is a harmless mistake if she is willing to join in the deed. *Davis* v. *Dean Vincent, Inc.,* 465 P2d 702 (Oreg. 1970).

9.06 The buyer

Just as a deed must have a grantee, so a contract must have a buyer. The buyer should be named in the contract. If there are two or more buyers and they wish to acquire title as joint tenants, it is necessary that they be so described in the contract. Otherwise serious difficulties may develop if one of the buyers dies before the deed is executed. The buyer should be an adult of sound mind.

9.07 Sale price—payment provisions

The contract of sale must state the sale price. A common fault in contracts is the failure to state precisely how the purchase price will be paid.

9.08 Property sold

Disputes over a deficiency in the quantity of land sold are common, especially in the case of farmland. The usual rule is that a deficiency in quantity is immaterial if the sale is *in gross.* A sale in gross is a sale of a specific tract of land by name or description. 1 ALR2d 18.

EXAMPLE: Seller contracts to sell to Buyer "the Evergreen Ranch in Coles County, Colorado, containing 640 acres, more or less, at a price of $500,000." A survey shows the ranch contains only 620 acres. No deduction will be allowed from the sale price. The sale was of the ranch, not of 640 acres. The fact that the price was a gross price, not a *per acre* price, helps establish this. 1 ALR2d 28. This rule will be applied unless the deficiency is very great. *Maxwell* v. *Reid,* 496 P2d 1320 (Kans. 1972). Deficiencies as high as 20 percent have been disregarded.

Where the sale is on a price per acre basis the buyer is sometimes given some sort of relief if there is a deficiency in quantity. 94 ALR3d 1091.

EXAMPLE: Seller contracted to sell to Buyer "the North seven acres of the Hawkins Tract at a price of $5,000 per acre." The deal was closed and $35,000 paid to Seller. Thereafter, it was discovered the tract conveyed was short three-fourths of an acre. Buyer can sue Seller for the deficiency. 153 ALR 37.

In an acreage sale it is best to insert a *usable acreage* clause.

CLAUSE: At a price of $_____ per usable acre, but if survey reveals acreage of less than _____ usable acres, buyer shall have the right to rescind within _____ days after delivery of copy of survey to seller. Areas falling in (1) open or dedicated public streets or ways, (2) recorded private easements of ingress, or (3) areas fenced by adjoiners are not deemed usable acres. All other acres are deemed usable.

The land sold necessarily includes all fixtures comprising part of the land. However, in the case of apartment buildings, hotels, and so on, there may be items of personal property used in connection with the land sold that might not be considered fixtures, such as furniture. If these items are also to go to the buyer, the contract should contain a provision to the effect that such personal property shall be transferred to the buyer at the time of the giving of the deed. In the absence of such provision, the buyer is not entitled to any items that are not fixtures.

On larger sales, industrial plants, for example, it may be prudent to break the sale price down into two parts, one price for the building and the rest for the chattels (machinery). The IRS has one depreciation rule on real estate (buildings) and another on equipment.

9.08(a) Description of the land sold

The contract must contain a reasonably certain description of the land sold. While the description need not be as formal as that contained in a deed, it must be sufficiently definite to identify the land sold with reasonable certainty. 23 ALR2d 6.

There are two views as to the sufficiency of a contract that contains some description of the property but that requires resort to oral testimony to identify the particular property intended to be sold. In states that take a strict view, such contracts are not enforceable.

> **EXAMPLE:** A contract described the land as "real estate situated in the County of Cook and State of Illinois, to wit: One five-room flat and two six-room flats at 3517 Palmer Street." The city in which the land was located was not mentioned. It was held that this description was too indefinite. *Herous* v. *Romanowski,* 336 Ill. 297, 168 NE 305 (1929). Since verbal evidence would be needed to establish the city and state in which the land is located, the contract is not sufficient. This is the rule followed in most states.

On the other hand, liberal courts enforce such contracts.

> **EXAMPLE:** A contract identified land as "305 S. Negley Avenue." Oral testimony was admitted to prove that the seller owned property of this address in Pittsburgh, Pa. *Sawert* v. *Lunt,* 360 Pa. 521, 62 A2d 34 (1948).

If the city and state are given, a description by street address is sufficient. 23 ALR2d 39. But it is preferable, of course, to use a correct legal description of the land sold.

Where a contract contains a defective street address description but also states that the legal description may be inserted later, the court decisions are conflicting. One line of cases states that the buyer can insert the proper legal description. *Schmalzer* v. *Jamnik,* 407 Ill. 236, 95 NE2d 347 (1950). Other courts hold the contract void. *Murphy* v. *Morse,* 96 Ga. App. 623, 100 SE2d 623 (1957).

Where the seller owns a house and vacant lot adjoining great care must be exercised in preparing the description. Likewise, care should be taken where the building has several addresses. *Goebel* v. *Benefit Tr. Life Insurance Co.,* 88 Ill. App.2d 19, 232 NE2d 211 (1967).

9.09   Completeness

In order to be enforceable, a contract must be complete in all its parts. All the terms of the contract must be settled, and none must be left to be determined by future negotiation. 68 ALR2d 1222.

> **EXAMPLE:** A contract called for a sale price of $75,000, $5,000 cash, "time of possession and balance of payment to be arranged at a later date." This contract is not enforceable even if the buyer wishes to pay cash. *Murphy* v. *Koll Grocery Co.,* 311 Ky. 771, 225 SW2d 466. Note that if the contract had simply stated a price of $75,000 and had said nothing regarding terms, the contract would have been good. The court would have read into the contract that a cash deal was intended, deal to be closed in a reasonable time. But since the parties intended something other than a cash deal, but left the exact terms unsettled, the contract was incomplete. A similar holding followed where a contract stated that balance of price was payable "by future agreement on or before January 1,

19—." *Bentzen* v. *H.N. Ranch,* 78 Wyo. 158, 320 P2d 440 (1958); 68 ALR2d 1221 (1958). The court held likewise where the contract stated that a price of $85,000 was payable "as per terms agreed on." *Roberts* v. *Adams,* 164 Cal. App.2d 312, 330 P2d 900 (1958). The same was held where the contract stated "balance in monthly payments." *Cefalu* v. *Breznik,* 15 Ill.2d 168, 154 NE2d 237 (1958). The court also held likewise where the contract said that the balance of $50,000 was payable "as lots are released at purchaser's convenience." *Edward H. Snow Co.* v. *Oxsheer,* 62 N.M. 113, 305 P2d 727 (1957).

In other words, where the written memorandum indicates on its face that parties intended additional terms that were to be negotiated at some future time, the contract is incomplete. The courts explain that they can enforce a contract that the parties have made but cannot make or complete a contract that the parties have failed to complete, by leaving some provisions for future bargaining. Quite commonly this rule is applied when it appears that some sort of credit sale was contemplated, but the terms were not agreed upon. Today's courts will supply minor terms that the parties have omitted. Corbin, *Contracts* § 1137; 11 Williston, *Contracts* (Jaeger ed.) § 1424.

If the contract calls for a purchase money mortgage but fails to specify the due date thereof, it is incomplete and cannot be enforced. *Sweeting* v. *Campbell,* 8 Ill.2d 54, 132 NE2d 523 (1956); 60 ALR2d 251. And where a contract provided that the seller would give the buyer a deed that would reserve a vendor's lien for the balance of the purchase price, and the contract further provided that "the rate [of interest] will be agreed upon later," it was too incomplete and indefinite to be enforced. *Hume* v. *Boyle,* 204 SW 673 (Tex. Civ. App. 1918).

9.09(a)   Certainty

In addition to being complete, the contract must be definite and certain. If the court cannot tell what the parties agreed upon, it cannot force them to carry out their agreement.

> **EXAMPLE:** Seller agreed to sell certain land to Buyer for $5,000, "one-half cash, balance one to four years, with interest at 7 percent." This contract is too vague and indefinite to be enforced. No one can be certain what the quoted portion means. *Crawford* v. *Williford,* 145 Ga. 550, 89 SE 488.

> **NEW DEVELOPMENTS.**   The law is changing. Previous strict requirements of completeness and certainty are being liberalized. The fact is that virtually no contract provides for the innumerable contingencies that might possibly occur. And since language is inexact at best and all of us have an imperfect command of the English language, the courts are confronted with a choice—namely, to enforce contracts entered into in good faith but imperfectly expressed or to refuse enforcement for defects in expression. The recent trend is toward the application of courageous common sense. Many contracts deemed too indefinite or incomplete under the older decisions would be enforced under today's decisions. Restatement, *Contracts* § 370; Restatement, *Contracts 2d* § 33; Corbin, *Contracts* § 95–102, 1137; Williston, *Contracts* § 37, 48, 1424; Murray, *Contracts,* § 27.

9.10 Type of title, deed, and evidence of title

There are three separate ideas that are sometimes confused.

EXAMPLE: A contract of sale is silent as to the *type of title* the buyer is to receive. In such case the buyer is entitled to a marketable title, free of all encumbrances. This will be explained later.

EXAMPLE: The contract is silent as to the *type of deed* the buyer is to receive. In most states the buyer must be content with a quitclaim deed.

EXAMPLE: The contract is silent as to the *type of evidence of title* (abstract, title policy) the buyer is to receive. In such case the buyer must procure his own evidence of title at his own expense.

9.10(a) Type of deed

A contract is enforceable even though it does not specify the type of deed to be given. Nevertheless, since there is a vast difference between a quitclaim deed and a warranty deed, the contract should specify the type agreed upon.

If the contract is silent regarding the type of deed to be given, in most states the seller need only give a quitclaim deed or a deed of bargain and sale without covenants. *Morris* v. *Goldthorp,* 390 Ill. 186, 60 NE2d 857 (1945); *Boekelheide* v. *Snyder,* 71 S.D. 470, 26 NW2d 74 (1947); *Vitra Seal Co.* v. *Jaycox,* 1 N.J.S. 560, 62 A2d 431 (1948); *Tymon* v. *Linoki,* 16 N.Y.2d 293, 213 NE2d 661 (1965); 16 ALR3d 1430. This does not excuse the seller from giving a marketable title. It simply means that once the title has been shown to be marketable, the seller may deliver a quitclaim deed and be rid of any possibility of future worry regarding presently unknown title defects.

It is best for the buyer to insist on a warranty deed. In a number of states, the mere fact that the buyer is content to take a quitclaim deed is enough to keep him from being a bona fide purchaser, and he will take the land subject to unrecorded deeds, mortgages, liens, and so forth.

EXAMPLE: Pursuant to a contract of sale Seller gave Buyer a quitclaim deed. Buyer then discovered that Seller had placed an unrecorded mortgage on the property. In some states a grantee in a quitclaim deed is not considered a bona fide purchaser and the unrecorded mortgage would be good against Buyer.

The deed should comply with the contract in all respects.

EXAMPLE: Seller contracts to sell to Husband and Wife in joint tenancy. He made the deed to Husband only. Wife is entitled to have the deed reformed to run to Husband and Wife as joint tenants. *Wahl* v. *Fairbanks,* 405 Ill. 290, 90 NE2d 735 (1950).

EXAMPLE: Seller contracts to sell to Buyer. The deed calls for a warranty deed. Nothing is said about encroachments. A survey shows the building encroaches 3 inches into the street. Seller wants to make his warranty deed subject to the encroachment. He cannot do so. The deed must follow the contract.

EXAMPLE: Seller contracts to sell to Buyer and to give Buyer a warranty deed. Actually Seller has the property in the name of Nominee, and offers Buyer a warranty deed signed by Nominee. Buyer need not accept it. 57 ALR 1507.

WARNING: One must not attach too much importance to the giving of a warranty deed. After all, I could sit down at this moment, write out, sign, and deliver to you a warranty deed purporting to convey to you the Merchandise Mart, the Tower of London, Westminster Abbey, and all the motels in the Holiday Inn chain. As a result of this activity you would own absolutely nothing. I cannot convey what I do not own. A warranty deed is like the frosting on a cake. It's nice to have if the grantor really owns the land. But, if you really want to know that I own what I am trying to convey, you must insist on receiving evidence of title, written proof that I really own the land I am attempting to convey. If the land is really owned by the grantor in the warranty deed, but the title search fails to show some unpaid real estate tax, unpaid mechanic's lien, and so forth, the warranty deed might help the grantee collect from the grantor the tax he is compelled to pay to protect his title. This however, is about all the warranty deed is useful for.

9.10(b)   Marketable title

Unless the contract provides otherwise, the seller must convey a marketable title. Such a title is also described as a *merchantable title.* This means that the seller must have a good title, free from liens, encumbrances, or defects other than those specified in the contract. As a general rule, every buyer of land has a right to demand a title that shall put him in all reasonable security against loss or annoyance by litigation. He should have a title that is free from doubt, one that will enable him not only to hold his land, but to hold it in peace and free from the hazard of litigation. If he wishes to sell the land, he should be reasonably sure that no flaw will come up to disturb its market value. *Firebaugh* v. *Wittenberg*, 309 Ill. 536, 141 NE 379 (1923).

SUGGESTION: The contract should contain a *subject clause* specifying the *permitted objections*. These are the objections the seller knows are against his title, usually those that were in existence when he bought the land, and usually of a character such that they cannot be removed, like building restrictions, and usually such that the buyer finds unobjectionable. As long as they are listed in the subject clause, they do not render title unmarketable.

In every state, and even in different localities within a state, lawyers have struggled to evolve lists of permitted objections appropriate to the locality. Such lists often find their way into printed contract forms prepared by bar associations, real estate boards, and title companies. Several dangers are present: (1) Since new laws are enacted constantly, there is always danger that a given form is outdated. (2) A form appropriate to one locality must not be used elsewhere.

(3) A form suitable for a home may be totally inapplicable to a purchase of vacant land or an office building.

At all events, in purchasing a home, the buyer ought not agree to accept a title that will be rejected by a lender who will seek FHA insurance or other federally related lenders. Let the contract include a clause as follows:

> **CLAUSE:** The purchaser does not agree to accept a title that fails to conform to current FHA general standards for single-family dwellings.

Law students are puzzled at times by an apparent conflict between two situations. They know that *recording imparts constructive notice.* All persons are deemed to know what the public records reveal. Why, then, they ask, is it customary to set forth in the contract of sale the encumbrances which the buyer must accept (*permitted objections*) in general form, such as building restrictions of record? The answer is, of course, that at this point practice and law differ. In point of fact, the parties cannot be certain what encumbrances exist *until the title search has been completed.* This search is made *after* a bargain has been struck and a contract signed. Meanwhile, the parties must agree on a list of *permitted objections* that neither party considers objectionable.

As can readily be seen, the rules of law that operate on a point that the parties have failed to cover in their contract are often hopelessly impractical. It is for this reason that lawyers and form writers constantly "draft around" these rules. And, of course, even the forms are often imperfect and require modification. This is usually the task of the lawyer. Real estate brokers or salesmen are, in many states, forbidden to change forms to fit the situation. This is considered the unauthorized practice of law.

One of the important functions of contracts, then, is to spell out the rights and duties of the parties so as to reach a result different from that offered by the rules of law. This is perfectly legal and is done constantly.

> **EXAMPLE:** In the contract of sale state that the seller will give a *warranty* deed.

> **EXAMPLE:** In the contract of sale list the encumbrances the seller is powerless to remove and which the buyer agrees to accept. Building restrictions contained in the plat of subdivision would provide an instance of this sort.

> **EXAMPLE:** In the contract of sale provide that within — days seller will deliver to buyer an updated abstract of title.

What form of deed the contract will specify is likely to depend largely on local custom. In the Midwest the general warranty deed is commonly specified. In New York and California the special warranty deed or grant deed is used. It is best to conform to custom unless some important considerations require one to do battle on this score.

The question of marketability of title must be disposed of before the deal is closed. In other words, if the buyer wishes to avail himself of his right to insist upon a marketable title, he must point out such defects as he discovers and must do this before he pays his money and receives his deed. Once the deal is closed, the money paid, and the deed delivered, the buyer cannot demand his money back if the title proves defective. 57 ALR 1261; 84 ALR 1025, 1027, 1032; 92 CJS 15; 92 CJS 559. However, if the buyer has received a warranty deed from the seller, he may sue the seller for damages, should the title prove defective.

9.10(b)(1) Marketable title—mortgages and other liens

Unless the contract provides otherwise, the buyer has the right to demand a title free and clear of all mortgages, tax liens, judgment liens, mechanics' liens, and all other liens. It is not sufficient for the seller to offer to deduct the amount of such liens from the purchase price. The buyer may reject the title unless it is actually cleared of such liens. Suppose, however, that there is a mortgage or other lien on the property, and the seller can arrange to have the mortgagee present at the closing of the deal, so that, at the closing of the deal, the mortgage will be paid in full out of the purchase money due the seller and the mortgagee will deliver a release of the mortgage to the buyer. Must the buyer go through with the deal in this manner if the contract does not require him to do so? In quite a number of states, the answer is in the affirmative. The seller's title is not considered unmarketable if he can arrange to have the owner of the mortgage, judgment, or other lien present at the closing of the deal, ready to turn over proper releases to the buyer on receiving payment of the amount due from the buyer. *Gibson* v. *Brown,* 214 Ill. 330, 73 NE 578 (1905); *Joslyn* v. *Irvin Dick Co.,* 168 Minn. 279, 209 NW 889 (1926); *Robeson-Marion Develop. Co.* v. *Powers Co.,* 183 SE2d 455 (S.C. 1971); *Sparks* v. *Helmer,* 142 Okla. 219, 286 Pac. 306 (1930). In other states, a contrary rule is followed. Any mortgage or other lien not mentioned in the contract must be cleared before the deal is closed. *Johnson* v. *Malone,* 252 Ala. 609, 42 So2d 505 (1949).

> **CLAUSE FOR SELLER'S BENEFIT:** If at the date of closing there is any mortgage encumbrance which the vendor is obligated to pay and discharge, the vendor may use any portion of the balance of the purchase price to satisfy the same, provided the vendor shall at closing of deal either (1) deliver to the purchaser an instrument in recordable form sufficient, in the judgment of purchaser's title company, to satisfy such encumbrance of record, or (2) deposit with the purchaser's title insurance company sufficient money required by it to insure the recording of such satisfaction and the issuance of title insurance to the purchaser free of any such emcumbrance, together with the mortgagee's letter indicating its willingness to accept such payment.

9.10(b)(2) Marketable title—easements

Easements render the title unmarketable, unless, of course, the contract requires the buyer to take title subject to easements.

NEW DIRECTIONS: In recent decisions, the title is not rendered unmarketable by the existence of *visible* and *beneficial* easement.

EXAMPLE: The contract is silent regarding easements. A utility company has an easement over the rear five feet of the land for an electric power line, and such a power line is, in fact, located on the rear five feet. The power line services the property in question. In many states, the title would be considered marketable. 57 ALR 1426.

SUGGESTION TO SELLER: Check your title insurance policy or other evidence of title. If it shows your title to be subject to an easement, state in contract that title will be subject "to easement recorded as Document No. 1234567."

SUGGESTION TO BUYER: Do not sign a contract stating that seller will deliver title subject "to easements of record." This would obligate you to take title subject to a recorded easement for a one-hundred-foot highway running right through the middle of the house. Insist that the contract specifically describe the easements to which the title is subject and read them over before you sign the contract.

9.10(b)(3)   Marketable title—building restrictions

Often the use to which a tract of land may be devoted is restricted by building restrictions contained in recorded deeds or subdivision plats. Unless the contract provides otherwise, the buyer is not required to accept a title encumbered with restrictions as to the character of the buildings that may be erected, the use to which the property may be put, and so on, even though such restrictions actually enhance the value of the property.

EXAMPLE: Seller contracts to sell Buyer a vacant lot in a high-class residential subdivision. The contract does not mention restrictions. In the recorded plat of the subdivision, there is a restriction providing that only single-family dwellings may be erected in the subdivision. Buyer may reject the title. 57 ALR 1414.

Suppose the contract requires the buyer to accept title subject to "building line and building restrictions," but it appears that the building on the property violates existing restrictions. The buyer may decline to go through with the deal, for a *violation of a restriction* is a defect or encumbrance separate and distinct from the restriction itself.

EXAMPLE: A contract required the buyer to accept title subject to building and use restrictions. There was a building restriction prohibiting the erection of buildings within five feet of any side line. The buildings actually extended into the prohibited area. It was held that the buyer could refuse to go through with the deal. *Herb* v. *Severson,* 32 Wash.2d 159, 201 P2d 156 (1948); *Lohmeyer* v. *Bower,* 170 Kans. 442, 227 P2d 102 (1951).

SUGGESTION TO BUYER: Never sign a contract which states that title will be subject to "restrictions of record." This obligates you to take title subject to any restriction, no matter how absurd, even a restriction that the only building permitted on the land is a chicken coop. If the seller's title insurance policy is available, look at it. If it shows a restriction, go to the title company or the recorder's office and read the restriction. If you have no objection to it, let the contract read that title will be "subject to restriction recorded as Document No. 123456." Where the contract must be signed at a time when information as to existing building restrictions is not available, and the land is improved with a building that is the principal subject matter of the sale, you might employ the following clause: "Subject to covenants and restrictions of record, provided same are not violated by the existing improvements and the use thereof." When you are buying *vacant* land you *must* insist on reading the restrictions in full before signing the contract.

9.10(b)(4) Marketable title—zoning and building code violations

Building restrictions imposed by deeds or plats must be distinguished from zoning and building ordinances. Such ordinances, though they may greatly restrict the use that may be made of the land, do not render title unmarketable. Generally, the attitude of the courts is that zoning and building ordinances are part of the law of the land, and all persons are supposed to take notice of them. 39 ALR3d 370. Ignorance of the law excuses no one. Suppose that the premises contain actual, existing *violations* of zoning or building ordinances. Here the rule is different. In most of the recent decisions, courts have held that substantial existing violations of *zoning ordinances* render title unmarketable. 5 *American Law of Property* § 11.49; *Lohmeyer* v. *Bower,* 170 Kans. 442, 227 P2d 102 (1951); *Mayer* v. *De Vincentis,* 107 Pa. Super. 588, 164 Atl. 111 (1933); *Hartman* v. *Rizzuto,* 123 Cal. App.2d 186, 266 P2d 539 (1954); 39 ALR3d 375.

EXAMPLE: A building containing three apartments was erected in an area where the ordinance prohibited construction of a building containing more than two apartments. The court held that the buyer could terminate the contract and obtain return of his down payment. *Oates* v. *Delcuze,* 226 La. 751, 77 So2d 28 (1954).

In many cities, violations of building ordinances (like those forbidding basement apartments, requiring certain minimum sanitary arrangements, requiring separate exits for each apartment, requiring fireproof material, etc.) now entail drastic punishment, for cities have come to recognize that the fight against the slum is a fight for survival. Building ordinance violations, like zoning ordinance violations, are being recognized as flaws in the marketability of title, for they impose on a purchaser the same hazards of litigation that the rule of marketability of title was designed to avoid. *Brunko* v. *Pharo,* 3 Wis.2d 628, 89 NW2d

221 (1958) noted, 1958 *Wis. L. Rev.* 641; *Bronen* v. *Marmer,* 206 N.Y.S.2d 909 (1960). *Contra: Stone v. Sexsmith,* 28 Wash.2d 947, 184 P2d 567 (1947); *Ableman* v. *Slader,* 80 Ill. App.2d 94, 224 NE2d 569 (1967).

The prudent buyer will insist that the contract of sale provide that the seller will deliver the property "free from all violations of zoning and building ordinances," and a check with city officials for such violations should be made before the deal is closed. The seller will not be allowed to avoid by trickery or subterfuge his responsibility for ordinance violations.

> **EXAMPLE:** The sale involved a house with an illegal basement apartment. The seller could not bring the building into compliance by tearing out the illegal apartment, for what the contract really contemplates is that the seller will get a permit from the city legalizing the condition as it was when the contract was signed. As it stands, the title is unmarketable. *Hammer* v. *Michael,* 243 N.Y. 445, 154 NE 305 (1926). See 39 ALR3d 362.

Advertising for sale a building that contains ordinance violations may constitute a fraud upon the buyer.

> **SUGGESTION TO LAWYERS:** A comparable problem arises when a warranty deed is given that makes no mention of zoning or building code violations. Some courts say that the grantor is not liable. *Domer* v. *Sleeper,* 533 P2d 9 (Alaska 1975); *Marathon Builders Inc.* v. *Polenger,* 263 Md. 410, 283 A2d 617 (1971). Other courts hold the grantor liable. *Wilcox* v. *Pioneer Homes, Inc.* 41NCA 140, 254 SE2d 214 (1979).

REFERENCES ON ZONING AND BUILDING CODE VIOLATIONS: 24 Albany L. Rev. 167; 27 Rocky Mt. L. Rev. 255; 1957 Wis. L. Rev. 204 (nonconforming use).

9.10(b)(5) Marketable title—leases and tenancies

Unless the contract so provides, the buyer need not accept a title subject to existing leases, or even to existing tenancies, without leases. *Haiss* v. *Schmukler,* 201 N.Y.S. 332. If such leases or tenancies exist, the contract should provide that the title is subject to such leases or tenancies.

> **SUGGESTION TO BUYER:** Do not sign a contract to accept title subject to *existing leases and tenancies.* The existing leases may be very favorable to the tenant and disadvantageous to the property owner. The seller should therefore be required to include a schedule, either in the contract or in a separate document, listing the expiration date, tenants, and rentals on all existing leases and tenancies, together with a statement as to whether the leases include an option to renew or to purchase the property.

9.10(b)(6) Marketable title—encroachments

Encroachments are of three kinds: (1) The building on the land sold encroaches on neighboring land. (2) The building on the land sold encroaches on adjoining streets or alleys. (3) Buildings on adjoining land encroach upon the land sold. 47 ALR2d 331.

When the seller's buildings extend over and upon neighboring land, the factor that renders title unmarketable is the danger that the neighbor may obtain a court order directing removal of the offending portion of the structure, a task that may involve great expense; or the neighbor may institute litigation in an effort to obtain such an order, and the buyer will be put to the expense of defending the litigation. This is in harmony with the principle that a title is not marketable if there is an appreciable risk of litigation. *Very slight* encroachments will not render the title unmarketable, as where a wall of the building on the premises sold extends three-fourths of an inch on neighboring land. *Traxler* v. *McLeran,* 116 Cal. App. 226, 2 P2d 553 (1931). The reason such property remains marketable is that, when (1) the encroachment of my building on your land is slight, (2) the cost of removal is great, and (3) the benefit to you from removal of the building is slight, courts will not compel removal of the encroachment. *Nitterauer* v. *Pulley,* 401 Ill. 494, 82 NE2d 643 (1948). Also, when the building that encroaches on neighboring land is old or dilapidated, or a temporary structure of small value, or a structure that is removable at only slight effort or expense, the title is deemed marketable. With respect to permanent structures, it is hard to draw the line between objectionable and unobjectionable encroachments. The encroachment of a house one and one-half inches on neighboring land has been held to render title unmarketable. *Stokes* v. *Johnson,* 57 N.Y. 673.

When buildings on neighboring land encroach on the premises being sold, courts are more liberal. At the worst, the buyer will be deprived of some portion of the land that the seller has agreed to sell. If the area occupied by the encroaching building is insignificant when compared with the total area of the land being sold, the title is marketable. *Merges* v. *Ringler,* 54 N.Y.S. 280.

When buildings on the land sold extend over adjoining streets or alleys, as in the case of buildings extending over and upon neighboring privately owned land, there is danger that a suit will be instituted to compel removal of the encroachment. Title is unmarketable. Still, if the encroachment is trivial, so that action by the city authorities is highly improbable and it is unlikely that a court would order the encroachment removed, the title is marketable.

> **EXAMPLE:** A building encroached two inches on an adjoining street. The title was held to be marketable. *Mertens* v. *Berendsen,* 213 Cal. 111, 1 P2d 440 (1931).

Suppose the contract provides that the seller agree to deliver a title "subject to questions of survey" or "subject to such a state of facts as an accurate survey would show." Such clauses are inserted to relieve the seller of all responsibility with respect to encroachments. If the existence of encroachments is revealed, the buyer must nevertheless go through with the deal. *McCarter* v. *Crawford,* 245 N.Y. 43, 156 NE 90 (1927).

Suppose the contract requires the seller to deliver title "free from all encumbrances and encroachments." Here the existence of trivial encroachments, such as would ordinarily not render title unmarketable, will nevertheless justify the buyer's rejection of the title.

9.10(b)(7)   Marketable title—chattels

Many sales of land specifically include valuable chattels, as, for example, when a hotel is being sold. The buyer is entitled to marketable title to the chattels. *Peters* v. *Spielvozel,* 163 So2d 59 (Fla. 1964).

9.10(b)(8)   Marketable title—miscellaneous defects

There are many other defects or encumbrances that may render a title unmarketable. For example, a deed signed by some prior landowner may be defective in that the property is not properly described therein, or a signature may be lacking, or the grantor's wife may have failed to sign the deed. Court proceedings on which the title depends, such as mortgage foreclosures, sales by guardians, and the like, may have been defectively conducted. Estates of deceased landowners may have been improperly probated. It is impossible to enumerate within the allotted space the many defects that may render a title unmarketable. Marketability of title plays an important part in those situations where the buyer, after having signed a contract to purchase the land, regrets his bargain and wishes to get out of the deal. His attorney will then subject the title to a minute scrutiny, hoping to find some defect that renders the title unmarketable, so that his client may declare the contract at an end and obtain a return on his down payment.

9.10(b)(9)   Marketable title—title insurance

The fact that a title company is willing to insure the seller's title does not make it marketable.

EXAMPLE: Seller entered into a contract to sell real estate to Buyer. The contract required Seller to furnish a clear policy of title insurance. The title search revealed a recorded easement. The title company was willing to issue a clear policy. Buyer was permitted to back out of the deal. Buyer is entitled to a marketable title and title insurance. *New York Investors, Inc.* v. *Manhattan Beach Bathing Parks Corp.,* 243 N.Y.S. 548, 30 Columb. L. Rev. 1215.

SUGGESTION TO SELLER: Let the contract provide that the title policy is conclusive evidence that the title is good as therein stated but it shall not be evidence of any matters not insured by said policy. This relieves the seller of the obligation to deliver a marketable title. This gets rid of the flyspecking present in marketable title law.

9.10(b)(10)   Marketable
title laws

With each passing year it has grown increasingly difficult to prove that any given title to land is marketable. Year by year the chain of deeds, mortgages, wills, and other recorded matters relating to the title, beginning with the original grant from the government, grows longer and more complex. In consequence, abstracts of title and title searches grow longer, more difficult, and more complex. Many more opportunities present themselves for technical errors that impair the marketability of title. For these difficulties a solution had to be found. It has, indeed, been found in a number of states. In these states (Illinois, Indiana, Iowa, Massachusetts, Michigan, Minnesota, Nebraska, North Dakota, Ohio, South Dakota, and Wisconsin, for example) new laws have been passed to promote the marketability of title. In general, laws such as this select a particular period of time. In Illinois, for example, the period is forty years. If an examination of the public records shows that for the last forty years title to a particular tract of land has passed from one person to another in a connected fashion, that this connected chain of title culminates in a deed to X, and that X is in peaceable possession of the land in question, X will be deemed to have good and marketable title to that tract of land free and clear from any adverse claims to the title that antedate the forty-year period. This does not mean that all claims that are forty years old or more are automatically wiped out. Each of these marketability laws provides a period of time during which a person claiming an interest that is more than forty years old (or whatever the statutory period may be) may record an affadavit or other claim stating the nature of his interest in a particular piece of land. In this fashion, any claim to the title of land must appear on the records within the last forty years, or it is automatically outlawed. Consequently, a person searching the title to the land need only search the title during the past forty years, and if he finds a connected chain, he need not concern himself with recorded matters that antedate the forty-year period. Each of these marketability laws lists certain interests that are not affected or outlawed by the legislation.

> **EXAMPLE:** A common provision is to the effect that a person claiming an easement need not record his claim of easement if the existence of such an easement is revealed by a physical examination of the land itself. Thus if a neighbor claims party wall rights or an easement for a driveway extending over the premises, it is fairly clear that a mere glance at the property will reveal the existence of such easement claims. Therefore they need not be rerecorded.

Another common exception relates to claims of the United States government. No state has the power or right to pass laws that extinguish the rights of the United States government. But whatever the claim may be, if it does not fall within the list of claims not affected by the legislation, it is outlawed unless a document in proper form showing the existence of such claim is recorded within the forty-year period.

REFERENCES: 53 Cornell L. Rev. 45; 2 Drake L. Rev. 79; 47 Iowa L. Rev. 413; 46 Ky. L. J. 605; 56 Mich. L. Rev. 225; 51 Minn. L. Rev. 356; 50 Marq. L. Rev. 15; 29 N. D. L. Rev. 265; 44 N. C. L. Rev. 99; 34 Okla. B. J. 2357; 1957 U. Ill. L. F. 491; 13 U. Miami L. Rev. 51; 4 Washburn L. J. 240; 1942 Wis. L. Rev. 258; 11 Wyo. L. J. 19; 71 ALR2d 846; Basye, *Clearing Land Titles* §§ 171–189 (2d ed. 1970).

9.10(c) Time of existence of good title

Ordinarily the seller need not have good title on the date of the contract. It is sufficient if he has good title at the time fixed for delivery of the deed, or even later, for example, at the time the court, in a specific performance suit, orders the contract to be enforced. *Gibson* v. *Brown,* 214 Ill. 330, 73 NE 578 (1905).

If the contract provides that time is of the essence and also provides that the seller will furnish the buyer an abstract of title or other evidence of title within a specified period of time, the seller must meet this deadline, or the buyer will have the right to declare the contract at an end.

9.10(d) Evidence of title

It is important to distinguish between the seller's duty to deliver good title and his duty to furnish evidence that his title is good. As above stated, unless the contract provides otherwise, the seller must furnish the buyer a *marketable title.* But if the contract does not require him to do so, the seller is under no obligation to furnish the buyer *any evidence that the title is good.* The buyer makes his own title search unless the contract specifies otherwise.

9.10(d)(1) Time for furnishing evidence of title and curing defects in title

If the contract requires the seller to furnish evidence of title, but does not fix a time limit for the furnishing and examination of the abstract or other evidence of title, it is assumed that a reasonable time was intended. In such case:

1. The seller has a reasonable time to furnish the buyer the abstract or other evidence of title.

2. The buyer has a reasonable time to examine the abstract and point out defects in title.

3. The seller has a reasonable time to eliminate or cure defects in title disclosed by the abstract or other evidence of title.

To eliminate uncertainties and speculation by either party on the rise or fall of the value of the property before choosing to perform his part of the contract, the contract should:

1. Fix the time allowed the seller to furnish the buyer evidence of title.

EXPLANATION: When the contract requires the seller to furnish evidence of title by a day named and provides that time is of the essence, and the title evidence is not furnished by the day named, the buyer may rescind, i.e., declare the contract terminated, and may recover his deposit. *Johnson* v. *Riedler,* 395 Ill. 412, 70 NE2d 570 (1941). Most forms of contracts fix a specific time for furnishing the evidence of title and provide that time is of the essence.

2. Fix the time allowed the buyer to examine the abstract and require him to point out any defects in title within the time limited, failure to do so to constitute an acceptance of the title as good.

3. Fix the time allowed the seller to cure defects in title.

4. Fix a time within which the buyer must choose to accept or reject a defective title that the seller cannot cure within the time allowed him.

9.11   Earnest money

Earnest money is a deposit or down payment made by the buyer as a guaranty that the contract will be performed on his part. If he does perform, it applies as a part payment of the purchase price. If he defaults, it is retained by the seller. Usually, the contract specifically permits the seller to retain the earnest money where the buyer defaults. But even in the absence of such a provision, a buyer who is in default cannot recover his earnest money from the seller. *Zersky* v. *Sheehan,* 413 F2d 481 (1969); *Bruce Builders Inc.* v. *Goodwin,* 317 So2d 868 (Fla. 1975); 31 ALR2d 8. Courts have allowed the seller to retain rather substantial down payments; for example, $300,000 on a sale price of $3,000,000, and $35,000 on a sale price of $140,000. Corbin, *The Right of a Defaulting Vendee to the Restitution of Installment Unpaid,* 40 Yale L. J. 1013 (1931). But retention of an earnest money deposit of $30,000 on a sale for $95,000 is unconscionable. *Hook* v. *Lomar,* 320 F2d 536 (5th Cir. 1968).

SUGGESTION TO SELLER: The seller should, for his protection, require a deposit large enough to cover the broker's commission, the expense of the title search, and the compensation to the seller for the loss of his bargain should the buyer default.

SUGGESTION TO BUYER: Provide that the earnest money shall be held in escrow by some third person pending the closing of the deal to insure that the buyer will experience no difficulty in obtaining a return of his deposit should it prove impossible for the seller to deliver clear title. *Gauss* v. *Kirk,* 77 A2d 323 (D.C. 1950).

SUGGESTION TO BUYER: If you put up a check as earnest money, be sure there is money in your bank account to cover it. If the seller attempts to have the check certified, and the bank refuses because funds are lacking, the seller then has an excuse that gives him the right to refuse to carry out the deal. *Gallinero* v. *Fitzpatrick,* 267 NE2d 649 (Mass. 1971).

SUGGESTION TO BUYER: If the seller insists that his broker hold the earnest money, let the contract provide that if the broker fails to return the money to the buyer when the buyer is entitled to it, the seller will pay the amount of the earnest money to the buyer. This will force the seller to think twice about entrusting a large amount of money to an individual. Banks, title companies, and trust companies charge a very small fee for holding earnest money deposits.

With respect to earnest money there is a common misconception shared by the seller and his broker. They tend to view the earnest money as belonging to the seller. This is not the case.

EXAMPLE: Buyer pays Seller earnest money but Seller's title proves unmarketable. Obviously, Seller must refund Buyer's earnest money. This suffices to show that the money is held by Seller for the benefit of both parties at least until Seller shows that he is able to perform. 40 Yale L. J. 1030. Until then Seller's right to the earnest money is inchoate, that is, it has not yet ripened. 35 ALR2d 1384, 1379, 1380.

9.12 Mortgages and financing in real estate sales

In the financing of real estate sales several possibilities are present:

1. The land may have no mortgage on it, and the buyer may be ready to pay cash. No mortgage figures in the sale of the land.

2. The land may have no mortgage on it, but the seller may be willing to accept part cash and to take back a purchase money mortgage for the balance of the purchase price. For example, an insurance company owns a building that it has acquired by foreclosure of a mortgage. It will wish to sell the land, since it is not in the real estate business, but since it also wishes to keep its money in good investments, a purchase money mortgage may be the ideal situation for both seller and buyer.

3. The land is clear of mortgages, but the buyer will need to mortgage the property in order to raise the full purchase price.

4. The land is subject to an existing mortgage, and the buyer is willing to buy the property subject to such existing mortgage.

5. The land is subject to an existing mortgage, but it is too small, or the payments are not convenient for the buyer, so that it will be necessary for the buyer to put a new mortgage on the property for an amount and payable on such terms as will meet his needs. This means that the sale involves paying the existing mortgage and simultaneously placing a new mortgage on the property.

6. The sale may be by an installment contract with clause reserving right to seller to mortgage the land, buyer to take title subject to the mortgage.

7. The sale may be by an installment contract with provision that buyer will receive deed when specified amount is paid in, buyer then to give seller mortgage for balance of purchase price.

8. The sale may be by an installment contract with no mortgage provisions.

Special laws. In Maryland, a law provides that when the purchaser in an installment contract has paid 40 percent of the purchase price he is entitled to demand a deed upon executing a purchase money mortgage to the seller for the balance. 13 Rutgers L. Rev. 625.

Unless the contract provides otherwise, the buyer need not accept title subject to a mortgage. If there is a mortgage on the land and the buyer is to accept the land with the mortgage remaining unpaid, the contract should specify: (1) that the land is being sold subject to such mortgage; (2) the amount remaining unpaid thereon; (3) whether or not the buyer *assumes and agrees* to pay the mortgage, since if he does, he becomes personally liable to the mortgagee for the mortgage debt. If he does not *assume and agree* to pay the mortgage, he may lose the land by foreclosure should he default in his mortgage payments, but no personal judgment can be rendered against him. If the contract calls for the buyer to take the land subject to a mortgage but misdescribes the mortgage, the buyer can back out of the deal. *Crooke* v. *Nelson,* 195 Iowa 681, 191 NW 122 (1922).

9.13 Contingent contracts

Often a clause will be inserted in a contract making it subject to some contingency, so that if the specified event does not occur, the deal is off and the buyer gets back his down payment. Usually such clauses are inserted at the buyer's request. One example would be a clause making the contract contingent on the buyer's ability to procure a mortgage loan of a specified sum. Or the contract may be contingent on the buyer's ability to procure a transfer to himself of the seller's liquor license. Or the contract may be contingent on the rezoning of the premises within a specified time. 39 ALR3d 385. For example, if a buyer needs the property for an industrial plant but it is presently zoned for residential purposes, he will insist that the contract have a provision rendering it void unless rezoning is obtained within a certain number of days.

At times these contingency clauses tend to be rather vague. Nevertheless some courts will enforce them.

EXAMPLE: Where the contract called for a soil compaction report satisfactory to the buyer, the court held that this meant a report satisfactory to a reasonable person. *Collins* v. *Vickter Manor,* 47 Cal.2d 875, 306 P2d 783 (1957).

Some, but not all, modern decisions seem to sanction a good bit of indefiniteness in the contingent clause.

EXAMPLE: The contract stated it was contingent on the buyer's procuring a mortgage loan of a stated sum "with interest at current prevailing rate." This was held to be sufficiently definite. *Barto* v. *Hacks,* 124 Ga. App. 472, 184 SE2d 188 (1971).

EXAMPLE: A contract of sale for $28,000 stated it was contingent on the buyer obtaining a mortgage of $_____. The court held that a mortgage for a "reasonable amount" was intended, and where the buyer tried to get a mortgage of $21,000 and failed, the contract was at an end. *Grayson* v. *LaBranche,* 225 A2d 922 (1967).

9.13(a) Contingent contracts—financing

The buyer must make a reasonable effort to procure financing. *Fry* v. *George Elkins Co.*, 327 P2d 905 (Cal. 1958). What defines a reasonable effort is not always clear. A buyer who fails to make a reasonable effort is guilty of *bad faith.* As a result the contingency clause becomes void and the buyer will lose his earnest money.

If the contract is contingent upon the buyer's procuring a mortgage of a specified amount, and he makes *no effort* to procure one (as is likely to occur when the buyer has changed his mind about buying the property), the clause is waived, and the seller is entitled to forfeit the buyer's earnest money. *Huckleberry* v. *Wilson*, 284 SW2d 205 (Tex. 1955). The buyer must act in good faith.

It is best that the contract give details of the mortgage such as interest rate, time of payment, and so forth. Often the contract gives the buyer ten days to procure financing, and if he fails the seller is then given ten additional days to procure financing for the buyer. A seller may procure a mortgage loan of the desired amount for the buyer and the buyer reject it in horror because the interest rate is too high. Obviously, all such details should be covered in the clause. If, however, the details are omitted, the courts are likely to insist that the terms of the offered mortgage be "reasonable"; otherwise the buyer is not required to accept it. *Lach* v. *Cahill*, 138 Conn. 418, 85 A2d 481 (1951). *Chambers* v. *Jordan*, 262 A2d 505 (Md. 1970). Minds differ so much as to what is reasonable that controversy and litigation easily develop in such a situation.

> **SUGGESTION TO SELLER:** Also tie the contingent clause into the printed clause of the contract form. The contract may give the buyer *thirty* days in which to procure a mortgage of a specified amount. Yet the printed portion of the contract may state that the seller must deliver to the buyer evidence of seller's good title within *twenty* days of the date of the contract. Why should the seller have his title examined when he does not even know that he has a deal with the buyer?

If the contract is contingent on the buyer's obtaining a mortgage, describing it adequately, and if the buyer acting in good faith cannot procure the mortgage, he is entitled to a return of his earnest money deposit. *Levicki* v. *Chrachol*, 56 Ill.App.2d 54, 205 NE2d 491 (1965).

All contract clauses contingent on obtaining financing are being revised at present. It is almost impossible to obtain the old type of level interest rate financing. If the contract is contingent on obtaining the new type of mortgage discussed in the mortgage chapter, the advice of an experienced real estate lawyer is needed. Aiken, *"Subject to Financing" Clauses in Interim Contracts for the Sale of Realty*, 43 Marq. L. Rev. 265 (1960); 62 *id.* 123; 78 ALR3d 880.

9.13(b) Contingent contracts—subject to resale

A new type of contingency clause has made its appearance in this period of difficult financing.

EXAMPLE: Broker finds Purchaser, who has $15,000 cash to apply on a sale price of $100,000. Purchaser, of course, insists on a clause making the contract contingent on his ability to get a loan of $85,000. Seller is unwilling to take his home off the market while Purchaser hunts down financing of this amount. He therefore is willing to sign the contract only if the contract is subject to sale to a third party who firms up his financing prior to Purchaser's obtaining his commitment. Purchaser desperately needs a place to live. He will agree to such a clause. Obviously any loan application he signs should permit Purchaser to recover his application fee if the deal falls through because another buyer (who has a larger down payment) can obtain a loan commitment more rapidly.

Frequently clauses of this type have a "kickout" provision which saves the contract for the buyer, if he waives the contingency.

EXAMPLE: Buyer and Seller enter into a real estate contract for the purchase of Seller's house. This contract is contingent upon Buyer selling his existing home. Seller will go along with this as long as a firmer deal does not come along. If it does, Seller may notify Buyer that he has an offer from another buyer. Buyer then has a stated, usually one- or two-day period of time to decide whether to waive the contingency. If the contingency is waived, Buyer must go through with the deal or lose the earnest money, whether Buyer sells his existing home or not. If Buyer elects not to waive the contingency, the seller is allowed to accept the offer of the new buyer and the contract between Buyer and Seller becomes void. Buyer gets his earnest money back at that point.

9.13(c) Contingent contracts—approvals

Many contracts for the purchase of homes are signed on Sunday, when advice of legal counsel is not available. It seems advisable for the parties to insert some clause making the terms of the contract, other than price, subject to the approval or amendment by a lawyer. Also, the buyer often recognizes that he is unable to determine the physical condition of the property. He needs the help of an expert. All of this simply reflects the fact that a buyer needs expert advice. *Indoe* v. *Dwyer*, 424 A2d 456 (N.J. 1981). One such clause follows:

This contract, except as to price and financing terms (if any), is contingent upon approval by the respective attorneys for purchasers and sellers within three (3) business days of the date hereof. The parties agree that such approval shall be deemed to have been given, and this contingency satisfied or waived, unless an objection or amendment or addition or other express statement withholding approval is made in writing within said three day period.

9.14 Possession and rents

The general rule of law is that the right to possession of land follows the legal title. Since the purchaser does not acquire the legal title to the land until he receives his deed, as a rule he is not entitled to possession until that time. 56 ALR2d 1272. The contract, however, may expressly authorize the buyer to take possession before he receives his deed. Such a provision should normally be included in an install-ment contract, for in such a contract, a purchaser usually expects to take posses-sion long before he is ready to receive his deed. Also, the contract may by impli-cation confer the right of possession on the buyer, as where it contains a provision requiring the buyer to keep the buildings in repair or to give up pos-session in case of default.

The party who is entitled to possession is entitled to the rents of the land. Ordinarily, therefore, rents falling due before the seller gives the buyer a deed belong to the seller, and rents due after the delivery of the deed are payable to the buyer.

9.15 Taxes

Unless the contract provides otherwise, the seller must give the buyer good title free and clear of tax-es that were a lien at the time the contract was made. In fact, if the seller remains in possession after the contract is made, and taxes become a lien while the seller is in possession, the seller must pay these taxes. However, if the buyer goes into possession and taxes thereafter become a lien, the buyer must pay these taxes. To eliminate questions, the contract usually specifies the taxes to which the land will be subject when the deed is made.

9.16 Insurance and risk of loss

It sometimes happens that before the deal is closed the building is destroyed or damaged by fire or other casualty. In some states, the loss so caused falls on the buyer. In other words, the buyer must go through with the deal and pay the full contract price, even though the building has been de-stroyed. 27 ALR2d 466; 27 ALR3d 572; 51 Ill. B.J. 124; 52 *id* 464. This risk is not limited to fire. It includes damage from flood, windstorm, vandalism, boiler destruction, hurricane, erosion, subsidence, collapse of retaining wall, and freez-ing of an orange grove. Friedman, *Contracts and Conveyances of Real Property* § 4.11 (3d ed. 1975). But most states give the buyer the benefit of the seller's insurance. *Id.* But in an increasing number of states, including California, Con-necticut, Illinois, Kentucky, Maine, Massachusetts, Michigan, New Hampshire, New York, Oregon, Rhode Island, South Carolina, South Dakota, and Wiscon-sin, laws or court decisons put the risk of loss on the seller, so that if a substan-tial loss by fire or other casualty occurs before the buyer has been given a deed to the property, the buyer may cancel the deal and obtain return of his down payment. However, an important factor in some of these states is the fact of pos-session. The one in possession is in a better position to prevent fires. *Skelly Oil Co.* v. *Ashmore*, 365 SW2d 582 (Mo. 1963). Hence in these states, if the buyer is put in possession before the deal is closed, you will find the courts or the laws assigning this as a reason for putting the risk of loss back on the buyer.

In all states the risk of loss falls on the seller where: (1) The contract specif-ically provides that risk of loss pending closing of the deal rests on the seller. (2)

The seller does not have a good marketable title at the time of the loss, the reason being that it is unfair to put the risk of loss on a buyer when the seller is in no position to perform his obligations under the contract. *Eppstein* v. *Kuhn,* 225 Ill. 115, 80 NE 80 (1906). (3) The seller is at fault in causing the delay in closing the deal, and during this delayed period a loss occurs. (4) The loss is due to the carelessness of the seller, as when he leaves the house during a cold spell without draining the heating system and all the radiators are cracked by ice formation. 3 Corbin, *Contracts* 661.

9.17 Prorating or apportionment

Provision is frequently made for prorating, adjustment, or apportionment of rents, taxes, insurance, premiums, water taxes, interest accrued on mortgage indebtedness, personal property taxes on personal property transferred to the buyer, gas and electric bills, janitor's salary, management fees on current rent collections, and charges on service contracts, such as exterminator or scavenger service. It is also customary to provide that fuel on hand shall be purchased by the buyer at current prices as of the proration date. Although it is usual to prorate certain items not mentioned in the contract, it must be remembered that, in the event of controversy, the party contending that an item should be prorated will be unable legally to compel proration in the absence of provision in the contract therefor. *Lathers* v. *Keogh,* 109 N.Y. 583, 17 NE 131 (1888); *Antietam-Sharpsburg Mus.* v. *William H. Marsh, Inc.,* 249 A2d 221 (Md. 1969); *Wilson* v. *Campbell,* 425 SW2d 518 (Ark. 1968). A special prorating clause is needed where there are percentage leases, since the actual rental will not be known until after the deal is closed.

9.18 Date

The contract need not be, but usually is, dated.

9.19 Signature

As heretofore pointed out, the contract must be signed by the party against whom enforcement of the contract is sought. Of course, in practice the contract is almost invariably signed by both seller and buyer.

Suppose land is owned jointly by *A* and *B. C* negotiates with A for the purchase of the property and agrees with *A* that the land will be sold for the sum of $10,000. A contract is prepared, designating *A* and *B* as sellers and *C* as buyer. *A* and *C* sign the contract; *B* refuses to sign. Is the contract binding on *A*? No, for the contract shows on its face that a sale was intended only if both landowners agreed. *Madia* v. *Collins,* 408 Ill. 358, 97 NE2d 313 (1951); 154 ALR 778; 92 CJS 547.

9.20 Contracts signed by agents

A person may authorize an agent to enter into contracts on his behalf for the purchase or sale of real estate. In many states, this authorization must be in writing, and in all states it is customary to employ a written authorization. Such an agent is called an *attorney in fact,* and the document granting this authority is called a *power of attorney.*

9.21 Seal

A seal is not necessary to the validity of a contract.

9.22 Delivery

Suppose you list your land with a broker for sale and he finds a buyer interested in its purchase but who does not wish to pay the price you are asking. The buyer prepares and signs a contract of sale stipulating a lower price. This is an *offer.* He hands the contract to the broker, who hands it to you. You sign the contract and return it to the buyer. This is an *acceptance.* The contract is now in force. Suppose, however, that you simply hold on to the contract, hoping that a higher offer will appear, and refuse to answer the buyer's telephone calls. This last situation poses the questions: (1) Must the buyer be *notified* that his offer has been accepted? In other words, can he legally withdraw his offer at any time before he is *notified* that the offer has been accepted? (2) Is delivery necessary to the validity of a contract? The buyer, you will notice, is in an awkward spot. He cannot risk signing a contract to buy some other house, for if he does, he may find himself obligated to buy two houses. Some courts protect the buyer and allow him to revoke his offer in this last situation, stating either that the acceptance is ineffective until the buyer is notified thereof or that delivery is necessary for a written contract to be binding. *Hollingshead* v. *Morris,* 172 Mich. 126, 137 NW 527 (1912). However, there are also contrary decisions. 1 Corbin, *Contracts* 93, 208.

> **SUGGESTION TO BUYER:** Let the contract be prepared in duplicate. The buyer signs both duplicates. Each duplicate contains a provision that the buyer's liability, if any, is terminated and his down payment returned, unless a duplicate signed by the seller is delivered to the buyer within three days after the date of the contract. The buyer hands both duplicates to the seller but retains a carbon copy, so that he can always prove his nonliability, if he fails to receive a signed duplicate within the specified time.

9.23 Acknowledgments

An acknowledgment is not necessary, although it is desirable since it simplifies proof of the contract in any suit brought thereon. If the contract is to be recorded, acknowledgment is necessary in nearly all states.

9.24 Witnesses

If the contract is not acknowledged, it should, as a practical matter, be witnessed, although this is not necessary as a matter of law. The fact that the signatures are witnessed simplifies use of the contract in any litigation that may develop.

9.25   Recording

Some contracts will go so far as to include a clause providing that the contract is void if the buyer records it. A buyer who is hopelessly in default will sometimes record the contract, hoping thereby to cloud the seller's title and to obtain a return of part of the purchase price paid. In view of the public policy behind recording law, such provisions are of doubtful validity, but their use may well dissuade the buyer from recording. 12 Wayne L. Rev. 402.

9.26   Effect of contract—interest of purchaser

The signing of a contract for the sale of land does not give the buyer legal title to the land. Ownership can be transferred to the buyer only by a deed. However, the buyer does acquire an interest in the land. This interest is known as equitable title.

The equitable title of the buyer results from the doctrine of equitable conversion. *Shay* v. *Penrose*, 25 Ill.2d 447, 185 NE2d 218 (1962); 91 CJS *Vendor and Purchaser* § 106. In most states this equitable title arises the moment the contract is entered into.

> **EXAMPLE:** Seller enters into an installment contract with Buyer. Buyer dies without a will, leaving Heir as his only heir. Administrator is appointed administrator of Buyer's estate. The equitable interest of Buyer passes to Heir, as real estate. 33 CJS *Executors and Administrators* § 112. Suppose Seller dies and *ABC Co.* is appointed his administrator. ABC Co. will be entitled to collect the contract payments. 33 CJS *Executors and Administrators* § 112. Since Buyer was the equitable owner of the land, the courts will, for most purposes, treat Seller's interest under the contract as personal property, going to his administrator.

As a result of this rule, a contract purchaser can mortgage his contract interest by means of a real estate mortgage. 73 ALR2d 1400.

9.27   Effect of deed

When the deal is closed and the seller's deed delivered to the buyer, the deal is regarded as consummated. The contract of sale has served its purpose. It is *merged* in the deed. 38 ALR2d 1310. The contract no longer exists. For this reason, if matters remain to be attended to after closing of the deal, it is best that they be set forth in the deed. This is particularly important as to title matters, for the buyer waives his right to cancel the contract because of defects in title if he accepts and pays for a deed while the title is defective or encumbered. 84 ALR 1001, 1031. However, there are some exceptions to the merger rule. In particular, when the contract calls for something to be done after the deal is closed, delivery of the deed does not extinguish that aspect of the contract.

> **EXAMPLE:** The contract required the seller to lay water mains and sewers after closing of the deal. The deal was closed, and the deed delivered to buyer. Thereafter, the seller failed to lay the water mains and sewers. The buyer filed a

damage suit against the seller, and the seller was held liable. *McMillan* v. *American Suburban Corp.,* 136 Tenn. 53, 188 SW 615. The same would be true where the contract requires the seller to build a house on the land sold. 84 ALR 1023. If the contract warrants that the building is in sound condition, this warranty survives the closing of the deal, for that obviously was what the parties intended. *Levin* v. *Cook,* 186 Md. 535, 47 A2d 505 (1946). Contract provisions as to the date on which possession will be turned over to the buyer are not merged in the deed. In all these cases the buyer's only remedy, if the seller fails to perform, is to sue the seller for damages. He cannot sue to get his money back. *De Bisschop* v. *Crump,* 24 F2d 807 (1928).

Also when the deal is closed and the deed accepted by the buyer-grantee, all questions of *marketability of title* are at an end. 66 C.J. 847, 1480; 84 ALR 1025, 1027, 1032; 57 ALR 1261. Of course, a grantee who receives a warranty deed can sue the grantor for damages if a title defect shows up; but he cannot get his money back. The buyer's right to sue the seller for the seller's misrepresentations is not affected by the closing of the deal. Normally the buyer does not discover these misrepresentations until after he has taken possession.

RECAPITULATION: Thus, it can be said with respect to merger:

1. That the obligations of the seller to furnish a title of a particular character, or evidence of such title, ends with the closing of the deal.
2. That the obligations of the seller to perform acts after closing (such as landscaping) do not end with closing.
3. That the buyer's rights with respect to the seller's misrepresentations or nondisclosure do not end with closing, since normally they are not discovered until after the buyer takes possession.

9.28   Assignment of the contract

The buyer may assign his interest in the contract. By virtue of the contract, the buyer has the right to demand a deed to the property on performing his part of the contract. He may sell and transfer his right to a third party, which is accomplished by means of a brief instrument called an *assignment.* Such third party is called the *assignee.* The assignee has the right to make the payments required by the contract and to demand a deed from the seller. In other words, the assignee steps into the shoes of the buyer and may compel the seller to perform his part of the contract.

However, the assignee does not become personally liable to the seller for payment of the purchase price, unless the assignment provides that the assignee *assumes and agrees to pay* the purchase price. *Lisenby* v. *Newton,* 120 Cal. 571, 52 Pac. 813 (1898).

Of course, the buyer cannot escape personal liability for payment of the purchase price by assigning the contract. He remains liable to the seller notwithstanding the assignment. If the rule were otherwise, a buyer could always rid himself of a burdensome contract by assigning it to a pauper.

Installment contracts quite commonly provide that there can be no assignment without the written consent of the seller.

9.29 Deed by seller to stranger

When the seller, after entering into the contract, sells and conveys the land to some third party, the question arises as to whether the buyer under the contract can compel such third party to give him a deed to the land on payment of the contract price. The buyer can compel such third party to give him a deed on payment of the contract price in the following cases:

1. When the contract was recorded prior to the making of the deed to the third party.
2. When, though the contract was not recorded, the buyer took possession of the land prior to the making of the deed to the third party.
3. When, even though the contract was recorded and the buyer did not take possession of the land, the third party actually knew of the earlier contract at the time he received his deed.

If the case does not fall within these three rules, the buyer cannot compel the third party to give him a deed. In other words, he has lost all his rights in the land. However, the buyer may then sue his seller and recover from him any amounts paid on the purchase price.

If the contract requires the seller to give a warranty deed, the buyer need not accept a warranty deed signed only by the seller's grantee. The seller must also join in the deed. *Crabtree* v. *Levings*, 53 Ill. 526 (1870).

9.30 Time for performance

The contract should specify the date on which the deal is to be closed. If the contract does not specifically fix the time when it is to be performed, it will be implied that it is to be performed within a reasonable time, and the purchase price must be paid at that time. Most contracts fix a specific time for the performance of all acts thereunder. If the contract provides that *time is of the essence* each act required by the contract must be done promptly at the time specified. In a cash sale, where time is of the essence, if either party fails to perform promptly he will be unable to obtain specific performance.

EXAMPLE: Contract called for earnest money down payment, balance to be paid within five days after seller's title was shown to be good, and time to be of the essence. Seller delivered evidence of good title on August 5. Buyer did nothing. On August 19, seller served notice on buyer to close deal within five days. Buyer again did nothing. On September 10, buyer tendered balance of purchase price. Seller refused to accept. Buyer now filed suit for specific performance and the court refused to grant it. Buyer was in default and time was of the essence. *Johnson* v. *Riedler,* 395 Ill. 412, 70 NE2d 570 (1946).

9.31 Remedies of the seller—remedies other than forfeiture or foreclosure

If the buyer fails or refuses to perform, the seller, in lieu of declaring a forfeiture, may pursue one of the following courses:

1. The seller may *rescind* the contract. *Rescission* is not the same as *forfeiture. Coe* v. *Bennett,* 46 Idaho 62, 266 Pac. 413 (1928). By rescinding, the seller declares the contract at an end and surrenders all rights thereunder. Both seller and buyer must be restored, as far as possible, to the situation existing before the contract was made. The seller, on rescinding, must give back to the buyer the payments he has made, less a fair rent for the time the buyer has been in possession. *Hillman* v. *Busselle,* 66 Ariz. 139, 185 P2d 311 (1947). The right to rescind does not depend upon any provision in the contract. However, most contracts give the seller the right to declare the contract forfeited if the buyer defaults. Forfeiture is a right expressly reserved in the contract itself. *Realty Securities Corp.* v. *Johnson,* 93 Fla. 46, 111 So 532 (1927). By declaring a forfeiture, the seller terminates the contract but retains all payments previously made by the buyer, since this right is expressly conferred by the contract. The seller may thereupon file a suit to clear his title of the cloud created by the forfeited contract. *Ibid.*

Some states allow the seller to rescind, apply the earnest money in reduction of his damages, and sue the buyer for any other damages he has sustained. Dobbs, *Remedies* 855 (1974). This is a sensible rule. *Anderson* v. *Long Grove Country Club Estates,* 111 Ill. App.2d 127, 249 NE2d 343 (1969).

2. In some states, the seller may tender a deed to the buyer and then sue the buyer for the purchase price.

3. The seller may sue the buyer for damages.

4. The seller may sue the buyer for specific performance of the contract.

5. The seller may simply retain the earnest money.

As to forfeiture, see Ch. 22.

9.31(a) Remedies of the buyer

In case of the seller's refusal or failure to perform, the buyer may pursue one of the following courses:

1. He may *rescind,* that is, declare the contract terminated, and recover his deposit. To rescind is the buyer's normal remedy when the land has decreased in value. One difficulty here is that the seller usually is reluctant to give back the buyer's deposit. The buyer, of course, has the right to file a suit against the seller and obtain a judgment, which can be enforced in the usual ways, by levy on property, by garnishment, and so forth. However, while the suit is pending, the seller may very well decide to sell the particular land to someone else and then spend or secrete the money.

2. The buyer has a lien on the land as security for repayment of purchase money paid in and may enforce such lien if the seller is unable or unwilling to convey good title. 33 ALR2d 1384. A buyer who wishes to obtain return of his down payment from a defaulting seller would be well advised to file a suit to enforce his purchaser's lien, for this ties

up the seller's property and prevents him from selling the land to others. This is not true if the buyer merely sues the seller for a money judgment.

3. The buyer may sue the seller to compel *specific performance* of the contract, that is, to compel the seller to give him a deed on receiving payment of the purchase price. The buyer will resort to this remedy when he wants the land for some particular purpose, for example, to keep out a competitor, or when he anticipates that the land will appreciate in value. In general, specific performance is a more effective remedy than a suit for money damages, since damages are always hard to prove and judgments for money are hard to collect.

4. The seller, of course, cannot compel the buyer to accept a bad title. But sometimes the buyer wants to go through with the contract and the seller refuses. The seller's title may be clouded with some unpaid tax, unpaid mortgage, or easement. To make things more difficult for the buyer, the seller refuses to make any effort to eliminate these defects. Here the buyer may wish to file a suit for specific performance and ask the court to make deduction from the purchase price because of the defects in title.

EXAMPLE: The contract price is $10,000. An examination of title reveals the existence of $1,000 in unpaid taxes. The court will order specific performance on the buyer's depositing $9,000 in court for the seller if the seller refuses to pay the taxes. This remedy of the buyer is called *specific performance with an abatement from the purchase price.*

5. Where the seller will not or cannot go through with the deal, the buyer may sue the seller for *damages.* In such an action, the buyer ultimately will receive a judgment for money damages. In the meantime, however, while the suit is pending, the seller is at liberty to sell the land to others, and any buyer who gets a deed before the buyer obtains his judgment takes the land free of the buyer's claims.

9.31(b) Remedies— restitutionary damages— promissory estoppel

On occasion, *even where a contract has not been signed,* there will be a liability for damages.

EXAMPLE: Hoffman and his wife owned a small store. Red Owl, a national franchiser, advised Hoffman to sell his store, promising to find a party to buy some land, build a bigger building and lease it to the Hoffmans with an option to purchase. The Hoffmans would receive a Red Owl franchise. All this was arranged orally. The Hoffmans sold their store in reliance on Red Owl's promises. Red Owl refused to go through with the deal. Red Owl was held liable for all the damages the Hoffmans suffered. Red Owl made a promise knowing the Hoffmans would rely on it. Under modern ethical concepts of the law (promissory estoppel) the promisor is liable for the damages his promisee incurs. Although the promises were made to Hoffman only, Red Owl could foresee that his wife would also rely on Red Owl's promise. Hence they are liable to her as well. *Hoffman* v. *Red Owl Stores Inc.,* 26 Wis.2d 683, 133 NW 267 (1965). Lawyers often speak of this as *detrimental reliance.*

REFERENCES: 77 Harv. L. Rev. 401; 51 Cornell L. Q. 351.

9.31(c) Remedies— election of remedies

Some remedies are so inherently inconsistent that if a party chooses one he cannot resort to remedies he would otherwise have.

EXAMPLE: A seller in an installment contract elects to exercise his forfeiture clause. He cannot thereafter sue the buyer for payment of the purchase price. 91 C.J.S. § 376.

EXAMPLE: In some states an installment seller has a *statutory right* to cancel the contract by giving the buyer notice of his default and forfeiture. Thereafter he cannot sue the buyer for damages. *Zirinsky* v. *Sheehan,* 413 F2d 481 (1969).

9.31(d) Remedies of the seller and buyer— exclusiveness of the remedies spelled out in contract—choice of inconsistent remedies

In the case of a cash sale, even though the contract is silent on the point, the seller may, in the event of default by the buyer, retain the buyer's earnest money deposit. This is a form of forfeiture that is universally permitted. Often the contract specifically provides that in the case of the buyer's default the seller may declare the contract ended and keep the earnest money. This is not an *exclusive remedy*. 81 CJS 531; 32 ALR 584, 98 ALR 887. In other words, the seller, *in lieu of retaining the earnest money, has the right to sue the buyer for specific performance or for damages.*

But, the contract often provides that, in the event the seller's title proves defective, the buyer must either take the title *as is* or be content with a return of his earnest money deposit. This is then the buyer's exclusive remedy if the seller is *in good faith unable* to clear his title. *Old Colony Trust Co.* v. *Chauncey,* 214 Mass. 271, 101 NE 423 (1913); *Nostdal* v. *Morehart,* 132 Minn. 351, 157 NW 584 (1916). If the buyer wishes to accept title *as is,* he must notify the seller of his decision within the time allowed by the contract. *Miller* v. *Shea,* 300 Ill. 180, 133 NE 183 (1921). However, if the seller's title examination reveals defects that the seller could easily clear, but he refuses to do so because of his reluctance to go through with the transaction or if the seller knew his title was defective when he signed the contract of sale, then the clause is not deemed to provide an exclusive remedy, and the buyer may file for specific performance with an abatement from the purchase price or for damages. *Mokar Properties Corp.* v. *Hall,* 179 N.Y.S.2d 814 (1958). This clause protects the seller only where he is truly unable to deliver a clear title and was unaware of the defects in his title. *Blau* v. *Friedman,* 140 A2d 193 (N.J. 1958).

If a seller has a right to declare a *forfeiture* of the contract because of the buyer's default, and he does so, he cannot thereafter sue the buyer for damages or for the balance due on the purchase price. *Morey* v. *Huston,* 85 Ill. App.2d 195, 28 NE2d 44 (1967). 92 CJS 311. He must choose to forfeit *or* sue for damages or recovery of the purchase price. And if the seller files a suit to foreclose the contract, this automatically sets aside any forfeiture that the seller has previously declared because of the buyer's defaults. *Zumstein* v. *Stockton,* 199 Ore. 633, 264 P2d 455 (1953).

9.32   Abandonment

Through abandonment, either buyer or seller may lose his rights under the contract. If either party clearly shows by his acts that he does not intend to go through with the contract, the other party may assume that he has abandoned the contract. 68 ALR2d 581.

> **EXAMPLE:**   The buyer, under an installment contract, took possession of the premises. Later he fell far behind in his payments and eventually accepted a lease from the seller. When oil was discovered, he attempted to enforce the contract. The court held that his rights had been lost by abandonment. *Dundas* v. *Foster,* 281 Mich. 117, 274 NW 731.

9.33   Hardship

On occasion a court will refuse to enforce a contract where enforcement would cause undue hardship. See § 9.39.

9.34   Fairness and inadequacy of consideration

A contract for the sale of land will be enforced, regardless of whether the price is too high or too low. Although a person has made a very bad bargain, the courts will force him to carry out his contract.

> **EXAMPLE:**   The holder of a tax title to a tract of land went to the owner of the land and told him that his, the owner's, title was worthless, since the land had been sold for taxes. However, the tax title holder said he was willing to give the owner $125 for a deed to the land. The owner accepted the $125 and gave the tax title holder a deed. The land was worth about $3,200, and the tax title was really worthless. It was held that the deed would not be set aside. *Grant* v. *Fellows,* 58 Ill. 242 (1871).

However, if the price is far below the real value of the land, and the parties are not on equal terms, as when the buyer is an experienced businessman and the seller is ignorant, mentally feeble, or inexperienced, the court will refuse to compel the seller to give a deed.

> **EXAMPLE:**   Shortly after the Chicago fire, the owner of certain lots in Chicago, a weak-minded man who was ignorant of the value of the land and of business generally and who was unable to understand English well, was persuaded by a shrewd man to sell the lots for $21,000. The lots were worth much more, and their value was rapidly rising. Owners of adjoining lots had just made arrangements to build on these adjoining lots. These facts were known to the buyer but not to the seller. The court refused to compel the seller to give a deed. *Fish* v. *Leser,* 69 Ill. 394 (1873).

9.35 Mistake

The very word *contract* implies that there must be a meeting of the minds. Occasionally both parties to the contract are mistaken as to some matter. This is called a *mutual mistake*. When there is a mutual mistake, either party may cancel or rescind the contract.

> **EXAMPLE:** The owner of certain land verbally offered to sell the land for $6,000. The buyer misunderstood the price to be $3,000 and agreed. Under such misunderstanding the deed was executed and delivered. There was no meeting of the minds here, and the owner was entitled to a reconveyance. *Neel* v. *Lang,* 236 Mass. 61, 127 NE 512 (1920).

9.36 Misrepresentation and fraud

So many statements are made by each party in the course of a sale of land that almost always some untrue statement, called a *misrepresentation,* is made. If the misrepresentation is of some unimportant or trivial matter, generally speaking, it will not affect the contract. Such a misrepresentation is said to be immaterial. Suppose, however, that a misrepresentation is made as to some important matter. It is clear, first of all, that such a misrepresentation does not make the contract null and void. After the misrepresentation has been discovered, the party who was deceived may nevertheless wish to enforce the contract. He may do so. If the contract has not yet been performed—that is, the seller has not yet given a deed, and the buyer who was guilty of the fraud files a suit to enforce the contract, the other party may use the fraud as a defense to such a suit. He will bring to the court's attention the fact that the party who is bringing the suit made a misrepresentation as to an important matter, and the court will refuse to enforce the contract.

If the contract *has* been performed—that is, the seller has given the deed and the buyer paid the purchase price—and one party then discovers that an important misrepresentation has been made, he may file a suit to get his land back (rescission), if he was the seller, or get his money, if he was the buyer.

Remember that the buyer is seldom in a position to discover the seller's misrepresentation until he has taken possession of the property. And the buyer may rescind (get his money back) even if the misrepresentation was not intentional, which is rare.

Some matters with respect to which misrepresentation are common follow:

1. rents, profits, volume of business, or income of the property
2. location of boundaries of the property
3. area or frontage of the property
4. age of buildings on the property
5. drainage conditions
6. buildings erected on filled ground
7. true identity of purchaser
8. existence or nonexistence of encumbrances, such as tax liens, mortgages

A misrepresentation by the seller's broker is tantamount to a misrepresentation by the seller if the seller insists on trying to hold the buyer to the deal. 58 ALR2d 10; 61 ALR2d 1237. Likewise, the broker who makes a misrepresentation becomes liable to the purchaser for damages. *Sawyer* v. *Tildahl,* 148 NW2d 131 (1967). Each is liable for damages.

Where the seller is guilty of making a misrepresentation, the buyer has a choice of remedies. He may sue the seller for damages in an action called "deceit." Prosser, *Torts* 687. However, the problem here is that courts tend to require the buyer to show that the misrepresentation was *knowingly* made. The commonest misrepresentation is as to rents or income of the property. Obviously, such a misrepresentation is knowingly made. Alternatively, the buyer may sue to set the transaction aside and get his money back. This is a suit in equity. Equity does not require proof that the seller knew the representation was false.

However, modern decisions tend to abolish this distinction. If a material misrepresentation is made, the buyer is hurt to the same degree whether the misrepresentation is knowingly or innocently made. He ought to be allowed to select whatever remedy he chooses, including a suit for damages. *Miller* v. *Bare,* 457 F.Supp. 1359 (1978).

Today's courts are less concerned with sin (*intentional* misrepresentation) than economic harm.

9.36(a) Misrepresentation —opinion, value, and puffing

Misrepresentations of matters of opinion will not justify cancellation of the contract.

It is often difficult to distinguish an expression of opinion from a representation of a fact. For example, a misrepresentation by the seller's broker that *he now has a commitment from a mortgage house to make a loan of a certain sum on the property* allows the buyer to cancel the deal, but a statement by the broker that a loan of a certain amount *can be obtained* is simply his opinion and does not allow the buyer to back out if such a loan cannot be obtained. *Owen* v. *Schwartz,* 177 F2d 641 (1949). 14 ALR2d 1337.

A representation made by a *builder* will sometimes be held to be a representation of fact even though such a representation made by someone else would be a matter of opinion. *Pacesetter Homes Inc.* v. *Brodkin,* 85 Cal. Reptr. 39.

> **EXAMPLE:** A builder who owned the house he had constructed stated to a buyer that it was "well constructed in a good and substantial manner." This was untrue. The builder was liable for fraud. *Tate* v. *Jackson,* 22 Ill. App.2d 471, 161 NE2d 156 (1959). Likewise where the builder said "there will be no water in the cellar," he was liable for fraud. *Pietrazak* v. *McDermott,* 341 Mass. 107, 167 NE2d 166 (1960).

Value is usually a matter of opinion. Representations as to the value of the property, though greatly exaggerated, do not ordinarily justify a cancellation of the contract when the other party had an opportunity to learn the truth or falsity of the representations. If the buyer has an opportunity to examine the land, it is his duty to make use of this opportunity. He can then form an opinion as correct as the seller's as to the worth of the land.

Puffing is praise of the property by the seller couched in more or less general terms. Generally, the law requires the buyer to be wary of such puffing talk. Unwarranted praise that does not include concrete misrepresentations of specific facts does not entitle the buyer to back out of the deal.

EXAMPLE: The seller told the buyer that he "could not go wrong" in buying the house and that he "would never regret" the purchase. This is mere puffing. *Fegeas* v. *Sherrill,* 218 Md. 472, 147 A2d 223 (1958).

9.36(b) Misrepresentation as to zoning or building ordinances

When a seller makes a misrepresentation as to zoning or building ordinances affecting the property—for example, when the seller states that the land is in a district zoned for manufacturing, whereas it is in fact in a district zoned for stores—the buyer, upon discovering the facts, may sue the seller for damages. *Bobak* v. *Mackey,* 107 Cal. App.2d 55, 236 P2d 626 (1951); 175 ALR 1055.

In an effort to give greater protection to buyers against imposition, courts have evolved the idea of *tacit misrepresentation.* Under this doctrine, it is not necessary that the seller be guilty of a direct falsehood for a misrepresentation to exist. What he says and does may amount to a misrepresentation.

EXAMPLE: The seller showed the property to the buyer as a multiple-family dwelling and commented on the rents he collected. This was a *tacit representation* that the premises were legally usable as an apartment building, which was false, for such use violated the city ordinances. It was held that the buyer could rescind (declare contract void) on discovering the imposition. *Gamble* v. *Beahm,* 198 Oreg. 537, 257 P2d 882 (1953).

This would be true also if there is any statement in the contract or advertisement for sale that can be construed as representing that the existing use of the building is a *legal one,* as when the contract describes the building as a "store and dwelling" but such use is actually illegal. 27 Rocky Mt. L. Rev. 258; 1958 Wis. L. Rev. 641.

The fact that the zoning ordinance is a public document, available to all the public, is immaterial. The building may have been constructed before the ordinance was passed, for example. It would then be a legal nonconforming use. The buyer has a right to rely on the seller's representations as to zoning. Also, having told part of the story, for example, that there is a basement apartment, the seller must tell the rest, namely, that the apartment is illegal. The presence of zoning or building ordinance violations may render title unmarketable. Or it may give the buyer a right to sue the seller for damages.

9.36(c)   Right to rely upon a representation

Even a misrepresentation of a material fact will not always entitle the other party to cancel the contract. For example, some courts say that a buyer has no right to rely on a representation when the sources of information are equally available to both parties.

> **EXAMPLE:** Seller represented to buyer that the tax assessor had valued the property at a certain figure. Actually, the assessor's figure was a good deal lower. The court held that the buyer was not entitled to rely on this information since the tax assessor's valuation was a public record equally available to both parties. *Morel* v. *Masalski,* 333 Ill. 41, 164 NE 205 (1928).

Again, some courts say that the buyer is not entitled to rely on the seller's representation as to matters that would be disclosed by the buyer's inspection of the property.

> **EXAMPLE:** The seller made a false representation as to the volume of water and the daily flow in the well on the property. It was held that the buyer had no right to rely on this representation, for it was a matter than an inspection would reveal. *Hays* v. *McGinness,* 208 Ga. 547, 67 SE2d 720 (1951).

Along the same lines is the rule that the buyer cannot rely on the seller's representations as to the condition of the building when the buyer has actually made a careful inspection of the building, for in such case he is relying on his own observation, not on the seller's representation. 70 ALR 942. But if the buyer makes only a cursory or casual inspection, the rule does not apply, for in such case he is really relying on the seller's representations. 70 ALR 924. For example, where a buyer inspects the land but makes no attempt to check the seller's representations as to area, the buyer may rescind the contract if there is a misrepresentation in this respect. 54 ALR2d 690. But a buyer who learns of a defect, such as decay or crumbling of the foundation, has no right to make a merely casual inspection. He must make a careful inspection. *Carpenter* v. *Hamilton,* 18 Cal. App.2d 69, 62 P2d 1397 (1937).

> **NEW DIRECTIONS:** The rule forbidding a buyer to rely on certain representations made by the seller is a bad one. In effect, it legalizes fraud in many situations. Many courts have discarded this barbarous rule, and no doubt it will disappear in time. *Yorke* v. *Taylor,* 332 Mass. 368, 124 NE2d 912 (1955). No rogue should enjoy his ill-gotten plunder for the simple reason that his victim is by chance a fool.

When the parties are not dealing on equal terms, the party to whom a representation is made is usually justified in relying thereon.

> **EXAMPLE:** The seller was a real estate dealer, familiar with the locality, and the buyer was a laborer from the city, unacquainted with farming. The seller misrepresented the number and condition of fruit trees on the land. The buyer was entitled to rescind (cancel the contract), even though he had inspected the land. The seller had superior means of knowledge. *Mitchell* v. *Coleman,* 127 Ark. 373, 192 SW 231 (1917).

> **EXAMPLE:** A farm broker misrepresented to the buyer, who was a city rooming house operator, the amount of acreage in the farm. It was held that the buyer could rescind. *Owen* v. *Schwartz,* 177 F2d 641 (1949).

9.36(d) Misrepresentation —buyer's fraud

Fraud and misrepresentation on the buyer's part are uncommon. When they occur, the result is the same as where the seller is the guilty party. When the buyer has been guilty of fraud, the seller may either rescind the contract or sue the buyer for damages. 52 ALR 1153.

> **EXAMPLE:** Where the parties were negotiating for the sale of timber land, the buyer sent in a timber cruiser, who determined that there were in excess of 2,300,000 feet of timber in the tract. The buyer represented to the seller that the cruise disclosed the presence of 1,537,500 feet of timber. Later the seller discovered the misrepresentation. He may sue the buyer for fraud. *Heise* v. *Pilot Rock Lumber Co.,* 222 Oreg. 78, 352 P2d 1072.

> **EXAMPLE:** A buyer's misrepresentation of his intended use of the land gives the seller a right to rescind. 35 ALR3d 369.

9.36(e) Nondisclosure— *caveat emptor* or *caveat vendor*

The old law was *caveat emptor,* "let the buyer beware." The buyer had to investigate before buying. If he failed to discover defects in the building, that was his bad luck. Nowadays, the courts are getting away from this primitive rule.

> **NEW DIRECTIONS:** Many modern courts say that when the seller knows certain material facts relating to defects in the property being sold, and knows them not to be within the reach of reasonable inspection by the buyer, the seller is bound to disclose such facts to the buyer, and failure to do so renders the seller liable to damages. *Theis* v. *Heuer,* 280 NE2d 300 (Ind. 1972); *Sorrel* v. *Young,* 491 P2d 1312 (Wash.); *Jenkins* v. *McCormick,* 184 Kans. 842, 339 P2d 8; Prosser, *Torts* 697 (4th ed. 1971). Under the modern view, nondisclosure is often regarded as *misrepresentation by silence. Cooper* v. *Cordova Sand & Gravel Co.,* 485 SW2d 261 (Tenn. 1972); 80 ALR2d 1453.

EXAMPLES: The seller knew that the house being sold was inadequately based on filled earth. When the buyer discovered this, he was entitled to a return of his money on deeding the property back to the seller. *Rothstein* v. *Janss Inv. Corp.,* 45 Cal. App.2d 64, 113 P2d 465 (1941); *Wolford* v. *Freeman,* 150 Neb. 537, 35 NW2d 98 (1948); 80 ALR2d 1453; Prosser, *Torts* 698 (4th ed. 1971). The seller knew that the driveway of the premises was partly on adjoining property and failed to disclose this fact. Again, on discovering this, the buyer was entitled to a return of his money. *Dugan* v. *Bosco* (Del.), 108 A2d 586 (1954). Seller failed to disclose that the adjoining owner claimed two feet of the sixty-foot lot being sold. Buyer could rescind. *Hall* v. *Carter* (Ky.), 324 SW2d 410 (1959).

OTHER EXAMPLES: Seller failed to disclose the following defects and the court held it was fraud: (1) the house was built over a ditch covered with decayed timber; (2) a drain-tile ran beneath the house and caused water to accumulate; (3) the basement was subject to flooding; (4) rents charged were in excess of those allowed by law; (5) the house was in a slide area, dangerous to life; (6) there was a defective sewer installation potentially dangerous to health; 8 West. Res. L. Rev. 5; *Kaze* v. *Compton,* 283 SW2d 204 (Ky. 1954); *Lawson* v. *Citizens Bank,* 180 SE2d 206 (S.C. 1971). (Seller held liable for damages).

EXAMPLES: A developer–builder failed to disclose installation of an underground water conduit or irrigation ditch beneath the house. *Bethlahmy* v. *Bechtel,* 91 Idaho 55, 415 P2d 698 (1966), approved in *Tobin* v. *Paparone Constr. Co.,* 349 A2d 574 (N.J. 1975). A developer–builder failed to disclose to buyer that massive cracks in the foundation were concealed by plasterboard. *Haberman* v. *Greenaman,* 82 Misc.2d 263 (N.Y.). A broker and his seller knew that sewer backed up, inundating basement. They were under a duty to disclose this fact to buyer. *Shane* v. *Hoffman,* 324 A2d 532 (Pa.). A drain tile beneath the house caused water to accumulate. The seller was under duty to disclose. *Kaze* v. *Compton,* 283 SW2d 204 (Ky.). A seller failed to disclose termite infestation and was held liable. *Lorio* v. *Kaiser,* 277 So2d 633 (La. 1973). Foundation constructed with untreated concrete blocks below soil level and subsidence occurred. The seller held liable. *Jackson* v. *Goad,* 385 P2d 279 (N.M. 1963). A building was constructed by developer on filled land and there was no disclosure to the purchaser. The buyer could *rescind,* that is, terminate the deal and obtain the return of his money. *Sorrell* v. *Young,* 491 P2d 1312 (Wash. 1971). A house was in a slide area dangerous to life. No disclosure. The buyer could rescind and obtain the return of his money. *Henderson* v. *Johnson,* 403 P2d 669 (Wash. 1965). A developer filled in a gully with stumps and other rubble to a depth of twenty-five feet and concealed the fill. The house began to sink. Buyer could recover damages. *Lawson* v. *Citizens & Southern Nat'l. Bank,* 180 SE2d 206 (S.C. 1971). Lot on fill, soil saturated with oil, which precluded building of footings except at unreasonable cost. Seller liable. *Nolt* v. *Palumbo,* 383 P2d 1015 (Ore. 1963). A house was built over a dangerous and defective sewer. No disclosure. The buyer could rescind for fraud. *Lilley* v. *Copeland,* 399 SW2d 496 (Ark. 1966). Percolation tests revealed cellar could not be built. No disclosure. The seller was held liable. *Lodigiani* v. *Potter,* 170 NE2d 359 (1960). The seller encouraged a buyer in the belief that a fence marked the boundary of land although the boundary was 4 feet 3 inches short of fence. The court held that the buyer was entitled to claim up to fence, since seller owned that land. *Webb* v. *Culver,* 509 P2d 1173 (Ore. 1973). Seller and broker held liable for failure to disclose that easement existed over property. *Gilbey* v. *Cooper,* 310 NE2d 268 (Ohio). The buyer of a homesite discovered that the presence of salt water made growing of lawn impossible. Seller liable for damages. *Griffith* v. *Byers Const. Co.,* 510 P2d 198 (Kans. 1973). Seller failed to disclose that his garage was located partly on adjoining premises. Buyer could rescind. *Webb* v. *Culver,* 509 P2d 1173 (Ore. 1973). Seller failed to disclose that neighbor was planning to build tennis court. Held, fraud. *Tobin* v. *Paparone Const. Co.,* 349 A2d 574 (1975).

Some courts still cling to the old, primitive notions.

EXAMPLE: The buyer, after purchasing the house found it was infested with termites, a matter not readily disclosed by inspection. The court held that the seller had no duty to disclose this fact to the buyer. *Swinton* v. *Whittinsville Savings Bank,* 311 Mass. 677, 42 NE2d 808 (1942). Most courts today would allow the buyer to get his money back in these circumstances. *Fraser* v. *Amling,* 277 So2d 633 (La. 1973); *Phoenix* v. *Stevens,* 127 NW2d 640 (Iowa 1964); *Obde* v. *Schlemeyer,* 56 Wash.2d 449, 353 P2d 672 (1960); 22 ALR3d 972. Alternatively, he can sue the seller for damages.

Consider the case of a house infested with termites. Either the seller or the buyer must take the loss. The law cannot protect both. The seller knows what he is doing. He is unloading a defective product on an unsuspecting buyer. Most buyers lack the sophistication to get a termite inspection. The law is beginning to force the seller to disclose. If he does not, he can be sued for damages. *Hughes* v. *Stusser,* 415 P2d 89 (Wash. 1956); *Obde* v. *Schlemeyer,* 56 Wash. 2d 449, 353 P2d 672 (1960); *Fraser* v. *Amling,* 277 So2d. 633 (La. 1973); 22 ALR3d 972; Prosser, *Torts* 696 (4th ed. 1974). The decisions that protect the seller are surely singularly unappetizing cases.

Naturally, the seller is guilty of fraud if he deliberately hides a defect.

EXAMPLE: The basement of a house flooded from time to time. Before showing the house to the buyer, the seller washed and painted away the water marks. This is fraud. *Russow* v. *Bobola,* 2 Ill. App.3d 837. This is an example of the rule that fraud or misrepresentation can take place by acts as well as by words. *Batey* v. *Stone,* 192 SE2d 528 (Ga. 1972).

The buyer is ordinarily under no duty to disclose to the seller facts in his possession that increase the value of the property, such as the fact that oil has been discovered in the vicinity. 56 ALR 429. But the result is different where the seller is related to the buyer or is in a position of trust and confidence, as where the buyer is the seller's attorney, partner, and so forth. *Ibid.*

Of course, the seller must disclose to the buyer all matters covered by the Interstate Land Sales Act. 15 USCA § 1701.

NEW DIRECTIONS: The rule of seller liability for nondisclosure is applicable to sales of both new and used houses. The termite cases all involve *used homes*. A totally different situation is presented where a *developer–builder* is saddled with the *implied warranty* that began its existence when the courts began to hold that in every sale of a newly built residence by a builder–seller there is an *implied warranty* that the home was built in a workmanlike manner and is fit for habitation. Here the seller is held liable to the first purchaser without any requirement of proof *that he knew of the defect*. Obviously, since he built the house *it is almost certain that he knew of the defect. But that is not an element the buyer is required to prove and indeed it can be difficult to prove.*

9.36(e)(1)   Nondisclosure— violations of zoning and building ordinances

When a seller knows that the building sold violates a zoning or building ordinance, it is his duty, according to recent court decisions, to disclose that fact to the buyer, and if he fails to do so, he is liable for damages. *Barder* v. *McClurg,* 93 Cal. App.2d 476, 252 P2d 378 (1953); *Heckrotte* v. *Riddle,* 224 Md. 491, 168 A2d 879 (1961); 3 Okla. L. Rev. 435.

EXAMPLE: A builder violated the building code in that the wall studs of the building were spaced too far apart and plaster had been applied on an unauthorized base. The builder was under a duty to disclose these ordinance violations to the buyer, and, where he failed to do so, the buyer had the right to revoke the deal and obtain a return of his down payment. The fact that the buyer inspected the property was immaterial, for these are matters that no ordinary inspection is likely to reveal. Moreover, the seller has superior means of knowledge. *Milmoe* v. *Dixon,* 101 Cal. App.2d 257, 225 P2d 273 (1951). (Seller liable for damages.)

NEW DIRECTIONS: The modern view is that concealment is tantamount to actual fraud when the seller knows of facts that materially affect the desirability of the property and that he knows are unknown to the buyer.

Again, you will find more conservative courts following the old "let the buyer beware" line.

EXAMPLE: Seller failed to disclose that a septic tank did not comply with the building code. He was held not liable. *Egan* v. *Hudson Nut Products, Inc.,* 142 Conn. 344, 114 A2d 213 (1955).

9.36(e)(2)   Nondisclosure— half-truths

To tell part of the truth is often the same as telling a lie. If a man states a fact that by itself is true, he must tell all the other facts that qualify or modify the fact stated. Otherwise he will be liable for damages. *Franchey* v. *Hannes,* 207 A2d 268 (Conn. 1965). Prosser, *Torts* 696, (4th ed. 1974).

> **EXAMPLE:** The seller told the buyer that he personally constructed the building and that it was well built. He now has a duty to go on and state, if that is the case, that he built it without a building permit, for even a well-built structure may violate an ordinance, and costly alterations may be needed to bring the building into compliance with the law. *Milmoe* v. *Dixon,* 101 Cal. App.2d 257, 225 P2d 273 (1951). (Seller liable for damages.)

> **EXAMPLE:** The seller stated that the buyer could use all the water he wanted at a flat rate of $2.00 per month. It was held that the buyer could set the deal aside when he discovered that the water was never supplied by the water company between 7:00 P.M. and 7:00 A.M. *Simmons* v. *Evans,* 185 Tenn. 282, 206 SW2d 295 (1947).

> **EXAMPLE:** The seller of a hotel disclosed the amount of its income accurately, but failed to reveal that the source of the income was largely through the operation of a brothel. The seller is liable for fraud. *Ikeda* v. *Curtia,* 43 Wash. 449, 261 P2d 684 (1953).

> **EXAMPLE:** The seller had two engineers make a report on the property but disclosed only the favorable report to the buyer. Seller is guilty of fraud. *Gilbert* v. *Corlett,* 171 Cal. App.2d 116, 339 P2d 960 (1959).

9.37 Returning benefits received under the contract

If a party wishes to cancel a contract for fraud, he must offer to return whatever he has received under the contract.

> **EXAMPLE:** The buyer went into possession of the farm he had purchased and, after discovering a fraud, sold all the livestock on the farm. He could not rescind, since he could not return what he had received under the contract.

9.38 Ratification

If a misrepresentation is made, and the other party, after discovering the fraud, fails to take prompt action to call the deal off, he is said to ratify or approve the contract and thereafter cannot have it set aside.

> **EXAMPLE:** The seller of a saloon property told the buyer that the tenant in possession of the property was making money, when in fact the tenant was losing money and had lost over $4,000 in the business in the last four years. The seller also said that there was sufficient stock on hand in the saloon to run for thirty to sixty days, when the supply was in fact good for only three or four days. The buyer paid the purchase price and went into possession. He discovered the misrepresentation almost immediately, but remained in possession over seven months, try-

ing to make the business pay. It was held that this constituted a ratification of the contract, and the buyer was not entitled to get his money back.

9.39 Hardship

At times, if circumstances change after the contract is signed, and as a result it would be a substantial hardship to compel performance of the contract, the courts have refused to enforce it. 11 ALR2d 390.

> **EXAMPLE:** After the contract was signed the city rezoned the land for residence purposes. The buyer, as was known to seller, planned to erect a factory. The court refused to enforce the contract. *Clay* v. *Landreth,* 187 Va. 169, 45 SE2d 875 (1948). To some considerable extent, the concept of hardship is being replaced by the concept of unconscionability. See § 9.04 (a).

9.40 Liability for injuries

The matter of implied warranties of the building is one that deals with (1) new buildings erected by a merchant–builder and (2) damages suffered by the buyer because of defects in the building which the buyer must expend funds to repair. A different question is presented when the buyer (or a member of his family) or a member of the public suffers injuries because of a defect in the building or land sold.

The seller may be liable because he knew of a hidden defect that created a danger to occupants.

> **EXAMPLE:** Seller knows that there is a dangerous break in the flooring of a dark closet. Seller also knows that it is unlikely that Buyer will discover the danger. Seller fails to warn Buyer. Buyer's wife is injured while hanging clothes in the closet. Seller is liable. *O'Connor* v. *Altus,* 123 N.J. Super. 379, 303 A2d 329 (1973), citing Restatement *Torts* 2d § 353.

> **EXAMPLE:** There is an unused well on the property which Seller has covered with sod. Wife of Buyer steps on the sod and the rotten boards break, plunging her into the well. Seller is liable for failure to warn Buyer. *Cooper* v. *Cordova Sand Co., Inc.,* 485 SW2d 261 (Tenn. 1972).

> **EXAMPLE:** The building in question has a cornice that has been weakened by water freezing in the spaces between lengths of the cornice. There is an obvious danger to members of the public on adjoining sidewalks. Seller sells the property to Buyer. The cornice falls, injuring a pedestrian. Seller is liable because he sold a nuisance. Buyer is liable because he knowingly maintained a nuisance. *O'Connor* v. *Altus,* 123 N.J. Super. 379, 303 A2d 329 (1973), citing Restatement *Torts* 2d § 373; 58 Am.Jur.2d *Nuisances* §§ 50, 51.

It is evident that these rules greatly resemble those involved in landlord and tenant situations.

Except as above, an ordinary seller is not liable for defects or injuries occurring after the sale. *Kimberlin* v. *Lear,* 500 P2d 1022 (Nev. 1972).

REFERENCE: 48 ALR3d 1027.

9.41 Liability of vendor— installment contracts

Because installment contracts figure prominently in today's creative financing, they deserve a special glance. There is a recent decision.

EXAMPLE: Seller entered into an installment contract to sell to Buyer on May 1, 1963. Buyer moved in. On May 7, 1963, Buyer's daughter fell through a stair rail from which several slats were missing. The court held that Seller was not liable. No nuisance was involved. The defect was not hidden. *Anderson* v. *Cosmopolitan State Bank,* 54 Ill. 2d 504, 301 NE2d 296 (1973), criticized in 5 Loyola U. L. J. (Chicago) 669. An unspoken consideration here is that normally the seller cancels out his liability insurance when the deal is closed.

9.42 Liability of vendor— builder liability

Builder liability is discussed elsewhere. See Chapter 34.

9.43 Suggestions on contract draftsmanship

Preliminary observations. The goal to be achieved in drafting a contract of sale is twofold: (1) to draft a contract that the courts will enforce, since many contracts are so poorly drafted that courts cannot and will not enforce them; (2) after the seller and buyer have explored all aspects of the deal and reached an agreement as to all their rights and duties, to specify all the terms that the parties have agreed on, and to state them so clearly that there can be no controversy as to their meaning.

Parties. In general, the suggestions made regarding parties to deeds are applicable to contracts to parties.

Purchase price. State the purchase price and terms of payment, including prepayment privilege, if any, and acceleration clause, in complete detail and with utmost clarity. If sellers are joint tenants, state that price is payable to them "as joint tenants with right of survivorship and not as tenants in common or by the entireties."

Earnest money. For the seller's protection, the deposit should be adequate. Insist on a certified or cashier's check. Buyer should insist that money be held in escrow by a bank or trust company.

Purpose for which buyer is purchasing the property. Careful thought must be given to the purpose for which the buyer is purchasing the property. For example, it may be that the buyer intends to use the property for a purpose forbidden by the zoning ordinance. If so, the contract must contain a clause for the buyer's protection requiring an amendment to the zoning ordinance to be procured within a limited time, and in default thereof, the buyer to be entitled to cancel the contract and obtain a return of his money. If the contract is prepared and signed at a time when information concerning the provisions of recorded building restrictions or applicable zoning and building ordinances is unavailable, but the seller feels that neither restrictions nor ordinances will prevent use for the buyer's intended purpose, a clause may be added giving the buyer the right to terminate the contract within a specified time if it shall appear from recorded covenants, conditions, or restrictions, or from zoning or building ordinances, official maps or plans, or applicable statutes that the premises cannot legally be used for the intended purposes.

Description of the land. In considering the adequacy of the land description of the contract, the parties should consult also the specific suggestions hereinafter set forth.

Streets and alleys. The seller will usually have some right, title, or interest in and to the streets or alleys adjoining the premises sold, including private streets and vacated streets, and it is desirable that the contract of sale call for the seller to convey, without warranty, all such right, title, and interest.

Items to be conveyed to buyer or retained by seller. A contract for the sale of land obligates the seller to deliver title to the land and all fixtures, including the building, for it, of course, is a fixture, and fixtures are part of the land. Chattels, however, such as furniture, are not included, unless the contract expressly so provides. Any items that are clearly personal property might give rise to controversy.

Chattel clause. Together with the following chattels for which a bill of sale will be given at closing:

Air conditioning equipment, awnings, bar and bar stools, bookcases, cabinets, carpets (particularly stair carpets), chandeliers and lighting fixtures, clothes washer and dryer, crops, curtains, curtain rods, draperies, and other interior decorations, dryers, electric fans, electrical equipment, fireplace grates and andirons, dishwasher, doorbells and chimes, fuel, furniture, garage door openers and car units, garbage cans, garbage disposal, garden statuary, gas logs, high fidelity or stereo equipment that has been built in, ironing boards, lamps, lawn mowers, and garden equipment, linoleum, mirrors, perennial plants, refrigerators, rugs, screen doors, security systems, shelves, space heaters, sprinkling equipment, stokers, storm doors and windows, shrubbery, stoves, supplies, TV antennas and masts, tools and equipment (particularly janitor's tools), water softener, trade fixtures, venetian blinds, ventilators, wash tubs, water heaters, towel racks and bars, water meter, window shades, and window screens.

Easements. Does the buyer need an easement over adjoining land to provide access to the land purchased? If he does, let the contract provide for execution of an easement grant, and since the buyer will want an abstract or title insurance policy to evidence the seller's good title to the land sold, consider whether a similar precaution is not advisable as to the land over which the easement passes. Only the man who really owns the land can grant an easement over it. As a minimum, the contract should require the seller to warrant his title to the easement premises. Are there leases to tenants or fire insurance policies? Let the contract call for the assignment and delivery thereof to the purchaser. The contract should also require seller to assign to buyer any other items that buyer wishes to receive, e.g., service contracts (contracts with exterminators, scavengers, and so on), roof guaranties, or tenant's deposits.

Fixtures. What does the seller expect to retain after the deal is closed? Once the contract is signed, the seller is obligated to deliver to the buyer all fixtures, for they are legally part of the land. If the seller expects to retain attached machinery or other items that might be considered fixtures, provision to this effect should be included in the contract. If the seller needs to reserve an easement over the land sold, a provision to that effect should be included in the contract.

Encumbrances to which the title is to be subject and to which the buyer agrees. The seller should see that he has listed in the contract all the encumbrances or other defects in title that he does not propose to clear before the deal is closed. Most contract forms contain a printed list of common encumbrances, such as leases or building restrictions, but it is intended that the seller will add to this list as necessary. Suppose, for example, that the seller's title is subject to an easement. Is it mentioned in the contract? If not, and the buyer changes his mind and decides to back out of the deal, he may be able to do so because the title, as finally examined before the deal is closed, must reveal no encumbrances other than those listed either in general or in specific language in the contract.

The buyer should carefully analyze every encumbrance listed by the seller. For example, if in the contract he agrees to take subject to "existing leases," he must accept the property subject to any lease, no matter how ridiculously low the rent may be. If the contract says that the buyer will accept title subject to "building and other restrictions of record," "easements of record," and "mineral rights," as many printed forms provide, will any of these restrictions, easements, or mineral rights interfere with his building program, assuming that he is buying land to build on? Moreover, will some easement documents to which the land is subject obligate the buyer in some way as owner of this land? For example, an easement for road purposes may obligate me to keep my neighbor's road in repair. Similar personal liability provisions may be contained in restriction documents.

Mortgage provisions. These should be detailed and complete. For example, if the contract calls for a purchase money mortgage, are the amount, interest rate, maturity date, and form of mortgage clearly set forth? Similar details should be included in a clause giving the buyer the right to cancel if he cannot procure the mortgage of a specified amount, and in this clause also specify the time allowed to procure the mortgage. If land is being sold subject to a mortgage, specify the amount and whether or not the buyer assumes personal liability. If the seller has a mortgage on his land that must be released, the contract should provide that the seller will have the right to pay it off at the closing of the deal, using the buyer's sale price for this purpose, the seller to have the mortgagee present prepared to release the mortgage and surrender the canceled papers. Occasionally a seller in an installment contract wants to reserve the right to mortgage the land. In these cases the contract should: (1) give details of the loan, maximum amount, maximum interest rate, and so forth; (2) specify that the mortgage will be prior and superior to the rights of the contract buyer; (3) give the buyer the right to make the mortgage payments if the seller fails to do so and to deduct payments so made from his contract payments.

Evidence of title. The contract should provide: (1) What type of title evidence is to be furnished, title insurance, abstract, and so forth. (2) Who is to furnish and pay for same. (3) Time allowed: (a) for furnishing evidence of title, (b) for buyer to point out defects in title not permitted by the contract, (c) for seller's clearance of objections, and (d) for buyer to decide whether to accept title *as is* if objections cannot be cured. (4) If abstract of title is specified, for the seller's protection a clause should be included giving the seller the right to cure any of the buyer's objections to the title by delivery of a clear policy of title insurance. This may save the seller the time and expense of a quiet title suit when the buyer's attorney raises numerous unimportant objections to the title. (5)

The seller should not sign a form of contract that calls for title insurance if his land is registered under the Torrens system, for this will subject him to a double expense if the buyer insists on his contract rights.

Clearing title by escrow deposits. For the protection of the seller, the contract should contain a provision allowing the seller to leave money in escrow with some bank or title company if his title is not clear on the day that he must deliver clear title. Otherwise, a deal may fall through simply because a seller is not in a position to remove some trivial defect, such as a small mechanic's lien, within the time allowed for clearing title.

Chattel lien search. Specify if the seller is to furnish search for financing statements or other liens on personal property being sold, and if so, time allowed for same.

Building ordinance violations. If the seller is to furnish a formal, official report as to building code violations, cover this, including the time allowed for this purpose. The buyer should endeavor to have the contract provide that the seller "warrants the building on said premises is now and at the date of closing will be free and clear of all violations of laws and ordinances, and for breach of this warranty buyer may rescind this contract, before or after closing, or, at his election, may sue for damages."

Survey. If the seller is to furnish a survey, specify the time allowed for this and that it is to be satisfactory to the buyer's attorney. The time allowed for the buyer to raise objections based on the survey should tie into the time allowed the buyer for raising objections to the title. If the seller objects to paying for a survey, the buyer may decide to get one at his own expense. Is a survey necessary? Business judgment should be used in answering this question. For example, if *A* is buying a forty-year-old dwelling where the fences have also been up for that length of time, it is unlikely that any encroachment trouble will develop. Age has set the matter at rest. If, on the other hand, *A* is buying a recently erected commercial building that apparently extends to the property lines, a survey is definitely advisable, for the building may actually extend over property lines. Again, how can the buyer be sure that the legal description in the contract covers the property that the buyer has inspected and wants to buy? The only really satisfactory proof of this is a land survey. A survey is always advisable if new construction is contemplated, so that the building is set within the lot lines and within lines established by ordinances and private restrictions.

Building and other restrictions. If the seller wishes to place building restrictions on the land sold, he must make provision for this in the contract.

Risk of loss. Suppose the building is destroyed or damaged by fire or other casualty before the deal is closed. The right of the buyer to cancel the deal and his right to insurance money if he does not back out, should be covered.

Warranties of building. The buyer should try to get a clause in the contract stating that basement does not flood, building is free of termite infestation, roof does not leak, and heating plant and electrical system are now and at closing will be in good working order.

Miscellaneous documents to be furnished to the buyer. If a new building requires a certificate of occupancy or an approval by the underwriters of electrical installations, or if it is customary to obtain similar certificates with respect to plumbing and the like, the contract should provide that the seller will deliver these at the closing. In case of a new building, guaranties by the subcontractors are customary. There is usually a roof guaranty and a guaranty of the plumbing and heating equipment and electrical installations. The contract should provide that the seller will transfer and deliver these to the purchaser at the closing.

Installment contracts. The forfeiture clause is of the greatest importance here. Also cover the buyer's duty to pay taxes, carry insurance, and keep buildings in repair and free of mechanic's liens, restrictions on assignment of contract, and so forth. The seller should be given the right to declare the entire purchase price due if the buyer defaults. For the seller's protection provide that the buyer shall not assign the contract without the seller's consent. Also provide that the buyer is to pay taxes and furnish insurance with seller named in the policy. Buyer should agree to keep the premises in repair and in compliance with ordinances and laws, not to remodel without the seller's consent, and to keep the premises free from mechanic's liens.

Possession. Cover the date on which possession is to be given.

Leases. Provide for assignment to buyer of all seller's leases, including leases for advertising signs.

Concessionaire contracts. Provide for assignment of all such contracts.

Tenant's security deposits. Assignment of tenant's security deposits to buyer must be covered specifically.

Advance payments of rent. The contract should allow the buyer a credit against the purchase price where a tenant has already paid the seller the rent for the last several months of the term.

Prorated items. These should be covered in great detail to avoid arguments at closing over who pays for janitor's vacation pay, water bills, and so forth.

Income tax. The seller should consider whether an income tax savings will result if the property is sold under an installment contract rather than for cash.

Building construction. If the contract calls for construction of a building, many additional matters must be considered.

Documents. All miscellaneous documents that the buyer will need should be provided for in the contract. The seller is under no legal obligation to furnish any document that the contract does not call for.

Signatures, acknowledgment, witnessing. All the parties must sign, being careful to sign as their names appear on the contract. Witnessing and acknowledgment are desirable, so that the buyer may record the contract, for without witnessing and acknowledgment, the contract is not recordable in many states.

10 CLOSING REAL ESTATE TRANSACTIONS: LOAN CLOSINGS: ESCROWS

10.01 Sale closing defined   After the contract of sale has been signed, there are a number of details that must be attended to. For example, the title must be examined to determine if the seller really owns the property and what mortgages, liens, and restrictions exist. A survey must be ordered. The premises must be inspected to ascertain the presence of encroachments, unrecorded easements, and the unrecorded rights of parties in possession. At the end, the seller gives the buyer the deed, and the seller is paid the balance of the purchase price. All this is the process of "closing the deal." Often, much the same process is taking place with respect to the buyer's mortgage. So there will be a contemporaneous "mortgage closing" also.

While the two closings, sale and mortgage, involve a process that occurs simultaneously and may culminate in a single meeting when both transactions are finalized, the processes will be dealt with separately here. This is in recognition of the two distinct sets of relationships, which, although they involve the same subject matter, give rise to different rights and obligations.

10.02 The lawyer's role   The need for counsel in the real estate transaction can best be demonstrated by example.

> **EXAMPLE:** Buyer signed a contract to buy a corner vacant lot intending to erect a filling station thereon. He had no lawyer. The deal was closed. After closing, he discovered that the lot was zoned for single-family dwellings. Lawyers are taught to inquire into zoning.

> **EXAMPLE:** Buyer without consulting a lawyer, put down a payment of $15,000 on the purchase of a vacant tract. The contract was a preprinted form reciting that buyer would accept title subject to "recorded building restrictions." Buyer intended to erect a dog hospital. When the title search came out, it showed

recorded building restrictions that permitted only residential use. Buyer lost his $15,000. He had no use for a residence. Lawyers are taught to be wary of building restrictions.

Obviously, examples like these take place each year. They need not occur. The attorney is needed from the precontract stage through the closing. Many people fail to recognize this need until it is too late. This is particularly true in residential transactions, perhaps the largest, single transaction many people ever have in their lifetimes. Rather than rely upon the advice of counsel, many consumers eagerly execute the purchase contract and rely upon sheer luck to pull them through. Inflation has caused many "average" homes to have selling prices of six figures, but these buyers and sellers only rarely have representation when the blueprint for this transaction, the real estate sales contract, is executed. What is more incredible is the number of people who carry the transaction through to closing without counsel only to find to their chagrin that they were pennywise and dollar foolish.

10.02(a) Conflict of interest

It has long been a rule of legal ethics that a lawyer is forbidden from representing conflicting interests in a transaction without full disclosure and consent by all of the parties. This disclosure must not only be of the multiple representation, but also of the effect of this representation upon the exercise of the lawyer's professional judgment on behalf of each party. Disciplinary Rule 5-105. The real estate sales transaction is a somewhat frequent scene for this practice, as where a developer's attorney is automatically denominated as buyer's counsel as a form of repayment for services rendered to the developer. See *In re Kamp*, 194 A2d 236 (N.J. 1963). This activity may lead to professional sanctions being taken against the lawyer. *The Florida Bar* v. *Tietelman*, 261 So2d 140 (Fla. 1972). It may also have repercussions for the clients.

> **EXAMPLE:** A purchaser was entitled to rescind a real estate sales contract when he was represented by seller's counsel who failed to disclose to the purchasers the existence of a lien on the property. The court found this to be a material fraud on the part of the seller. *Holley* v. *Jackson,* 158 A2d 803 (Del. 1959).

Some lawyers are also real estate brokers and insurance brokers. They should maintain separate offices for each line of endeavor. The real estate brokerage, the insurance business, and the law practice must be operated completely separately. 48 Fordham L. Rev. 38 (1980).

REFERENCES: 68 ALR3d 697: Werner, *Real Estate Closings,* 5 (1979).

10.03 Matters to be considered before closing

10.03(a) Evidence of title

If the contract requires the seller to furnish an abstract or other evidence of title, he should do so *within the time allowed by the contract,* for if he fails to do so, a reluctant buyer may seize the opportunity to cancel the deal. If the seller is furnishing a title commitment, be sure it is a signed, original commitment. The buyer, in turn, should *within the time allowed by the contract,* draw attention to any defects in title not permitted by the contract. Otherwise he will be regarded as waiving such defects. The seller should then, *within the permitted time,* cure any defects pointed out by the buyer. When the contract specifies that the seller shall furnish an abstract of title showing clear title, the buyer has a right to insist that quitclaim deeds needed to clear the buyer's title objections be recorded in the recorder's office and included in the abstract of title. *Kincaid* v. *Dobrinsky,* 225 Ill. App. 85 (1922). When the contract calls for a title insurance policy showing clear title in the seller, the buyer has the right to insist that all unauthorized objections be cleared from the title policy by the seller.

See, generally, Werner, *Real Estate Closings,* Ch. 2 (1979).

The buyer should consider whether special coverage endorsements, i.e., zoning coverage or an encroachment endorsement, should be ordered from the title insurance company. Even though the contract does not require the seller to provide these special endorsements or the transaction may not be contingent upon the title company's willingness to issue such coverage, the buyer may be well advised to order the special endorsements that are appropriate for the transaction. See Werner, *Real Estate Closings,* 31–35 (1979).

10.03(b) Closing documents

Closing document preparation takes a great deal of time and care. In larger deals, it is usual for the closing documents to be identified in, or even made exhibits to, the real estate sale contract. In other transactions, the exact nature and form of the closing documents must be worked out as the closing approaches. Typical closing documents are:

1. Seller's affidavit. (If the transaction is going to be insured by a title insurance company, an ALTA Loan and Extended Coverage Owner's Policy Statement may be substituted.) See Werner, *Real Estate Closings,* 86–88 (1979) for a sample form. A misrepresentation in the affidavit will support an action for damages. *Somerset County* v. *Durling,* 415 A2d 371 (N.J. 1980).

2. Bill of sale for personal property.

3. Evidence of compliance with fire, health, building, and zoning laws and ordinances.

4. Bulk sales affidavit.

5. Chattel lien search.

6. Corporate resolutions.

7. Declaration of homestead.

8. Deed.

9. Indemnity agreements.

10. Insurance policy assignment, cancellation, or binder.

11. Minutes of the closing meeting.

12. Mortgages to be executed at the closing. A buyer who is taking subject to existing financing should obtain a copy of the outstanding mortgage and note. The buyer should also obtain all paid notes on existing mortgages which are assumed since the notes may be needed to obtain a release deed. The existing mortgagee should also give an estoppel statement showing the amount due on the existing mortgage so that it cannot later assert that a larger amount is due. If the buyer is taking title subject to an existing mortgage, the contract should be contingent upon, and the closing documents include, the lender's written consent to the sale if the mortgage has a due-on-sale clause.

13. Opinions of counsel regarding the validity of corporate documents, usury, zoning, etc.

14. Payoff statements on encumbrances to be paid at closing or loan status statements and lender's consents for loans to remain outstanding after closing. If the existing lender is consenting to the sale on the condition that the interest be increased, loan term altered, and the like, the documents recasting the loan must be drawn and executed.

15. Permits for curb cuts, awnings, etc.

16. Pest control report.

17. Plans and specifications. On big buildings, the buyer wants to get the plans that depict the building "as built." No building is ever built 100 percent according to the original plans. Pipes and conduits are often relocated when construction reveals that the planned locations are impractical.

18. Power of attorney.

19. Real estate transfer tax declaration or return.

20. Receipt for broker's commission.

21. Contracts for scavenger service, janitorial service, exterminator service, and the like and their assignment.

22. Soil test report.

23. Survey.

24. Tenant roster, rent roll, outstanding leases, assignment of leases, letter to tenants. Where a building is managed by a responsible management firm, buyers and lenders customarily accept a manager's letter as to apartment leases. On commercial properties, space leases are usually checked unless they are short-term office leases. The manager's letter always covers renewal options, purchase options, advance payments of rent, and security deposits.

25. Title evidence.

26. Warranties from the builder, roofer, appliance manufacturers, etc.

A full discussion of these and other closing documents can be found in Werner, *Real Estate Closings,* Ch. 3 (1979).

Since closings are apt to be fairly hectic, it is a good idea for the parties to submit to each other, in advance of closing, all the documents that will then be exchanged, such as the deed, mortgage note, survey, leases, assignments. The documents are then checked in the quietude of one's office and pencil initials are placed in a corner of the document. Further scrutiny of the form at the time of closing is then omitted though a check of signatures and acknowledgments will still be needed at that time.

10.03(c)   The survey

Check the date on the survey. A survey made ten years ago, for example, obviously will not cover buildings erected since then. Does the survey locate the property with reference to known monuments, such as government section corners? Does it show the location of all outbuildings? All neighboring buildings? Are all buildings, walks, and so on well within the lines of the lot on which they belong? Do any structures extend over the setback lines established by city ordinances or building restrictions? Does the survey show whether upper portions of the building (bay windows or eaves) extend over the lot lines? Are there possible subsurface encroachments, such as footings on the building, extending into adjoining land?

The certificate of the survey should also be checked for an express declaration that it is intended to be relied upon, and, if erroneous, can be sued upon by the buyer, his mortgagee, and their title companies. *Rozny* v. *Marnul,* 250 NE2d 659 (Ill. 1969); Note, 64 N.W.U.L. Rev. 903 (1961). See Kratovil, *Modern Real Estate and Documentation,* Ch. 7 (1975).

10.03(d)   Chattel lien search

If valuable chattels are included in the sale, a search of the Uniform Commercial Code records should be made for financing statements affecting such chattels. This search requires care. Code filings relating to fixtures, crops, and consumer goods (stoves, refrigerators, and other appliances found in the ordinary home) are found in some local office, often the recorder's office, but in some states in a department separate from the department where ordinary deeds are filed. Filings covering furniture and other chattels in a hotel or furnished apartment, or raw materials in an industrial plant, are likely to be found in some central office, usually that of the secretary of state in the state capitol.

10.03(e)   Ordinance violations search

If in the particular community it is possible to procure a title company or other search of city records as to building ordinance violations, this should be done. In lieu thereof, an architect or engineer should check the building carefully for violations.

10.03(f)   Inspection of the property by the buyer

Before closing the deal the buyer should make a careful physical check of the property. Possession imparts constructive notice. The buyer will take subject to the rights of the grantee in an unrecorded contract, or to other rights disclosed by occupancy. Tenants' leases should be checked for options to renew or to purchase. If the premises are occupied by tenants, their occupancy is notice of their rights. The buyer must not accept the seller's assurance that tenants are month-to-month tenants. He should check with the tenants. This check with the tenants will also determine what furniture, appliances, etc., the tenants claim belong to them.

> **EXAMPLE:** Seller is selling a furnished apartment building to Buyer. The entire building is under lease to Tenant. The lease has only one month to run, and Buyer plans to operate the building himself. Buyer inquires of Tenant and finds that Tenant owns all the furniture. Buyer must plan to acquire new furniture or plan to buy the old furniture from Tenant.

The buyer checks for the existence of unrecorded easements, for the buyer takes subject to unrecorded easements if their existence would be revealed by an inspection of the premises. Check to see whether this particular sale will result in the creation of any implied easements. Check to see whether rear or side exits run over adjoining property, thus making an easement necessary, and whether shutters open over adjoining premises. Check to see if heat is furnished by an adjoining building, thus making a written agreement necessary. Check for vaults, marquees, and so forth extending into public streets, which would make permits necessary. If you defer inspection until after the abstract or other evidence of title has been furnished, you can check to see whether the building violates any recorded building restrictions. It should be remembered that, even if the contract requires the buyer to take subject to "building restrictions," he is not required to take subject to violations of restrictions. Such violations constitute a separate and distinct defect in title. Check also for violations of zoning or building ordinances and for recent repairs or construction that might ripen into a mechanic's lien. If valuable chattels are included in the sale, inquire of the tenants whether they claim ownership of such chattels.

It is also customary to have an inspection shortly prior to the closing so that mechanical systems (heating, air conditioning, and so forth) can be checked to determine whether they are in operating condition and how they function. Sometimes the buyer may want an inspection by a qualified home inspection company. An appropriate contingency clause is often inserted in the contract, stating that the sale will close only if the inspection shows all systems in working order. Where other than single-family property is involved, it is customary for the buyer's engineer to make an inspection of the building. This is also a good time for the seller to set out the drawings, blueprints, plans and specifications, warranties, instruction manuals, and so forth for the buyer and his staff. If there is a reluctance on the seller's part actually to surrender these items until the sale actually closes, at least the buyer will know where to find these things when possession is obtained. Recent local laws call for the inspection of the premises by local officials prior to the closing. This results in some official determination that the property is in compliance with the current building code, i.e., that it has the required number of smoke alarms, etc.

10.03(g) Maintenance of property from date of contract to date of closing

It is the seller's responsibility to maintain the property in a reasonable manner between the date of contract and the date of closing. If he permits it to deteriorate, the buyer may sue him for damages even after the deal is closed. Goldberg, *Sales of Real Property* 442; 92 CJS *Vendor & Purchaser* § 286a.

10.03(h) Prior approvals

All will admit that it is better to take care, before closing, of questions of form and substance of the transaction documents. The questions, if they erupt at closing, can cause arguments and even failure to close. If the parties exchange unexecuted forms of these documents, problems can be ironed out in advance and approved documents can be initialed by the attorneys. Closing can then be devoted to ministerial acts and exchanges. If the documents are other than standard form, it is also good to have a title company officer check and initial them.

10.03(i) Closing agent

Closing practices vary from locality to locality, and even within the same county or city. In various areas, closings are conducted by lending institutions, title insurance companies, escrow companies, real estate brokers, and attorneys for the buyer or seller.

10.04 Bulk sales affidavits and notices

A sale of real estate may incidentally involve the sale of the entire stock of goods, wares, or merchandise of some retail establishment operated by the seller on the premises. It is necessary that such a sale comply with the local Bulk Sales Act, which usually involves giving notice of the pending sale to the creditors of the business so that they can protect their rights. UCC § 6-101 *et seq.*

10.05 Closing date

The contract of sale should fix a closing date, the time the deed is to be delivered, and the balance of the purchase price paid. If no closing date is fixed in the contract, it is presumed that the deal is to be closed within a reasonable time, and either buyer or seller may select a reasonable date and notify the other that he will be prepared to close at such time. Often one of the parties is not prepared to close on the date specified in the contract and requests an adjournment of closing. In such case, the other party, in granting the request for adjournment, specifies that the prorating or apportionment will be computed as of the original date or the adjourned date, whichever is more favorable to him. For example, if the adjournment is made at the request of the seller and the income of the building is greater than the carrying charges, the buyer will insist that the apportionment or prorating be computed as of the original date. The buyer will receive the rents from the date originally fixed for closing, and the seller will be entitled to interest on the unpaid balance of the purchase price and the purchase money mortgage from the original closing date. Of course, if the contract fixes a closing date and provides that time is of the essence, the party who is ready to close on the date fixed need not grant a request for an adjournment.

Some contracts fix a date that is to govern the prorating of apportionment, regardless of the date of the delivery of the deed. Other contracts provide that prorating or apportionment shall be computed as of the date of the delivery of the deed.

The buyer should not rely on any extension of time granted by the seller's lawyer or broker. Normally, neither of them has the power to grant extensions.

10.06 Matters to be attended to at closing

10.06(a) Title

The buyer should make a final check to see that the title is clear and subject only to the encumbrances permitted by the contract of sale. If the deal is not closed in escrow, an informal check should be made of the records to cover the period between the date of the abstract or title search and the date of the closing of the deal. Judgments or other liens may attach during the interval, and will, of course, be good against the buyer. The buyer should at least insist that the seller's attorney give him a written statement that he will not turn the buyer's check over to the seller until after the deed to the buyer has been recorded and the title searched to cover that date. Of course if the deal is closed in escrow, all danger from this source is obviated. If, by agreement, the seller is to clear certain objections after closing, the buyer should retain part of the purchase price, usually double the amount of the lien involved, to insure performance on the part of the seller.

10.06(b) Form and contents of documents involved

The documents should all be checked to see if they are in proper form and comply with the contract. For example, if the deed to be given is a warranty deed, the subject clause of the deed should be checked to make certain that it does not include any items that were not included in the subject clause of the contract. The deed should also be checked to see if the recorder of deeds will accept it for recording. For example, in many states, laws forbid "metes and bounds" subdivisions, that is, the division of a tract of land into plots for sale without the formality of recording a subdivision plat. The recorder will often reject such a deed, and the buyer is left with a deed that he has paid for but cannot record.

If, as is so often the case, the major portion of the purchase price is being furnished by the buyer's mortgage lender, the attorneys will make a final check of the mortgage and note to see that the principal amount, interest rate, and monthly payments are in accordance with the loan commitment. If this has not previously been attended to, a similar check should be made of the other loan documents, such as the assignment of rents or waiver of defenses.

10.06(c)   Water and other utility bills

The buyer should call for the production of paid water and other utility bills. If these bills have not been paid, service to the building may be cut off.

10.06(d)   Insurance premiums

The buyer should see that the seller's insurance premiums have been paid, since the seller will receive credit for insurance in the prorating.

10.06(e)   Production of seller's deed

The buyer should require the seller to produce the deed by which he acquired title. This affords some measure of protection against forgery and impersonation.

10.06(f)   Prorations or adjustments

Prorations or adjustments should be computed and a closing statement prepared.

10.06(g)   Payment of purchase price and delivery of documents

The balance due according to the closing statement should be paid and the documents to which each party is entitled delivered.

10.07   Closing statement— prorations

The contract of sale usually provides that various items shall be adjusted or prorated. Items not mentioned in the contract are nevertheless often prorated because of the prevailing local custom. *O'Donnell* v. *Lutter,* 156 P2d 958 (Cal. 1945); *Valley Garage, Inc.* v. *Nyseth,* 481 P2d 17 (Wash. 1971). This prorating, or adjustment, results in credits and debits against each party. These are usually shown on a closing statement, which is also called a settlement sheet. Forms of closing statements vary and may be imposed by a regulatory agency, i.e., HUD's RESPA mortgage closing statement. A form commonly used lists in one column all credits due the seller and in a separate column all credits due the buyer. The completed statement is approved by buyer and seller. An extended discussion of the closing statement and its elements can be found in Werner, *Real Estate Closings,* Ch. 4 (1979).

These calculations can be made with reference to the proration table found on page 184.

10.07(a)   Closing statement—credits due seller

The following are the usual credits due the seller:

1. Full purchase price.
2. Unearned insurance premiums.
3. Fuel on hand.

4. Any items paid by seller in advance, as water tax (if same has been so paid), prepayments on exterminator or other service contracts, prepayments on taxes and insurance made by seller to mortgagee under the terms of the mortgage, when such mortgage is to be assumed by buyer.

PRORATING TABLE FOR RENTS, TAXES, AND INSURANCE

Number of years, months and days	RENTS One Month Days to Month		TAXES & INS. One Year		INSURANCE Three Years			INSURANCE Five Years			Number of years, months and days
	30	31	Months	Days	Years	Months	Days	Years	Months	Days	
1	.0333	.0323	.0833	.0028	.3333	.0278	.0009	.2000	.0167	.0006	1
2	.0667	.0645	.1667	.0056	.6667	.0556	.0019	.4000	.0333	.0011	2
3	.1000	.0968	.2500	.0083	1.0000	.0833	.0028	.6000	.0500	.0017	3
4	.1333	.1290	.3333	.0111		.1111	.0037	.8000	.0667	.0022	4
5	.1667	.1613	.4167	.0139		.1389	.0046	1.0000	.0833	.0028	5
6	.2000	.1935	.5000	.0167		.1667	.0056		.1000	.0033	6
7	.2333	.2258	.5833	.0194		.1944	.0065		.1167	.0039	7
8	.2667	.2581	.6667	.0222		.2222	.0074		.1333	.0044	8
9	.3000	.2903	.7500	.0250		.2500	.0083		.1500	.0050	9
10	.3333	.3226	.8333	.0278		.2778	.0093		.1667	.0056	10
11	.3667	.3548	.9167	.0306		.3056	.0102		.1833	.0061	11
12	.4000	.3871	1.0000	.0333		.3333	.0111		.2000	.0067	12
13	.4333	.4194		.0361			.0120			.0072	13
14	.4667	.4516		.0389			.0130			.0078	14
15	.5000	.4839		.0417			.0139			.0083	15
16	.5333	.5161		.0444			.0148			.0089	16
17	.5667	.5484		.0472			.0157			.0094	17
18	.6000	.5806		.0500			.0167			.0100	18
19	.6333	.6129		.0528			.0176			.0106	19
20	.6667	.6452		.0556			.0185			.0111	20
21	.7000	.6774		.0583			.0194			.0117	21
22	.7333	.7097		.0611			.0204			.0122	22
23	.7667	.7419		.0639			.0213			.0128	23
24	.8000	.7742		.0667			.0222			.0133	24
25	.8333	.8065		.0694			.0231			.0139	25
26	.8667	.8387		.0722			.0241			.0144	26
27	.9000	.8710		.0750			.0250			.0150	27
28	.9333	.9032		.0778			.0259			.0156	28
29	.9667	.9355		.0806			.0269			.0161	29
30	1.0000	.9677		.0833			.0278			.0167	30
31		1.0000									31

Example:

Rent $135.00 per mo.
To find value of 23 days of a 31 day mo.
From Table:—
23 days = .7419
.7419 × 135.00 = $100.16

Example:

Taxes = 1215.12.
To find value of 7 mos. and 19 days
From Table:—
7 mos. = .5833
19 days = .0528
7 mos. 19 days = .6361
.6361 × 1215.12 = 772.95

Example:

3 Year Policy Premium = 58.75
To find the value of 1 yr. 3 mos. 11 days
From Table:—
1 yr. = .3333
3 mos. = .0833
11 days = .0102
1 yr. 3 mo. 11 days = .4268
.4268 × 58.75 = 25.07

Example:

5 Yr. Policy Premium 312.82
To find value of 3 yrs. 4 mos. 13 days
From Table:—
3 yrs. = .6000
4 mos. = .0667
13 days = .0072
3 yrs. 4 mos. 13 days = .6739
.6739 × 312.82 = 210.81

10.07(b) Closing statement—credits due buyer

The following are some of the credits due the buyer:

1. Earnest money.

2. Existing mortgages if the sale is for part cash and balance by assumption of existing mortgages.

3. Interest accrued and unpaid on existing mortgages that are to be assumed by the buyer.

4. Amount of purchase money mortgage if seller has agreed to receive such mortgage as part of the purchase price.

5. Unearned rents that have already been collected, since rents are usually collected on the first of the month. If the deal is closed after the first of the month, the buyer is, under most contracts, entitled to his proportionate part of the current month's rent collections. This includes unearned rent on leases of advertising space or advertising signs.

6. Deposits by tenants made as security for payment of rent for the last month of the lease.

7. Taxes. Since the seller has had possession of the rents of the property for prior years and for part of the current year, it is only fair that he pay all taxes for prior years and his proportionate part of the taxes for the current year, if these have not already been paid, and contracts usually so provide. In some localities, however, it is not customary to apportion current taxes. In periods of rising taxes, a clause in the contract may call for proration of taxes at a base in excess of the latest bill, for example, "107 percent of the latest available tax bill." As an alternative the contract may call for reproration of taxes if the actual bill, when finally received, exceeds the latest available bill substantially—say, by 10 percent or more. Without such provision, neither buyer nor seller can seek adjustment if the variation is costly. *3700 S. Kedzie Bldg. Corp.* v. *Chicago Steel Foundry Co.,* 156 NE2d 618 (Ill. 1959). Do not confuse taxes with special assessments. While the former may be proratable, the latter are not unless the contract expressly so provides. *Alder* v. *R. W. Lotto, Inc.,* 517 P2d 227 (Wash. 1973).

8. Items based on meter readings, such as water tax, electricity, and gas, if same are not paid in advance.

9. Wages and other charges accrued and unpaid, such as janitor's salary or scavenger service.

10. Release fee and recording charge, when buyer will record or obtain release of mortgage that seller should have removed from his title.

11. Condominium and PUD assessments must also be prorated with appropriate credits given to the buyer or seller. Werner, *Real Estate Closings,* 186 (1979).

10.07(c) Closing statement—other items

Some charges are allocated to either the seller or buyer, depending on the terms of the contract of sale, which are often dictated by local custom.

1. In the Midwest, the contract requires the title charges to be borne by the seller. These are therefore a debit against the seller. In New York, the buyer picks up this cost.

2. Who pays for the survey? This is a matter of negotiation. Most often the contract allocates this cost to the seller.

3. The chattel lien search fee, termite inspection cost, and deed tax are usually paid by the seller.

4. The buyer pays the recording fee for the deed and the contract usually requires the buyer to pay for the recording of any purchase money mortgage and the cost of title evidence covering that mortgage.

5. Escrow fees are often divided between the buyer and seller.

6. The broker's commission is usually paid out of the proceeds of sale and charged against the seller.

10.08 Matters to attend to after closing

After closing, the buyer should immediately record his deed and any release of mortgage obtained at the closing and have his evidence of title brought down to cover the closing date. The seller should record and insure any purchase money mortgage. The buyer's title insurance policy and the title policy covering the mortgage the buyer put on at closing should be issued as soon as possible. If this has not already been attended to, the seller should notify the janitor, building manager, scavenger, exterminator, and so forth of the termination of their employment and that he will no longer be responsible for their compensation. The buyer should: (1) have water, gas, and electric bills, and real estate tax books changed to his name; (2) arrange for janitor, scavenger, building manager, and other services; (3) obtain consent of insurance company to assignment of policy; (4) have mortgage loss clause attached to existing insurance policies if mortgage has been executed; (5) obtain workmen's compensation and employer's liability insurance, if necessary.

10.08(a) The closing letter

After the deal has been closed, the buyer's lawyer writes the buyer a closing letter. The letter encloses and describes the documents that the buyer is receiving and describes the documents that the mortgagee retains (fire insurance policy, abstract, etc.) and the documents that are still to come. For example, it takes the recorder of deeds a while to complete the recording of the deed. Once it is received from the recorder's office it will in turn be sent to the buyer.

The letter should suggest to the buyer what he is to do in the future—for example, giving the date on which tax bills should be received, retain the closing statement for income tax records, put the deed and title policy in a safe-deposit box, etc.

10.09 Mortgage closing defined

Just as a sale is closed by delivery of the deed to the buyer and delivery of the balance of the purchase price to the seller after examination of the title and disposition of other details, for the protection of buyer and seller, a mortgage transaction is closed by delivery of the mortgage and note to the lender and disbursement of the mortgage funds to the mortgagor after attending to the details that insure that the mortgagee has a good first lien on the property.

10.09(a) Borrower's concerns

In shopping for a lender, the borrower should have numerous areas of concern beyond the obvious questions of rate of interest, term of loan, points, and equity required. The borrower should also ask the lender the following questions:

1. Is the borrower required to carry life or disability insurance? Must he obtain it from a particular company? He may prefer no insurance or may wish to obtain it at a better premium rate elsewhere.

2. Is there a late payment charge? How much? How late may the payment be before the charge is imposed? The borrower should be aware that late payments may harm his credit rating.

3. If the borrower wishes to pay off the loan in advance of maturity (for example, if he moves and sells the house), must he pay a prepayment penalty? How much? If so, for how long a period will it apply?

4. Will the lender release the borrower from personal liability if the loan is assumed by someone else when the house is sold?

5. If the borrower sells the house and the buyer assumes the loan, will the lender have the right to charge an assumption fee, raise the rate of interest, or require payment in full of the mortgage?

6. If the borrower has a financial emergency, will the terms of the loan include a future advance clause, permitting him to borrow additional money on the mortgage after he has paid off part of the original loan?

7. Will the borrower be required to pay monies into a special reserve (escrow or impound) account to cover taxes or insurance? If so, how large a deposit will be required at the closing of the sale? May a savings account be posted in lieu of monthly impound payments? How large an account is needed? How long must it remain posted?

8. In looking for the best mortgage to fit the borrower's particular financial needs, the borrower may wish to check the terms and requirements of a private conventional loan versus a loan insured through the Federal Housing Administration or Farmers Home Administration or guaranteed by the Veterans Administration. The FHA, VA, and Farmers Home Administration loans involve federal ceilings on permissible charges for some settlement services, which may be of interest to the borrower. Ask lenders about these programs.

9. If the borrower is dealing with the lender who holds the existing mortgage, he might be able to take over the prior loan, in a transaction called "assumption." Assumption usually saves money in settlement costs if the interest rate on the prior loan is lower than that being asked in the market. In times of inflation in the housing market, a higher down payment might be required than if you had obtained a new loan. The borrower may want to ask the seller whether he would be willing to "take back" a second mortgage to finance part of the difference between the assumed loan and the sales price.

10.09(b) RESPA

The Real Estate Settlement Procedures Act, 12 USC § 2601, has caused a great deal of consternation among lenders, brokers and real estate attorneys.

In its present form, the act's primary impact upon the closing process is directed toward lenders of "federally related mortgage loans." These are loans that are both secured by a first lien on residential (one to four family) real properties and meet any one of the following four criteria: (1) the loan is made by a lender which has its deposits insured by or which is regulated by the federal government; or (2) the loan is insured, guaranteed, supplemented, or assisted under a federal housing or urban development program; or (3) the loan is intended to be sold to FNMA, GNMA, or FHLMC; or (4) the loan is made by any creditor who makes or invests in residential loans aggregating more than $1,000,000 per year. 12 USC § 2602. As you can see, the coverage of the act is very broad, with most lenders being made subject to its strictures.

The Act now requires: that most loans be closed through the use of the HUD settlement sheet, 24 CFR § 3500.8(d), which must be available to the borrower before the closing, 12 USC § 2603(b); that within three days of the application, the lender make a good faith estimate of likely settlement service charges, 12 USC § 2604(c) & (d), 24 CFR §§ 3500.6 & 3500.7(a); that the HUD booklet, *Settlement Costs and You,* be given to the borrower with the estimate. 12 USC § 2604.

The Act also limits impound or escrow accounts for the payment of real estate taxes and insurance. 12 USC § 2609.

See Kratovil and Werner, *Modern Mortgage Law and Practice* §§ 27.06 *et seq.* (2d ed. 1981), for a full discussion of the impact of RESPA upon lenders.

10.09(c)   Title defects

It is, of course, important to the mortgagee to be sure that his mortgage is a first lien on the land and that no title defects exist. Among the precautions he would take in this regard are the following:

1. Check mortgage for errors in filling blanks, signatures, witnesses, acknowledgment, etc. Have mortgage filed or recorded and bring abstract or other evidence of title down to cover the date of the recording of the mortgage before paying out. This will disclose any other liens that have appeared of record prior to the recording of the mortgage. Any such liens should be paid and released or subordinated to the mortgage. The prudent lender will weigh the true worth of the various means of evidencing title. Sophisticated lenders tend to insist on the ALTA mortgage title insurance policy. Among other advantages, it insures that the mortgage is valid and enforceable. It also insures against unfiled mechanics' liens, unrecorded leases, unrecorded easements, encroachments, and other questions of survey, and lack of legal access to the mortgage property. If the lender is forwarding funds to a title company's agent or its approved attorney, the lender should insist on receiving its *insured closing letter,* which insures the mortgagee against embezzlement of loan funds or the agent's failure to follow the mortgagee's directions. This, incidentally, insures the lender that all prior liens shown on the title search will be paid off, for all mortgagees directions require this, and the insured closing letter insures that this will be done. If the mortgage is being assigned to your company, require the title company to issue its endorsement to the mortgage title policy insuring the validity of the assignment and substituting the name of your company as the party assured.

2. Analyze all objections to the mortgagor's title disclosed by the examination of title. All defects in title should be cleared. If the title search reveals building restrictions or conditions, ascertain whether existing buildings violate such restrictions. Of course, copies of the instruments creating restrictions, easements, and so forth should be obtained and analyzed.

3. The mortgagee should inquire into the rights of parties in possession for the purpose of discovering unrecorded leases with options to purchase, unrecorded deeds and contracts, unrecorded easements, and so on. He must keep in mind the fact that the mortgagee, in nearly all states, takes his mortgage subject to the interests of all parties in possession of the premises.

4. The mortgagee should: (a) inspect the building carefully for signs of recent work, and if any appears, demand to see paid bills and demand mechanic's lien waivers for any substantial work, as in construction loans; (b) get affidavit from mortgagor that all work or materials furnished to premises have been paid in full, which, if false, will subject him to criminal prosecution; (c) if the building is occupied by persons other than the mortgagor (tenant, contract purchaser, and so on), see that notice of nonliability for mechanics' liens is posted on the property in the states where such notice is effective.

5. A survey should be obtained to determine whether any encroachments or other survey defects exist.

6. The mortgagee should obtain the usual mortgagor's affidavit to the effect that there are no judgments, bankruptcies, and so on against such mortgagor.

7. Within the time limits specified by the law and regulations, the lender must disclose to the borrower all matters required by the federal Truth-in-Lending Act (15 USCA §§ 1601–1665). See Kratovil and Werner, *Modern Mortgage Law and Practice,* § 4.13 *et seq.*

10.09(d) The loan closing statement

Seldom does the borrower receive the full amount of the mortgage loan. Various deductions are made for title searches, surveys, recording fees, and other items. Therefore, on disbursement of the loan, the mortgagee will prepare a loan settlement statement similar to that prepared in sales of land. This form should be used for three reasons: (1) it furnishes the borrower with a complete record of all disbursements made by the mortgagee from the proceeds of the loan; (2) it provides the mortgagee signed authorization by the borrower for all such disbursements and thus eliminates all possibility of any legal action that might be taken if the mortgagor claims improper charges were made against his loan; and (3) in those cases where there is no binding loan commitment, it fixes the date on which the mortgage becomes a lien on the land, since where there is no binding commitment, the mortgage does not become a lien on the land in some states until the date on which the loan is paid out to the mortgagor. In general, this settlement statement shows the full amount of the loan, and all deductions from it and their amount. It also shows the net amount available to the mortgagor and contains an acknowledgment by him that he has received that amount. The statement should be dated and signed by both mortgagor and mortgagee when the loan is closed.

There are many miscellaneous items that are debited to buyer as a borrower on the mortgage. Where the lender is a bank or savings and loan each item is one called for by the mortgagee's printed application form, which becomes part of the loan contract with the borrower. Where the mortgage will be a purchase money mortgage, perhaps the simplest practice is to use a printed loan application used by a savings and loan and doctor it to indicate that a purchase money mortgage is intended. Otherwise a lengthy rider will be needed on the sale contract. Of course, the borrower should always sign an acceptance of the application terms, which, of course, is an acceptance of the fees and deductions listed in the application. Among the items debited to the buyer as a borrower are the following:

1. Lenders usually require that borrowers pay at settlement the interest that accrues on the buyer's mortgage from the date of settlement to the beginning of the period covered by the first monthly payment.

EXAMPLE: Suppose settlement takes place on April 16. The buyer's first regular monthly payment takes place on June 1. This is done because a payment made on May 1 would collect May's interest in advance. Collecting interest in advance should be avoided as much as possible. On the settlement date the lender will collect interest for the period from April 16 to May 1. Collection of this interest in advance is customary. The June 1 payment will pick up the interest that accrued in May.

2. The lender's title protection is charged to the borrower.

EXAMPLE: In title insurance territory, two polices are issued, one to the buyer (the *Owner's Policy*) and one to the lender (the *Mortgage Policy*). The fee for the mortgage policy is a debit against the borrower.

3. On some mortgage loans the mortgagee insists on *Private Mortgage Insurance*. This insures the lender against loss if a foreclosure becomes necessary. The premium is debited against the borrower.

4. Most homebuyers take out a new *Homeowners' Policy* to cover fire loss, liability coverage, etc. The first year's premium is usually a debit against the borrower. The policy is held by the lender. It contains a clause making loss payable to the lender. See Ch. 12.

5. Some lenders insist that the monthly payment include one-twelfth of the estimated real estate taxes and hazard insurance premiums for the current year. These are called impounds. In these cases there is an initial payment called the *impound reserve* that is debited against the borrower.

6. There may be miscellaneous fees that are debits against the borrower.

EXAMPLE: Lender's attorney's fee, mortgage tax, fees for recording mortgage and accompanying documents, etc.

When mortgage money was readily available, these matters were routinely handled by skilled mortgage loan officers. Today, where the mortgage often runs to the seller, these matters are handled by the attorneys for the parties.

10.09(e) Zoning and building code violations   A check should be made for violations of local zoning and building ordinances which the mortgagee might be compelled to remedy at his own expense were he to acquire title by foreclosure.

10.09(f)   Insurance   Existing fire insurance policies should be checked to determine that the amounts thereof are adequate and that the policies are properly written with mortgage clause attached.

10.09(g)   Documents of the loan file   The mortgagee's loan file should include the following papers:

1. Application for the loan, signed by borrower, and copy of mortgagee's letter of commitment.

2. Plat of survey.

3. If the loan is made to finance the purchase of property, the mortgagee should have a copy of the contract of sale in his files. This will prove helpful in making an appraisal of property.

4. Appraisal.

5. Mortgage, mortgage note, chattel lien on personal property in building, and assignment of rents and leases.

6. Assignment of mortgage and waiver of defenses if loan was purchased from original lender.

7. Credit reports on the borrower.

8. Insurance policies, with mortgagee loss clauses attached.

9. Abstract and opinion, mortgage title policy, Torrens certificate, or other evidence of title.

10. Mortgagor's affidavit as to judgments, divorces, recent improvements, and other pertinent facts.

11. Copy of escrow agreement, if loan was closed in escrow.

12. Loan closing statement, including receipt for loan proceeds signed by borrowers.

13. If loan was a refinancing loan, the canceled mortgage and note that was taken up by the new loan.

14. If the loan is part of any federal program—i.e., VA guaranteed, FHA insured, or sold in the secondary market to FHLMC or some other similar purchaser—the special documents that make up such loan package and are required by those entities must be a part of the loan file. (*See,* e.g., The Mortgage Corporation, *Seller's Guide Conventional Mortgages* § 3.502.)

15. The requirements of any loan servicing contract relating to document retention must also be followed. Many of these servicing contracts require that the loan file be retained for a stated period after the loan is repaid.

16. Subordination of reverter if one was obtained. If any other prior mortgage or other lien was subordinated to the current mortgage, the subordination agreement, of course, should also be in the loan files.

17. Certified copy of corporate resolutions if mortgage was made by corporation. If property mortgage is all, or substantially all, of the assets of the corporation, resolutions by both directors and stockholders may be necessary.

18. Will, trust indenture, or other trust instrument, or copy of these, if mortgagor is a trustee.

19. Full copy of building restrictions affecting the mortgaged premises, particularly if loan is a construction loan.

20. Leases to key tenants and assignments thereof to mortgagee.

21. Necessary statements, waivers, and so forth necessary to document compliance with federal and state disclosure laws, the Real Estate Settlement Procedures Act (12 USCA § 2601 *et seq.*) and similar local laws. A discussion of these disclosure laws may be found in Barron, *Federal Regulation of Real Estate*.

10.10   Nature of escrow

A deed is delivered *in escrow* when it is deposited with a third person with directions to deliver the deed to the grantee only upon the performance of some condition set forth in the escrow instructions but not in the deed. The third person, to whom the deed is delivered, is called the *escrow holder, escrow agent,* or *escrowee.* The instructions defining the conditions to be performed prior to delivery of the deed to the grantee are called the *escrow agreement* or *escrow instructions.*

10.10(a)   Operation and purpose of escrows

A contract for the sale of land usually requires the seller to furnish an abstract or other evidence of title showing the condition of his title *on the date of the contract.* Suppose that on May 10, *R* agrees to sell certain land to *E* for $5,000. The contract is not recorded, and the seller remains in possession of the land. *R* orders an abstract or other evidence of title. This abstract is received by *R* on May 20. It does not, however, show the condition of the title on May 20, but on some earlier date, probably May 10. *E*'s lawyer completes his examination of the abstract on May 25 and finds title clear in *R* as of May 10. On May 26 *E* pays the money to *R,* and receives his deed. Then it develops that on May 11 the United States had filed an income tax lien of $1,000 against *R.* This is a lien on the land, like a mortgage. Other objections to the title, such as judgments, suits attacking title, or a mortgage, may also arise during this interval between the date of the contract and the recording of the deed. The seller may even die, leaving minor heirs, who obviously would be incapable of signing any deed.

In order to avoid these and other similar risks, sales may be closed in escrow as follows: Both the deed and the purchase price are delivered to some disinterested third party, often a title insurance company, with written instructions to record the deed, to order an examination of title, and, if the title shows clear *in the buyer,* to pay over the purchase price to the seller. The escrow agreement also provides that, if it shall appear that the seller's title is defective and the defects are not cured within a certain specified time, the buyer shall be entitled to the return of his money upon reconveying the title to the seller. In those cases where the seller has not recently had his title examined, the procedure is often divided into two steps. First, before the deed is recorded, the escrow holder is instructed to cause the seller's title to be examined down to the date of the contract. This first step may even be taken before the escrow agreement is signed. Then if title shows clear in the seller, the instructions provide that the deed be recorded and the examination of title brought down to cover the recording of the deed.

When the transaction follows the procedure above outlined, it is common for the grantee to deposit with the escrowee a quitclaim deed conveying the land back to the grantor. Then if the title proves defective, the quitclaim deed can be recorded by the escrowee so that the records will once more show title in the grantor.

Suppose that the title search shows an incurable defect in the seller's title. The escrow directions provide that the quitclaim deed from the buyer to the seller be recorded. This revests title in the seller. The directions provide that the buyer's money be returned.

Suppose that the difficulty consists of a large judgment against the buyer. Here the companion mortgage escrow cannot close because the mortgagee requires a mortgage on a clear title. Just as the buyer gave a reconveyance quitclaim deed, the mortgagee has deposited a release to be used to clear the title of the mortgage if the transaction has to be unwound. The recordation of the release, together with the quitclaim deed, returns the title to the status quo.

A question is always asked: How can the title company insure clear title in the seller after the transaction is unwound because of a judgment against the buyer which was shown by a title search after the deed to the buyer was recorded? The answer is that the buyer acquired only a conditional title. This title, by the very words of the escrow, will be defeated if the deal cannot close. Hence, when the buyer's title vanishes, the judgment lien against the buyer's interest vanishes.

The question is also asked: If the title shows clear in the buyer except for the seller's old mortgage, on what theory can the escrowee use the buyer's funds to pay the old mortgage? The answer is that as soon as the title shows clear in the buyer, subject only to the old mortgage, the seller's proceeds in the escrow belong to the seller. The escrow also contains an instruction to the escrowee to use enough of those proceeds to pay the old mortgage.

In counties where it is possible to examine titles very quickly, the procedure may follow these lines: The seller will have his title examined down to the date of the contract of sale. If title shows clear, the seller deposits his deed with a title company as escrowee. The escrowee orders a second examination of title to cover the period intervening between the date of the last examination and the close of recording hours on the day the deed is deposited. This examination can be made quickly, for it covers a period of only a few days. If title shows clear, the seller's deed is recorded the next morning the moment the recorder's office opens.

Under either system, the buyer's money is not paid to the seller until the buyer is assured of receiving clear title.

Escrow practices and the frequency of their use differ quite a bit from state to state. In many communities, escrows are virtually unknown. This is particularly true of small communities where seller and buyer know and trust each other. The danger here that the seller will make a deed or mortgage to some third person in order to get out of the deal is not so great as in large communities, where relationships are apt to be more impersonal. When a deal is closed without benefit of escrow, the buyer often requires the seller, at the time the deal is closed, to give an affidavit that he has not signed any deeds, mortgages, or contracts since the date of the contract of sale, and that since that date no judgments have been rendered against him.

Another benefit of the escrow is that if objections to the title that can be removed by use of the purchase money appear, such as judgments against the seller or unpaid taxes, the buyer may with absolute safety, after title is recorded in his name, allow the escrow holder to use part of the purchase money for the purpose of removing such objections. An escrow also protects the buyer against the seller's changing his mind and conveying the property to some third person in order to escape performance of the agreement. On the other hand, it assures the seller that the purchase price will be paid to him if the title is clear and enables a seller who has liens against his title to use the buyer's money to pay off such liens.

Escrows are also used in land assemblies. In this context, the seller who has given an option is required to put a deed in escrow to be given to the buyer upon the buyer's timely performance of the conditions of the option. Through this device the seller who learns that his deal is part of a large assembly is powerless to hold up the larger transaction having already given the deed to a neutral third party.

Even where a sale transaction is not closed in escrow, some of the closing proceeds are often put into an escrow to take care of some element of the seller's performance that remains incomplete, i.e., new construction that is not finished, damage to the property that occurred between the contract date and the closing date that is the seller's responsibility to repair.

10.10(b) Requirements of valid escrow

The following are the requirements for a valid escrow for the sale of land:

1. There must be a valid and enforceable contract for the sale of the land. *Johnson* v. *Wallden,* 173 NE 790 (Ill. 1930). The escrow agreement may in itself contain all the essential requirements of a contract of sale. *Wood Bldg. Corp.* v. *Griffitts,* 330 P2d 847 (Cal. 1958). The existence of a valid contract of sale, either in the escrow instructions or in a separate instrument, is, however, indispensable for a binding escrow. If this were not true, it would be possible to have what is in effect a contract for the sale of land without the written agreement that the law requires for land sales. *Campbell* v. *Thomas,* 42 Wis. 437.

EXAMPLE: Two landowners executed deeds to each other pursuant to an oral exchange agreement and delivered such deeds to an attorney with verbal directions to deliver each deed to the grantee named therein when each landowner had presented a receipt showing payment of back interest on existing mortgages. Before these receipts were delivered, one of the landowners demanded return of his deed. The court held that he was entitled to return of his deed. The contract of exchange was only oral and therefore unenforceable. *Jozefowicz* v. *Leickem,* 182 NW 729 (Wis. 1921).

2. The escrow agreement must contain a *condition,* something that must be done before the buyer's money is paid to the seller. The usual condition, of course, is the showing of clear title of record in the buyer, subject only to those objections listed in the contract of sale and escrow instructions.

3. The deed must be a good and valid deed.

4. The escrow holder must be some third person. Neither buyer nor seller may act as escrow holder.

10.10(c)   Contents of escrow agreement

The escrow agreement usually covers the following matters:

1. Names and signatures of buyer and seller and name of escrow holder.

2. Documents to be deposited by seller, such as deed, insurance policies, separate assignments of insurance policies, leases, assignments of leases, abstracts or other evidence of title, tax bills, canceled mortgage notes, notice to tenants to pay rent to buyer, and service contracts.

3. Deposits to be made by buyer, such as purchase price and purchase money mortgage, if any.

4. When deed is to be recorded, whether immediately, after buyer's check clears, or after seller furnishes evidence of good title at date of contract.

5. Objections to which buyer agrees to take subject.

6. Type of evidence of title to be furnished.

7. Time allowed seller to clear defects in title.

8. How and when purchase price is to be disbursed, with directions as to what items are to be prorated or apportioned if escrow holder is to do some prorating.

9. Directions to deliver deeds, leases, insurance policies, assignments of policy, and service contracts to buyer when title shows clear.

10. Return of deposits to the respective parties where title cannot be cleared.

11. Reconveyance by buyer to seller if deed to buyer has been recorded immediately on signing of escrow agreement and examination of title thereafter discloses seller's title was defective and cannot be cured.

12. Payment of escrow, title and recording charges, broker's commission, and attorney's fees.

While an escrow often takes the form of *instructions* by the buyer and seller to the escrowee, the legal fact remains that it is an agreement or contract, and is so referred to herein.

10.10(d)   Escrow is irrevocable

When a valid escrow agreement has been executed and the instruments provided for are delivered to the escrow holder, neither party can revoke the escrow and obtain return of his deposit. At times one party to a sale of land changes his mind and makes a demand on the escrowee for return of his deposit.

The escrowee is justified in refusing to comply with an unwarranted demand. If the situation is legally doubtful he may insist on a court adjudication of the rights of the parties. *Franks* v. *North Shore Farms, Inc.*, 253 NE2d 45 (Ill. 1969); *Cocke* v. *Transamerica Title Ins. Co.*, 494 P2d 756 (Ariz. 1972).

10.10(e)   Conflict between contract of sale and escrow agreement

Since the escrow is a means of carrying out the terms of the contract of sale, there should be no conflict between the two agreements. In the event of conflict, however, disposition of the deed and money deposited in escrow must be governed by the escrow instructions. *Widess* v. *Doane*, 112 Cal. App. 343, 296 Pac. 899 (1931).

10.10(f)   When title passes

Prior to the performance of the condition specified in the escrow, title to the land remains in the seller even though his deed to the buyer is recorded. Even an innocent purchaser or mortgagee from the grantee is not protected in such cases. *Osby* v. *Reynolds*, 103 NE 556 (Ill. 1913); *Clevenger* v. *Moore*, 259 Pac.219 (Okla. 1927).

> **EXAMPLE:**   An escrow agreement required the buyer to deposit the purchase price in escrow. Before this was done, the buyer persuaded the escrow holder to give him the deed, which the buyer thereupon recorded. He thereafter placed a mortgage on the property. When the seller discovered this mortgage, he filed suit, and the court canceled the mortgage as a cloud on his title, even though the mortgagee had acted in entire good faith. *Blakney* v. *Home Owners' Loan Corp.*, 135 P2d 339 (Okla. 1943).

However, if the grantor allows his deed to be recorded, an innocent purchaser from the grantee will usually be protected if the grantor has also allowed the grantee to take possession of the land, for in such case *both the records and the possession show the grantee as the apparent owner,* and an innocent purchaser from such grantee should be protected, for there is nothing to apprise him of the grantor's rights. *Mays* v. *Shields*, 45 SE 68 (Ga. 1903).

Immediately upon the performance of the conditions specified in the escrow agreement, ownership of the land passes to the buyer and ownership of the purchase price passes to the seller. Thereupon the escrow holder becomes the agent of the buyer as to the deed and of the seller as to the money. *Shreeves* v. *Pearson*, 230 Pac. 448 (Cal. 1924). Since at that moment the escrow holder holds the deed for the grantee, this is as though the grantee himself held the deed. Thus delivery of the deed has been completed, and actual manual delivery of the deed by the escrow holder to the grantee adds nothing to the grantee's title. *Shirley* v. *Ayers*, 14 Ohio 307. However, it is the practice to provide for a delivery of the deed by the escrow holder to the grantee. This is the so-called *second delivery.* Since ownership of the land remains in the seller until the conditions specified in the escrow instructions have been met and performed, then, even though a deed from seller to buyer has been recorded, the seller remains in possession, collects the rents, and pays taxes, until the escrow conditions have been performed.

Likewise if the building is destroyed or damaged by fire or other calamity before the terms of the escrow have been met and performed, the risk of loss falls on the seller, for he is still the owner of the land. The seller's insurance company is liable to him even though he has signed a deed to the buyer because the deed has not as yet taken effect. However, escrow companies carry blanket insurance to cover the situation where the seller's insurance company denies liability.

10.10(g)   Relation back   Where the grantor delivers a deed in escrow, then dies, and thereafter the condition of the escrow is performed, the deed is considered as passing title as of the date of the delivery of the deed to the escrow holder. It is said that the title *relates back* to such time.

> **EXAMPLE:** *R* enters into a written contract to sell land to *E*. *R* signs a deed to *E* and delivers this deed to *X* as escrowee. *E* also deposits the purchase price with *X*. *X* records the deed under escrow instructions, which provide that the purchase price is to be paid to *R* when an examination of title shows the title clear of all objections. Before the examination is completed, *R* dies, leaving minor children as his heirs. Thereafter the title examination is completed and shows clear title in *E*. The deed is good, since the transfer of title to *E* relates back to the time when *R* was alive.

The same is true when the seller marries or becomes insane after delivering a deed in escrow.

If the *grantee* dies after the deed has been delivered in escrow, and the condition of the escrow is thereafter performed, the deed will be treated as relating back to the delivery in escrow and may be delivered to the grantee's heirs. *Prewitt* v. *Ashford,* 7 So 831 (Ala. 1890).

The rule that title relates back to the time of the original delivery of the deed to the escrowee is confined to the examples given above. In other situations, *transfer of ownership of the land takes place as of the time when the terms and conditions of the escrow are performed,* illustrated by the defalcation cases. For example, if the escrowee absconds with the buyer's purchase money before the terms and conditions of the escrow have been performed, the loss must fall on the buyer, because *at the time of the defalcation the purchase money still belongs to the buyer. Hildebrand* v. *Beck,* 236 Pac. 301 (Cal. 1925); 39 ALR 1080. On the other hand, if the terms of the escrow have been performed and thereafter the escrowee absconds with the money, the loss falls on the seller, because *after the escrow terms have been met and performed, the money on deposit belongs to the seller. Lechner* v. *Halling,* 216 P2d 179 (Wash. 1950); *Lawyers Title Ins. Co.* v. *Edmar Const. Co.,* 294 A2d 865 (D.C. 1972).

Thus, if a lender is a party to an escrow and the escrowee embezzles the mortgage money before the title has been cleared as required by the escrow instructions, the mortgage funds still belong to the mortgagee, and therefore he must suffer the loss of his funds and cannot collect from the mortgagor even though he holds the mortgagor's promissory note. *Ward Cooke, Inc.* v. *Davenport,* 413 P2d 387 (Oreg. 1966).

10.10(h) Mortgages

Since a mortgage does not become a lien until a debt which the mortgage secures exists, mere recording of a mortgage does not create a lien. Liens attaching to the land *prior to the time that the mortgage money is disbursed to the mortgagor may obtain priority of lien* over the mortgage. But if the mortgagee deposits his mortgage money in escrow, with directions to pay the money over to the mortgagor if an examination of title shows the mortgage as a first lien on the date of its recording, then immediately upon the recording of the mortgage its position as a first lien is established. Payment into escrow is treated as payment by the mortgagee to or for the benefit of the mortgagor. Thus there are mortgage escrows as well as sale escrows.

Again, there are cases where a buyer is borrowing money to complete his purchase. The mortgagee does not want his money paid out until title shows clear in the buyer, who is the mortgagor. The seller will not want to give a deed until and unless he is assured of receiving the purchase price. This difficult situation is easily taken care of through an escrow. The deed, mortgage and mortgage money are deposited with an escrowee under written instructions to record the deed and mortgage and pay the mortgage money to the seller if the title examination shows the mortgage as a first lien. The interests of all parties are protected.

EXAMPLE: The contention has been advanced by the creditors of the mortgagor that they can garnishee such funds. The courts have rejected this contention. Kratovil & Werner *Modern Mortgage Law and Practice,* § 25.34 (2d ed. 1981). The same result occurs where creditors attempt to garnishee construction money held by the mortgagee. The funds cannot be garnisheed.

10.10(i) Long-term escrows

In the West and Southwest, the long-term escrow is used in the financing of real estate. This operates somewhat as follows: *A,* a land owner, enters into a contract to sell the land to *B. B* is unable to pay the full price at once. *A* desires to retain control of the land so as to insure the payment of the price in full or the restoration of the land to him. *A* therefore executes a deed of the land to *B* and places the deed in the hands of *C,* as escrowee, to be delivered to *B* on full payment of the price by *B* to *C.* If *B* makes timely payment of the price to *C,* the latter will hand the deed to *B. C* will also pay the money to *A.* If *B* fails to make such payment, *C* will be under a duty to return the deed to *A.* Bogert,

Trusts and Escrows in Credit Conveyancing, 21 *Ill. L. Rev.* 655 (1927). The disadvantages of this arrangement are as follows:

1. Until completion of the payments, the public records show title in *A,* and this gives *A* the opportunity to defraud *B* by making a deed or mortgage to some third person who is unaware of the contract's existence. *Waldock* v. *Frisco Lumber Co.,* 176 Pac. 218 (Okla. 1918). This would not be true if the contract were recorded or if the buyer went into possession of the land.

2. The depositary may deliver the deed to the buyer notwithstanding the fact that he has not completed his payments, and recording of this deed will cloud the seller's title.

3. Default on the buyer's part after he has made substantial payments may result in a lawsuit against the depositary. *Phoenix Title & Trust Co.* v. *Horwath,* 19 P2d 82 (Ariz. 1933).

4. In some states a buyer in an escrow deal takes subject to judgments rendered against the seller while the deal is in escrow but before the purchase price is fully paid and the deed recorded. *May* v. *Emerson,* 96 Pac. 454 (Oreg. 1908); 117 ALR 69, 85–88. The danger from this risk is increased when the escrow extends over a long period of time. In addition to the danger of judgments, there is the danger that, while the escrow is running, federal income tax liens may be filed against the seller or the seller may go into bankruptcy. Kratovil and Werner, *Modern Mortgage Law and Practice* § 39.11 (2d ed. 1981).

The use of the long-term escrow is spreading to all parts of the country. To avoid becoming involved in forfeiture proceedings, the escrowee often insists that after a lapse of 6 days without any payments by the buyer, the escrowee may return the seller's deed to him. The seller then proceeds to declare the forfeiture.

10.11 Closer's liability

Whether the closing is conducted by an escrowee, lending institution, or lawyer, the closer may incur liability for improper or mistaken performance of its closing duties.

EXAMPLE: Where an escrowee breaches the escrow instructions, the escrowee will be liable for damages proximately caused by the breach.

EXAMPLE: Where a lender fails to obtain the proper insurance coverage for a buyer who has instructed the lender to obtain the insurance, the lender will be liable. *Parnell* v. *First Fed. Sav. & Loan Assn.,* 336 So2d 764 (Miss. 1976); *Taylor* v. *Colonial Sav. Assn.,* 533 SW2d 61 (Tex. 1976).

11 EVIDENCE OF TITLE: TITLE INSURANCE: ABSTRACTS

11.01 Historical background

It is obvious that a purchaser of land cannot merely rely upon the fact that he receives a warranty deed as conclusive evidence that he is receiving good title. For example, anyone could give a deed to the Merchandise Mart in Chicago. That deed would give no title whatsoever. It would merely give the grantee the right to sue the grantor, a right that may be quite empty.

So there has arisen the practice of furnishing evidence of title to the buyer. The form of this evidence of title is agreed upon in the contract of sale. Since the nature of title evidence varies from area to area, it may be necessary for the buyer and seller to conform their needs to the customs of the area where the land lies. Generally speaking, in large-scale transactions, the mortgage lender dictates the nature of the evidence of title because it has the largest stake in the transaction. Often, the lender requires title insurance.

In all events, the history of the development of title evidence is interesting and useful. In the early days of this country, the nation was predominantly agricultural. Transfers of ownership were infrequent. Indeed, farmers tended to hold the land in the family, passing it from generation to generation. Hence the land record books in the county courthouse were not numerous, and it was easy for a lawyer to go to them to examine the title to a particular tract of land.

Also, going back to the old days, when villages were relatively small, business was done largely on a first-name basis. The lawyer for the buyer in a real estate transaction would go to the courthouse to examine the land records. He would have a friendly conversation with the recorder of deeds who was thoroughly familiar with everything that had happened in the courthouse in recent memory. The recorder could probably tell the lawyer what transactions there were relating to the land in question. The lawyer would then make a formal check of the land records. He would then go to the tax office and again have an informal talk with the tax collector followed by a quick search of the tax records. The lawyer would then return to his office and prepare an opinion of title which would reflect the result of his searches. The whole process was quite informal.

However, as time went on, other factors caused this friendly format to become more formalized. One of these factors was the opening of the Erie Canal in 1825. When that occurred, it became possible for ships to move from the Atlantic seaboard through the Great Lakes to Chicago. It was also no longer necessary for people traveling westward to use the ancient Indian trail roads that were at times impassable. This in turn created a flow of commerce that sharply increased land values and a good deal of land speculation resulted. As a result, land transactions became numerous and the land record books in the courthouse multiplied. The number of recordings increased again when railroads began to enter the picture. The speculation became feverish. It was no longer easy for a lawyer to check the growing number of land records. It was no coincidence that abstract offices began to open at this time.

As recorders would leave their elected office, they would often open an abstract office near the courthouse. A courthouse man would be hired to make trips to the recorder's office to note all documents filed in the public record on a particular day. He would also check the tax records to determine what tax sales or payments were made. He would then return to the nearby abstract office and enter those transactions in the abstract company's books. These entries were made in a far more convenient form than existed in the courthouse. For example, suppose that we are involved in a sale of Lot 1 in Block 1 in Sheffield's Addition to Chicago. The abstractor would open a page in his book with that particular description at the top of the page, and every transaction involving that particular lot would be entered in chronological order on that page. This was done in anticipation of future title examination orders that might be placed with this abstractor.

When the lot was being sold, the contract of sale would call for the seller to furnish the buyer an abstract of title. At that time, the abstractor would look at his books and make a list of all the transactions appearing on that particular page. This list is sometimes referred to as a "chain." The chain would be taken to the courthouse and very brief copies of each instrument appearing in the chain would be made. The abstractor would then prepare a brief history of the title beginning with the first grant from the United States. Each transaction would appear in chronological order but in a highly abbreviated form. Today, many abstractors prepare their abstracts by photocopying each document in the chain of title. This is the *abstract* that is referred to in this chapter. The abstract would be handed to the buyer's attorney for examination and the preparation of an *opinion of title.* This was a very important step forward in the process of examining and evidencing title. The lawyer was liberated. He could examine the title to the property in the comfort and convenience of his office by merely using the abstract.

For many years the abstract system worked very well. Indeed, it is still used in the agricultural parts of the Midwest. However, from time to time, defects in the abstract system came to light.

> **EXAMPLE:** Owner is selling an apartment building that is encumbered with a $200,000 mortgage. Owner could, of course, clear the mortgage by paying it off. But, for a much lesser cost, Owner could merely forge the lender's execution of a mortgage release and record the document. While this apparently rids the record title of the mortgage, the release is really a nullity. Buyer would actually be acquiring the property subject to the $200,000 mortgage.

Many other such defects came to light. These are the "hidden risks" that are referred to in this chapter. Abstracts did not protect against these hidden risks.

Beginning around 1880, the abstractors took on an additional chore. They would prepare their abstract as usual. An in-house attorney would examine the abstract and render his title opinion. Then the abstractor would issue an insurance policy insuring the purchaser of the property that he was acquiring good title to the property. In this fashion, the insurer took the risk of forgeries, misrepresentation of marital status, and so on, the so-called hidden risks.

We can see that the actual events that took place in this country changed the character of the evidence of title that was used in this country. In the beginning, the attorneys went to the courthouse and searched the title. This practice is still followed to a considerable degree along the Atlantic seaboard. Then as land transactions multiplied and land records grew too numerous, the abstract of title came into use because lawyers were unwilling to spend the time in the courthouse to examine the records. Then, as the defects in the abstract system became evident, the abstractor moved into the title insurance business.

In the early days of title insurance, the abstractor was unwilling to inspect the property. Nonetheless, there are certain defects in title that do not appear on the public records, but appear only from an examination of the property itself. For example, if the property is occupied by a purchaser under an unrecorded contract, the contract will be valid and binding on any other purchasers because possession imparts constructive notice of the possessor's rights. See § 7.05(a). Also, if there is an unrecorded easement crossing the property, it will be valid and binding against a purchaser. Also, if there are any encroachments, such as the encroachment of my building onto the adjoining property, the encroachment will not appear from the public records, but may be revealed only by a survey. Because of this, the title insurance policies set up certain exclusions for those facts that could be found only upon an examination of the property, such as the unrecorded rights of parties in possession. The title insurer refused to insure against title defects that could not be seen from a review of the public records because the title insurer did not visit the premises to look for such defects.

However, as time went on, purchasers of title policies came to demand more protection. As a result, the title insurance companies, which had replaced the abstractor–insurer, began to inspect the property to determine if the exceptions relating to parties in possession, encroachments, unrecorded easements, and mechanic's liens could be removed.

As the title insurance companies began this practice, they also discovered the need for other special coverage. For example, if a building violates a building restriction, a special endorsement could be given insuring the purchaser against loss arising by reason of this violation. Many such situations developed, and the title companies proceeded to develop numerous special coverage endorsements. Taking for example a recent development, title companies are willing to insure that a condominium unit conforms to the state statute relating to the creation of condominiums.

Finally, title insurers formed the American Land Title Association (ALTA), a national trade association, and a degree of uniformity in title policies and endorsements made its appearance.

11.02   Abstract

As discussed, an abstract is a history of the title to a particular tract of land. It consists of a summary of the material parts of every recorded instrument affecting the title. It begins with a description of the land covered by the abstract, which description is called the *caption,* or *head,* of the abstract, and then proceeds to show, usually in chronological order, the original government grant and all subsequent deeds, mortgages, release deeds, wills, judgments, mechanics' liens, foreclosure proceedings, tax sales, and other matters affecting the title.

Of course all these items are shown in a highly abbreviated form. In fact, usually a bare outline of the deed, mortgage, or other instrument is shown. "Fine print" provisions are omitted altogether or summarized in a few words. The manner in which the instrument was signed is now shown unless there is some irregularity in this respect. If the acknowledgment is in due form, the abstractor merely indicates that the instrument was acknowledged. A purchaser or mortgagee may rely on the abstractor to draw attention to these irregularities, since where an abstract purports to state the substance of a deed, mortgage, or other instrument, and there is nothing on the face of the abstract to indicate an error, the customer is justified in assuming that no irregularity exists in those portions of the document that the abstractor has omitted from his abstract. *Equitable B. & L. Assn.* v. *Bank of Commerce & Trust Co.,* 102 SW 901 (Tenn. 1907).

The abstract concludes with the *abstractor's certificate.* This discloses what records the abstractor has examined and, what is more important, what records he has *not examined.* For example, some abstractors will not examine records located outside of the county seat, and their certificates reflect that fact. In such case, it is necessary to supplement the abstract by obtaining the necessary searches. If an abstractor certifies that he has made no search of federal court proceedings affecting the property, it will be necessary to write to the clerk of the district court, who will supply the search for a small charge. The certificate also shows the date covered by the abstractor's search of the records. Because of the unavoidable delay intervening between the filing in the recorder's office of a particular day's deeds and mortgages and the entry of the same on the abstractor's books, the abstractor is not in a position to certify on any particular day as to the status of the record title on that day. His certificate will certify today as to the status of the record title on some previous day.

11.02(a) The abstractor

Abstracts are prepared by public officials, lawyers, and abstract companies. In some states, an abstractor is required to post a bond to protect all those who rely on his abstracts against any loss resulting from a lack of care or skill on his part. Many abstractors keep their own books. They take great pride in their "abstract plant," and, in many communities, the abstractor's records are more accurate than the public records. Other abstractors prepare their abstracts from the public records.

Since abstracting is a profession requiring much legal knowledge and careful research, a prudent purchaser or mortgagee will rely only on abstracts furnished by abstractors possessing the requisite skill, care, and experience. The financial responsibility of the abstractor and the existence and limits of his *errors and omissions insurance* are likewise important, since if an error is made in preparing the abstract of the title to a valuable tract of land, there should be no doubt as to the ability of the abstractor to respond in damages.

11.02(a)(1) Abstractor's liability

The abstractor is in no sense a guarantor of title. He merely undertakes to exercise due care in the preparation of his abstract. He renders no opinion as to the title. If he includes in his abstract all recorded instruments affecting the title, and, as a consequence, the abstract discloses a fatally defective title, the abstractor has fully discharged his responsibilities. But, if an intending purchaser orders an abstract prepared and the abstractor negligently omits therefrom a mortgage, judgment, or other lien that the purchaser is thereafter compelled to pay, the purchaser can obtain reimbursement from the abstractor. 28 ALR2d 891. The abstractor's liability may also extend to third persons not parties to the contract for abstracting services. 34 ALR3d 1122.

> **EXAMPLE:** Purchasers relied upon an abstract prepared for sellers by abstract company. The court held that the purchasers could recover even though the abstract was prepared before the contract of purchase. *Williams* v. *Polgar,* 204 NW2d 57 (Mich. 1972).

To be safe, it is best for anyone who relies upon the abstract to have it certified to that person, and to the purchaser's mortgagee.

11.03 Examination of title

The mere fact that a purchaser or mortgagee has received an abstract of title affords him no protection. In fact, examination of the abstract may disclose that the title is hopelessly clouded. Hence, after an abstract has been prepared by a reliable abstractor and certified so that the buyer or mortgagee can rely thereon, it should be delivered to a competent attorney for examination. This attorney will thereupon examine the abstract and prepare his *opinion* as to the title, which will show the name of the titleholder and all defects and encumbrances disclosed by the abstract.

11.04   Certificate of title

In some localities the making of an abstract is dispensed with. The attorney merely examines the public records and issues his certificate, which is his opinion of title based on the public records that he has examined. Like an abstractor, such an attorney is liable only for damages occasioned by his negligence. 59 ALR3d 1176. The same is true when a certificate of title is issued by a title company. *Lattin* v. *Gillette*, 30 P 545 (Cal. 1892); *Bridgeport Airport Inc.* v. *Title Guaranty & Trust Co.*, 150 A 509 (Conn. 1930).

11.05   Risks involved in relying on record title

There are certain defects in title that even a perfect abstract or certificate of title will not disclose because these hidden defects or hidden risks cannot be discovered by an examination of the public records. These hidden risks include:

1. *Forgery.* A deed in the chain of title may seem entirely regular but may nevertheless be a forgery. Such a deed is totally void and a purchaser or mortgagee of such title is not protected. Likewise, a forged release of mortgage does not discharge the mortgage lien.

EXAMPLE: Suppose that you own some land and someone forges your signature on a deed purporting to deed the land to him or even to some innocent person to whom the forger represents that he is the real owner. Obviously, you would expect the law to protect you, even as against an innocent purchaser. It does. Or suppose that you owned a mortgage of $100,000 on an apartment building, and the apartment owner signed your name to a release purporting to discharge this mortgage. Even if the land were sold to an innocent purchaser, you would expect the law to permit you to foreclose your mortgage. It does.

2. *Insanity and minority.* A deed or release of mortgage executed by a minor or insane person may be subject to cancellation by subsequent court proceedings.
3. *Marital status incorrectly given.* A deed or mortgage may recite that the grantor or mortgagor is single, whereas in fact he may be married. This may later result in a dower or other claim by his spouse.

EXAMPLE: *H* owns an apartment building and is married to *W,* but is separated from her. *H* has an opportunity to sell the building to you at a good price, and does so. *H* signs *W's* name to the deed. Her dower remains outstanding, and if *W* survives *H,* she will be able to force a sale of the building and her dower rights will be paid her out of the sale price.

4. *Defective deeds.* A recorded deed may never have been properly delivered. For example, it may have been found by the grantee among the grantor's effects after the grantor's death and then placed on record. Such deeds, of course, pass no title.

EXAMPLE: *A* owns an apartment building. He is a bachelor. He shares a safe-deposit box with his nephew, *X*. *A* dies. *X* opens the box and finds a deed from *A* to *X* to the apartment building, with a note pinned to it, stating that *A* wants *X* to have the building. *X* records the deed. The deed is void. The mere fact that the deed was recorded after *A*'s death discloses that there is something wrong with the deed.

There are many other defects in title that the public records do not disclose.

There are also certain other risks not of a legal character that are encountered when a deal is closed in reliance on a certificate of title or abstract and opinion. One of these risks is the risk of unwarranted litigation attacking the title. A landowner's title may be good as a matter of law, but if some other person entertains the notion that he has some title to, or interest in, the land, he may institute litigation asserting his supposed rights, and such litigation, even though successfully defended, may prove costly. Again, a competent attorney examining an abstract for a purchaser may reach an entirely correct opinion that the title is good. But when the purchaser, in turn, is selling or mortgaging the land, the attorney for the subsequent buyer or mortgagee may arrive at a different conclusion. This may necessitate the institution of litigation to clear the title. It is this fear of objections to the title by some subsequent examiner that prompts attorneys to scrutinize abstracts closely and raise every technical objection apparent therefrom. This practice is known as *fly-specking.*

11.06   Title insurance

It is the function of title insurance to shift or transfer to a responsible insurer risks such as those mentioned in the preceding section. Title insurance is a contract to make good a loss arising through defects in title to real estate or liens or encumbrances thereon. *Beaullieu* v. *Atlanta Title & Trust Co.,* 4 SE2d 78 (Ga. 1939). As a rule, a title company will not insure a bad title any more than a fire insurance company would issue a policy on a burning building. However, title companies disregard many of the technical objections that would be raised by an attorney examining an abstract. If an examination of the title discloses that good title is vested in a particular person, the company will issue its policy whereby it agrees, subject to the terms of its policy, to indemnify such person against any loss he may sustain by reason of any defects in title not enumerated in the policy and to defend at its own expense any lawsuit attacking the title where such lawsuit is based on a defect in title against which the policy insured.

11.06(a)   The title insurance policy

Title companies issue both *owner's policies* and *mortgage policies,* the latter being known also as *loan policies.* The owner's policy is usually issued to the landowner himself. Mortgage policies, of course, are issued to mortgagees. Unlike other types of insurance policies, which insure for limited periods of time and are kept in force by periodic payment of renewal premiums, an owner's title insurance policy is bought and paid for only once, and then continues in force without any further payment until a sale of the property is made. At that time, the title is examined to cover the period of time since the issuance of the policy, and a new policy is issued to the purchaser. A charge is usually then made for the issuance of this new policy.

It may help you understand title insurance if you compare it with fire insurance.

> **EXAMPLE:** *X* buys a home and the deed to *X* is received on April 1, 1980. He receives a title insurance policy insuring his title as of April 1, 1980. On the same day he takes out a one-year fire insurance policy. The title insurance policy insures *X* against any defects in title not shown in the policy where such defects occurred *on or prior to April 1, 1980.* No annual premium need be paid. As to fire insurance, that policy insures against any fire damage *occurring after April 1, 1980.* Annual premiums must be paid to keep the policy in force.

The mortgage policy terminates when the mortgage debt is paid. However, if the mortgage is foreclosed, then the protection of the mortgage policy continues in force, protecting against any defects of title that existed on, or prior to, the date of the policy. In both policies, the company usually undertakes, subject to the terms of its policy, to defend at its own expense any lawsuit attacking the title where such lawsuit is based on a defect in title against which the policy insures. This is one of the attractive features of title insurance to property owners, since "nuisance" litigation affecting real estate is quite common and is expensive to defend, even though not well founded. A policy of title insurance usually shows the name of the party insured and the character of his title, which is usually fee simple title, although title policies are also issued on other interests, such as leaseholds or easements. It also contains a description of the land and, if the policy is a mortgage policy, a description of the mortgage. The policy lists those matters which affect that particular tract of land, such as any mortgage, easement, lien, or restriction thereon. Like other insurance policies, it contains printed conditions and stipulations.

Common printed exceptions found in owner's policies relate to the rights of parties in possession and questions of survey. Often real property is in the possession of those whose rights are not disclosed by the records. Common instances are tenancies under oral or unrecorded leases and rights of those in possession under unrecorded contracts of purchase. When no survey has been furnished the company, it has no means of knowing what encroachments exist, if any. The policy will therefore be subject to encroachments and other matters that a survey would reveal, also the rights of persons in possession claiming under some unrecorded document.

11.06(b)   Title insurance— residential policy

In 1980, a new residential form of owner's title insurance was introduced. This policy, issued only to consumers for residential transactions, is a dramatic innovation for two reasons. First, it is written in "plain language" in response to laws in some states that require insurance policies to be written in clear and understandable language. Second, the new policy offers expanded coverage to the homebuyer. This additional coverage includes:

> 1. Protection against unrecorded matters such as survey problems, unrecorded easements, and unrecorded mechanic's liens.
> 2. As a protection against the effects of inflation, the policy amount will automatically increase by 10 percent per year for the first five years of coverage.
> 3. Insurance for actual loss incurred as a result of the forced removal of the existing structure because it extends onto adjoining land or onto any easement or because it violates a restriction shown in the policy or because it violates the zoning law.
> 4. Insurance against actual loss incurred if the insured cannot use the land for a single-family residence because such a use violates a restriction shown in the policy or an existing zoning law.
> 5. In the event that the insured cannot use any of the land because of a claim against the title, the insurer will repay the insured for rent paid until the cause of the claim is removed.

11.06(c)   Title insurance— endorsements

Where the evidence of title reveals defects not permitted by the sale contract (or permitted by the contract only where title insurance thereover is available), the parties may choose to avail themselves of title insurance coverage afforded against the potential loss or damage which could be incurred by the existence of such defects. Also, the insured may desire greater coverage than that given by the standard form of policy. Title companies offer such endorsements to cover encroachments, restrictions, foundations, zoning, and the like.

11.06(d)   Title insurance— leasehold policies

Suppose a tenant is about to take a lease on a store, theater, restaurant, or other commercial location in which he plans to make a substantial investment for remodeling. Just as a buyer of land needs to know that his seller has a good, clear title, this tenant needs to know that his landlord has a good, clear title to the leased premises and that the tenant will not be dispossessed in the middle of his lease by foreclosure of mortgages or other liens on the landlord's title. Contracts for such leases are drawn along the lines of a contract for the sale of land. They require the landlord to have his title examined and to furnish the tenant a *leasehold policy* issued by a title company insuring the validity of the tenant's lease free from mortgages or other encumbrances. Also, when the leasehold is the security for a mortgage, the lender will require a leasehold loan policy.

In 1975, ALTA promulgated standard forms of leasehold owners and loan policies. Prior to that time various title companies insured leaseholds by "doctoring up" regular owner's and loan policies. The new policies define the insured leasehold estate to include the right of possession for the term of the lease subject to the conditions of the lease. The policies also describe a method of evaluating the leasehold estate and lists the items of incidental damage which will be paid if the insured is forced to surrender occupancy of the premises due to matters insured against.

11.06(e)   Title insurance–easement policies

Suppose you are selling me a tract of industrial property that has access to a railroad by means of an easement for a spur track over adjoining land. The validity of the easement is just as important to me as the fact that you have good title to the land I am buying. I will therefore insist that the policy you furnish me insures the validity of the easement.

11.06(f)   Title commitments

Suppose that *A* had purchased some land in 1940 and had recieved a title policy at that time. He is now selling this same land to *B*. Naturally, *B* would not want to rely on such an outdated document. Therefore, the contract of sale will call upon *A* to have the title company bring its title search down to the present date, which they will do. The title company will issue a *commitment* obligating the company to issue its policy to *B* subject only to the matters shown in the commitment. If any defects appear on the commitment that the seller must clear up—unpaid back taxes, for example—the seller pays off the item, receives paid tax bills or other documents, and exhibits them to the title company, which thereupon stamps the item "waived." When the title is clear, the land is conveyed by the seller to the buyer, the deed recorded, and a title policy issued in the name of the buyer.

11.07   The Torrens system

In a few counties in the United States, there is, in addition to the system of transferring title under the Recording Acts, a system known as the *Torrens system*. Under the Recording Acts, when a deed is made conveying land, the grantee in the deed usually takes it to the recorder's office and leaves it there for recording. The recorder makes a copy of the deed, places this copy in record books, which are available to the public, and returns the original deed to the grantee. The recorder does not pass upon the validity of the deed. If the grantee wishes to satisfy himself that he has received a good title, he may obtain title insurance, an abstract and opinion of title, or a title certificate.

The Torrens system operates quite differently. A landowner who wishes to register his land under the Torrens system first obtains a complete abstract of title to the land. He then files in the proper public office an application for the registration of title. This application lists the names of all persons who appear to have any interest in the land. These names are obtained from the abstract and from an investigation of the possession of the premises. The application constitutes the filing of a lawsuit against all persons named therein, and any person wishing to contest the applicant's claim of title may do so on receiving notice of the filing of the application. If the applicant is successful in proving that he is the owner of the land, the court enters an order so finding and also stating the mortgages, liens, restrictions, and so on to which said title is subject. The court also orders an official known as the *Registrar of Titles* to *register* such title. The registrar then makes out a *certificate of title,* showing the title as found by the court. These certificates are bound up in books and are public records. At the same time that the registrar makes out the original certificate, he makes out a *duplicate certificate of title,* which he delivers to the owner.

When a tract of land has been registered under the Torrens system, no subsequent transaction binds the land until such transaction has also been registered. When the land is sold, the deed itself does not pass ownership of the land. The deed must be taken to the registrar's office, and if the registrar is satisfied that the deed is valid, he cancels the old certificate of title and issues a new one to the grantee. It is this *registration* that puts ownership in the grantee. The deed is not returned to the grantee but remains in the registrar's office. In other words, the registrar of titles, unlike the recorder of deeds, investigates to determine the validity of the transfer, and only after he is satisfied that the transfer of title is valid will he issue a new certificate in the grantee's name. Thus, as to Torrens land it is said that "title passes by registration, not by deed." Likewise, a mortgage is not effective against the property until the registrar has checked it as to form and signature and entered it on the certificate of title. However, the registrar does not check on or guarantee the essential validity of the mortgage, for example, to see whether or not the mortgage money has been paid out or whether the interest is usurious. No judgment or other lien is valid against Torrens property until a copy has been filed in the registrar's office and the lien noted on the certificate of title.

Use of the Torrens system is largely confined to a few metropolitan areas, Boston, Chicago, Duluth, Minneapolis–St. Paul, and New York City.

In Chicago, the Torrens system has worked so poorly that the Illinois legislature now permits no new Torrens filings and has recently enacted legislation allowing owners of Torrens property to withdraw from the system.

The Torrens certificate purports to be conclusive proof that the title is as therein stated. As in the case of other evidences of title, there are exceptions and objections that the Torrens certificate does not cover. These vary somewhat from state to state. Unlike a policy of title insurance, the Torrens certificate does not require the registrar to assume the defense of litigation attacking the title of the registered owner. The property owner must defend the litigation at his own expense, and if he is successful, he cannot obtain reimbursements from the registrar for the expenses of the litigation.

12 INSURANCE

12.01 In general   In the past, insurance was purchased in pieces. A fire policy with extended coverage was bought from one carrier, a liability policy from another, and so on. Today, coverage on homes is offered in a package best exemplified by the homeowners' policy. Nonetheless, a historical perspective is in order.

12.02 Development of standard fire policy   The need for fire insurance first became apparent after the Great Fire of London in 1666. However, the policies that came into use in England following that catastrophe contained numerous and varied fine-print exceptions that led to much litigation and disappointment on the part of the policyholders. These conditions also prevailed in America, and, in 1873, agitation for a standard policy led to the adoption of a standard policy form in Massachusetts. In 1886, New York adopted a standard policy form, which was revised by a law effective in 1918. This policy still strongly favored the insurer, and in 1943, New York adopted a revised form more favorable to the insured. This form has been widely adopted in this country, and the discussion in this chapter is largely keyed to this form of policy.

12.03 Hazards covered— fire loss   The policy covers direct loss and damage *caused by fire*. Loss and damage caused by hazards *other than fire* must be covered by riders attached to the policy, or by separate insurance. Among the hazards *not* covered by the fire policy are:

> 1. Explosion damage. If an explosion not caused by fire occurs on the premises and no fire results, none of the damage is covered. If a fire starts *first* and the fire causes an explosion, all loss is covered whether due to fire or explosion, for the fire is the cause of

212

the loss. 82 ALR2d 1128. If an explosion occurs first and fire results, the policy covers the damage caused by the fire but not the damage caused by the explosion.

2. Water damage not resulting from a fire, as damage from water seepage in a basement or from a leaking sprinkler system.

3. Windstorm damage. As in the case of explosions, if a fire results from windstorm damage, the fire loss is covered by the policy.

4. Loss from hail, riot, civil commotion, aircraft, and many other hazards.

Breakage, water damage, and damage from chemicals caused through efforts to extinguish the fire are considered to be caused by fire and are therefore covered by the policy.

12.03(a) Extended coverage endorsement

A rider attached to the fire policy on payment of an extra premium is known as an *extended coverage endorsement.* Its content varies according to locality, but it often covers loss from windstorm, hail, explosion, riot, civil commotion, aircraft, vehicles, and smoke from friendly fires, except those in fireplaces. The windstorm damage coverage of the extended coverage endorsement does not cover rain, snow, or other water damage as such, except where caused by or resulting from windstorm or another peril specified in the extended coverage endorsement.

EXAMPLE: In a heavy rain, the sewer backs up and floods the basement of your house. The damage is not covered by the extended coverage endorsement.

EXAMPLE: A tornado tears off a roof and the debris breaks water pipes. The water rushes out of the pipes, causing damage. All the damage is covered by the insurance, for the basic cause of the entire loss is the windstorm.

EXAMPLE: A hailstorm breaks windows, and the rain and wind sweep in, causing damage. All the damage is covered, because the original cause is a hailstorm, which is a peril specified in the extended coverage endorsement.

Damage caused by explosion of a steam boiler on the premises is not covered. Damage caused by vehicles driven *by the landowner* is not covered, but if, for example, a delivery truck entering a side drive runs into the house this damage is covered.

12.03(b) Hazards covered—homeowners policies

For many years after the adoption of the New York 1943 form, the traditional fire insurance policy was offered as a basic form of coverage, which together with a rider or endorsement covered loss by windstorm and other perils. In recent times, however, this policy has been largely replaced in home insurance by the package of coverage offered in the homeowners policy. The current forms of homeowners policies do away with fine print, long sentences, and lawyers' language opting for a booklet type of presentation with readable type, simple sentences, and the absence of hypertechnical language.

There are two basic types of homeowners policies. One is the old-fashioned *"named peril"* policy. This form lists the risks or perils insured against. There are presently two forms of this policy, the HO-1 and the HO-2. The HO-1 covers losses caused by the following perils:

Fire or lightning
Windstorm or hail
Explosion
Riot or civil commotion
Vehicles
Smoke
Vandalism and malicious mischief
Theft
Breakage of glass

The HO-2 form expands the coverage of the HO-1 form and also insures against losses caused by:

Falling objects
Weight of ice, snow, or sleet
Collapse of a building or any part of a building (71 ALR3d 1072)
Accidental discharge or overflow of water or steam
Sudden and accidental tearing apart or bulging of a heating, air conditioning, or hot water system
Freezing of plumbing, heating, air conditioning system, or household appliance
Sudden and accidental damage from artifically generated electrical current

The HO-3 is an "all-risk" policy. In this format, instead of enumerating the perils insured against, it insures against all perils except those listed as uninsured risks. 88 ALR2d 112.

Because inflation has pushed sky-high the cost of replacing furniture and personal valuables, such as hi-fi equipment and cameras, renters tend to carry renters insurance, form HO-4. This covers loss or damage by fire and other hazards or theft and also liability for personal injuries sustained in the rented areas by third persons (guests, delivery men, etc.). Insurance is available to cover replacement cost. This is a recent development and should be checked with your agent. The older policies allow the company to deduct depreciation in value and can virtually render hazard insurance valueless.

> **EXAMPLE:** The depreciation tables makes a fifteen-year-old sofa virtually valueless although it may cost $500 to replace.

The HO-6 condominium owner's policy covers the condominium unit and personal property in the same basic fashion as the HO-2 coverage. All-risk coverage is also available for the condominium owner.

Consistent with the concept of providing homeowners with a package of insurance, the HO policies provide other coverages that are a natural part of a full package of protection for homeowners. These coverages include:

12.03(b)(1) Personal property coverage

This coverage extends to the homeowner's personal effects, i.e., furniture, stereo equipment, color TV, clothes, etc. The policy coverage on valuables such as jewelry, furs, silverware, etc. is very low. The insurance agent should be consulted for a special policy or floater covering valuables. Sophisticated homeowners have inventoried and photographed these items for use in claiming loss and to help the insurer recover the stolen articles. An appraisal is a requirement to recovery of insurance on valuables such as furs, jewelry, antiques, fine paintings, etc. An appraisal will also help the insured make his claim if the property is stolen.

Scheduling of personal property removes the restrictions caused by the formula coverage built into the policy for personal property. Typically, unscheduled personal property is covered to the extent of 50 percent of the coverage on the building. The face of the policy so states. Therefore a policy with $50,000 in coverage on the building would provide $25,000 of coverage for unscheduled personal property. Those formulas are inapplicable to scheduled personal property, which has its own value statement unrelated to the amount of coverage on the building.

12.03(b)(2) Liability coverage

In addition to providing coverage for the building and its contents, the homeowners' policies provide liability coverage for bodily injury and property damage to others arising out of the insured's negligence. This coverage applies to accidents occurring both on and off the insured premises and extends to damages caused by members of the insured's family who live with the insured and the insured's pets. Typically, the coverage is for a low amount. It can be increased by endorsement.

12.03(b)(3) Medical payments

The liability insurance protects the insured for damages which he causes to someone else. Medical payment coverage defrays the cost of injuries that occur through no one's fault, events that are purely accidental. This coverage, usually $5,000 per person and $25,000 per accident, is available for injuries occurring to anyone other than the insured and the insured's family.

The popularity of certain forms of coverage varies from region to region. For example, in the Midwest, earthquake coverage is cheap but practically never purchased. In California it is popular, and its price varies depending upon the type of structure and locale.

In making the decision as to which coverage is appropriate, it is good to note that the disparity in price between the premiums for the least comprehensive and most comprehensive homeowner's policies is relatively minor. The extra coverage is usually well worth the few extra dollars spent. Be watchful also to increase coverage as you increase value to your property. For example, if there is a room addition, the policy should be appropriately endorsed.

Some property is in slum or riot-prone areas where insurance is not ordinarily available. A federal program, the FAIR plan, exists to provide coverage for these properties. Insurance agents know all about it.

12.03(c) Hazards covered—hostile and friendly fires

The fire policy does not cover damage caused by smoke from a fire that is confined to the place where it is intended to be. Such a fire is called a *friendly fire.* Damage caused by smoke and soot issuing from a defective furnace is not covered. Damage caused by steam escaping from heat pipes is not fire damage, since the fire is a friendly one. But if the fire, though originally kindled in a stove, furnace, or fireplace, escapes, it becomes a hostile fire, and loss caused is covered by the policy. Nor is it ncessary that the hostile fire be on the premises covered by the policy.

> **EXAMPLE:** If my neighbor's house catches fire and the heat destroys the paint on the wall of my house, this is fire damage, covered by my policy, even though my building does not catch fire.

Damage from smoke or soot is covered if it is caused by a hostile fire.

12.03(d) Hazards covered—rent loss and business interruption

Since the policy covers fire damage to the *building,* it does not cover loss of rents when a rental building is rendered untenantable by fire, nor does it cover loss of *profits* when operation of a business is interrupted by fire. Both items can be covered by riders attached to the policy or by separate insurance such as rent insurance and business interruption insurance.

12.04 When protection attaches

It often takes some time for a formal policy of insurance to be prepared and forwarded to the insurer. Hence oral coverage is perfectly valid, pending the issuance of the policy. This gives the insured the coverage of the standard policy subject to its terms and conditions. *Bersani* v. *General Accident, Fire & Life Assur. Corp.,* 330 NE2d 68 (N.Y. 1975). Oral coverage is usually confirmed by letter.

12.05 Description of the property insured

The property insured should be accurately described in the policy, and all policies applying to the same property should contain identical descriptions.

The street address of the property is often used in insurance policies.

There has been a tendency in recent times, however, to insist on the insertion of a full legal description so that there will be no dispute as to the property covered. This is particularly true with respect to houses recently constructed which often do not have a street address at the same time the policy is written.

12.06   Insurable interest

The insured must have some insurable interest in the property. Otherwise the policy is void. Persons having an insurable interest include both buyer and seller in a contract for the sale of land, mortgagor, mortgagee, part owner, trustee, receiver, and life tenant.

12.07   Interest covered by policy

The present form of policy is an *interest policy*. It protects only the party insured and covers only the financial loss suffered by the insured, which can never be more than the value of his interest in the property and which may be less than the actual damage to the building.

> **EXAMPLE:** A bachelor buys a home and takes out a policy in his name. He then marries and has the home placed in joint tenancy. He now owns only a half interest in the home and could collect no more than half of any loss. Suppose further that a loss occurs after the husband's death. Here his entire interest in the property has passed to his wife, but she has no insurance whatever.

Insurance does not pass with the property. It insures the person, not the property.

Where land is owned by co-owners, insurance taken out by one of them, unless it is expressly written to insure all co-owners, does not benefit the other.

> **EXAMPLE:** *H* and *W*, husband and wife, owned their home in joint tenancy. They became estranged. *H* took out a policy in his name only for the full value of the property. Then he died. *W* has no right to collect on this insurance. *Russell* v. *Williams,* 374 P2d 827 (Cal. 1962).

The lesson is clear: Make sure that the property insurance tracks with the ownership of the property unless you are intending to insure only a partial interest.

Since insurance does not cover the building, but only the interest of the insured in the building, and persons other than the insured cannot collect on the policy, persons having liens on insured property are not covered by the insurance.

> **EXAMPLE:** A city has no right to have insurance money applied to payment of delinquent real estate taxes, which are a lien on the insured property. *Shelton* v.

Providence Washington Ins. Co., 131 SW2d 330 (Tex. 1939). Nor can a mechanic's lien claimant become entitled to fire insurance proceeds. 9 ALR2d 307.

Insurance taken out by a tenant does not benefit the landlord, nor does the landlord's insurance benefit the tenant. Insurance taken out by a builder does not benefit the landowner. *Russell* v. *Williams,* 374 P2d 827 (Cal. 1962).

12.08 Acts of the party insured

Naturally, where the party insured causes the loss, as when the building is set on fire to collect the insurance, the insurance company is not liable.

12.09 Unoccupancy clause

The policy provides that the insurer shall not be liable while the building is vacant or unoccupied beyond a period of thirty consecutive days. The words *vacant* and *unoccupied* are not synonymous. *Vacant* means without inanimate objects; *unoccupied* means without animate occupants. A dwelling is unoccupied when it has ceased to be a customary place of habitation or abode and no one is living in it. Thus, if furniture remains in the building, it is not vacant, but if the owner has left the dwelling with the intention of permanently residing elsewhere, the building is unoccupied, and the insurance may become void. *Vandalism coverage* usually ceases if the building is unoccupied for thirty days.

Because the danger of vandalism has greatly increased in recent times, insurance companies are enforcing this clause. This requires that the owner obtain an endorsement waiving the clause or provide an occupant if a lengthy absence is planned.

12.10 Increase of hazard

The policy provides that the company shall not be liable for any loss occurring while the hazard is increased by any means within the control or knowledge of the insured. The operation of this clause is restricted to physical changes in the building or in the use or occupancy of the premises. Any alteration or change in the building or in the use of the property that will increase the risk of loss violates this clause if it is of a more or less permanent nature. 28 ALR2d 762.

> **EXAMPLE:** The following operations increase the hazard and invalidate the insurance: (1) Tenant began operating a still. (2) Owner turned off a sprinkler system. (3) Owner brought fireworks on the premises. (4) Owner began use of a room as a tinshop.

But doing something that involves risk, that is a more or less normal and expected routine operation, is not considered an increase of hazard that invalidates the policy, for example, using a torch to burn off old paint preparatory to repainting. 28 ALR2d 771. Also, the increase of the hazard must contribute to or cause the loss. *Northern Assurance Co.* v. *Spencer,* 246 F.Supp. 730 (1965).

12.11 Double insurance   Unless a policy endorsement provides otherwise, the insured may procure additional insurance. However, the liability of each company is limited to the proportion of the loss that its insurance bears to the total insurance covering the property. Thus, if the same property is insured in two companies through two policies of $5,000 each, and if a loss of $2,000 occurs, the maximum liability of each company would be $1,000.

The insured should check to see that all portions of all policies covering the same property read exactly alike.

12.12 Amount recoverable   When insurance is bought, the insured is concerned with two things. First, what hazards or risks are covered? Second, what amount will the insurance company pay if a loss occurs? The premium is based upon many factors, but it is primarily determined by the combination of these factors. Obviously, it is the amount of coverage that sets the maximum limit on a claim.

Aside from the amount of coverage purchased, the amount that the insurance company will pay is determined by whether the policy calls for the loss to be measured by the *actual cash value method* or the *replacement cost method*.

Under the still-used 1943 New York Standard Policy, the measure of loss is the "actual cash value of the property at the time of loss," but not more than the cost to replace or repair the damaged property. Thus, if the actual cash value of the loss was $1,000, but the cost to replace was $700, the insurance company would pay $700, not $1,000.

While the term "actual cash value" is easy to say, its meaning is not always easy to determine. Indeed, the courts have found three different ways to apply this term as a measure of loss. Some courts hold that actual cash value is determined by subtracting the fair market value of the property after the loss from the fair market value of the property before the loss. Other courts have adopted the cost of repair or replacement less depreciation formula. Yet other courts use the broad evidence rule that takes all factors into consideration, i.e., obsolescence, utility of buildings, depreciation, market value, etc. Cozen, *Measure and Proof of Loss to Buildings and Structures Under Standard Fire Insurance Policies—the Alternatives and Practical Approaches,* 12 Forum 647 (1976); Dykes, *"Actual Cash Value"; the Magic Words—What Do They Mean?,* 16 Forum 391 (1981); 8 ALR4th 533.

Replacement cost insurance can be obtained by adding an endorsement or rider to the standard fire policy. Under this coverage, the insured is paid the actual cost of replacing or restoring the building. 66 ALR3d 885. This method eliminates the guesswork and argument involved in agreeing upon the application of the actual cash value standard.

The modern homeowners' form of policy provides replacement coverage for the buildings, but not the personal property. Chattels are covered on an actual cash value basis unless a personal property replacement cost endorsement is purchased. This endorsement will not cover fine paintings, antiques, jewels, etc. They must be insured under a special schedule or floater.

The replacement cost coverage of the homeowners' policy is conditioned upon the property being insured for 80 percent of its replacement cost. This provision and the coinsurance clause, § 12.13, require the insured to be watchful of the amount of insurance purchased so as always to have the required percentage of coverage.

The amount of coverage purchased is also important because other coverages, i.e., liability, personal property, and medical payments, are set at percentages of the building coverage. The insured should compare his needs for these coverages to the amounts set by the application of these formulas. Most notably, an inventory of personal property should be made and compared to the amount of personal property insurance to determine whether the amount of insurance is sufficient.

The amount of coverage is reduced by the payment of a loss.

> **EXAMPLE:** The insurance company's payment of a $1,000 loss on a $5,000 policy reduces the amount of coverage outstanding to $4,000.

Some policies have riders that automatically restore the original insurance amount, and the modern homeowners' policy expressly provides that loss payments will not reduce the policy limits.

If only part of the building is destroyed, but rebuilding the structure is prohibited by law (as where the building is a nonconforming use under the zoning ordinance), the loss is treated as total and the insured is allowed to collect the full face amount of the policy up to, but not exceeding, the full value of the building before the fire loss occurred. *Metropolitan Mutual Fire Ins. Co.* v. *Carmen Holding Co.*, 220 A2d 778 (Del. 1966). However, it is customary to add a rider extending the policy to cover such loss.

12.13 Coinsurance clause

Very few fires or other casualties cause a total destruction of the property. Insureds are aware of this fact. If it were not for the coinsurance clause the insured might be inclined to take part of the risk of total loss while passing the first layer of loss, where most losses will fall, to the insurer. To prevent this ploy and to encourage insurance to the full value of the property, insurance companies have added the coinsurance clause. This provision requires the owner to keep the property insured to a prescribed level, often 80 percent of the replacement value, if insurance benefits are to be paid in full. The customary use of the 80 percent coinsurance factor stems from the fact that generally only 80 percent of a building's value is destructible. The masonry, foundation, underground utilities, and the like will remain even after a catastrophe. If the owner insures for less than the stated percentage, the coinsurance clause operates to reduce the amount of loss payable to the insured.

> **EXAMPLE:** Assume an 80 percent coinsurance clause, a building worth $10,000, and insurance in the amount of $4,000. The most the insurance company will pay is 50 percent of any loss. The same formula applies to rent loss coverage.

Typically, the insurance value of new buildings is easily determined. The older the building gets, however, the easier it is to fall inadvertently into a coinsurance problem. To avoid this, some insurance companies have adopted the use of *automatic increase endorsements* or the *agreed amount clause.* Through the latter device, the insurer agrees that the amount of insurance coverage satisfies the coinsurance requirement. Without these provisions, the owner should obtain a replacement cost appraisal from a real estate appraiser or from the insurance company, to be sure that the coverage meets the 80 percent requirement.

12.14 Mortgage interests

Both the mortgagor and the mortgagee have an insurable interest. Both interests may be, and usually are, covered in one policy. But each may take out a separate policy. This right is of value to the mortgagee when the mortgagor has defaulted in his mortgage payments and declines to take out insurance since he feels that he will lose the property anyway. If the mortgagee obtains his own insurance with his own money and a loss occurs, the mortgagor is not entitled to the insurance money. If the insurer pays off the mortgage in such case, he is entitled to an assignment thereof and may foreclose. Of course the mortgagee's recovery is limited to the balance due on the debt, for that is the measure of his interest in the property.

On the other hand, in the absence of any clause in the mortgage requiring the mortgagor to insure for the mortgagee's benefit, the mortgagee is not entitled to insurance money paid under a policy obtained by the mortgagor in his own name and at his own expense. 9 ALR2d 299. However, most mortgage forms require the mortgagor to keep the buildings insured for the benefit of the mortgagee, and if a loss occurs in such case, the mortgagee is entitled to have insurance money applied in reduction or payment of the mortgage debt. *Sureck* v. *U.S. Fidelity & Guaranty Co.,* 353 F.Supp. 807 (1973). Where a mortgage containing a covenant to insure is assigned, a right to the insurance proceeds is created in the assignee. *Kintzel* v. *Wheatland Mutual Ins. Assn.,* 203 NW2d 799 (Iowa 1973).

12.14(a) The mortgage clause

Formerly it was customary for the mortgagor to take out insurance in his own name and, with the insurer's consent, to assign the policy to the mortgagee. This did not adequately protect the mortgagee. He simply stood in the mortgagor's shoes, and if the mortgagor violated the conditions of the policy so that it became void, the mortgagee was unable to collect the insurance. For example, if the mortgagor committed arson, the policy became void. The same result followed where the *open mortgage clause* was used. This clause simply stated that loss, if any, was payable to the mortgagee *as his interest shall appear,* which still left the mortgagee's insurance subject to be destroyed by the ignorance, carelessness, or fraud of the mortgagor. *Central National Insurance Co.* v. *Manufacturer's Acceptance Corp.,* 544 SW2d 362 (Tenn. 1976). Hence the *mortgagee loss clause,* also known as the *New York, standard, or union loss clause,* was developed. *Syndicate Ins. Co. v. Bohn,* 65 Fed. 165 (1894). This clause, now in general use, provides that the insurance shall not be invalidated by acts of the mortgagor. Under this clause, if the mortgagor does any act that would ordinarily make the policy void, for example, commits arson or brings dynamite on the premises, *such act merely makes the policy void as to the mortgagor, but the insurance remains in force for the benefit of the mortgagee. City-Wide Knitwear* v. *Safeco Ins. Co.,* 366 N.Y.S.2d 81 (1973). When such a clause is used, there are really two separate contracts, one between the insurer and the mortgagor and the other between the insurer and the mortgagee, and most matters that would invalidate the first of these contracts leave the second intact and in full force.

Since the standard mortgage clause is a separate contract between the mortgagee and the insurer giving the lender coverage that is separate from the homeowner's, it follows that many acts that invalidate the homeowner's coverage do not affect the lender's coverage. Thus, the mortgagee's protection continues even where:

- the policy is canceled without the mortgagee's consent. *Mutual Creamery Ins. Co.* v. *Iowa Nat. Ins. Co.,* 294 F.Supp. 337 (1969). Do not confuse cancellation with expiration. If the policy expires, the mortgagee is not entitled to any special notice and the mortgagee's protection ends. 60 ALR3d 164.
- the mortgagor increases the hazard in the use of the property without the mortgagee's knowledge, for example, by storing flammable substances.
- the mortgagor is negligent or intentionally damages the insured property. This is very important to the lending industry at a time when arson is a national problem.

EXAMPLE: *John Smith* takes out fire insurance with *ABC Co.* on a home he occupies. He mortgages the home to *XYZ Mortgage Co.* and the standard mortgage clause is attached to the fire policy. Needing money desperately, *John Smith* sets fire to his home. It is destroyed. This act of *John Smith* precludes him from collecting on the insurance if the arson can be proved. But *XYZ Mortgage Co.* will collect insurance up to the amount remaining due on the mortgage. Its separate contract (the mortgagee loss clause) is not affected by *Smith's* acts.

There are limits on the protection afforded by the mortgagee loss clause. The mortgagee must notify the insurer of any change in ownership of the property that comes to the knowledge of the mortgagee. The mortgagee is also bound by the coinsurance clause and any limitation periods in the policy upon the time in which a suit on the policy may be brought. *Greater Providence Trust Co.* v. *Nationwide Ins. Co.,* 355 A2d 718 (R.I. 1976).

Since the mortgage clause is a separate and independent contract of insurance, the name of the mortgagee as party insured must be stated in the mortgage clause. *Pacific Ins. Co.* v. *R. L. Kirmsey Cotton Co.*, 151 SE2d 541 (Ga. 1966). And if the mortgage is released and a new mortgage placed on the property, then a new mortgagee clause must be issued even though the mortgage runs to the same mortgagee who was covered by the previous mortgage clause. *Attleborough Sav. Bank* v. *Security Ins. Co.*, 46 NE 390 (Mass. 1897). The homeowners' policy provides for the opposite result. Coverage runs to the named mortgagee under "present or future mortgages."

12.14(a)(1)   The mortgage clause—foreclosure

The mortgagee loss clause continues to protect the lender after foreclosure. *Northwestern Nat. Ins. Co.* v. *Mildenberger*, 359 SW2d 380 (Mo. 1962). But see *Consolidated Mortgage Corp.* v. *American Sec. Ins. Co.*, 244 NW2d 434 (Mich. 1976), which requires notice to the insurer of the foreclosure. The mortgagee that takes a deed in lieu of foreclosure also has continued protection. *Union Central Life Ins. Co.* v. *Franklin County Farmers Mutual Ins. Assn.*, 270 NW 398 (Iowa 1936). But see *Insurance Co.* v. *State Savings & L. Assn.*, 425 F2d 1180 (7th Cir. 1970). These statements must be taken with a grain of salt, as the following points out.

A serious problem exists as to the rights of the mortgagee after the foreclosure sale. In most cases the mortgagee is the highest bidder at the foreclosure sale, and he usually bids an amount close to the amount of his mortgage debt. In a number of cases the courts have stated that this amounts to a satisfaction or payment of the mortgage debt in the amount of the sale price. The thinking here is that if a third party had been the successful bidder, his cash money would have gone to the mortgagee in reduction of the mortgage debt, and the result should be the same where the mortgagee "bids his mortgage" at the foreclosure sale. The consequence is that if a fire occurs after the foreclosure sale, the mortgagee recovers at a maximum the difference between the foreclosure sale price and the amount due on the mortgage debt, which difference is usually a trifling amount. *Northwestern Nat. Ins. Co.* v. *Mildenberger*, 359 SW2d 380 (Mo. 1962). *Whitestone S. & L. Assn.* v. *Allstate Ins. Co.*, 270 NE2d 694 (N.Y. 1971). Other courts say that the mortgagee should be allowed full recovery where a mortgagee loss clause exists. *Trustees of Schools* v. *St. Paul Fire & Marine Ins. Co.*, 129 NE 567 (Ill. 1921); *City* v. *Magnur*, 329 NE2d 312 (Ill. 1975).

> **SUGGESTION:** The mortgagee should procure a new policy or a rider to the existing policy the moment he has made his successful bid at the foreclosure sale.

A distinction should be made with respect to the sequence of events, namely: (1) If the foreclosure sale takes place and *thereafter* a fire loss occurs, the mortgagee is usually able to collect full insurance. The mortgagee's rights are fixed as of the time of the foreclosure sale. (2) If, however, the fire loss occurs, and *thereafter* the foreclosure sale is held, arguably the mortgagee made his foreclosure bid with his eyes wide open, and the decisions tend to hold that the foreclosure sale paid off and satisfied the mortgage debt to the extent of the foreclosure sale price, so that the mortgagee can collect insurance only to the extent of the deficiency, which is usually a nominal amount. 8 Fordham Urban L. J. 857 (1979). This reasoning is technical and unappetizing. No one explains why an insurance company that has collected premiums for the entire loss should not pay it. An insurance company that denies liability on technical grounds deserves to have this fact widely publicized. Once the courts wake up, this miserable rule should disappear. Meanwhile, mortgagees must protect themselves.

12.15 Contracts for the sale of land

When a landowner takes out insurance and thereafter contracts to sell the land to a purchaser, the sensible course is to have the insurance endorsed to cover both parties as their interests may appear. Then, in case of serious loss, the company will pay the seller the balance due on the contract, and the balance will be paid to the buyer.

When a policy taken out by the buyer is payable to the seller, and a fire occurs and the company pays the unpaid balance of the purchase price to the seller in satisfaction of the insurance claim, all rights of the seller in the property are extinguished, and the company is not entitled to any assignment of the contract. *Fields* v. *Western Millers Mutual Fire Ins. Co.*, 37 N.Y.S.2d 757 (1942). The buyer is entitled to a deed to the land since the insurance money has paid the purchase price. *Dysart* v. *Colonial Fire Underwriters*, 254 Pac. 240 (Wash. 1927).

When the buyer takes out a policy with loss payable to the buyer and seller as their interests may appear, and thereafter the seller declares the contract forfeited because of the buyer's default in his payments, the seller is still covered by such insurance. *Aetna Ins. Co.* v. *Robinson*, 10 NE2d 601 (Ind. 1937). And mere default in his payments does not terminate the buyer's insurance. He remains covered until the seller declares a forfeiture of the contact.

Suppose the contract of sale (as is customary in installment contracts) requires the buyer to take out insurance for the benefit of seller and buyer, but the buyer takes out insurance in his own name only. If a loss occurs, the courts will require the buyer to carry out his contract by forcing him to apply his insurance money in payment of the contract price due to the seller. *American Equitable Assurance Co.* v. *Newman*, 313 P2d 1023 (Mont. 1957); 64 ALR2d 1416.

It now seems clear that where a landowner has entered into a contract of sale and a fire occurs after the buyer has substantially reduced the balance due, the seller may nevertheless collect for the full amount of the loss.

> **EXAMPLE:** *A* took out a fire insurance policy and thereafter contracted to sell the land to *B*. When the contract had been paid down to $16,000, a fire loss occurred. *A* was allowed to collect $46,750 in fire insurance. *First National Bank* v. *Boston Ins. Co.*, 160 NE2d 802 (Ill. 1959); *Edlin* v. *Security Ins. Co.*, 269 F2d 159 (1959).

Although a contract-of-sale endorsement can be obtained to add the purchaser as an insured, no satisfactory standard form endorsement for the homeowners' policy exists to protect the installment contract seller.

> **EXAMPLE:** Seller enters into an installment contract to sell a home to Buyer. The existing homeowners' policy was written to insure Seller. A new policy is written to insure the Buyer, but with an endorsement making loss payable to Buyer and Seller, as their interests may appear. Buyer commits arson and the building is totally destroyed. Seller may be unable to collect on the insurance. *Langhorne v. Capitol Fire Ins. Co.,* 44 F.Supp. 739 (D. Minn. 1942).

This is a rerun of the mortgagor–mortgagee problem before the standard mortgagee loss clause was developed. See § 12.14(a). For proper protection, a *manuscript endorsement* should be used. This is a tailor-made endorsement used when no adequate printed form is available. It should state that no acts done or suffered by the buyer will in any way affect or impair the coverage to the seller.

12.16   Assignment

Assignment of the policy does not render the policy void, but the assignment itself is not valid except with the written consent of the company. For this reason, when the policy is assigned in connection with a sale and deed by the seller of all his title to the property, the seller could not collect on the policy for a subsequent loss since after sale he has no insurable interest in the property. Nor could the buyer collect if the assignment had not been consented to by the company. In other words, hazard insurance does not "run with the land." It must be assigned to the buyer for the buyer's protection. *Eastway Const.* v. *New York Property Underwriting Assn.,* 382 N.Y.S.2d 949 (1976). The prudent buyer will procure oral coverage and/or a binder giving protection until the assignment is consented to.

The right to the insurance proceeds is assignable *after loss. Travelers Indemnity Co.* v. *Isseal,* 354 F2d 488 (1965).

As a practical matter the problem of assignment has become less significant in recent years. Frequently, the seller's policy, because of its schedule of personalty, is appropriate only for the seller and is canceled upon closing. Similarly, the buyer must tailor his protection and seek his own coverage, possibly written by the family insurance man. Always oral coverage and/or a binder should be obtained to procure coverage until the new policy is issued.

12.17   Liability insurance

A building owner and lessee must carry liability insurance to protect them against loss caused to someone as a result of their involvement with the real estate.

> **EXAMPLE:** A customer who slips on the threshold and breaks a leg will sue the building owner and the tenant who runs the store.

Obviously, an injured party will sue everyone involved with the property. It is best to have coverage if for nothing more than protection against the costs of defending a case of this type.

12.17(a)   Liability insurance for contractors

A liability policy issued to a general contractor is likely to contain exclusions colloquially referred to as "x," "c," and "u." The "x" exclusion excludes liability for blasting. An endorsement can be obtained deleting this exclusion. The "c" exclusion excludes liability for collapse of building, and coverage for this liability should be purchased. The "u" exclusion excludes liability for damage to underground facilities such as conduits and sewers. Coverage should be obtained.

Completed operations insurance covers liability for a completed job.

> **EXAMPLE:** A contractor completes a bridge and later it collapses, causing bodily injury and property damage.

In general, a mortgage lender wants to see that all proper insurance is obtained.

> **EXAMPLE:** Lender is lending money on a large construction loan, with Contractor acting as general contractor. A bridge built by Contractor in another state collapses. With no insurance coverage, Contractor goes broke. A new contractor must be found and costs go up astronomically.

12.18   Builder's risk insurance

Builder's risk insurance is fire and extended coverage insurance for a building under construction. In its natural state, the amount of coverage under this form of policy increases as the building is completed. Today, a completed value form is available from the very outset of construction. This form eliminates the need to report construction progress. Also, in its natural state, builder's risk insurance will not cover an occupied project. An endorsement can be obtained, either at the outset of the job or at completion to give this coverage.

12.19   Business interruption insurance

This type of insurance protects from loss of income and continuing expenses when a business property is destroyed or damaged. There are two kinds of business interruption insurance. The "gross earnings" form pays an amount roughly equal to the gross earnings lost while business was interrupted. This coverage puts the insured business in the place it would have been if the business continued. It pays lost profits only to the extent that profits would have been earned. If losses would have been sustained, no payment is made under the insurance policy. Proving the amount of loss under this form is fairly complicated. Another form of business interruption insurance is the *valued* form under which the insurer and the insured agree at the time the policy is issued on the duration and amount of coverage.

> **EXAMPLE:** You take out a policy that pays $1,000 per week for a period of not more than six months while your plant is shut down by fire damage. There is a fair amount of guesswork in this type of coverage.

By writing to the INA Corporation, 1600 Arch Street, Philadelphia, Pa., 19101, you can get the booklet, *Business Interruption Insurance.* The bigger your operation, the more desirable it is to consult an insurance counselor before making a decision. His services are especially valuable in helping you determine the type and amount of insurance to purchase.

> *REFERENCE:* Miller, *Business Interruption Insurance: A Legal Primer,* 24 Drake L. Rev. 799 (1975).

12.20   Rent loss insurance

Rent loss insurance is the landlord's equivalent to business interruption insurance. It pays the landlord's loss due to the uninhabitability of the property by paying the gross rentals lost less variable expenses not incurred.

> **EXAMPLE:** A fire made a section of an office building untenantable. Rent loss amounted to $1,000 per month. Variable expenses relating to the damaged units were reduced because less janitorial services were needed and fewer utility users were occupying the property while repairs were made. This saved $150 per month in those expenses. The rent loss policy will pay $850 per month.

12.21   Public insurance adjuster

Some insureds who have suffered a loss immediately turn to the insurance adjuster for expert help in gathering the evidence of the extent of loss. For a fee of usually 10 percent of the recovery from the insurance company, the adjuster will prepare inventories of damaged property, determine the extent of seen and unseen damage, calculate the cost of repair and replacement, and the like. Adjusters also have access to a group of support personnel, expert engineers, architects, appraisers, and others who aid in determining the loss.

> *REFERENCES:* American Bar Assn., *Annotations to the Homeowners' Policy* (1980), offers summaries of all major cases applicable to the homeowners' policy decided prior to 1980. American Bar Assn., *Property Insurance Annotations— Fire and Extended Coverages* (1979), presents annotations of cases relating to the 1943 standard fire insurance policy and extended coverage endorsement decided prior to 1977. Cotton, *Insurance Coverage for the Real Estate Venture,* 14 Practical Lawyer 13 (March 1973). *Couch on Insurance,* 2d ed., is a multivolume set covering all areas of insurance law.

13 LAND ACQUISITION AND ASSEMBLY

13.01 In general One intending to build upon or develop vacant land must acquire it. The suggestions made in the chapters on contracts of sale and land development are, of course, applicable to the process of land acquisition. The mechanics of land acquisition and assembly call for special expertise.

13.02 Precautions prior to undertaking assembly Before undertaking a land assembly, the developer routinely visits with the title company and gets an idea of the ownerships involved. Obviously, it is easier to assemble three or four ownerships than thirty or forty ownerships. He also can get some idea as to the existence of building restrictions or easements that might thwart his building plans.

13.03 Gaps and gores It is often necessary to acquire and assemble the lands of several adjoining landowners, for example, for a subdivision, or a factory site. Here the danger is that the descriptions used may leave small gaps between the parcels.

> **EXAMPLE:** Buyer proposes to acquire the Northwest Quarter of Section 10 in a government township. He assumes that it contains exactly 160 acres, which it theoretically should contain. Actually, of course, owing to inaccuracies in surveying there is no such thing as a perfect quarter section, and it happens that his quarter section contains 161 acres. Suppose, then, that Buyer acquires from Seller #1 the "east eighty acres" of the quarter section and gets a deed from Seller #2 to the "west eighty acres" of the quarter section. This leaves a one-acre strip between the two eighty-acre tracts. Buyer thus does not acquire title to this strip.

These small strips between parcels are called *gores.*

This suggests the need for a *boundary survey* to be made by a surveyor before the contract is signed, so that the buyer's earnest money is not tied up until it can be seen that there are no gaps or gores.

Where one seller owns all the parcels being acquired, the surveyor can be asked to furnish a *perimeter description.* This is a description that describes the entire tract being acquired by metes and bounds. (See § 5.02). Then the survey will be made while the title is being examined, and if gaps or gores are revealed, the buyer can report the title as unmarketable. Alternatively, the buyer can insist that the title company insuring the title furnish a special endorsement insuring *contiguity* of all the several parcels, in which case the buyer again can back out of the deal if the title company refuses to insure contiguity.

13.04 Nominees

Land is often acquired in the name of a nominee, often a skilled negotiator from a local real estate firm. This is done because asking prices soar when it becomes known that some well-known company is acquiring land in the area. The nominee need not disclose that he is acting for an undisclosed principal. 32 Iowa L. Rev. 790 (1947). But if the seller inquires, the nominee must not misrepresent the identity of the purchaser, for if he does, the seller has the right to terminate the contract because a material misrepresentation has been made. Friedman, *Contracts and Conveyances of Real Property* § 2.2 (3d ed. 1975); 121 ALR 1162; 35 ALR3d 1374. Indeed, if such misrepresentation is made, the seller can have his deed set aside even after the deal has been closed, so long as he acts promptly on learning of the misrepresentation. The nominee must refrain from misrepresenting the use to which the property will be put. 35 ALR3d 1369.

> **EXAMPLE:** Nominee went to Seller and persuaded Seller to sell a vacant lot adjoining Seller's home. He stated that he planned to build a house. When it later developed that Nominee was buying on behalf of a church, the deed was set aside. *Keyerleber* v. *Euclid Congregation,* 143 NE2d 313 (Ohio 1957); 6 ALR2d 812.

This rule has special force where the seller retains some land and the buyer intends to devote the land to some offensive use, such as a junkyard, cemetery, or bar. 35 ALR3d 1370.

If the seller has turned down an offer made by the developer, use of a nominee thereafter is precluded. 6 ALR2d 812.

> **EXAMPLE:** Buyer offered to buy Seller's lot. Seller refused to deal. Buyer hired Nominee to buy the lot. Buyer can have his deed to Nominee set aside. *Gloede* v. *Socha,* 199 Wis. 503, 226 NW 950.

If bad blood or previous dealings lead a buyer to believe that the seller will not sell to him, it is useless to hire a nominee. The seller can have the deal set aside. 6 ALR2d 814; 35 ALR2d 1374.

There seems to be some advantage in having the developer form a straw corporation with some bland name to acquire the land. This would be a wholly-owned subsidiary of the developer. The subsidiary could then hire the nominee, who if asked, or even if not asked, could truthfully state: "I'm working for *Real Estate Associates, Inc.*"

Where it is decided to attempt a secret assembly, some developers use a different nominee, lawyer, and real estate broker for each acquisition.

Obviously, a nominee who has no judgments or other liens against him should be used. Often a bachelor is employed, for then no spouse's rights questions arise.

At times the nominee will request that his employer sign an indemnity agreement protecting the nominee against liability by reason of his ownership of the land.

13.04(a)   Written authority

Because an agent's authority to buy land must be in writing in some states, there should be a written contract of employment.

13.04(b)   Trust declaration by nominees

The nominee routinely signs a brief trust agreement reciting that he is acquiring the land and will hold it in trust for _____ (the developer). This is acknowleged, just as a deed is acknowledged, but it is not recorded. This is an indispensable document, for example, if the nominee dies while the ownership of the land stands in his name. It is especially important in land assemblies that may take a long period of time. Some developers also require the nominee to sign an unrecorded quitclaim deed as soon as he acquires ownership of a parcel.

13.05   Escrows

A seller who senses that he is not dealing with the real purchaser may become uneasy.

To quiet his fears the deal should be closed in escrow.

> **EXAMPLE:** Nominee tenders a contract of sale to Seller, with a provision therein that the entire purchase price will be held by *ABC Bank* under an escrow agreement providing that Seller gets the entire purchase price or gets ownership of his land back just as it was before the contract was signed.

13.06   Subdivision trusts

In Arizona extensive use is made of the *subdivision* trust.

> **EXAMPLE:** Seller enters into a contract to sell vacant land to Buyer for $100,000. Buyer pays $20,000 down. Seller now makes a deed of the land to

ABC Title Co. in trust. Seller is the first beneficiary of the trust and Buyer is the second beneficiary. The trustee files a plat of subdivision. Buyer engages in sales of lots. Lot buyers make their payments to *ABC Title Co.* which remits to Seller and Buyer according to a schedule with a minimum amount due periodically. The lot buyers receive their deeds from *ABC Title Co.* Ultimately Seller is paid the balance of the purchase price. If sales collapse and Buyer cannot meet the schedule of payments, Seller can declare a forfeiture of Purchaser's interest. Thereupon *ABC Title Co.* deeds the unsold lots to Seller. Carlock, *The Subdivision Trust—A Useful Device,* 5 Ariz. L. Rev. 2 (1963).

13.07   Land trusts

The land trust is an ideal vehicle for land assemblies. It enables the developer to acquire the individual parcels in the name of a trust company.

13.08   Holding agreements

In California and Nevada a device somewhat similar to the land trust is used, called a *holding agreement.*

13.09   Purchase money mortgage

Often a developer buying a farm will be able to persuade the farmer to take back a purchase money mortgage for a good part of the purchase price. In such case the contract of sale must contain two clauses.

> **CLAUSE:** This clause requires the farmer to join in the plat of subdivision. All plat statutes require all mortgagees to join in the subdivision plat. Otherwise, foreclosure of the mortgage would wipe out the streets dedicated by the plat.

> **CLAUSE:** This clause requires partial release of the mortgage as a lot is sold to a home buyer. This is necessary because the home buyer also needs to get a mortgage, and his lender will want his mortgage to be a first mortgage.

Of course, the contract must be quite detailed as to the terms of the mortgage.

If the developer plans to put construction mortgages on the property, a further clause is needed.

> **CLAUSE:** This clause subordinates the purchase money mortgage to any construction mortgage put on by the developer. This is done because the construction lender will want a first mortgage on the property. Caution is needed in drafting this clause. If it does not give enough standards or terms of the construction mortgage, it will be unenforceable. See Kratovil & Werner, *Modern Mortgage Law and Practice,* Ch. 30. (2d ed. 1981).

If there are barns or other buildings on the land sold, the contract and mortgage should give the developer the right to demolish them. A mortgagee can block demolition of buildings on mortgaged land unless the mortgage provides to the contrary.

13.10   Options

Options are often used in land acquisitions.

EXAMPLE: Buyer plans a site that requires assembly of ten separately owned tracts of land. Buyer hires agents who procure options on all ten tracts of land. If Buyer is unable to obtain options on all ten tracts, Buyer allows all options to lapse. If all ten options are procured, Buyer exercises all options.

13.11   Taxes

Assessors usually assess farmland considerably lower than subdivided land. This suggests that the development proceed in stages, if this is possible. Leave as much as you can in farmland until you are ready to go forward with subdivision and sale. And if you plan a commercial area, postpone platting this until you are ready to build, for the tax assessor will assess commercial land higher than residential land or farmland.

13.12   Leasehold acquisitions

Obviously, acquisition of a leasehold presents problems different from those involved in acquisition of outright ownership.

EXAMPLE: Condominium Developer acquires a leasehold. He then discovers that local law does not permit condominium developments on leaseholds.

EXAMPLE: Co-op Developer acquires a leasehold and erects a high-class apartment building. He encounters sales resistance. Prospective tenants point out that as the mortgage on the leasehold is reduced by payment, the equity of the apartment owner becomes so substantial that it becomes difficult to sell the apartment for cash and mortgage financing on a co-op is virtually unobtainable. This makes it almost necessary for the ground lease to contain some provision for the landlord joining in the ground lessee's financing. Obviously, there is a problem here.

14 CO-OWNERSHIP

14.01 In general

Once people decide to own property jointly, they must decide upon the form of their co-ownership. Should they form an artificial entity—i.e., a corporation, partnership, or trust—or should they hold their property in their own names? If they choose the latter approach, should they own the property as joint tenants or tenants in common? If they are married, what of the impact of tenancy by the entireties, community property, or other laws dealing with marital rights? In determining what form of ownership to use, the parties must consider, among other things, the income tax and estate planning consequences of the various forms of ownership. These decisions are not easily made and are not entirely legal in nature. The law tells the parties the consequences of their actions; the parties must then choose which consequences they want.

As indicated, a person can be the sole owner of a tract of land or may own the land with others. Where there are two or more co-owners they are known as *co-tenants*. There are different kinds of co-ownerships, or co-tenancies, as they are called. Persons may own the land as *joint tenants*, as *tenants by the entireties*, or *as tenants in common*.

14.02 Joint tenancy— tenancy in common distinguished

When a deed is made to two or more persons who are not husband and wife and nothing is said in the deed concerning the character of the tenancy created by the deed, the grantees acquire title as tenants in common. That is, on the death of either party, his interest in the real estate will go to his heirs if he dies without leaving a will, or, if he leaves a will, to the persons named therein.

EXAMPLE: Seller conveys land to Brother #1 and Brother #2. Since the deed is not in joint tenancy form, Brother #1 and Brother #2 are tenants in common. Brother #1, a widower, dies without a will, leaving Child #1 and Child #2 as his only children. Brother #2, Child #1, and Child #2 own the land as tenants in common, Brother #2 owning a half and Child #1 and Child #2 each a fourth.

If, however, the deed runs to two or more persons as joint tenants, a different rule applies. While both joint tenants are alive, they are co-owners of the land, but as soon as one dies, his title passes automatically to the surviving joint tenant.

> **EXAMPLE:** Seller makes a deed of his land to *A* and *B* as joint tenants. *A* dies. *B* succeeds to *A*'s interest and becomes the sole owner of the property.

Although a will of the decedent does not alter this result, and probate proceedings are not necessary to vest the survivor with complete ownership, careful estate planning is necessary because inheritance and estate taxes may result from the automatic transfer of the property to the surviving joint tenant. See § 14.06

Any number of persons may hold real estate in joint tenancy.

> **EXAMPLE:** Seller makes a deed to *A, B, C,* and *D,* as joint tenants. *D* dies. *A, B,* and *C* now own the land as joint tenants. *A* dies. *B* and *C* own the land as joint tenants. *B* dies. *C* is now the sole owner.

For the impact of community property law on these rules, *see* § 14.13 *et seq.*

14.02(a)   Abolition of survivorship

Some states have enacted laws that purport to abolish the joint tenant's right of survivorship, so that on the death of a joint tenant, his share goes to his heirs or to the persons named in his will, just as if a tenancy in common had been created. See Ariz. Rev. Stat. § 33–431; Fla. Stat. Ann. § 689.15. However, even in these states, the right of survivorship is not absolutely prohibited. If the deed to the joint owners expressly states that upon the death of one owner, the property shall go to the surviving grantee, the right of survivorship will be enforced. *Chandler* v. *Kountze,* 130 SW2d 327 (Tex. 1939); 69 ALR2d 1058.

14.02(b)   Joint tenancy— creation

To create a joint tenancy, a deed must state that the grantees are acquiring title as joint tenants. The actual language used varies somewhat from state to state, but it is best to use comprehensive language in creating a joint tenancy. 46 ALR2d 523.

> **SUGGESTED FORM:** To *A* and *B* as joint tenants with the right of survivorship, and not as tenants in common or as tenants by the entirety, or as community property.

A deed to persons who are husband and wife poses special problems. It may create a tenancy by the entireties. 32 ALR3d 570. It may create community property. But if it does neither of these things and is not a joint tenancy deed, the husband and wife are tenants in common.

> **EXCEPTION:** In Wisconsin, a deed to husband and wife creates a joint tenancy unless the deed states otherwise.

A joint tenancy may also be created when the parties have ineffectively attempted to create a tenancy by the entireties.

Rather frequently today we find a husband and wife helping a newly married son or daughter to buy a house. Often the two couples buy a two-apartment dwelling for their joint occupancy, each couple acquiring a one-half interest in the property. The old couple wants their half interest held in joint tenancy, but does not want the young couple to have any interest in the old couple's half. The young people feel the same about their half. Each couple wants its half to be in joint tenancy, so that when one dies the surviving wife or husband will own the entire half interest, but they want a tenancy in common as between the two half interests. To accomplish this, it is best to use two separate joint tenancy form deeds, one going to each couple. Before the land description in each deed, insert, "An undivided one-half interest in . . ." Thus, each couple will have its own deed. If one of the owners dies, the surviving spouse will own a one-half interest in the property as the surviving joint tenant. The others continue to own their half as joint tenants. The two halves are as separate for this purpose as if they were separate tracts of land.

A similar problem results when friendly couples purchase property together.

> **EXAMPLE:** John Jones and Mary Jones, his wife, and Henry Brown and Susan Brown, his wife, are friends. They decide to invest in real estate and buy a twelve-unit apartment building together. They take title as "John Jones and Mary Jones, as joint tenants as to an undivided one-half interest, and Henry Brown and Susan Brown, as joint tenants as to an undivided one-half interest."

Of course, the parties should have a written agreement spelling out their respective rights and duties. This agreement should address: upkeep and maintenance obligations, occupancy rights of the parties, rights to rents and profits of the property, debt service obligations, buy-out obligations, right of first refusal, and the like.

In states that have abolished survivorship rights in joint tenancies, some special problems exist.

> **EXAMPLE:** In a state where the law states that the right of survivorship in joint tenancies is abolished, Seller makes a deed to Husband and Wife "as joint tenants

with the right of survivorship and not as tenants in common." Husband dies. Wife takes all as the survivor. However, the cases are not in agreement as to the nature of the interest created by the deed. One line of cases says that a joint tenancy was created by agreement of the parties. It becomes an ordinary joint tenancy. In other states it creates an estate for lives with the right of survivorship. Neither party can sever it by deed as can be done in an ordinary joint tenancy. It is an indestructible right of survivorship. *Anson* v. *Murphy,* 32 NW2d 271 (Neb. 1948); *Bernhard* v. *Bernhard,* 177 So2d 565 (Ala. 1965). Statutes of the type discussed will likely disappear in time. They cause difficulties with common, necessary joint tenancies, such as those in bank accounts.

14.02(b)(1) The four unities

Not every deed that describes the grantees as joint tenants is sufficient to create a joint tenancy. In the creation of a joint tenancy, there must be present the four unities of time, title, interest, and possession. That is, the joint tenants must have one and the same interest, acquired by one and the same deed, commencing at one and the same time; and they must hold by one and the same undivided possession.

> **EXAMPLE:** Owner owned a tract of land. Thereafter, he married and executed a deed to himself and his wife "as joint tenants." No joint tenancy was created by this deed. Owner and his wife did not acquire title at the same time or by the same conveyance, since Owner had owned the land long prior to the making of the deed. The unities of time and title were not present. The deed actually created a tenancy in common. Owner and his wife should have conveyed title to a third person, and this third person should have thereupon reconveyed the title to Owner and his wife as joint tenants. *Deslauriers* v. *Senesac,* 163 NE 327 (Ill. 1928).

Pointless technicalities like these are going out of fashion. Hence in many states laws have been passed under which a deed by a landowner to himself and another as joint tenants creates a good joint tenancy. See, e.g., Cal. Civ. Code § 683; Ill. Rev. Stat. Ch. 76, § 1b.

For reasons relating to community property, dower, and homestead, the landowner's spouse should join in the deed. One often sees a landowner and his wife conveying to themselves as joint tenants, and the whole thing, though odd, is quite legal in most states. 44 ALR2d 605.

When a deed reveals an intention to create a joint tenancy, but fails to for some technical reason, some modern courts tend to show little patience with the old technicalities and give the property to the survivor, even though a true joint tenancy has not been created.

> **EXAMPLE:** A husband who owned some land in his own individual name signed a deed conveying a half interest in this land to his wife, the deed stating that they were to hold the land as joint tenants. Obviously this is no way to create a joint tenancy, for the four unities are lacking. Nevertheless, on the death of the

husband the court awarded the entire property to the surviving wife. *Runions* v. *Runions,* 207 SW2d 1016 (Tenn. 1948). There can be a right of survivorship even though the land is not owned in joint tenancy, which is something of a subtle distinction but has the happy result of achieving what the parties wanted.

It is impossible to make a deed to *A* of a one-fourth interest in the land and to *B* of a three-fourths interest to hold as joint tenants. A deed creating joint tenancies must give the joint tenants equal shares as to the property conveyed in joint tenancy. This does not prevent a joint tenant from owning a different and distinct interest in the land.

> **EXAMPLE:** *X* conveys a half interest to *A* and a half interest to *A* and *B* as joint tenants. This is perfectly valid. *In re Galletto's Estate,* 171 P2d 152 (Cal. 1946).

14.02(c)   Severance of joint tenancy

There is nothing sacred about a joint tenancy. Either joint tenant has the right to break the joint tenancy as he wishes. 64 ALR2d 918. Certain actions will break the joint tenancy and convert it into a tenancy in common even against the wishes or without the knowledge of the other parties.

1. A conveyance by a joint tenant to a third party destroys the joint tenancy.

> **EXAMPLE:** *A* conveys to *B* and *C* in joint tenancy. *C* conveys his half of title to *D*. *D* thereafter conveys this interest back to *C*. *C* dies. His title passes to his heirs, not to *B*. The conveyance from *C* to *D* severed or terminated the joint tenancy. The joint tenancy was not revived by the reconveyance. At *C*'s death, *B* and *C* were holding title as tenants in common. *Szymczak* v. *Szymczak,* 138 NE 218 (Ill. 1923). It is not necessary that *B* be informed of the fact that *C* is breaking the joint tenancy. *Burke* v. *Stevens,* 70 Cal. Reptr. 87 (1968).

Where there are three or more joint tenants, and only one makes a deed to a third party or to one of the other joint tenants, some highly technical problems are encountered.

> **EXAMPLE:** *A, B* and *C* own land as joint tenants. *C* conveys his third to *D*. *A* and *B* continue to hold their two-thirds as joint tenants. *Morgan* v. *Catherwood,* 167 NE 618 (Ind. 1929); *Hammond* v. *McArthur,* 183 P2d 1 (Cal. 1947).

> **EXAMPLE:** *A, B,* and *C* own land in joint tenancy. *A* conveys to *B* by quitclaim deed. *B* and *C* continue to own a two-third interest in the land in joint tenancy, and *B* owns a one-third interest as tenant in common. *Shelton* v. *Vance,* 234 P2d 1012 (Cal. 1951); *Jackson* v. *O'Connell,* 177 NE2d 194 (Ill. 1961).

> **EXAMPLE:** *A, B,* and *C* own land in joint tenancy. *C* conveys one-twentieth of his interest to *X*. *A* and *B* continue to own their two thirds in joint tenancy. *C* and *X* are tenants in common. *Giles* v. *Sheridan,* 137 NW2d 828 (Neb. 1968); Swenson & Degnan, *Severance of Joint Tenancies,* 38 Minn. L. Rev. 466, 472 (1954).

This severance occurs notwithstanding the fact that the deed was not recorded. *Carmack* v. *Place,* 535 P2d 197 (Colo. 1975).

2. An involuntary transfer of title will sever a joint tenancy.

EXAMPLE: *A* and *B* hold title as joint tenants. *A* goes into bankruptcy. Under the old bankruptcy law, title to all of *A*'s property was automatically transferred to the bankruptcy trustee. This transfer severed the joint tenancy. *In re Victor,* 218 F.Supp. 218 (S.D. 111. 1963). Whether the same result will follow under the new bankruptcy law is not entirely clear. Rather than transferring the debtor's property to the bankruptcy trustee, the new law creates a bankruptcy estate when the bankruptcy case has begun. 11 USC § 541.

The actions of creditors of one of the joint tenants can also sever the tenancy.

EXAMPLE: *A* and *B* hold title as joint tenants. Creditor obtains a judgment against *A,* and a sheriff's sale is held to obtain money to pay the judgment. Buyer purchases the property at the sheriff's sale and obtains a sheriff's deed. This severs the joint tenancy. Buyer and *B* now hold as tenants in common. However, the rendition of a judgment against one joint tenant and the making of a levy on his interest will not sever a joint tenancy. *Van Antwerp* v. *Horan,* 61 NE2d 358 (Ill. 1945); *Hammond* v. *McArthur,* 183 P2d 1 (Cal. 1947); *Eder* v. *Rothamel,* 85 A2d 860 (Md. 1953). It has even been held that a sheriff's sale under such a judgment does not sever the joint tenancy and that the joint tenancy is not severed until a sheriff's deed issues. If the joint tenant against whom the judgment was rendered dies before the sheriff's deed issues, the other joint tenant takes all the property free and clear of the judgment creditor's rights. *Jackson* v. *Lacey,* 97 NE2d 839 (Ill. 1951).

3. In title and intermediate states, a mortgage executed by one of the joint tenants severs the joint tenancy, notwithstanding the fact that the mortgage is subsequently paid and released by the mortgagee. 64 ALR2d 918.

Mattis, *Severance of Joint Tenancies by Mortgages: A Contextual Approach,* 1 So Ill. U. L. J. 27 (1977).

EXAMPLE: *A* and *B* hold title as joint tenants. *A* executes a mortgage on his half of the title and thereafter pays off the mortgage, which is released. Thereafter, *B* dies. *B*'s half of the title passes to his heirs, not to *A*. *A*'s mortgage severed the joint tenancy.

But a mortgage executed by *both* joint tenants does not sever the joint tenancy.

EXAMPLE: *A* and *B* hold title as joint tenants. They both join in a mortgage. Thereafter, *A* dies. *B* takes title as the surviving joint tenant. 64 ALR2d 918, 935.

The cases do not agree as to the effect of a mortgage by one joint tenant in a lien state. *People* v. *Nogarr,* 330 P2d 858 (Cal. 1958); Comment 11 Stan. L. Rev. 574 (1959).

EXAMPLE: *H* and *W* owned land in joint tenancy. *H* gave a mortgage on his interest to *E* without the knowledge of *W. H* died. The mortgage was thereby terminated. It attached only to an interest that would itself terminate unless the mortgagor survived his joint tenant. *D.A.D. Inc.* v. *Moring,* 218 So2d 451 (Fla. 1969). This is the better rule in lien states, but not all will follow it.

4. A contract by one joint tenant to sell or convey his interest in the land to a third person will operate as a severance of the joint tenancy. *Naiburg* v. *Hendriksen,* 19 NE2d 348 (Ill. 1939).

EXAMPLE: *A* and *B* own land in joint tenancy. *A* enters into a contract to sell his half interest to *C.* The joint tenancy is severed. Suppose *B* dies, for example. His half goes to his heirs.

5. If one joint tenant files a partition suit against the other, and a partition decree is entered, the joint tenancy is severed. *Schuck* v. *Schuck,* 108 NE2d 905 (Ill. 1952); *Hammond* v. *McArthur,* 183 P2d 1 (Cal. 1947).

6. A husband and wife own land in joint tenancy. One files a divorce suit against the other. A divorce decree is entered. It orders the land sold and the proceeds of sale divided between them. The joint tenancy is now severed. Baade v. *Ratner,* 359 P2d 877 (Kans. 1961). Indeed, if a husband and wife own land in joint tenancy and they enter into a separation agreement providing that the land will be sold when the divorce decree is entered and the proceeds of sale divided between them, this agreement will sever the joint tenancy. *Carson* v. *Ellis,* 348 P2d 807 (Kans. 1960).

7. A simple, written, signed, and recorded declaration by one joint tenant that the tenancy has been severed has been held sufficient to terminate the joint tenancy, thereby converting it into a tenancy in common. *Hendrickson* v. *Minneapolis Fed. S. & L. Assn.,* 161 NW2d 688 (Minn. 1968). This is a pretty liberal decision and has been criticized. It is safer to have the party deed out to a dummy and have the dummy deed back.

8. Any agreement between the joint tenants that shows an intention to treat the land as a tenancy in common will cause a severance. 64 ALR2d 941.

9. In one or two states the making of a lease by one joint tenant severs the joint tenancy. *Alexander* v. *Boyer,* 253 A2d 359 (Md. 1969).

There are other events that do not break the joint tenancy:

1. A will by the deceased joint tenants.

EXAMPLE: *A* and *B* own land as joint tenants. *A* makes a will giving all his property to *C. A* dies. *B* takes all the joint tenancy property, and *C* gets no part of it. *A's* will does not break a joint tenancy. *Eckardt* v. *Osborne,* 170 NE 774 (Ill. 1930).

2. A lien created against one of the joint tenants.

EXAMPLE: *A* and *B* own land as joint tenants. A judgment lien, internal revenue lien, or other lien is filed against *A* only. *A* dies before he has lost his title through enforcement of the lien. *B* takes the entire title free and clear of the lien. In other words, if *A* is a joint tenant, a lien against him attaches not to the land but to *A's interest in the land,* which is an interest that will be totally extinguished if *A* dies before *B* does, so long as the parties are joint tenants when *A* dies. One who has a lien on *A's* interest ordinarily can have no greater rights than *A* has, and if *A's* rights will be extinguished by his breach, so will the lien. 134 ALR 957.

3. An easement created by one joint tenant only.

EXAMPLE: *A* and *B* own land as joint tenants. *A* alone signs an easement grant to *C,* and *A* dies before *B* does. *B* then owns the entire title free and clear of the easement.

4. Dower and curtesy of a spouse of a deceased joint tenant.

EXAMPLE: If *A* and *B,* both married men, own land as joint tenants, and *A* dies first, his wife has no dower in the land because at *A's* death all his title to the land is extinguished, leaving nothing to which dower can attach.

5. Divorce. State laws differ on the subject of divorce.

EXAMPLE: In some states, a divorce does not break a joint tenancy. Where no specific law exists, if *H* and *W* own land as joint tenants, are divorced, and if nothing is said in the divorce decree about the property, the joint tenancy is unbroken. Suppose that *H* thereafter marries another person, *X. H* dies before *W* does. *W,* the former wife of *H,* takes the entire property, and *X* takes nothing. *H* could have prevented this by breaking the joint tenancy by deed. On the other hand, in some states the entry of a divorce decree automatically converts the joint tenancy into a tenancy in common. This is by virtue of special laws.

6. The making of a lease by one of two joint tenants does not sever the joint tenancy. *Tindall* v. *Yeats,* 64 NE2d 903 (Ill. 1946); *Hammond* v. *McArthur,* 183 P2d 1 (Cal. 1947); *Tennet* v. *Boswell,* 18 Cal. 3d 150, 554 P2d 330 (1976). *Contra: Alexander* v. *Boyer,* 253 A2d 359 (Md. 1969). See Note 7 Baylor L. Rev. 97 (1955); Comment 25 Cal. L. Rev. 203 (1937). The court decisions holding that a lease severs a joint tenancy are absurd.

EXAMPLE: *H* and *W,* husband and wife, own an apartment building in joint tenancy. *H* manages the building and signs the leases to the tenants. It is absurd to hold that the joint tenancy is broken.

7. One joint tenant files a partition suit against the other, but one of them dies before a partition decree is entered. The survivor takes all as surviving joint tenant. 129 ALR 813.

8. A deed by one joint tenant to himself does not sever the joint tenancy because it is nothing but an empty ceremony. *Clark* v. *Carter,* 70 Cal. Reptr. 923 (1968), and the

contrary has also been held. Minonk State Bank v. Grassman, 432 NE2d 386   (Ill. 1982). See 7 ALR4th 1268.

9. Where one of two joint tenants grants a life estate to another this does not sever the joint tenancy. *Hammond* v. *McArthur,* 183 P2d 1 (Cal. 1947).

10. The mere granting of an option to purchase by one joint tenant does not sever the joint tenancy. *Alexander* v. *Boyer,* 253 A2d 359 (Md. 1969).

REFERENCE: Severing Joint Property Interests, 16 Real Prop., Prob. & Tr. J. 435 (1981).

14.02(d)   Disadvantages of a joint tenancy

Rather frequently, when title is held in joint tenancy by a husband and wife and one of them dies, the survivor, impressed with the simplicity of transfer of ownership on the death of a joint tenant, ponders the advisability of creating a new joint tenancy in which the surviving spouse will be joint tenant with one of the spouse's children. This has certain disadvantages. Such a deed cannot be unmade without the consent of both parties. Suppose that the surviving spouse and the child named as joint tenant quarrel, which is not uncommon. Indeed, the mere fact that the parties share ownership of the real estate seems to trigger quarrels. The child may file a partition suit and put property up for sale. Thus, the surviving spouse may find himself or herself without a place to live. Perhaps judgments may be rendered against the child, and creditors will force the property to a sale. Many lawyers counsel the surviving joint tenant to avoid setting up a joint tenancy such as this. Where a will is made, it can always be changed. It gives no one any right in the property until the landowner dies. Perhaps this may strike a cynical note, but the fact remains that when there is a will rather than a deed, there is much less likelihood of family quarrels.

14.02(e)   Joint tenancy— creditors' rights

A judgment or other lien creditor against one joint tenant's interest is in a somewhat fragile position.

If the lien is not transformed into ownership, as for example by an execution sale, before the death of the debtor joint tenant, the interest of the lienor is cut off. The deceased joint tenant's interest vests in the surviving joint tenant free of the lien. To an opposite effect, if the other joint tenants die before the debtor joint tenant, the lien will spread to the entire fee interest that vests in the surviving debtor joint tenant upon the death of the other joint tenants.

> **EXAMPLE:** *A* and *B* own Blackacre as joint tenants. Creditor obtains a judgment lien against *A.* The following results are possible: (1) if *A* dies before levy and execution sale, Creditor's lien is extinguished and *B* acquires Blackacre free of Creditor's lien; (2) if *B* dies before levy and execution sale, *A* owns a 100 percent interest in Blackacre which is entirely subject to Creditor's lien; (3) if Creditor levies, executes, and purchases at the execution sale, the joint tenancy is severed and Creditor and *B* own undivided one-half interests in Blackacre.

14.03   Tenancy by the entireties—in general

In Arkansas, Delaware, District of Columbia, Florida, Hawaii, Indiana, Kentucky, Maryland, Massachusetts, Michigan, Mississippi, Missouri, New Jersey, New York, North Carolina, Oklahoma, Oregon, Pennsylvania, Rhode Island, Tennessee, Utah, Vermont, Virginia, and Wyoming, a form of joint tenancy, known as tenancy by the entireties, exists. This is a tenancy that exists only where the co-owners are husband and wife, and it is based upon the common law notion that they are one person, and each are holders of the entire estate. Unlike a joint tenancy, no words are necessary to create such a tenancy.

EXAMPLE: In a tenancy by the entireties state, *X* makes a deed to *H* and *W*, husband and wife. Nothing is said as to the character of their co-ownership. They are tenants by the entireties.

EXCEPTION: In Kansas, Kentucky, Massachusetts, Mississippi, Montana, Oklahoma, Rhode Island, Utah, and Virgina, laws have been passed stating that the deed must expressly show an intention to create a tenancy by the entireties. 52 Mich. L. Rev. 804.

Tenancy by the entireties resembles joint tenancy in that upon the death of either husband or wife the survivor automatically acquires title to the share of the deceased spouse.

Tenancy by the entireties differs from joint tenancy in that neither spouse has the power to defeat or sever the tenancy by any deed or mortgage to a stranger made without the signature of the other spouse. *Hoffman* v. *Newell*, 60 SW2d 607 (Ky. 1932).

EXAMPLE: A deed is made to a husband and wife, nothing being said as to the character of their tenancy. Thereafter, the husband makes a deed that purports to convey his interest in the land to *X*. The wife does not join in this deed. Thereafter, the husband dies. The wife now has full title to all the land. *X* has nothing.

However, a deed by both husband and wife will, of course, give the grantee good title.

As long as the marriage exists neither spouse may have a partition of the estate by the entireties. *Lawrence* v. *Lawrence*, 190 A2d 206 (N.J. 1963).

EXAMPLE: *A* and *B* hold property as *tenants in common*. If they disagree upon the disposition of the property, they can ask the court either to physically divide the property between them (this is called partition in kind) or sell the property and divide the proceeds. This relief is not available to *tenants by the entireties*.

EXAMPLE: Where *H* and *W* hold property as tenants by the entireties and *W* sues *H* for divorce, *H* can ask that the court, if a divorce is allowed, divide the property or sell it and divide the proceeds. *Bastians* v. *Bastians,* 321 N.Y.S.2d 480 (1971).

Tenancy by the entireties is not recognized in community property states.

14.03(a) Creation of tenancy by the entireties

In the states where tenancies by the entireties are recognized, there is much difference of opinion as to the legal effect of a deed to a husband and wife that describes the grantees as joint tenants. In some states, Indiana, Maryland, New Jersey, New York, and Wyoming, for example, such a deed creates a joint tenancy rather than a tenancy by the entireties. *Witzel* v. *Witzel,* 386 P2d 103 (Wyo. 1963). But in most of the states that recognize tenancies, such deeds are held to create a tenancy by the entireties. *Hoag* v. *Hoag,* 99 NE 521 (Mass. 1912); 161 ALR 470. If a joint tenancy is desired, the deed should always state that the grantees are "joint tenants and not tenants in common or by the entireties." This should avoid litigation over the issue.

However, when a deed to a husband and wife describes them "as tenants in common," such a deed is almost universally regarded as creating a good tenancy in common rather than a tenancy by the entireties.

For the creation of a tenancy by the entireties, it is necessary that the grantees be husband and wife. If they are not husband and wife, even express language in the deed declaring an intention to create a tenancy by the entireties will not create such a tenancy.

14.03(b) Defective tenancy by the entireties as creating a joint tenancy

Tenancy by the entireties exists only as between husband and wife. A deed to parties who are not husband and wife creates some other kind of tenancy even though a tenancy by the entireties is specified.

EXAMPLE: A deed to *A* and *B,* who claimed to be, but were not, husband and wife, recited that it was made to them as tenants by the entireties and not as tenants in common. Since this revealed a general intention to create survivorship rights, but could not create a tenancy by the entireties, the parties not being husband and wife, the court held that a joint tenancy was created. *Morris* v. *McCarthy,* 32 NE 938 (Mass. 1893); *Coleman* v. *Jackson,* 286 F2d 98 (1960); *Righter* v. *Righter,* 275 A2d 4 (Pa. 1971); Kepner, *The Effect of an Attempted Creation of An Estate by the Entirety in Unmarried Persons,* 6 Rutgers L. Rev. 550 (1952); Note 37 Notre D. Law 441 (1962); Note 37 Cornell L. Q. 316 (1952).

EXAMPLE: In New Hampshire and Wisconsin, which do not recognize tenancy by the entireties, a deed to husband and wife "as tenants by the entireties" creates a joint tenancy. *In re Ray's Will,* 205 NW 917 (Wis. 1925); 1 ALR2d 247.

> **EXAMPLE:** A deed to two sisters "as tenants by the entireties" has been held to create a joint tenancy. *In re Richardson's Estate,* 282 NW 585 (Wis. 1938). Likewise this was true where the deed was to two brothers. *Penn. Bank & Tr. Co.* v. *Thompson,* 247 A2d 771 (Pa. 1968).

However, in most states a deed to *H* and *W*, describing them as tenants by the entireties or as husband and wife creates only a tenancy in common if they are in fact not married. *Pierce* v. *Hall,* 355 P2d 259 (Oreg. 1960); 9 ALR4th 1189.

> **EXAMPLE:** A deed was made to Charles Smith and Julia Smith, *husband and wife.* Actually they were not married. Julia died. Charles, describing himself as a "surviving spouse," made a deed to a purchaser. Then three sisters of Julia appeared and claimed her half of the property as her heirs. They succeeded. Only a tenancy in common existed and Charles was not even an heir. *Thurmond* v. *McGrath,* 334 N.Y.S.2d 917 (1972).

14.03(c) Tenancy by the entireties—deeds between spouses

Suppose a husband or wife owns land in his or her own name, or they own land as tenants in common. They wish to put the land in their names as tenants by entireties. The traditional way of accomplishing this is to have the husband and wife join in a deed to a straw man, or nominee, and such nominee then deeds the land back to the husband and wife as tenants by the entireties. Just as in the case of joint tenancies, the old rule is: In order to have a good tenancy by the entireties, the husband and wife must acquire title by the same deed, and the dummy conveyance satisfies this requirement.

Just as in the case of joint tenancies, recent laws and court decisions allow a husband or wife to create a tenancy by the entireties without deeding out to a dummy. In these states, among which are Arkansas, Florida, Massachusetts, Michigan, Missouri, New Jersey, New York, Oklahoma, Oregon, Pennsylvania, Rhode Island, Tennessee, and Utah, if the husband owns land and wishes to create a tenancy by the entireties with his wife, he makes out a deed running to himself and his wife "as tenants by the entireties, and not as joint tenants or as tenants in common." Phipps, *Tenancy by Entireties,* 25 Temple L. Q. 24, 43 (1952); 44 ALR2d 598. For reasons relating to dower and homestead, the wife should join in this deed as co-grantor.

However, in a few other states it has been held that it is still necessary, if a good tenancy by the entireties is to be created, that the husband landowner and his wife join in a deed to a third person, who thereupon conveys to the husband and wife. This practice should be followed unless it is clear that your state has abolished the need for a third-party conveyance.

When land is held in tenancy by the entireties, a deed by the husband to the wife gives her good title even though she does not join in the deed to herself. The same is true of a deed by the wife to the husband. 8 ALR2d 634.

14.03(d) Tenancy by the entireties—deeds, mortgages, leases, rents, and brokers' listings

As a rule, a deed or mortgage of property owned in tenancy by the entireties must be signed by both husband and wife.

In most states, when a tenancy by the entirety exists, a deed to a stranger signed by the husband or wife alone is void. Phipps, *Tenancy by Entireties,* 25 Temple L. Q. 24, 46 (1952). In a few states, the deed is given some effect, but the effect, varies from state to state. It may grant a share of the rents or may be operative if the grantor survives the other spouse. In any event, in all states the deed becomes void if the spouse who did not join in the deed survives the spouse who conveyed.

Both parties should sign any lease. In many tenancy by the entirety states, husband and wife have equal rights to rents and possession, and any lease must be signed by both. Phipps, *Tenancy by Entireties,* 25 Temple L.Q. 26, 46 (1952); 141 ALR 202.

Certainly this is the impact of new laws designed to equalize the rights of the wife and those of the husband. Mich. Stat. Ann. § 26.210(1).

If the husband alone lists property with a real estate broker for sale, he will be liable for a commission if the broker finds a buyer. It is no defense that the wife failed to sign. *Taub* v. *Shampanier,* 112 Atl 322 (N.J. 1921).

14.03(e) Tenancy by the entireties—creditor's rights

In most tenancy by the entireties states, a judgment creditor of either husand or wife alone can acquire no rights by a sheriff's sale of the land. Since neither husband nor wife alone can make a voluntary sale of his or her interest in the land, an involuntary or forced sale of the interest of either husband or wife alone cannot be valid. 75 ALR2d 1175. In a few states, Arkansas, New Jersey, New York, and Oregon, for example, a husband's interest can be sold by the sheriff under a judgment against the husband alone, but the sheriff's deed will automatically become void if the wife survives the husband. The wife then remains the sole owner, free of the judgment. Phipps, *Tenancy by Entireties,* 25 Temple L. Q. 24, 39 (1952); 75 ALR2d 1183.

Of course if the judgment is against both husband and wife, the land may be sold by the sheriff, provided it is not their homestead.

As above stated, in most of the tenancy by entirety states, the rents of the land belong to the husband and wife jointly. Therefore a creditor of either the husband or wife alone cannot reach the rents, income, or crops of the land.

> **EXCEPTIONS:** In Arkansas, New Jersey, New York, and Oregon, creditors of either the husband or wife are allowed to reach the debtor's share of the rents, income, or crops of the land. In Massachusetts and North Carolina, creditors of the husband, but not those of the wife, may reach all the income of the land held in tenancy by the entireties while the tenancy continues. Phipps, *Tenancy by Entireties,* 25 Temple L. Q. 24, 39 (1952). *See* 8 Rutgers Camden L. J. 707, 714; 1 Wayne L. Rev. 105

14.03(f) Tenancy by the entireties—divorce

A divorce converts a tenancy by the entireties into a tenancy in common. Some states, however, have an opposite rule which holds that divorce changes a tenancy by the entireties to a joint tenancy with the right of survivorship. *Shepherd* v. *Shepherd,* 336 So2d 497 (Miss. 1976).

14.04 Murder—joint tenancies and tenancies by the entireties

When one joint tenant or tenant by the entireties murders his co-tenant and later is convicted of such murder in a court trial, one of three results is possible.

1. The murderer will, despite his crime, take the entire property by virtue of his right of survivorship. This is a bad rule that is certainly doomed to disappear.

2. The murderer, because of his crime, loses all his interest in the property, and the heirs of the murdered co-owner take the entire property, which rule is followed in Minnesota and Wisconsin. *Vesey* v. *Vesey,* 54 NW2d 385 (Minn. 1952); *In re King's Estate,* 52 NW2d 885 (Wis. 1952).

3. The murder is regarded, in legal effect, as converting the tenancy into a tenancy in common, so that the murderer retains his half interest, and the heirs of the murdered co-tenant take the other half. This rule is followed in most states. *Abbey* v. *Lord,* 336 P2d 226 (Cal. 1959); *Bradley* v. *Fox,* 129 NE2d 699 (Ill. 1955); Note, 5 DePaul L. Rev. 316 (1956).

Of course if in the murder trial the killer is acquitted—on the ground of self-defense, for example—the killing is not murder but justifiable homicide, and the survivor will take the entire property even though he caused the death of his co-tenant.

14.05 Contracts of sale— joint tenancies and tenancies by the entireties

A contract to sell property owned in tenancy by the entireties obviously should be signed by both husband and wife. If it is not, the buyer will be unable to obtain specific performance, though the seller who signed might be liable for damages. *Cartwright* v. *Giacosa,* 390 SW2d 204 (Tenn. 1965).

In tenancy by the entireties states, when a landowner signs a contract to sell his land to a husband and wife, the buyers hold the contract interest as tenant by the entireties, so that if either dies before the deal is closed, the seller's deed should be made to the survivor. *Comfort* v. *Robinson,* 118 NW 943 (Mich. 1908).

If the state does not recognize tenancy by the entireties or community property, a contract to sell land to *H* and *W,* who are husband and wife, creates a tenancy in common in the contract interest. If *H* dies, his contract interest passes to his heirs or devisees, and the seller must not make the deed to *W* alone. Obviously when an installment contract is involved, it may take years to pay up, and the death of one of the buyers is a distinct possibility.

SUGGESTED FORM: To avoid the endless complications of tenancy in common or necessity of probate, suggest to buyers that they agree to buy the land "as joint tenants with the right of survivorship, and not as tenants in common nor by the entireties nor as community property."

Of course if land is owned in joint tenancy, all owners must join as sellers in any contract to sell the land.

Where a husband and wife enter into a contract to sell their land, and one of them dies before the purchase price is fully paid, questions arise as to who gets the balance of the purchase price, the surviving spouse or the estate of the decedent. Where the sellers held the land in joint tenancy or tenancy by the entireties some courts hold that the right to the money goes to the survivor just as though there were a right of survivorship as to the contract price. *Watson* v. *Watson,* 126 NE2d 220 (Ill. 1955); *Hewitt* v. *Biege,* 327 P2d 872 (Kans. 1958); *DeYoung* v. *Mesler,* 130 NW2d 38 (Mich. 1964). *In re Maguire's Estate,* 296 N.Y.S. 528 (1937).

EXAMPLE: *H* and *W,* joint tenants, enter into a contract to sell their land to *X.* After a few payments are made on the contract, *H* dies leaving a will giving all his property to children by a former marriage. *W* will get the entire remainder of the purchase price.

There are cases taking a contrary view.

EXAMPLE: *H* and *W,* joint tenants, entered into a contract to sell land. *H* dies. His heirs got his share of the sale price. In a few states sale proceeds are treated as though held in tenancy in common. *Register of Wills* v. *Madine,* 219 A2d 245 (Md. 1966). *In re Baker's Estate,* 78 NW2d 863 (Iowa 1956); *Buford* v. *Dahlke,* 62 NW2d 252 (Neb. 1954). These cases are poor law.

EXAMPLE: *H* and *W,* tenants by the entireties, entered into a contract to sell land. *H* died. His heirs got his share of the purchase price. *Panushka* v. *Panushka,* 349 P2d 450 (Oreg. 1960); Note, 14 Vand. L. Rev. 687 (1961). This result is dictated by the rule in some tenancy by the entireties states which do not recognize this type of tenancy in money or *personal property.*

Once again, the sellers can take the uncertainty out of this eventuality by agreeing in advance as to the disposition of these proceeds.

Of course once the money has been paid by the buyer to the sellers, the cash money, even if held intact by the sellers in a joint safe-deposit box, is owned by them in tenancy in common. *Ill. Public Aid Commission* v. *Stille,* 153 NE2d 59 (Ill. 1958).

Suppose that the sellers are tenants by the entireties. They give a deed to the buyer and take back a purchase money mortgage. Some states hold that the mortgage is owned as tenants by the entireties. *Ciconte* v. *Barba,* 161 Atl. 925

(Del. 1932). Others hold that the mortgage is owned in tenancy in common. *Webb* v. *Woodcock,* 290 Pac. 751 (Oreg. 1930); 64 ALR2d 8.

The problem extends even to condemnation awards.

> **EXAMPLE:**   *H* and *W* owned land in tenancy by the entireties. The city con-demned the land and deposited $100,000 as a condemnation award. *H* died. *W* takes the entire award as the surviving tenant by the entireties. *H's* other heirs take nothing. *Smith* v. *Tipping,* 211 NE2d 231 (Mass. 1965); *In re Idlewild Airport,* 85 N.Y.S.2d 617 (1948).

Community property states present special problems.

> **EXAMPLE:**   In a community property state, *H* and *W,* joint tenants, entered into a contract to sell land. The proceeds of sale are community property. *Smith* v. *Tang,* 412 P2d 697 (Ariz. 1966).

The problem also exists with respect to the proceeds of fire insurance poli-cies.

The better rule is that the money goes to the survivor. Had the parties been asked about this when they received their deed, virtually all would have been astonished to hear any question raised as to the right of the survivor to get the money. This intention ought to be controlling.

> **SUGGESTION:**   Let the contract read that the price is payable to the sellers *as joint tenants with the right of survivorship and not as tenants in common nor as tenants by the entireties nor as community property.*

It seems rather odd that the courts seldom mention a rule of contract law that on the death of one of several promisees (sellers) the survivor or survivors have the right to collect from the promisor (buyer). The estate of the deceased promisee collects from the surviving promisees unless the contract shows that the parties had some contrary intention. Murray, *Contracts* (2d ed. of *Grismore on Contracts,* 1974) § 274. In other words, the situation lends itself to contract law rather than property law.

Suppose that a contract of sale names the buyers as joint tenants. Their rights *as between themselves* are established as soon as the contract is signed.

> **EXAMPLE:**   Seller contracts to sell a home to Husband and Wife, as joint ten-ants. Husband persuades Seller to make the deed run to Husband only. Wife dis-covers this. She is entitled to a court order reforming the deed to run to Husband and Wife as joint tenants. *Remus* v. *Schwass,* 406 Ill. 63, 92 NE2d 127 (1950).

14.06 Inheritance and estate tax—joint tenancy and tenancy by the entireties

The automatic transfer of title to the surviving joint tenant or tenant by the entireties upon the death of a co-owner is subject to state inheritance and federal estate tax if the deceased owner's estate is in excess of the exemptions allowed by law. See *Powell on Real Property* §§ 619 & 623.1.

The rules in this regard are simple. The entire value of the property is included in the decedent's estate for estate tax purposes. 11 USC § 2040(a).

> **EXAMPLE:** *A* and *B* own property as joint tenants. The property is worth $100,000. One of the owners dies. The decedent's estate will include the entire $100,000 value of the property.

There are two exceptions to this rule. First, the decedent's estate shall not include that portion of the value of the property actually purchased by the survivor's contribution.

> **EXAMPLE:** *A* and *B* acquire Blackacre as joint tenants. They pay $50,000 for the property, each contributing $25,000. The property appreciates in value to $100,000 at the time of *A*'s death. Only $50,000 will be included in *A*'s estate, the other one-half interest was bought and paid for by *B*.

The second exception relates to joint interests created between a husband and wife alone, i.e., a tenancy by the entireties or a joint tenancy with the husband and wife as the only joint tenants. In this instance, there is no estate tax on the death of the first spouse, but, for people of means, estate tax problems could crop up on the death of the survivor. Proper estate tax planning must take place before the property is purchased.

14.07 Tenancy in common

Co-owners who are not joint tenants, tenants by the entireties, or owners of community property are tenants in common. Their shares need not be equal. For example, one co-owner may have an undivided one-tenth interest and the other the remaining undivided nine-tenths interest. They need not have acquired their titles at the same time or by the same instrument.

Tenancies in common often occur when title is acquired by descent or will.

> **EXAMPLE:** *X*, a widower, dies without a will, leaving his children, *A, B,* and *C,* as his only heirs. The children own *X*'s real estate as tenants in common.

> **EXAMPLE:** *X*, a widower, dies leaving a will, by which he gives his land to his children, *A, B,* and *C,* in equal shares. They own the land as tenants in common.

Tenants in common are entitled to share the possession and rents of the property according to their shares in the property. Except for their sharing of possession and rents, however, the situation is almost as if each tenant in common owned a separate piece of real estate. Each tenant in common may convey or mortgage his share, and the share of each tenant in common is subject to the lien of judgments against him.

Upon the death of a tenant in common, his share goes to his heirs or the parties named in his will. Also, only the decedent's share of the property is included in his estate.

14.08   Partition

If tenants in common, or joint tenants, for that matter, wish to terminate their joint possession of the land, any of the co-tenants may file a suit to partition the real estate. The court will appoint commissioners to divide the land into separate tracts according to the shares of the co-tenants, so that each will become the sole owner of the tract set aside for him. If the land cannot be divided in this manner, the court will order the land sold and will divide the proceeds of the sale among the co-tenants according to their respective interest.

> **EXAMPLE:** *A* dies owning a tract of land improved with a single-family dwelling and leaving no widow and no will, but leaving as his heirs a son, *B,* and two grandchildren, *C* and *D,* who are children of a deceased son, *E. B* owns one-half of the title, and *C* and *D* own one-fourth each. *B* files a partition suit against *C* and *D.* The courts finds, as it obviously must, that the land cannot be divided among the three tenants in common. It orders the land sold at public auction, whereupon the same is sold to *F,* the highest bidder, for $6,000. *B* receives $3,000 from the proceeds of the sale, and *C* and *D* each receive $1,500.

Partition can, of course, be accomplished by the voluntary action of all co-owners without the necessity of court proceedings. Frequently this action is impossible, since many co-ownerships involve minor heirs, who cannot participate in voluntary partition.

As a rule, community property and land held in tenancy by the entireties are not subject to partition during the continuance of the marriage. *Stanley* v. *Mueller,* 350 P2d 880 (Oreg. 1960); *Lawrence* v. *Lawrence,* 190 A2d 206 (N.J. 1963).

14.09   Rights and obligations of co-owners

Co-owners must, as a rule, contribute ratably toward payment of taxes, special assessments, mortgages, and repairs of the property. 48 ALR2d 1305. If one co-owner, through refusal of the other co-owners to contribute, is compelled to pay more than his share of the necessary expenses, he thereby acquires a lien analogous to a mortgage lien on the shares of the other co-owners, and he may foreclose such lien if they persist in their refusal to contribute. *Cal-*

cagni v. *Cirino,* 14 A2d 803 (R.I. 1940). But one co-owner cannot purchase the property at a mortgage foreclosure sale or tax sale of the land and thus acquire a title that would enable him to oust the other co-owners. The title thus acquired is acquired for the benefit of all co-owners if they seasonably contribute their respective proportions of the expense incurred by the tenant who purchased the outstanding title. *Laura* v. *Christian,* 537 P2d 1389 (N.M. 1976).

If one co-owner collects all the rents but does not himself occupy the land, he must account to the other co-owners for their share of the rents. *Thompson* v. *Flynn,* 58 P2d 769 (Mont. 1936). A few states have laws making a co-owner liable to the other co-owners for rent where he alone occupies the land, collecting no rent therefrom. *Hazard* v. *Albro,* 20 Atl. 834 (R.I. 1890). But in many states, a co-owner who personally occupies the premises and does not rent them out is not liable to the other co-owners for the rental value of the premises unless he has agreed to pay them rent or has forcibly kept them out of possession. *Burk* v. *Burk,* 22 So2d 609 (Ala. 1945). But, a co-owner who exclusively possesses the premises must bear the entire burden of taxes, repairs, and mortgage interest payments. *Clute* v. *Clute,* 90 NE 988 (N.Y. 1910).

14.10   Grants by one co-tenant

Obviously a mortgage signed by only one of the co-owners does not bind the others. It creates a lien only on the interest of the one who signs. *Rostan* v. *Huggins,* 5 SE2d 162 (N.C. 1939). Likewise, a judgment, federal lien, or other lien against one of the co-owners creates no lien on the shares of the others. The lessee of one co-tenant becomes, for the term of the lease, a co-tenant of the nonjoining owners. *Garland* v. *Holston Oil Co.,* 386 SW2d 914 (Tenn. 1965). The actions of the nonjoining co-tenants may amount to a ratification, thereby estopping them from denying the validity of the lease even as against their interest.

> **EXAMPLE:** *H* and *W* owned recreational property. *H* leased the property to *T.* *W* knew of lease renewals and received some rent payments. The court held that *W* acquiesced in *H's* leasing of the property and was estopped from denying the validity of the lease. *Gleason* v. *Tompkins,* 375 NYS2d 247 (1976).

14.11   Bankruptcy of co-tenant

Where land is owned by two or more persons in any kind of co-tenancy, and one of the co-tenants goes bankrupt, the bankruptcy court has the power to sell all of the property. 11 USC § 363(f). The obvious reason is that it is almost impossible to sell a fractional interest in property. Because of this eventuality, great care must be used in selecting co-owners.

14.12   Federal tax liens

Where two or more persons own land as co-tenants, and a federal lien (for unpaid income tax, for example) is filed against one co-tenant, the federal government may force a sale of the entire property. *U.S.* v. *Kocher,* 468 F2d 503 (2d Cir. 1972). The portion of the sale proceeds that is attributable to the interest of the delinquent taxpayer goes to the government and the remainder goes to the other co-tenants. Again, this is evidence that one must use care in choosing investment partners. However, in most states where tenancy by the entireties is recognized, and a creditor of one spouse cannot reach any share of the property, the federal lien does not attach at all if it is against only one spouse. Plumb, *Federal Tax Liens* 37 (3d ed. 1972).

14.13   Community property—in general

The community property system is of Spanish origin and obtains in states that were subject to Spanish influence, namely, Arizona, California, Idaho, Louisiana, Nevada, New Mexico, Texas, and Washington. The law of these states recognizes two kinds of property that may belong to the spouses in case of marriage—the *separate property* and the *community property.* The separate property of either husband or wife is what he or she owned at the time of marriage and what he or she acquired during marriage by inheritance, will, or gift. The separate property of each spouse is wholly free from all interest or claim on the part of the other and is entirely under the management and control, whether by deed, mortgage, will, or otherwise of the spouse to whom it belongs. All other property is community property.

14.13(a)   Theory of community property

It is the theory in these states that the husband and wife should share equally property acquired by their joint efforts during marriage. Thus, the husband is as much entitled to share equally in acquisitions by the wife through her industry as she is entitled to share equally in acquisitions by the husband, and each spouse owns one-half of all that is earned or gained, even though one earned or gained more than the other or actually earned or gained nothing. *See* Cal. Civ. Code § 5105.

14.13(b)   Property acquired during the marriage

Property *purchased* with separate funds is the separate property of the purchaser, whereas property purchased with community funds is community property.

Property acquired by *purchase* during the marriage is ordinarily presumed to vest in the husband and wife as community property, regardless of whether the deed is made to the husband, wife, or both. Under the community property system, the ownership of property does not depend upon the question of who happens to be named as grantee in the deed.

In California prior to January 1, 1975, and in New Mexico prior to July 1, 1973, it was provided that real estate conveyed to a married woman in her own separate name was presumed to be her separate property. So far as the husband and wife are concerned, this presumption can be destroyed by proof that the property was purchased with community funds and that the placing of title in the wife's name was not made with the intention of making a gift to her. Such property is community property. But the presumption that the property is the separate property of the wife and can be sold or mortgaged without the husband's signature is conclusive in favor of purchasers and mortgagees dealing with the wife in good faith and for a valuable consideration. *Fulkerson* v. *Stiles,* 105 Pac. 966 (Cal. 1909).

Except possibly in Louisiana and Texas, a husband and wife may by agreement change the status of property from separate to community property or from community to separate property. Income tax returns are often received as evidence of such agreements.

A deed by the husband to the wife raises a presumption that this was intended to convert the land into her separate property. But this presumption can be rebutted. 41 CJS *Husband & Wife* § 491(c).

In Arizona, California, Idaho, New Mexico, Texas, Washington, and Nevada, a deed to husband and wife as joint tenants makes the property the separate property of each, which property they hold in ordinary joint tenancy. *Collier* v. *Collier,* 242 P2d 537 (Ariz. 1952); *Siberell* v. *Siberell,* 7 P2d 1003 (Cal. 1932). However, oral evidence can be admitted in court to show that the husband and wife really intended this to be community property, and such intention will prevail. *Gudelj* v. *Gudelj,* 259 P2d 656 (Cal. 1953). In New Mexico, the opposite is true. A deed to a husband and wife in joint tenancy gives them the land as community property, unless evidence can be found that the parties did not intend the land to become community property. *In re Trimble's Estate,* 253 P2d 805 (N.M. 1953).

It is difficult, however, to present briefly an accurate picture of the law in community property states relative to joint tenancies. The law is complex and some standard treatise should be consulted. Baxter, *Marital Property* § 18.5 (1973); 21 Natural Resources J. 593. Only one thing seems clear, namely, the fact that the deed runs to the husband and wife as joint tenants will not prevent a court from holding that the land is held as community property. In states other than California, the claim of community ownership seems to be favored despite the joint tenancy form of the deed.

A husband may transfer his interest in community property to his wife and it will become her separate property. Baxter, *Marital Property,* § 20.1 (1973). A like result occurs where the land is purchased with community property and the husband directs that the land be conveyed to the wife. *Id.* § 20.2.

A gift made to both spouses is community property.

14.13(c) Deeds and mortgages of community property

In all community property states both husband and wife must sign if the property constitutes their home.

In any event, it is desirable and customary in most states for the husband and wife to join in any deed of any kind of land. And their joining is legally necessary where the land conveyed is occupied by the parties as their home. In most community property states that require the wife's consent to a deed of community property, the wife's signature is also needed for a valid contract to convey community property. *Rundle* v. *Winters,* 298 Pac. 929 (Ariz. 1931); *Chapman* v. *Hill,* 137 Pac. 1041 (Wash. 1914); *Elliott* v. *Craig,* 260 Pac. 433 (Idaho 1927); *Adams* v. *Blumenshine,* 204 P 66 (N.M. 1922). The wife should also join in all but short-term leases of community property. *Bowman* v. *Hardgrove,* 93 P2d 303 (Wash. 1939).

> **NEW DIRECTIONS:** The aspects of the community property system that give sole control to the husband are invalid on constitutional grounds. The battle is being fought both in the state legislature and the courthouse.

See Kirchberg v. *Feenstra,* 101 S.Ct. 1195 (1981); *Powell on Real Property* § 626(2); 15A Am. Jur. 2d *Community Prop.* § 78.

14.13(d)   Wills and descent of community property

The descent of community property when there is no will varies from state to state. It must be remembered in this connection that, regardless of the legal title, each spouse owns one-half of the community property.

In some community property states, in the absence of a will that specifies another disposition of the property, the surviving spouse succeeds to the decedent's share of the community property. In other states the decedent's share goes in whole or in part to his or her descendants. All community property states recognize the right to make a will by the first spouse to die.

14.13(e)   Dower and curtesy

Neither dower nor curtesy exists in community property states.

14.13(f)   Divorce and separation

On entry of a divorce decree, the court usually divides up the community property between the spouses. And even without a divorce, the spouses may in most states enter into an agreement dissolving the community and dividing their property.

14.14   Dower—in general

Dower is the interest in the real estate of the husband which the law in many states gives to the widow to provide her with a means of support after her husband's death. It is a life estate in one-third of the lands that the husband owned during the continuance of the marriage relation. *Dickson* v. *Ind. Bank,* 348 A2d 26 (R.I.). The requirements for dower are: (1) a valid marriage; (2) that the husband own the land during the continuance of the marriage relation; and 3) that the husband die prior to the death of the wife.

The right of dower originated in early times when a man's wealth consisted largely of real estate. Many states have recognized the widow's need for more than a life estate in the husband's realty and have passed laws that give the widow a share in her husband's estate. See *Powell on Real Property* § 213. These laws vary from state to state.

In all states laws have been enacted that alter the old rules concerning the rights of one spouse in land owned by the other. These laws must be consulted.

14.14(a)   Inchoate and consummate dower

During her husband's lifetime, the wife's rights consist merely of the possibility that she may become entitled to her dower. Until his death, the wife's dower is said to be *inchoate.* It is not such an interest that the wife can convey to a stranger, nor can it be sold at a forced sale to pay the wife's debts. The right can be released, however, as where the wife joins in her husband's deed of the property to a third party.

Should the wife predecease her husband, even this incipient right is automatically extinguished. Thus, if her husband has previously conveyed his land without obtaining her signature on the deed, the grantee's title becomes perfect upon the wife's death before her husband's. It is as though her dower had never existed.

On the husband's death, her dower becomes *consummate.* It has ripened into something that she is certain to enjoy.

If the husband conveys his land without his wife joining in the deed, and the wife survives her husband, she then becomes entitled to her dower. The fact that the purchaser from the husband acted innocently does not protect him.

> **EXAMPLE:** *H,* a married man, buys Lot 1. He becomes estranged from his wife, *W. H* sells and conveys Lot 1 to *E,* describing himself as "a bachelor." *E* believes this representation. Later *H* dies and *W* survives him. She can now go into court and obtain her dower rights.

> **EXCEPTION:** In some states, Massachusetts, for example, dower exists, but if the husband conveys the land in his lifetime without his wife's signature, her dower in that land is wiped out.

14.14(b)   Assignment of dower

On the husband's death, one-third of the land that the husband owned during the marriage and in which the wife did not release her dower (which includes the land owned by him at the time of his death and also the land that he conveyed during the marriage without obtaining her signature) is set apart for the widow, usually by court order. This is called *assignment of dower.* In this third, the widow has an ordinary life estate. She may occupy the land herself or rent it to a tenant. On her death, all her rights therein are terminated.

If the land cannot be divided, the widow may be given one-third of the rents for her lifetime as her dower, *Shilowitz* v. *Shilowitz,* 291 A2d 383. Or, in many states, the land will be sold and a portion of the proceeds allotted to her.

In any case, if the husband is indebted at the time of his death, the widow's dower rights are superior to any claims of his creditors in and to the land. This is one of the important characteristics of dower.

14.14(c)   Joint tenancy and dower

Although a widow has dower in lands owned by her husband in tenancy in common with others, there is no dower in a joint tenancy.

> **EXAMPLE:**   Two men, *A* and *B,* hold title in joint tenancy. *A* is married to *C,* and *B* is married to *D. A* conveys to *X. A*'s wife, *C,* does not join in the deed. Ordinarily when a wife does not join in her husband's deed, her dower remains outstanding, but here no dower remains outstanding in *C* because *A* held title as a joint tenant. However, *B,* and *X* now hold title as tenants in common, and their wives have dower in the real estate. *Johnston* v. *Muntz,* 4 NE2d 826 (Ill. 1936).

> **EXAMPLE:**   *H* and *W,* husband and wife, own land in joint tenancy. *H* conveys his half interest to *X. X* takes this interest free of any dower rights of *W,* because when *H* signed the deed, he was a joint tenant and there is no dower in a joint tenancy. *Laterza* v. *Murray,* 2 Ill. 2d 219, 117 NE2d 779 (Ill. 1954). However, *H* now has dower in *W's* half interest.

14.14(d)   Mortgages and other liens

When a wife fails to join with her husband in the execution of a mortgage on the husband's land, any title acquired through foreclosure of such mortgage will be subject to the wife's dower in states where dower is recognized. *Thomas* v. *Thomas,* 18 S2d 544 (Ala. 1944). An opposite result occurs where the mortgage provides the purchase money for the property mortgaged. *Frederick* v. *Emig,* 57 NE 883 (Ill. 1900). The same results follow in some states that have substituted some ownership share for dower but requires the wife to join in any deed in order to release her ownership share. And the same result follows in many states where the husband has curtesy, dower, or an ownership share in the wife's real estate and fails to join in her mortgage. Obviously where land is owned by either husband or wife, it will usually be necessary for the spouse to join in any mortgage on the land.

Dower is subject to any liens or encumbrances to which the land was subject at the time of the marriage or at the time the husband acquired title.

> **EXAMPLE:**   *A* buys a tract of land on which there is a mortgage. On foreclosure of this mortgage, the dower of *A*'s wife will be extinguished.

> **EXAMPLE:**   *H* places a mortgage on his land and thereafter marries *W. W's* rights again are subject to those of the mortgagee, and foreclosure will extinguish her rights.

> **EXAMPLE:**   *X* obtains a judgment against *H,* a landowner. Thereafter, *H* marries *W. W's* dower is subject to the lien of *X's* judgment. But if a judgment is ren-

dered against a married man, as a rule any sheriff's sale under such a judgment will be subject to the wife's dower. *Seibert* v. *Todd,* 9 SE 822 (S.C. 1889).

14.14(e)   Leaseholds

The leasehold interest of a tenant under his lease is personal property, and since dower is a right that attaches to real estate only, a tenant's wife has no dower in the leasehold. 173 ALR 1260. Ordinarily a tenant may assign his leasehold without the wife's signature when no homestead rights are involved.

14.14(f)   Contract for sale of land

If a husband signs a contract for the sale of land, but his wife does not, she cannot be compelled to join in the deed to the buyer and her dower will remain outstanding. Obviously, any prudent buyer will insist that the wife sign the contract. Dower acquired by a landowner's spouse after he has signed a contract of sale, however, does not affect the rights of the contract purchaser.

> **EXAMPLE:** *H,* a bachelor, signs a contract to sell land to *B.* Thereafter, *H* marries *W.* When the last of the purchase price is paid, *W* refuses to sign the deed to *B.* Nevertheless, *H*'s deed to *B* gives *B* good title to the land, free of the wife's dower. Her dower was subject to the contract, *J. J. Newberry Co.* v. *Shannon,* 167 NE 292 (Mass. 1929); 63 ALR 136.

14.14(g)   Release of dower

The widow is entitled to have dower assigned out of any land conveyed, mortgaged, or leased by her husband during the marriage without her signature. Hence, it is important that the landowner's wife release her dower by joining with him in any deed, mortgage, or lease of his land.

Even if a grantor or mortgagor describes himself in the deed or mortgage as a bachelor or widower, and the grantee or mortgagee honestly believes that the grantor's marital status is as he describes it to be, the wife, should the grantor or mortgagor actually have one, is entitled to dower in the land if she survives the grantor or mortgagor. However, in a number of states, the widow's dower is limited to the land owned by the husband *at the time of his death,* so that any deed made by him in his lifetime defeats her dower even though she did not sign the deed. And in some states, a woman who is residing outside of the state at the time her husband makes a deed to land within the state has no right of dower even though she does not sign the deed.

14.14(h)   Dower—election

Many states give the widow, at her husband's death, a right to elect between her dower or some ownership (fee simple) share of the land.

14.14(i)   Dower—fee title given in lieu of dower

In a number of states, a widow is given a share in fee simple of her deceased husband's land in lieu of dower. Instead of acquiring merely a life estate, she may become the owner of one-third, or some other fraction, outright of her husband's land on his death. Remember that dower is only a life estate.

The law of some of these states gives the widow's share only in lands that the husband owned *at his death.* Thus, the widow has no claim whatever upon land conveyed by the husband during his lifetime and without the wife's signature. In other states that give the widow an ownership share in lieu of dower, the widow is entitled to her share in any land conveyed by the husband in his lifetime without her signature. Obviously in these last states, the wife's signature is necessary on any deed, mortgage, or contract of sale given by the husband.

14.14(j) Curtesy

In some states, a widower has a life estate known as *curtesy,* in the lands owned by his wife during their marriage. 100 U. Pa. L. Rev. 196. It is somewhat analogous to the widow's dower, but there are these points of difference:

> 1. In some curtesy states, a child must be born to the couple for this interest in land to arise. Most laws have abolished this requirement.
>
> 2. The widower's curtesy, according to the old English law, was a life estate in all the land owned by the wife during the marriage, as contrasted with the one-third allowed the widow as her dower. In most of the curtesy states, however, the husband's share has been reduced by modern laws to some fraction, such as one-third.

In a number of states the husband is given dower instead of curtesy.

Whenever a husband has dower or curtesy, obviously he should join in the wife's deed, mortgage, or contract of sale of her property. However, in some states, a deed given by the wife conveying her own land bars the husband's curtesy even if he does not join in the deed.

In a number of states, a surviving husband is given a share in fee simple of the wife's lands in lieu of curtesy. In some of these states, for example, the widower's share is limited to the land that the wife owned at her death. He has no claim whatever upon land conveyed by her in her lifetime without his signature.

In still other states that give the widower an ownership share in lieu of curtesy, the widower is entitled to his ownership share in any land conveyed by the wife in her lifetime without his signature.

Many states that give a widower curtesy or dower allow him, at the wife's death, to choose an ownership share instead.

14.14(k) Divorce

Divorce terminates dower, curtesy, and their statutory substitutes. Some state laws provide however that a divorce bars only the dower or curtesy of the spouse for whose fault the divorce was obtained.

> **TIPS FOR LAWYERS:** The Uniform Marriage and Divorce Act has been adopted in a number of states. It provides for an equitable division of property on

divorce without regard to marital fault. This eliminates the phony adultery and cruelty charges that formerly characterized divorce. *Kujawinski* v. *Kujawinski,* 71 Ill. 2d 563, 376 NE2d 1382 (1978). As to real estate owned separately by one of the spouses, such as land owned by the spouse before marriage, that spouse may sell and convey the land before divorce without obtaining the signature of the other spouse. *Ibid.* This rule applies as soon as divorce proceedings have been filed. *Cady* v. *Cady,* 581 P2d 358 (Kan. 1978). Of course, this does not apply to the marital home. In all states having homestead laws, such a deed requires both signatures. See 68 Ill. B. J. 320, 698.

14.15   Homestead

When a family owns and occupies a tract of land as its home, in many states that portion of the tract which does not exceed in area or value the limit fixed by law for homesteads is the family homestead, and certain rights, called homestead rights, are created therein. These homestead rights may, of course, extend to the entire tract if it is within the area and value limits fixed by law.

There are three principal motives behind the various state homestead laws. One is the protection of the family against being evicted from their home by enforcement of the claims of creditors. The homestead portion of the tract of land is protected against sheriff's sales on a judgment against the landowner.

The second object of the homestead laws is to protect the wife against the husband. The lawmakers thought it would be a good idea if the husband were not allowed to sell his own home if the wife was opposed to the idea. Evidently, the theory was that the old home should not be disposed of until a new home suitable for the family had been provided. To accomplish this result, the lawmakers provided that the husband could not convey good title to his own home unless his wife signed the deed. It is therefore necessary that both husband and wife join in any deed or mortgage of homestead property, except, of course, a purchase money mortgage.

As a final protection of the wife against the husband and his creditors, the homestead laws provided some protection for the widow after the death of her husband. This was necessary because dower did not afford the widow adequate protection. Dower does not give the widow any right to the occupation of any real estate until a particular tract of land has been set apart or assigned to her as dower. Immediately upon the husband's death, the widow might be subject to eviction from the home. Protection was afforded by the laws providing for the widow's homestead. Even a husband who has quarreled bitterly with his wife cannot legally deprive her of this protection. A final development in this direction was the *probate homestead,* which created a home for the widow in land that the husband had never occupied as his home. In this regard, the widow's rights are superior to the rights of any creditor of the deceased husband. Land so occupied by the widow cannot be sold to pay the deceased husband's debts.

The homestead here discussed exists only under state laws and has nothing to do with the Federal Homestead Law.

For a valid deed or mortgage of the homestead, it is necessary that both husband and wife join in the same deed or mortgage. The wife is thus protected against the improvidence of the husband. In some states, it is necessary that the deed or mortgage of the homestead contain a clause expressly releasing or waiving all homestead rights, and in many states a deed or mortgage of the homestead land must be acknowledged in order to be valid.

14.16 Unmarried cohabitants

Recent years have seen an increase in the number of instances where individuals have established housekeeping units without the benefit of formal marriage. This may cause problems.

> **EXAMPLE:** *A,* a bachelor, and *B,* a spinster, buy a house. The deed simply runs to them as *A* and *B*. Both sign the mortgage required for part of the purchase price. Both contribute to the cash payment, since both have jobs. There is no contract between them. *A* dies. *B* is a stranger and inherits nothing from *A*. Still *B* must continue making payments on the mortgage to prevent foreclosure.

Of course, the parties can quite simply solve this problem.

> **EXAMPLE:** In states where joint tenancy is recognized, *A* and *B* can have the deed run to them as joint tenants.

And in states that recognize tenancy by the entireties and joint tenancy, some courts come to the rescue.

> **EXAMPLE:** *A* and *B,* unmarried persons, buy a home and the deed runs to them "as tenants by the entireties." Some states will treat this as a joint tenancy.

Except in those jurisdictions which still recognize common law marriage, dower, curtesy, spouse's rights statutes, and the law relating to distribution of property upon divorce are inapplicable to unmarried cohabitants. *Hewitt* v. *Hewitt,* 394 NE2d 1204 (Ill. 1979). But see 81 ALR3d 6; 81 ALR3d 110; Comment, 1978 So. Ill. U. L. J. 423, relating to the rights of a putative spouse. 3 ALR4d 13.

Various reasons have been given by courts in the various states in refusing to recognize property rights in unmarrieds. The most extreme of these is the courts' refusal to enforce contracts relating to property rights of unmarried persons who live together. Courts in other states will honor the contract if it is properly drawn.

Some courts make a distinction between cases involving parties who honestly thought they were married and those who know full well that they were not married. Evans, *Property Interests Arising from Quasi-Marital Relations,* 9 Cornell L. Q. 246 (1924).

EXAMPLE: *M,* thinking his divorce from *F* is final, engages in a marriage ceremony with *W.* Both *M* and *W* intend to marry and have otherwise complied with
all form requirements. The failure of *M* to be finally divorced from *F,* however,
rendered the marriage of *M* to *W* a nullity. This is a *putative* marriage and *M* and
W are *putative husband and wife.* The courts will treat their property as if they
were husband and wife.

EXAMPLE: *M* and *W* decide to live together and engage in sexual relations
without the benefit of any formal marriage. The older decisions refer to this as
concubinage. Some courts refuse to recognize property rights by either in the
property of the other.

There are various grounds for awarding property rights to the parties of a
nonmarital relationship. Primary among them is the *express agreement.* The parties
may expressly agree to pool their assets and share in their accumulations, enter
into a partnership or joint venture agreement, or exchange property for services. An express agreement is certainly the preferable course of action, since
they are almost always enforced by the courts if sexual conduct is not mentioned
in the contract. Unfortunately, most cohabitants do not have the foresight to enter into such agreements. This is folly especially where substantial assets are involved.

This problem has been the subject of much discussion. 19 Duq. L. Rev. 199
(1980); 16 J. Family Law 331 (1978); 15 *id.* 350; 24 Loyola L. Rev. 128 (1978);
61 Neb. L. Rev. 138; 53 Wash. L. Rev. 145 (1977); 23 Wayne L. Rev. 1305; 12
Willamette L. J. 453 (1976); 13 New England L. Rev. 453.

It is preferable that such agreements be in writing. The intent of the parties
and the terms of the agreement are more easily proved. Oral agreements are
nonetheless enforceable. *Marvin* v. *Marvin,* 557 P2d 106 (Cal. 1976). While
these agreements are sometimes subject to the defense of illegality as encourag-
ing immorality, they will only be declared invalid where sexual services are the
principal consideration. Courts frequently hold, however, that if the woman
makes a financial contribution, she will be protected.

EXAMPLE: *M* and *W* lived together for seven years. All property acquired during this period was taken in *M*'s name. At the outset of the relationship, *M* and *W*
orally agreed that while the parties lived together they would combine their efforts and earnings and would share equally in all accumulations as a result of their
individual or combined efforts. *W* also agreed to render services as companion
and homemaker. *M* agreed to provide for *W*'s financial support and needs for the
rest of her life. *W* gave up a lucrative singing career to devote her time to her
household responsibilities. During the period of cohabitation, and as a result of
their efforts and earnings, *M* and *W* acquired substantial property in *M*'s name.
The relationship then came to an end. The court allowed the enforcement of this
oral contract even though sexual relations may have been involved. *Marvin* v.
Marvin, 557 P2d 106 (Cal. 1976).

There are other grounds for awarding property to the parties to a nonmarital relationship. The courts may struggle to find some sort of partnership, trust, or gift as grounds for allocating property rights between the parties. These courts try to allow the bargain of the parties to be enforced rather than allow one of the parties to be deprived of what was jointly accumulated. *Latham* v. *Latham,* 547 P2d 144 (Oreg. 1976). Modern courts will try to enforce the reasonable expectations of the parties. *Carlson* v. *Olson,* 256 NW2d 249 (Minn. 1977). The decisions go so far as to order specific performance of an oral promise to convey real estate. *Tyranski* v. *Piggins,* 205 NW2d 595 (Mich. 1973).

Older decisions that deny protection to the unmarried woman no longer appear to be valid. The courts should be free to inquire into the conduct of the parties to determine whether their conduct demonstrates an implied contract or implied agreement of partnership or some sort of trust. Also, the older barrier against recovery for the reasonable value of services rendered may well be removed. *Marvin* v. *Marvin,* 557 P2d 106 (1976).

Unmarried cohabitants are vulnerable where a zoning ordinance forbids occupancy of homes by unrelated persons. Granting that these ordinances were aimed at communes, they have been used against unmarried cohabitants.

14.16(a) Tandem houses

There is a strong trend toward the construction of the tandem house. This is a house with a master bedroom and bath at opposite ends of the home, with a living room and kitchen between. Two unmarried persons join in the purchase of the home. They share the use of the kitchen and living room. This is done so that the cost of the home can be shared. Home prices are simply too high for either party to handle the deal alone.

Obviously, again a detailed agreement is needed, covering joint payments on the mortgage, taxes, insurance, repairs, effect of either party's failure to make his contribution; an option by *A* to buy out *B* if *B* decides to move; a veto by *A* of a purchaser produced by *B* if *B* decides to move and *A* cannot buy him out but objects to the purchaser tendered by *B;* house rules on cleaning shared quarters, hours for playing hi-fi, etc. The zoning must be checked carefully to see if it permits occupancy by unrelated persons. See § 26.30(c). The arrangement has a growing popularity among senior citizens.

14.16(b) Homosexuals

No dependable statement can be made regarding the property rights of cohabiting homosexuals. Arguably, express agreements between them relating to their property rights should be enforced. Public policy, however, may stand in the way. *Jones* v. *Daly,* 176 Cal. Reptr. 130 (1981); Baxter, *Marital Property* § 35.15 (pocket part 1980).

REFERENCES: The authorities on the rights of unmarried cohabitants are many. Baxter, *Marital Property* § 35.15 (1980 pocket part); Burch, *Property Rights of De Facto Spouses Including Thoughts on the Value of Homemaker's Services,* 10 Fam. L. Q. 101 (1976); Evans, *Property Interests Arising from Quasi-Marital Relations,* 9 Cornell L. Q. 246 (1924); Kaminski, *Joint Tenancy and a Residential Mortgage: An Unmarried Couple's Estate Tax Problem,* 69 Ill. B. J. 706 (1981); 50 Ind. L. J. 389 (1975); 3 ALR4th 13. Numerous articles deal with the leading case involving movie star Lee Marvin. 90 Harv. L. Rev. 1708; 16 J. Family L. 331; 8 New Mexico L. Rev. 81; 30 Okla L. Rev. 494; 17 Santa Clara L. Rev. 947; 11 Suffolk L. Rev. 1327; 10 S.W.U. L. Rev. 699; 52 Tul. L. Rev. 188; 46 U. Cinn. L. Rev. 924; 53 Wash. L. Rev. 145; 23 Wayne L. Rev. 1305; 65 Cal. L. Rev. 937.

15 REAL ESTATE FINANCE—MORTGAGES

15.01 Mortgage defined A mortgage may be defined as a conveyance of land given to secure the payment of a debt. On analysis, this definition discloses the existence of two elements: (1) Like a deed, a mortgage is a conveyance of land. (2) However, the intention is not, as in the case of a deed, to effect a sale of land, but to provide security for the payment of a debt.

15.02 History of mortgage law The history of mortgage law is the history of hundreds of years of ceaseless struggle for advantage between borrowers and lenders. The lawbooks reflect the constantly shifting fortunes of this war. Occasionally, the battle has gone in favor of the lenders. More recently, however, the consumerism wave has resulted in court decisions and new laws favorable to the borrowers. The tide of battle, as it has many times in the past, has shifted in the borrowers' favor. To understand how the modern mortgage developed out of these centuries of struggle is to take a long step forward toward understanding modern mortgage law. Much of our mortgage law comes to us from England. In that country, mortgage arrangements of various kinds existed even in the Anglo-Saxon times before the conquest of England by William the Conqueror in 1066. However, it will suffice for our purposes to begin with the mortgage of the fourteenth century. This document was a simple deed of the land, running from the borrower (mortgagor) to the lender (mortgagee). All the ceremonies needed for a full transfer of ownership took place when the mortgage was made. The mortgagee became the owner of the land just as if a sale had taken place. However, this ownership was subject to two qualifications:

1. The mortgagee, as owner, could oust the mortgagor, take immediate possession of the property, and collect the rents. However, the rents so collected had to be applied on

the mortgage debt. For this reason, the mortgagee often permitted the mortgagor to remain in possession.

2. The mortgage described the debt it secured and stated a date of payment, known as the *law day.* The mortgage gave the mortgagor the right to pay the debt on the law day. If he did so, the mortgage provided that it was thereby to become void. This provision was known as the *defeasance clause,* for payment of the debt on the law day defeated the mortgage and put ownership back in the mortgagor.

In early times, the courts enforced the mortgage as it was written. Foreclosure proceedings did not exist. Failure to pay the mortgage debt when due, termed a *default,* automatically extinguished all the mortgagor's interest in the land.

15.03 The equity of redemption

For many years no one dreamed of questioning this scheme of things. Then, slowly at first, and later in greater numbers, borrowers who had lost their property through default began to seek the assistance of the king. A typical petition by such a borrower would set forth the borrowing of the money, the making of the mortgage, the default in payment, and the resulting loss of the land. The petition would continue with the statement that the borrower now had funds and offered to pay the mortgage debt in full, with interest. The petition would then ask that the king order the mortgagee, who now owned the land, to accept the proffered money and convey the land back to the borrower. The king had little time or inclination to tend to these petitions personally, and so he habitually referred them to a high official, the lord chancellor. Since the king was the fountain of all justice, it was the chancellor's duty to dispose of these petitions justly and equitably, according to good conscience. This he did. In cases of hardship or accident, for example, where the mortgagor had been robbed while on his way to pay the debt, the chancellor would order the mortgagee to accept payment of the debt from the borrower and to convey the land back to the borrower. A mortgagee who refused to do as he was told was sent to jail. In time, by about the year 1625, what had begun as a matter of grace on the part of the king had developed into the purest routine. Borrowers filed their petitions directly with the chancellor, who was now functioning as the judge of a court, and with regularity his order was issued commanding the mortgagee to reconvey. Thus, a new and very important right was born, the right of the mortgagor to pay his debt even after default and in this manner to recover his property. This right came to be known as the *equitable right of redemption,* or the *equity of redemption.* Later the courts held that the mortgagor could sell this equitable right of redemption, that he could dispose of it by his will, and that if he died leaving no will the right could be exercised by his heirs. You will perceive that as a result of these developments, the mortgagor, even after default, retained very important rights in the land. Technically the mortgagee became full owner of the land upon default, but practically the mortgagor could now be regarded as the owner even after default, since he could reacquire ownership by exercising his equitable right of redemption.

15.03(a)   Waiver of right of redemption

The mortgagees reacted to the development of the equitable right of redemption by inserting clauses reciting that the mortgagor waived and surrendered all of his equitable rights of redemption. The courts, however, nipped this idea in the bud by holding that all such clauses were void. This result was based upon the courts' feeling that it was their duty to protect the needy borrower who would sign anything. This rule flourished and exists in full vigor today. Any provision in the mortgage purporting to terminate the mortgagor's ownership in case of failure to make payments when due is against public policy and is void. *Once a mortgage, always a mortgage.* It cannot be converted into an outright deed by the mere default of the mortgagor. No matter how the mortgage seeks to disguise an attempted waiver of the equittable right of redemption, the courts will strike it down.

> **EXAMPLE:** At the time the mortgage was made, the mortgagor signed a deed conveying the property to the mortgagee. He then delivered the deed to a third person in escrow with directions to deliver the deed to the mortgagee in case of default in the mortgage payments. This deed and escrow were held invalid as an attempted waiver of the equitable right of redemption. *Plummer* v. *Ilse,* 82 P. 1009 (Wash. 1905); *Hamud* v. *Hawthorne,* 338 P2d 387 (Cal. 1959).

15.03(b)   Clogging the equity

Other means were invented to in some way hamper the exercise of the equitable right of redemption. Rather than waiving the right, mortgagors executed documents which limited the manner of exercise of the right of redemption. Courts would not allow arrangements where the right of redemption could only be exercised for a certain period after law day or only by the mortgagor himself. Osborne, *Handbook on the Law of Mortgages* §§ 96 and 97 (2d ed. 1970). The courts will also use their powers to invalidate any agreement whereby the mortgagee oppresses or takes unconscionable advantage of the mortgagor. 55 Am. Jur. 2d *Mortgages* § 514; 59CJS *Mortgages* § 113. See also § 16.06(c).

> **EXAMPLE:** Owner mortgaged his Lot 1 to Lender. Lender demanded and received from Owner an option to buy Owner's Lot 2. When Lender sought to exercise this option, Owner resisted and litigation ensued. The court held the option void. *Humble Oil & Refining Co.* v. *Doerr,* 303 A2d 898 (N.J. 1973). A mortgagee is entitled to payment of the mortgage debt. He cannot take advantage of the mortgagor by compelling him to grant "collateral advantages."

15.04   Development of foreclosure

The efforts of the courts to rescue the mortgagor in turn placed the mortgagee at a disadvantage. The mortgagee, it is true, became the owner of the land when the mortgagor defaulted, but he could not be certain he would remain the owner, for the mortgagor might choose to redeem. To remedy this situation a new practice sprang up. Immediately upon default in payment of the mortgage debt, the mortgagee would file a petition in court, and the judge would enter an order, called a decree, allowing the mortgagor additional time to pay the debt. If he failed to pay within this time, usually six months or a year, the decree provided that his equitable right of redemption was thereby barred and foreclosed. Thereafter he could not redeem his property. Thus developed the *foreclosure suit,* a suit to bar or terminate the equitable right of redemption.

The method of foreclosure just described is known today as *strict foreclosure.* It is still used in Connecticut and Vermont and occasionally elsewhere.

The next development was foreclosure through public sale. The idea emerged that in mortgage foreclosures, justice would best be served by offering the land for sale at public auction, for if at such sale the property sold for more than the mortgage debt, the mortgagee would be paid his debt in full and the surplus proceeds of the sale would be salvaged for the mortgagor. This method of *foreclosure by sale* is the most common method of foreclosure in America today. This development constituted another major victory for the mortgagor. More important still, it led to another and even greater victory for the borrowers. As the practice of foreclosure by sale grew more common, the view began to emerge that the mortgage, despite its superficial similarity to a deed, was really not a deed of conveyance but only a *lien* on the land—that is, merely a means of bringing about a public sale to raise money for the payment of the mortgage debt.

15.05   The institutionalization of mortgage law

Mortgage lending has also progressed from pre–World War I days when the majority of mortgage lenders were individuals to a time when lenders are primarily institutions. Mortgage lending today also takes place against the backdrop of the secondary mortgage market and mortgage-backed securities that give virtual anonymity to the ultimate investor and isolation between it and the borrower. This evolution has taken mortgage processing from an individual-to-individual context to a context where the borrower deals with an ethical and highly skilled professional lender. Kratovil, *Mortgage Law Today,* 13 John Marsh. L. Rev. 251 (1980).

While first mortgage lending has become institutionalized and federalized, creative financing has given rise to much second mortgage lending by individuals. This is discussed in Ch. 21.

15.06   Federalization of mortgage law

The federalization of mortgage law has been accomplished by direct federal legislation such as the Real Estate Settlement Procedures Act, the Equal Credit Opportunity Act, etc. and by the involvement of the U.S. Department of Housing and Urban Development (HUD) largely through the Federal Housing Administration (FHA). HUD attempts to help people purchase homes on a sound basis. Under the HUD system, a homebuyer makes a small downpayment and obtains a mortgage loan for the balance of the purchase price. The loan is made by a bank, savings and loan association, mortgage banker, or other HUD-approved lender and is insured by HUD. This insurance protects the lender against loss on the loan which in turn allows the lender to be more liberal in granting the loan—thereby extending home ownership opportunities to families that would otherwise be unable to buy a home.

Through a similar program, the Veterans Administration (VA) guarantees loans made to veterans.

The Federal Home Loan Bank Board (FHLBB), regulating federal savings and loan associations, and the Controller of the Currency, regulating national banks, have also had an impact on lending practices of those lenders as do the federally regulated instrumentalities of the secondary market.

All of these programs have their own sets of standards and regulations which have played a large role in shaping underwriting requirements, the terms of loan documents and foreclosure practices to align mortgage practices with federally sponsored social goals.

REFERENCE: Weimer, Hoyt, & Bloom, *Real Estate,* Ch. 16 (7th ed. 1978).

15.07   Secondary mortgage market

The mortgage industry today is divided into two markets, the primary market of loan originators and the secondary market of investors that purchase the loans from the originators, holding them in a loan portfolio for a long-term investment. This secondary market has several benefits, both for the investors and the housing industry alike. First, it provides liquidity in that an investor in a mortgage security has a ready market for the sale of that asset. Second, it tends to moderate dips in the flow of mortgage capital allowing lenders to sell portfolios of loans to replenish their supply of funds. Third, it moves capital from one area of the country to another. And fourth, it permits investor portfolio diversification. Dennis, *Fundamentals of Mortgage Lending* 108 (1978).

One of the principal participants in the secondary mortgage market is the Federal National Mortgage Company (FNMA), sometimes called "Fannie Mae." FNMA was begun in 1938 as a corporation wholly owned by the federal government. In 1968, FNMA was split into two separate corporations. One, the Government National Mortgage Association (GNMA), sometimes called "Ginnie Mae," continues to be wholly owned by the federal government. The other,

FNMA, became a privately owned, federally chartered corporation subject to federal regulation. FNMA is the largest supplier of mortgage funds for homes and apartments, purchasing these loans from the originator thereby giving the lender funds to lend again. FNMA has long specialized in buying FHA insured or VA guaranteed loans, but it also buys large quantities of conventional loans that are not backed by the government. FNMA either holds the mortgages in its own portfolio or sells them to investors. All the while, the loan is typically being serviced by the originating lender or some other local entity.

GNMA is organized a bit differently. It is still a government agency, but it buys pools of mortgages and holds them as security for certificates that are issued to investors.

> **EXAMPLE:** Mortgage Banker has originated a volume of mortgages that are sold to GNMA. GNMA gets the funds to make this purchase by selling certificates, *mortgage-backed securities,* that may be purchased by investors with as little as a $25,000 minimum investment.

The pools are made up of FHA and VA mortgages and the investors' security lies both in the mortgages backing the pool and the full faith and credit of the United States Treasury that also guarantees payment. Every month, the investors receive a check that represents one month's interest on the remaining balance plus repaid and prepaid principal. These securities are held primarily by large investors such as banks, savings and loan associations, credit unions, and pension funds. Over $100 billion of such securities have been issued.

The Federal Home Loan Mortgage Corporation (FHLMC), sometimes called "Freddie Mac," buys conventional, nongovernment insured, mortgages in the secondary market. These mortgages are also placed in pools and certificates backed by these pools are sold to investors who ultimately receive the payments made by the mortgagors.

Investors in the secondary market are not all government related entities. Pension funds, insurance companies, and others also play a role as mortgage loan buyers. Some lenders have attempted to make their own mortgage pools selling shares in that pool, or using the pool as collateral for mortgage backed bonds. See, generally, Kratovil & Werner, *Modern Mortgage Law and Practice,* §§ 29.04 *et seq.* (2d ed. 1981); 13 ABA Real Ppty. Prob 2 T. J. 1011 (1978).

REFERENCE: FNMA, *A Guide to Fannie Mae* (1979).

15.08 Title and lien theories

The relatively recent view that the mortgage is not really a conveyance of land but only a lien, has reached its fullest development in the agricultural and western states. Certain states, called *title theory states,* still take the older view that a mortgage gives the mortgagee some sort of legal title to the land. In other states, called *lien theory states,* the view that the mortgagee has the legal title is entirely superseded by the view that he has merely a lien to secure his debt: Some states take a position midway between these two views. These are called *intermediate states.*

It is not possible, however, to draw any hard and fast line between these groups of states, since vestiges of title theory will be found in lien theory states, and many title theory states have adopted rules developed by lien theory courts. The differences in point of view are of importance in determining the mortgagee's rights with respect to possession and rents of the mortgaged property.

15.09   Types of mortgages

There are several different types of mortgage instruments. Those commonly encountered are regular mortgages, deeds of trust, equitable mortgages, and deeds absolute given as security for debts.

15.09(a)   Regular mortgages

The ordinary printed form of mortgage encountered in most states today is referred to herein as the regular mortgagee. It is, in form, a deed or conveyance of the land by the borrower to the lender, followed or preceded by a description of the debt and including a provision to the effect that such mortgage shall be void on full payment of such debt. The content of the additional paragraphs of "fine print" varies considerably.

15.09(b)   Deeds of trust

The regular mortgage involves only two parties, the borrower and the lender. In the trust deed, also known as the deed of trust, the borrower conveys the land, not to the lender, but to a third party, a *trustee,* in trust for the benefit of the holder of the note or notes that represent the mortgage debt.

The deed of trust form of mortgage has certain advantages: the chief one is that in a number of states it can be foreclosed by trustee's sale under the power-of-sale clause without any court proceedings. The power of sale trust deed is used in Alabama, Alaska, California, Colorado, District of Columbia, Mississippi, Missouri, Montana, Nebraska, Nevada, New Mexico, North Carolina, Oregon, Tennessee, Texas, Virginia, Washington, and West Virginia.

15.09(c)   Equitable mortgages

As a general rule, any instrument in writing by which the parties show their intention that real estate be held as security for the payment of a debt will constitute an equitable mortgage, capable of being foreclosed in a court of equity.

EXAMPLE: A landowner borrowed money from a mortgagee giving a promissory note to evidence the debt. On this note the borrower placed the following recital: "This note is secured by a real estate mortgage on . . ." (here followed a description of the land). No separate mortgage was executed. The court held that the note itself, with the quoted endorsement, constituted an equitable mortgage on the land, for it clearly expressed an intention that the land should stand as security for the debt. *Trustees of Zion Methodist Church* v. *Smith,* 81 NE2d 649 (Ill. 1948).

An instrument intended as a regular mortgage, but which contains some defect, may also operate as an equitable mortgage.

EXAMPLE: When, through inadvertence, a trust deed altogether omitted the name of a trustee, it was obviously ineffective to transfer title or create a power of sale in any one since it lacked a grantee. However, it was sustained as an equitable mortgage, which could be foreclosed by means of a foreclosure suit. *Dulany* v. *Willis,* 29 SE 324 (Va. 1898).

15.09(d) Deeds absolute given as a security

Often when a landowner borrows money he gives as security an absolute deed to the land. By "absolute deed" is meant a quitclaim or warranty deed such as is used in an ordinary land sale. On its face, the transaction looks like a sale of the land. Nevertheless, the courts treat such a deed as a mortgage where the evidence shows that the deed was really *intended* only as *security for a debt.*

EXAMPLE: Owner owns a home, which is already mortgaged to a bank. He needs money for medical expenses and goes to his brother, Lender, for a loan of $1,000. Lender loans Owner the money but insists that Owner sign a simple promissory note and give a quitclaim deed to his home. It is agreed orally that if the debt is paid when due, Lender will quitclaim the property back to Owner. Owner fails to pay the debt. Lender is not the owner of the land. He merely holds a mortgage on it, which he must foreclose. And remember that all the world has notice of the true nature of his deed, for undoubtedly Owner will remain in possession, and possession imparts constructive notice.

A deed such as that described in the above example is regarded by the courts as an attempt to "waive the equitable right of redemption." The courts often use the maxim, "Once a mortgage, always a mortgage." It cannot be converted into a conveyance of absolute ownership by mere default. Hence it becomes necessary for the courts to go back to the very beginning of the transaction. The task is a simple one. Either the deed was *then intended* as an absolute *transfer of ownership* (as in a land sale), or it was *then* intended merely to provide *security to a lender.* So the court listens to all the testimony regarding the beginnings of the transaction. Oral testimony is received as to what was said and done. And the court hears testimony as to what occurred thereafter. Usually it is child's play to distinguish between a deed intended to transfer absolute ownership and one that was merely intended to provide a lender with security.

The following circumstances are usually considered:

1. Adequacy of consideration. If Owner conveys land worth $10,000 and receives only $5,000, the indication is that the transaction is a mortgage. Normally land will sell for its full value.

2. Prior negotiations between the parties. When Owner applies to Lender for a loan and the transaction is consummated by Owner giving Lender a deed to the land, this tends to show that the transaction is a mortgage. It is as if Lender had said: "I will lend you the money, but give me a deed as security." Of course, if it appears that Lender rejected the application for a loan, this tends to show that the transaction is a sale. It is as if Lender had said: "I will not loan you any money, but I am willing to buy your land."

3. Subsequent conduct of the parties. If Owner receives money from Lender and gives Lender a deed to Owner's land, but Owner thereafter remains in possession, paying taxes, insurance premiums, and so on, this tends to show that the transaction is a mortgage, for in a normal land sale the buyer takes possession.

4. Possession. If the transaction is merely a security transaction, almost invariably the borrower retains possession of the land, and his possession gives the whole world notice of the fact that the deed was merely a security deed and that foreclosure must take place.

If the court construes the transaction to be a deed given as security for a debt, the mask of the sale transaction is stripped away and the mortgage aspects of the transaction are exposed. This means that the grantor/borrower has redemption rights according to state law. He may repay the debt and demand reconveyance of the property just as in the case of an ordinary mortgage. If the debt is not paid, the grantor/lender must foreclose just as if a regular mortgage had been made.

The return going to the lender/grantee is also measured against the usury laws to determine whether the charges assessed against the borrower resulted in a greater return than authorized by law. *Schulte* v. *Franklin,* 633 P2d 1151 (Kans. 1981). A return greater than the usury laws permit tends to stamp the transaction as a disguised loan.

Another result of a deed being held to be a security device lies in the fact that truth-in-lending requirements may be applicable. See § 15.13(g). If the proper disclosures were not made, the truth-in-lending penalty provisions may be invoked against the lender. *Long* v. *Storms,* 622 P2d 731 (Oreg. App. 1981).

REFERENCE: Cunningham & Tischler, *Disguised Real Estate Security Transactions as Mortgages in Substance,* 26 Rutgers L. Rev. 1 (1972).

Note, there is a second type of deed absolute problem. It is described in § 15.40.

15.10 Sale and leaseback

This form of transaction typically involves a landowner in need of funds to use in its business. While the landowner cannot give up use of its business property, the landowner can give up ownership of the property. An investor is found to buy the property at its full value and lease the property back to the seller. Hence the term *sale and leaseback.* There are other frequently found characteristics of this form of transaction. The seller–lessee is usually a retailer or industrial concern of high credit standing. The lease is usually for a term of twenty to thirty years and the seller–

lessee is usually given options to renew the lease and to purchase the property. The rental on the original term pays the buyer an amount equal to the purchase price plus a return higher than could be obtained on a conventional mortgage. The lessee is required to pay all real estate taxes, fire insurance, repairs, and so forth in a "net" rental arrangement. There are some variations on the sale and leaseback pattern.

> **EXAMPLE:** *XYZ Hamburgers,* a chain, spots a good location. *ABC Realty Investment Trust* buys the land, finances construction through an affiliate, and leases the location to *XYZ Hamburgers.*

The attraction of this type of transaction to the seller–lessee lies in the fact that he gets the full value of the property instead of the smaller amount that he could obtain on a mortgage, and he is under no obligation to repay this amount if he is willing to forego his repurchase of the land. In other words, he is not saddled with a debt, as he would be if he had made a mortgage on his land. Note, of course, the seller–lessee may have a continuing rental payment obligation. The advantage to the buyer is that foreclosure is not necessary if default is made in the rent payments, since the transaction is a sale and lease, not a mortgage.

Use of this device in a modified form is common today. An industrial corporation wants money to use in its business. It sells its plant to an investor, receiving the full cash value. The investor then leases the land back to the industrial corporation. Hence the term *sale and leaseback.*

Among the advantages to the lessee of such an arrangement are the following:

> 1. A tax advantage. In computing its income for income tax purposes, the lessee deducts its rent payments under the lease. Were the transaction a mortgage, the only permitted deductions would be interest and depreciation. Also, if the building is not newly constructed, it may be that the current value and sale price are substantially less than the price paid when the seller–lessee bought the building, and the sale to the investor represents an income tax loss to the seller–lessee.
>
> 2. By selling the property for its full value to the lessor, the lessee obtains much more cash money than it could raise on a mortgage, for no mortgagee will loan up to 100 percent of the value of the property.
>
> 3. Existing mortgages, corporate charters, debenture agreements, or other documents binding on the lessee may place restrictions on its right to borrow money. Since a lease is not a loan, the leaseback arrangement provides a method of getting around these restrictions.

The chief disadvantages to the lessee are:

> 1. If the building goes up in value, the investor, not the lessee, will reap the benefit of this increase once the lease expires.
>
> 2. The lessee has all the burdens of ownership, for the lease requires the lessee to pay taxes, insurance, and so on. But the lessee lacks the freedom of action that an owner

enjoys. Under the terms of the lease, the lessee cannot sell the leasehold without the consent of the investor. Even if the investor consents, there are many prospective purchasers who are reluctant to buy leaseholds. Moreover, the lessee cannot tear down or remodel buildings as business needs dictate unless the investor consents. Likewise, to erect new buildings would be foolish, for they would belong to the landlord at the end of the lease period.

Formerly, the sale and leaseback had the advantage over a mortgage in that the mortgage debt would always be shown on the debtor's balance sheet as a liability, while the lease obligation would not be shown at all or would only be shown as a footnote. In 1976, the accounting rules changed to require that fixed and certain lease liabilities be shown as liabilities.

15.10(a) Sale and leaseback—consequences of transaction being set aside

The sale and leaseback transaction is indeed very complex and is a financing vehicle. It must be distinguished from a deed absolute to secure a debt. *Matter of Kassuba*, 562 F2d 511 (7 Cir. 1977). Merely labeling a transaction a sale and leaseback will not make it immune from attack and when the transaction is attacked, the courts will carefully analyze the relationship between the seller–lessee and the buyer–lessor to determine whether a sale really occurred or whether the transaction is really a mortgage. *Burton* v. *Smith*, 357 So. 2d 324 (Ala. 1978). If the transaction is found to be a mortgage, consequences befall both the seller–lessee and the buyer–lessor. The relationship of mortgagor–mortgagee with its requirement of foreclosure and redemption rights replaces the relationship of landlord and tenant with its quick possessory remedy of forcible entry and detainer. Usury law may come into play as a standard for evaluating the fairness of the return to the buyer–lessor who has unexpectedly found itself in the role of lender. The income tax treatment that both parties had used and anticipated will not be available, and, indeed, past years' tax returns will have to be amended.

As can be seen, the transaction is quite complex and should only be entered into after careful consultation with an experienced counsel and tax advisor. The consequences of a mistake can be awesome.

15.10(b) Sale and leaseback—recent developments

In the case of a sale and leaseback where the rent provision contained an escalator clause tied in some way to the inflationary spiral, rentals have increased at times to a point where the transaction is no longer favorable to the tenant. Deals that looked bad for the investor in the late 1960s are now looking better. In some cases, the investor is selling the shopping center or other property back to the tenant at a profit and deferring the capital gains tax by exchanging a "like kind" property of comparable value.

REFERENCE: Kratovil and Werner, *Modern Mortgage Law and Practice,* Ch. 23 (2d ed. 1981). See § 23.03(a) of that text, discussing *Frank Lyon* v. *U.S.,* 435 U.S. 561, commented on in 49 J. Taxation 42 (1978); 56 Taxes 618; 6 R.E.L.J. 199 (1978).

15.11 Vendor's lien reserved by deed

In some states, a seller, in lieu of taking back a mortgage from the buyer, expressly reserves in his deed to the buyer a lien on the land to secure payment of the balance of the purchase price. Such a lien is called a *vendor's lien.* It is really a mortgage.

EXAMPLE: *A,* a landowner, conveyed to *B* by a warranty deed that warranted that title was free from all encumbrances excepting three certain notes executed by *B,* for which a vendor's lien was retained until said notes and the interest thereon should be fully paid. The court held that this clause created a lien on the land. Such a lien is regarded as partaking of the nature of an equitable mortgage. This device is governed by the same rules as a mortgage and may be foreclosed as such. *Crabtree* v. *Davis,* 186 So 734 (Ala. 1939); *Lusk* v. *Mintz,* 625 SW2d 774 (Tex. 1981).

Such a lien enjoys priority over subsequent liens and encumbrances and, like a purchase money mortgage, has priority over prior judgments against the purchaser. The grantee under such deed does not become personally liable for the purchase money unless he has signed a promissory note, as in the above example, or otherwise obligated himself personally to pay the debt. And a purchaser from such grantee does not become personally liable to the holder of the vendor's lien unless by his deed he assumes and agrees to pay the unpaid balance of the debt. The debt may be assigned, and the assignee will have the right to foreclose the lien.

15.12 Purchase money mortgages

Purchase money mortgages taken back by sellers provide a major form of real property financing in periods of tight credit. In such times, this form of financing vehicle provides the basis of most forms of creative financing that allows property to be sold. See Ch. 19.

15.13 Application and commitment

A mortgage transaction usually begins with an application for a loan. The application serves a double purpose: (1) it is a source of information on which the lender will base his decision as to making the loan; and (2) it defines the terms of the loan contract. The application is usually made on the mortgagee's preprinted form and signed by the prospective borrower. After investigating the prospective borrower's financial circumstances and appraising the real estate, the lender may write the applicant a letter stating that the loan application has been accepted. This letter is sometimes referred to as a *commitment*. This will usually result in a contract for the making of a mortgage loan.

Technically, the application is an *offer* by the mortgagor to give a mortgage and note on the terms specified in the application. The commitment is an *acceptance* of the offer, *Burns* v. *Washington Savings*, 171 So2d 322 (Miss. 1965), which, under basic contract law, creates a contract. If the letter of commitment makes any changes in the terms, it is technically a *counteroffer*. There is no contract in this instance unless the applicant agrees to the new terms, which he may do by writing the word "accepted" and his signature on the mortgagee's letter of commitment. To the lawyer this is the typical "offer and acceptance" problem.

Since the application and commitment define the terms on which the loan is to be made and constitute a contract that neither party can change or add to without the other's consent, the application should state the terms in detail. Indeed, a failure to include essential terms, will lead a court to hold that no binding contract came into existence. *Calosso* v. *First National Bank,* 143 So2d 343 (Fla. 1962). All contracts must be complete and certain. The mortgagee will of course want to see to it that the offer and acceptance contain various other clauses which may or may not be essential to the formation of a contract. Included among these other terms is the agreement of the borrower to sign a note and mortgage in a certain specified form; the borrower's agreement to furnish evidence of title and survey at his expense; the borrower's agreement to sign chattel security documents and to sign an assignment of leases and rents; provisions for deducting title and other charges from the proceeds of the loan; provisions that the lender shall have possession of the fire insurance policies and shall have the power to determine the quality and quantity of coverage afforded by those policies.

In periods of high or rising interest rates, many lenders will write a "commitment" letter approving the borrower and all loan terms except the interest rate. The letter states that the loan will carry the interest rate prevailing when the loan closes. This may not be a contract. An essential term, the price that the lender will charge, has yet to be agreed upon.

15.13(a)   Commitment fees   Quite commonly, in larger loans, the borrower pays a commitment fee which is refundable only if he performs his part of the bargain.

> **EXAMPLE:**   *R* procured a commitment from *E* for a mortgage loan on a shopping center. The commitment was contingent upon *R's* procuring eight leases with major tenants. *R* paid *E* a commitment fee. *R* was able to procure only six leases. *E* could keep the fee. *Boston Road Shopping Center* v. *Teachers Ins. & Annuity*

Assn., 11 NYS2d 831 (1962). *Accord, White Lakes Shopping Center, Inc.* v. *Jefferson Standard Life Ins. Co.,* 490 P2d 609 (Kans. 1971); 93 ALR3d 1156.

15.13(b) Damages

A lender will be liable to the borrower for damages if the lender does not live up to the commitment. *St. Paul at Chase Corp.* v. *Manufacturer's Life Ins. Co.,* 278 A2d 12 (Md. 1971); *Liben* v. *Nassau S. & L. Assn.,* 337 NY2d 310 (1972); 36 ALR 1408; 4 ALR4th 682.

> **EXAMPLE:** Lender commits to loan Borrower $1,000,000 at 12 percent interest. Lender refuses to make the loan when the time for funding arrives. Borrower obtains a loan from Banker at 14 percent interest. Lender is liable to Borrower for the 2 percent interest differential. *Pipkin* v. *Thomas & Hill, Inc.,* 258 SE2d 778 (N.C. 1979).

Although it is generally held that specific performance will not be granted for a contract to loan money, an argument can be made for the opposite result. Draper, *The Broken Commitment: A Modern View of the Mortgage Lender's Remedy,* 59 Cornell L. Rev. 418 (1974). In fact, there have been some cases with rather unusual circumstances that have resulted in specific performance being granted against the lender. *Vandeventer* v. *Dale Construction Co.,* 534 P2d 183 (Oreg. 1975); 82 ALR3d 1116.

> **EXAMPLE:** Owner gives Lender #1 a mortgage which is a construction loan to build an office building. Lender #1 makes the loan in reliance on Lender #2's commitment to make a new mortgage when the building is completed, the funds to be used to pay Lender #1's mortgage. When the building is completed, the mortgage market and office building market are dead. Funds are simply unobtainable elsewhere. Specific performance can be used to force Lender #2 to go through with his commitment.

15.13(c) Flood insurance

Mortgages must not only be concerned with the creditworthiness of the applicant and the value of the security, they must also consider the impact of the Flood Disaster Protection Act 42 USCS §§ 4001 *et seq.* The act requires that the lender determine whether the property is in a flood-prone area, notify the purchaser of such hazard and require flood insurance, if it is available.

A problem exists in that flood insurance is not automatically available to all applicants, but rather it is only obtainable in those communities which qualify and participate.

15.13(d) Discrimination in the application process

By enacting the Equal Credit Opportunity Act, 15 USCS §§ 1691 *et seq.,* Congress has acted to make credit available with fairness, impartiality, and without discrimination on the basis of race, color, religion, national origin, sex, marital status, or age. While marital status inquiries are not absolutely prohibited to the mortgage lender, 12 CFR § 202.4(c)(1), only the terms "married," "unmarried," or "separated" may be used. 12 CFR § 202.4(c)(2). The thought is that other inquiry is not directed toward an applicant's creditworthiness. The creditor cannot discount the income of an applicant or an applicant's spouse solely because it is derived from part-time employment, but the probably continuity of such income may be considered. 12 CFR § 202.5(e). Inquiries into the birth control practices and child-bearing intentions of the applicant are forbidden. 12 CFR § 202.4(h). 13 J. of L. Reform 102 (1979).

15.13(e)   Redlining   Both the states and the federal government have enacted laws as a reaction to some lenders' practice of automatically rejecting loans to be secured by property located in certain parts of a metropolitan area. Basically, these laws require the disclosure or reporting of various types of application and commitment data by census tract or some other defined geographical area. 12 USCS §§ 2801 *et seq;* Ill. Rev. Stat. 1975 ch. 95, § 201. At least one state, New Jersey, has, however, enacted a law prohibiting redlining and fining those guilty of violations. Aside from the reporting aspects, redlining has been held to constitute discrimination under the Fair Housing Act. *Laufman* v. *Oakley Bldg. & Loan Assn.*, 44 L.W. 2381 (USDC S. Ohio 1976).

The great issue here is whether the states may enforce their requirements against federally chartered lenders who are complying with the federal law. It has now been decided that any such enforcement will only be done by the federal authorities and the state authorities cannot act. *Conference of Federal Savings & Loan Associations* v. *Stein*, 604 F2d 1256 (9th Cir. 1979), aff'd. 445 U.S. 921, 63 L. Ed.2d 754 (1980).

REFERENCES: Duncan, Hood, and Neet, *Redlining Practices, Racial Resegregation and Urban Decay: Neighborhood Housing Services as a Viable Alternative,* 7 Urban Lawyer 510 (1975); Earthman, *Residential Mortgage Lending: Charting a Course Through the Regulatory Maze,* 29 Vand. L. Rev. 957 (1976).

15.13(f)   Denial of loan application   Under some state and federal laws, a lender must advise a loan applicant of the denial of the application and give the applicant a statement of the reasons for the denial. 15 USC § 1691.

15.13(g)   Truth-in-lending   The Federal Truth-in-Lending Act, 15 USC §§ 1601 *et seq.*, was enacted to give the consumer a disclosure of various credit terms to enable him to shop several lenders to obtain the best deal possible. The required disclosures include: the annual percentage rate; the number, amount, and due dates of scheduled payments; the amount of any balloon payments; the conditions of refinancing; the amount of the late payment charge; a description of any security interest; whether after-acquired property will be subject to the security interest; a description of any prepayment penalty; and the amount of any escrow account required for the payment of taxes, insurance, and the like. 12 CFR § 226.8. Special disclosures are also needed of the provisions of a variable rate or graduated payment mortgage.

If the required disclosures are not given, the borrower may sue the lender for civil penalties and in some cases to rescind or set aside the transaction. Kratovil and Werner, *Modern Mortgage Law and Practice* §§ 4.13 *et seq.* (2d ed. 1981).

15.13(h)   False applications   In today's world of tight money and high interest rates, many borrowers are tempted to falsify their loan applications in order to get a loan or to get the loan at more favorable terms.

> **EXAMPLE:** A borrower may state that he is paying a 20 percent downpayment when really the seller is receiving 10 percent in cash and taking back a second mortgage for 10 percent of the purchase price. Some buyers and sellers go so far as to have two sets of documents, one stating the form of the transaction as the lender wants to see it and the other stating the form that the transaction really takes.

> **EXAMPLE:** A borrower will state his intent to occupy the property when he has no real intent of living there.

These kinds of false statements are violations against the state law, and if a federal instrumentality is involved, federal law. See e.g., 18 USC §§ 1010–1014; Ill. Rev. Stat. Ch. 38, § 17–1(c).

15.14   Mortgage forms and practice   In the field of residential mortgage, both homes and apartments, mortgage forms follow the forms and practice set forth by FNMA, FHLMC, FHA, and VA. The old diversity of forms has vanished. Moreover, the details of mortgage practice are set forth in the detailed Servicer's Guides—for example, those of FHLMC and FNMA. The capable legal and lending personnel of these agencies have set forth in detail requirements that offer a mortgage practice guide of the very highest quality. Moreover, these guides furnish invaluable advice to the attorney involved in real estate transactions.

> **EXAMPLE:** These guides set forth a list of technical objections to title that are nevertheless deemed unobjectionable to a prudent lender. Thus they provide a parallel to the Title Standards adopted by title lawyers in the various states. It must be kept in mind that lenders always regard themselves as potential owners of the property. Foreclosures do take place. The superiority of the federal manuals lies in their domination of the mortgage market. If you buy a federally acceptable title, you can obtain federally related lending.

EXAMPLE: If you represent a purchaser of a condo unit or a unit in a PUD you will routinely study the federal manual to make sure that your unit will qualify under the federal manuals. In the process you will be making an analysis that represents the finest judgment that those with greatest experience and expertise have brought to bear on the problem.

It is for the foregoing reasons that the authors have concluded that much of our everyday real estate law and practice will be found in the federal manuals.

15.15   Private mortgage insurance

Beginning in 1957, Mortgage Guaranty Insurance Corporation (MGIC), a corporation of Wisconsin, began a program of insuring mortgage loans that has since generated many competitors. Through this program, the borrower, for an initial premium of one-half of 1 percent of the original loan balance and subsequent annual premiums of one-quarter of 1 percent of the loan balance, buys a policy that insures the lender that the loan will be repaid. In this way, first-time homebuyers who have not saved enough for a 20 percent down payment or who want to retain some of their savings are able to purchase a home with a down payment of 10 or even 5 percent.

This coverage gives the lender insurance that the top layer of 20 or 25 percent of the debt will be repaid. Obviously, full coverage is not necessary. Resort to the security should bring about the repayment of most of the debt. In only the most unusual of default situations will the lender need insurance for more than 25 percent of the debt.

EXAMPLE: Borrower falls into default on a $60,000 mortgage. Lender is protected by private mortgage insurance for 20 percent of the debt or $12,000. Lender forecloses, takes title to the property as the successful bidder at the foreclosure sale, and sells the property for $57,000. A claim is made to the private mortgage insurance company for the $3,000 deficiency.

Today there are many companies that issue such insurance.

15.16   The mortgage note

After the mortgagee has given his commitment to make the loan, the mortgagor signs a promissory note and mortgage. The mortgage stands as security for payment of the note. *The chief function of the note is to make the mortgagor personally liable for payment of the mortgage debt.* If the mortgagor signs such a note and then decides that he does not want the building, he cannot simply abandon the property and move elsewhere. Wherever he goes he takes his personal liability with him, and if the mortgage is foreclosed, the mortgagee can obtain a personal judgment against him for any deficiency between the foreclosure sale price and the amount of the mortgage debt. Armed with such a judgment, the mortgagee can garnishee the mortgagor's wages or have his other property sold to pay the balance due.

15.16(a) The mortgage note—negotiability

If a note is properly drawn, it can obtain the legal status of *negotiability.* This means that it can pass from the original creditor to a holder in due course. While the debtor may have had some defenses against the original creditor, i.e., the full debt was not disbursed, those defenses will not work against the holder in due course.

In 1976, regulations of the Federal Trade Commission (FTC) became effective to cure abuses of this system by preserving consumer claims and defenses against the sellers of certain consumer goods and lenders who financed those transactions. 16 CFR § 433 *et seq.* This regulation prevents the assignee from becoming a holder in due course to thwart the defenses available to the borrower. This regulation has application to lenders on mobile homes sold without the land and classified as personal property and lenders financing home improvement contracts.

> **EXAMPLE:** Before the FTC regulations became effective, a home improvement contractor and a homeowner would make an agreement for the installation of some siding. Part of the agreement would be a promissory note secured by a mortgage. The siding would prove to be defective, but because the contractor had assigned the note to a bank-holder in due course, the defenses that the homeowner had against the contractor would not be available when the bank began suit to collect on the note. The FTC regulation now requires that the note contain a notice that any holder is subject to the claims and defenses which the debtor could assert against the contractor. This makes the assignee of the note subject to the same defenses to collection that were available against the contractor.

An entirely different problem is posed by the new mortgages where interest rates vary from time to time as selected indexes move up and down. It seems doubtful that those mortgage notes are negotiable. *A. Alport & Son Inc.,* v. *Hotel Evans, Inc.,* 317 N.Y.S.2d 937 (1970). The importance of negotiability appears to be diminishing.

15.17 Parties to the mortgage

The borrower, who corresponds to the grantor in a deed, is known as the *mortgagor.* The lender, who corresponds to the grantee in a deed, is known as the *mortgagee.* It is important that the names of the parties be given accurately and fully in the mortgage. The marital status of the mortgagor, as *bachelor, spinster,* or *widower,* should be recited. The same considerations that require the grantor's spouse to join in his deed require the mortgagor's spouse to join in his mortgage. A mortgage by a minor or an insane person is subject to the same objections that exist in the case of deeds. A mortgage by a corporation must be authorized by proper corporate resolutions, which should show that the money is being borrowed for proper corporate purposes. In general, the requirements relative to the grantor and grantee in a deed are applicable to the mortgagor and mortgagee in a mortgage.

15.18 Foreclosure provisions and power of sale

Provisions are usually included in the mortgage for the foreclosure thereof, and, in states permitting foreclosure by exercise of power of sale, the power of sale is fully set forth in the mortgage. See § 24.05.

15.19 Waiver of homestead and dower

In some states, a mortgage on homestead land must include a clause releasing and waiving homestead rights. Again, in some states, a mortgage signed by the spouse of the mortgagor should contain a clause stating that such spouse thereby waives all dower as against the mortgagee.

15.20 Execution

The mortgagor and his spouse should sign the mortgage. Some states require that the word "SEAL" appear after their signatures. A corporation should always affix its corporate seal. In some states witnesses are required. The mortgage should also be acknowledged and delivered to the mortgagee.

15.21 Recording

As a practical matter, a mortgage must be recorded, since an unrecorded mortgage is void as to subsequent purchaser, mortgagees, or, in some states, judgment creditors who are ignorant of the existence of such mortgage. It is important that the mortgage be filed or recorded as soon after its execution as possible.

As a general rule, the priority of successive liens often is determined by priority of recording, the first mortgage recorded being a first lien on the land, the second mortgage recorded being a second lien, and so on. The importance of early recording thus becomes obvious, since foreclosure of a first mortgage will wipe out and extinguish all junior liens, such as second mortgages.

In states that have mortgage taxes, the recorder will want proof that the tax was paid.

15.21(a) Master mortgage

To save recording expenses, mortgagees have turned to the *master mortgage.* A mortgage lender records his usual mortgage form with none of the blanks filled in. This is the *master mortgage.* Thereafter each mortgage recorded by the mortgage company simply refers to the book and page of the master mortgage for the fine-print provisions, enabling the mortgagee to get all the necessary recordable data of each mortgage in a one-page document. Laws permitting this have been enacted in many states.

15.22 Debt—in general

In order for a mortgage to exist there must be a debt for the mortgage to secure. Without the debt there is nothing to secure, and the mortgage has no effect. Ordinarily, the debt takes the form of an obligation to pay money such as a promissory note or a bond which may or may not be negotiable. This is not necessarily so, however, and the debt may be in the form of any contractual relation.

The requirement of a debt is not a requirement that there be *personal liability* for the payment of the debt. It is competent for the parties to make any bargain on this subject as they please. They may agree that the mortgagee will look only to the real estate as security for repayment of the loan. *Gagne* v. *Hoban,* 159 NW2d 896 (Minn. 1968). In such case, the mortgagee cannot obtain a personal judgment or deficiency decree against the mortgagor should the mortgaged land prove insufficient to satisfy the mortgage debt.

The mortgage lien is measured by the amount of the mortgage debt. Thus if a mortgage recites a debt of $10,000, but actually only $5,000 is loaned, the mortgage stands as security for only $5,000. Likewise, the mortgage lien diminishes as the mortgage debt is reduced by payment. Thus if a mortgage of $10,000 is paid down to $5,000, the mortgage lien is reduced accordingly, and if the mortgagee thereafter loans the mortgagor additional funds, these additional funds are not secured by the mortgage unless the mortgage contains a clause covering *future advances.*

15.22(a) Debt—history of debt payment structure of home loans

Prior to the Great Depression first mortgages on homes were usually payable in five years, with one principal note and ten interest coupons due semi-annually. When the maturity date arrived, quite commonly the mortgagor made a nominal payment on principal, and the balance was extended. The extension agreement was recorded. Evidently, no one was greatly concerned about ultimate repayment of the principal. Second mortgages were common. They were used where the purchaser of the home lacked funds to make the required down payment. Many second mortgages were sold to individuals, who purchased them because of the higher return they provided.

Following the crash of 1929, many mortgages went into foreclosure. Banks closed. Mortgage funds dried up.

The Roosevelt administration put the FHA insurance program in place. Mortgage lenders could loan money safely once more on homes, since the loan was insured by a federal agency. But FHA insisted that the mortgage be amortized. Monthly payments were made, so that a constant reduction of the portion devoted to interest assured ultimate repayment of the principal. To be sure, few mortgages ran their full course, since homes are sold at intervals, perhaps seven years, and at each sale, the existing mortgage is commonly repaid through funds obtained by the purchaser on a new mortgage.

While this amortization mortgage served the country well and is still in use, other forms of mortgage adapted to an inflationary economy have been created. These are discussed elsewhere. See Ch. 16.

15.22(b) Debt—personal liability

Of course, the parties are at liberty to make any agreement they wish concerning personal liability.

> **EXAMPLE:** The borrower's personal liability may be limited to rents collected, the theory being that this prevents the borrower from milking the property. Kratovil & Werner, *Modern Mortgage Law and Practice* § 10.04(b) (2d ed. 1981). Or liability may be limited to defaults occurring during the first three years.

15.22(c) Debt—priority of lien

Any discussion of mortgage debt inevitably involves questions of priority of lien. Often there will be two or more liens against the same property.

> **EXAMPLE:** Owner mortgages his property to Lender #1 in 1971 and then mortgages the same property to Lender #2 in 1972. If both mortgages are valid and both are properly recorded, Lender #1's mortgage is a first lien, and if he is compelled to enforce it by foreclosure, he will extinguish Lender #2's mortgage, which is a subordinate or inferior lien. Of course, Lender #2 has the right to pay Lender #1's mortgage to prevent this extinguishment and to foreclose for the amounts due on both mortgages. It is said, in such circumstances, that Lender #1 enjoys priority of lien. Lender #2's lien is subject to Lender #1's.

The same situation exists when the liens are of different kinds.

> **EXAMPLE:** Lender acquires a mortgage lien on the property in 1978. Creditor acquires a judgment lien on the same property in 1979. Mechanic acquires a mechanic's lien on the property in 1980. Normally, these liens have priority according to the time they attach to the land. First in time is first in right. There are, however, many exceptions to the rule.

15.22(d) Debt—description of debt

A mortgage must in some way describe and identify the debt that it is intended to secure. 145 ALR 369; 89 ALR3d 937, 938, 939. The character and amount of the debt must be defined with reasonable certainty in order to preclude the parties from substituting debts other than those described. *Bowen* v. *Ratcliff,* 39 NE 860 (Ind. 1895). Otherwise, in some states, subsequent mortgagees, purchasers, or judgment creditors will acquire rights superior to those of the mortgage. 2 *Merrill on Notice* § 1090 (1952); 5 *Tiffany on Real Property* § 1407 (1939).

> **EXAMPLE:** Owner borrows $10,000 from Lender and gives Lender his note therefor. To secure the loan, Owner gives Lender a mortgage, but the mortgage does not recite the amount of the loan. The mortgage is recorded. Thereafter, Creditor obtains a judgment against Owner. Creditor's judgment is a prior lien, coming in ahead of Lender's mortgage. *Bullock* v. *Battenhousen,* 108 Ill. 28 (Ill. 1883). See also *Flexter* v. *Woomer,* 197 NE2d 161 (Ill. 1964).

The mortgage need not state the maturity date of the debt. 1 *Jones on Mortgages* 549, 559 (8th ed. 1928). *Contra: Sullivan* v. *Ladden,* 125 A. 250 (Conn. 1924). However, it is advisable that it do so. Similarly, the mortgage need not state the interest rate. *Metropolitan Life Ins. Co.* v. *Kobbeman,* 260 Ill. App. 508 (1931).

Where the note provides for future advances, the mortgage should state the maximum amount of future advances that the mortgage will secure. *Northridge Bank* v. *Lakeshore Commercial Finance Corp.,* 365 NE2d 382 (Ill. 1977).

15.22(e)   Debt—future advances—obligatory advances

A mortgage debt is rarely created at the same instant that the mortgage is signed. Normally, the mortgagor will receive his money sometime after the signing and recording of the mortgage. The question that arises is whether the mortgage has priority over junior mortgages, judgments, and other liens that may attach to the land before the money is paid out. The problem usually arises in three situations:

> **EXAMPLE:** An ordinary mortgage loan is applied for. The mortgage is executed and recorded. Payment of the mortgage money to the mortgagor is delayed pending the completion of a title search. A judgment or other lien attaches to the land after the recording of the mortgage. Thereafter, the mortgagee's title search is completed, but since the search covers only the date of the recording of the mortgage, the mortgagee is unaware of the judgment. Thereafter, the mortgagee pays out the mortgage money to the mortgagor. Discussion follows.

> **EXAMPLE:** An ordinary mortgage loan is made and the mortgage money is properly paid out to the mortgagor. The mortgage contains a provision to the effect that it also secures future advances to the mortgagor not in excess of $2,000, or some other sum. This is called an *open-end mortgage.* A year or so after the mortgage has been made, the mortgagor applies to the mortgagee for additional funds and receives an additional loan of $2,000. Before he receives his money, a judgment or other lien attaches to the land. The mortgagee pays out the $2,000 in ignorance of the existence of the judgment lien. Discussion follows.

> **EXAMPLE:** A construction loan is involved. The mortgage doles out the mortgage money as the building goes up, and before construction is completed other liens attach to the land. Discussion follows.

Where a mortgagee is obligated, by contract with the mortgagor, to advance funds to be secured by the mortgage, such mortgage will be a valid lien from the time of its recording, as against all subsequent encumbrances, even though the mortgage money is paid to the mortgagor after such subsequent encumbrances have attached to the mortgaged land. This holds true even though the mortgagee is actually aware of the existence of the subsequent encumbrances at the time he pays out the mortgage money. 80 ALR2d 191, 196, 199, 217, 219. Such advances are called *obligatory advances.* Because of the mortgagee's obligation to pay out the money, the mortgage debt is regarded as being in existence from the time of the contract. The obligation is usually created in one of two ways: (1) where the mortgagor has made written application for a mortgage loan and the mortgagee is contractually obligated to go through with the transaction; (2) where a construction loan is involved, the obligation is usually created by a construction loan agreement, which is an agreement entered into between mortgagor and mortgagee when the purpose of the loan is to provide funds for the construction of a building. This agreement authorizes the mortgagee to disburse the mortgage funds as the building goes up and seems to obligate disbursement. See Kratovil & Werner, *Mortgages for Construction and the Lien Priorities Problem—The "Unobligatory" Advance,* 41 Tenn. L. Rev. 311 (1974). It also binds the mortgagor to complete the erection of the building and to turn over to the mortgagee for disbursement such money as the mortgagor is furnishing from his own funds toward the erection of the building. The agreement also authorizes the mortgagee to act as the mortgagor's agent in dealing with the contractor and subcontractors. This agreement should dovetail into the construction contract between the mortgagor and his builder, so that the builder will not be clamoring for money at a time when the mortgage is not yet required to pay out funds.

Let us return to consideration of the application and commitment. It is not always easy for mortgage men to think of these documents as creating a contract for a loan so that the money subsequently advanced is an obligatory advance, and yet a simple illustration will prove that is the case.

> **EXAMPLE:** *A* applies to *ABC Corp.* for a $1,000,000 mortgage loan at 15 percent interest on his hotel building. The corporation gives a commitment to make this loan. Thereafter, *ABC Corp.* refuses to honor its commitment. *A* goes to *XYZ Corp.,* which gives him a loan on the same property at 16 percent interest. Without the slightest doubt, *ABC Corporation* is liable to *A* for the difference between 15 percent and 16 percent interest over the life of the loan. This is so because *ABC Corp.* broke its obligation to loan the funds to *A* at 15 percent.

Of course, in all states expenditures made by the mortgagee to preserve the lien of his mortgage, such as payments made by the mortgagee on delinquent real estate taxes that the mortgagor has failed to pay, are considered obligatory expenses, and the mortgagee has the same lien for such advances as he has for his original debt.

15.22(f) Debt—future advances—optional advances

Suppose that the mortgage does not absolutely bind the mortgagee to fund the mortgage debt. Advances under such a mortgage are called *optional advances.* Despite the fact that such mortgage is duly recorded, it is by no means certain that it will operate as a lien from the date of its recording as against all other liens attaching after that date. The argument that can be made against the mortgage is that a mortgage is a conveyance to secure a debt and that without a debt there is no mortgage. It must therefore follow that *until* the money has actually been advanced to the mortgagor no legal mortgage exists, for until that time the mortgagor owes no money to the mortgagee, and therefore no debt exists. In the case of obligatory advances, the courts dispose of the argument by saying that since the mortgagee must at all events loan the money, as he has contracted to do, for all practical purposes the debt exists as soon as the obligation to make the loan is created. Since this obligation is normally created, either by application and commitment or by a construction loan agreement, an obligatory advance mortgage is good against the whole world, including subsequent lienors, from the date the mortgage is recorded. As to mortgages where the mortgagee has not entered into a binding contract to advance the funds, the problem is far more complex, as the ensuing discussion of the open-end mortgage reveals.

Note that the same debtor and creditor may have both secured and unsecured relationships.

> **EXAMPLE:** Lender gave Owner a loan secured by a mortgage. This defines the extent of the secured relationship between Lender and Owner. Lender may later extend other credit to Owner that is completely unrelated to the mortgage. Unless the mortgage has an anaconda or dragnet clause the other advance would be unsecured.

15.22(g) Debt—future advances—open-end mortgages

The open-end mortgage provides that the mortgage secures not only the original note and debt, but also any additional advance that the mortgagee may choose to make to the mortgagor in the future. This means that if in the future, the mortgagor wishes to borrow additional funds for the addition of a room or garage or for some other purpose, he can borrow this money from the mortgagee if the latter sees fit to lend it. The advantages are obvious. The expense of executing a new mortgage is obviated. The mortgagee's security is enhanced by the additions or repairs. Recourse to short-term high-rate consumer financing is eliminated.

Clearly, the open-end mortgage is an optional advance mortgage. That is, the mortgagee is under no legal obligation to loan the additional funds. The problem here is one of intervening liens.

> **EXAMPLE:** Owner borrows $10,000 from Lender #1 on January 31 and gives Lender #1 a future advance type (open-end) mortgage. The mortgage is duly recorded. On July 1, Owner borrows $1,000 from Lender #2 and gives him a junior mortgage on the land, which he records. On December 1, Owner comes to Lender #1 and borrows an additional $1,000 under the future advance clause of the mortgage. Will this new advance, with the original first mortgage amount, enjoy priority over the junior mortgage of July 1, or will the July 1 mortgage enjoy priority over the new advance so that it is in effect a third mortgage on the property? In a majority of the states, the additional advance will enjoy priority over the

intervening lien, the junior mortgage of July 1, unless Lender #1 has actual knowledge of the second mortgage when he gave Owner the advance. In Illinois, Michigan, Ohio, and Pennsylvania, a mortgagee must, before making an optional future advance, search the records for intervening liens. Record notice of intervening liens is enough to give the intervening lien priority over the additional advance. 138 ALR 566. In these states title companies make special, inexpensive title searches to cover mortgages that propose making additional advances.

A mortgage secures only the debt described therein. Hence, a mortgage designed to secure optional future advances should draw attention to that fact. The older decisions are somewhat liberal in this regard. 5 DePaul L. Rev. 76, 80 (1955); 81 ALR 631. However, since the open-end mortgage has become popular, the notion that such mortgages should describe such future advances seems to be winning acceptance. At a minimum today, for safety's sake, the mortgage should specify the upper limit of the future advances to be made.

NEW LAWS: A great many states have enacted laws governing open-end mortgages. In Rhode Island, for example, an open-end advance that does not exceed $3,000 has the same priority as the original mortgage.

It is necessary also, that the future advances fall within the description thereof given in the mortgage.

EXAMPLE: If the mortgage, by its terms, secures future advances made to the mortgagors, an advance made to one of the mortgagors probably is not secured by the mortgage. *Capocasa* v. *First Nat. Bank,* 154 NW2d 271 (Wis. 1967). Likewise, an advance made to a grantee of the mortgagors might not be secured by the mortgage unless the mortgage so provides. *Walker* v. *Whitemore,* 262 SW 678 (Ark. 1924).

Finally, the documents evidencing the future advance should refer to the mortgage, so that it is evident that such advances were meant to be advances secured by the mortgage.

WARNING: If the mortgage makes no reference to future advances, any later document securing future advances must be executed and acknowledged like an original mortgage, recorded, and the title searches brought down to cover recording, for it is, in legal effect, a new mortgage on the property.

HUD MORTGAGES: Additional FHA insurance is available to cover additional advances for improvement or repair of property subject to FHA insured mortgages which contain open-end advance provisions. The advance must, however, be made for improvements on repairs which substantially protect or improve the basic livability or utility of the property, and the additional advances, when added to the unpaid balance of the original principal obligation, cannot exceed the amount of the original principal obligation unless the mortgagor certifies that the advance will be used to finance the construction of additional rooms. 12 USC § 1715 p.; 24 CFR § 203.44.

NEW LAWS: Some states, Florida, for example, require that a mortgage given to secure future advances so state. Fla. Stat. Ann. § 697.04(1). Other states provide that the mortgage lien shall not exceed at any one time the maximum amount stated in the mortgage. Kans. Stat. Ann. § 9-1101(4). Some states expressly allow revolving credit type future advances clauses. Fla. Stat. Ann. § 697.04(1).

EXAMPLE: Lender lends money to Owner under a revolving-credit-advance type of mortgage which states that no more than $15,000,000 may be outstanding at any one time. The initial advance is $5,000,000 and interim advances bring the total to the $15,000,000 mark. Owner repays $5,000,000. Under the common law, this payment extinguishes the lien to the extent of $5,000,000. If the lender wanted to advance additional funds he would have to put on a new mortgage and be subject to intervening interest holders to the extent of any subsequent advances. Under this statutory scheme, however, Lender may advance more money, not exceeding $15,000,000 total, and rely upon the security and priority of the original mortgage.

15.22(h) Debt—anaconda clause

One type of future advance clause is called the *anaconda clause.*

EXAMPLE: A mortgage from Owner to Lender secures a promissory note of Owner for $10,000 and all other obligations of Owner owned by Lender. Here Lender can buy up Owner's other obligations, perhaps at a steep discount, and enforce the mortgage for the face amount of all such debts in addition to the $10,000. 172 ALR 1079. The clause is also called a *dragnet clause.*

The courts are hostile to these mortgages and construe them strictly.

EXAMPLE: Husband and Wife give Lender a mortgage securing a note and all other obligations of Husband and Wife acquired by Lender. Lender bought a note signed by Husband only. The court held that this note was not secured by the mortgage. It was not an obligation of Husband and Wife. 172 ALR 1101.

In order for this type of clause to include other indebtedness, the second indebtedness must have been reasonably within the contemplation of the mortgagor and mortgagee at the time of the mortgage transaction. *Airline Commerce Bank* v. *Commercial Credit Corp.,* 531 SW2d 171 (Tex. 1975); 3 ALR4th 690.

EXAMPLE: This clause in a normal mortgage transaction will not be allowed to embrace a claim for damages for breach of contract.

In all mortgages securing future advances, the lender's title insurance policy must be analyzed to make certain it insures the priority of such advances. Urban, *Future Advances & Title Insurance,* 15 Wake Forest L. Rev. 329 (1979).

15.22(i)   Debt—guarantees

Many mortgages are signed by corporations having little capital. It is advisable to have the debt guaranteed personally by the principal shareholders. Prior to making the loan, the lender should obtain dependable financial statements and should analyze these statements carefully. And the guarantee should be prepared by a competent lawyer.

> **EXAMPLE:** *ABC Corp.* mortgages its land to Lender and signs the customary mortgage note. Guarantor, a shareholder, signs a guarantee. Later, the loan gets into trouble and the borrower and Lender recast the loan, reducing the monthly payments and extending the date of final maturity. This discharges Guarantor's liability unless he consents to the recasting. Hence, the guarantee must contain an agreement by Guarantor that recasting of the loan will not affect his liability.

The practical question relates to the efficacy of the guarantee. Experience shows that it is effective. The guarantee, being a personal liability, appears on Guarantor's financial statements. If the loan goes into default, this is a black mark that will seriously affect Guarantor's ability to obtain credit. He will struggle to prevent this. And if there is a loan workout, he will come up with a financial contribution in order to procure a release of his guarantee.

15.23   Participations

The mortgagee may sell a share of his mortgage to a third party. This is called a participation.

> **EXAMPLE:**   Owner gives a mortgage to Lender for $100,000. Lender, the *lead*, sells a 50 percent interest in the mortgage to Participant. Nothing is recorded as to this participation and no notice is given to Owner. There is a participation agreement between Lender and Participant, outlining Lender's rights and duties. But as to the rest of the world, it is as if Lender remained the full owner of the mortgage.

> **EXAMPLE:**   In the foregoing example, Owner and Lender conspire to defraud Participant. Lender records a release of the mortgage, and Owner sells the land to Bona Fide Purchaser. The mortgage is extinguished. All Participant can do is sue Owner and Lender.

REFERENCE: Armstrong, *The Developing Law of Participation Agreements,* 23 Bus. Law. 689 (1968).

The Bankruptcy Act protects a participant against any claim by the trustee in bankruptcy of the lender. 35 Bus. Law. 1648 (1980). This was an open question under the old Bankruptcy Act. Kratovil and Werner, *Modern Mortgage Law and Practice* § 33.09 (2d ed., 1981).

15.24   Description of the mortgaged property

An accurate description of the mortgated land is of great importance Even greater care must be exercised in this regard than is necessary in the case of deeds, since a purchaser usually goes into the possession of the land under the deed and thereby gives all the world notice of his rights, whereas a mortgagee rarely goes into possession and therefore depends entirely on the recording of the mortgage to give subsequent purchasers and mortgagees notice of rights.

When a mortgage is foreclosed, the mortgagee should be in a position to take over the mortgaged building as a functioning and operating unit. This is something to be considered at the time the mortgage is made. For example, if the building contains personal property necessary for its proper functioning, such as furniture in a furnished apartment building, some arrangement must be made to enable the mortgagee to take over these items in the event the mortgage is foreclosed. To accomplish this, it may be necessary to have the mortgagor sign a financing statement and security agreement under the Uniform Commercial Code on such personal property; for a real estate mortgage, although it covers fixtures, does not cover personal property.

In the *package mortgage* method of financing, the home loan also finances the purchases of equipment such as stoves, refrigerators, dishwashers, or washing machines which are essential to the livability of the property. Following the legal description in the mortgage is a clause containing a general catchall enumeration of the common items and a provision reciting that all such items are fixtures and therefore part of the real estate. The package mortgage attempts to make specific articles fixtures by means of an agreement between the mortgagor and mortgagee, even though in the absence of such agreement, the articles would be chattels. The practical advantages of this course are obvious. Installation of such equipment by the builder makes the house more salable. Moreover, it enables the prospective homebuyer to finance the initial purchase of such equipment at a lower interest rate and over a longer term than if the purchase were made separately from a department store. The legal objection to the use of the real estate mortgage to cover these articles has yet to be fully tested in the court. Kratovil, *Fixtures and the Real Estate Mortgage,* 97 U. Penn. L. Rev. 180, 210 (1948); 6 Kans. L. Rev. 66 (157).

When the article is actually removed from the mortgaged premises and then sold to a bona fide purchaser, it is then to all appearances a chattel, and in some states such a purchaser will acquire good title to the article. If this were not the law, any purchaser of chattels would incur the risk of losing them if it should later develop that they were wrongfully removed from mortgaged land. In other states, the real estate mortgagee is permitted to reclaim such articles, even when he finds them in the possession of an innocent purchaser. And generally a purchaser of such articles who buys them while they are still installed on the mortgaged land will not be protected. *First Mortgage Bond Co.* v. *London,* 244 NW 203 (Mich. 1932); *Dorr* v. *Dudderar,* 88 Ill. 107 (1878). To prevent such articles from passing into the hands of a bona fide purchaser, mortgagees have initiated the practice of pasting a notice directly on the equipment stating that the article is covered by the real estate mortgage. Purchasers of articles so marked would not be protected if they saw the notice, since they would not be bona fide purchasers.

Since it is by no means certain that, even with elaborate fine-print clauses, the real estate mortgage alone will afford the mortgagee protection against the removal of readily removable articles, many mortgagees insist upon a separate security agreement and financing statement under the Uniform Commercial Code. In other words, where chattels form a substantial part of the mortgage security, the mortgagor will give the mortgagee a security agreement, and both will sign a financing statement which will be filed with the appropriate chattel filings under the Uniform Commercial Code.

15.25   Interest

The mortgage should state the rate and time of payment of interest, though failure to do so will not invalidate the mortgage.

15.25(a)   Interest—usury

At one time, most states had laws fixing the maximum rate of interest that may be charged. These laws, which find their origins in Old Testament times, were designed to protect the needy unsophisticated borrower from crafty and knowledgeable lenders. Time and upward pressure of interest rates brought exceptions to these laws.

There is no reason to protect knowledgeable and sophisticated borrowers, so exceptions were made for loans to corporations and businesses. There is likewise no need to protect the public from well-regulated, responsible financial institutions, so loans made by such lenders, i.e., savings and loan associations, were exempted from the usury laws of some states. As market interest rates pushed upward against antiquated usury ceilings, state legislatures reacted by legislating higher interest rate limits or floating maximum rates that are set periodically by reference to various economic indicators.

The national mortgage market was a confusing hodgepodge of usury laws and exemptions. Mortgage funds in states with below-market levels of interest flowed to other states where higher yields were available. This artificial disruption of the availability of funds was harmful to potential homebuyers in states with low interest rate ceilings and frustrated national housing programs and policies.

Finally, in 1980, the federal government reacted by preempting state usury laws to the extent that they apply to most first mortgages on residential real property. 12 USC § 1735F-7; 12 CFR § 590.

Another section of this federal legislation preempts state usury laws applicable to business or agricultural loans of $25,000 or more. 12 USC § 86a. This section, rather than eliminating usury interest rate ceilings on such loans, imposes a federal limit of 5 percent above the Federal Reserve discount rate on ninety-day commercial paper unless state law permits a higher rate. Presently, this preemption is set to expire on April 1, 1983. 12 USC § 86a. The federal government has given the states until April 1, 1983, to enact a law overriding these preemptions. Some states, e.g., Colorado and Massachusetts, have enacted such override legislation. See Depository Institutions Deregulation and Monetary Control Act of 1980. Pub. L. 96-221 § 501 *et seq. See also* 1981 Ariz. St. L.J. 211 (1981).

REFERENCE ON USURY LAW: Kratovil and Werner, *Modern Mortgage Law and Practice,* Ch. 13 (2d ed., 1981).

15.25(b)   Exceptions to the federal preemption

The federal statute that preempts state usury laws has no application to some state aspects of finance charges, such as late charges, prepayment charges, attorneys' fees, etc. It also applies only to first mortgages, not second mortgages.

It does, however, specifically sanction floating interest rates in loans made by institutions.

It does apply to first liens on co-op stock and to first liens on mobile homes.

The law does preempt state laws prohibiting a lender from charging points.

A simple assumption of an old mortgage is not affected by the federal law.

Since the law covers federally insured lenders, it affects nearly all state banks and state chartered thrift institutions.

15.26   Escrows

A subject of much recent litigation, legislation, and writing is the so-called *mortgage escrow* or *impound* which lenders establish to insure payment of taxes and insurance premiums. For many years, this device was an effective and virtually unchallenged tool which lenders used to insure that necessary payments were made. Of late, however, consumer groups have taken to the courtroom and statehouse to correct some alleged abuses that may have crept into the use of this form of escrow. The attack has been primarily aimed at attempting to force the lender to limit the size of or pay interest on the impounded amount. The judicial response has been almost universally that the lender does not have to pay interest absent a statute, regulation, or mortgage provision to the contrary. *Sears* v. *First Federal Sav. & L. Assn.,* 275 NE2d 300 (Ill. 1971); *Tierney* v. *Whitestone Savings & Loan Assn.,* 83 Misc.2d 855 (N.Y. 1974). *Contra, Derenco, Inc.* v. *Benjamin Franklin Federal Sav. & L. Assn.,* 577 P2d 477 (Oreg. 1978). Borrowers then addressed their pleas to legislatures and found that the response was more favorable to the borrowers' situation. Perhaps the most significant factor in the ability of the legislature to respond was the fact that, as opposed to the courts which were called upon to act in the face of a contract binding upon the mortgagor and mortgagee, the legislation enacted takes prospective effect only, operating on transactions entered into after its effective date.

NEW LAWS: The states enacted various types of laws relating to such escrow accounts. Some laws require that lenders pay interest on the funds. See Cal. Civ.

Code § 2943. Others limit the size of the impound, Neb. Leg. Bill 502, Laws of 1976, or provide that the borrower be allowed the option of pledging an interest bearing savings account in lieu of the monthly escrow payment. Ill. Rev. Stat. 1975 Ch. 95, § 101 *et seq.* The Real Estate Settlement Procedures Act falls into the category of those laws which limit the size of accounts held by lenders in connection with federally related mortgage loans. 12 USCS § 2609.

Here, as in many areas of mortgage law, a controversy is raging over whether state law is applicable to govern the conduct of federal savings and loan associations. So far, the rule seems to be that state laws requiring the payment of interest on impounds are inapplicable to federal savings and loan associations. *First Fed. Sav. & Loan Assn.* v. *Greenwald,* 591 F2d 417 (1st Cir. 1979).

Some creditors of borrowers have attempted without success to garnishee monies paid into these funds by borrowers. Kratovil and Werner, *Modern Mortgage Law and Practice,* § 25.34 (2d ed., 1981).

> *REFERENCES:* The subject of interest in these escrows or impounds has attracted considerable comment. 54 Boston U. L. Rev. 516 (1974); 25 Catholic U. L. Rev. 102; 12 Creighton L. Rev. 697 (1978); 25 Me. L. Rev. 315; 41 Mo. L. Rev. 133; 23 Syracuse L. Q. 352 (1974); 7 Urb. Law 702; 50 ALR3d 697.

15.27 Real estate taxes

Especially in connection with parcels having an irregular shape, some question may arise as to whether the mortgaged land is identical with the land on which the real estate bill issues. This is due to the fact that tax authorities attempt to shorten the description. Some competent person must determine that the two descriptions cover the same identical tract of land. Federal lenders want such proof.

15.28 Leases antedating mortgage

It is important to distinguish between the rights of a tenant under a lease made prior to the mortgage and those of a tenant under a lease made subsequent to the mortgage. When the lease is made subsequent to the mortgage, the mortgagee can, by foreclosing his mortgage, extinguish the rights of the tenant under his lease. When the lease antedates the mortgage, the mortgagee must respect the tenant's rights, and regardless of foreclosure, the tenant cannot be evicted prior to the expiration of the lease, unless, of course, he fails to pay his rent.

Again, *in title intermediate theory states,* if the lease antedates the mortgage, then immediately upon the mortgagor's default, the mortgagee may serve a demand upon the tenant that he pay all rents to the mortgagee. Thereafter, the tenant must pay all rents to the mortgagee. *King* v. *Housatonic R. R. Co.,* 45 Conn. 226; L.R.A. (1915C) 200. Of course the tenant may continue to pay rents to the mortgagor until such demand has been served upon him.

In *lien theory states,* the mortgagee ordinarily is not entitled to make such a demand on the tenant. L.R.A. (1915C) 200.

15.29 Leases subsequent to mortgage

Obviously, a mortgagor cannot make any leases that will give the tenant greater rights than he, the mortgagor, possesses. Most important, where the lease is subsequent to the mortgage it is inferior to the mortgage, and the mortgagee can extinguish the lease if and when he forecloses his mortgage. Likewise, in *title and intermediate states,* the mortgagor has no right to retain possession after default. Tenants who occupy by virtue of leases made after the making of the mortgage also have no right to retain possession of the premises after the mortgagor's default, and the mortgagee may evict such tenants. To avoid eviction, the tenant, upon the mortgagee's making demand for possession, may agree to pay rent to the mortgagee, and the mortgagor will have no right to collect further rent from such tenant. *West Side Trust & Savings Bank* v. *Lopoten,* 358 Ill. 631, 193 NE 462; *Del-New Co.* v. *James,* III N.J.L. 157, 167 Atl. 747; *Anderson* v. *Robbins,* 82 Maine 422, 19 Atl. 910. One disadvantage of this course is that such action automatically terminates the lease, and the tenant becomes a tenant either from month to month or from year to year. *N.Y. Life Ins. Co.* v. *Simplex Products Corp.,* 135 Ohio St. 501, 21 NE2d 585; *Gartside* v. *Outley,* 58 Ill. 210. If the lease is one favorable to the landlord, the mortgagee will prefer to have a receiver appointed, since in many states the receiver can hold the tenant to his lease.

In *lien theory states,* in the absence of some provision in the mortgage, the mortgagee is not entitled to collect rents even under leases made after the making of the mortgage.

When the lease is favorable to the landlord, a mortgagee will attempt to preserve the lease even though he wishes to consummate foreclosure of the mortgage. In some states, Florida, New Jersey, and New York, for example, a mortgagee may, if he so wishes, leave unaffected by his foreclosure a lease that was executed subsequent to the mortgage, and the mortgagee, on acquiring title by foreclosure, may hold the tenant on such lease. 109 ALR 457. In other states, completion of the foreclosure automatically wipes out any lease made after the mortgage and thus relieves the tenant of further liability. 109 ALR 455. In these states, there is nothing that the mortgagee can do to keep the lease alive after foreclosure.

Many lawyers feel that an express provision in the lease that it will survive foreclosure if the mortgagee desires will be valid, even as to a junior lease. Alternatively, the tenant and mortgagee might enter into a separate agreement that they will sign a new lease on the old terms if the old lease is extinguished by foreclosure. Or as a further alternative the mortgagee and lessee may sign a subordination, under which the lease is made prior and superior to the mortgage. Bear in mind that many mortgage loans today are made in reliance on the financial strength and pulling power of the tenant, and loss of that tenant could be disastrous.

15.30   Possession and rents   The difference in viewpoint between title theory and lien theory states is of greatest importance with respect to the mortgagee's right to the possession and rents of the mortgaged property. To illustrate the significance of this statement, let us list, in chronological order, some important dates in a defaulted mortgage transaction: (1) the date when the mortgage is signed by the mortgagor; (2) the date when the mortgagor first defaults; (3) the date when the mortgagee files his foreclosure suit; (4) the date of the foreclosure sale; and (5) the date when the statutory redemption period expires and the mortgagee receives the deed under which he becomes the owner of the mortgaged property.

Let us first make our broad generalizations and thereafter list the particular points of difference that exist. In general, the title theory states regard the mortgage as retaining some of its early character; that is, they view it as a conveyance of the land, so that immediately on the signing of the mortgage, the mortgagee has the right to take possession of the property and collect the rents thereof. On the other hand, the lien theory states regard the mortgage as merely creating the right to acquire the land through foreclosure of the mortgage so that the mortgagor remains the full owner of the land with the right to possession and rents until the statutory redemption period has expired and the foreclosure deed has issued to the mortgagee. In other words, at its most extreme, this difference in point of view represents to the mortgagee the difference between dates (1) and (5) in the above list so far as the right to possession and rents is concerned. In title states, therefore, rents are an important part of the mortgagee's security. In lien states, this is not so. *Grether* v. *Nick*, 213 NW 304, 215 NW 571 (Wis. 1927).

Now let us analyze the situation in somewhat greater detail, from the point of view just expressed:

1. In a number of title theory states, Alabama, Maryland, and Tennessee, for example, the mortgagee, immediately upon execution of the mortgage, has the right to take possession and collect the rents of the mortgaged property. *Darling Shop Inc.* v. *Nelson Realty Co.,* 79 So2d 793 (Ala. 1953). The right exists even though the mortgage is silent on this point. There are two exceptions: (1) in recent times laws have been passed in some title states giving the mortgagor the right of possession until default occurs—in effect, these laws convert such states into intermediate states; (2) many mortgage forms used in title states give the mortgagor the right of possession until default.

2. In intermediate theory states, Illinois, New Jersey, North Carolina, and Ohio, for example, the mortgagor has the right of possession until his first default, but after default the mortgagee has the right to take possession.

3. In lien theory states, in the absence of a contrary provision in the mortgage, the mortgagor is entitled to possession and rents at least until the foreclosure sale.

4. In some lien theory states, either by express provision in the mortgage or by a separate assignment of rents signed at the time that the mortgage is signed, the mortgagor may give the mortgagee the right to take possession and collect rents as soon as a default occurs, and such provisions are valid. *Penn Mutual Life Ins. Co.* v. *Katz,* 297 NW 899 (Neb. 1941); *Kinnison* v. *Guaranty Liquidating Corp.,* 115 P2d 450 (Cal. 1941); *Dick & Reuteman Co.* v. *Jem Realty Co.,* 274 NW 416 (Wis. 1937). However, some of

these lien theory states make special rules as to owner-occupied homes. In New York, for example, a homeowner cannot be compelled to pay rent pending foreclosure. *Holmes* v. *Gravenhorst*, 188 NE 285 (N.Y. 1933).

5. In other lien theory states, the provisions described in number 4 are considered void as against public policy. *Rives* v. *Mincks Hotel Co.,* 30 P2d 911 (Okla. 1934); *Hart* v. *Bingham,* 43 P2d 447 (Okla. 1932). In some states that formerly took this view (for example, Minnesota, Washington, Oregon), statutes have been enacted validating the assignment of rents.

6. In all states, if the mortgagor, after defaulting in his mortgage payments, voluntarily turns over possession to the mortgagee, the mortgagee has the legal right to remain in possession. Notice that in number 5 it is the provision binding the mortgagor to give up possession *at some future time* when default occurs that is held void. The same agreement made *after default* is valid. The mortgagee is then called a *mortgagee in possession.*

7. Whenever a mortgagee takes possession before he has acquired ownership of the property by foreclosure, the rents he collects must be applied in reduction of the mortgage debt. A mortgage does not become the owner of the property by taking possession. Foreclosure is still necessary.

8. Whenever a mortgagee has the right to possession and fails to exercise that right, allowing the mortgagor to remain in possession and to collect rents, the rents so collected belong to the mortgagor.

9. In many states, there is a statutory period of redemption. No general rule can be laid down as to the right of possession during this period, for each state has its own rule.

15.30(a) Practical aspects of the problem

A mortgage lender seeks a regular return on a safe investment and does not wish to assume the responsibilities of management. A lender is most unlikely to make a loan that will require him to go into immediate possession of the land, and this right is, therefore, seldom exercised. On the mortgagor's default, however, it is imperative that prompt action be taken to seize the rents so that they will not be diverted to the mortgagor's own personal use. An eviction suit to enforce the mortgagee's right to possession is often a long, drawn-out affair, especially when the mortgagor is interposing all the legal obstacles available to him. However, if the mortgagee files a foreclosure suit, he might be able to have a receiver appointed, and this is the course usually preferred. Other technical reasons exist for preferring the remedy of receivership.

Courts differ as to the grounds for appointment of a receiver. Some say it is enough that the property be inadequate security for the mortgage debt. Other courts require a showing that the security is inadequate and that the mortgagor is insolvent. Still others appoint a receiver only when the property is in danger of destruction. 26 ALR 33.

15.30(b) Rent reductions, lease cancellations, and advance payments of rent

A problem of considerable importance is the extent to which a receiver or a mortgagee entering into possession is bound by rent reductions, prepayments of rents, and lease cancellations effected by the mortgagor for a cash consideration. Such agreements are standard devices by which hard-pressed mortgagors pocket the future earning capacity of the land and deliver to the mortgagee the empty shell of the mortgaged asset. Again, differences exist between title theory and lien theory states. The rules are quite complex. See Kratovil & Werner, *Modern Mortgage Law and Practice* § 20.07(a) (2d ed., 1981).

15.30(c)   Assignment of leases and rents

At the time the mortgage is signed, the mortgagee should require the mortgagor to sign a separate assignment of leases and rents. This document assigns to the mortgagee the mortgagor's interest in all existing leases, all leases to be executed in the future, and all rents falling due after the date of the mortgage, as additional security for payment of the mortgage debt. Lawyers have found that there is magic in the argument that the mortgage creates a lien on the land and that the assignment creates a lien on the rents. *Franzen* v. *G. R. Kinney Co.,* 259 NW 850 (Wis. 1935); 50 Harv. L. Rev. 1322 (1937). All existing tenants are notified of the making of the assignment. The assignment is recorded. *Franzen* v. *G. R. Kenney Co.,* 259 NW 850 (Wis. 1935); *Fidelity Bankers Life Ins. Co.* v. *Williams,* 506 F2d 1242 (1974); 75 ALR 268. The problem arising in connection with an assignment of leases and rents are also complex. See Kratovil & Werner, *Modern Mortgage Law and Practice,* §§ 20.07 *et seq.* (2d ed. 1981) (cited with approval in *Butner* v. *U.S.,* 440 U.S. 48 (1979); Gose, *Assignment of Leases and Rents,* 3 ALI–ABA Course Materials 87 (1978).

15.30(d)   Active assignment of leases and rents

In recent times mortgage lenders have turned to a device that has certain advantages where a building is to be constructed with mortgage funds for a high-credit tenant. As soon as the lease is made, the landlord assigns his interest in the lease and all rents thereunder to the mortgage lender. The assignment calls for the mortgage lender to begin collecting rents *immediately* on completion of the building. The lease refers to the assignment, and it also is recorded, thus making certain that the mortgagee's rights are treated as recorded rights, good against the whole world. The lease is a "net" lease under which all taxes, insurance premiums, and so forth are borne by the lessee, and no burdens or payments are borne by the lessor or the mortgagee. The rent payments exactly equal the mortgage payments. A mortgage accompanies the transaction, but the main security is the assignment. The loan is for the full cost of construction of the building. With a high-credit tenant a lender can lend with complete security on a transaction of this sort. The assignment is good against a subsequent bankruptcy of the lessor. It also prevails over subsequent federal liens, subsequent creditors of the mortgagor, subsequent attempts of the mortgagor to cancel the lease or obtain prepayment of the rent. In short, virtually nothing can occur that will prevent full collection by the lender.

NEW DIRECTIONS: The existence of a critical housing shortage has given rise to legislation protecting tenants from eviction or rent increases. The question arises over whether the rights of tenants whose leases or tenancies are subject to a mortgage being foreclosed can seek the protection of these laws. One court has held that these laws apply only to the traditional landlord proceeding against the traditional tenant and not to the mortgagee asserting its right against junior tenants. *Guttenberg S. & L. Assn.* v. *Riviera,* 428 A2d 1289 (N.J. 1981). This victory may be shortlived. Indeed, in communities where tenants have a strong voice, such as Santa Monica, California, an ordinance may well be passed making future mortgages on multifamily property subject to the rights tenants would have against their landlord.

REFERENCE: Randolph, *The Mortgagee's Interest in Rents: Some Policy Considerations and Proposals,* 29 Kans. L. Rev. (1980).

15.31 Acceleration

The mortgage and mortgage note usually provide that in case of any default the entire principal sum shall become immediatly due and payable. This clause is known as the *acceleration clause.* If it is not present, the mortgagee must file separate foreclosure suits as each installment of the mortgage debt falls due and is defaulted. Manifestly, the acceleration clause is one of the most important terms of the mortgage.

There are two kinds of acceleration clauses, automatic and optional. The theory of the automatic clause is that the happening of the event, *ipso facto,* advances the maturity of the debt. The optional clause, as its name implies, merely gives rise to the ability of the lender to call the debt due. The latter form is preferable as it obviates those problems caused by accidental or minor defaults while it gives the lender the ability to protect its interest.

While we usually think of acceleration in terms of payment-type defaults, mortgages usually are so drafted as to allow acceleration for nonmoney-type defaults, and courts have allowed a mortgage to accelerate because of a mortgagor's failure to keep a building in repair, 69 ALR3d 773, or failure to keep insurance in force. 69 ALR3d 774.

The operation of the acceleration clause upon the borrower's default may bring about a harsh result. Some courts, even when confronted with minor deviations caused by the borrower's mistake or inadvertence, find themselves powerless to avoid the strict application of the mortgage language. Other courts, finding themselves not so hamstrung, have gotten around the language either by holding its operation to be unconscionable in the given instance or by deeming some act of the mortgagee to have negated the impact of the language. *Continental Bank* v. *Eastern Ill. Co.,* 37 Ill. App. 3d 148, 334 NE2d 102 (1975); Rosenthal, *The Role of Courts of Equity in Preventing Acceleration Predicated upon a Mortgagor's Inadvertent Default,* 22 Syr. L. Rev. 897 (1971).

EXAMPLE: Where an acceleration is declared only because of the mortgagor's failure to pay real estate taxes, the courts will allow the mortgagor to cure this default before foreclosure is filed. *Kaminski* v. *Longon Pub Inc.,* 301 A2d 769 (N.J. 1973); 31 ALR 731.

EXAMPLE: Acceptance of past-due interest payments may operate as a waiver of the mortgagor's right to accelerate upon a prior default. 97 ALR2d 997. This result is especially a reality in view of today's stress upon not treating the mortgagor unconscionably.

It is clear that consumerist, proborrower judicial attitudes have no use for the older decisions.

NEW DIRECTIONS: Courts have begun to set accelerations aside on the ground of unconscionability. This is a new ball game. *Federal Home Loan Corp.* v. *Taylor,* 318 So2d 203 (Fla. 1976); *Miller* v. *Pac. First Fed. S. & L. Assn.,* 545 P2d 546 (Wash. 1976); *Streets* v. *MGIC Mtg. Corp.,* 378 NE2d 915 (Ind. 1978).

In other instances courts have refused to follow the letter of the acceleration clause.

EXAMPLE: A mortgage and note provided that in case of default the mortgagee could declare an acceleration "without notice to the mortgagor." The court set aside an acceleration declared without notice to the mortgagor. *White* v. *Turbidy,* 183 SE2d 363 (Ga. 1971). This is contrary to earlier decisions on this point. There is, however, a strong trend of statutes and case law to require such a notice. In effect, this gives the mortgagor an opportunity to cure defaults. A mortgagor must be given notice of an intended acceleration and a reasonable time to cure defaults. *Haase* v. *Blank,* 187 NW 669 (Wis. 1922). Some states allow the foreclosure suit to stand as notice of the mortgagee's election to accelerate, *Home Federal Savings & Loan Assn.* v. *LaSalle National Bank,* 264 NE2d 704 (Ill. 1970), but better practice is to give formal notice, and such action is mandatory when foreclosure is by power of sale. *Crow* v. *Heath,* 516 SW2d 225 (Tex. 1974). *Contra, S & G Investment Inc.* v. *Home Federal Savings & Loan Assn.,* 505 F2d 370 (D.C. Cir. 1974).

EXAMPLE: A mortgagee had been in the habit of accepting tardy payments. The court held that he could not accelerate without giving the mortgagor a reasonable opportunity to pay. *Stinemeyer* v. *Wesco Farms, Inc.,* 487 P2d 65 (Oreg. 1971).

NEW LAWS: Legislatures in California, Colorado, Illinois, Minnesota, New York, Oregon, and other states have passed laws which, within defined time limits, give the borrower the right to cure defaults by paying the sums necessary to make the mortgagee whole. This right of the borrower to reinstate the mortgage will be found in the FNMA mortgage form.

15.31(a)   Acceleration— owner occupancy clause

Many mortgage loans are made on the premise that the property that secures the loan be owned occupied. This requirement is made upon the belief that such loans are safe because owner–occupants are more likely to protect their homes. In times of a credit crunch, mortgage loans for non-owner-occupied residential property become scarce or impossible to obtain. Sometimes a better interest rate is available to the owner–occupant–borrower than the borrower who will not occupy the property. Investors, not deterred by possible criminal sanctions, falsify their loan applications to get these few loans or better terms.

To counter this threat, some lenders have begun using a mortgage clause that will allow the lender to declare an acceleration of the debt upon the borrower's failure to occupy the property. These clauses are valid. *Investors Savings and Loan Assn.* v. *Ganz,* 416 A2d 918 (N.J. 1980).

15.32   Deed of mortgaged premises

Generally, when mortgaged land is sold, the mortgage is paid and released during the process of sale for the reason that the existing mortgage usually does not meet the financing requirements of the buyer. For example, if land is sold for $15,000 and there is an existing mortgage of $13,000, which has been paid down to $6,000, the buyer will want a new mortgage of more than $6,000. Thus, it becomes necessary to retire the old mortgage in the process of closing the sale. However, it is perfectly possible to sell mortgaged land without providing for retirement of the old mortgage. For example, where *A* owns land worth $15,000 on which there is a mortgage securing a debt of $5,000, the arrangement between seller and buyer can be that there will be a payment to the seller of the sale price ($15,000) less the amount of the mortgage debt ($5,000), in this case, $10,000. Obviously, the understanding here is that the buyer will pay the balance of the mortgage debt. In this situation, where the buyer is to pay the mortgage debt when and as it matures, the deed from the seller to buyer may take one of the following forms:

1. The deed may provide that it is subject to the mortgage, which the purchaser assumes and agrees to pay. This is called an assumption clause.
2. The deed may merely recite that the property is subject to the mortgage.
3. The deed may be a quitclaim deed with no subject clause.

The following rules apply:

1. When the deed of the mortgaged premises recites that the grantee *assumes and agrees to pay* the mortgage or *assumes* the mortgage, it imposes on the grantee personal liability for the payment of the mortgage debt. The mortgagee when he forecloses may obtain a deficiency judgment or decree against such grantee when the sale price is less than the amount of the debt. In this way the mortgagee may obtain a personal judgment

against such grantee for the difference between the amount of the foreclosure sale and the amount of the mortgage debt.

2. Where the deed merely recites that the land is taken "subject to" the mortgage, the grantee is usually not personally liable for the payment of the mortgage debt. *Pearce* v. *Desper,* 144 NE2d 617 (Ill. 1957).

3. Where the mortgagor enters into a contract to sell merely his equity over and above the mortgage and thereafter gives the buyer a quitclaim deed, the buyer does not become personally liable to the mortgagee.

15.33 Assumption

Because of the shortage of mortgage money, the sale of mortgaged properties subject to an existing mortgage is commonplace today. In the trade's jargon it is referred to as an *assumption.* The deal has become complex. The mortgage is checked for the presence of a due-on-sale clause. If such a clause is present, a legal judgment must be made as to the necessity for the lender's consent.

In any case it helps to have the lender's consent. An arrangement can be made for a release of the mortgagor's personal liability and the assumption by the buyer of the liability for the mortgage debt. This is called a *novation.*

The documentation can also provide that if the buyer fails to make the mortgage payments and the original borrower's personal liability has *not* been released, the original borrower can pay the lender and receive an assignment of the mortgage. In this way the original borrower recoups his loss.

Funds for such a purchase may be available, since the borrower, on becoming the owner of the first mortgage, can subordinate it to a new mortgage. A deal such as this is usually closed in escrow.

Legal advice is needed by the lender as to the effect of releasing the borrower's liability on FHA, VA, or PMI insurance and on the liability of guarantors.

If the mortgage has been assigned, obviously all decisions are made by the assignee.

When property is sold subject to a first mortgage, whether or not the buyer assumes or merely takes subject to that mortgage, the buyer should check to see if the mortgage has a future advance clause. If so, the buyer must give the first mortgagee notice of his rights and get the lender's assurance that no additional advances will be made to the original debtor. Otherwise, the lender may make further advances to the borrower even after the conveyance of the property by the borrower to the buyer thereby further encumbering the buyer's property. *Commercial Bank* v. *Readd,* 242 SE2d 25 (Ga. 1978). See also Ch. 18.

15.34 Assignment of mortgage

Often a mortgagee wishes to sell his mortgage. In fact, many mortgages are originated for prearranged purchasers. The manner in which the transfer may be accomplished depends upon whether the mortgage in question is a deed of trust or regular mortgage. A deed of trust is usually given to secure a negotiable note which passes from hand to hand, very much as money. Such a note may be payable to the bearer. In that case, merely handing the note to the purchaser will be sufficient to transfer title thereto. Endorsement is unnecessary. If the note is payable to the order of a named person, that person must endorse the note over to the purchaser. In the case of a deed of trust securing negotiable notes, a sale of the mortgage is affected by properly transferring the notes by delivery or endorsement, depending on the character of the note.

In the case of a regular mortgage, it is necessary to execute an assignment, which is a brief form reciting that the mortgagee, the assignor, transfers and assigns the mortgage and mortgage note to the purchaser thereof, the assignee. The mortgage is identified by a recital of the names of the parties thereto, its date, the recording date, the book and page where the mortgage is recorded, and so on. The assignment should be signed by the mortgagee, acknowledged, delivered to the assignee, and recorded. The mortgage note, too, should be endorsed or delivered to the assignee along with the original mortgage.

The mortgage cannot be assigned except in connection with a sale of the mortgage debt. The reason for this is that the mortgage is incidental to and exists only for the purpose of securing payment of the debt. A person who does not own the mortgage debt can have no reason for obtaining the mortgage and any attempt to assign the mortgage without a transfer of the debt is a nullity. *Commercial Products Corp.* v. *Briegel,* 242 NE2d 317 (Ill. 1968). The assignee of the mortgage must insist on receiving the mortgage note, since if the mortgagee has already transferred the mortgage note to someone else, he can no longer make a valid assignment of the mortgage.

On the other hand, whatever is sufficient to transfer the mortgage debt will transfer a mortgage given to secure it. This is because the debt secured by the mortgage is the principal thing and the mortgage is a mere security for its payment. Thus, if a regular mortgage secures a note, its transfer without an assignment of the mortgage will give the transferee the right to foreclose the mortgage. But as a practical matter, for the assignee's protection, it is necessary to obtain an assignment of the mortgage. The reason for this is that in the case of a deed of trust securing negotiable notes, everyone is supposed to know that it is likely that the notes will be sold. However, in the case of a regular mortgage securing a note payable to the mortgagee, unless an assignment of the mortgage is filed in the recorder's office, subsequent purchasers or mortgagees of the mortgaged premises are entitled to assume that the mortgagee continues to hold the mortgage note.

EXAMPLE: Owner executed a regular mortgage or Lender #1 to secure a note payable to Lender's order. Lender #1 endorsed the note to Assignee but no assignment of the mortgage was recorded. Thereafter, Owner sold the mortgaged land to Lender #1, and Lender #1 entered a satisfaction of the mortgage on the public records. Lender #1 then mortgaged the land to Lender #2. It was held that Lender #2's mortgage was a first mortgage on the land, since when Lender

#2 took his mortgage on the land, the earlier mortgage appeared from the public records to have been released by the apparent owner thereof. *Bowling* v. *Cook,* 39 Iowa 200.

When the mortgage secures a nonnegotiable note, a purchaser of the mortgage takes it subject to all defenses to which it was liable in the hands of the original mortgagee. *Holly Hill Acres Ltd.* v. *Charter Bank,* 314 So2d 209 (Fla. 1975). This means that if the original mortgagee has been guilty of fraud or some other conduct that would make it impossible for him to foreclose the mortgage, any person to whom he sells the mortgage will also be unable to foreclose.

EXAMPLE: Owner mortgages his land to Lender to secure a nonnegotiable note for $5,000, but Lender never pays out the money to Owner. Lender sells the mortgage to Assignee. Assignee will be unable to foreclose the mortgage.

In time, American mortgage bankers began the experiment of having the mortgage secure a negotiable note. The experiment proved highly successful. In all states except Illinois, Minnesota, and Ohio, it is now the rule that *a holder in due course* of a negotiable note secured by a mortgage, that is, one who buys the note and mortgage in good faith before the debt is overdue and without knowledge of any infirmities, takes the mortgage as well as the note, free from defenses that would have been available to the mortgagor against the original mortgagee. The theory is that negotiable notes, like money, should pass freely from hand to hand, without the necessity of any inquiry by purchasers thereof as to the possible invalidity of the paper. And since the mortgage is a mere security for the note, it should enjoy the same protection that the law accords to the note.

EXAMPLE: Owner gave Lender a mortgage securing a negotiable note for $50,000, but never received any money from Lender. Lender sold the note and mortgage to Assignee before the due date of the note. Assignee can foreclose the mortgage even though Owner never received the mortgage money. As an innocent purchaser of a negotiable note, Assignee is protected against any defenses that exist between Owner and Lender.

A purchaser of a mortgage can also be protected against unknown infirmities existing as between the mortgagor and the original mortgagee by insisting that he be furnished a statement signed by the mortgagor stating that he has no defenses to the enforcement of the mortgage. This document is variously called a *waiver of defenses, estoppel certificate, no set-off certificate,* or *declaration of no defenses.* Under standard mortgage practice, it is addressed to "all whom it may concern" and is signed by the mortgagor at the time the mortgage is signed.

The practical effect of a waiver of defenses is to give the assignee a legally enforceable mortgage even though the mortgage does not secure a negotiable note and the mortgagee could not have successfully foreclosed. For example, if the mortgagee had paid out no money or had received payment in full, he could not foreclose. But an assignee who receives a waiver of defenses can foreclose, since he received the mortgagor's written assurance that the mortgage is valid and enforceable. 59 CJS 531; 110 ALR 457.

> **EXAMPLE:**   Owner gave Lender a mortgage securing a note for $50,000, but never received any money from Lender. Lender sold the note and mortgage to Assignee before the due date of the note. Lender also delivered to Assignee a waiver of defenses signed by Owner. Assignee can foreclose the mortgage even though Owner never received the mortgage money. As an innocent purchaser relying on a waiver of defenses, Assignee is protected against any defenses that exist between Owner and Lender.

Before purchasing a mortgage, one should always check the public records for any prior recorded assignment of the mortgage, since in many states, where there are two or more assignments of the mortgage by the mortgagee, the first recorded assignment prevails.

The assignee should also obtain the mortgagee's evidence of title, assignment of chattel security agreements, if any, and other such papers.

The assignee of a mortgage may foreclose for the full amount due on the mortgage even though he purchased at a discount. 2 Jones, *Mortgages* § 997 (1928).

15.34(a)   Notice of assignment

The purchaser of a note secured by either a regular mortgage or deed of trust should always give personal notice to the mortgagor that he has purchased such note. If he fails to do so, and the mortgagor afterward in good faith makes a payment to the original mortgagee, this payment will reduce the mortgage debt accordingly. This rule is generally followed where the mortgage note or bond is nonnegotiable.

Except in Illinois and Minnesota, it is the rule that the purchaser of a negotiable note need not notify the mortgagor of his purchase, and if the mortgagor continues to make payments to the original mortgagee, he cannot claim that the mortgage debt has been reduced thereby. This places the burden on the mortgagor of demanding production of the mortgage note and endorsement of each payment thereon.

In Illinois and Minnesota, even where the mortgage secures a negotiable note, the mortgagor may continue to make payments to the original lender until he receives notice of the assignment. *Napieralski* v. *Simon,* 64 NE 1042 (Ill. 1902). The Illinois–Minnesota rule is based on the inconvenience to the mortgagor of requiring production of the mortgage paper each time a payment is made on the mortgage debt.

Whenever notice of assignment is necessary, the notice should be given personally to the mortgagor. Merely recording an assignment of the mortgage ordinarily will not suffice. The mortgagor should not be subject to the burden of making constant searches of the records to see if the mortgage has been assigned, especially since it requires little effort for the assignee to serve a personal notice on the mortgagor. 89 ALR 196. However, any purchaser of the property from the mortgagor is usually required to take notice of such a recorded assignment. *Erickson* v. *Kendall*, 191 P 842 (Wash. 1920).

15.35   Payment

The mortgagor, to release himself from personal liability on his note, must see that he pays the money to the holder of the note. This is also true of any purchaser of the mortgaged premises. He is bound at his peril to pay the debt to the one entitled to receive payment. Upon paying the mortgage note, the party should demand that the canceled note be delivered to him. This prevents any further transfer or negotiation of the note and is of particular importance where payment is made prior to the maturity of the note.

Payment also has the effect of destroying the mortgage lien to the extent of such payment. When the mortgage is paid in full, the lien is ipso facto extinguished. *American National Insurance Co.* v. *Murray*, 383 F2d 81 (5th Cir. 1967). However, it is customary to record a release, satisfaction, or discharge of the mortgage in order to clear the public records in the recorder's office.

15.35(a)   Payment to agent

A mortgagor, before making payment to an agent of the mortgagee, should ascertain the agent's authority by inquiring of the mortgagee or by requiring the agent to produce a power of attorney from the mortgagee. *Coxe* v. *Kriebel*, 185 A 770 (Pa. 1936).

15.35(b)   Payment—joint mortgagees or joint sellers

Where a husband and wife own land jointly, sell it, and take back an installment contract or purchase money mortgage, the rule is that payment to either party is good payment. 70 CJS Payment § 4, 59 CJS *Mortgages* § 446. The party receiving payment can give a release of the mortgage. One would think that the buyer would feel more comfortable if this is spelled out in the documents. Of course, if the check is made payable to both, a different problem arises, namely, whether one party can endorse the other party's name. Again, the documents should cover this.

15.35(c)   Prepayment of mortgage debt

In the absence of an agreement to the contrary, the mortgagee has a contractual right to have his money earning the stipulated interest for the agreed period. *Dugan* v. *Grzybowski*, 332 A2d 97 (Conn. 1973). The mortgagor has no right to insist upon making payment before maturity, even by offering to pay the principal and all interest to the maturity date. *Peter Fuller Enterprises Inc.* v. *Manchester Sav. Bank*, 152 A2d 179 (N.H. 1959). Accordingly, it is to the mortgagor's advantage to provide in the mortgage and the mortgage note that the debt is payable *on or before* the due date, *Fortson* v. *Burns*, 479 SW2d 722 (Tex.

1972), or that the debt is payable in monthly payments of a stated sum *or more,* or payments are to *not less than* a given amount. *Peters* v. *Fenner,* 199 NW2d 795 (Minn. 1972). Also, a specific clause may be inserted conferring upon the mortgagor the privilege of prepaying the mortgage debt. This is known as a *prepayment privilege.* In corporate trust deeds securing issues of bonds, the comparable provision is that providing for *redemption* of bonds prior to their stated maturity dates. Such provisions enable the mortgagor to refinance when money is cheaper or to retire the mortgage where he has entered into a contract of sale that requests him to deliver title free and clear of any mortgage.

Occasionally a mortgagor whose mortgage does not have a prepayment clause, defaults in his payments hoping to force the mortgagee to accelerate. Thereupon, he reasons, he can pay off the mortgage. The trouble is, it will not work. The mortgage usually has a clause in it stating that if the mortgagor defaults, the mortgage may foreclose as to the defaulted payments only, subject to the continuing lien of the mortgage as to the remainder of the debt. Thus, all the mortgagor succeeds in doing is to incur attorneys' fees and foreclosure costs.

Where a mortgagor takes advantage of a mortgage provision which allows prepayments on any monthly payment date and suddenly becomes pinched for ready cash, he may contend that he has the right to skip payments until the prepaid amount is exhausted. This contention will not prevail. In effect the prepayments are applied against the last payments falling due. *Smith* v. *Renz,* 265 P2d 160 (Cal. 1954). Some recent cases hold that where the mortgagor has been making prepayments, he will not be in default until these prepayments have been exhausted by application to current payments. *Bradford* v. *Thompson,* 470 SW2d 633 (Tex. 1971).

NEW LAWS: Various forms of limitations on prepayment penalties have found their way into the fabric of mortgage law. In some states prepayment penalties may only be exacted during the initial years of the loan, Cal. Civ. Code. § 2954.9, or if the interest exceeds a certain rate, prepayment penalties are absolutely forbidden. Ill. Rev. Stat. 1975 Ch. 74 § 4.

FEDERAL MORTGAGES: HUD mortgages are usually required to carry a provision which permits the mortgagor to prepay and the imposition of a prepayment penalty is prohibited. See, e.g., 24 CFR §§ 203.22(b) and 234.37(b). FHLBB regulations provide that borrowers may prepay their home mortgage loans without a penalty unless there is an express penalty provision in the loan contract. Even when the penalty provision is expressed, it cannot exceed six months advance interest. 12 CFR § 545.6–12(b).

Other typical approaches to the prepayment problem include:

1. Mortgage provisions that set out a sliding scale with either no prepayment allowed or a larger penalty imposed on prepayment during the early years of the mortgage and a decreasingly burdensome penalty as the mortgage matures.

2. The giving of a notice of intention to prepay prior to prepayment.

3. The allowance by some mortgagees of prepayment without penalty upon the sale of a house where the buyer finances his purchase through the same mortgagee, or where the mortgagor finances his new home through the same mortgagee.

15.35(d) Payment—late charges

A *late charge* is, as the name implies, a customary charge made by the lender for the expense involved in processing and pursuing late payments. 63 ALR3d 50. If reasonable, it is valid and devoid of the taint of usury. However, some states place a limit on the amount that can be charged. FHA limits the late charge to 4 percent of the payment, the FHLBB and FHLMC limit the charge to 5 percent of the late payment, and FNMA requires a late charge of at least 4 percent.

15.35(e) Payment—balloon

The balloon note takes one of a few general forms. The note may call for interest-only payments until its due date. Alternatively, the note may call for regular amortization payments under a typical term, say, twenty-five years, but the entire debt is payable in a much shorter period. Under any format, the principal is due in a relatively short period of time, say, one to five years. These notes fell into disfavor after the Great Depression when many balloons fell due, but could not be refinanced. Today's alternative financing vehicles have resulted in a comeback for the balloon note. Even the FHLBB has lifted its prohibition against savings and loan associations making balloon loans. 12 CFR § 541.6 *et seq.*

In the now typical institutional residential loan with a balloon payment, the lender will discuss refinancing alternatives with the borrower shortly before the balloon is due. The borrower is usually given the opportunity to refinance at the going rate.

Alternatively, he can refinance with another institution, but seldom takes this course, since home interest rates tend toward uniformity and the costs of refinancing would eat up any of the benefits of a lower rate charged by another lender.

The advantage to the lender is great. The transaction is much simpler than any VRM or RRM. And the lender need not cope with the statutes and court decisions that have weakened the due-on-sale clause.

The advantage to the borrower is that he is not locked into a long-term loan at a high rate of interest. Moreover, institutional lenders treat their borrowers fairly. Any renewal will be a fair one.

The obvious danger to the borrower is that at the end of three years the lender may be in such bad shape financially that it is granting no renewals. If times are really bad, other lenders have no money to lend. Foreclosure could result. This is unlikely. A weak financial institution is usually merged into a stronger one under pressure from the FDIC or FSLIC.

15.35(f)   Payment—final payment

When a final payment has been made on a mortgage, the landowner should insist on receiving a receipt stating that payment in full has been made. The landowner should also insist on receiving: a release in recordable form satisfying the mortgage of record; the canceled mortgage and note; all evidence of title and other loan documents held by the lender; and an endorsement from the hazard insurance company stating that the mortgage loss clause (giving the name of the lender as an additional party insured) has been released. This last requirement is quite important. Lacking this endorsement, the insurance company will make any check for loss payable to the mortgagee as well as the landowner. The owner then must go through the bother of obtaining the old lender's endorsement on the check, a task that may take some time.

15.36   Limitations

In all states, a promissory note ceases to be enforceable after a certain time if no payments are made thereon. Such a note is said to be barred by limitations. The period varies from state to state. In most states, the fact that the mortgage note is barred by limitations only prevents the obtaining of a personal judgment on the note and does not prevent foreclosure of the mortgage. But in other states, the mortgage is automatically barred whenever the mortgage note is barred.

In many states, if a period of twenty years elapses after the maturity date of the mortgage note, the mortgage is presumed to be paid. The mortgagee, however, may overcome this presumption by providing that the mortgage has not been paid, but has been kept alive by partial payments of principal or interest thereon. Since this rule makes it dangerous to disregard even an old recorded mortgage, some states go further and provide by law that after a stated period of time, the mortgage becomes void. The period varies from state to state. In Michigan it is thirty years; in Kentucky, fifteen years.

15.37   Extension agreements

Where the mortgagor and mortgagee agree to extend the maturity date of the mortgage note, the priority of the mortgage over those who took their interest between the recordation of the mortgage and the execution of the extension agreement remains undisturbed. The same is true when the earlier mortgage or note is replaced by another bearing a later maturity date. A different result follows, however, where in addition to merely extending the maturity date, the extension works a prejudice against the interests of the intervening interest holders.

> **EXAMPLE:** As a result of an economic downturn, mortgagor's business activity and profits are sharply reduced. To cope with this problem, mortgagor and mortgagee agree to alter the payoff schedule on the mortgage covering mortgagor's plant. It is agreed that principal payments would be deferred for eighteen months, mortgagor only being required to pay interest for that period. The ulti-

mate maturity date is thereby extended eighteen months. Priority over junior mortgagees remains the same. This is a valid extension.

EXAMPLE: Mortgagor and mortgagee agree to extend the maturity date and increase the interest rate. This agreement results in a split priority for the mortgage over junior lienors. To the extent of the unpaid principal and original interest, the mortgage is senior; to the extent of the increased interest, the priority will date from the modification date. This agreement results in a highly unusual priority problem: (1) the original mortgage principal and interest will have a first lien; (2) the second mortgage will take second place, subject only to (1) above; (3) the increased interest will have a third lien on the property. *Bowen* v. *American Arlington Bank,* 325 So2d 31 (Fla. 1975).

A question arises whether the first mortgagee can overcome this handicap by language inserted in the first mortgage. No case has been discovered indicating that this can be done. Probably it is impossible. The granting of the extension is like an "optional advance."

REFERENCE: Kratovil and Werner, *Mortgage Extensions and Modifications,* 8 Creighton L. Rev. 595 (1975).

HUD MORTGAGES: Where the mortgagor defaults because of circumstances beyond his control, he may enter into a forbearance agreement wherein mortgage payments may be altered or suspended for a specified period. 24 CFR § 203.340. Also, HUD may approve a modification of the amortization provisions by recasting the balance due over the original term of the mortgage or an extended term. 24 CFR § 203.342. Recent cases have held that the HUD insured mortgagees must seek to aid the distressed debtor and, absent such efforts, foreclosure is not allowed. *FNMA* v. *Ricks,* 83 Misc.2d 814 (N.Y. 1975).

15.38   Release, satisfaction, or discharge of mortgage

Although the payment of the mortgage debt discharges the mortgage, it nevertheless remains on the public records as a cloud upon the title until it has been released. The common method of releasing a mortgage or deed of trust is by execution, acknowledgment, delivery, and recording of a *release deed,* also variously called *satisfaction, discharge,* or *deed of reconveyance,* executed under seal by the trustee or mortgagee.

These formalities are necessary even though full payment has the effect of extinguishing the lien of the mortgage. Payment is not revealed by the public records and without the recordation of a properly executed satisfaction or release deed, the mortgage remains a defect in title.

15.38(a)   Partial release

When a mortgage conveys several distinct tracts of land, it is often provided in such a mortgage that on payment of a certain specified portion of the debt the mortgagor shall be entitled to a release of the mortgage as to a certain tract of land. Such a release is known as a partial release. In the absence of such a provision, the mortgagor is not entitled to any release of the mortgage except upon full payment of the mortgage debt. When a blanket mortgage is placed on an entire subdivision, such a provision is indispensable, since otherwise the subdivider could not furnish lot purchasers with clear title to their lots.

15.38(b)   Partial release schedule

Typically, the release clause will contain a schedule showing what lots may be released and the amount of payment for the lot or lots released. This must be set forth in accurate detail. *White Point Co.* v. *Herrington,* 73 Cal. Reptr. 885 (1968).

15.38(c)   Default

Unless the mortgage provides otherwise, the mortgagor can legally insist on a partial release even if he is in default in his mortgage payments. 41 ALR3d 7; 59 CJS 759. Hence it is best for the mortgagee to insist on a clause preventing this result.

> **CLAUSE:**   No partial release will be issued if an uncured default in payment of principal or interest or breach of covenant exists hereunder.

15.39   Marshalling of assets

There is danger to a first mortgagee who releases part of the land where junior liens may exist.

> **EXAMPLE:**   Owner mortgages Lots 1 and 2 to Lender #1. Owner thereafter mortgages Lot 1 to Lender #2. Lender #1 knows about the mortgage to Lender #2. Despite this, on Owner's request, Lender #1 releases Lot 2 from Lender #1's mortgage, thereby throwing all the burden of Lender #1's mortgage on Lot 1. This may cause Lender #1 to lose part or all his priority over Lender #2 as to Lot 1. Kratovil & Werner, *Modern Mortgage Law and Practice* § 16.04 (2d ed. 1981). Hence every mortgage should contain a clause designed to prevent this result.

> **CLAUSE:**   The mortgagee reserves the right to release any part of the mortgaged premises from the lien of this mortgage or to release the personal liability of any person for the debt hereby secured without regard to the effect upon junior liens or encumbrances.

15.40   Deed by mortgagor to mortgagee

Earlier, the deed absolute problem was described. There is a second type of deed absolute problem. At times a mortgagor will find that he is unable to pay the mortgage debt. In this event, the mortgagee may, of course, foreclose the mortgage. Foreclosure, however, usually costs the mortgagee time and money. He may wish to make some arrangement with the mortgagor for acquiring ownership of the land without the necessity of foreclosure. This is accomplished by means of an agreement between mortgagor and mortgagee whereby the mortgagor agrees to sell the land to the mortgagee for a small sum of money, and the mortgagee, in return, agrees to cancel the mortgage debt. The mortgagor thereupon gives the mortgagee a deed, and the mortgagee cancels the notes and releases the mortgage. The courts are inclined to be suspicious of such transactions, since the mortgagee is in a position to exert pressure on the mortgagor. To give validity to such a sale by the mortgagor, it must appear that the conduct of the mortgagee was, in all things, fair and frank and that he paid for the property what it was worth, and that he did not coerce the mortgagor into signing the deed. In order to protect himself, a mortgagee entering into such a transaction should take the following precautions:

1. He should examine the title to the land to make sure that no other liens, such as judgments or junior mortgages, attach to the land after the date of the mortgage.

2. A written contract should be entered into between the mortgagor and mortgagee. This contract should show that it was the mortgagor, not the mortgagee, who proposed the transaction. This renders it difficult for any court to hold that the mortgagor was coerced, since the agreement itself shows that he took the initiative in the transaction. The contract should also provide that the deed is given in full satisfaction of the mortgage debt. *Rooker* v. *Fidelity Trust Co.,* 109 NE 766 (Ind. 1915). In some states the same result is accomplished by putting a clause in the deed or in a separate affidavit.

3. The mortgage should be released and the mortgage and mortgage note canceled. If the mortgage debt is not canceled, courts tend to regard the deed as merely additional security for the debt rather than an outright sale of the mortgagor's equity. 129 ALR 1495.

4. The mortgagee should not enter into any contract to resell or reconvey the land to the mortgagor, though he may safely give the mortgagor an option to repurchase the premises. 129 ALR 1473.

HUD MORTGAGES: A mortgagee in a HUD mortgage may acquire the security from a mortgagor by a deed in lieu transaction if the following conditions are met: (1) the mortgage must be in default at the time the deed in lieu is executed and delivered. (2) The credit instrument must be canceled or surrendered to the mortgagor and the mortgage must be satisfied of record. (3) The mortgagor must give a warranty deed and convey good marketable title. 24 CFR § 203.357.

As you can see, this section presents a problem much like that presented in § 15.09(a). The problem is one of determining whether the deed is actually given with the intention to transfer the absolute ownership of the land or was given primarily as additional security, without the intention of extinguishing the mortgage.

15.41 Federal forms

Mortgage "law" cannot be discussed in light of cases and statutes alone. The mortgagor and mortgagee make the "law" applicable to their transaction by the execution of the documents in the mortgage package. As the federal government has dominated the residential mortgage industry, so has it dominated the wording of the mortgage documents. This influence comes from both the standards imposed by statutes and regulations discussed in the earlier sections of this chapter, and from the promulgation of uniform instruments. FNMA and FHLMC have jointly drafted these documents with the aid and assistance of some of the nation's leading authorities on mortgage law and practice and these forms must be used if the lender intends the loan to be sold in the secondary market.

The documents contain provisions uniform throughout the country and also are individually tailored for use in the various states and include both a note and mortgage or deed of trust. Also available are riders for the mortgage documents where the mortgaged property is a unit in a condominium or planned unit development.

The substance of some of the uniform provisions of these forms follows:

1. Borrower is entitled to prepay the principal obligation in whole or in part.

2. Borrower must pay monthly payments to the lender for the establishment of escrow accounts for the payment of taxes. Unless the agreement between borrower and lender, or the applicable law requires, lender shall not be required to pay borrower interest on the funds so held.

3. Borrower must pay all taxes, assessments, liens, and so forth levied against the property and perform all of the obligations imposed by any declaration of covenants relating to a condominium or planned unit development.

4. Borrower must not commit waste or permit deterioration of the property.

5. Borrower must keep the property properly insured.

6. Borrower agrees in advance to extension and modifications of the mortgage obligation granted to any successor in interest of the borrower.

7. Lender may waive the right to accelerate upon a sale of the property if the credit of the purchaser is satisfactory and the rate of interest to be paid by the purchaser to the lender is agreed upon. If such waiver is given and the buyer executes an assumption agreement which is accepted by the lender, the lender shall release the borrower from liability.

REFERENCES ON MORTGAGE LAW AND MORTGAGE LENDING: Britton and Kerwood, *Financing Income-Producing Real Estate* (1977); Dennis, *Fundamentals of Mortgage Lending* (1978); Jones, *A Treatise on the Law of Mortgages* (8th ed. 1982); Kratovil and Werner, *Modern Mortgage Law and Practice* (2d ed., 1981); Osborne, Nelson, and Whitman, *Real Estate Finance Law* (1979).

16 REAL ESTATE FINANCE— NEW FORMS OF MORTGAGES

16.01   In general

Since the 1930s, home financing has been largely done by the use of long-term fixed interest loans. These loans were made for twenty- to thirty-year terms and at interest rates that remain fixed for the life of the loan. For decades, this was acceptable to lenders because interest rates moved gradually and loans were repaid as an increasingly mobile population sold their homes before the loans matured.

As we moved through the 1970s, a great upheaval occurred in mortgage law and practice. Inflation in home prices and rising interest rates have driven the price of housing to a point that many first-time homebuyers are forced to abandon or postpone their home purchase plans.

> **EXAMPLE:**   In 1975, a home may have sold for $50,000, had real estate taxes of $1,000, and hazard insurance premiums of $150. A 9 percent, thirty-year, conventional mortgage with 20 percent down would have resulted in a mortgage payment of $322, which when added to one-twelfth of the taxes and insurance would require a monthly payment of $417.84. Under then existing mortgage underwriting guidelines (annual housing payments should not exceed one-fourth of annual income), a person making $20,000 per year would qualify for the mortgage loan. Let's assume that the house doubled in price and was for sale in 1981 for $100,000; real estate taxes increased to $1,500 per year; hazard insurance premiums increased to $225; and interest increased to 17 percent. The monthly mortgage payments on a thirty-year conventional 80 percent loan at 17 percent interest (assuming such loan was available) would be $1,140.80, which when added to one-twelfth of the real estate taxes and insurance premiums would produce a monthly payment of $1,284.55. To qualify for this loan under traditional standards, the homebuyer would need an annual income of $61,700. Some lenders have relaxed their qualifications to require that housing costs not exceed one-third of annual income. Even if this standard is used, the borrower must have an annual income of $43,300.

Some states invalidated the due-on-sale clause that lenders relied upon to call in funds from lower rate mortgages. Borrowers devised clever ways to conceal the sale of their homes from lenders so as not to trigger the due-on-sale clause. The continued existence of these long-term, low-rate, fixed interest mortgages has caused lenders great losses.

The concept of *negative spread* has been used to describe the loss that lenders have been taking on loans that are earning less than the amount of interest that lenders are paying. For example, savings and loan associations made billions of dollars of fixed rate loans during the 1970s at 7 to 10 percent. While the lenders are locked into the interest rates prescribed in these mortgages, their depositors are not. Depositors become careful shoppers for the best interest rates possible. This has forced lenders to try to attract funds with higher rates thus raising the average cost of funds to the lenders. This average often exceeded the return being earned on the lenders' portfolio of loans.

These factors have resulted in two fundamental changes in mortgage lending practices. For borrowers, a new type of loan had to be developed that would give the borrower a lower monthly payment in the earlier term of the loan and then increase as the loan matures. For lenders, a loan that allowed interest rate movement as interest rates increased was needed. Alternatively, lenders sought some of the appreciation that property owners enjoy. Indeed, these two goals have been achieved by the implementation of new lending programs that in various ways give the desired results to both borrowers and lenders.

These various documents are generally called *alternative mortgage instruments* (AMIs) or adjustable rate mortgages (ARM). Such mortgages may be found in combination with one another, taking features of one plan and combining them with features of another plan to give both the borrower and the lender the aspects of today's mortgages that they want.

Most of the discussion in this chapter will be keyed to the FHLBB AMI programs as they appear to either be the dominant programs or are models for other programs. There are, however, special state statutes authorizing various AMI programs, and the Comptroller of the Currency has promulgated a set of AMI regulations for national banks. The differences in all of these laws and regulations are not dramatic and it is expected that competition will compel substantial similarity among all mortgagees in the same community.

16.02 Negative amortization

Several ARM loan formats involve *negative amortization.*

EXAMPLE: In the typical loan, each monthly payment consists of two parts. One part is allocated to the interest due for the month. The remainder is allocated to reduce the principal. Suppose in a given ARM the interest moves up and down as interest rates on ninety-day Treasury bills move up and down. The interest rate on Treasury bills swings sharply upward. The entire monthly payment may be insufficient to pay the interest. If the amount of the monthly payment remains unchanged, the unpaid portion of the interest is added to the principal. With each monthly payment, the amount of the mortgage debt increases.

This creates several issues that must be resolved. The loan-to-value ratio increases making the loan riskier from the lender's standpoint. Many states prohibit the charging of interest on interest as occurs in the negative amortization situation. The increased principal may not have the same priority over intervening lien claimants as the original principal.

As is obvious, negative amortization that occurs where the early monthly payments are insufficient to pay the *interest* accrued that month presents a special problem. The mortgage tells us that the unpaid part of the interest is added to the principal. Under the decisional law this is illegal in some states. Kratovil & Werner, *Modern Mortgage Law and Practice* § 12.02 (2d ed. 1981); 45 Am.Jur.2d *Interest and Usury* §§ 76,77. The federal usury preemption does not solve the problem. It is not a usury question at all. It stems from the fact that the law frowns on compounding of interest. It does not invalidate the mortgage. In over half the states, it is simply not permitted. As to FHA loans under § 245, there is a specific federal preemption, and most GPM loans fall under that section.

As to FHA insured mortgages the regulations provide: "The mortgage may provide that any interest which accrues and which is unpaid pursuant to a financing plan approved by the Secretary shall be added to the principal obligation of the mortgage." 24 CFR § 234.75.

It would seem that, since interest becomes part of the principal, interest accruing thereafter will accrue on the new principal, so that true compounding takes place.

It seems reasonably clear that interest that accrues on a GPM offers less of a threat or danger to the borrower than does an ARM. From the outset, the borrower can compute the "worst case" that will occur under a GPM because the mortgage places an upper limit on the interest charged. This is not possible in an ARM. It is the ARM, therefore, that offers the greatest danger.

16.03 Interest rate adjustable loans

As is evident from the frequent newspaper accounts of the problems, many mortgage lenders have found that they can no longer lend on the basis of a fixed interest rate paid by the borrower while the interest rates they pay to their depositors on certificates of deposit swing upward and downward. Lenders have become convinced that the interest rate paid by the borrower must move up and down as the market forces interest rates paid to depositors to move up and down. In short, an adjustable interest rate loan is needed. Many forms of loans have developed to give lenders some ability to adjust the interest rate during the life of the loan. Although these loans have many names, variable rate mortgages (VRMs), renegotiable rate mortgages (RRMs), rollover mortgages (ROMs), adjustable mortgage loans (AMLs), and the like, they all have the common quality of allowing for a change in prevailing market interest rates paid to depositors to be passed on to the borrower. Where that is the case, the loans go by the generic term of adjustable rate mortgages (ARMs). These loans tend to insure a positive spread for the lenders and transfer to borrowers the risk of increases in market interest rates.

Before a borrower assumes that some form of adjustable loan is the only form of loan available, shopping is needed. Some lenders still make fixed rate loans, but they may charge a premium interest rate for such a loan. The borrowers must weigh the alternatives. If the borrower agrees to accept an ARM, he should not assume that all ARMs are the same. Borrowers should shop and analyze the differences between ARMs offered by various lenders. Inquire about many factors:

1. How are interest rate adjustments put into effect? Does the monthly payment change, the principal amount of the loan change, or the maturity of the loan change?

2. Will the interest rate move up and down according to some index, such as the interest paid on Treasury bills?

3. How frequently will rates change? As the index changes? Every month? Every six months? Every year? Every five years?

4. Are there minimum and maximum limits on interest rate movements?

5. What period of notice must be given to the borrower before a change will be allowed?

6. Are the borrowers charged a fee upon adjustment of the interest rates or refinancing with the same lender?

7. Must the lender offer to refinance at the conclusion of each adjustment period?

8. What index is used to determine the extent of any rate change?

9. Over what period is the loan amortized?

10. Is the loan prepayable at any time? If so, the borrower is free to take advantage of other financing that may become available.

11. What happens if the selected index pushes the monthly payments so high that all of the payment must be allocated to interest, thus forcing the debt to accumulate? See §16.03(i).

12. Are the mortgages acceptable to the secondary market?

13. Is a fixed rate loan available? If so, compare the projected payments on the fixed rate loan to the projected payments on the variable rate loan. Of course, some assumptions will have to be made to make this comparison, and assumptions of economic expectations are often wrong, but some comparison is needed if an informed decision is to be made.

EXAMPLE: Assume a $50,000 mortgage available as a thirty-year fixed rate mortgage at 18 percent or as a thirty-year variable rate mortgage at an original rate of 17 percent with interest rates that can increase by no more than one-half of 1 percent every six months. Assume also that the borrower intends to keep this house for only three years. Under the fixed rate loan, the monthly payment would be $753.50 and after three years the monthly payments would total $27,126, of which $26,958.50 would have gone to the payment of interest. If we assume that the variable rate loan had one maximum interest rate increase after the first and second years, monthly payments would be $713 for the first year, $732.14 for the second year, and $751.84 for the third year for a total of $26,363.79, of which $26,207.45 would have gone to the payment of interest. The total payments under the fixed rate mortgage are $762.21 more than under the variable rate mortgage and the interest paid under the fixed rate mortgage exceeds that paid under the variable rate mortgage by $751.05. Obviously if the assumptions are varied, the results will vary, but the mathematics should be worked out to demonstrate the impact of the various formats to the borrower.

14. Is it possible that reasonably foreseeable increases in interest rates will cause the periodic payments to increase to such a level that will be only burdensome to the buyer?

15. How long does the borrower intend to hold the loan?

16.03(a)   Risks in adjustable rate mortgages

It is obvious that the ARM creates risks not present in the older mortgages. These risks include: (1) The inability of the borrower to handle payment increases, where an increase in the market interest rate compels an increase in the size of the monthly payment. (2) The erosion of the equity due to negative amortization.

These risks can be minimized for the borrower by the inclusion in the mortgage of a stated maximum on the permitted increase in interest.

The lender's risk can be controlled by insistence on private mortgage insurance.

These loans must be looked at very carefully by borrowers. Gone are the days when every payment went to reduce the loan balance and increase the borrower's equity. The addition of amounts to principal can have a long-term impact on the borrower's financial planning and should not be taken lightly. Borrowers must carefully study these loans and shop for alternatives. Shopping for mortgage loans was always possible theoretically. In practice, it seldom occurred. The brief time allowed for closing a deal compelled the buyer to take the first loan offered, and competition assured that this would be much the same as any other loan offered. This is no longer true. A borrower might be able to live with *Index A*, but not *Index B*.

16.03(b)   Variable rate mortgages (VRM)

The VRM is the most basic ARM and is almost standard in commercial and construction lending. These loans are usually tied to a prime rate, have no limit on interest rate movements, and cause the interest rate to increase or decrease simultaneously with movements in the prime rate.

Until not too long ago, the VRM was only used in commercial transactions. Indeed, it was largely forbidden in most consumer mortgages. The FHLBB, regulating federal savings and loan associations, largely outlawed VRMs for those lenders until 1978 and 1979. Similarly, many states had statutes that prohibited interest rate increases during the life of the loan. Recent interest rate history has mandated the change in these laws that has occurred since 1978. With the change in the law, the fixed rate mortgage has lost its dominance of the mortgage market to such an extent that some say it will become extinct.

16.03(c) Rollover mortgage

In the renegotiable rate loan, or rollover, the *interest rate* is set for a period of time, say three to five years, at which time the loan falls due. But the monthly payments are fixed as though the loan would mature on a thirty-year schedule. Once the initial loan term is up, the loan is renegotiated in that the borrower may seek financing elsewhere, or, if the lender permits, renew the loan at the original lender's new rate. This plan has been used in Canada for some time. However, in recent years it has pushed Canadian mortgage payments so high that foreclosures have skyrocketed.

16.03(d) Adjustable mortgage loans (AMLs)

The Federal Home Loan Bank Board (FHLBB) has enacted a regulation giving federal savings and loan associations very flexible authority to make loans that permit the adjustment of interest rates over the life of the loan. 12 CFR § 545.6-4a. These loans may use any interest rate index as long as it is readily verifiable by the borrower and is not within the control of the lender, i.e., not that lender's prime rate. Adjustments caused by movement of the index may be made by increasing or decreasing the payments, the outstanding balance, the loan term, or all of these factors. There is no limit on the amount of interest rate increase or decrease that may be made at any one time or over the life of the loan, and there is no limit on the frequency of adjustments. These loans must be prepayable at any time without penalty and must not have a term longer than forty years.

16.03(e) ARM—index

The selection of the index is an important aspect of this form of loan. At each adjustment date, the difference between the index at the date of the mortgage, or the last adjustment, and the index at the adjustment date is added to or subtracted from the mortgage rate.

> **EXAMPLE:** The mortgage is dated January 30, 1982. At that date, the index specified in the mortgage documents was 12.75 percent. On July 30, 1982, the next specified adjustment date, the index moved to 13.25 percent. The mortgage rate would move up 0.50 percent (13.25 percent minus 12.75 percent). If the original interest rate on the mortgage was 14 percent, the new mortgage rate would be 14.5 percent.

From the lender's point of view, the index should reflect the lender's cost of funds, i.e., the index should move up and down as the lender's cost of funds increases and decreases. From the borrower's point of view, an index that could move up so fast as to outstrip the borrower's ability to pay the loan should be avoided. Both borrowers and lenders are concerned with the volatility of the index. Does it quickly respond to changes in short-term interest rates or does it reflect long-term interest rate trends?

Selection of the index, although subject to some negotiation or at least shopping on the part of the borrower, is initially the lender's decision. Federal savings and loan associations may choose any index that is readily verifiable and out of the association's control. Of course, the prudent borrower will go to an association that uses the index that he prefers. On ARM home loans, national banks must choose (1) the monthly average contract interest rate charged by all lenders on mortgage loans for previously occupied homes, (2) the monthly average yield on U.S. Treasury securities adjusted to a constant maturity of three years, or (3) the monthly average of weekly average auction rates on six-month U.S. Treasury bills. 12 CFR § 29.4(2).

It seems appropriate at this point to explain the nature of these instruments. Treasury bills are short-term U.S. government IOUs maturing in three, six, or twelve months. They are sold at a discount rather than at face or par value.

> **EXAMPLE:** An auction price of three-month Treasury bills may be $96.562 per $100 of face value giving an investor an effective yield of 14.28 percent.

Treasury notes and bonds are longer maturity debt instruments of the U.S. government that pay the investor a fixed interest on a semiannual basis. These instruments may be sold either at a discount or a premium thereby yielding the investor more or less than the stated interest.

> **EXAMPLE:** The U.S. Treasury auctions a two-year note with a stated interest rate of 8.5 percent at $99.802 per $100 of par value. The effective annual yield to the investor is 8.61 percent.

If the index is based upon short-term rates such as three- or six-month Treasury bills, it will move up and down faster than if it is based on long-term rates. Conversely, an index based upon longer maturity securities such as three- or five-year U.S. Treasury notes is slow moving and will not rise or fall as quickly as market rates may move.

The Average Cost of Funds to FSLIC insured associations is computed semiannually, and its use allows lenders to tailor loan terms to their costs. From a borrower's point of view, this is probably a bad index today. The elimination of regulated ceilings on the interest paid to depositors will contribute to a probable continued and fast-paced rise in this index for the immediate future.

The National Average Mortgage Contract Rate for Major Lenders on the Purchase of Previously Occupied Homes is computed monthly by the FHLBB. Although many lenders seem to pick this rate as an ARM index, it does not reflect the lender's cost of funds. As a long-term rate, it moves slowly and is an advantage to borrowers in times of rising interest rates, but, once rates peak out, it will also move down slowly as rates decline.

All of these indexes fluctuate constantly and are published in financial newspapers and magazines.

The mortgage documents must specify which index has been selected.

16.03(f) ARM—limits on interest rate movement

To control the degree of interest rate movement and to keep borrowing costs controllable for borrowers, some loans have limits upon the degree of increase or decrease during any prescribed period and over the life of the loan. By using a "worst case" forecast, a lender and borrower can at least project interest payments.

> **EXAMPLE:** A $50,000 interest-only payment loan with a three-year balloon and an original rate of 17 percent had a variable interest rate provision but called for interest rate adjustments every six months and limited increases to one-half of 1 percent per six-month period. The borrower could project that the interest costs would not exceed $708.33 per month for the first six months, $729.17 per month for the second six months, $750 per month for the third six months, $770.83 per month for the fourth six months, $791.67 per month for the fifth six months, and $812.50 per month for the last six months of the loan.

The borrower's cash flow and cash needs can be projected and an appropriate budget worked out. If interest rates do not increase to such a degree so as to cause the rate to increase to these maximum levels, so much the better for the borrower.

Borrowers should carefully analyze the possible size of payments under these loans. Those with little discretionary income available for the payment of housing costs may have difficulty meeting future increased payments brought about by increases in interest rates.

> **SUGGESTION:** Books are available that give pages of tables covering every conceivable interest rate fluctuation. Every person interested in real estate must have such a book.

Federal savings and loan associations have no limit on interest rate adjustments, but national banks cannot adjust the loan rate by more than one point for every six months of the loan's life.

Competition will probably compel lenders to state maximums for each adjustment period or over the life of the loan. FNMA and FHLMC will probably insist on such limits.

16.03(g) ARM—frequency of adjustment

Depending upon the type of loan and its documentation, the interest rate may fluctuate simultaneously with interest rate index changes or only after a stated period, i.e., six months, two years, etc. In commercial mortgages, particularly construction loans, the loan rate often moves as the prime rate moves. As can be guessed, the frequency of adjustment is high in these types of loans.

In home loans, federal savings and loan associations can adjust the interest rate as often as the movement of the index justifies adjustment. Of course, frequent adjustments may be too costly for the lender to implement. National banks can adjust the rate only upon intervals of at least six months.

Competition will probably force lenders to state a period during which a given rate must remain in force.

16.03(h) ARM—direction of interest rate movements

The loan documents may provide that the interest rate may move both up and down with index movements. Are interest rate movements optional with the lender? Must the rate move down if the index moves down? The loan documents must answer these questions. In some cases, the law requires downward movement if the index moves down, as is the case with federal savings and loan associations.

16.03(i) ARM— implementing adjustments

While often a change in the interest rate will be reflected in the level of monthly payments, other methods can be used to accommodate the interest rate change.

The term of the loan can be extended, thereby keeping the monthly payment level and reducing the amount of the payment that goes to repay principal. Obviously, this method has limits. The FHLBB ARM regulation requires that the term not exceed forty years. 12 CFR § 545.6-4a(b)(2). Mathematically, it may not be possible to stretch the term to a length that will pay off the debt.

Lastly, the loan principal may be increased by keeping the payment level at the initial amount and adding any unpaid interest to the principal of the loan.

> **EXAMPLE:** Assume an $80,000 ARM on a $100,000 home at an original rate of percent with an original amortization period of thirty years with interest rate adjustments every three years and no limit on the amount of the adjustment. The initial payment would be $948 per month. That would reduce the loan balance to $79,352.80 after three years. If the index increases to cause the loan rate to go to 16 percent, the interest payment alone on that balance would be $1,058.03. If the payment were to remain constant at $948 per month for the second three-year period, negative amortization would occur.

Because the mathematics of upward interest rate adjustments can create such a large mortgage debt, many lenders periodically reset the payoff schedules to fully amortize the loan over the remaining term. The FHLBB requires this to be done every five years. 12 CFR § 545.6-4a(b)(2). In a period of rising interest rates, this can greatly increase the monthly payment. National banks must limit negative amortization to 10 percent of the original principal amount of the loan.

16.03(j)   ARM—effect of variable rate clauses on parties secondarily liable

Frequently, mortgages have parties secondarily liable, with the borrower being primarily liable for payment of the debt. For example, in major transactions, it is not uncommon to have guarantors for the principal's obligation of payment of the debt. Similarly, endorsers and assignors may have secondary liability. Under traditional theories, an alteration of the obligation between the principal and the creditor will discharge the obligation of the secondarily liable parties. This should present no great difficulty in the variable rate mortgage context since careful draftmanship, even where the increase in the interest rate is optional, can continue the obligation of these parties notwithstanding the increase in the burden upon the primary debtor. Barnett, *Alternative Mortgage Instruments: How to Maintain Secured Lender's Status*, 96 Banking L. J. 6, 31 *et seq.* (1979).

16.03(k)   ARM—due-on-sale clause

FNMA and FHLMC require that the due-on-sale clause be in all ARMs that they purchase. The form of this clause embodied in the FNMA and FHLMC uniform instruments gives the lender the right to call the loan due upon sale or to review the credit of the new owner who assumes the loan after an adjustment in the interest rate.

16.03(l)   ARM—secondary mortgage market

The sale of ARMs in the secondary mortgage market has met some resistance. Investors are especially wary of loans that lack certainty in their terms, or result in negative amortization as in an ARM and GPM. Indeed, as of this printing, FHLMC will not purchase any ARM loans with a negative amortization feature and will only purchase ARMs that use the "contract Interest Rate, Purchase of Previously Occupied Homes, National Average for all Major Types of Lenders" published by the FHLBB as the index. FNMA will purchase ARMs that have adjustment periods of from six months to five years, based on the movement of five different, but widely published, indexes of interest rate changes. It will also consider purchasing other forms of ARMs on a case-by-case basis.

16.04   Loans that provide lower payments at the beginning of the loan and higher payments thereafter

In many instances, the borrower must have a lower payment at the outset of the loan to afford the house of his choice. Before selecting such a loan, the parties should look at the following:

1. Has the program been fully explained? Does the borrower understand exactly what the payments will be as the loan matures?

2. Does the borrower expect his income to increase as the payments are scheduled to increase? If not, are alternate payment schedules available that are more in line with the borrower's expected cash flow increases?

3. If the loan has an interest rate adjustment feature, the borrower has all of the same concerns of a borrower under an ARM. See § 16.03 *et seq.*

16.04(a) Graduated payment mortgage (GPM)

The graduated payment mortgage is characterized by lower payments during the initial period of the loan and higher payments thereafter. Theoretically, as the borrower's income increases, payments increase. The payment graduation schedule and the interest rate are set at the outset of the transaction. While payments on this mortgage are lower during the initial years, the period payments level off at a higher plateau than for a comparable level payment mortgage. The total amount paid on this type of mortgage exceeds the amount that would be paid on a level payment mortgage of the same amount for the same period of time.

> **EXAMPLE:** A borrower under a 30-year, 8½ percent, $30,000 GPM with payments increasing by 5 percent a year for the first five years with level payments thereafter, would make monthly payments of $190.83 during the first year, $200.37 during the second year, $210.39 during the third year, $220.91 during the fourth year, $231.96 during the fifth year, and $243.56 thereafter. Foster, *The HUD Graduated Payment Mortgage Experiment,* I AMIRS V–Table 1 (1977). A level payment mortgage of the same amount would have monthly payments of $230.68. If both the GPM and the level payment mortgages run to maturity, the borrower under the GPM plan will make principal and interest payments totaling $85,724.28 and the borrower under the level payment plan will make principal and interest payments totaling $83,044.80, $2,679.48 less than under the GPM plan.

The increase in periodic payments in the years after the loan is originated can cause strains upon the ability of the borrower to make payments if expected increases in income do not occur or inflation in other areas of the economy causes unexpected strains on the borrower's income stream.

A feature of this type of financing device is that initial payments are not of sufficient size to fully pay the interest that accrues during any month. To the extent that the initial payment is insufficient in this regard, additional principal is created. Thus, in the early stages of the payment schedule, the debt increases rather than decreases. This is called *negative amortization.*

If the price of the home does not increase at an acceptable pace, the negative amortization feature of a GPM can cause the borrower an out-of-pocket expense upon the sale of the property. Frequently, these mortgages are low down payment loans and the "thin equity" of the borrower is made even thinner by operation of the negative amortization aspect. Selling costs can quickly erode whatever equity there is.

The advantages of negative amortization in a GPM are great.

EXAMPLE: On a $50,000 GPM mortgage bearing an initial 14 percent interest the borrower can qualify with a salary of $19,768. On a fixed rate mortgage the salary needed would be $25,768.

And if the borrower can expect salary increases of 10 percent annually, obviously the mortgage payments should take a decreasing percentage of income.

EXAMPLE: Various computations have been made showing that an expected GPM mortgage that will take 50 percent of the borrower's income in the first year will take only 21 percent of his income in the tenth year. This points up an obvious economic fact. The danger of default is in the early years of the loan. But housing is a categorical imperative. One must live somewhere. Veterans have been paying over 40 percent of their income on VA financed housing, and in some areas (San Francisco) the average homeowner pays over 50 percent of his income for housing.

Lenders view negative amortization *arising from a GPM* as acceptable because the amounts of the increase are known at the outset. A borrower can from the outset judge his capacity to pay during the life of the loan. But negative amortization *arising from variable interest rates* is harder to pin down. It is considered unsafe by some unless the mortgage fixes a maximum beyond which it cannot push the payments, and this maximum is one the borrower can handle.

16.04(b) Graduated Payment Adjustable Mortgage Loans (GPAMLs)

Federal savings and loan associations are authorized to make loans that combine the features of both the AML and GPM. 12 CFR § 545.6-4b. FHLBB regulations are quite flexible on these loans and largely incorporate the AML requirements. The GPAML has the added feature that the payment at the outset may be insufficient to fully amortize the principal. Lenders are given almost complete freedom to arrange payment schedules during the first ten years of the loan, but by the end of the tenth year, the scheduled payments must rise to a level sufficient to amortize the then existing interest rate and principal over the remaining term of the loan. Thereafter, the payment amount must be adjusted at least every five years to a level sufficient to fully amortize the loan. Because interest rate adjustments may be made on a GPAML from time to time, the payment amount, loan balance, or loan term may increase or decrease as these adjustments are made.

Of course, the entire formula for increases and decreases in the payment levels, loan term, and loan balance together with the formula for the implementation of interest rate increases must be spelled out in the original loan documents.

This is but a prominent example of the combined forms of AMIs that are now appearing. This form gives consumers the feature of lower payments during the initial loan term, increasing at somewhat programmed levels as the loan matures. At the same time, lenders get the benefit of the ability to adjust interest rates to keep their loan portfolio in line with current rates.

16.04(c) Pledged account loans

By pledging a savings account or other fund to a lender and giving that lender the ability to draw upon that account to supplement monthly payments during the early stages of the loan, the borrower achieves the goal of reducing payments during the initial term of the loan by using withdrawals to supplement the borrower's payment. During the early part of the loan, the withdrawals are larger, reducing on a programmed basis as the loan matures and as the payments made by the borrower increase. The lender gets the combined security of the real estate and the savings account. Federal savings and loan associations are allowed to make these loans, but the loan shall not exceed the appraised value of the real estate and the savings account. Federal savings and loan associations are allowed to make these loans, but the loan shall not exceed the appraised value of the real estate and the savings account must belong to the borrower, a member of the borrower's family, or the borrower's employer. 12 CFR § 545.6-2(a)(5).

16.04(d) GPM—form

Mortgage and note should state that the size of the monthly payment increases periodically and should contain a provision such as, "From time to time, deferred interest shall be added to the principal balance outstanding on this loan." This statement is made necessary by state laws requiring the character of the debt or mortgage to be reflected in the recorded documents. Other state laws require that the maximum amount to be advanced or secured by the mortgage be stated. Careful draftsmanship can solve these problems. An unsolvable problem is created by state laws that limit the time for making advances if they are to have priority over intervening liens. Barnett, *Alternative Mortgage Instruments: How to Maintain Secured Lender's Status,* 96 Banking L. J. 6, 17 (1979).

16.04(e) GPM—the due-on-sale clause

The due-on-sale clause presents special difficulties in this form of transaction. A buyer will have to be uniquely qualified to "fit" into the then existing stage of the payment schedule that was originally tailored for the needs of some other borrower. It may be possible that the borrower is qualified to meet the monthly payment level at the time that a sale of the property occurs, but a question remains as to the buyer's potential income increases necessary to meet larger future payments.

16.04(f) GPM—truth-in-lending

The truth-in-lending laws require the disclosure of the graduated payment feature by a statement of the contemplated payment schedule and the effective interest rate that results from deferring interest payments.

16.04(g)   GPM—usury problems

The GPM may cause usury problems. If state law or policy forbids interest on interest and thus interest is treated not as being on an increased principal amount but rather as additional interest, the effective rate of interest will be increased and state usury laws could be violated. 37 ALR 325, 345 suppl. by 76 ALR 1484, 1487.

> **EXAMPLE:**   The GPM is made at 10 percent, the maximum allowable interest rate. If state law will not recognize the concept of increasing the principal and charging interest on the increased principal, the effective rate of interest will be increased above 10 percent, and the usury law will be violated, absent of course any federal preemptive law applying to the situation.

16.05   Reverse annuity mortgages (RAMs)

Over the past years, inflation in home values has greatly built up the net worth of many older people. Many of the same people are, however, in a cash flow bind since they cannot spend the wealth that is accumulated in their property without selling the property. The RAM allows the landowner to convert equity in property to cash flow while retaining ownership and use of the property. Through this device, the lender, securing its position by a mortgage on the property, either makes periodic advances to the borrower or advances a sufficient amount to purchase an annuity that will make periodic payments to the borrower. Of course, there are variations on these themes and combinations of the two.

Because the RAM increases the encumbrances on the property, it may have great effect upon the net value of small estates and later estate plans. Obviously, consultation is needed with the estate planner if a RAM is contemplated. Great caution must be exercised by borrowers since the older population is at a state of life where financial errors of judgment can have serious consequences. The borrower also faces the risk that he will outlive the loan term only to be saddled with a heavy debt burden.

Because these instruments turn non-liquid real estate into a stream of funds for the borrower's use, the borrower does not receive "earned" income so as to disqualify him from eligibility for social security payments and medicare. The payment stream could, however, disqualify the borrower from Medicaid and Supplemental Income for the Aged, Blind and Disabled. Edwards, *Reverse Annuity Mortgages,* III AMIRS XIX–12 (1977); Ege, *Legal Implications of the Alternative Mortgage Instruments, id.* at XX–29. This can obviously have a devastating effect upon a needy borrower, and is a step which should be taken only after all alternatives are explored.

The borrower and lender must also address the question of whether the lender will advance additional principal to pay real estate taxes and insurance premiums on the property.

Lenders will typically want the borrower to retain a significant equity in the home so that the borrower has an economic compulsion to maintain the property. This equity is then a form of wealth that can be passed on to heirs while the elderly provide themselves with supplemental income during retirement. The lender must be watchful of loan-to-value problems as the debt increases. The loan must be structured with this problem in mind. Perhaps payments can be allowed until the loan-to-value ratio reaches a given point and the open-end advance clause drafted to allow additional advances as the property increases in value.

Federal savings and loans are authorized to make these loans that provide for periodic payments to homeowners based upon their accumulated equity. The payments are made directly by the lender to the homeowner or are made through the purchase of an annuity from an insurance company. The loan becomes due on a specified date after disbursement of the entire principal of the loan or when a specified event occurs such as the sale of the property or the death of the borrower. The interest rate may be fixed or may be adjusted periodically. Since these are rather new forms of loans with far-reaching consequences for borrowers, they are given a seven-day cooling-off period between the issuance of the commitment and the making of the loan. 12 CFR § 545.6-4(c).

16.05(a) RAM—discrimination

If these loans are extended only to older borrowers, the lender may be subject to discrimination claims under the Equal Credit Opportunity Act as discrimination against the young borrower. Ege, *Legal Implications of the Alternative Mortgage Instrument,* III AMIRS XX-33 (1977).

16.05(b) RAM—truth-in-lending

Truth-in-lending disclosures must be made of the fact that the entire principal and any deferred interest are due at the conclusion of the loan term.

16.05(c) RAM—due-on-sale clause

Because of the peculiar tailoring of these loans to the needs of the individual borrower, the due-on-sale clause should be utilized and enforceable. On the other hand, the lender relies heavily upon the property as security for the loan rather than the creditworthiness of the borrower. Some have suggested that the due-on-sale clause in a RAM should be as enforceable as under a regular mortgage. The question remains to be resolved by the courts or the legislators.

16.05(d) RAM—negotiability and the secondary market

If the borrower has the option of stopping additional advances under the rising debt version of the RAM, the loan may be nonnegotiable under the Uniform Commercial Code since the amount due is uncertain. UCC § 3-104, 3-112, and 3-119. Secondary market activity in these instruments is inhibited because of the need of the purchaser to fund the

additional advances, negative amortization, and because of the potentially imminent payment of a fully funded RAM.

16.05(e)   RAM—income tax consequences

Borrowers must concern themselves with the income tax aspects of the fixed-debt RAM, balancing
the taxable portion of the gross annuity against the
interest expense deduction. The borrower must keep in mind the standard deduction and the exemptions which effectively allow some income to go untaxed.
Under the rising debt variation, the principal payments to the borrower are tax
free but the interest deductions would not be allowed to a cash basis taxpayer
until the interest is paid, usually at death. To a like effect, a cash basis lender will
not report the interest income until it is paid, while the accrual basis lender has
interest income without cash flow. Rev. Rul. 80-248, 1980 I.R.B. No. 37 at 10.

16.06   Shared appreciation mortgages (SAMs)

Over the past several years, inflation has greatly
enhanced the return to developers and project
owners while decreasing the economic return to
the lender that has financed the equity buildup. Traditional permanent lenders,
recognizing this, have altered their investment philosophy by seeking out new
investment devices, including the outright purchase of a property, the partial
purchase of a property, short-term loans, contingent interest provisions, indexed interest, and SAMs.

In the SAM, the lender, as an inflation hedge, obtains a share of the appreciation of the property that is security for the debt. This is done in one of two
general formats. In one, the lender finances the property, usually at below market rates, and at the same time takes an ownership interest in the property. In
the other format, the borrower promises to pay the lender *contingent interest,* that
is, interest that is payable only out of appreciation in the value of the property
or, in the case of income property, out of the owner's proceeds from the operation of the property.

Where the contingent interest format is used, the lender must be careful in
defining the income that is subject to the contingent interest application and establish a system to carefully monitor the income to determine that the proper
amount of contingent interest is in fact being paid.

While SAMs are becoming an important form of financing for commercial
projects, they are developing very slowly as forms of residential financing. This
is so even though the lower interest rate means that buyers will have an easier
time qualifying for the loans.

16.06(a)   SAM—refinance provisions

Some SAMs require a sale or refinance after a few
years, often five or ten years, to "buy out" the
lender's position. How is the value to be deter-
mined if the property is not sold? How are improvements to be factored into the
valuation? How is the lender to be paid its share of the appreciated value of the

property, by a cash payment or by addition to the loan principal? If the latter method is chosen, will the borrower be able to meet the debt service requirements of the larger loan?

16.06(b) SAM—ownership considerations

Any lender embarking on a SAM program must consider the impact of the essential change in the nature of its status. Owners have liability for the operation of the property, different insurance needs, care that their partner is fairly accounting for the property's revenues, etc. The lender is also in a somewhat dangerous position, because of the potential that junior lien claimants may contend that the quasi-equity position of the lender destroys any priority rights available to the lender upon foreclosure as against the junior lien claimant.

> **EXAMPLE:** Buyer and Lender enter into a transaction where Lender finances the acquisition of a home and certain improvements (room additions and new roof) to be placed in the home. Through the shared equity device, these improvements will work to the Lender's benefit in that the value of the home will be increased. Even though the law of the state where this loan is made allows a true "Lender" priority interest in this regard against mechanic's lien claimants, that priority protection is not available to an owner. If the loan goes into default, mechanic's liens arising out of these improvements will be alleged to be prior to the owner/Lender's interest.

16.06(c) SAM—clogging the equity

The old theory of clogging the equity has moved into the limelight with the SAM loan.

> **EXAMPLE:** The SAM provides that the lender will receive contingent interest in the form of 40 percent of the profit on the sale of the mortgaged property in addition to the interest stated in the note.

> **EXAMPLE:** As a hedge against inflation, the lender on a commercial property obtains an option to purchase the property.

The application of this ancient doctrine may invalidate the mortgagee's option or right to contingent interest. The theory is that the lender is exacting a *collateral advantage* in addition to the interest specified in the loan or somehow making the transaction more than a mortgage that can be repaid, returning the borrower to the position that it was in before the loan was made. This very complex problem is explained in Kane, *The Mortgagee's Option to Purchase Mortgaged Property,* in A.B.A. Real Prop., Prob. & Tr. L. Sect., *Financing Real Estate During the Inflationary 80s* (Strum ed. 1981).

This ancient rule should not find application in a transaction negotiated between a large developer represented by a team of experts and a large lender represented by a team of experts. These sophisticated parties should have the complete freedom to contract for the result they want in light of the economic realities they find in the marketplace.

REFERENCES: *Mac Arthur* v. *North Palm Beach Utilities Inc.,* 202 So2d 181 (Fla. 1967); *Smith* v. *Smith,* 82 NH 399, 135 A25 (1926); *Hopping* v. *Baldridge,* 130 Okla. 226, 266 P2d 469 (1928); *Coursey* v. *Fairchild,* 436 P2d 35 (Okla. 1967); *Griffin Co.* v. *Chicago,* 52 Ill. 130 (1869); 59 CJS *Mortgages* § 113; 55 Am.Jur. 2d *Mortgages* § 85, § 514; 2 Harv. L. Rev. 459, 472. See also § 15.03(b)

16.07 Convertible mortgages

A variation of the SAM is the convertible mortgage that gives the lender an option to convert the mortgage into a full or partial ownership share. Once again, the owner typically gets a less than market rate loan, but gives up the right to some of the appreciation of the property if the lender elects to convert from lender's to owner's status.

16.08 Equity investments

Vast sums of institutional funds, including pension funds, are being attracted to real estate. The difference today lies in the fact that these funds are coming in the form of an equity investment rather than a loan secured by the real estate. These investments may take many forms: purchase of 100 percent of the equity in the project, joint venture, sale and leaseback, convertible mortgage, and the like. Nellis and Hastie, *Real Estate Joint Ventures in the 80s,* in A.B.A. Real Prop., Prob. & Tr. L. Sect., *Financing Real Estate During the Inflationary 80s* (Strum ed. 1981), Roegge, Talbot, and Zinman, *Real Estate Equity Investments and the Institutional Lender: Nothing Ventured, Nothing Gained,* 39 Fordham L. Rev. 579 (1971).

16.09 Deferred interest mortgage (DIM)

In the DIM, early payments not only fail to contribute to the amortization of principal, but also fail to cover all of the accrued interest. This then results in negative amortization and the interest on interest problems.

16.10 Interest-only mortgage

Under the interest-only mortgage, early payments do not contribute to the amortization of principal but fully pay any accrued interest. Either the mortgage is payable at a stated date, perhaps three or five years from its creation, or principal amortization is deferred until such later date.

Federal savings and loan associations are authorized to make loans that provide for the payment of interest only for an initial period of not longer than five years and then subsequent monthly installments adequate to amortize the debt within a forty-year loan term. 12 CFR § 545.6-2(a)(4)(iii). These loans may also be combined with any authorized AMI plan.

16.11   Balloon loans   Balloon loans are structured in one of two general ways. The loan is for a short term, with the payments including either interest-only or interest and principal amortized over a longer term with the whole loan payable at the end of the shorter term. At that time the loan is either renegotiated, refinanced, or paid off. This is really a form of ARM, giving the lender the chance to adjust the interest rate to current market conditions every three to five years.

The FHLBB has recently authorized federal savings and loan associations to make balloon loans with a maturity of up to forty years. 12 CFR § 545.6-2(a)(4). The comment on the regulation observes that the medium-length balloon would be the most attractive to the secondary market. The balloon loan will be subject to the 95 percent loan-to-value limitations applicable to home loans generally, but nonamortized balloon loans are subject to a 90 percent loan-to-value limitation.

The regulation also permits the use of a combined ARM–balloon mortgage, but the ARM feature will be permitted only on partially amortized balloon loans. The dangers of default on a straight five-year balloon with negative amortization are obvious.

16.12   Call provisions   In order to be able to raise interest rates as needed, lenders have been including mortgage clauses that permit the lender to *call the loan,* that is, to declare the entire principal due.

FNMA insists on such a provision in Arizona, Arkansas, California, Colorado, Florida, Georgia, Illinois, Iowa, Michigan, Minnesota, Mississippi, New Mexico, New York, Ohio, Oklahoma, South Carolina, and Washington, states that in some way fetter the due-on-sale clause. The theory is that ordinarily a mortgage loan is paid off in about seven years. Lenders made loans on this expectation. But inflation has led sellers and buyers to resort to all sorts of expedients to keep old loans alive. To counter this move, FNMA refuses to buy a loan in these states unless it is made callable after seven years.

16.13   Interest on interest   The negative amortization feature of an ARM and GPM creates a legal problem of charging interest on interest.

> **EXAMPLE:** To the extent that any monthly payment does not fully pay the interest due on the principal for that month, an addition to principal is made. Interest for the next month is then charged on the new principal balance which includes the amount added after the application of the last payment.

This practice is prohibited as being against the public policy of many states. *See* generally, *Hochmark* v. *Richler,* 26 P 818 (Colo. 1891); *Rose* v. *Bridgeport,* 17 Conn. 243 (1845); *Cox* v. *Smith,* 1 Nev. 161 (1895); *Abramowitz* v. *Washington Cemetery Assn.,* 51 A2d 461 (N.J. Ch. 1947); Ark. Stat. Ann. § 68-606; Ann.

Comm'l Code of Md. § 12-306(b)(1); Mo. Rev. Stat. § 408.080 (allows compounding once per year); 37 ALR 325, 332 suppl. by 76 ALR 1484, 1485. *But see Greer* v. *Greer,* 108 P2d 398 (Ariz. 1940); 37 ALR 325, 327 suppl. by 76 ALR 1484, 1485. This should not be confused with the allowable process of settling an overdue debt by an agreement which capitalizes past due interest and charges interest on the new principal amount including that past due interest. *Hamilton* v. *Stephenson,* 55 SE 577 (Va. 1906); 37 ALR 325, 328 suppl. by 76 ALR 1484, 1485.

> **EXAMPLE:** *A* loaned *B* $10,000 for one year with interest at 10 percent per annum. At the end of the year, *B* owed *A* $11,000, the $10,000 principal originally advanced and $1,000 in interest. *B* was unable to pay at that time, but, if given the chance, had a reasonable opportunity of fully repaying the debt upon the successful conclusion of a business transaction. *A* and *B* agreed and a new note was executed for the $11,000 debt (the $11,000 being the principal on the new obligation, the amount upon which interest would be charged) with interest at 10 percent per year. This device is perfectly valid. It is distinguished from the graduated payment mortgage system which at the outset creates a program for automatically increasing the principal each month by the amount of unpaid interest and charging interest for that month on the increased principal amount.

The interest on interest prohibition is becoming less of a problem in the ARM and GPM setting as some states have enacted statutes to facilitate the making of such mortgages. See, e.g., Ill. Rev. Stat. Ch. 32 § 794(e). These statutes generally exempt ARMS and GPMs from the interest on interest rule. See, e.g., Burns Ind. Stat. Ann. § 28-1-21.5-7(b). Minn. Stat. Ann § 47.201. This is obviously an area where federal preemption was necessary.

16.14 Intervening liens

While it is a simple task for the borrower and lender to allow the property to stand as security for additional debt created by the negative amortization feature of the AMI plan, the retention of priority over other lien claimants for that additional debt is another matter. This is especially a problem where the GPM, ARM, and RAM are used. As long as the "advances" or additions to principal caused by the negative amortization are obligatory on the part of the lender, the priority of the AMI will be preserved against intervening lien claimants. Kratovil and Werner, *Modern Mortgage Law and Practice* § 11.02 (2d ed., 1981).

However, since under the ARM the lender has the option of increasing the interest rate, the priority for the negative amortization cannot be upheld under the obligatory advance theory. At least one state has statutorily removed this problem for lenders, as does the FHLB Bd. regulation governing GPMs made by federal associations. Burns Ind. Stat. Ann. § 28-1-21.5-7(c); 12 CFR § 545.6-4(b)(3). Under these laws and regulations, the increased principal created by negative amortization is given first-lien status.

To the extent that regulations or statutes do not protect the priority of these loans for the amount of this additional principal, mortgagees are well advised to fully spell out the negative amortization features of the loan in the recorded mortgage. In this way, junior lien claimants are put on notice of the exact nature and possible size of the ARM debt. If they take their position in the face of these recorded disclosures, it seems that they should not be able to achieve priority over all or part of the ARM.

Does this potential non-first-lien position for the increased interest disqualify the loan from its federal preemption of state usury laws? If so, the interest at the higher level upon renegotiation may be usurious if it exceeds state-imposed limits.

Most title companies will insure against loss of priority on ARMs and GPAMs if the recorded mortgage gives the proper disclosures such as those embodied in the new adjustable rate riders adopted by FNMA and FHLMC for attachment to their uniform loan documents. There are several forms of endorsements for title insurance policies in AMI situations. Be sure to study the various forms available in your community and get the best coverage possible. See Goode, *ALTA Endorsements,* 42 Mtg Banking 33 (1982).

16.14(a) Face amount of mortgage exceeded

In states that tend to confine the mortgage debt to an amount equal to or less than the face amount of the mortgage, there is some danger that negative amortization that brings the debt above this figure might be invalidated to that extent.

16.15 Usury

An adjustable mortgage may become usurious if the index carries the rate over the usury limit. *Kin-Ark Corp.* v. *Boyles,* 593 F2d 361 (10th Cir. 1979). Another court has held that usury is not present even though the variable rate provisions at times carry the loan rate above the legal maximum if the parties contracted in good faith and without the intent to avoid the usury laws. *McConnell* v. *Merrill, Lynch Pierce, Fenner & Smith,* 146 Cal. Reptr. 371 (1978). See, *generally,* Werner, *Usury and the Variable-Rate Mortgage,* 5 RELJ 155 (1976). This is the better view.

Absent an exemption or preemption, the lender must include a provision in the loan documents that the interest rate will not increase to a level above the maximum rate allowed by law.

16.16 Negotiability

The concept of negotiability protects a holder in due course of a promissory note from defenses that may be available against the original creditor. The ARMs are often, almost by definition, evidenced by nonnegotiable (as opposed to nonmarketable) notes. Where the sum is uncertain, as in the ARM, and where the buyer of the loan must refer to something outside of the note itself, i.e., the index, to determine the interest rate, the note is not a negotiable instrument.

16.17   Federal preemption

Federal preemptive intervention in the modern mortgage context really began in the mid-seventies when Congress preempted the application of state usury statutes to some loans. This preemption was later embodied in the more far-reaching usury law preemption of the Financial Institutions Deregulation and Monetary Control Act of 1980. Pub. L. No. 96-221, 94 Stat. 132 (1980). See 37 Bus. Law. 747, 1079 (1982).

The preemption of state interest rate limits is only one aspect of mortgage law that was in need of federal preemption if a national program of ARMs was to be successful. State laws on interest on interest, clogging the equity, and lien priority needed to be made uniform and receptive to economic changes that require changes in mortgage practice and mortgage law.

Regulations applicable to federal savings and loan associations were adopted to preempt state laws that directly or indirectly restrict an association's ability or right to make loans authorized by federal regulations. See, e.g., 12 CFR §§ 545.6-4(a)(2) & 545.6-4a(a)(2). While this broad preemption will probably be the subject of much litigation, it is the stated intent of the FHLBB to free the loans that it authorizes from the hampering effect of state law. FHLBB Res. No. 81-206 (4/23/81).

It is clear that the federal preemption will shield the authorized loans from the application of state laws that would otherwise invalidate the loan or any of its terms.

> **EXAMPLE:** State laws prohibiting the collection of interest on interest would be inapplicable to loans made under programs authorized by the FHLBB.

It is less clear that the regulation gives first-lien status to additions to principal that are caused by the negative amortization features of ARMs and RAMs. Note that the regulation expressly gives first-lien status to interest capitalization resulting from the negative amortization feature of a GPM, 12 CFR § 545.6-4(b)(3), but the regulations on AMLs, GPAMs, and RAMs are curiously silent on this specific issue.

16.17(a)   Federal preemption–parity

Since the laws of many states placed impediments on the enforceability of some AMI features, it was necessary to federally preempt the application of those laws to federally related lenders. This left other lenders at a competitive disadvantage as compared to the federal lenders. Some states have responded by enacting *parity* or "wild card" laws that give these other lenders the powers of federally regulated lenders. See, e.g., Ill. Rev. Stat. Ch. 32, par. 706(c) & Ch. 16 1/2, par. 105(11). It seems that these laws should give the non-Federal lenders both the power to make AMIs authorized to federal lenders and the same immunity from the application of usury, interest on interest, clogging the equity, and lien priority rules afforded to federal lenders under the federal preemptive laws and regulations.

In the wild rush to give state institutions powers like those of federal institutions, little attention has been paid to the old problem of "referential legislation," that is, state legislation that fluctuates in its impact as federal legislation permits. Older lawyers raised eyebrows on laws of this sort, contending a state cannot delegate its powers to the federal government. *People* v. *Downes*, 212 NW2d 314 (Mich).

16.18   Income tax consequences

These new forms of mortgages cause federal income tax rules to be applied in a slightly different manner than in the case of a fixed rate mortgage. The chief impact is the result of negative amortization on a cash basis taxpayer.

As with loans such as an ARM and GPM, all interest accruals are not paid on a monthly basis. Unpaid accrued interest may be added to the loan balance as a result of the negative amortization feature of these loans. For the cost basis taxpayer–borrower, this means that only the interest actually paid is deductible for federal income tax purposes. The interest that is deferred will not be deductible until it is actually paid, an event that may occur gradually over the later life of the loan or suddenly, if the loan is refinanced or the property sold.

Under the SAM, the rule is applied in the same way to cause the deductibility of contingent interest to be deferred until the sale of the property when the contingent interest is actually paid to the lender. If the SAM is set up to give the "lender" an interest in the property, as opposed to contingent interest on the loan, a payment of interest will not occur on the sale. No deduction will result to the borrower for the lender's share of the sale proceeds. The borrower's selling price will of course be reduced by the lender's share, thereby resulting in less gain or perhaps even a loss to the seller–taxpayer upon the sale of the property.

The income tax implications of the SAM are quite complex and depend in large measure on the personal status of the borrower. Levine, *Tax Implications of Shared Appreciation Mortgages,* 59 Taxes 487 (July 1981).

16.19   Mortgage tax

There is the possibility, in all states that impose a mortgage tax, that the capitalized or deferred interest in a negative amortization situation would be subject to a mortgage tax.

16.20   Mortgage backed securities

Not too long ago, the funds for making mortgage loans came largely from depositors in savings institutions and purchasers of life insurance. To a great extent, that has now changed. The secondary mortgage market is the great provider of lendable funds. The mortgage investor, be it an individual or a large financial institution, purchases a mortgage backed security, thereby generating the capital for mortgage loan originators.

EXAMPLE: A lender will originate $50,000,000 of mortgage loans on uniform documents, and using uniform underwriting techniques. These loans will be placed in a pool and securities or bonds backed by the pool will be sold to investors. Instead of buying a particular loan or group of loans, the investor buys an undivided interest in the pool or a bond or debt obligation of the lender that is secured by the lender's mortgagee's interest in the loans that make up the pool. The investor then receives payments of interest and principal as the borrowers make their payments. The lender continues to service the loans.

Investors in these securities have the opportunity to choose among several investments.

EXAMPLE: A pension fund has millions of dollars to invest. It may select from many investments, i.e., General Motors bonds, Treasury securities, mortgage backed securities, etc., depending upon its investment goals and its evaluation of the various securities.

Because mortgage backed securities are only one of several possible alternative investments, mortgage securities must be competitive with other securities that are also trying to attract investor dollars. In a real sense, homebuyers compete with corporations for credit.

There are two basic types of mortgage backed securities. In one type, the *pass-through certificate,* the originator–servicer simply passes through to the investors the principal and interest payments made by the mortgagors. Since this security is in reality a participating interest in a pool of mortgages, it is treated as a sale of assets on the originator's balance sheet rather than a liability. The other type is a *mortgage backed bond,* or the originating lender's promissory notes, which are secured by the mortgages in the lenders' pool. The difference between the two lies in the fact that, in the mortgage backed bond, the investor has the originating lender's promise to pay while in the pass-through security the investor has an interest in the lender's loan portfolio.

16.20(a) GNMA guaranteed mortgage backed securities

The Government National Mortgage Association (GNMA) pools large groups of mortgage loans and issues mortgage backed securities based on those loans to investors.

A specialized vocabulary has arisen around these investments. *Modified pass-through securities* provide for regular payment to the investor of principal and interest whether or not the mortgagors have paid the issuer. If the mortgagors of the mortgages making up the mortgage pool have not made their payments, the deficiency must be made up by the issuer. GNMA backs up the issuer's obligation in this regard.

EXAMPLE: Issuer offers a $100,000,000 offering of fully modified pass-through mortgage backed securities. The mortgages in the pool are assigned to a trustee for the benefit of GNMA. Pension funds, insurance companies, and the like buy up the issue and expect monthly payments due from the mortgagors, plus a pro rata share of any prepayments. Let's say the expected monthly payments of principal and interest from the mortgagors should be $825,000. If the mortgagors do not make their payments in a timely fashion, the issuer, or upon the issuer's default, GNMA, must make up any default. Thus, if only $800,000 in monthly payments is received from mortgagors, the $25,000 will have to be paid by the issuer or GNMA.

GNMA guarantees the payment of these securities, a guarantee that is backed by the full faith and credit of the United States government.

16.20(b)   FHLMC guaranteed securities

The Federal Home Loan Mortgage Corporation (FHLMC) provides funds for its secondary market purchase activities by selling *Participation Certificates* (PCs) and *Guaranteed Mortgage Certificates.* The PCs are undivided interests in groups or pools of specified first mortgages with a *modified pass-through* feature. This means that the FHLMC guarantees the timely payment of interest and the full return of principal.

The mortgage certificates pay interest semiannually and annually pay investors any principal repaid by the borrowers. FHLMC guarantees these payments and agrees to repurchase any certificates that are still outstanding after twenty-five years.

16.20(c)   Other mortgage backed securities

Private corporations have seized upon these devices for funding of mortgage lending activities. These devices involve the assignment to a trustee-servicer of a group of mortgages totalling more than 100 percent of the total offering and a promise in the nature of a fully modified pass-through obligation. This promise is limited, however, to the extent of payments received under partial mortgage guaranty insurance policies. This insurance is typically purchased in an amount equaling 5 percent of the offering.

Some federal savings and loan associations have issued *mortgage backed* bonds. These instruments are secured by a pool of mortgages often all FHA insured or VA guaranteed; they are not of the pass-through variety. This means that the bonds are debt obligations of the association secured by the "mortgage assets." The instruments do not give the investor an ownership interest in the mortgage collateral. Adams, *The Thrifty Seek Capital with Mortgage Backed Bonds,* 6 #1 R. E. Rev. 38, 39 (Spring 1976).

Indeed, even some homebuilders have raised mortgage funds for their homebuyers by issuing such securities.

16.20(d)   Tax-exempt municipal mortgage bonds

Some cities have issued tax-exempt bonds and made the proceeds available through mortgage lenders who act as loan originators and servicers. Because of the tax exemption that these bonds carry, and thus the lower cost of these mortgage funds, the interest rate on these mortgages is generally lower than on other mortgages. Some cities have earmarked a portion of such funds for problem areas. Others have permitted condominium speculators to borrow these funds. Some programs put income limits on the loan applicants. Others do not.

While bond payments are generated by the mortgage payments made by borrowers, bond investors are cautioned that the full faith and the credit of the local governments do not stand behind these devices.

These devices were the center of controversy. Since they increase the supply of tax-exempt bonds, it was thought that the interest rates for all such offerings would be pushed up. The Internal Revenue Service was upset over the loss of tax revenue that will result from this additional supply of tax-exempt investments. Congress reacted by enacting the Mortgage Subsidy Bond Tax Act of 1980, Internal Rev. Code § 103A *et seq.*, which greatly limits the eligibility of potential borrowers and bans the issuance of tax-exempt bonds after December 31, 1983.

REFERENCES ON MORTGAGE BACKED SECURITIES: Strine, *New Commercial Devices—Mortgage Backed Securities,* 13 R.P.P. & T.J. 1011 (1978). 1979 FNMA General Counsel's Conference 5 *et seq.*

REFERENCES: Gobel and Miller, *Handbook of Mortgage Mathematics & Finance Tables* (1981). A.B.A. Real Prop., Prob. & Tr. L. Sect., *Financing Real Estate During the Inflationary 80s* (Strum ed. 1981). This book is a must for every real property lawyer. HUD, *Alternative Mortgage Instruments Research Study* (1981). PLI, *Mortgages and Alternative Mortgage Instruments* (Sweat, Chmn. 1981). Public Information Dept., Fed. Res. Bank of N.Y., *The Arithmetic of Interest Rates* (1981). Brodkey, *AMIs: Let the Lawyers Work Out the Details,* 45 Legal Bull. 133 (May 1979). Kaplan, *Alternative Mortgage Instruments, the FHLBB Study,* in 1977 *FNMA Gen. Counsel's Conf.* 157.

---

17 REAL ESTATE FINANCE— DUE-ON-SALE CLAUSE

17.01 In general   The most controversial clause in mortgage law today is the due-on-sale clause. Let us begin with a
simple, early version of this clause:

> In case of a sale of the mortgaged premises without the written consent of the
> mortgagee, the entire principal of the mortgage debt shall, at the election of the
> mortgagee, become immediately due and payable.

A word or two of history is needed. The mortgage lending that took place
prior to the Great Depression was essentially balloon-note financing based on a
bricks-and-mortar appraisal of the property. During the bad years of the Depression, mortgage lending ground to a halt. After President Roosevelt took office in
1933, there was a modest revival of home mortgage lending sparked by the introduction of FHA mortgage insurance and the creation of the federal savings
and loan associations.

A new concept found its way into mortgage lending, namely, that the loan
should be an amortized loan made to a creditworthy borrower. The borrower
would have to be one who could "qualify" financially for the loan. As a corollary,
the lender argued that he should be able to prevent the passing of the mortgaged property into the hands of an owner who was not creditworthy, who
might allow the property to run down. Toward that end, the lenders began to
insert the due-on-sale clause in their mortgages. Even FHA used the clause.

For many years the clause gave no difficulty. However, when inflation and
interest rates began to skyrocket, a new problem developed. The thrift institutions found themselves saddled with old, low-interest loans. At the same time
they were compelled to pay high rates of interest on certificates of deposit. Ultimately, the thrift institutions began to run into the red, as is presently the case.

Another unforeseen factor made its appearance. In the normal situation, when a home was sold, the old mortgage was paid off and the buyer obtained a new mortgage to finance the deal. Hence a mortgage with a stated maturity of thirty years would normally be paid off in seven years, the average period a home is owned before it is sold by its purchaser. But as high interest rates appeared, sellers and buyers bent their efforts toward keeping the old, low-interest-rate mortgage in force.

> **EXAMPLE:** Owner mortgages his home to Lender in 1970 for $50,000 at 8 percent interest. In 1978 the mortgage has been paid down to $45,000. Owner is selling his home to Buyer for $70,000. Buyer would like to pay $25,000 in cash and buy the home subject to the old mortgage. As can be seen, in normal times the old mortgage would have been paid off and a new mortgage made at a current rate of interest. Lender threatens to invoke the due-on-sale clause. Buyer does not wish to run this risk. He accepts a new mortgage from Lender at 12 percent interest.

Because the consumer movement gathered strength after 1965, many lawsuits developed concerning the use of the clause to exact high interest rates. In a number of states, courts held that the due-on-sale clause could not be invoked where the buyer was creditworthy. Other courts chose to permit lenders to enforce the clause in these circumstances. A few states (Iowa and Minnesota, for example) enacted statutes emasculating the clause. As is evident, a bitter controversy is raging. A recent decision sustaining the clause and arguing cogently for that position is *Occidental S. & L. Assn.* v. *Venco Partnership,* 293 NW2d 843 (Neb. 1980). A recent case going the other way is *Continental Fed. S. & L. Assn.* v. *Felter,* 546 P2d 1013 (Okla. 1977). The authorities are collected in 69 ALR 3d 713 (1976).

This, however, is merely the beginning. Other issues have surfaced.

17.02 Federal preemption

Some lending corporations are organized under state law, others under federal law. To a considerable but poorly defined extent the federal lenders are governed by federal law. Federal savings and loans are largely governed by federal laws and federal regulations. For many years they have used and enforced the due-on-sale clause.

Federal regulations have stated unequivocally that enforcement of this clause is a federal matter. Nevertheless, beginning in 1976, California took the position that the clause could not be enforced by either federal or state institutions where the buyer was creditworthy. A number of states passed laws incorporating this point of view or their courts chose to follow the California reasoning.

Stripping away the legalities, the problem can be viewed as a contest between federal power and state power or as a contest between economic interests. The lenders want to enforce the clause on any sale of the mortgaged land, for this enables them to raise the interest rates above old existing impossibly low rates, like 8 percent or 10 percent. Real estate brokers want the clause nullified, since, in creative financing, a house with a 10 percent mortgage is easy to sell.

At all events the Supreme Court decided that federal savings and loan associations in invoking the due-on-sale clause were immune from state regulation or court interference. *Fidelity Fed. S & L Ass'n.* v. *De la Cuesta,* 102 S.Ct. 3014 (1982). Of the many articles previously written on the subject, only a few had anticipated this result. (See Kratovil, *A New Dilemma for Thrift Institutions: Judicial Emasculation of the Due-on-Sale Clause,* 12 John Marshall J. of Practice & Procedure 299 (1979); Kratovil, *Epilogue: Wellenkamp* v. *Bank of America,* 15 J.M.L. Rev. 435 (1982).)

In the last week of September 1982, Congress enacted a law dealing with the due-on-sale clause. The Supreme Court's decision that neither state laws nor court decisions can limit a federal savings and loan association's enforcement of the due-on-sale clauses in their mortgages gave the *federal* associations a competitive advantage over state associations. Congress has now passed a law allowing all lenders to exercise the due-on-sale clauses in their mortgage documents. The law does encourage lenders to permit assumptions at the rate specified in the existing mortgage or at a rate that is no higher than the average between the rate of existing mortgage and the market rate.

This law will not apply to mortgages orginated or assumptions made after a state has prohibited or limited due-on-sale clauses and before October 22, 1982. Until October 22, 1985, each *state* that presently restricts the due-on-sale clause in some way is given the power to enact a law to extend, outlaw, or modify due-on-sale clauses in mortgages. Garn St. Germain, Depository Institutions Act of 1982, section 341.

As can be seen, the federal government has made it clear that states will not be allowed to tinker with mortgages running to federal savings and loan association. And since this is true, the states will be reluctant to do anything that places state lenders at a competitive disadvantage. A big step forward has been taken.

The many sales that were put together in the thought that the old mortgage would remain carrying its old, low interest rate are now up for scrutiny. Federal lenders will not demand higher interest on these older mortgages. Most of these cases will be compromised on the basis of a "blended interest rate."

On another front, buyers who bought without any warning of this problem will look around for somebody to sue. Lawyers and brokers who failed to warn of this problem may find themselves sued for malpractice.

17.03 Events that trigger the clause

Another bitter controversy rages concerning whether an installment contract for the sale of land triggers the due-on-sale clause. Most older versions of the clause spoke in terms of a "sale" of the property. Some courts have held that an installment sale is indeed a sale. It is a sale on credit, but it is a sale. *Mutual Fed. S. & L. Assn.* v. *Wis. Wire Works,* 239 NW2d 20 (Wis. 1976); *Century Fed. S. & L. Assn.* v. *Van Glann,* 144 N.J. Supp. 48, 364 A2d 588 (1976); *First Fed. S. & L. Assn.* v. *Kelly,* 312 NW2d 476 (S.D. 1981); *Kemp* v. *Empire Assn.,* 635 P2d 269 (Colo. 1981); *Dobitz* v. *Oakland,* 561 P2d 441 (Mont. 1977); *Bellingham* v. *First*

Fed. S. & L. Assn., 553 P2d 1090 (Wash. 1976). Other courts appear to feel that only a cash sale triggers the clause. *Chopan* v. *Klinkman,* 330 So2d 154 (Fla. 1976); *Nichols* v. *Ann Arbor Fed. S. & L. Assn.,* 250 NW2d 804 (Mich. 1977).

Another facet of the problem involves the situation when the mortgagor is a corporation. A transfer of stock by the sole stockholder creates a problem. So does a transfer by the corporation to its sole stockholder. *Fidelity Land Development Corp.* v. *Richter & Sons,* 377 A2d 691 (N.J. 1977); *Nichols* v. *Evans,* 401 N.Y.S.2d 426 (1978); 98 Banking L.J. 300. Here a useful analogy exists. Many leases forbid assignment without the consent of the landlord, but a transfer of a corporate tenant's stock does not require consent. *Rubinstein Bros.* v. *OLE of 34th Street, Inc.,* 421 N.Y.S.2d 534 (1979); *Dodier Realty* v. *St. Louis Nat. Baseball Club,* 361 Mo. 981, 238 SW2d 321 (1951); 37 Va. L. Rev. 1003; 34 ALR2d 695. The stock transfer should not trigger the clause.

A transfer by partners into the partnership name should not trigger the clause. *Webber* v. *Rosenberg,* 318 Mass. 768, 64 NE2d 98; *Princeton Bank & Tr. Co.* v. *Berlex,* 394 N.Y.S.2d 714 (1977).

Similarly, a question arises where the mortgagor conveys the land to a trustee and then assigns the beneficial interest of the trust to a purchaser. It has been held that this is a subterfuge. It triggers the clause. *Williams* v. *First Fed. S. & L. Assn.,* 651 F2d 910 (4th Cir. 1981). Likewise a deed by the trustee to the beneficiary triggers the clause. *Damen S. & L. Assn.* v. *Heritage Bank,* 103 Ill. App. 3d 301 (1982).

Again, suppose the mortgagors are father and son, and the father makes a gratuitous deed to his son. It would seem that the clause is not triggered. There appears to be no law. *But see Ray Ford* v. *Louisiana S. & L. Assn.,* 380 So2d 1232 (La. 1980).

Likewise, a deed by one spouse to the other does not trigger the due-on-sale clause. *Mills* v. *Nashua Fed. S. & L. Assn.,* 433 A2d 1312 (N.H. 1981).

17.04 Owner occupancy clause

At times in states where the due-on-sale clause can be enforced, the seller and buyer will deliberately refrain from seeking the lender's consent, hoping that the lender will not detect the sale.

To counter this threat, and to simplify the problem of proof, some lenders have begun using a mortgage clause that will allow the lender to declare an acceleration of the debt upon the borrower's failure to occupy the property. These clauses have been held valid. *Investors Savings and Loan Assn.* v. *Ganz,* 416 A2d 918 (N.J. 1980).

As is evident, it is simple to determine that the premises are occupied by one other than the mortgagor. It is harder to determine that a sale has taken place.

This parallels the lease draftsmanship experience, where the clause forbidding assignment or sublease without the lessor's consent has been expanded to forbid occupancy by one other than the tenant.

17.05   FNMA attitudes

As is well known, despite the fact that thirty-year mortgages have been common for years, very few of such mortgages stayed on the books for that length of time. In fact, the average family lives in its home just about seven years, when it is sold. When mortgage money was plentiful, every sale involved a refinancing. As interest rates began to creep upward, every effort was bent toward keeping the old, low-interest mortgage alive. This defeated the mortgagee's expectation of refinancing. FNMA is endeavoring to revive this seven-year refinancing practice by requiring the mortgages it buys to have a seven-year call provision inserted by agreement, if there is a doubt of the enforceability of the clause in a particular state.

This requirement is not applied to federal savings and loan mortgages, since FNMA believes federal law preempts state law as to the due-on-sale provisions in such mortgages. Nor is this requirement applied in states that give full recognition to the due-on-sale clause. And it is inapplicable to the adjustable rate mortgage since such a mortgage automatically adjusts its interest rate to the market.

17.06   Form of due-on-sale clause

To eliminate some of the controversies, FNMA–FHLMC have drafted broad form clauses. The multifamily residence form is as follows:

19. **TRANSFERS OF THE PROPERTY OR BENEFICIAL INTERESTS IN BORROWER; ASSUMPTION.** On sale or transfer of (i) all or any part of the Property, or any interest therein, or (ii) beneficial interests in Borrower (if Borrower is not a natural person or persons but is a corporation, partnership, trust or other legal entity), Lender may, at Lender's option, declare all of the sums secured by this Instrument to be immediately due and payable, and Lender may invoke any remedies permitted by paragraph 27 of this Instrument. This option shall not apply in case of

(a) transfers by devise or descent or by operation of law upon the death of a joint tenant or a partner;

(b) sales or transfers when the transferee's creditworthiness and management ability are satisfactory to Lender and the transferee has executed, prior to the sale or transfer, a written assumption agreement containing such terms as Lender may require, including, if required by Lender, an increase in the rate of interest payable under the Note;

(c) the grant of a leasehold interest in a part of the Property of three years or less (or such longer lease term as Lender may permit by prior written approval) not containing an option to purchase (except any interest in the ground lease, if this Instrument is on a leasehold);

(d) sales or transfers of beneficial interests in Borrower provided that such sales or transfers, together with any prior sales or transfers of beneficial interests in Borrower, but excluding sales or transfers under subparagraphs (a) and (b) above, do not result in more than 49% of the beneficial interests in Borrower having been sold or transferred since commencement of amortization of the Note, and

(e) sales or transfers of fixtures or any personal property pursuant to the first paragraph of paragraph 6 hereof.

The language of a suggested due-on-sale clause has been discussed. Squires, *A Comprehensible Due-on-Sale Clause (with form)*, 27 Practical Lawyer, No. 1, p. 67 (April 1981). The author recommends use of the New York plain language form, but makes some suggestions for improving even this excellent form. There are some unusual decisions dealing with form problems.

> **EXAMPLE:** It has been held that the due-on-sale clause, to be legally effective, must appear in the mortgage note as well as in the mortgage. *2140 Lincoln Park West* v. *American Nat. Bk. Tr. Co.*, 88 Ill. App.3d 660, 410 NE2d 990; 63 Chicago Bar Record 16.

17.07 Acceleration statutes

A number of states, Delaware, for example, have statutes dealing with acceleration.

> **EXAMPLE:** The Delaware statute forbids acceleration declared because the lender deeds himself insecure. This type of clause is borrowed from chattel mortgage financing, where it was formerly quite common. Such a clause would seem to bar use of the due-on-sale clause to accelerate where the lender feels the buyer is not creditworthy.

17.08 Economic duress

Where the lender knows of a pending sale, but fails to invoke the clause until closing time, he may face a claim of economic duress. *Leben* v. *Nassau S. & L. Assn.*, 34 N.Y.2d 671, 312 NE2d 180, 356 N.Y.S.2d 671 (1974).

17.09 Estoppel

Where the lender knows of the sale in 1977 but waits until 1979 to assert his rights, he is barred by estoppel and laches. *First Nat. Bank* v. *Brown*, 412 NE2d 1078 (Ill. App. 1980).

17.10 Installment contract provisions

In some instances the seller and buyer may deliberately take the risk involved in failing to obtain the lender's consent. In such case there are agreements to be made concerning allocation of risk if the lender discovers the sale and elects to foreclose. Liss, *Drafting Around the Mortgage "Due on Sale" Clause in the Installment Contract*, 62 Chicago Bar Record 312 (May–June 1981). For example, the costs of refinancing must be allocated. Payment of taxes and hazard insurance premiums must be covered. The article cited furnishes a suggested clause.

17.11 Tax-free bonds

A special form of the due-on-sale clause may be encountered. Many state and local governments have established programs to help low-income and moderate-income individuals obtain housing. These programs are financed with bonds exempt from federal taxes. The federal law (Title X 1-A, Pub. L. 96–499) requires the bond-issuing authorities to take action assuring that the loans be assumed only by those eligible for assistance. The authority may, therefore, place a restriction in the mortgage allowing acceleration if the mortgage is assumed by an ineligible party.

REFERENCES: Kratovil, *A New Dilemma for Thrift Institutions,* 12 John Marshall J. 299 (1979); Enforcement of Due-on-Transfer Clause, 13 ABA R.P.P.&T.J. 891 (1978); 16id. 291 (1981); 31 U. Fla. L. Rev. 933 (1979); 36 Wash. & Lee L. Rev. 1121 (1979); 13 So. Tex. L. J. 296, 306; 29 U. Miami L. Rev. 584; 24 Wayne L. Rev. 971; 64 Cal. L. Rev. 753; 22 Hastings L. J. 431; 20 S. Dak. L. Rev. 329 (1975); 55 N. C. L. Rev. 310 (1977); 47 Miss. L. J. 331 (1976); 96 Banking L. J. 300 (1981) (good); 10 Colo. Law. 972 (1981).

18 REAL ESTATE FINANCE— SALE SUBJECT TO EXISTING MORTGAGE

18.01 In general

For economic rather than legal reasons, a home sale has in the past usually involved the paying off of the old mortgage and the obtaining by the buyer of a new mortgage.

> **EXAMPLE:** In 1975 Owner buys a home for $80,000 and gives a mortgage to Lender for $70,000 to finance the purchase. In 1981 Owner is selling to Buyer for $120,000. Buyer needs a loan of $100,000. Buyer obtains this loan from Lender #2. In the closing of the deal, the old mortgage is paid off.

Today mortgages are difficult to obtain. For this reason, the parties are likely to attempt to work out the deal in such a way that the old mortgage remains. It is not paid off. There is a fringe benefit if this can be done. The old mortgage may carry a lower interest rate, say 11 percent. A new mortgage could carry an interest of 16 percent.

The first question, then, is this: Is it legally permissible to sell property without paying off the old mortgage? The answer is that this can legally be done except where the old mortgage contains an enforceable due-on-sale clause. For convenience, the due-on-sale clause is discussed in a separate chapter (see Chapter 17). In this chapter, it is assumed that (1) the old mortgage is *assumable,* that is, it contains no enforceable due-on-sale clause; or (2) the old mortgage contains an enforceable due-on-sale clause but the mortgage lender has consented to the sale.

18.02 Personal liability of seller to lender after sale

Where Owner mortgages his land to Lender, as has previously been stated, he customarily signs two important documents, namely, a promissory note and a mortgage securing the note.

The promissory note creates personal liability from Owner to Lender. If Owner sells the property to Buyer, Lender is not involved. His rights are not affected. Owner's personal liability to Lender continues. Lender's mortgage is unaffected.

All mortgage lenders have a printed form available that will change this. The form is designed for the signatures of Owner, Lender, and Buyer. It releases Owner's liability as of the date of his deed to Buyer. In turn, Buyer accepts personal liability to Lender for the balance of the mortgage debt. This is a commonplace transaction. Sometimes it is called a *novation agreement.* From the seller's point of view, this is the best possible result. See § 15.33.

Concerning the personal liability of the buyer for payment of the mortgage debt, certain distinctions must be kept in mind.

In the first place, regardless of personal liability, if the old mortgage is not paid off in the process of closing the sale, the old mortgage remains, and if the payments on the mortgage are not made, the old mortgage can be foreclosed. The question here discussed, then, is whether in addition to foreclosing the mortgage, the mortgagee can obtain a personal judgment against the buyer.

> **EXAMPLE:** The mortgage is in the sum of $80,000. The foreclosure sale price is $75,000. This is considered a part payment of the mortgage debt. Thus the mortgage debt, after the foreclosure sale, is $80,000 minus $75,000, or $5,000. Can the mortgage lender obtain a judgment against the buyer? If he can, he can levy on the buyer's automobile, his bank account, his appliances, etc.

Absent in novation agreement there are two important documents that bear on this issue: the contract of sale and the deed to the buyer.

> **EXAMPLE:** Owner owns a home. It is mortgaged to Lender. The contract of sale and the deed to the Buyer both recite that the land is subject to a mortgage to Lender, which Buyer does *not* assume or agree to pay. Here the only relevant documents state unequivocally that Buyer does not assume liability for the mortgage debt. Buyer has no personal liability for that debt.

> **EXAMPLE:** Facts as in previous example, except that both documents provide that Buyer *does* assume and agree to pay the mortgage debt. Even though Lender, the mortgagee is not a party either to the contract of sale or the deed, Buyer becomes personally liable to Lender. The theories differ from state to state. The favorite theory is that Lender is the third-party beneficiary of a contract between Owner and Buyer. Buyer's liability to Lender attaches when Lender learns of the transaction and determines to hold Buyer liable.

> **EXAMPLE:** Facts as in previous example, but contract and deed simply state that land is being conveyed "subject to" the described mortgage. The phrase that Buyer does assume and agree to pay the mortgage is absent. In all but one or two states, Buyer has no personal liability for the mortgage debt.

> **EXAMPLE:** Facts as in first example, but neither the contract nor deed says anything about the mortgage. Again, Buyer has no personal liability for the mortgage debt.

See Kratovil and Werner, *Modern Mortgage Law and Practice,* Ch. 15 (2d ed., 1981).

Much of this discussion is quite academic in a number of states. During the Great Depression, personal judgments in favor of mortgagees bankrupted many persons.

EXAMPLE: In 1933 a mortgage for $100,000 is foreclosed. The foreclosure sale price is $5,000. The mortgagee obtains a personal judgment against the mortgagor for $95,000. This struck many legislatures as disgraceful. In many states, laws were passed totally abolishing deficiency decrees.

In addition, there are factors today which diminish the importance of personal liability. Before a foreclosure is begun, the lender makes every attempt to work the situation out without foreclosure. If the mortgage can be recast, with lower monthly payments that the landowner can handle, that will be done. If recasting the mortgage will not help, the majority of the deals are worked out by a deed in lieu of foreclosure, which, of course, includes a release of all personal liability.

18.03 Protection of seller–mortgagor

Where mortgaged land is sold without paying off the mortgage, it is necessary to provide carefully for the protection of the seller–mortgagor. As has been stated, the seller–mortgagor cannot get rid of his personal liability to the mortgagee merely by selling the mortgaged land. Now let us take a close look at an example previously given.

EXAMPLE: Owner owns a home. It is mortgaged to Lender. Owner sells the home to Buyer. In the contract of sale and deed it is stated that the land is subject to a described mortgage which Buyer assumes and agrees to pay. In a situation like this, the law creates a scheme of priorities, so far as personal liability is concerned. It is said that Buyer is primarily liable to Lender and Owner is secondarily liable to Lender. This is the first step in applying the law of *subrogation.* If Lender chooses to pursue Owner, when default occurs, and succeeds in collecting the balance of the mortgage debt from Owner, then Owner steps into Lender's shoes as mortgagee. Owner can foreclose the mortgage against Buyer. This is for the reason that, as between Owner and Buyer, Buyer should have paid the mortgage debt. The result would be the same if the deed merely stated that the land "is subject to" the described mortgage without adding words of assumption. Here the courts say that use of the "subject clause" makes the land the primary fund for the payment of the mortgage.

All this is well and good, but it is better to have this and more in black and white. A carefully prepared document is needed, signed by Owner and Buyer when the sale to Buyer is made. It provides that if Owner is compelled by Lender to pay the mortgage debt, Owner is entitled to foreclose the mortgage against Buyer. But it goes further. It requires Buyer to pay the real estate taxes, keep up the insurance, keep the building in repair, etc. If Buyer fails to make these expenditures, Owner is permitted to do so, and to add such amounts to the mortgage. Owner is permitted to buy the mortgage at a discount, and to enforce it for the full amount of the debt.

If the buyer is not to assume personal liability *to the mortgagee* for the mortgage debt, that ought to be spelled out clearly. Caution suggests the addition of a clause that the contract is only for the benefit of the parties thereto and not for the benefit of any third parties. This prevents the mortgagee from contending that one or more provisions of the sale contract were intended for the mortgagee's benefit.

18.04 Personal liability of buyer to seller

Let us go back to an example previously given.

> **EXAMPLE:** Owner owns a home. It is mortgaged to Lender. Owner sells the home to Buyer. In the contract of sale and deed it is stated that the land is subject to a described mortgage, which Buyer assumes and agrees to pay. This is a promise that makes Buyer personally liable to Lender when Lender learns of the transaction. But this promise runs to Owner, so Buyer also becomes personally liable to Owner.

What this means, in practical effect, is that if Lender and Buyer get together to work out a deed in lieu of foreclosure, it will also be necessary to get Owner into the deal. Lender will release Owner's personal liability to Lender, and Owner will release Buyer's personal liability to Owner. Kratovil and Werner, *supra*, § 40.04.

18.05 Assumptions and interest rates

Where there is an existing mortgage, there are two situations that bear upon the interest rates of new financing.

> **EXAMPLE:** The existing mortgage contains an enforceable due-on-sale clause. It bears a below-market interest rate, say 12 percent. The new purchaser wishes to assume this mortgage. He requests the lender to consent to the sale. The lender agrees to give its consent if the borrower will agree to hike the interest rate to 14½ percent, which is midway between the old rate of 12 percent and the current market rate of 17 percent. Both parties benefit by the deal.

> **EXAMPLE:** The facts are as in the preceding example, except that there is no due-on-sale clause but the purchaser needs a larger loan. Again, the parties work out the deal at 14½ percent. Again, both parties benefit.

FNMA has been active in promoting programs of this sort.

19 REAL ESTATE FINANCE—
PURCHASE MONEY MORTGAGES

19.01 In general

The purchase money mortgage is a venerable mortgage instrument.

> **EXAMPLE:** Seller conveys his home to Buyer for $60,000, Buyer paying $20,000 cash, and giving Seller a mortgage for the balance of $40,000. Notice that no outside bank is present in the transaction. Seller holds the mortgage and collects mortgage payments. The only cash involved is the $20,000 down payment. This is currently being called by realtors the *take-back* mortgage. It is estimated that almost half the sales of used homes involve such a mortgage. Its use is likely to grow.

Second mortgages given by second mortgage lenders have terms and bear interest according to current market conditions. The purchase money mortgage, in contrast, is given because the seller wants to sell the property. He will quote terms that enable him to sell, often with interest well below the market. Of course, the seller may balance this off by increasing his quoted sale price. To some extent the seller can increase his sale price and reduce the interest rate to minimize the impact of federal income tax, subject to the problem of imputed interest.

19.02 Legal advantages of take-back mortgage

The take-back mortgage is a favorite of the law.

> **EXAMPLE:** Seller sells his home to Buyer. Buyer is married to Wife, who is insane. Buyer needs a home for his children. Wife's signature would ordinarily be needed on any mortgage, as is true in most states involving home mortgages. Buyer gives a take-back mortgage to Seller. It is good as gold without Wife's signature.

EXAMPLE: Seller is selling his home to Buyer. Buyer has had a tussle with the IRS and they have filed an income tax lien against his assets for $10,000. Buyer is contesting this lien. Ordinarily, this lien would cloud Buyer's title. But his purchase money mortgage to Seller has priority over the earlier IRS lien.

REFERENCE: Kratovil and Werner, *Modern Mortgage Law and Practice* § 19.04 (2d ed., 1981).

At times a third-party financial institution is advancing the money to pay the seller and wishes to claim the legal benefits given the purchase money mortgage. The law permits this. 59 CJS *Mortgages* § 231(c).

19.03   Income tax advantages of take-back mortgage

The take-back mortgage offers certain income tax advantages.

EXAMPLE: Seller bought an apartment building in 1976 for $200,000. He is selling it to Buyer in 1983 for $300,000. He has an obvious capital gain. But if Seller takes a down payment, say $25,000, and takes back a mortgage for $275,000 payable over a five-year period, Seller can spread his gain and his tax over the entire five-year period.

There are also income tax pitfalls.

EXAMPLE: In the last example, suppose the parties agree that the mortgage debt shall bear 2 percent interest. This is an obvious subterfuge. Today there is no such thing as a 2 percent interest rate. The parties have jiggled the principal and interest to reduce Seller's interest income to 2 percent. This will not work. 33 Am.Jur.2d Federal Taxation § 2900 *et seq.* At least 9 percent interest must be charged. If less is charged you pay tax on 10 percent interest (imputed interest).

19.04   Usury and the purchase money mortgage

There has been previous discussion of the juggling of interest rates and the amount of mortgage debt where a purchase money mortgage is involved. The same juggling process gives rise to a usury problem.

EXAMPLE: Seller sells his home to Buyer for $100,000. Buyer pays $20,000 in cash and gives Seller a purchase money mortgage for $80,000. Obviously, the figures can be juggled. Seller can quote a price of $105,000, with a 10 percent interest rate, or a price of $100,000 with a 14 percent interest rate, having income tax consequences in mind. If the 14 percent exceeds the usury rate, it has nevertheless been held that there is no violation of the usury law. *Mandelino* v. *Fribourg,* 23 N.Y.2d 145, 242 NE2d 823 (1979), 20 Syracuse L. Rev. 762; 91CJS *Usury* § 18; 45 Am. Jur2d Interest & Usury § 126; 91ALR 1105 (listing conflicting decisions). The philosophy here is that the parties can and do juggle the two components of the transaction, price and interest rate, and the economic consequences to the buyer are the same. Bear in mind that this problem often arises on second mortgages and that the usury law is usually different from that governing first mortgages.

19.05 Flexibility of take-back mortgage

The take-back mortgage is just as flexible as the parties wish to make it.

> **EXAMPLE:** Seller is selling Buyer a block of stores and taking back a purchase money mortgage, payable in monthly payments. The parties can agree that the monthly payments will fluctuate as cash flow fluctuates.

The mortgage can also provide for lower payments during the first three years of the loan, as is commonly done where a "buy-down" exists.

19.06 Discounting the take-back mortgage

The seller most often chooses to hold the take-back mortgage to maturity. After all, it's well secured. But if he needs to convert the take-back mortgage into funds, he will probably have to discount it.

> **EXAMPLE:** Seller sells his home to Buyer for $80,000. Buyer pays $20,000 cash and gives Seller a purchase money mortgage for $60,000, bearing 12 percent interest. A year later, Seller needs money. He sells the mortgage to Mortgage Investor, who will only pay $50,000 for the mortgage. This gives Mortgage Investor an effective annual yield of about 19 percent. This is the big disadvantage of the take-back mortgage. Investors who buy individual mortgages want substantial returns and insist on this discount.

19.07 FNMA purchase

FNMA issues its private regulations from time to time. Under current regulations it will buy take-back mortgages as funds are available for this purpose. Inquiry should be made at a bank or savings and loan and they will advise you as to the terms on which such sales can currently be made.

19.08 Hazard insurance

Like any other mortgagee, the take-back mortgagee should insist that the standard mortgagee loss clause be attached to the fire insurance policy. The mortgagee may insist on holding the policy.

19.09 Due-on-sale clause

The due-on-sale clause has previously been discussed.

Before any property can be sold without paying off the existing mortgage, such mortgage must be studied to see if it contains a due-on-sale clause. If it does, the mortgagee's consent to the transaction must be obtained unless the transaction falls in a category where the due-on-sale clause is inapplicable.

EXAMPLE: In California the due-on-sale clause cannot be invoked if the buyer is truly creditworthy. The theory is that the lender is not hurt by such a sale. A number of states have emasculated the due-on-sale clause. Always the state law must be checked.

In any case, a seller selling with a take-back mortgage should insist that his mortgage contain a due-on-sale clause. The clause should be a broad form clause, covering such matters as installment contracts.

19.10   Balloon notes

Perhaps the most popular device in the arsenal of creative financing draftsman is the balloon note. The mortgage is drafted with monthly payments as though the loan were to run for the usual thirty years. But at the end of, say, three years the entire debt falls due. This is the *balloon.*

The philosophy is that over the short run mortgage money will become more plentiful and interest rates will come down. This philosophy is open to question.

The depression experience with such notes was so bad that savings and loan associations were forbidden to use balloon notes. Some states, such as Florida, have statutes that forbid certain types of balloon notes. *O'Neil* v. *Lorain Nat. Bank,* 369 So2d 378 (Fla. 1979). Consumer organizations oppose them. 1976 Am. Bar Found. Res. J. 35, 43. Regulation Z of the Federal Truth-in-Lending Act requires disclosure of the balloon. *Ibid.* at 84.

The danger, of course, is that the borrower will be unable to borrow funds elsewhere to pay the balloon and the holder of the mortgage will be in a position to exact harsh terms for a renewal. Also, borrowers under balloon notes will have to go into the market to compete with homebuyers and other borrowers when the balloon comes due. It is uncertain what that market will be when those loans are sought. Alternatively, the borrower will approach the seller for an extension. The seller–lender will then have much more bargaining power. He does not have a house to sell. There is no reason then for the seller–mortgagee to settle for a below-market interest rate. He may not want to give the extension, at any rate.

19.11   Call provisions

As an alternative to the balloon note, there is the call provision which gives the mortgage holder the right to declare the entire debt due and to foreclose if alternative financing is available on reasonable terms and the borrower refuses to avail himself of it. A form of such clause is found in Kratovil & Werner, *Modern Mortgage Law and Practice* § 19.09 (2d ed. 1981).

19.12   Deficiency judgments

During the land sales boom of the 1920s, vacant land was sold at insane prices and huge purchase money mortgages were signed. When the Great Depression of 1929 began, thousands of mortgagors were subjected to large judgments obtained by the noteholders for a deficiency. These borrowers were forced into bankruptcy. As a reaction, many laws were enacted forbidding deficiency judgments in purchase money mortgages. 1960 Duke L. J. 1.

19.13 Form of take-back mortgage transaction

The take-back mortgage documents do not differ greatly from normal real estate mortgage transactions. There is a mortgage, a promissory note, and, where appropriate, an assignment of leases and rents. If the mortgage is a junior mortgage, as is often true, the clauses needed in a junior mortgage are inserted.

19.14 Equity finance-out

Under a variation of the take-back mortgage, the seller places a second mortgage against the property to finance out much of his equity and then carries back a purchase money mortgage.

> **EXAMPLE:** John and Mary Homeowner purchased their home in 1972 for $45,000, giving a $35,000 mortgage which is paid down to $30,000 in 1981 when the home is worth $100,000. The Homeowners seek to sell. Because conventional financing is unavailable, the Homeowners decide to engage in some creative financing. They place a $35,000 second mortgage against the home. Of course, this mortgage has no due-on-sale clause, but it is a short-term loan. The Homeowners have now taken $35,000 of their equity (more than they have invested) out of the home. They then go to sell the house, subject to the existing financing and with a purchase money mortgage. Under this format, the purchase money may be paid as follows:
>
> | | | |
> |---|---:|---:|
> | Purchase Price | | $100,000 |
> | Buyer's down payment | $ 20,000 | |
> | Subject to first mortgage | 30,000 | |
> | Subject to second mortgage | 35,000 | |
> | Purchase money mortgage to seller | 15,000 | |
> | | $100,000 | $100,000 |

The due date on the purchase money mortgage and the existing mortgages should not coincide since this will cause the buyer to refinance both at the same time, a task that may be impossible. The purchase money mortgage may also contain a subordination provision to allow the refinancing of the prior mortgages as they come due. This clause should be rather tightly drafted to allow the refinancing only if it does not prejudice the purchase money mortgagee, as would occur if the underlying debt was increased or the interest rate on the refinanced debt was raised.

A tight subordination clause, strictly enforced by the purchase money mortgagee, can be a key factor in causing the refinancing of all three mortgages. For example, if financing is not available at a rate equal to or lower than the prescribed limit of the subordination clause, the buyer may have no choice but to refinance all debt. This is good for the seller–purchase money mortgages since it frees his funds to be invested as he chooses.

19.15   Truth-in-lending

When the purchase money mortgagee–seller is the typical homeowner who is not in the business of buying and selling real estate, the federal truth-in-lending law and other disclosure type statutes such as RESPA do not apply. 12 USCA § 2603.

19.16   Recitals

Every purchase money mortgage ought to recite that it is a purchase money mortgage. And the deed to the buyer ought to recite that the grantor is taking back the mortgage as a purchase money mortgage. A purchase money mortgage, after all, enjoys priority over certain judgments, liens, dower, and homestead. The public records ought to reveal the true character of the mortgage so that the mortgagee is in a position to claim those benefits.

19.17   Co-ownership problems

Where a husband and wife own land as joint tenants or as tenants by the entireties, and they sell the land on an installment contract or take back a purchase money mortgage, questions arise as to the nature of their interest in the proceeds of sale.

> **EXAMPLE:**   Husband and Wife own Lot 1 in joint tenancy. They enter into an installment contract to sell Lot 1 to Buyer. This contract creates a new "chose in action," namely, a right to receive the purchase money. The question that arises is this: Is this "chose in action" owned in joint tenancy or in tenancy in common? The same question arises where a purchase money mortgage is involved. The decisions are in wild conflict. See § 14.05.

> **SUGGESTION:**   If a joint tenancy is wanted, let the contract provide that the purchase price is payable to Husband and Wife as *joint tenants with the right of survivorship and not as tenants in common or as community property.* If a tenancy by the entireties is wanted, let the contract of sale, mortgage, and mortgage note read that the funds are payable to Husband and Wife *as tenants by the entirety and not as joint tenants or as community property.* Some states do not permit a tenancy by the entireties in personal property such as mortgages. 41 CJS *Husband & Wife* § 35.

19.18   Payment—joint mortgagees or joint sellers

Where a husband and wife own land jointly, sell it, and take back an installment contract or purchase money mortgage, the rule is that payment to either party is good payment. 70 CJS *Payment* § 4; 59 CJS *Mortgages* § 446. The party receiving payment can give a release of the mortgage. One would think that the buyer would feel more comfortable if this is spelled out in the documents. Of course, if the check is made payable to both, a different problem arises, namely, whether one party can endorse the other party's name. Again, the documents should cover this.

19.19 Contract provisions   There are a number of legal problems involved in drafting a contract of sale where the seller is to take back a purchase money mortgage.

> **EXAMPLE:** The contract of sale calls for the seller to take back a mortgage of $30,000 but states no interest rate, manner of payment, etc. The contract cannot be enforced if either party chooses to resist enforcement. It is "incomplete." *Sweeting* v. *Campbell,* 8 Ill.2d 54, 132 NE2d 523 (1956); 60 ALR2d 251.

Any contract of sale that calls for a purchase money mortgage must spell out the protection the mortgagee is to receive. Traditionally, the buyer pays for title insurance, recording of the mortgage, mortgage tax if any, filing fees for any chattel lien or assignment of rents, and the like.

20 REAL ESTATE FINANCE—
WRAPAROUND MORTGAGES

20.01   In general   The wraparound mortgage, sometimes known as the *all-inclusive deed of trust,* made its appearance in large-scale commercial financing. It is a second mortgage, but a special type of second mortgage. The typical second mortgage is one that is added onto land already subject to an earlier encumbrance. The face amount of the wraparound mortgage represents the total of the existing first mortgage and the new money advanced under the wraparound. This compares to the face amount of a typical mortgage that states only the amount advanced under the junior mortgage. Since the debt stated in the wraparound mortgage is the total of the first and second mortgage debts, the wraparound lender charges interest on this total. This creates a yield far greater than the yield on an ordinary second mortgage.

Also, because the debts are aggregated in this fashion, the wraparound mortgagee collects payments sufficient to pay the payments due on the first and second mortgages. And the wraparound lender pays to the first mortgagee the payments due on the first mortgage.

EXAMPLE: Owner mortgages a shopping center to Lender #1 for $5,000,000 at 8 percent interest. Over the course of years, the loan has been paid down to $4,000,000. Owner now would like to borrow an additional $5,000,000 and the present value of the shopping center will support such a loan. The going rate of interest is 17 percent. Owner gives Lender #2 a second mortgage in the amount of $9,000,000 but Lender #2 only advances $5,000,000. Owner pays 17 percent interest on the entire $9,000,000 debt as part of the debt service on the $9,000,000 debt, Lender #2 acting as an intermediate collection agent for the servicing of the first mortgage to Lender #1. In this way, Lender #2 deducts the amounts due Lender #1, including amortization of principal and the interest payment of 8 percent and pays those monies to Lender #1. Lender #2 retains the 9 percent difference between the interest on the first mortgage and the interest payable on the wraparound. The result is a yield to Lender #2 of approximately 24 percent.

Under some forms of the wraparound mortgage, the full amount stated as the debt is not advanced to the borrower at the time the loan is made. Rather, the wraparound loan funds will be advanced as payments are made to reduce the amount of the first mortgage. Eventually, the underlying mortgage is paid and the payments are then all directed to retire the wraparound.

For the life of the wraparound, there is the danger that other liens will attach to the property and assert priority. To meet this danger, the wraparound lender relies heavily on the theory of subrogation. This is a legal doctrine under which one who pays money on a senior lien is often entitled to claim the benefit of the priority enjoyed by the senior lien.

> **EXAMPLE:**   At the time the mortgage to Lender #2 is executed, Owner and Lender #2 enter into an agreement providing that Lender #2 will be subrogated to Lender #1's prior lien position as to all payments made by Lender #2 to Lender #1. This is called *conventional* subrogation or subrogation by agreement. It is a technical concept, but is widely recognized. It gives Lender #2 all the priority that Lender #1's mortgage enjoys over intervening liens, that is total priority. Osborne, Mortgages § 282 (2d ed. 1970).
>
> Also the mortgage to Lender #2 provides, as it invariably will, that all payments made by Lender #2 to Lender #1 shall be protected and secured by the mortgage to Lender #2 to the same extent as any previous disbursements and advances made by Lender #2. This is valid and binding. *Boone* v. *Clark,* 129 Ill. 466, 21 NE 850 (1889). This is the rule of *tacking.* Mortgagees often pay real estate taxes and insurance premiums under such covenants, and the courts hold that such payments give the mortgagee a lien equal in dignity to the mortgage debt. *Reisman* v. *Jacobs,* 107 Ga. App. 200, 129 SE2d 338 (1962).

The wraparound today is used in residential financing as well as in commercial financing. In either case the objective for the lender is an increased yield, while the benefit to the borrower is a lower overall financing cost than would be obtained through complete refinancing. It often develops that the underlying loan is not prepayable, or has such a low interest rate that prepayment is undesirable. The borrower arranges a wraparound loan package that has higher than normal yield to the seller–lender, while allowing the buyer–borrower to pay a lower rate than if the property was refinanced.

> **EXAMPLE:**   The rate on the underlying mortgage is 8 percent. Existing rates are 17 percent. The balance on the underlying mortgage is $50,000. The purchase price of the property is $100,000. The buyer can pay $20,000 down. Charging 15 percent, the seller finances the difference between the underlying loan balance and the down payment. The seller makes no actual advance of money, but sells the property, taking the down payment of $20,000 and obtaining a yield in excess

of 15 percent, while the buyer, in effect, pays 2 percent below the market rate. The seller's yield is calculated as follows:

Interest on wraparound ($80,000 × 15%) $12,000
Interest on underlying ($50,000 × 8%) 4,000

Interest differential to wraparound lender $ 8,000

$$\frac{\$ 8,000 \text{ Interest differential}}{\$30,000 \text{ Amount "advanced"}} = 26.66\%$$

The seller also gets the benefit of the use of the installment method of reporting gain for income tax purposes.

20.02 Usury

Unless the borrower is exempt from usury laws (e.g., when the borrower is a corporation), or if the lender is exempt (e.g., when the lender is a bank) or the loan is exempt (e.g., when the loan is a business loan), the transaction may come within the prohibitions of local usury law. If there is no local exemption (see e.g., La. Rev. Stat. § 3504B which exempts wraparound mortgages from the usury laws if the interest rate charged against the face amount of the mortgage is not beyond the usury level), the question of usury may arise, especially if local law prohibits the lender from *receiving* more than the statutory maximum.

Beyond the statutory interest rate limitations, the common law prohibition against the exaction of unconscionable interest must be recognized and dealt with. While the stated interest rate is always under the statutory limit, the effective yield to the lender may increase the interest received by the lender on the funds actually advanced beyond the legal limit. This results from the lender's receipt of interest at the stated rate on the amount actually advanced plus the spread between the stated interest and the interest remitted to the first lienholder. Comment, 21 UCLA L. Rev. 1529, 1532 *et seq.* (1974); Note, 1972 Duke L. J. 785.

20.03 Wraparound documents

For lenders who do not hold the original first-lien mortgage, certain borrower controls must be built into the wraparound mortgage instrument to prevent possible deterioration of the wraparound loan's first-lien status or its high yield.

The most important wraparound mortgage "clause" is the cross default provision. This is protective language, such that a default of the wraparound mortgage is considered a default of the first mortgage. This provision prevents the borrower from entering into an agreement with the first lender to keep the first lien current while defaulting on the wraparound mortgage. Likewise, any default on the first mortgage should be a default on the wraparound mortgage.

The borrower should not be allowed to prepay the first mortgage. This will protect a high wraparound yield.

REFERENCES: Galowitz, *How to Use Wraparound Financing,* 5 Real Est. L. J. 107 (1976) (discusses mathematics involved). Gunning, *The Wrap-Around Mortgage,* 2 Real Est. Rev. 35 (1972). Yield Table for Wrap-Around Mortgages, Financial Pub. Co., 82 Brookline Ave., Boston, Mass. 02215. Comment, *The Wrap-Around Mortgage: A Critical Inquiry,* 21 U.C.L.A. L. Rev. 1529 (1974). The Magic Wrap Yield Charts, M.G.I.C., MGIC Plaza, Milwaukee, Wis. 53202. Kratovil and Werner, *Modern Mortgage Law and Practice* §§ 24.11 *et seq.* (2d ed., 1981).

21 REAL ESTATE FINANCE— JUNIOR MORTGAGES

21.01 In general
There is generally no legal limit on the number of mortgages a landowner can place on his property. Ordinarily, these mortgages will be ranked according to time under the legal rule that *prior in time is prior in right.*

> **EXAMPLE:** Owner owns a home and mortgages it to Lender #1 in 1978. The mortgage is duly recorded. In 1979, Owner mortgages the same home to Lender #2. The mortgage is duly recorded. The mortgage of 1978 is a *first lien* on the property. The mortgage of 1979 is a *second lien.* If both mortgages go into default, both will be foreclosed. But foreclosure of the first lien wipes out the second lien. Lender #2 can prevent this by paying off Lender #1's lien. But if he doesn't do this, Lender #2's mortgage will be extinguished. That is why Lender #2's mortgage is customarily referred to as a *junior lien.* Foreclosure of Lender #1's mortgage (the senior lien) extinguishes the junior lien.

As is evident, the risk involved in lending on a second or junior mortgage is greater than in lending on a first mortgage. For this reason the interest rate is generally higher on a second mortgage. The usual rule governing all investments is that where the risk is greater, the return is higher. Conversely, where the return is high, be suspicious: the risk is greater. Also, customarily the junior mortgage has a shorter maturity than a first mortgage. The philosophy is that risk is reduced by compelling retirement of the junior debt over a shorter span of time.

Obviously, a junior mortgage is made only when there is an *equity* over and above the first mortgage.

> **EXAMPLE:** Owner buys a home in 1978 for $80,000. He borrows $70,000 from Lender #1 and gives Lender #1 a first mortgage on the home. In 1982 the

home value has risen to $100,000. Owner borrows $10,000 from Lender #2 and gives Lender #2 a second mortgage. The mortgage debts aggregate $80,000, but the combined loan-to-value ratio is 80%. This is safe, conservative lending.

21.02   Form and contents of second mortgage

A second mortgage routinely contains clauses designed to protect the lender against the first mortgage. Some typical clauses are:

1. That the borrower will keep up the payments on the first mortgage and if he fails to do so, the second mortgage may make these payments and add the sums so paid to his second mortgage debt.

2. That the second mortgage may, with the consent of the first mortgagee, buy the first mortgage at a discount and add the full face amount of the first mortgage to the second mortgage debt.

3. That if the borrower defaults in his first mortgage payments, the second mortgagee may declare an acceleration of the second mortgage debt and foreclose the mortgage.

4. That the surplus proceeds of any foreclosure sale over and above the amount needed to pay the first mortgage debt are assigned to the second mortgage. This is particularly helpful where a third party is the successful bidder at the foreclosure sale and bids more than enough to pay the first mortgage.

5. A covenant by the borrower reciting the total amount unpaid on the first mortgage and stating that no default exists under the first mortgage.

6. That the borrower will forward to the second mortgagee any notices received by the borrower from the first mortgagee or any public body. This enables the second mortgagee to prevent foreclosure of the first mortgage in some cases. The second mortgagee can make the payments on the first mortgage. Or if a public body is threatening action to close down the building for code violations, the second mortgagee can give the city assurances that all violations will be corrected.

7. That foreclosure of the first mortgage does not extinguish personal liability of the mortgagor on the note secured by the junior mortgage. 59 CJS *Mortgages* §§ 523, 704.

21.03   FNMA

FNMA has begun a program for purchasing second mortgages originated both by regular institutional lenders and by home sellers who have taken back a second mortgage to help finance the sale of their home. Where the seller is to be the originating lender, FNMA requires that an FNMA approved lender handle the appraisal, credit check, and other aspects of the loan's origination and continue to service the loan after its sale to FNMA. The FNMA requirements are detailed and should be complied with.

21.04   Right to pay senior mortgage

If a first mortgage is not in default, a junior mortgagee has no right to compel the first mortgagee to accept full payment. *Gregory* v. *Suburban Realty Co.*, 292 Ill. 568, 127 NE 119 (1920).

21.05 Foreclosure agreement with first mortgagee

The second mortgagee may dicker with the first mortgagee and obtain a written agreement that the first mortgagee will give the second mortgagee a notice of any proposed first mortgage foreclosure. And even without the first mortgagee's consent, the second mortgagee may, in some states, record a notice requesting that he be notified of any foreclosure. This is done routinely in California, for example, where a deed of trust with power of sale is the common mortgage instrument and foreclosure is by the trustee's exercise of the power of sale without any court proceedings.

21.06 Subordination provisions

Second mortgages usually contain a clause that if it becomes necessary to refinance the first mortgage, the second mortgagee will subordinate his mortgage to the new first mortgage. Because of the technicalities involved in all subordinations, this clause must be set forth in detail. See Kratovil and Werner, *Modern Mortgage Law and Practice* chs. 30 and 38 (2d ed., 1981).

> **EXAMPLE:** In 1975 Owner mortgages his land to Lender #1 for $100,000 with 11 percent interest. In 1981 Owner gives a second mortgage to Lender #2 for $20,000 with 16 percent interest. A clause is included that Lender #2 will subordinate to any refinancing mortgage paying off Lender #1's mortgage. In 1982 Owner gives a refinancing mortgage to Lender #3 bearing 16 percent interest. A dispute will surely arise. Lender #2 will argue that a "refinancing" should bear the same interest as the loan refinanced. Lender #2 will also argue that his mortgage is not subordinated to any commissions, points, attorneys' fees, title charges, etc. Subordinations are usually interpreted rather narrowly. Draft the clause broadly.

21.06(a) Subordination to institutional mortgages

An agreement in a junior mortgage to subordinate the mortgage to a refinancing of the existing first mortgage is, at times, qualified so that the subordination will run in favor only of an institutional lender. There is widespread respect for regulated institutional lenders (bank, savings and loans) and a belief that any mortgage to such an institution will have reasonable rates and terms.

Where the new loan runs to an institutional lender, the second mortgagee may be willing to agree that the new loan will be larger than the existing first mortgage and at a higher rate of interest.

21.07 First mortgage provisions

Many corporate first mortgages contain clauses dealing with second mortgage financing.

> **EXAMPLE:** Owner gives a first mortgage to Lender in 1982 on his office building. Almost certainly this mortgage will contain a clause providing that Owner will place no second mortgage on the property and that if this clause is violated, Lend-

er may declare his mortgage debt due and foreclose. This is the "due-on-encumbrance" clause. Some states, California, for example, have laws covering this situation.

The philosophy here is that placing a second mortgage on the property has two adverse consequences to the first mortgage, namely: (1) places an undue financial burden on the borrower and may create a default in the first mortgage payments, and (2) the second mortgagee may take action that will destroy leases that could be valuable to the first mortgagee.

Interestingly, in the numerous articles and decisions that discuss the due-on-sale clause there is no discussion of the corporate mortgage. One can conclude that the courts are compartmentalizing mortgage law. They are developing rules for home mortgages that have no application to corporate mortgages.

21.08 Statutes governing junior mortgages

There are, of course, a variety of state laws governing junior mortgages.

EXAMPLE: Some statutes define consumer loans (e.g., loans for home repairs) and declare the mortgage void if made by an unlicensed lender. The philosophy here is that the state has a duty to the small borrower to see that reputable firms engage in second mortgage lending. Small borrowers usually do not consult lawyers. The opportunity to charge exorbitant fees is present. *Stubbs* v. *Security Discount Co.,* 407 A2d 1269 (N.J. 1979).

Or a law may forbid banks or insurance companies to make second mortgages. *National Bank* v. *Mathews,* 98 U.S. 62 (1878); *Jurgens* v. *Cobe,* 99 Ill. App. 156 (1900). Or the law may require a second mortgage to be so labeled in big print, so that any buyer of the paper will know he is buying a second lien. Ill. Rev. Stat. Ch. 121 1/2 § 137.3(k).

A number of states have statutes invalidating certain junior mortgages.

EXAMPLE: The defendants became indebted to plaintiff's assignor for purchase of an automobile secured by installment sale and security agreement and collaterally secured by real estate mortgage. At issue was whether or not the mortgage is good under the Secondary Mortgage Loan Act. It was held that a real property mortgage may not be taken as additional security under the Retail Installment Sales Act. A mortgage on real estate given by the retail installment buyer in connection with the financing of an automobile is null and void and will be ordered discharged of record. *Girard Acceptance Corp.* v. *Wallace,* 76 N.J. 434, 388 A2d 582 (1978).

Various securities laws affect junior mortgages. There are consumer protection laws, protecting homeowners against sharp practices, such as kickbacks by building contractors to lenders. Some such laws declare the junior mortgage void. *Stubbs* v. *Security Discount Co.,* 407 A2d 1269 (N.J. 1979). Today's lawmakers regard the highly regulated first mortgage lenders as responsible lenders, who can be trusted not to take advantage of borrowers. They tend to regard junior mortgage lenders as less reliable. They impose more stringent regulation.

21.09 Second mortgage companies

In many areas second mortgage companies are quite active. They are licensed. Ill. Rev. Stat. Ch. 16½ Par. 601 *et seq.* They will buy second mortgages, usually at a substantial discount. This means that a home seller who takes back a purchase money mortgage must be prepared to suffer a loss if he is forced to sell his mortgage. These mortgage companies also carry on an active business selling second mortgages to investors. If I buy a second mortgage from a mortgage company, I will ordinarily enter into a written agreement with the company under which it collects the payments, checks the property to see that the first mortgage payments, taxes, and insurance premiums are paid, and in general maintains supervision of the loan, for which it receives a "service charge."

21.10 Prepayment

It is customary in some areas for a second mortgage to carry a prepayment privilege clause that stipulates a penalty of some sort, perhaps 80 percent of six months' interest, if the loan is prepaid. In Los Angeles, 80 percent of second mortgages are prepaid, reports one company. This produces a substantial return to the lender. Some second mortgages, especially purchase money mortgages, contain a clause requiring prepayment when regular bank financing is available. No prepayment penalty is charged. The terms of the financing are spelled out in detail.

Some states, Georgia, for example, permit junior mortgage lenders to use an add-on interest rate.

> **EXAMPLE:** In an add-on loan a borrower who borrows $100 has the interest (say 9 percent) added on immediately so that his monthly or weekly payments include payments on the principal of $109 rather than one of $100. Obviously, the yield to the lender is in excess of 9 percent.

These loans, it is evident, collect at the outset, interest for the entire life of the loan. If the loan is prepaid, the portion of interest for the period from payment to maturity is technically unearned.

Some states, Georgia and Alabama, for example, require the application of the Rule of 78's in such a case. This is a complex rule that provides for rebate of part of the unearned interest. *Winkle* v. *Grant National Bank,* 601 SW2d 559 (1980). It is not well adapted to long-term loans.

Take the last example and suppose that the note has a prepayment privilege. Suppose that the borrower prepays on June 30, 1982. It is obvious that the $9.00 interest was intended to be spread over the entire year of 1982. Hence that portion representing interest from July 1, 1982, to December 31, 1982, is unearned.

Under this artificial rule, you divide the loan into 78 parts, allocating 12 to January, 11 to February, and so on, with 1 allocated to December.

You treat 12/78s of the interest of $9.00 as being earned in January, an additional 11/78s as being earned in February, and so on. If you add 12–11–10–9–8–7–6–5–4–3–2–1, you arrive at the sum of 78. Hence, the name of the rule.

Hence, in our case you would take July (6), August (5), September (4), October (3), November (2), December (1), and add them, which equals 21. Now take 21/78 of the $9.00. This is the refund to which the prepaying debtor is entitled.

21.11   Interest rates

Local law concerning interest rates must be carefully analyzed where interest rates are concerned. State usury laws and the Uniform Consumer Credit Code come into play.

21.12   Rents

In large mortgages on commercial property the first mortgagee may insist that any junior mortgage provide that all rents collected by the junior mortgagee shall be held in trust for the first mortgagee and applied on the first mortgage debt.

21.13   Open-end senior mortgage

While the danger does not appear to be great, there is at least a possibility that where there is an open-end senior mortgage, advances may be made under the senior mortgage that could prime the junior mortgage. It is therefore advisable for the junior mortgagee who finds such a first mortgage on the public records to notify the first mortgagee of the making of the second mortgage. This will protect the second mortgagee against such advances.

21.14   Condo assessments

A common provision in condo declarations is that the lien of assessments shall be subordinate to institutional *first* mortgages. Of course, the lien of assessments, since it relates back to the recording of the condo declaration, will enjoy priority over the lien of a junior mortgage. *Washington Fed. S. & L.* v. *Schneider,* 408 N.Y.S.2d 588 (1978).

22 REAL ESTATE FINANCE— INSTALLMENT CONTRACTS

22.01 In general
Probably the most popular form of creative financing is the installment contract, sometimes called the *land contract* or *contract for deed.* In one variation or another the installment contract is a ready alternative when regular financing becomes too expensive or impossible to obtain. Witness the period beginning in 1979 when tens of thousands of deals were closed on installment contracts.

Before signing an installment contract, the seller should remember that he is going into the credit business. For this reason, the seller should do the same evaluation of the buyer as a lender does in the loan underwriting process. Is the buyer creditworthy? A credit check must be made. Does the buyer have the income to make the periodic payments as they come due? Check the buyer's annual income by inquiry of his employer or a review of his income tax returns. A good real estate broker can be of great help to the buyer in attending to these details and in evaluating the information.

Perhaps the best way to understand the installment contract is to review its terms.

22.02 Broker's commission
Where the broker's listing contract permits an installment contract (as distinguished from a cash sale) or the seller decides to accept an installment purchaser, the broker's commission is earned once the contract is signed.

> **SUGGESTION TO THE SELLER:** In the listing contract provide for the commission to be payable in installments. The buyer doesn't want to pay a full commission if the buyer defaults in the early months of the sale.

22.03 Spouse's signature
Both sellers and spouses should join in the contract of sale because of marital and homestead rights.

22.04   Purchaser as joint tenants

Where a husband and wife are buying it is probably wise to have them purchase as joint tenants or as tenants by the entireties. Over the relatively long life of the contract, one of the buyers may die.

22.05   Balloons

Many installment contracts call for a balloon, or contain a call provision, making the entire balance due after a short period, say three years. This poses a problem to the buyer. Will financing be available then?

22.06   Title search

The seller is allowed to perfect his title at any time before the date set for the giving of the deed. 109 ALR 242. This is bad from the buyer's viewpoint.

> **SUGGESTION TO THE BUYER:** Require that a preliminary contract be signed. In this procedure the installment contract will not be signed until the seller's title has been examined and found to be acceptable to the buyer. Or combine the preliminary contract into the final installment contract. Where title is examined before the installment contract binds the purchaser, some form of title insurance is available everywhere.

22.07   Assignment by buyer

In order to control the occupancy of the property, the seller may wish to include a clause forbidding assignment of the contract by the buyer without the seller's consent. Such a clause is valid. *Immel* v. *Travelers Ins. Co.,* 373 Ill. 256, 26 NE2d 114 (1940).

Where an assignment is made, thought should be given to the liability of the assignee. By the weight of authority, a mere assignment does not create a personal liability of the assignee to the seller. *Quest* v. *Robinson,* 71 Ill. App.3d 678, 318 NE2d 1335 (1980). In a few states, the assignee does become so liable. *Rose* v. *Vulcan Materials Co.,* 194 SE2d 521 (N.C.), (citing authorities pro and con). Of course, if the seller's consent is needed, he may insist that the assignee sign an instrument assuming personal liability in consideration of receiving the seller's consent. In some instances the seller has consented to an assignment containing the language that the assignee "assumes" the contract. This is sloppy draftsmanship.

Clauses forbidding assignment of the contract by the buyer do not prevent the buyer's signing an installment contract to sell his interest. Such a contract is called a *subpurchase. Covington* v. *Clark,* 346 P2d 225 (Cal. 1959). *Lake Shore Club* v. *Lake Front,* 398 NE2d 893 (Ill. App. 1979). *See also* 4 Stanf. L. Rev. 443; 100 U. Pa. L. Rev. 1073; 27 Univ. N.Y. L. Rev. 174; 3 Utah L. Rev. 257 (all dealing with subpurchase contracts).

In point of fact, the restriction on assignment can take one of three forms, namely: (1) The contract contains a covenant not to assign. Presumably, for a breach of this covenant the remedy would be a suit for damages. (2) The contract may state that the making of an assignment without the required consent makes the *assignment* void, or (3) makes the *contract* void at the option of the injured party. Murray, *Contracts* § 305, p. 623 (1974). It is therefore important to frame the clause carefully, selecting the particular choice with care. Again, in states where forfeitures are frowned upon, and this is a long list of states, one is permitted to wonder if option (3) is a realistic option.

Actually, a fourth option exists, namely, inclusion of a due-on-sale clause that is triggered either by an assignment or subpurchase contract.

22.08 Recording Some printed forms forbid the recording of the contract. There is some doubt as to the validity of such a clause. Illinois forbids this clause in residential contracts. Ill. Rev. Stat. Ch. 29, par. 8.12.

22.09 Interest rate In one creative financing plan, the installment contract price bears 14 percent interest, but only 10 percent is paid for a period of time. The remaining 4 percent is allowed to accrue. This allows the buyer time to fix up the building. If it is an apartment building, he may be able to sell it at a profit to a condo converter and pay off all accruals.

22.10 Prorations Normally, the contract gives the buyer the right of possession as soon as both parties sign it. Thereafter, the contract requires the buyer to pay taxes, insurance, and so forth. Hence the contract should require that all such items be prorated as of the date of the contract.

22.11 Prepayment privilege The buyer will insist that the contract give him the right to prepay the installment balance of the purchase price. If the contract does not expressly give this privilege, the contract balance cannot be prepaid. *Burns* v. *Epstein,* 413 Ill. 476, 109 NE2d 774 (1952). Sellers are concerned about the income tax impact of prepayment and may require deferred payments. Sellers may even exact a stiff prepayment penalty. Courts will uphold it if it is reasonably related to the seller's risk of incurring increased income tax liability. *Williams* v. *Fassler,* 167 Cal. Reptr. 545 (1980).

22.12 Impounds We are encountering many installment contracts in home sales where the contract requires the buyer to make monthly payments that include one-twelfth of the yearly real estate tax and fire insurance premium. This, of course, is a common provision in home mortgages. In such case, failure of the buyer to include these *impound payments* in his monthly remittance would be a default under the contract and might eventually lead to a forfeiture.

22.13   Acceleration clause

From the seller's point of view, it is desirable that an installment contract authorize the seller to declare the entire purchase price due in case of default. Otherwise, a chronically delinquent buyer can drive a seller to distraction by curing his defaults each time the seller serves notice on him of the seller's intent to declare a forfeiture.

> **EXAMPLE:**   Owner contracts to sell real estate to Buyer, purchase price of $20,000 payable in monthly installments. Buyer is constantly late in making payments. The contract contains an acceleration clause. Owner sends Buyer notice to cure all his defaults within thirty days, otherwise Owner will declare the entire purchase price due. This is permitted under the acceleration clause. After acceleration has taken place, Owner is in a position to forfeit unless Buyer can come up with the entire purchase price. This is helpful in getting rid of the chronic delinquent. But, as in the case of mortgage law today, the seller must not exercise his rights unfairly.

The acceleration clause is commonly regarded as valid. *Benincash* v *Mihailovich,* 188 NW2d 136 (Mich. 1971). However, it is probably necessary for the seller to give the purchaser notice to cure his defaults and a reasonable time to do so. *Brannock* v. *Fletcher,* 155 SE2d 532 (N.C. 1967). And if the seller accelerates unfairly, courts will set the acceleration aside.

> **EXAMPLE:**   The seller cannot declare an acceleration where there is an honest dispute as to the amount due. *Moore* v. *Bunch,* 185 NW2d 565 (Mich. 1971).

22.14   Insurance

It seems wise for the contract to spell out all the appropriate insurance requirements and to require the buyer to furnish evidence periodically that the insurance is in force. Both seller and buyer should have liability coverage. To be sure, the brunt of liability will fall on the buyer–occupant, but the seller may be named a defendant in personal injury suits, and an insured seller will be entitled to have the insurer defend the lawsuit without charge. The hazard insurance should have a "manuscript" rider covering both seller and buyer.

> **SUGGESTION TO THE SELLER:**   Draft a paragraph for the insurance endorsement stating that acts of the buyer (arson, for example) will not invalidate seller's coverage. Existing forms of this rider are inadequate.

22.15   Income tax

The income tax benefits of an installment sale are well known. Spreading the seller's capital gain on the sale over a period of years can be quite beneficial. To avoid income tax, sellers often will increase the sale price but reduce the interest rate. At times the interest rate is reduced to some absurd figure like 2 percent. This will not work. IRS will catch this and penalize you. Charge at least 9 percent. 26 USCA § 483.

22.16 Judgments against seller—equitable conversion

In many states the buyer is regarded as the equitable owner of the property. In these states, commonly the interest of the seller is a bare, naked, legal title. Judgment liens against the seller do not attach to such a title. 87 ALR 1505, 1512. The state law must be checked. Some contract forms contain a provision that the purchaser acquires no title, legal or equitable, until the sale price is paid in full. The validity of these clauses has been sustained. *Cox* v. *Supreme S. & L. Assn.,* 126 Ill. App.2d 74 (1970) (holding valid clause that buyer acquires no interest in land until contract price is paid in full).

This clause is objectionable to the purchaser and should be deleted. It negates the equitable conversion that would result from the signing of the contract and deprives the purchaser of the protection this doctrine provides against judgments against the seller.

At times, during the life of the contract, the buyer will learn that a judgment or other lien has, in fact, been filed against the seller. This raises a problem of great difficulty. The seller may, in good faith, be appealing or otherwise contesting the lien. But the buyer is put to the hazard of continuing his payments on a title that may be clouded when it is conveyed to him. Some relief is obtained by a clause providing that in such cases the buyer may elect to make his payments to a bank in escrow for both parties until assurances have been given, satisfactory to buyer's attorney, that these liens will not affect the buyer's title. However, there is no device that is really satisfactory to both parties. A long-term escrow may help if accompanied by a title policy protecting the buyer against future liens. Or the title may be placed in a trust at the time the contract is signed with directions to the trustee to give a deed to the buyer when the last payment is made.

Again, a title company may be persuaded to give the buyer a clear policy on the theory that, in states where equitable conversion exists, the seller holds a naked legal title in trust for the buyer and such a title is not subject to judgment liens. *Reuss* v. *Nixon,* 272 Ill. App. 219; *Lynch* v. *Eifler,* 191 Ill. App. 344; 87 ALR 1505, 1515.

22.17 Mortgages

Both seller and buyer have interests that may be mortgaged. *Tanglewood Land Co.* v. *Boyd,* 256 SE2d 270 (N.C. 1979).

As to the seller's interest, the contract should provide that the buyer's interest is subordinate to any mortgage that does not exceed the balance due on the contract or the interest rate or monthly payments stated therein; likewise, that in case of any default in the mortgage, the buyer may make the payments on the mortgage and such payments shall reduce the contract balance.

As to the buyer, a clause is needed under which the seller joins in the mortgage or subordinates his interest thereto. Some rehab contractors accept a mortgage on the buyer's interest only. This is legally valid, but unsound. If the buyer's interest is terminated for default, this wipes out the mortgage.

REFERENCES: *Nelson* v. *Bailey,* 54 Wash.2d 161, 338 P2d 757, 73 ALR2d 1400 (1959); *Simonson* v. *Wenzel,* 27 N.D. 638; 147 NW 804, LRA 1918C 780 (1914); *Eade* v. *Brownlee,* 29 Ill.2d 214, 193 NE2d 786 (1963) (all holding that contract purchaser has interest that may be mortgaged).

Norlin v. *Montgomery,* 367 P2d 621 (Wash. 1962) (seller's interest is not subject to mortgages executed by buyer).

Eade v. *Brownlee,* 29 Ill.2d 214, 193 NE2d 786 (1963); and *Miles Homes* v. *Grant,* 134 NW2d 569 (Iowa 1965) (both holding buyer's mortgagee not entitled to notice of forfeiture). *Contra: Kendrick* v. *Davis,* 452 P2d 222 (Wash. 1969). As to notice to lien creditors of buyer generally, see *Hayes* v. *Carey,* 287 Ill. 774, 122 NE 524 (1919); *MGIC Mtg. Corp.* v. *Bowen,* 572 P2d 547 (N.M. 1977).

Knauss v. *Miles Homes Inc.,* 173 NW2d 896 (N.D. 1970) (holding that purchaser's mortgage is necessary party to seller's suit to quiet title).

87 ALR 1505, 1515; 43 Mo. L. Rev. 371; and 45 Wash. L. Rev. 645, all dealing with situation where after installment contract is recorded the seller mortgages his interest, and issue is whether buyer can claim priority over mortgage for payments made after he learns of the mortgage.

22.18 Escrows

In some states it is the practice to have the seller deposit his deed in escrow with a bank or trust company. This is done at the time the contract is signed. The bank is directed to collect the payments on the contract and to deliver the deed to the buyer when the last payment is made. 21 Ill. L. Rev. 655. In this manner one avoids the problem of the death of the seller during the life of the contract.

22.19 Bankruptcy of seller

The new Bankruptcy Act protects a buyer in possession against the bankruptcy of the seller. The former Bankruptcy Act did not. The buyer should insist that the title policy issued when the contract is signed contain affirmative protection against the seller's bankruptcy. Then if the bankruptcy court attempts to reach the asset, the title company will defend the buyer. The buyer must be in possession to receive this protection.

22.20 Building code violations

Laws will be encountered that require an installment seller, prior to signing of the contract, to furnish information as to reported building code violations. Ill. Rev. Stat. Ch. 29, §§ 8.31, 8.32. A question remains as to the liability of the seller for building code violations that develop later. The buyer, of course, is liable, since he has possession and control of the building. *Cox* v. *Supreme S. & L. Assn.,* 126 Ill. App.2d 293, 262 NE2d 74 (1970). However, the code language may be broad enough to impose liability on the seller as well. *Cocanig v. City of Chicago,* 21 Ill.2d 464, 173 NE2d 482 (1961); *City of Chicago v. Porler,* 26 Ill. App. 2d 323, 168 NE2d 468 (1960). Of course, the seller will be liable to the city for building code violations existing when the contract was signed. *Cox v. Supreme S. & L. Assn.,* 126 Ill. App.2d 293, 262 NE2d 74.

In some states the fines for building code violations are substantial. Obviously, the seller should require the buyer to keep the building free from building code violations and make violation of this agreement grounds for forfeiture. He should retain the right to make reasonable inspections of the building and exercise this right. If substantial code violations appear, he should declare the contract forfeited.

22.21   The forfeiture process

Every installment contract contains a forfeiture clause. If the buyer fails to meet his payments, this clause gives the buyer the right to terminate the contract and to retain the payments the buyer has made. This is what lawyers call an *agreed remedy.* It exists only if the forfeiture clause is found in the contract. *Realty Securities Corp.* v. *Johnson,* 93 Fla. 46, 111 So 532 (1927). In this respect forfeiture differs from *rescission.* Rescission is a right the courts give the seller even where the contract is silent. The seller may terminate the contract if the buyer fails to meet his payments, but should "restore the status quo." This means he should return to the buyer the payments made by the buyer. Obviously, the seller wishes to keep those payments. Hence the importance of the forfeiture clause. By declaring the contract forfeited, the seller terminates the contract and retains all payments previously made by the buyer. 77 Am.Jur.2d *Vendor and Purchaser* § 500.

Just as we so often find that tenants do not pay their monthly rent exactly on the day it is due, so we often find that purchasers under installment contracts do not pay their payments exactly on the day they are due, or they may from time to time make payments of less than the amount due. The overwhelming majority of installment sellers go along with the buyer, hoping that he will ultimately be able to straighten out his finances. Ultimately, the seller may decide that he can no longer be indulgent. Then he faces a problem that his own indulgence has created.

EXAMPLE: An installment contract provided that time was of the essence, but the seller often accepted payments after the dates fixed for payment. This constituted a waiver of the provision that time was of the essence. The reason is that the seller, by accepting payments after the dates fixed, had led the buyer to believe that he would not insist on the provision that payments must be made strictly on the specified dates. It would therefore be highly unjust to permit the seller suddenly to declare a forfeiture of the contract for the buyer's failure to pay one of the installments promptly. *Fox* v. *Grange,* 261 Ill. 116, 103 NE 576 (1913); 31 ALR2d 55, 85.

The seller may *revive* the provision that time is of the essence. He may serve a *warning notice* on the buyer that in the future he will insist on strict performance of the contract according to its terms, and thereafter the buyer must make his payments promptly or the seller may declare a forfeiture. This warning notice must be followed by a declaration of forfeiture if the buyer fails to cure his defaults within the allotted time. Such a warning notice must not be a mere dun. It must state unequivocally that the contract will be forfeited if the defaults are not cured within the specified time. *Monson* v. *Bragdon,* 159 Ill. 61, 42 NE 383 (1895). Many printed contract forms contain a provision that acceptance of late payments shall not constitute a waiver of the provision that time is of the essence. Some courts refuse to give this provision effect. *Morrey* v. *Bartlett,* 288 Ill. App. 620; *Scott* v. *Cal. Farming Co.,* 4 Cal. App.2d 232, 40 P2d 850 (1940). In many states, a warning notice must always be given before an installment contract is forfeited. *County of Lincoln* v. *Fischer,* 216 Oreg. 421, 339 P2d 1084 (1954); 31 ALR2d 14.

It is obvious that forfeiture involves a number of steps. The first step is the giving of notice to the purchaser, as has been stated. Where there are two or more purchasers, each is entitled to his or her separate notice. In short, the seller should never send a notice addressed to "Mr. and Mrs. John Smith."

Sending a notice to the wrong address is a fatal defect if the seller knows the correct address. *Kingsley* v. *Roeder,* 2 Ill.2d 131, 117 NE2d 82 (1954).

If the purchaser has assigned his interest to a third party, or placed a mortgage on his interest, obviously the better practice is to serve all notices on all such parties. Whether failure to so notify these parties will invalidate the forfeiture is a difficult question to answer. *Eade* v. *Brownlee,* 29 Ill.2d 214, 93 NE2d 786 (1963) (purchaser's mortgagee not served). *Holiver* v. *Dept. of Public Works,* 127 NE2d 790 (Mass. 1955); *Stannard* v. *Marboe,* 159 Minn. 119, 198 NW 127 (1924) (purchaser's mortgagee must be given notice); *Miles Homes Inc.,* v. *Grant,* 134 NW2d 569 (Iowa 1965) (purchaser's mortgagee not entitled to notice). *Kendrick* v. *Davis,* 452 P2d 222 (Wash. 1969) (purchaser's mortgagee is entitled to notice); *MGIC Mtg. Corp.* v. *Bowen,* 91 N.M. 200, 572 P2d 547 (1977) (purchaser's judgment creditor not entitled to notice); *Hayes* v. *Carey,* 287 Ill. 274, 122 NE 524 (1919) (purchaser's judgment creditor not entitled to notice).

In earlier times, it was the practice to insert a clause in the installment contract that mere default would of itself work a forfeiture of the contract. Such clauses were once held valid. *Realty Securities Corp.* v. *Johnson,* 93 Fla. 46, 111 So 532 (1927); 66 CJ 769; 91 CJS *Vendor and Purchaser* § 139. In this day and age, where not only the contract but the conduct of the parties must be conscionable, it is doubtful that such a provision would withstand attack. *See however, Sturm* v. *Heim,* 95 Ariz. 300, 389 P2d 702 (1964) (doubtful that this decision would withstand attack today).

In some states the forfeiture procedure is set forth in state laws rather than in the contract. *Sanchez* v. *Brandt,* 567 SW2d 254 (Tex. 1978).

22.21(a)   Trifling defaults

At times the buyer will argue that forfeiture ought not be permitted where the default is trifling in amount.

> **EXAMPLE:**   A buyer in a $30,000 contract deliberately defaulted in a payment of $10.48. The court sustained the forfeiture. Where a default is deliberate, the buyer is, in effect, demanding a reduction in the sale price. He cannot force this decision on the seller. *Miller* v. *American Wonderlands,* 275 NW2d 399 (Iowa 1979).

But where there are minor defaults not due to stubborn defiance, the courts often set aside or refuse forfeiture. *Fisel* v. *Yoder,* 320 NE2d 783 (Ind.).

22.21(b)   Forfeiture procedure—acceleration improper

For some unexplained reason, many installment contracts lack an acceleration clause. In such case, a seller seeking to decalre a forfeiture may demand payment of only those installments that are delinquent. However, on occasion a seller will, quite improperly in such cases, declare an acceleration in his notice of his intention to declare a forfeiture. By the better view this is a fatal defect. The forfeiture must be set aside. *Rader* v. *Taylor,* 333 P2d 480 (Mont. 1959). A buyer facing a demand for the entire balance due will, when he is having a hard time making the regular monthly payments, throw up his hands in despair. It is unfair to give him the impression that he can save his interest only by paying the entire balance due.

However, a mere mistake in the forfeiture notice does not invalidate it.

> **EXAMPLE:**   Seller demands payment of $500 in his forfeiture notice. Actually, the correct amount is $450. This does not invalidate the forfeiture. *Rader* v. *Taylor,* 333 P2d 480 (Mont. 1959) (dissenting opinion citing *Forest Preserve Co.* v. *Miller,* 379 Ill. 375, 41 NE2d 526).

22.21(c)   Forfeiture procedure—declaration of forfeiture

Of course, following the seller's notice to the buyer to cure defaults or suffer a forfeiture, the seller must declare the forfeiture. A forfeiture cannot be made in the seller's mind. It must be communicated to the buyer. *Lovins* v. *Kelly,* 19 Ill.2d 25, 166 NE2d 69 (1960). If, and only if, the contract requires it, the declaration of forfeiture must be recorded. *Tobin* v. *Alexander,* 380 NE2d 45 (Ill. 1978).

22.21(d)   Forfeiture procedure—recovery of money paid by buyer

Even where a forfeiture has been declared, the buyer's rights may be revived. This occurs where the seller waives the forfeiture by conduct indicating that he considers the contract still in force, as by negotiating with the buyer concerning the title of the property, possible repurchase by the seller, extension of time of payment, and the like. 107 ALR 345. All owners of the land must join in the notice of forfeiture. 66 CJ *Vendor and Purchaser* § 62 p. 762.

Where a recorded contract has been properly forfeited, the seller can obtain a court decree declaring the buyer's rights terminated.

Where the buyer is in military service, the contract cannot be forfeited without a court order. The court may either postpone the forfeiture or order the repayment of prior installments before permitting forfeiture of the contract.

In California, Georgia, Montana, South Dakota, Wisconsin, and Utah, a purchaser whose contract has been forfeited is allowed to get back the amount he has paid, less a reasonable compensation to the seller for the use of his land. Illinois, Iowa, and Minnesota allow the purchaser to cure his defaults within a specified grace period and thus preserve this contract. Arizona also provides a grace period that increases in proportion to the amount paid on the contract. 13 Rutgers L. Rev. 624; 24 Mo. L. Rev. 244. In Florida, Indiana, and Maryland, the contract must be foreclosed like a mortgage. *Mid-State Inv. Corp.* v. *O'Steen* (Fla.) 133 So2d 455; *Stendzel* v. *Marshall,* 301 NE2d 641 (Ind. 1973). However, in most states, the forfeiture provisions in the contract will be enforced. *Coe* v. *Bennett,* 46 Idaho 62, 266 Pac. 413 (1928); 31 ALR2d 38, 71.

Perhaps the most important clause in an installment contract, from the seller's point of view, is the forfeiture clause.

In various circumstances, courts will allow the buyer to recover a portion of the purchase price he has paid. 4 ALR4th 993.

22.21(e)   Relief against forfeiture—forfeiture and damages

Courts will on occasion set aside a forfeiture of an installment contract. 55 ALR3d 10; Restatement, *Contracts,* §§ 275, 276. The more money the buyer has paid in, the more likely the court is to do this. Where the buyer has made substantial improvements, he is quite likely to obtain this sort of relief. *Krentz* v. *Johnson,* 36 Ill. App.3d 142, 343 NE2d 165 (1976). The more lenient the seller has been in accepting short payments or delayed payments, the greater the likelihood that the forfeiture will be set aside. *Krentz* v. *Johnson, supra.* Where the buyer's breach consists of failing to make repairs, the seller's notice must give him a reasonable time to make repairs. Otherwise the forfeiture cannot stand. *Reeploeg* v. *Jensen,* 490 P2d 445 (Wash. 1971). Where the forfeiture notices were sent to the wrong address, the forfeiture cannot stand. *Kingsley* v. *Roeder,* 2 Ill.2d 131, 117 NE2d 82 (1954). Whenever it would be unreasonable to let the seller keep the buyer's payments and oust him from the land, the forfeiture is set aside. *McWilliams* v. *Urban Land Co.,* 194 NW2d 920 (Mich.). In such cases the court may order foreclosure by sale, which gives the buyer a right to redeem. *Ruhl* v. *Johnson,* 159 Neb. 810, 49 NW2d 687 (1951). Where the buyer's payments amount to little more than the rental value of the land he has occupied, his case for relief is poor. But where the seller is himself in default, any forfeiture he declares will be set aside.

Some states that normally allow the remedy of forfeiture, nevertheless insist on foreclosure where the buyer has paid in substantial amounts.

EXAMPLE: Court refused forfeiture and ordered foreclosure where buyer had paid in 30 percent of sale price. *Morris* v. *Weigle,* 383 NE2d 341 (Ind. 1978).

Some courts put this on the ground that a forfeiture in such case is *unconscionable. Williams* v. *Havens,* 444 P2d 132 (Idaho 1968). Other courts state that forfeiture in such cases "shocks the conscience of the court." *Kay* v. *Wood,* 549 P2d 709 (Utah 1976); *Jenkins* v. *Wise,* 574 P2d 1337 (Hawaii 1978). Of course, some courts are more liberal with purchasers than others. It is not possible to state a definite rule as to what investment will protect a buyer against forfeiture. *Clements* v. *Castle Mtg. Service Co.,* 382 A2d 1367 (Del. 1977).

REFERENCES: The question of a defaulting buyer's right to recover his earnest money or other purchase money paid has been the subject of many articles: 24 Mo. L. Rev. 244; 47 So. Cal. L. Rev. 201; 25 Southern L. Rev. 387; 1950 U. of Ill. L. Forum 249; 12 U. of Detroit L. J. 59; 19 U. of Miami L. Rev. 552; 20 id. 1. The great leading article is Corbin, *The Right of a Defaulting Vendee to the Restitution of Installment Unpaid,* 40 Yale L. J. 1013 (1913).

22.21(f)   Remedies of seller—foreclosure

A seller may file a foreclosure suit if the buyer defaults. The foreclosure may be a *strict foreclosure. Walker* v. *Runnenkamp,* 373 P2d 559 (Idaho 1962); 77 ALR 282. In such a foreclosure, the purchaser will be given a period of time to pay up, and if he fails to do so, his rights are extinguished. Or the court may order a foreclosure sale of the land. 77 ALR 276. If foreclosure is by sale, some states allow some sort of redemption period. 51 ALR2d 672. Other states allow no redemption period.

As in the case of forfeitures, the court may hold in foreclosure cases that the seller has waived the contract provision that time is of the essence.

EXAMPLE: Seller entered into an installment contract with Buyer. It contained an acceleration clause. From time to time Buyer was delinquent in his payments and Seller wrote him dunning letters. Finally, Seller, in exasperation, declared all the contract price due and filed a suit to foreclosure. Buyer tendered all his back payments into court. The court dismissed the foreclosure. *Stinemeyer* v. *Wesco,* 487 P2d 65 (Oreg. 1971).

NEW DIRECTIONS: This last example is new law but is likely to become the law in many states. In this age of consumerism, the courts, in their desire to ameliorate hardships, are quite likely to set aside accelerations.

23 REAL ESTATE FINANCE—MISCELLANEOUS DEVICES—GROUND LEASES

23.01 Ground rents—in general

Ground leases as a method of real estate finance have been commonplace in Maryland, Pennsylvania, and Hawaii and the practice is spreading.

23.01(a) Ground rents— the Maryland system

In Maryland, leases are used in the *ground rent* method of financing. The chief characteristics of the Maryland ground rent leases are: (1) the landowner leases the land to the lessee for a period of ninety-nine years; (2) with a provision for the perpetual renewal of the lease from time to time as each ninety-nine-year period draws to a close, upon payment of a small sum of money called a *renewal fine;* (3) the lessee agrees to pay a certain sum of money (usually semiannually) as ground rent; and (4) the lease contains a provision that if the lessee makes default in his ground rent payments, the lessor may declare the lease void and evict the lessee. The lessee also agrees to pay the taxes on the property, and they are assessed to the lessee. The interest acquired by the lessee under the lease is regarded as personal property. His wife or widow has no dower in the leasehold estate. Prior to 1884, the ground rents reserved by such leases were not redeemable by the lessee unless expressly so stipulated in the lease; but in that year and by subsequent laws, it was provided that the lessee, in leases subsequently executed, could pay the lessor the value of the lessor's interest and thus *redeem* the rent and become the owner of the property. The original lease and assignments thereof must be executed, acknowledged, and recorded in the same manner as deeds. The leasehold estate is subject to the liens of judgments against the lessee. In practical economic effect, the relation of the lessee to the property is that of the owner of the land subject to the payment of the annual rent and the taxes; and his economic relation to the owner of the ground rent is much like that of a mortgagor paying interest on a debt where the principal never matures so long as the mortgagor pays the interest and taxes. The technical relation between the owner of the rent and of the leasehold is that of landlord and tenant. *Jones* v. *Magruder*, 42 F.Supp. 193.

Such ground rents are bought and sold in Baltimore the same way mortgages are dealt in.

23.01(b) Ground rents— improved property

A Maryland case (*Packard* v. *Corporation for Relief of Widows*, 77 Md. 240, 26 Atl. 411) describes the operation of the ground rent system in a sale of improved property.

> **EXAMPLE:** Landowner sold and conveyed his land to Buyer for $4,500. Buyer immediately leased to Tenant for a consideration of $1,000 cash, and rent payable at $210 which capitalized at 6 percent equals $3,500. Thus, a margin of $1,000 was left to protect Buyer against loss in case he should be compelled to take the property back. It was held that this was not a mortgage, but was merely a ground rent.

The court pointed out, however, that in legal contemplation this lease was not a mortgage, since, while the lessee had the privilege of redeeming, he was not obliged to do so. Thus there was lacking the relation of debtor and creditor which is the distinguishing characteristic of mortgage transactions.

23.01(c) Ground rents— redemption

Originally, ground rents were divided into redeemable and irredeemable rents. An irredeemable rent was one in which there was no provision in the lease allowing the lessee to buy the land. A redeemable lease contained an option permitting the lessee to purchase the land on payment of a stipulated price. Legislation was passed in 1884 and subsequent years making redeemable all ground rents thereafter created. Thus, under laws passed in 1900 all long term ground rents created thereafter are redeemable, at the option of the tenant, for a sum of money equal to the capitalization of the rent at a rate not exceeding 6 percent. However, irredeemable ground rents existing prior to the passage of these laws are still not subject to redemption. And, as heretofore pointed out, the landlord cannot compel the tenant to redeem.

23.01(d) Ground rents— Pennsylvania system

In Pennsylvania, ground rents are created by a deed of the land which conveys the legal title to grantee subject to the payment of rent to the grantor. *Jones* v. *Magruder*, 42 F.Supp. 193. A subsequent purchaser of the land must pay the rent thus stipulated, but he does not become personally liable therefor unless his deed provides that the grantee assumes and agrees to pay such rent. However, the grantee in the original deed remains liable for rents accruing even after his sale of the land. If default is made in payment of ground rent and the owner of the land obtains a judgment therefor, a sheriff's sale under his judgment wipes out all encumbrances and titles arising subsequent to the creation of the ground rent. Pennsylvania also has passed laws providing for the redemption of ground rents. *In re Crean's Estate,* 321 Pa. 216, 183 Atl. 915.

23.01(e) Modern developments in ground rents

Today's ground lease financing is a relatively simple transaction.

> **EXAMPLE:**   Builder builds a home on a lot he owns. He enters into a contract of sale and lease with Tenant, the purchaser. The contract calls for the usual title search. When that shows clear title in Builder, he is required at closing to give Tenant a deed to the *building* and a long lease of the land. The lease includes an option to purchase the land. The option price steps up each year, so that the annual increase in option price reflects the appreciation in land value and also exerts pressure on Tenant to buy as soon as he can command the resources. The lease is usually at a flat rental for fifteen years. The contract requires Tenant to execute a mortgage to *ABC Co.,* the company financing the transaction. By means of the mortgage, Tenant mortgages his leasehold estate and his option to purchase. Builder joins in the mortgage or signs a separate document subordinating his ownership interest to the mortgage. This process is called "bringing the fee under the mortgage." *See* Kratovil and Werner, *Modern Mortgage Law and Practice* Ch. 30 (2d ed. 1981). The result is that if the mortgage is foreclosed, *ABC Co.* acquires full ownership of the land. But since Tenant initially acquired only a lease of the land, he is permitted to make a substantially smaller down payment. But because Builder joins in the mortgage, the lender has total security. If Builder is in need of cash (as builders often are), he can make up a package of twenty or more such homes and sell the land to a syndicate at a discount.

The leasehold mortgage in this form can be sold to FHLMC.

The ground lease viewed from the land developer's perspective is a different and far more complex transaction. Kratovil, *Modern Real Estate Documentation,* Ch. 34.

23.02 Sale and management agreement— "earn outs"

An owner of an existing commercial property (e.g., shopping center, office building) may, for a variety of reasons, choose to sell the asset. Yet he may wish to extract some further benefit from the property, for example, through a long-term (five years) management agreement. The buyer may be willing to agree to such an arrangement because the seller has general expertise in the field and his intimate knowledge of the project, its tenants, its legal and construction problems. Such an arrangement may be attractive to foreign investors who wish to avoid intimate involvement with daily management problems. It may also be attractive to pension funds. Such funds are no longer content with mortgage investments, since the interest return dwindles in value as inflation continues, while pension compensation must keep pace with inflation.

The management agreement may be tailored so that the buyer sets financial goals the project is expected to achieve, and the seller's continuing as manager is contingent on achievement of these goals. This would be particularly true of new projects.

New projects may be initiated for the express purpose of selling the completed project and the signing of a management agreement.

The contract of sale may provide for an adjustment in the sale price to take place after the closing of the deal. This adjustment may take place whether or not the seller retains a management position. It would be logical to use this "earn out" provision where the seller retains a management position and can control the economic destinies of the project. The adjustment will be in the form of seller's participation in the earnings of the project based on economic achievements set forth in the contract. The situation offers problems, since a seller retaining management control has an incentive to manipulate the project so as to reflect cash flow or rental achievements that will trigger his participation in the earnings. This suggests that the buyer may need to have some control over the management operation. This, in turn, poses other problems. If the two parties share control, the deal begins to look like a partnership or joint venture (with the attendant liabilities) and the seller–manager looks less like an independent contractor.

A like problem arises if the seller's share of the earnings is abnormally large. This again suggests joint venture.

Also, a seller may be liable to the buyer on some fraud or securities law theories.

23.03 Pledge of beneficial interest

In states that recognize the validity of the land trust there is a mode of financing that offers many advantages.

EXAMPLE: Owner owns Blackacre. He conveys it in 1979 to *XYZ Trust Co.,* as trustee, using a typical land trust documentation. The trust agreement designates Owner as sole beneficiary. Under the land trust documentation the beneficial interest is deemed personal property. In 1982, Owner wishes to borrow money. He applies to *ABC Bank* for a loan. The loan is worked out as a pledge of the beneficial interest. Owner executes a collateral note to the bank. This is a lengthy promissory note well known to all bankers who lend money on corporate stock as collateral. Technically, it is a pledge of personal property. It contains provisions authorizing the bank, in the event of default, to declare an acceleration of the debt, to hold a pledgee's sale in its own offices, and to bid at its own sale. As security, Owner assigns his beneficial interest to the bank. This assignment is on a form furnished by the bank. It is lodged with *XYZ Trust Co.* As is evident, since the bank now appears on the trust company's records as the purported owner of the beneficial interest, the trust company will not execute any deeds or mortgages or honor any further assignments of the beneficial interest without the bank's consent. The property is "locked up." In case of default, the bank holds a quick pledgee's sale under the Uniform Commercial Code and bids in the beneficial interest. It places Blackacre up for sale. It finds a purchaser. It directs *XYZ Trust Co.* to make a deed to the purchaser at the closing of this sale and this is done. Everything is accomplished quickly and inexpensively. Nothing relating to the loan appears on the public records.

There is one warning. This type of deal will not work where the landowner deeds the land into the trust and simultaneously pledges the beneficial interest. This is treated as an attempted waiver of the equitable right of redemption, and under ancient principles of mortgage law the whole transaction is deemed a real estate mortgage. But those who deal in real estate find it convenient to keep their real estate holdings in a land trust. Hence this rule is no inconvenience.

REFERENCES ON PLEDGES OF LAND TRUST BENEFICIAL INTEREST: Horney v. *Hayes,* 11 Ill.2d 178, 142 NE2d 94 (1957) (60 Ill. B. J. 268, 55 Chicago Bar Rev. 64) (pledge of existing beneficial interest is valid as pledge of personal property); *Quinn* v. *Pullman T. & S. Bank,* 98 Ill. App.2d 402, 240 NE2d 791 (1968) (pledge made simultaneously with creation of land trust is ineffective as a pledge).

23.04   Vendor's lien reserved by deed

In some states, a seller, in lieu of taking back a mortgage from the buyer, expressly reserves in his deed to the buyer a lien on the land to secure payment of the balance of the purchase price. Such a lien is called a *vendor's lien.* It is really a mortgage.

EXAMPLE: Landowner conveyed to Buyer by a warranty deed which warranted that title was free from all cumbrances excepting three certain notes executed by Buyer, for which a vendor's lien was retained until said notes and the interest thereon should be fully paid. The court held that this clause created a lien on the land. Such a lien is regarded as partaking of the nature of an equitable mortgage. It is really a mortgage and is governed by the same rules as a mortgage, and must be foreclosed as such. *Crabtree* v. *Davis,* 237 Ala. 264, 186 So 734 (1939).

Such liens are governed by many of the rules applicable to mortgages.

EXAMPLE: A promissory note was given by the buyer to the seller for part of the purchase price, and the deed recited that a purchase money lien was retained for the payment of the note. The court held that the fact that the payee of the note was not mentioned in the deed did not invalidate the deed. But under Kentucky law the deed must recite the amount of purchase price remaining due if the lien is to be valid against subsequent creditors and purchasers of the property. *Campbell* v. *Salyer,* 290 Ky. 493, 161 SW2d 596 (1942).

Such a lien enjoys priority over subsequent liens and encumbrances, and, like a purchase money mortgage, has priority over prior judgments against the purchaser. The grantee under such deed does not become personally liable for the purchase money, unless he has signed a promissory note or otherwise obligated himself personally to pay the debt. And a purchaser from such grantee does not become personally liable to the holder of the vendor's lien unless by his deed he assumes and agrees to pay the unpaid balance of the debt. The debt may be assigned, and the assignee will have the right to foreclose the lien.

23.05   Buy-down

Developers have engaged in the practice of "buying down" the buyer's interest rate. The developer pays a lump sum or agrees to pay a stated sum to a lender who agrees to finance the buyer's purchase. If the developer is committing to pay instead of paying, he may deposit a sum in the lender's savings account deposits as security for his advancing funds. The developer's money operates as an inducement to the lender to reduce the borrower's interest payments for a period of time, often three years.

Often, this is done on a sliding scale. The largest reduction in the buyer's interest rates occurs in the first year and the smallest in the third year. The obvious purpose here is to "hook" the buyer. Most people tend to think of their problems *now*, not three years from now.

At the end of the third year the mortgage payments move up to the market rate. Or in some cases there is a balloon at the end of the third year and the buyer must refinance.

The economic philosophy urged in justification is that in three years interest rates will have moved down to a manageable level.

Some concern has been expressed about this practice. The ads in the newspapers tell the public that the interest rate is a comfortable 11 ½ percent, for example. But in fine print that follows we are told that this is for the first three years. Especially if there is a balloon, there is some concern that consumer type litigation may result.

The opinion has been expressed that the amounts paid by the developer to the lender are tax deductible.

FHA mortgages with a three-year minimum buy-down have been approved by HUD. GNMA will issue guaranteed securities secured by FHA buy-down mortgages. FNMA will purchase buy-downs. It is comforting, in a way, to see this government stamp of approval placed on the buy-downs. No doubt courts will be strongly impressed by this approval if the buy-downs come under fire.

24 REAL ESTATE FINANCE—FORECLOSURE AND REDEMPTION

24.01 In general

After default, today's lender exhausts all possibility of effecting a "workout," extension of time, moratorium on payment, sale of the property to a creditworthy buyer, deed in lieu of foreclosure, and the like. Any of these is preferable to foreclosure. If these alternatives fail, and foreclosure becomes necessary, it is, of course, handled according to local law. Even after foreclosure has begun, a workout is possible until a foreclosure sale has taken place. Even after the foreclosure sale, perhaps half of the states allow the owner a period of redemption, permitting the borrower to retain ownership of the property until that period has expired. The foreclosure and redemption process are technical "lawyer law" problems.

As to the "workout" by agreement of a large, defaulted mortgage, see Kaster, Hershman, and Roegge, *Realty Interests Default and Rescue*, PLI (1974).

24.02 Types of foreclosures

Methods of foreclosure vary from state to state. A common method involves a court proceeding filed by the mortgagee, called a foreclosure suit. In such suits the court orders a public auction sale of the property, and the sale is held by an officer of the court. Up to the time of the foreclosure sale, the mortgagor, his wife, any junior mortgagee, or even the mortgagor's tenant may come in, pay off the mortgage, and stop the foreclosure. This, you will remember, is the equitable right of redemption. In states that have statutory redemption, the highest bidder at the foreclosure sale usually receives a certificate of sale reciting that he will be entitled to a deed if no redemption is made. In states that do not have a statutory redemption period, the highest bidder receives a deed to the land, and this deed gives him ownership of the mortgaged land, free and clear of the rights of the mortgagor.

24.03 Statutory redemption

The equitable right of redemption is cut off by a sale under a foreclosure judgment, or decree, since that was the object of the foreclosure suit. After the foreclosure sale, in many states, an entirely different right arises, called the statutory right of redemption. Laws providing for statutory redemption give the mortgagor and other persons interested in the land, or certain classes of such persons, the right to redeem from the sale within a certain period, usually one year, but varying in different states from two months to two years after the sale.

Most statutory redemption laws were passed in a time when America was predominantly agricultural. Most mortgagors were farmers. When the weather was bad, crops failed, and foreclosures followed. It seemed logical to suppose that the next year might bring better weather and good crops. Hence laws created the statutory redemption period, usually one year, and usually the law was so worded that the mortgagor had the right to possession during that year.

At the expiration of the redemption period, if redemption has not been made, the purchaser at the foreclosure sale receives a deed from the officer who made the sale.

Statutory redemption is usually accomplished by payment to the officer who made the sale of the amount of the foreclosure sale plus interest. After redemption the mortgagor holds the land free and clear of the mortgage.

In a number of states there is no statutory redemption after sale. Immediately after the foreclosure sale a deed is given to the purchaser, and he thereupon acquires ownership of the land. In states that do not permit redemption after the foreclosure sale, provision is often made for postponing the sale in some way in order to permit the mortgagor to effect a redemption or discharge of the mortgage prior to the foreclosure sale.

24.04 Deficiency judgment

A mortgage foreclosure sale is regarded as a payment of the mortgage debt in an amount equal to the sale price. If the foreclosure judgment, or decree, finds that there is $5,000 due to the mortgagee on his mortgage, and the property is sold for $4,500, the mortgage debt is thereby reduced by $4,500, leaving a deficiency of $500 due the mortgagee. Since by virtue of the promissory note that usually accompanies a mortgage, the mortgagor becomes personally liable to the mortgagee for the mortgage debt, the mortgagee is entitled to a personal judgment against the mortgagor for the amount of the deficiency.

In many states, laws have been passed limiting the mortgagee's right to a deficiency decree.

24.05 Foreclosure by exercise of power of sale

In many states, mortgages may be foreclosed by exercise of a power of sale without resort to any court proceedings. If the mortgage is, in form, a trust deed, a provision will be found therein conferring on the trustee the power to sell the land in the event of a default in the mortgage payments. If the instrument is a regular mortgage, the power of sale is conferred on the mortgagee. However, in Colorado, the power of sale must be exercised by an official known as the public trustee, and in Minnesota, the sale is made by the sheriff or his deputy.

In states where this method of foreclosure is employed, the mortgage or trust deed spells out the events of default that will give the trustee or mortgagee power to sell the premises, and it also sets forth the notice of sale that must be given and the other formalities that must be complied with in making the sale. The state law may also specify the notice of sale that is to be given. In some states, personal notice to the mortgagor is necessary, but in others, advertisement is sufficient. Some state laws provide that a notice of default must be recorded and a stated period of time must elapse thereafter before the sale is held. This gives the mortgagor a final opportunity to pay his debt.

At one time, concern was expressed over the validity of the power of sale in the aftermath of United States Supreme Court decisions which held that pre-judgment seizures of chattels violated the due process clause of the fourteenth amendment. See, e.g., *North Georgia Finishing, Inc.* v. *Di-Chem, Inc.,*, 419 U.S. 601 (1975). The debate centered on whether power-of-sale foreclosures of real property were constitutional in the absence of prior notice and a hearing for the benefit of the defaulting mortgagor. Recent cases have upheld the nonjudicial power-of-sale foreclosure process. *Flagg Bros.* v. *Brooks,* 436 U.S. 149; 56 L. Ed. 2d. 185; 28 De Paul L. Rev. 523; 27 Kan L. Rev. 674 (1978). This is a necessary decision. The incredible inflation of home prices requires that expensive time-consuming judicial foreclosures end.

While the consumer movement has not ultimately prevailed in the courtroom in this area of the law, the earlier court decisions and consumer lobbies have succeeded in enacting amendments to the power-of-sale foreclosure laws of the various states. The new laws have been generally directed toward requiring that the borrower and other parties with an interest in the real estate be given a more effective notice of the impending foreclosure.

> **EXAMPLE:** Prior law in Texas merely required the posting of a notice of the foreclosure at three public places for three weeks prior to the sale. Obviously, this method is not the best reasonable method of notifying the debtor of the foreclosure sale. The amendment to that law requires the posting of such notices at the local courthouse and a certified mail notice to the debtor. Vernan's (Texas) Ann. Civ. St. Art. 3810.

Unless the mortgage allows him to do so, the mortgagee cannot purchase the property at his own foreclosure sale, either in his own or his wife's name, or in the name of some third party, and if he does so, the sale may be set aside. *Mills* v. *Mutual B. & L. Assn.,* 6 SE2d 549 (N.C. 1940). The trustee in a deed of trust is likewise forbidden to purchase at his own foreclosure sale. However, the holder of the note secured by a deed of trust is permitted to purchase at the trustee's sale. Deed of trust forms usually expressly permit the trustee to bid at the foreclosure sale, and such provisions are valid. Experience indicates that there will be fewer lawsuits attacking a foreclosure sale if the sale is held by some impartial individual. A lender who uses some individual in his employment as trustee in his deeds of trust often finds it expedient to appoint some disinterested third party as trustee if foreclosure becomes necessary.

The sale is usually at public auction, and a deed is executed to the highest bidder. Whether or not redemption is allowed depends on the local law.

24.06 Foreclosure by other methods

Other methods of foreclosure—strict foreclosure, foreclosure by entry and possession, and foreclosure by writ of entry—are allowed in a small number of states. These involve technical procedures that are only of local interest.

24.07 Foreclosure— conscionable conduct

No matter what the method of foreclosure may be, lenders must always be mindful that today's courts protect consumers, and in the mortgage transaction the borrower is the consumer. Evidence of the protection given to borrowers may be found in recent cases requiring lenders to ascertain the reasons for default and make a concerted effort to avoid foreclosure by voluntary forbearance or recasting the mortgage. *FNMA* v. *Bryant,* 378 NE2d 333 (Ill. 1978); *Hamm* v. *Taylor,* 429 A2d 946 (Conn. 1981); 1976 Utah L. Rev. 327; *FNMA* v. *Ricks,* 372 N.Y.S. 485 (N.Y. 1975). While these cases may apply to a particular class of lenders (FHA and VA mortgagees) and have been undercut by subsequent proclamations by the Department of Housing and Urban Development, the decisions once again announce to lenders that conduct toward borrowers must be conscionable or foreclosure will not be allowed. Kratovil, *Mortgage Law Today,* 13 John Marsh L. Rev. 251, 265 (1980).

EXAMPLE: Borrower lost his job and fell four payments in arrears on his mortgage. Lender began foreclosure proceedings whereupon Borrower once again employed, tendered the past due payments. Lender refused the tender because it did not include the attorney's fees incurred in beginning foreclosure. Foreclosure would not be allowed as Lender's conduct was unconscionable. *Brown* v. *Lynn,* 385 F. Supp. 986. (1974).

REFERENCE: 53 Chi-Kent L. Rev. 703 (1976).

These decisions are reflections of not only the law but also the "fireside equity" practiced by many judges when they sit in foreclosure courts. Frequently, foreclosure will not be allowed unless the borrower is at least three or four payments behind and good faith settlement negotiations have produced no results.

24.08 Foreclosure sale— bankruptcy problems

Recently, federal courts have introduced a new uncertainty into foreclosure law.

EXAMPLE: Land worth $200,000 was mortgaged to secure a $75,000 debt. The loan falls into default and foreclosure occurs with the mortgagee being the purchaser at the foreclosure sale. The mortgagee's successful bid was the amount of the mortgage debt including principal, interest, and foreclosure costs. The lender thereby acquires property supposedly worth $200,000 for only slightly more than $75,000.

If the debtor goes into bankruptcy shortly after the foreclosure sale, the interest of the mortgagee, now owner of the property, may be in jeopardy. The trustee in bankruptcy has the duty to enlarge the bankrupt's estate by attempting to return to the estate any property that was conveyed for less than full value. The trustee will attack the foreclosure sale as a fraudulent transfer (it being for less than the value of the property) to return the property to the estate.

This attack is based upon the provision of the bankruptcy law that avoids a transfer made within one year of the bankruptcy filing if the debtor received less than a reasonably equivalent value. 11 USC § 548 (a) (2) (A). In some recent decisions decided under the old bankruptcy law, a court has accepted the trustee's arguments. *Abramson* v. *Lakewood Bank*, 647 F2d 547 (5th Cir. 1981); *Durrett* v. *Washington Nat. Ins. Co.*, 621 F2d 201 (5th Cir. 1980). It is thought that this same result will follow under the new bankruptcy law.

These decisions are subject to criticism on several grounds. First, if a debtor has any equity in the property, he will generally try to sell the property or borrow against it to cure the default and save the equity. If the sale or refinance cannot be accomplished, the indications are that there is no real value over the encumbrances. Second, foreclosure sales are advertised public sales. The failure of bidders to bid over the mortgage debt is the best evidence that the foreclosure sale brought a reasonably equivalent value in exchange for the property at that time and under those circumstances.

24.09 Foreclosure— bankruptcy stay

Bankruptcy proceedings are designed to collect the debtor's assets and then either liquidate the debtor's estate or restructure the debt payment schedules to allow the debtor to continue. Under either course of action, the bankruptcy trustee needs time to study the value of these assets. When the bankruptcy petition is filed, however, the debtor is usually in the midst of lawsuits and foreclosures caused by defaults on his loans and accounts. To give the bankruptcy trustee the time needed to inventory and evaluate the assets, the bankruptcy law provides that the filing of the bankruptcy stays or prohibits the commencement or continuation of any proceedings against the bankrupt, including the enforcement of liens against the debtor's property. 11 USC §362 (a). The stay stops such foreclosures until the creditor successfully petitions the court to vacate or modify the stay.

24.10 Mortgagee as purchaser at foreclosure sale

For several reasons, the mortgagee is often the only bidder at the foreclosure sale. The mortgagee is allowed to bid up to the amount of the mortgage debt without producing any cash. The reason is obvious. If he were to pay cash, the officer holding the sale would have to hand the cash back to him in payment of the mortgage debt, for after all, the sale is held to raise money to pay the mortgagee. Again, in states that have redemption laws the highest bidder will not get ownership of or possession of the property until the redemption period is over, and then only if no redemption is made. Land speculators, who are the chief bidders at public land sales, are unwilling to have their money tied up for long periods with such uncertainty as to ultimate ownership of the property.

24.11 Mortgagee as owner

Whenever and however the mortgagee becomes the owner of the property (either by foreclosure or deed in lieu of foreclosure), he must take all the precautions that an owner takes.

Immediately after the foreclosure sale, existing insurance policies must be indorsed to give protection to the mortgagee as an owner, or new policies must be obtained. Reliance on the old policy may be misplaced, since satisfaction of the debt by purchaser at the foreclosure sale or in the deed in lieu transaction satisfies the mortgage debt and may simultaneously extinguish the lender's protection. *Whitestone Savings & Loan Assn.* v. *Allstate Ins. Co.,* 270 NE2d 694 (N.Y. 1971). The necessity of other insurance such as liability, workmen's compensation, dram shop, and so forth should be determined. Since foreclosure usually extinguishes any leases entered into after the mortgage, new arrangements should be entered into with the tenants. *Kage* v. *1795 Dunn Road, Inc.,* 428 SW2d 735 (Mo. 1968). A new owner's title insurance policy should be obtained, and the currency and amount of real estate taxes and assessment payments should be examined. Inquiry should be made of the desirability of retaining or releasing the building manager. The building itself should be inspected for conditions potentially dangerous to tenants, compliance with local, state, and federal safety laws as they apply both to employees and others, and conditions that could damage the building or hinder its marketability.

REFERENCE: Kratovil and Werner, *Modern Mortgage Law and Practice,* Ch. 41, "Foreclosure," (2d ed. 1979).

---

25 LAND USE CONTROLS— BUILDING RESTRICTIONS

25.01 Private and public controls distinguished

Use of land is controlled in two ways, namely, through *private* controls and through *public* controls.

EXAMPLE: *A* buys 100 acres of farmland and divides it into 100 residential lots by means of a recorded plat of subdivision which specifies that all lots must be used only for the construction of single-family dwellings. This is *private* control of use of land by means of building restrictions.

EXAMPLE: The city of *X* adopts a zoning ordinance by which part of the city is zoned for residential use, part for stores, and part for industry. This is *public* control of land use.

Private land use controls rest on the philosophy that where private ownership of land is recognized, as it is in America, ownership of land includes the right to sell it on such terms as please the landowner, including the right to restrict the future use of the land in some way that seems desirable *to the seller.*

There is a parallel, but quite different philosophy, namely, that use of land must be controlled, not in the interest of private individuals as such, but in the public interest. Both methods coexist under our American law with some overlapping and some conflict.

Historically, private controls antedate public controls by many years. Hundreds of years ago in England, a landowner might have given away his land and included some whimsical or capricious requirements in his gift that, while legally enforceable, contributed nothing toward the practical control of land use.

EXAMPLE: Gifts on the following conditions were sustained by the courts: that the donor reside in the house on the land; that donee would lose the land if he were educated abroad; that donee must always write his name "T. Jackson Mason''; that the minister of donee's church always wear a black gown in the pulpit. 65 U. of Pa. L. R. 527.

If you bought a home in those early days, there was nothing to prevent your neighbor from constructing a slaughterhouse, tannery, or other offensive use adjoining your dwelling. Thus matters continued until 1848, when the courts first evolved the idea that if a land developer deeds out all the lots in the subdivision with identical restrictions providing, for example, that only single-family dwellings are permitted in the subdivision, *any lot owner can obtain a court order preventing any other lot owner from violating this restriction.* This was one of the great milestones in the history of law.

While this innovation was truly of immense importance, and remains so, certain problems arose.

> **EXAMPLE:**   A plat of subdivision provides that only single-family residences shall be erected in the subdivision, and houses are built and sold in reliance on this restriction. *X* buys land across the street from the subdivision and erects a tannery thereon. There is nothing the homeowners can do.

For this reason, much later, and not really effectively until 1926 when the United States Supreme Court first sustained the validity of zoning ordinances, a new kind of land use control came into being, namely, a system of *public controls,* implemented by a *zoning ordinance* allocating permitted uses to the various areas of the city. This was and is a far more effective system of land use controls, one that controls the entire area of the city. In an area the city has zoned as residential only, which may and usually does embrace an area greatly exceeding in extent the area one private developer might acquire and restrict, all homeowners are protected against offensive uses.

This development, however, has not rendered private building restrictions obsolete.

> **EXAMPLE:**   *A* land developer acquires 40 acres of land in an area zoned by the city for single-family residences. He records a plat of subdivision which contains restrictions that no residence shall be erected costing less than $75,000. This the city cannot do. Yet it definitely restricts the occupancy of the area in a way that seems desirable to the developer and his customers.

25.02 Private restrictions in general

Private restrictions fall into five main categories:

1. Whimsical or capricious restrictions imposed by the seller because of some whim or prejudice, such as a restriction that neither tobacco nor liquor shall be used on the premises sold or that there shall be no card playing on the premises.

2. Covenants for the benefits of land sold or land retained. These last are restrictions imposed by a landowner who owns two adjoining tracts of land and sells one of them.

> **EXAMPLE:** *A*, owning Lots 1 and 2, with a house on Lot 1, sells vacant Lot 2 with a clause in the deed that no building shall be erected in the front thirty feet of the lot. This protects the view from the front of *A*'s house. Or *A* could have sold the house lot, with a restriction that no buildings shall be erected on the front thirty feet of the lot retained.

3. Restrictions imposed by a subdivider or land developer with a view to making the subdivision attractive, such as a restriction that only single-family dwellings shall be erected in the subdivision. This is the most important category. These are the restrictions that create a *general plan.*

4. Affirmative covenants running with the land, discussed later herein.

5. Conditions. These are restrictions providing for a reverter of title if they are violated. They also are discussed later.

25.03   Creation of general plan restrictions

In order to attract lot purchasers, a subdivider or land developer often evolves a building scheme or general plan for restricting the lots in the tract undergoing development to obtain substantial uniformity in building and use. For example, the plan often contemplates that only residences shall be erected, thus excluding stores and industrial uses. The effect is to create a restriction that any lot owner may enforce against any other lot owner. Restrictions upon the use of property, imposed as a part of general plan for the benefit of all lots, give to the purchaser of any lot a right to enforce such restrictions against the purchaser of any other lot. Such restrictions are enforced on the theory that each purchaser buying with knowledge or notice of the general plan impliedly agrees to abide by the plan. 26 CJS *Deeds* 167.

> **EXAMPLE:** The map or plat of a certain subdivision provides that all the subdivision lots shall be used for residence purposes only. *A*, one of the lot owners, seeks to open a store on his lot. Any lot owner can obtain an injunction preventing *A* from using his lot for store purposes.

25.03(a)   Notice of general plan

It must be stressed at this point that there are two important ingredients here. (1) The *general plan* created by the uniform restrictions. (2) Notice of the general plan created on recording, usually of the plat or declaration of restrictions.

General plan restrictions were originally created by incorporating identical restrictions in all deeds by the subdivider. *Field Ppties, Inc.* v. *Fritz,* 315 So2d 101 (Fla. 1976); 4 ALR2d 1364. This is not the usual practice today. The character that a particular development is to assume is planned at the same time that the acreage is first subdivided into building lots. The subdivider incorporates in the recorded plat or map of the subdivision itself uniform restrictions to which all lots are subject. Clearly the plan is general. *Case* v. *Morisette,* 475 F2d 1300 (1973). It is best to have each deed state, "subject to restrictions in recorded plat." And since every lot purchaser must take notice of the recorded plat, he has constructive notice of the restriction. Therefore any lot owner may enforce the restriction against any other lot owner. Recently these building schemes have become so elaborate that there is not enough room for them on the plat or map. Hence the restrictions are set up in a recorded *declaration of restrictions* recorded simultaneously with the plat and referred to in the plat. Legally this is as though the restrictions had been set forth in the plat. Subsequently, as sales of the lots are made, the deeds contain clauses stating that the land is subject to such recorded restrictions. Kratovil, *Building Restrictions: Contracts or Servitudes,* 11 John Marshall J. 465 (1978).

Of course, the privilege of creating restrictions is by no means confined to subdividers. Any landowner is at liberty to insert restrictions in his deed when he sells and conveys the land. An enforceable restriction may be inserted in a contract for the sale of land. The landowners in a particular area may enter into an agreement subjecting their land to restrictions.

25.03(b)   Enforcement of general plan restrictions

If a general plan restriction is violated, the court will issue an order (injunction) forbidding the violation. Anyone who disobeys the order can be jailed. Structures erected in violation thereof can be ordered demolished. *Stewart* v. *Finkelstone,* 206 Mass. 28, 92 NE 37 (1910). The general plan creates rights known as *equitable servitudes.* The *benefit* and *burden* of those equitable servitudes attaches to each lot in the subdivision. For a general plan restriction to be enforced, the one seeking enforcement need only show that the violator purchased his lot with notice of the restriction, either from a recorded document or from actual knowledge of the restriction. The question as to enforcement of a general plan type restriction, then, arises when one lot owner attempts to violate a restriction, and another lot owner seeks a court order prohibiting such attempted violation. The court will ask two questions: (1) Is there a general plan? (2) If there is, did the violator purchase his land with actual knowledge or with notice from the public records of the existence of the general plan? If the answer to these questions is in the affirmative, the restriction will be enforced, except in the situations hereafter discussed.

As to who may enforce a general plan restriction, any lot owner, or his tenant or mortgagee, or contract purchaser may do so. 51 ALR3d 556; 26 CJS *Deeds* § 167. As long as the subdivider owns any lot in the subdivision he can enforce the restriction. However, when he has sold the last lot, he no longer has any economic interest to protect. Nearly all courts say that he thereupon loses his right to enforce. *Kent* v. *Koch,* 333 P2d 411 (Cal. 1958); *Canel Coal* v. *Indiana,* 78 Ind. App. 115, 134 NE 891 (1922).

The conscientious developer continues to want orderly development of his subdivision even after his last lot is sold. He will therefore create a home owners' association in the form of a nonprofit corporation at the time he creates his subdivision. The plat or declaration of restrictions confers on this association the right to enforce the general plan restrictions. As lots are sold, the lot owners become members of this association. They pay dues to the association, and a fund is thus formed to finance, among other things, a lawsuit if a violation of the restrictions is threatened. This device is valid. *Neponsit Property Owners Assn.* v. *Emigrant Industrial Svgs. Bank,* 278 N.Y. 248, 15 NE2d 793 (1938); *Merrionette Manor Homes Impt. Assn.* v. *Heda,* 11 Ill. App.2d 186, 136 NE2d 556 (1956).

25.03(c) Interpretation of general plan restrictions

The problem of framing restrictions that will carry out the intention of the subdivider is a difficult one. Much litigation has centered around this point. 20 Am.Jur.2d 752; 26 CJS *Deeds* § 164.

25.03(c)(1) Location restrictions

When the plat or map of a subdivision shows a line designated as a building line extending across the front portion of the subdivision lots, this is sufficient to create a building line restriction. No substantial parts of buildings may then be erected beyond the building line. Building line restrictions may also be created by restrictions in the deed. The purpose of a building line is twofold: to insure a certain degree of uniformity in the appearance of the buildings and to create a right to unobstructed light, air and vision. The fact that a small porch, awning, stoop, steps, or an overhanging bay window extends beyond the building line will not constitute a violation of the restriction.

In dealing with the interpretation of building restrictions, keep in mind that the courts are trying to discover and give effect to the intention of the subdivider. Where he leaves his intention in doubt, the court faces a difficult problem. It must be as practical as possible. Common sense must be applied. The literal language of the restriction must often be disregarded. Certainly, common sense dictates that minor violations of restrictions must be disregarded. The problem concerns where to draw the line. What, for example, is a "small porch"? However, a so-called bay window that is really the front wall of the house is a violation of the restriction. 55 ALR 332, 172 ALR 1324. Likewise, a carport is part of the house and is a violation. *Garden Oaks* v. *Gibbs,* 489 SW2d 133 (Tex. 1972).

CAUTION: When a restriction provides that no building shall be erected within a certain number of feet of the street line, it is the line where the lot meets the street that is meant. In other words, some plat of a subdivision shows this particular lot as fronting on some street. Where the lot ends, the street begins. Often enough, to be sure, the city paves only the middle part of the street strip, and laymen sometimes speak of this as the "street," which is erroneous. The street extends to the lot line and includes not only the roadway, but also the parkway or planted area, if any, sidewalks, if any, and so on. Building line restrictions are measured from the true street line, not from the curb line. *Trunck* v. *Hack's Point,* 204 Md. 193, 103 A2d 343 (1954).

25.03(c)(2)   Incidental use   A use purely incidental to a permitted use is permitted.

> **EXAMPLE:**   Shop in hotel. *Blakely* v. *Gorin,* 313 NE2d 903 (Mass. 1974).

25.03(c)(3)   Residence   Many restrictions provide that "the land shall be
purposes   used for residence purposes" or that "only residences shall be erected on this real estate." Under this type of restriction, any kind of building devoted exclusively to residence purposes may be erected, including a duplex house or an apartment building. 14 ALR2d 1376. If the restriction permits construction of only "private," "single," or "detached" residences, only single-family dwellings are permitted. *Flaks* v. *Wichman,* 128 Colo. 45, 260 P2d 737 (1953). But the renting of homes will be permitted. *Gilbert* v. *Shenandoah Valley Assn.,* 592 SW2d 28 (Tex. 1979).

25.03(c)(4)   History of   When the general plan restriction was born in
apartment role   1848, apartments were virtually unknown in most of America. The first apartments in Chicago, for example, appeared in the 1870s. In Detroit the first apartment was built in 1892. It is not surprising, then, that the early restriction schemes, those antedating 1880, were drawn by subdividers and their lawyers on the blissful assumption that all that was needed was protection of homes against *factories.* When the construction of apartments began, it was discovered that the early restriction schemes were lacking in protection against *apartments.*

If the owner occupies his residence, he may take in lodgers. *Shaver* v. *Hunter,* 626 SW2d 574 (Tex. 1981). However, if the building is completely converted into a boarding house, the restriction is violated, for this is a business rather than a residential use. Use of the premises as a tourist home also violates a residential restriction. *Deitrick* v. *Leadbetter,* 175 Va. 170, 8 SE2d 276 (1940). If the restriction provides that the premises shall be used only as a residence for *one private family,* this will prevent the letting of rooms to lodgers. *Sayles* v. *Hall,* 210 Mass. 281, 96 NE 712 (1911). It will also prevent the doubling up of two or more families. *See* 21 ALR3d 641 (incidental or accessory uses).

25.03(c)(5)   Tandem house   A new type of home is making its appearance as a result of rising construction costs. It has a bedroom and bath on each of opposite ends of the home. In between is a shared kitchen and living room. The home is purchased jointly by those who regard this as purely a sharing of costs. Obviously, it cannot be constructed where the restriction permits only one family.

25.03(c)(6)   Dwelling   Restrictions sometimes limit use of the land to *dwelling purposes.* 38 ALR3d 1419. In Illinois, New Jersey, North Carolina, Ohio, and Pennsylvania, such restrictions do not prohibit the erection of apartment buildings since apartment buildings are "dwellings." *Leverich* v. *Roy,* 338 Ill. App. 248, 87 NE2d 226 (1949); 14 ALR2d 1376. However, in Massachusetts, Michigan, and New Hampshire, apartments are not considered to be *dwellings.* Townhouses are not "dwellings." *Shapiro* v. *Levin,* 223 Pa. Super. 536 (1973).

25.03(c)(7) Condominium   A multifamily condominum is a violation of a restriction that forbids apartments. It is not a group of single-family dwellings. 65 ALR3d 1212.

25.03(c)(8) Form   A good residential restriction might read as follows:

> **SUGGESTED FORM:** Only one detached single-family dwelling and private attached garage appertaining thereto shall be erected on each lot. No use shall be made of said premises except such as is incidental to the occupation thereof for residence purposes by one private family residing in a detached, single-family dwelling.

This form has the following advantages: The phrase "single-family dwelling" keeps out apartments and other multiple dwellings. Single dwellings will not do the trick because in some states, a restriction against single dwellings does not prohibit a duplex or apartment.

Vocabulary is important. A *duplex* consists of two single-family dwellings, each on its own lot, but sharing a party wall that straddles the line between the lots. A duplex is permitted on land restricted to residence purposes. 99 ALR3d 985. A *bi-level* is a two-story house designed for occupancy by one family. A *two-flat* is a building with two apartments, one above the other, designed for occupancy by two families. A two-flat is not a single-family dwelling. 14 ALR2d 1376. The use of the word "detached" keeps out duplexes or row houses. The stipulation as to occupation by one private family keeps out lodgers and prevents doubling up of families.

If a restriction merely specifies the type of building that can be built but is silent regarding the use of the building, an argument may be advanced that the building can be used for any purpose. As a rule, courts try to give effect to the obvious intention by holding that use of the structures must conform to the purposes for which it was erected. 155 ALR 1000.

> **EXAMPLE:** A restriction provided that "no structure shall be built except for dwelling purposes." A dwelling was erected. Later, the owner of the dwelling attempted to use it as a beauty parlor. The court held that the building could be used only for dwelling purposes. *Holderness* v. *Central States Finance Corp.,* 241 Mich. 604, 217 NW 764 (1928). Obviously, the restriction was badly drafted. If it had been properly drafted, litigation could not have arisen. Accord: *J. T. Hobb & Son* v. *Family Homes,* 274 SE2d 174 (N.C. 1981).

The restriction should restrict the use of the *land* as well as use of the *building.* If the restriction deals only with use of the building, the argument may be advanced that any use of the land is permitted. *Albrecht* v. *State Highway Commission,* 363 SW2d 643 (Mo. 1963). Again, courts will usually come to the rescue by holding that the intention was to restrict use of both building and land.

> **EXAMPLE:** A restriction provided that no building erected on the land should be used for any purpose other than as a private dwelling place. The landowner attempted to use the vacant land as a parking lot. He contended that the restriction applied only to the use of buildings and therefore did not apply to vacant land. The court held that it was the intention to restrict use of both building and land. *Hoover* v. *Waggoman,* 52 N.M. 371, 199 P2d 991 (1948); 155 ALR 528, 1007. It has even been held that a restriction calling for only one detached *single-family* dwelling per lot impliedly forbids occupancy by two families. *Freeman* v. *Gee,* 423 P2d 155 (Utah 1967).

25.03(c)(9)   Family

A few liberal decisions hold that a group of mentally retarded persons living together constitutes a "family." *Malcolm* v. *Shamic,* 290 NW2d 101 (Mich. 1980). *State* v. *District Court,* 609 P2d 245 (Mont. 1980). *J.T. Hobb & Sons* v. *Family Homes,* 274 SE2d 174 (NC 1981); 71 ALR3d 725.

25.03(c)(10)   Duplex

Often one will hear the argument that a duplex is really two single-family dwellings connected by a party wall with one building on each lot. *Stephenson* v. *Perlitz,* 537 SW2d 287 (Tex. 1976); *Easterly* v. *Hall,* 182 SE2d 671 (S.C. 1971). To keep out duplexes, it is therefore advisable to have your restriction read that only one *detached* single-family dwelling may be built on each lot. *Freeman* v. *Gee,* 423 P2d 155 (Utah 1967); 99 ALR 3d 985.

25.03(c)(11)   Business purposes

When the restriction forbids use of the premises for business purposes, the following are not permitted: gasoline filling stations, billboards, and parking for business purposes. Especially in older deeds, one is likely to find restrictions prohibiting use of the property for a "trade or business." Suppose a doctor uses a room of his home as an office for the practice of medicine. This would not violate such a restriction because the practice of medicine is not a *trade* or *business;* it is a *profession. Auerbacher* v. *Smith,* 19 N.J. Super. 191, 88 A2d 262 (1952); 21 ALR3d 641.

25.04   Senior citizens

There are, of course, numerous subdivisions restricted to senior citizens. This is accomplished by means of general plan type restrictions in a declaration of restrictions. They are valid. *Riley* v. *Stoves,* 526 P2d 747 (Ariz. 1974); 68 ALR3d 1239.

SUGGESTION TO DRAFTSMAN: Since the old law frowns on restrictions on the *sale* of land, frame your restrictions in terms of restrictions on *occupancy* since these present no legal problem. Because of the desperate housing shortage and the tendency of condo developers to bar occupancy by children, the argument is being made that barring children is illegal. This is an unresolved issue. A genuine senior citizens community will probably survive attack. 100 ALR3d 241. *See* § 32.03 (d).

25.05 Defective restrictions

Many restrictions are so poorly drafted that they fail to achieve their main purpose.

EXAMPLE: A restriction provided that "no flat roof dwelling house shall be erected." Since no other type of building was mentioned, a flat roof church could be erected. *Corbridge* v. *Westminster,* 18 Ill. App.2d 245, 151 NE2d 822 (1958).

You can see that many restrictions, particularly the older ones, are negative in form. They contain enumerations of prohibited uses, such as apartments and businesses. Such devices are doomed to failure. In the first place, nobody ever makes the list of excluded uses long enough, and nobody, of course, can cover the uses that do not even exist today but will crop up in the future. This is why, particularly for residential property, modern restriction plans simply specify the one type of permitted use, that is, "only detached single-family dwellings shall be constructed, and the premises shall be used only as a residence for one private family."

25.06 Plans of buildings

Often a scheme of restrictions provides that no building shall be erected until the plans and specifications therefor have been approved by the developer or subdivider. Such provisions are valid, but any refusal to approve plans will be set aside by the courts if such refusal is capricious, arbitrary, or unreasonable. *Hannula* v. *Hacienda Homes,* 34 Cal. App.2d 442, 211 P2d 302 (1949); 19 ALR2d 1268; 47 ALR3d 1232.

25.07 Ingress and egress for a prohibited use

Occasionally, a lot in a restricted residential subdivision is acquired by one who seeks to use it for the benefit of nonresidential land outside the subdivision. This is not permitted.

EXAMPLE: A plat restriction permitted only residential use of the lots. *X*, who owned a restaurant across the street from the subdivision, bought three lots in the subdivision, meaning to use them for access to the restaurant and parking. The court prohibited this. *Bennett* v. *Consolidated Realty Co.,* 226 Ky. 747, 11 SW2d 910, 61 ALR 453 (1928); 25 ALR2d 904.

25.08 Modification, extension, and release of general plan restrictions

If the right to modify general plan is not reserved in the deeds, plat, or declaration, it takes a unanimous vote of all lot owners (probably also their mortgagees) to modify or release the restrictions. *Steve Vogli & Co.* v. *Lane,* 405 SW2d 885 (Mo. 1966); 4 ALR3d 570. This is rarely obtainable.

> **EXAMPLE:** All owners but one signed a release of the restrictions. He was entitled to enforce the restrictions. *Evangelical Church* v. *Sahlem,* 254 N.Y. 161, 172 NE 455 (1930).

In recent restriction plans, subdividers have often included a clause giving themselves the right to waive or dispense with the restrictions as to some or all of the lots. This is dangerous. A number of courts have held that such a provision destroys the uniformity necessary to a general plan, and therefore the restrictions cannot be enforced by one lot owner against another. 19 ALR2d 1282.

When the right to modify the restrictions is reserved to the developer by the deeds, plat, or declaration, he may validly exercise this right. *McComb* v. *Harly,* 132 N.J.Eq. 182, 26 A2d 891; 4 ALR2d 570.

In providing for periodical extensions and modifications of the restrictions in the declaration, thought must be given to the voting arrangements.

> **EXAMPLE:** There is a difference between "the owners of a majority of the lots" and "a majority of the lot owners."

Where the right to modify restrictions is reserved in the plat, declaration of restrictions or deeds, any modifications voted by the required majority must be general in their nature.

> **EXAMPLE:** A majority of the landowners voted to take one lot out of the restrictions so that a filling station be erected on it. This was invalid. *Riley* v. *Boyle,* 434 P2d 525.

Any amendment must be reasonable and must leave the plan basically intact. *Flamingo Ranch Estates* v. *Sunshine Ranchers,* 303 So2d 665 (Fla. 1974).

25.09 Mortgage foreclosure

One must exercise care concerning any mortgage that is recorded prior in time to the declaration of restrictions.

> **EXAMPLE:** Owner records a construction mortgage on some vacant but subdivided land to Lender. Thereafter Owner records a declaration of restrictions. He sells a few lots, and deeds are recorded to the buyers. Then he defaults on his mortgage, which is foreclosed. The restrictions are wiped out by the foreclosure.

Boyd v. *Park Realty Corp.,* 137 Md. 36, 111 A 129 (1920); *Saín* v. *Silvestre,* 144 Cal. Reptr. 478 (1978).

The construction mortgage should have stated that it was subject to a declaration of restrictions to be recorded later, or simultaneously with the recording of the declaration of restrictions Lender could have recorded a subordination of his mortgage to the restrictions.

25.10   Minor violations

Earlier, it was stated that courts will not force removal of trivial encroachments. A court is a tribunal where revenge or punishment in the way of reprisal has no place. *Kajawski* v. *Null,* 177 A2d 101 (Pa. 1962). The courts will "balance the equities." *De Marco* v. *Palazzolo,* 209 NW2d 540 (Mich. 1973). If an unintentional minor violation of a restriction is involved, the courts will not compel its removal. This has been explained in connection with location restrictions. The same rule applies to other violations.

> **EXAMPLE:** A restriction limited the height of buildings to twenty-five feet. By mistake, a landowner erected a building that was twenty-six feet high. The court refused to compel him to remove the offending one foot.

> **EXAMPLE:** At times a lot owner will build his home so that it extends slightly over the front building line established by the building restrictions. In the process of balancing the equities, the court will consider that compelling removal of three or four inches of a home is a disastrous burden, but such removal does little for the neighbor. Removal is rarely ordered. Note that encroachments *on a neighbor's land* of three or four inches are serious. Encroachments over a *building line* are less serious.

25.11   Factors that render general plan restrictions unenforceable

In considering what factors render restrictions unenforceable, it is necessary, first of all, to distinguish between restrictions that do not provide for a reverter of title and those that do. We consider first the general plan type restrictions, which are traditionally enforced by means of an injunction, or court order, forbidding violation. Such orders are not granted lightly. Various circumstances are considered by the courts in determining whether such an order should be granted.

25.11(a)   General principles

In determining the legal duration of a restriction, which is the subject matter of much of this section, keep in mind that courts are practical. Even if the restriction recites that it will exist "forever," courts are likely to terminate it when it has become useless. *Ferguson* v. *Zion Ev. Church,* 190 P2d 1019 (Okla. 1948).

25.11(b) Change in neighborhood

A court will not, as a rule, enforce a restriction by injunction when the neighborhood has so changed in character and environment as to make it unfit to continue the original use. 4 ALR2d 1111; 53 ALR3d 492; 26 CJS *Deeds* § 171. The court will "balance the equities." That is, it will not grant an injunction that will do the plaintiff little good but will do the defendant great harm.

> **EXAMPLE:** A restriction provides that lots in the subdivision shall be used only for residence purposes. Gradually the neighborhood changes character, and stores and factories creep in. This often happens because no single homeowner wishes to incur the expense of hiring an attorney and litigating the right of his neighbors to violate the restrictions. When it becomes impossible to characterize the area as residential, courts will refuse to enforce the restriction on the ground that it is no longer possible to carry the original plan into effect. However, if the change in neighborhood affects only a part of the subdivision while the remainder is unchanged, the restrictions may be enforced in the area that remains unchanged. *O'Neill* v. *Wolf*, 338 Ill. 508, 170 NE 669. Suppose *A* owns a house in a restricted subdivision, but six blocks away, a number of violating structures are erected. *A*'s acquiescence in these violations will not bar him from stopping a violation next door to him or in the same block. In other words, these previous violations are so remote from him that they do not constitute a change in his immediate neighborhood, nor could *A* be charged with undue neglect in enforcing his rights. *Meek* v. *Yarowsky*, 236 Mich. 251, 210 NW 226.

A question on which the courts are not in agreement relates to changes that occur outside the subdivision.

> **EXAMPLE:** A plat restriction limits the subdivision to residential uses. As the surrounding area changes, many stores are built across the street from the subdivision. Some courts insist that the front tier of lots in the subdivision must hold the line and the restrictions continue in force. *Knolls Assn.* v. *Hinton*, 389 NE2d 693 (Ill. App. 1979); *Oritz* v. *Jeter*, 479 SW2d 752; 2 Am. Law Ppty. § 9.39. Since it is not always easy to get people to buy homes across the street from the stores, other courts will allow changes of this nature to sway them in refusing enforcement of the restrictions. *Hecht* v. *Stephens*, 464 P2d 258 (Kans. 1970); *Exchange Nat. Bank* v. *City of Des Plaines*, 336 NE2d 8 (Ill. 1975).

The effect of the enactment of a zoning ordinance that conflicts with the building restrictions is considered elsewhere. *See* § 26.32.

25.11(c) Numerous violations

Even when the restricted neighborhood has not changed its general character, the right to enforce a particular restriction may be lost by abandonment. When the property owners in the subdivision have violated the restrictions and the violations have been so general as to indicate an abandonment of the original general plan, the restrictions will not be enforced. The reason for this is that the purpose of the restriction can no longer be carried out. It would be an injustice to a property owner to compel him to conform to a restriction that most of the other owners have violated when such enforcement would be of no benefit to the party seeking to enforce the restriction.

> **EXAMPLE:** A building line was established across a block consisting of fifteen lots. On nine of the lots, buildings were erected that extended across the building line. The owner of a lot that had remained vacant began construction of a building that would also violate the building line. The owner of another vacant lot sought a court order to prevent this violation. The court order was refused. The value of the building line had been destroyed by the numerous violations. *Ewersten* v. *Gerstenberg,* 186 Ill. 344, 57 NE 1051 (1900).

25.11(d) Abandonment

Even in the absence of numerous violations a landowner's acquiescence in violations of restrictions may render restrictions unenforceable. Restatement, Property § 561; 26 CJS *Deeds* § 169.

> **EXAMPLE:** A plat restricts all the lots to single-family dwellings. Without protest by others, *A* builds an apartment building on Lot 5 and *B* builds an apartment building on Lot 7. *X* now seeks to build an apartment building on Lot 6, which is sandwiched between the existing apartments. He may do so.

And there may be a *partial abandonment.* This leaves the remainder of the restrictions enforceable. *Donahoe* v. *Marston,* 547 P2d 39 (Mont. 1976).

> **EXAMPLE:** A plat restriction provided that all lots were to be used for residence purposes and only single-family dwellings could be erected. A number of two-flats were erected. Now one lot owner wishes to put in a store. He cannot do so. *Noyes* v. *McDonnell,* 398 P2d 838. Likewise minor violations of a building line furnish no excuse for major violations. *Carter* v. *Conroy,* 544 P2d 258 (Ariz. 1976).

25.11(e) Violations by party who seeks to enforce restriction

One who violates a nonreverter type restriction in some substantial degree or manner cannot procure a court injunction restraining the violation of the restriction by others. Restatement, Property § 560; 26 CJS *Deeds,* § 169, p. 1163; 4 ALR2d 1142.

> **EXAMPLE:** A plat restriction permits only single-family dwellings to be erected. *A* constructs a two-flat. His neighbor, *B,* now seeks to erect a three-flat. *A* cannot prevent this.

25.11(f) Delay in enforcing restrictions

Where a nonreverter type restriction, as distinguished from a condition, is involved, a person wishing to prevent a violation must act promptly.

EXAMPLE: A subdivision plat contains a nonreverter type building restriction forbidding the construction of anything but single-family dwellings. *X*, who owns a house in this subdivision, observes that *Y*, another lot owner, is erecting a filling station. After construction of the station has been completed, *X* files a suit to have it demolished. The court will refuse to interfere. *X* has been guilty of undue delay. 12 ALR2d 394; 36 ALR2d 861, 870. Lawyers call such delay *laches*.

25.11(g)   Restrictions about to expire by lapse of time

Many restrictions specifically state a time limit for their expiration. Suppose construction of a building that violates the restriction is begun a year or so before the restriction has expired by lapse of time. Here the courts may refuse to enforce the restriction for the simple, practical reason that to do so would be of little practical benefit.

25.11(h)   Statutes of limitations

In some states laws have been enacted limiting the period of time for bringing a suit for *violation* of a building restriction.

EXAMPLE: In Missouri, such a suit must be brought within two years after the date the restriction was violated. Sec. 516.095 Mo. Stat. New York has a two-year limitation on building line violations and in Massachusetts, the period is six years. In Massachusetts, building restrictions unlimited in duration expire after thirty years. Basye, *Clearing Land Titles* § 143 (2d ed. 1970). In Colorado a suit to enforce a restriction must be brought within one year from the date of violation. *Wolf* v. *Hallenbeck,* 123 P2d 412 (1942).

25.11(i)   State laws placing time limits on enforcement of restrictions

A number of states—Arizona, Georgia, Massachusetts, Michigan, Minnesota, Rhode Island, and Wisconsin, for example—have enacted laws providing that after the lapse of a stated number of years restrictions become unenforceable; *Payne* v. *Borkat,* 261 SE2d 393 (1979); *Baker* v. *Seneca,* 116 NE2d 325 (Mass); Basye, *Clearing Land Titles* § 143 (2d ed. 1970). And in all states having marketability of title laws, restrictions will expire after the permitted time unless kept alive by new recording as provided in the law. *Semachko* v. *Hopko,* 301 NE 2d 560 (Ohio 1973).

25.11(j)   Other factors

Courts are more merciful when the violation is not willful but is due to accident or mistake, as where my surveyor makes an error, and as a result my building extends over a building line. They are also more merciful toward minor violations than they are toward major violations. Of course, if the party seeking to enforce the restriction has said or done something that would encourage me to go ahead with the violation, he will get no help from the courts.

25.12 Conditions

A condition is a restriction that is coupled with a *reverter clause.* This clause provides that if the restriction is violated, ownership reverts to the grantor in the deed.

> **EXAMPLE:** Owner deeds a lot to Buyer with a provision forbidding sale or use of intoxicating liquor on the lot and that in case of violation, ownership reverts to Owner. In time the premises are sold to Buyer #2, who puts in a drugstore with a liquor department. Owner files a suit. The court will give the property back to Owner.

The outstanding characteristic of a condition is the fact that if it is violated, the grantor may get his land back by filing a suit to obtain possession. He need not pay any compensation for it. Any mortgages or other interests in the land created after the creation of the condition are extinguished if the condition is enforced, again without payment of compensation to the mortgagee. This rule operates so harshly that courts are reluctant to construe a provision as a condition. In nearly all states, if the restrictive provision is followed by a clause providing that in the event of a violation of the restrictions the title to land shall revert to the grantor in the deed, the restrictive provision is a condition. If the deed contains no reverter clause, that is, a clause providing for a reverter or forfeiture of title in the event of violation of the restrictions, the restrictive provision is usually a covenant. The nomenclature employed by the parties is by no means decisive as to the character of the restriction created.

> **EXAMPLE:** A deed contained this clause: "These presents are upon the express condition that the said premises shall not be used or occupied as a tavern or public house." There was no reverter clause. It was held to be a covenant. *Koch v. Streuter,* 232 Ill. 594, 83 NE 1072 (1908). Violation would not cause a reverter.

Occasionally, the condition is referred to herein as a *reverter type restriction.*

25.12(a) Enforcement of conditions

When a condition (that is, a reverter type of restriction) occurs in a deed but the condition forms no part of any general plan, enforcement is relatively simple. The condition can be enforced by the grantor in the deed, or, if he is dead, by his heirs. Other lot owners in the same subdivision cannot enforce the condition.

Suppose, however, that X subdivides a tract of land and in selling the lots includes in each deed an identical condition. Here the problem grows far more complex. One thing is clear. The same building restriction may be both a condition and a restriction. For example, if the restriction sets forth that it is a covenant and restriction on behalf of all lot owners in the subdivision and in addition, that the grantor may declare a reverter if the restriction is violated, then, of course, any lot owner can enforce the restriction by injunction, treating it as a nonreverter type general plan restriction, but the grantor may also enforce it by declaring a reverter of title. *O'Malley* v. *Central Church*, 67 Ariz. 254, 194 P2d 444 (1948). Suppose, however, that one can deduce the existence of a general plan only from the fact that the conditions in all deeds happen to be identical. There is no language indicating that the provision is also to be treated as a covenant in favor of other lot owners. Here some courts are willing to allow other lot owners to enforce the condition on the theory that a covenant in their behalf must have been intended. *Northwestern Imp. Co.* v. *Lowry*, 66 P2d 792; (Mont. 1937); *Sayles* v. *Hall*, 210 Mass. 281, 96 NE 712 (1911); *Simon* v. *Henrichson*, 394 SW2d 249 (Tex. Civ. App. 1965); *Genske* v. *Jensen*, 188 Wis. 17, 205 NW 548 (1925). Other courts see only what is on the printed page. Since the provision reads like a simple condition, only the grantor or his heirs are permitted to enforce it. *Werner* v. *Graham*, 181 Cal. 174, 183 Pac. 945; *Whitton* v. *Clark*, 112 Conn. 28, 151 Atl. 305 (1930); *Finchum* v. *Vogel*, 194 So2d 59 (Fla. 1966); *Goodman* v. *Bingle*, 48 SW2d 432 (Tex. Civ. App. 1932).

A recorded condition can be enforced against any subsequent purchaser or mortgagee of the land. Enforcement of a condition by the grantor in the deed containing the condition, or by his heirs, if he is dead, extinguishes all subsequent titles and rights in the land.

> **EXAMPLE:** Seller conveys a lot to Buyer #1 with a condition in the deed that the premises shall not be used for the sale of liquor. The deed provides that in the event of violation of this provision, title to the property shall revert to Seller. Buyer #1 sells and conveys the property to Buyer #2, who places a mortgage thereon to Lender. Thereafter, Buyer #2 leases the building to Tenant and the latter uses the property for the sale of liquor. Seller brings suit to recover the land on the ground that the condition has been violated. Seller will be allowed to recover the land and all buildings erected on it without payment of any compensation, and will have good title free and clear of the mortgage and lease.

For the above reason, mortgagees are often reluctant to loan money on land that is subject to a condition. In fact, many insurance companies, which are authorized by law to loan money on first mortgages only, cannot legally make a loan on land that is subject to a condition. The problem may be handled in a number of different ways.

> 1. The person who has the right to enforce a reverter (the grantor in the deed creating the condition, or his heirs) may always release the reverter outright to the landowner.
> 2. The person who has the right to enforce a reverter may *subordinate* this right to a mortgage by a document stating that the reverter right is *subject* to the the mortgage. If the subordination is unequivocal, the mortgagee, when he forecloses, completely extinguishes the condition.
> 3. Many subdividers who place conditions in their deeds also include provisions in their deeds stating that the reverter right is subordinate to all mortgages. These provisions are broad in their terms and protect any mortgagee who may take a mortgage on the land.
> 4. In some instances title companies will insure against loss caused by a reverter of title.

25.12(b) Factors that render conditions unenforceable

In many states, especially where older court decisions are still followed, the factors discussed above that would prevent enforcement of a *nonreverter type* restriction have little application to conditions, that is, *reverter type restrictions.* For example, in nearly all states, the grantor in a deed containing a condition, or his heirs, if he is dead, has the right to enforce a condition even though the neighborhood has so changed that enforcement is of little practical utility. In one or two modern states, however, the change of neighborhood rule is now also applied to conditions, and conditions will not be enforced where the neighborhood has changed. *Letteau* v. *Ellis,* 122 Cal. App. 584, 10 P2d 496 (1932); *Cole* v. *Colorado Springs,* 381 P2d 13 (Colo. 1963); *Koehler* v. *Rowland,* 275 Mo. 573, 205 SW 217 (1917); *Towsend* v. *Allen,* 250 P2d 292 (Cal. 1953).

Again, in every state, laws exist allowing a certain time, often as long as twenty years, for the bringing of a suit to declare a reverter of title and to enforce a condition. This period of time runs not from the date of the deed containing the condition, but from the date the condition is violated. Often situations arise where, after the condition has been violated, no action has been taken to enforce the condition, and the landowner continues in possession, perhaps for several years. Mere delay in enforcing a condition, so long as the period allowed by law has not expired, does not, in most states, bar enforcement of a condition. But if the one who has a right to declare a reverter stands idly by, apparently acquiescing in the violation of the condition, sees valuable improvement being made by the landowner and delays proceedings to enforce the condition until after the improvements have been completed, some modern courts feel that this conduct is so unfair to the landowner that they refuse to enforce the condition. 39 ALR2d 1111.

25.12(b)(1) Reverter acts

In some states laws have been passed outlawing conditions after a certain specified period of time has elapsed from the date of their creation. *Trustees* v. *Batdorf,* 6 Ill.2d 486, 130 NE2d 111 (1955); *State Highway Div.* v. *Tolke,* 586 P2d 791 (Ore. 1978); *Caldwell* v. *Brown,* 553 SW2d 692 (Ky. 1977); 87 ALR3d 1011. *But see Bd. of Educ.* v. *Miles,* 15 N.Y.2d 364, 207 NE2d 181, criticized in 1965 *Law Forum* 941. Marketability of title laws also have this result.

25.12(b)(2) Nominal conditions

A number of states have statutes that conditions may be disregarded when they become "merely nominal" or "without substantial benefit to the parties." Basye, *Clearing Land Titles* § 143 (2d ed. 1970).

> **EXAMPLE:** A subdivider deeded out all lots with a reverter clause against trade or business. After he had deeded out all lots he could not enforce the condi-

tions. They had only nominal value to him. He could not be hurt by violations. *Ingersoll Engineering Co.* v. *Crocker,* 228 Fed. 845 (Mich. 1915).

25.12(b)(3) Acquiescence in violations

Sometimes a general plan is revealed by the existence of identical conditions in deeds. In such case, if the owner of the reverter right follows a course of conduct that results in numerous violations of the conditions, he will, in some states, be denied the right to enforce any of the conditions. 39 ALR2d 1133.

> **EXAMPLE:** A subdivider sold all the lots in the subdivision by deeds containing conditions against sale of intoxicating liquor. Later, he voluntarily released this clause as to a number of lots, and saloons were built on the released lots. He was refused the right to enforce any of the unreleased conditions. *Wedum-Aldahl Co.* v. *Miller,* 18 Cal. App.2d 745, 64 P2d 762 (1937).

It can be seen that while the older and stricter court decisions freely allow the enforcement of conditions, the modern decisions are beginning to apply to conditions the same rules that they apply to nonreverter type restrictions.

25.13 Covenants running with the land

The topic covered in this section is best explained by an illustration.

> **EXAMPLE:** Seller owns two adjoining lots, Lots 1 and 2. Seller sells Lot 1 to Buyer, and in the deed he inserts a clause stating that Buyer covenants to keep in repair the fence between the two lots. Lot 2 enjoys the *benefit* of this covenant. Lot 1 bears the *burden* of the covenant. Any subsequent owner of Lot 1 must comply with this covenant and will be liable to pay damages to the owner of Lot 2 if he fails to do so. Any subsequent owner of Lot 2 will be able to enforce this covenant. *Such an affirmative covenant runs with the land,* much in the same fashion as an appurtenant easement runs with the land, the *burden* of the covenant running with Lot 1 and the *benefit* running with Lot 2.

Courts are somewhat reluctant to see land burdened with covenants that impose *personal liability* on subsequent owners, for such covenants tend somewhat to restrict salability of such land. These requirements are of diminishing importance today, for most covenants relating to land are *negative covenants,* that is, covenants *restricting the use of land, and these are enforced today by means of injunctions rather than damage suits.*

> **EXAMPLE:** A subdivider sells all lots in the subdivision by deeds providing that only single-family dwellings can be erected. Buyer #1 buys a lot and attempts to build a store. Buyer #2, another lot owner, obtains a court order forbidding such construction.

In issuing such orders, courts ignore all the technicalities that surround damage suits. As long as a property owner bought his land with notice, either actual or from the public record, that the land was bound by a covenant, he is subject to court injunctions compelling obedience. In modern times, in other words, the old-fashioned method of enforcing covenants by damage suits that may not be decided by a jury until years after the suit has been filed, and then may offer only a slim chance of persuading a jury or collecting the damages a jury may award, has given way to the new, effective method of enforcing a restrictive covenant by a judge's injunction order that may issue within a few days after suit is filed. *Affirmative covenants,* such as those requiring payment of assessments for maintenance of common grounds in a planned unit development, still pose the problems relating to covenants running with the land.

25.14   Racial restrictions

Racial restrictions, that is, restrictions prohibiting use of occupancy by, or sale of, the land to persons other than members of the Caucasian race are discussed elsewhere.

25.15   Suggestions

If you are about to buy real estate, you are concerned with several questions about restrictions: (1) Do any restrictions exist that will hamper or prevent the use you intended to make of this land or prevent construction of the building you have in mind? (2) What does the contract of sale say about restrictions? (3) Assuming that you are buying improved real estate and therefore have no building problem, are there reverter clauses in the restriction under which you may lose your title or that may hamper your financing of the real estate? (4) If there are restrictions, and the restrictions are desirable from your point of view, do you get the right to enforce them against other property owners?

In answering question 3 above, keep in mind that if there is a condition containing a reverter clause, and some prior owner violated the clause by constructing the wrong type of building or by committing some other violation, the grantor in the deed containing the condition has the right to take the property away from you.

In answering question 4 above, keep in mind the rules stated in the text. Lot owners get the best protection when the restrictions are incorporated in the map or plat of the subdivision, since this leaves no room for doubt that there is a general plan. The lot owners get the least protection in cases where the restrictions are imposed by the subdivider, who includes conditions in his deed to the lot owners. Except in a few states, only the subdivider or his heirs can, as a rule, enforce such conditions, and the subdivider is likely to lose interest once he has sold all lots in the subdivision. Also, when the subdivider has created conditions, the lot owners must be prepared to go to him each time they mortgage their lands and buy from him a subordination of reverter. Mortgagees usually insist on this protection, and lot owners have no recourse but to pay for it.

If you are attempting to obtain the release of a restriction, you must keep in mind the rules regarding the persons who may enforce the restriction. For example, if you buy a lot in a subdivision and the plat or map of the subdivision contains a restriction that only single-family dwellings shall be constructed, it is a waste of time to obtain the consent of the owners of the two neighboring lots to the construction of a two-flat building, because any lot owner in the subdivision can block construction of such a building.

26 LAND USE CONTROLS—ZONING AND BUILDING ORDINANCES

26.01 In general
Zoning is a very difficult subject to master for several reasons. Each tract of land is unique. My house or lot usually differs in some way from my neighbor's house or lot. As will be seen, the court tailors its decision to the particular tract of land. Again, most real estate law goes back hundreds of years, and much of it has remained relatively stable. The law of deeds and easements, for example, changes very little. But zoning really dates back only to 1926. Prior to that time it was considered illegal. In 1926 the United States Supreme Court held that zoning was valid. Since that time, moreover, the country has changed. The inner city is blighted, and is surrounded by suburbs determined to keep things as they are in their particular suburb. Some courts sustain the suburban officials in this effort.

> **EXAMPLE:** A village "zoned out" apartments, limiting construction to single-family dwellings. The court sustained this zoning. This effectively limits occupancy to middle-class or well-to-do people, because poor people cannot afford to own homes erected on expensive suburban land. However, another court ruled that if there was enough vacant land for apartments, the village must zone some of it for apartments. The village cannot "zone out" the poor.

Remember that there are fifty states. Each is at liberty to adopt its own views because the United States Supreme Court has largely chosen to ignore zoning in recent years. The Supreme Court changes its mind frequently, and when this occurs, the "constitution" changes. This is also true of the state courts.

> **EXAMPLE:** New Jersey court decisions were formerly quite favorable to the suburbs. Now they are leading the fight to open the suburbs to the poor.

Reading zoning decisions is a difficult task. The court must give a reason for its decision. But often the decision does not state the real reason. At times one can glean from the language of the decision the feeling that the court suspected that the developer had improperly influenced the zoning officials to get a zoning change. Obviously, the court, in striking down the change, will state a "legal reason" for its decision, not the real reason. The financial rewards in zoning changes are very great and people succumb to temptation. A tract of land may increase its value twentyfold or more if the zoning is changed.

The decisions, it is evident then, are far from harmonious. Judges are people. By and large they are well-to-do. Many own their own homes. Many live in the suburbs. Unconsciously perhaps, this creeps into judicial thinking.

Nevertheless, there are some rules, and the areas of conflict can be explored.

26.01(a)   Types of litigation situations

Although there are many variations on this theme, there are several *main* types of zoning litigation situations.

> **EXAMPLE:**   A developer buys land in a residential suburb and seeks a zoning change to permit construction of an apartment and store complex. The village refuses. The developer goes to court.

> **EXAMPLE:**   In the example given above, suppose the village chooses to change the zoning and permit the complex to be constructed. Now the neighbors go to court to block construction.

> **EXAMPLE:**   A developer wishes to develop an area in a village, and the village refused rezoning because it is financially unable to supply needed expansion of schools, sewer, water, and so forth. The developer goes to court.

26.02   History

The first zoning ordinance was adopted by New York City. Its purpose was to prevent the garment district from spilling over into the fashionable Fifth Avenue shopping area. But the real history of zoning began in 1926, when the Supreme Court held zoning valid. *Village of Euclid* v. *Ambler Realty Co.,* 272 U.S. 365, 47 S.Ct. 114, 71 L. Ed. 303 (1926). Historically, the Village of Euclid was founded by some land surveyors who liked the location they had surveyed and named the town after their favorite mathematician. Today, "cooky cutter" zoning that divides the municipality into rigid zones with rectangular lots in each zone, as was done in the Village of Euclid, is derisively referred to as "Euclidean zoning."

Early zoning ordinances generally divided the city into three zones: residential, commercial, and manufacturing. Only residences were permitted in residence districts. Both stores and residences were allowed in commercial zones. All types of uses were permitted in manufacturing zones. Attached to the ordinance was a map showing zone boundaries.

Since only residential uses were permitted in residential zones, residential use came to be known as a *preferred use.* All other zones were *cumulative zones* in that they permitted residences in commercial zones, for example, and stores and residences in industrial zones.

Modern zoning ordinances usually create a greater number of classifications. Residential districts may be divided into single-family districts and multiple-family districts. Multiple-family zones may be divided into *walkups* and *high-rise* (elevator building) zones. Commercial zones may be divided into retail and wholesale districts, industrial zones into heavy and light industry zones. Small stores may be permitted in apartment buildings and planned unit developments.

Originally, all states enacted *zoning enabling acts* which granted zoning power to their cities and villages and laid down the ground rules. Today many cities have *home rule* powers and need not obey the state zoning enabling act.

26.03   Future of zoning

The criticism of zoning has been bitter and continuous. Zoning practice has wandered far away from the original zoning dream of orderly land use. The abuses have occurred mainly in the suburbs. Suburbs tend to adopt "wait and see" zoning. Vast vacant areas are zoned for agriculture or for five-acre residential lots. The authorities know full well that few developers can live with such zoning. But they want to wait and see what kind of developers appear to request rational zoning amendments. And if they must wait for a protracted period, the homeowners in the suburb make no protest. They are satisfied with things as they are. They would like to keep new construction to an absolute minimum. The difficulty, of course, lies in the fact that the growing population of this country must live somewhere. Also lower income families ought to be able to locate near the industries that have moved from the cities to the suburbs. Moreover, the charge is frequently made that zoning is a tool used to exclude minorities from the suburbs.

Thus, the major battle has shifted to the area of rezoning. Request is made for an amendment to the zoning ordinance. The suburb refuses to rezone. Litigation results.

Some of this litigation is described under the title *exclusionary zoning.*

Some is described in the chapter on land development, where *no-growth* strategies are discussed.

Some is discussed in the chapter on *racial discrimination.*

However, some practical tools are surfacing. In 1979 California enacted a law authorizing local governments to enter into agreements with developers. Once an agreement has been entered into, the developer is guaranteed against subsequent harassment by zoning or building code changes. 13 Urb. Law 44.

The federal government is advocating general adoption of a somewhat similar system. *Streamlining Land Use Regulation,* published by HUD, November 1980. This excellent report owes much to the American Planning Association and the Urban Land Institute.

Obviously, this field is in utter turmoil. The decisions are conflicting.

26.04   Noncumulative zoning

Attempts are being made now to have zoning ordinances that do more than keep industries and stores out of residential zones. They are being used to exclude residences from commercial and industrial zones. Ordinances zoning certain areas exclusively for industrial purposes are fairly widespread and are valid. *Roney* v. *Board of Supervisors,* 138 Cal. App.2d 740, 292 P2d 529 (1956); *People ex rel.* v. *Morton Grove,* 16 Ill.2d 183, 157 NE2d 33 (1959); *Lamb* v. *City of Monroe,* 358 Mich. 136, 99 NW2d 566 (1959). Obviously, it is just as injurious to the welfare of the community to permit residential development of land needed for industrial expansion as it is to permit industrial expansion in residential neighborhoods. We must remember that in our growing country the supply of usable land is limited, and zoning is the chief tool that communities utilize to insure wise use of our limited land areas.

Some early decisions held such noncumulative zoning invalid. It is unlikely that any of these rulings would stand today.

Interestingly, there is a trend away from noncumulative or exclusive zoning.

EXAMPLE: Today you will find many mixed use zones. Stores are common in planned unit developments. In large planned developments you will find office buildings and theaters.

26.05   Zoning—validity—in general

Determining the validity of zoning is basically a state court function. The United States Supreme Court determined the *general validity* of zoning in *Village of Euclid* v. *Ambler Realty Co.,* 272 U.S. 365, 71 L. Ed. 303 (1926). It then decided that a state, acting under its police power, could compel a landowner to accept a substantial reduction in his land value as long as there was a corresponding benefit to the public. Thereafter, in *Nectow* v. *Cambridge,* 277 U.S. 183, 72 L. Ed. 842 (1928) the Supreme Court decided that while a zoning ordinance could be valid *in general* it might work such a hardship as to a particular tract of land that it would be held invalid *as applied to that tract of land.*

EXAMPLE: A zoning ordinance zoned a small tract of land for residential purposes. This tract of land was cut off from other residential lots by railroad tracks and by the intersection of diagonal streets was entirely surrounded by property zoned for industrial use; and was practically worthless as residence property. The *zoning map,* in other words, put the land in the wrong zone. It was held that the zoning ordinance was not valid *as applied.* Insofar as the zoning ordinance limits property to a use that cannot reasonably be made of it, it is invalid. *Tews* v. *Woolhiser,* 353 Ill. 212, 185 NE 827 (1933). This is a court decision. It is *not* rezoning.

Having laid down some general principles, the Supreme Court thereafter refused to decide zoning cases, leaving the problem of deciding validity to the state courts. Thus, in discussing the validity of a zoning ordinance, we are discussing its validity *as applied to a particular tract of land.* Each of the fifty states is pretty much at liberty to decide that issue under its own state constitution. The fact that most state constitutions are modeled after the federal constitution is no guaranty of uniformity. Far from it, for judges are people. The decisions exhibit a wild diversity, because judges entertain diverse views on what is proper zoning.

In the ordinary zoning case, we are dealing with a particular tract of land. In general, the landowner is trying to put in an apartment, a planned unit development, a mobile home court, an industrial plant, and opposition is encountered. There are some approaches to this problem that reveal a degree of uniformity. Since the validity of zoning in general is beyond question, most of the litigation, then, is over amendments or "rezoning" of a particular tract of land. Or else, a landowner attacks the zoning *map* that is attached to every zoning ordinance. He argues that his land is placed by the *map* in the wrong type of zone. Unsuitable zoning is illegal zoning.

There is an unspoken balancing process at work. The court considers the proposed rezoning. Is the new proposed use nuisancelike so that it is sure to be harmful to its neighbors? The odds are against it, if it is. Is it relatively benign, like a strictly residential planned unit development? Its chances are good. Does it fit well into the pattern of existing uses so that its neighbors will not suffer too much? Very likely it will prevail. And so on.

26.05(a)   Validity—factors to be considered

In dealing with zoning validity one is faced with a variety of situations, namely: (1) the attack may be leveled against the entire ordinance which is a rarity; (2) the attack may be leveled against the zoning ordinance *as applied* to a particular tract of land, as in *Tews* v. *Woolhiser;* (3) the attack may be leveled against the *granting or refusal* of: (a) an amendment to the ordinance (rezoning); (b) a variance; or (c) a special exception.

Passing for a moment item (1) above, the factors to be considered in all these situations are these:

1. The character of the neighborhood.

EXAMPLE: One who seeks to thrust an apartment, industrial plant, or mortuary in the midst of a neighborhood of single-family dwellings will not succeed. Conformity to surrounding uses is one of the objectives of sound zoning.

2. The extent to which property values are diminished by the particular zoning restriction and the extent to which the public is benefited.

EXAMPLE: An area is zoned single-family, but one vacant lot sits between two nonconforming apartments. No one thinking realistically would erect a house on this site. The owner must be permitted to erect an apartment. Under the concept of the police power, a landowner cannot be compelled to accept a harmful and sharp reduction in land value unless there is some corresponding benefit to the public. Here it is obvious that the vacant lot has zero value if zoned single-family. No public purpose is served. The land must be rezoned.

EXAMPLE: In the leading case of *Village of Euclid* v. *Ambler Realty Co.,* 272 U.S. 365 (1926), the village enacted a zoning ordinance under which Ambler's tract of sixty-eight acres fell into a single-family zone. This reduced its value from $10,000 per acre to $2,500 per acre. Nevertheless, there were residences to the east and west of the property, so that the zoning did indeed benefit large segments of the public. A landowner can be compelled to accept a reduction in land value if the ordinance is reasonable and there is a *benefit to the public.*

The philosophy here is that in a democracy the people grant to various legislative bodies the power to enact laws. But inherent in this grant of power is the limitation that the power must be exercised reasonably.

Another way of stating this rule is that the ordinance must not be *confiscatory as applied to the land in question.* A zoning decision by the authorities will not be held confiscatory unless the land cannot yield a reasonable return if used only for the purposes permitted in the zone. If the land is in a residential zone, this requires proof that residential development is not feasible and that use of the property for any of the permitted purposes in the zone is likewise not feasible. *Wackerman* v. *Town of Penfield,* 366 N.Y.S.2d 718 (1975).

And if the use being made of the land approaches the nuisance type of use, the court will sanction substantial destruction of land value. The theory is that no one has a constitutional right to operate a nuisance.

EXAMPLE: Where the ordinance in effect stopped the operation of an existing brickyard, diminishing land value by over 90 percent, the ordinance was sustained. The brickyard was surrounded by residences. *Hadacheck* v. *Sebastian,* 239 U.S. 394 (1915).

3. The extent to which removal of the existing limitation would affect the value of other property in the area.

EXAMPLE: The general area in question was generally vacant and far removed from any residential area. The land must be rezoned to permit the landowner to build an outdoor theater. The restriction in the ordinance against theaters had no *beneficial effect* whatsoever on the surrounding property. *People ex rel* v. *Village of Skokie,* 408 Ill. 397, 97 NE 310 (1951).

EXAMPLE: In an area zoned for heavy industry, it was irrational to single out the petroleum industry and exclude it. The area was already permeated with odors from existing, legal plants. *Tidewater Oil Co.* v. *Mayor & Council of Carteret,* 193 A2d 413 (N.J. 1963). Here we find no *benefit to the public.*

4. The suitability of the property for the zoned purpose.

EXAMPLE: The land was zoned single-family but was located in a district predominantly business and industrial and was worth ten times more for these purposes than as residential. The zoning is invalid as applied to this tract of land. Here the harm to the landowner is great, and there is no benefit to the public. *Galt* v. *County of Cook,* 405 Ill. 396, 91 NE2d 395 (1950).

5. The existing uses and zoning of nearby property.

EXAMPLE: *Tews* v. *Woolhiser, supra,* is a good illustration of this rule.

6. The length of time under the existing zoning that the property has remained unimproved considered in the context of land development in the area.

EXAMPLE: A tract of land was a vacant island surrounded by business buildings. It was zoned for parking. As such it remained in use as a parking lot for twenty-five years, although its value for office building use would be much greater. The ordinance was held invalid as applied to this land. *Vernon Park Realty* v. *City of Mount Vernon,* 307 N.Y. 493, 121 NE2d 517 (1954). As to this land the ordinance was *confiscatory.* Such well-located property would normally be developed in much less than twenty-five years. While a zoning ordinance need not zone property for its *highest and best use* (a phrase invented by land appraisers), this is a factor to be considered. Moreover an unspoken factor here is that cities often provide municipal parking lots and here, in effect, the city is forcing the landowner to furnish a public service. The land is reasonably adapted to office-building use. No reason can be given why it was not so zoned. Certainly its use for this purpose would be compatible with existing uses.

EXAMPLE: The land in question was zoned for residential use. For twenty years it remained vacant. During that period, development was totally stagnant. The only buildings in the area were a cow stable, a dairy farm, and a city incinerator. The property was worthless for residential purposes. The court held that the zoning was invalid as applied to the land. *Arverne Bay Cons. Co.* v. *Thatcher,* 278 N.Y. 222, 15 NE2d 587 (1938).

7. The relative gain to the public as compared to the hardship imposed on the landowner.

EXAMPLE: Some of the examples given above illustrate this principle aptly. Indeed, the example last given is an excellent illustration.

8. A city cannot validly zone private land for what are essentially public purposes.

EXAMPLE: City rezoned certain land for school purposes. *City of Plainfield* v. *Borough of Middlesex,* 69 N.J.S. 136, 173 A2d 785 (1961). City rezoned certain land as a wildlife preserve. *Morris Co. Land Imp. Co.* v. *Parsippany-Troy Hills Twp.,* 40 N.J. 539, 193 A2d 232 (1963). Both ordinances are invalid as applied.

EXAMPLE: Land cannot be zoned to remain a forest preserve. *MacGibbon* v. *Board of Appeals,* 340 NE2d 487 (Mass. 1976).

26.05(b) Validity—reasonableness as a test

In recent times, much of the technical verbiage of the older cases has disappeared. The real test of the validity of zoning is its *reasonableness.* Disregard "taking property," "confiscatory zoning," and instead ask the question: Is the zoning totally unreasonable? An ordinance requiring all building lots in Manhattan to be of a minimum size of one hundred acres would be totally unrealistic. Our forefathers gave our legislatures the police power, that is, the power to pass laws, but not to act indiscriminately. If the regulation is totally unreasonable as applied to particular land, it is invalid. *Fred F. French Inv. Co.* v. *City of N.Y.,* 39 N.Y.2d 587, 350 NE2d 381 (1976). Viewed in this light, the task of the courts becomes a good deal simpler and a good deal more sensible. When a court holds that a particular zoning decision is invalid *as applied* to a particular tract of land, it is holding that *in the circumstances* the zoning is unreasonable.

26.05(c) Validity—federal courts' role

As has been stated, this country has a federal Constitution. In determining whether a zoning law or local activity violates the federal Constitution, the United States Supreme Court has the final word. However, even if that court should hold that the federal Constitution has not been violated, that decision is of minor consequence in zoning law. Each state has its own constitution. What *that* constitution permits is determined by the *state courts.* Thus, an ordinance held "valid" by the Supreme Court is valid only so far as federal law is concerned. The State Supreme Court may hold the very same ordinance *invalid* as a violation of the *state constitution,* which becomes the final and binding decision. The federal court decisions get the headlines, but, in point of fact, they are of relatively minor importance. The United States Supreme Court has tended to ignore zoning altogether and, when it chooses to decide a zoning case, it takes such a liberal view that land developers have little to fear from the federal courts. Thus, it has been said that, "the exercise of sound discretion does not, of course, always require a slavish adherence to federal constitutional minimums." *State* v. *Smith,* 347 A2d 816 (N.J.). The United States Supreme Court has, in fact, encouraged the state courts to exercise their independence. *Oregon* v. *Hass,* 420 U.S. 714, 719, 46 L. Ed. 2d 313 (1975).

26.05(d) Validity—judgment declaring zoning invalid

It is commonplace, of course, for a landowner to file a suit to have zoning declared invalid as to his land. Suppose he wins. The court must then make a further decision. (1) It can declare the zoning invalid as to the land and go no further. The land is then unzoned. A factory could be built. (2) Or suppose the landowner wants to erect an apartment. The court can rezone the land for apartment use. Purists dislike this approach. Zoning and rezoning are jobs for the legislature. (3) Or the court can send the case back to the city with an order that the land be rezoned. *Zaagman* v. *City of Kenwood*, 223 NW2d 146 (Mich. 1975); 25 S.D.L. Rev. 116.

26.06 Rezoning— referendum

The Supreme Court has held that the federal Constitution is not violated by making rezoning subject to referendum approval by the people of the municipality. *City of Eastlake* v. *Forest City Enterprises, Inc.,* 416 U.S. 668, 96 S.Ct. 2358, 2361 (1976). This leaves the state courts free to deal with this problem as they choose. Some courts will follow the Supreme Court's view that this is simply returning power to the people. Other courts will hold the referendum device illegal.

> *REFERENCES:* 10 Akron L. Rev. 557 (1977); 28 Case W. L. Rev. 41 (1977); 82 Dick. L. Rev. 99 (1977); 23 Loyola L. Rev. 243 (1977); 91 Harv. L. Rev. 1528; 55 N.C.L. Rev. 517 (1977); 5 Fordham Urb. L. J. 141; 72 ALR3d 1030.

26.07 Zoning exactions

The subject of *forced dedication,* whereby the municipality approves a plat only if the developer agrees to exactions of some sort, donation of land to the public, for example, occurs in connection with plat approval. *See* § 27.04 *et seq.* Some municipalities make the same kind of exactions a condition to granting rezoning or a zoning variance or special exception.

This, predictably, will receive a mixed response in the courts. Most decisions will be favorable if the exaction is reasonable in the circumstances. *Sommers* v. *City of Los Angeles,* 62 Cal. Reptr. 523 (1967); *Board of Education* v. *Surety Developer,* 63 Ill.2d 193, 347 NE2d 149 (1975). *Unreasonable* exactions are a sneaky way of blocking development. They are invalid. *James City & County* v. *Rowe,* 216 Va. 128, 216 SE2d 199 (1975).

26.08 Senior citizens

It has been held to be unlawful to zone out senior citizens. *Shepard* v. *Woodland Twp. Planning Bd.,* 128 N.J. Super. 379, 320 A2d 191 (1974). It has also been held invalid in some states to limit occupancy to senior citizens.

> **NEW DIRECTIONS:** The better modern rule is that a municipality may limit a particular residential zone to senior citizens. Their needs, curb ramps for wheelchairs, for example, are largely peculiar to the elderly. They need a zone that caters to their needs. *Taxpayers Assn.* v. *Weymouth Tp.,* 71 N.J. 249, 364 A2d 1016 (1976); *Hinman* v. *Planning and Zoning Comm.,* 26 Conn. Supp. 125, 214 A2d 131 (1965); *Maldini* v. *Ambro,* 36 N.Y. 481, 33 NE2d 403 (1975).

> *REFERENCES:* 31 Ark. L. Rev. 707 (1978); 5 Fla. St. U. L. Rev. 423 (1977); 76 Mich. L. Rev. 64 (1977); 6 Urb. Law. 685; 83 ALR3d 1084, 1103.

26.09 Children   Zoning that restricts units available to families with children has been held invalid. *Duggan* v. *County of Cook,* 60 Ill. App.2d 107, 324 NE2d 406 (1975); *Malino* v. *Mayor of Glassboro,* 116 N.J. Super. 195, 281 A2d 401 (N.J. 1971); 24 De Paul L. Rev. 784 (1975). Ultimately, this law will have to be reconciled with the decisions sanctioning communities for senior citizens only. *See* §§ 25.04 and 32.03(d).

26.10 Churches   It is well established that a zoning ordinance must not exclude churches or synagogues from residential districts. 74 ALR2d 377.

26.11. Schools   *Public* schools, of course, are not subject to zoning ordinances. *Hall* v. *City of Taft,* 47 Cal.2d 177, 302 P2d 574 (1956). The only controversy, then, relates to *private* schools. The courts are not in agreement on this question. The more general view is that private schools, like churches, cannot be excluded from residential areas. *Roman Catholic Welfare Corp.* v. *City of Piedmont,* 45 Cal.2d 32, 289 P2d 438 (1955). 11 *Miami L.Q.* 68.

26.12 Prohibitory zoning   Two techniques are available when a village wishes to exclude unwanted uses, such as oil drilling. For example, the zoning ordinance may explicitly prohibit drilling for oil or extraction of minerals. 10 ALR3d 1241. Whether the exclusion will stand up depends on the circumstances surrounding the particular tract of land.

> **EXAMPLE:** A landowner whose land adjoined the city dump applied for rezoning that would permit oil drilling. Refusal of rezoning was held invalid *as applied* to this land. How could oil drilling possibly debase an area next to the city dump? 10 ALR3d 1241.

> **EXAMPLE:** A landowner applied for rezoning to permit oil drilling. His land was so close to the city water well that it created danger of contamination. Refusal of rezoning was sustained *as applied.* 10 ALR3d 1241.

As can be seen in both examples, the court considered the validity of the zoning *as applied* to the particular tract of land.

Another technique simply fails to provide a home in the ordinance for the unwanted uses. *Hohl* v. *Leadington,* 37 N.J.L. 271, 181 A2d 150 (1962); *Wiley* v. *County of Hanover,* 163 SE2d 160 (Va. 1968). The result is the same regardless of the technique involved.

A valid approach to this problem resorts to the *as applied* test.

> **EXAMPLE:** In Skokie, a suburb of Chicago, in an area then far from any residences, the zoning ordinance was amended to exclude motion picture theaters. It

was held to be invalid *as applied,* and an outdoor movie theater was permitted. *People ex rel.* v. *Village of Skokie,* 408 Ill. 397, 97 NE2d 310 (1951).

EXAMPLE: In another case involving a county zoning ordinance, the area in question was bounded by a railroad and a highway, and nearby uses consisted of a farm, a car dealership, industry, a par-three golf course, and a quarry. Refusal of a special exception for a trailer park was reversed by the court. Such action was invalid *as applied* to this land. The court stated that denial of a special exception must bear some reasonable relationship to the public welfare, and that the gain to the public here would be small as balanced against the hardship to the landowner. *Pioneer T. and S. Bank* v. *McHenry County,* 41 Ill.2d 77, 241 NE2d 454 (1970).

EXAMPLE: The village totally excluded trailer parks. The court pointed out that such a blanket exclusion could not stand up because it disregarded the circumstances surrounding each tract of land in the village. The court pointed out that the facts might establish that a trailer park is a legitimate use somewhere in the village. The court observed that the total exclusion of a legitimate use carries with it the duty to provide a zoning board hearing in which a landowner could test the legitimacy of the exclusion, presumably via the special exception technique. Should the city fail to provide such a hearing then, the court held, the court must provide a judicial special exception technique to determine whether the use should be allowed. In such hearings it might be established that the exclusion *as applied* bore no substantial relation to the public health, morals, and welfare. *High Meadows Park* v. *Aurora,* 112 Ill. App.2d 220, 250 NE2d 517 (1967).

A balancing test has been suggested. Note: Legitimate Use Exclusions Through Zoning: Applying a Balancing Test, 57 Cornell L. Rev. 461 (1971). Under this test the court would consider the character of the community. For example, mobile homes are appropriate in rural areas. Also to be considered is the strain on utilities, transportation, and municipal services. The court should consider the availability of alternatives to exclusion, such as regulation. Hardship to the landowner is to be considered, particularly loss of profits. Also to be considered is the possibility of relocating the use elsewhere in the region. The standard test as to whether the prohibition bears a reasonable relation to public health, safety, welfare is applicable. The court should consider the present character of the community and its plans for the future.

26.13 Development control zoning—sewer, water, and school problems—downzoning

In many cases villages have refused to rezone single-family zones to apartments or other such uses and have given as a reason the shortage of sewer, water, or school facilities. Or the village may engage in *downzoning.*

EXAMPLE: The village rezoned *A's* land from multifamily dwelling to a single-family dwelling because it lacked sewer facilities. This was held invalid.

Westwood Estates v. *Village of South Nyack,* 23 N.Y.2d 424, 244 NE2d 700 (1969). To like effect are *Appeal of Gersh,* 437 Pa. 237, 263 A2d 395 (1970) and *McGibbon* v. *Board of Appeals,* 340 NE2d 487 (Mass. 1976).

EXAMPLE: The town increased minimum lot size from 35,000 square feet to three acres and six acres because of lack of sewer facilities. The court upheld the ordinance but admonished the city that the change must be temporary only. *Steel Hill Development Inc.* v. *Town of Sanbornton,* 469 F2d 956 (1972). This is also *downzoning.*

It can be seen from the examples given that the efforts of some villages are bent toward holding the population stable, keeping things "as they are now," barring developers who bring in a new, unwanted population. And yet, at times, a genuine health problem or school problem exists. The cases, of course, are in utter confusion.

EXAMPLE: Downzoning by rezoning commercial to residential has been sustained. *Shelburne Inc.* v. *Conner,* 315 A2d 620 (Del. Ch. 1974). But rezoning of a single block to "zone out" apartments has been rejected as "spot zoning," *G. & D. Holland Const. Co.* v. *City of Maryville,* 12 Cal. App.2d 989, 91 Cal. Reptr. 227 (1970).

EXAMPLE: The desire of the villagers to keep the village rural does not justify increasing the minimum lot area from one to two acres and the minimum lot frontage from 100 to 200 feet. *Kavenesky* v. *Zoning Board,* 160 Conn. 397, 279 A2d 567 (1971); *Oakwood at Madison, Inc.* v. *Twp. of Madison,* 283 A2d 353 (N.J. 1971).

See 31 Hastings L.J. 103; 5 R.E.L.J. 311.

The situation seems to break down into several sharply conflicting points of view, namely: (1) the village cannot use its shortage of facilities as an excuse for refusal to grant proper rezoning. *Appeal of Kit Mar Builders Inc.,* 439 Pa. 466, 268 A2d 765 (1970); (2) the shortage in facilities is one factor that may be considered in refusing rezoning to the developer. *Adams* v. *Reed,* 123 So2d 606 (Miss. 1960); (3) the village may impose a zoning freeze of *limited* duration so long as it has a program for correcting the problem.

As can be seen, blanket, haphazard, unplanned restrictions, especially those of indefinite duration, are likely to be held invalid. However, if the development control zoning is carefully planned and is limited in time, it will be sustained by the courts.

NEW DIRECTIONS: The town of *X* adopts a zoning amendment under which erection of homes by a merchant builder would require a special permit. The standards for the issuance of special permits are framed in terms of the availability to the proposed subdivison of five essential facilities or services, specifically: (1) public sanitary sewers or approved substitutes; (2) drainage facilities; (3) improved public parks or recreation facilities, including public schools; (4) state, county, or town roads (major, secondary, or collector); and (5) firehouses. No special permit issues unless the proposed residential development has accumulated fifteen development points, to be computed on a sliding scale of values assigned to the specified improvements under the statute. Subdivision is thus a function of immediate availability to the proposed plat of certain municipal improvements, the avowed purpose of the amendments being to phase residential development to the town's ability to provide the above facilities or services. This was held valid. *Golden* v. *Planning Board of Town of Ramapo,* 30 N.Y.2d 359, 285 NE2d 291 (1972). This is a celebrated case, and the technique is likely to be used in many areas. This is *phased development zoning.*

As is evident, there are a number of factors to be considered. Perhaps the most important factor is one rarely mentioned in the court cases, namely, the suburbs want to stay the way they have been. They wish to exclude newcomers. But if all villages exclude all newcomers, where is our growing population to find homes? The other factor is that many suburbs are truly ill equipped to handle a sudden surge of population growth. But the villages have dragged their heels. They refuse to build schools or sewers, hoping to use this as an excuse to bar the newcomers. Another factor is the publicity given to federal court decisions. These decisions are virtually meaningless. All they hold is that this or that ordinance violates or does not violate the federal constitution. Any state court is at liberty to decide the question in a diametrically opposite fashion so long as it decides it on state constitutional grounds.

All one can say is that as of this moment the trend seems to be toward the rule that these real or fancied shortages may enable a village to declare a brief moratorium on development, but sooner or later land that is suitable only for homes will be developed for homes. The villages cannot block this indefinitely.

REFERENCES: The problem of phased development or "sequential controls" is discussed at length in Freilich and Ragsdale, *Timing and Sequential Controls,* 58 Minn. L. Rev. 1009 (1974). See also Note, *Ramapo Township's Time Controls,* 47 N.Y. U. L. Rev. 724 (1972). See Ch. 27.

26.14 Downzoning

At times a village will rezone land from a high-value use, like commercial, to a low-value use, like homes. This is *downzoning.* See § 26.13.

26.15 Bulk zoning

Bulk zoning is zoning that regulates the size and shape of the buildings to be erected and their location on the land. The purpose of this type of zoning is to control population density, open space, and access to daylight and air. The ordinance requires that any building erected must leave specified areas along the front, side, and rear of the lot which must not be built upon.

The energy crisis will affect both lot size and building size. Large lots and large residences are energy wasteful. Predictably, municipalities are going to reduce lot size, building size, and required open space around buildings. *Zero lot lines* will appear. Where these appear, a building will be placed so as to touch the lot line. Air space around the home wastes energy. Small homes with one solid, windowless wall are cheaper to build and use less land and energy.

26.16   Single-family zones

It is axiomatic that in single-family zones only one house per lot occupied by a single family will be permitted. But as times change, customs change. Many couples choose to live together today without marrying. So the zoning definition of a "single family" has tended to change. Thus the area of controversy.

A well-known case on family zoning is *Village of Belle Terre* v. *Boraas,* 416 U.S. 1, 39 L.Ed2d 797 (1974). Here a zoning ordinance restricted residence in the entire community to single-family dwellings and prohibited occupancy by more than *two unrelated persons,* while permitting occupancy by any number of persons related by blood or marriage. The ordinance was sustained. The quietude of the single-family dwelling area and its benefits for the rearing of children were pointed out. The decision has been criticized. 1977 U. of Ill. L. Forum at 917.

The family is perhaps the most revered institution in American life. Hence, any ordinance that forbids members of the same family to live together is invalid.

> **EXAMPLE:**   A grandmother cannot be prohibited from living with her grandson. A brother and sister must be allowed to live together. Zoning cannot slice into the family itself. *Moore* v. *City of East Cleveland,* 97 S.Ct. 1932, 52 L.Ed.2d 531 (1977). As an example, when a family's breadwinner dies, the broader family comes together for mutual assistance. The law cannot forbid this. The law protects the "extended family."

Litigation involving single-family zoning ordinances is common. Although there appear to be almost endless differences in the language used in these ordinances, they contain three principal types of restrictions. First, they define the kind of structure that may be erected on vacant land. Second, they require that a single-family home be occupied only by a "single housekeeping unit." Third, they often require that the housekeeping unit be made up of persons related by blood, adoption, or marriage, with certain limited exceptions. Although the legitimacy of the first two types of restrictions is well settled, attempts to limit occupancy to related persons have not been successful. The state courts have recognized a valid community interest in preserving the stable character of residential neighborhoods that justifies a prohibition against transient occupancy. Nevertheless, in well-reasoned opinions, the courts of Illinois, New York,

New Jersey, California, Connecticut, Wisconsin, and other jurisdictions have permitted unrelated persons to occupy single-family residences notwithstanding the existence of an ordinance prohibiting, either expressly or implicitly, such occupancy. *Moore* v. *City of East Cleveland,* 52 L.Ed.2d 531 (1977).

> **NEW DIRECTIONS:** The old-fashioned single-family dwelling zone is virtually obsolete. The housing shortage will continue for years. The tandem house is designed for occupancy by two unrelated persons. See § 14.16(a). Unrelated widows and widowers are living together to share expenses. Over 500,000 homes have illegal apartments for lodgers. In time, these will be legalized. As housing costs creep up to 60 percent of annual income (as in San Francisco) laws must change to reflect the drastic changes in the American scene.

> *REFERENCES:* The subject of family zoning has been quite fully explored. 11 Calif. W. L. Rev. 85; 23 Catholic L. Rev. 118; 23 Cleve. St. L. Rev. 354; 60 Cornell L. Rev. 299; 58 *id.* 138; 27 Drake L. Rev. 565; 13 Family L. J. 78; 13 Family L. Q. 1; 88 Harv. L. Rev. 13, 119; 6 Hofstra L. Rev. 1087; 23 Hastings L. J. 1459; 72 Mich. L. Rev. 508; 9 U. San Francisco L. Rev. 391; 19 Vill. L. Rev. 819; 71 ALR3d 693. See § 26.30(c).

26.17 Apartments

The leading case on zoning held that apartments may be excluded from single-family dwelling zones. *Village of Euclid* v. *Ambler Realty Co.,* 272 U.S. 365 (1926). The state courts have followed a like rule.

> **EXCEPTION:** A tract of land can be so located that *as applied* to that tract single-family zoning would be invalid, for example, a single lot located in a single-family zone between two large nonconforming use apartments.

> **EXCEPTION:** Courts following the exclusionary zoning theory force the city to make room for apartments.

26.18 Accessory uses

Every zoning ordinance recognizes that certain uses different from, but incidental to, the main use prescribed in the zone are normal. Such uses are legalized under the name *accessory uses.* Many accessory uses are found in residential zones.

> **EXAMPLES:** Coin-operated washing machines and dryers in apartment buildings, also pay telephones, postage vending machines, swimming pools, and skating rinks for which a charge is made, milk vending machines, etc., are accessory uses. *Newark* v. *Daly,* 85 N.J.S. 55, 205 A2d 459 (1964). Likewise, a food shop in a large apartment hotel is often permitted. A private garage on the rear of a residential lot is universally permitted. A doctor expects to see patients in his home even though he lives in a residential area.

26.19   Incentive zoning

A rather recent development in zoning law is incentive zoning. This is a type of zoning calculated to induce the landowner to introduce amenities the city deems desirable. This type of zoning employs the Floor Area Ratio concept (F.A.R.).

> **EXAMPLE:** The floor area ratio of a building is the ratio which the floor area within the building bears to the area of the lot occupied by the building. For example, a building occupying 40,000 square feet of lot area in a zone allowing an F.A.R. of 10:1 could have 400,000 square feet of total floor area in all the stories of the building. But if, for example, the building is located in San Francisco, an F.A.R. bonus is given if the building affords direct access to the rapid transit system, and in such case it would be allowed additional square feet of floor area. 21 Syracuse L. Rev. 895. In short, F.A.R. establishes a relationship between total land area and total floor space. Thus, under a F.A.R. regulation of 1:1, a developer could build a one-story structure covering the whole lot, a two-story structure covering half of the lot, or a four-story structure covering a quarter of the lot. Bartke & Lamb, *Upzoning,* 17 William & Mary L. Rev. 701, 705.

An extremely imaginative type of incentive zoning was developed in connection with the Lincoln Center for Performing Arts in New York City. The district zoning permitted developers 20 percent more floor space on provision of certain amenities, notably, pedestrian malls, galleries, covered plazas, and pedestrian-oriented circulation improvements. Elliott & Marcus, *From Euclid to Ramapo: New Directions in Land Development Controls,* 1 Hofstra L. Rev. 56. See also 21 Syracuse L. Rev. 895; 17 Wm. & Mary L. Rev. 701.

26.20   Change of neighborhood

A change of neighborhood may invalidate existing zoning. *Manger* v. *City of Chicago,* 257 NE2d 473 (Ill. 1970).

> **EXAMPLE:** In an area zoned single-family the authorities made no effort to enforce the zoning. Stores crept in everywhere so that the few remaining vacant lots were surrounded by stores and were totally unfit for residential use. The area had become a business area. The village must permit stores on the vacant lots. *Scott* v. *Springfield,* 83 Ill. App.2d 31, 226 NE2d 57 (1967); *Vigilant Investors Corp.* v. *Hempstead,* 34 App. Div. 2d 990; 312 N.Y.S.2d 1022 (1970).

The same result occurs where the city affirmatively causes the situation.

> **EXAMPLE:** The city fathers handed out variances so liberally that nonconforming stores in the area were allowed to expand all over the area. The few remaining lots cannot be held to single-family dwelling use. *Metrop. Bd. of Zoning Appeal* v. *Sheehan Const. Co.,* 313 NE2d 78 (Ind. 1974).

26.21   Nonconforming uses

All zoning ordinances make some provision for continuation of nonconforming uses.

EXAMPLE: To invalidate an existing store use in a residential area would be unconstitutional deprivation of property. This is a simple proposition.

There is a second type of problem involved here.

EXAMPLE: An area is zoned for multifamily dwellings. A developer buys it and obtains a permit to construct an apartment. The neighbors become aware of the situation and persuade the village to rezone the area to single-family dwellings. *If construction has not yet begun,* there is, as yet, most courts say, no nonconforming use. Perhaps the developer can attack the new zoning on other grounds, but not on the ground that he has a nonconforming use.

Virtually all courts agree that *if construction has begun* under a valid permit nonconforming use status has been achieved and construction may be completed even though the zoning is amended after commencement of construction and forbids erection of such a structure. *Lutz* v. *New Albany City Plan Comm.,* 101 NE2d 187 (Ind. 1951). The construction must be done in good faith and not hastily, simply to obtain nonconforming use status. In New York the construction must be substantial. *Reichenbach* v. *Windward at Southhampton,* 364 N.Y.S.2d 283 (1975).

A generous court has accorded nonconforming use status after a permit has been issued, survey made, site cleared, and ground leveled. *Griffin* v. *Martin County,* 157 Cal. App.2d 507, 321 P2d 148 (1958). Some courts have held that nonconforming use status was not attained where permit was issued, building plans made, and construction mortgage signed. *Paramount Rock Co.* v. *County of San Diego,* 40 Cal. Reptr. 74, 180 Cal. App.2d 217. *Contra: Hull* v. *Hunt,* 55 Wash.2d 492, 331 P2d 856 (1959).

Zoning ordinances, in permitting nonconforming uses, permit ordinary repairs to be made, but they sometimes forbid *structural alterations* of a nonconforming building. A structural alteration is such as would change the physical structure of the building or would change an old building in such a way as to convert it into a new or substantially different structure.

EXAMPLE: *A* operated a milk plant which was a nonconforming use in a residential zone. His attempt to replace decayed wooden walls with brick walls was a prohibited structural alteration. *Selligman* v. *Von Allmen Bros. Inc.,* 297 Ky. 121, 179 SW2d 207 (1944). 87 ALR2d 99.

Nonconforming uses, it is felt, should be gradually eliminated. *Cole* v. *City of Battle Creek,* 298 Mich. 98, 298 NW 466 (1941). The theory is that zoning seeks to safeguard the future in the expectation that time will repair the mistakes of the past. However, the treatment a particular nonconforming use will receive if it seeks to increase or change its use appears to vary considerably owing to differences in zoning ordinances. 87 ALR2d 4.

Once a nonconforming owner abandons the use of his property for a non-conforming purpose, he loses his right to make a nonconforming use of the property and must thereafter use it only in conformity with the uses allowed to other properties in the neighborhood. Were the law otherwise, an owner could keep his property in a nonconforming class forever.

> **EXAMPLE:** The owner of a nonconforming slaughterhouse took down the smokestack and definitely discontinued the slaughterhouse business. He thereby lost his right to make a nonconforming use. *Beyer* v. *Mayor of Baltimore,* 182 Md. 444, 34 A2d 765 (1943). Also where an old nonconforming house trailer was sought to be replaced by a new one, the change was refused because the old use had been abandoned. *Town of Windham* v. *Sprague,* 219 A2d 548 (Maine 1966).

But a mere temporary discontinuance of the nonconforming use, as when a landowner is temporarily unable to procure a tenant, will not constitute an abandonment of the right to resume such use. *Landay* v. *MacWilliams,* 173 Md. 460, 196 Atl. 293 (1938). 114 ALR 993.

If a nonconforming building is either fully or partially destroyed by fire or other casualty, many ordinances forbid rebuilding.

Recently, ordinances have been passed that attempt to place a time limit on the right to continue a nonconforming use. To the extent that the *amortization ordinances* prohibit continuance of the nonconforming use after the useful economic life of the building has come to an end, most courts would consider them valid. 42 ALR2d 1146.

The rule of invalidity *as applied* is, as one might expect, applied to amortization of nonconforming uses. Thus, the court must consider: (1) the nature of the surrounding neighborhood to determine whether discontinuance of the use will have any beneficial impact and to determine if the nonconforming use, in fact, conforms to other nearby use; (2) the value and condition of the improvements on the premises to determine the quantum of damage if use is discontinued; (3) the cost of relocation and all other costs of relocating the business; (4) whether the time allowed permits the landowner to make plans for the future of his business. *Harbison* v. *City of Buffalo,* 4 N.Y.2d 553, 152 NE2d 42, 176 N.Y.S.2d 598 (1958).

26.22 Amendments and rezoning—spot zoning

Amendments to the zoning ordinance are constantly being sought by landowners whose land will thereby become more valuable. For example, land is more valuable for industrial or commercial purposes than it is for residential purposes, so rezoning of residential land for industrial purposes will greatly increase its value. Some of such rezoning is invalid. Particularly objectionable is *spot zoning,* where the city, by amendment of its ordinances, singles out and reclassifies one piece of property in a particular zone without any apparent basis for such distinction. 51 ALR2d 267; 48 Ore. L. Rev. 245.

> **EXAMPLE:** A zoning ordinance was amended to permit construction of a mortuary in a residential district. This was held invalid as spot zoning. *Mueller* v. *Hoffmeister Undertaking Co.,* 343 Mo. 430, 121 SW2d 775 (1938). 51 ALR2d 263.

Spot zoning rules. The following are some of the circumstances that will validate rezoning that, on the surface, appears to be "spot zoning."

> **EXAMPLE:** A large area was rezoned for shopping center purposes because it was at the hub of a natural traffic concentration pattern. *Temmink* v. *Baltimore County,* 205 Md. 489, 109 A2d 85 (1954). Traffic is the key to this problem. The same approach is applicable to supermarkets. *State* v. *East Cleveland,* 169 Ohio St. 375, 160 NE2d 1 (1959).

> **EXAMPLE:** Zoning of all four corner lots in a large residential district for commercial uses. Here the need for service business in a residential area is the key. *Marshall* v. *Salt Lake City,* 105 Utah 111, 141 P2d 704 (1943).

> **EXAMPLE:** Rezoning to permit apartments in an area of older homes, thus increasing tax revenues of city. *Rodgers* v. *Village of Tarrytown,* 302 N.Y. 115 (1951).

> **EXAMPLE:** Rezoning to get needed electrical substation in a residential area. *Holt* v. *City of Salem,* 192 Oreg. 200, 234 P2d 564 (1951).

As can be seen, illegal spot zoning is basically a reclassification of a small area in such a manner as to disturb the surrounding neighborhood. It is a discordant and unneeded use. None of the examples fall in this category.

Where a real change in circumstances has taken place since the original ordinance was passed, an amendment that conforms the ordinance to the new circumstances will be valid.

> **EXAMPLE:** At the time the original zoning ordinance was adopted, the only structure in an area zoned industrial was a factory. Thereafter, many single-family residences were built in the area, but no new factories. To protect the homeowners, the area was rezoned for residential purposes, the old factory remaining as a nonconforming use. This is valid rezoning. *Atlantic Coast Line R.R. Co.* v. *Jacksonville,* 68 So2d 570 (Fla. 1953).

> **EXAMPLE:** Where an urban redevelopment displaced many families, creating a need for many units to house those displaced, a single-family dwelling zone could be revised to permit apartments. *Malafronte* v. *Planning Board,* 230 A2d 606 (Conn. 1967).

EXAMPLE: *X* owned an area that was zoned commercial. A large city park was opened across the street. The city rezoned the area for apartments. This change in circumstances makes the rezoning valid. *People ex rel* v. *City of Chicago,* 2 Ill.2d 350, 118 NE2d 20 (1954).

Or where the original zoning was a mistake the city can in most states correct the error.

EXAMPLE: A lot that was unsuitable, because of topography and soil conditions, for single-family dwellings was included in a single-family dwelling zone. To correct this error, the lot was rezoned for apartments. This is valid. *Eggebeen* v. *Sonnenburg,* 239 Wis. 213, 1 NW2d 84 (1941).

An amendment to the zoning ordinance will not be valid if it zones an area for a purpose for which it is in no way adapted so that the area becomes useless.

EXAMPLE: In an area almost completely industrial, the city rezoned a portion for apartment purposes, hoping thereby to keep the area vacant until funds could be raised to buy it for a city playground. The rezoning is invalid.

Where the amendment to the zoning ordinance is in the nature of a comprehensive revision of the earlier zoning ordinance, there is a strong presumption of its validity. The suspicion with which courts view amendments to a zoning ordinance is confined to individual piecemeal amendments. *City of Baltimore* v. *N.A.A.C.P.,* 221 Md. 329, 157 A2d 433 (1960).

The courts have been liberal in sustaining rezoning of large portions of residential areas to permit shopping centers. 51 ALR2d 263; 76 ALR2d 1172.

Spot zoning violates both the federal and state constitutions because it results in unequal treatment for persons similarly situated. *Sinn* v. *Selectmen,* 357 Mass. 606, 259 NE2d 557 (1970). Beyond that, it is plainly unreasonable.

26.22(a) Zoning— amendments—reliance rule

In a number of states the rule is followed that protection ought to be given by the courts to those who bought land in reliance on existing zoning and that zoning must not be changed unless some change in neighborhood has taken place. *Northern Trust Co.* v. *Chicago,* 4 Ill.2d 432, 123 NE2d 330 (1954). 91 Harv. L. Rev. 1494.

EXAMPLE: An area is built up with homes. There are a few scattered lots. One lot owner has his lot rezoned for apartments. The courts will invalidate this rezoning.

26.22(b) Amendments— after permit issued or applied for

The city can, in some states, amend the zoning after a building permit has been applied for *but before it has been granted.*

> **EXAMPLE:** After *X* had applied for a permit to build a building that complied with a zoning set back line of 24 feet, the city passed an amendment changing the setback to 49 feet. The court sustained refusal of the permit. *Builders Const. Co.* v. *Daly,* 10 N.J. Misc. 861, 161 Atl. 189 (1932). Until construction begins, the property has not achieved status as a *nonconforming use.*

However, in other states courts will strike down an eleventh-hour attempt to block construction where a landowner has in good faith made plans and applied for a permit in reliance on an existing ordinance. These same courts, however, may sanction the refusal of a permit where the landowner is attempting to rush through a permit in the knowledge that the city is working on an amendment that would block the intended construction, *CT&TCo.* v. *Village of Palatine,* 22 Ill. App.2d 264, 160 NE2d 697 (1959). Note, Ex post facto zoning, 1971 *Urban Law Annual* 63.

If a landowner receives a building permit and commences substantial construction in reliance thereon, the city cannot amend the ordinance so as to block the construction described in the permit. *Prescault* v. *Wheel,* 132 Vt. 247, 315 A2d 244 (1974). Basic fairness is becoming the test.

> **EXAMPLE:** *X* applied for and received a permit to build an apartment. He graded, excavated, and put in a foundation. The city then attempted to rezone the area to exclude apartments. *X* can go forward with his building. *Deer Park Civic Assn.* v. *City of Chicago,* 347 Ill. App. 346, 106 NE2d 823 (1952).

REFERENCES: 50 ALR 3d 596; 49 *id* 13; 49 *id* 1150.

26.22(c) Amendments— conditional

At times a city has rezoned land with a condition in the ordinance that a certain type of building would be erected. Older decisions frowned on this. Cities, they said, should not bargain for legislation.

> **NEW DIRECTIONS:** Recent decisions sustain conditional amendments.

> **EXAMPLE:** A zoning amendment was granted on condition that the land be used for a synthetic gas production plant. It was held valid. *Goffinet* v. *Christian County,* 65 Ill.2d 40, 357 NE2d 442 (1976); 70 ALR3d 125. This is simply a matter of contract zoning now. See § 26.28. As this grows more common, villages will be better able to control the quality of new construction. Of course, there will be decisions still that resist the idea. *Ziemer* v. *County of Peoria,* 33 Ill. App.3d 612, 338 NE2d 145 (1975).

Where the landowner fails to meet the conditions, the village may return to the original zoning.

> **EXAMPLE:**   The village rezoned residential to industrial on condition that the property be improved with an industrial plant. He failed to comply. The village zoned the land back to residential. *McGowan* v. *Cohalan,* 361 NE2d 1025 (N.Y. 1971).

The problem here resembles the problem created by contract zoning. See § 26.28.

26.22(d)   Amendments— rezoning procedure

When a municipality passes an ordinance of general application, such as a law fixing a maximum speed limit, ordinarily this does not require notice to anyone unless some state law requires it. However, where *rezoning* of a tract of land is involved, that is, amending the zoning ordinance or the zoning map, the latest court decisions regard this more in the nature of a lawsuit between the owner of the land and his neighbors. Of course, every lawsuit requires notice to the landowners affected and gives them an opportunity to be heard. Recently, progressive courts have held that as a matter of constitutional law an ordinance rezoning land requires notice to the neighbors and an opportunity to state their objections. *Fasano* v. *Board of Commissioners,* 264 Oreg. 575, 507 P2d 23 (1973); *Snyder* v. *City of Lakewood,* 592 P2d 371 (Colo. 1975); *Fleming* v. *City of Tacoma,* 81 Wash.2d 292, 502 P2d 331 (1972); *West* v. *City of Portage,* 221 NW2d 303 (Mich. 1974).

> **EXAMPLE:**   In an area zoned single-family and improved largely by residences, one landowner proposes that the city rezone his land to multifamily. His neighbors must be given notice, and a hearing must be held. Many ordinances routinely provide for such notice and hearing. And the notice given must be a reasonable notice.

> **EXAMPLE:**   A zoning ordinance provided that the zoning ordinance could be amended by publication of notice in a newspaper. This is invalid. Neighboring landowners can easily be found and given notice by name and by mailing. *American Oil Corp.* v. *City of Chicago,* 331 NE2d 67 (Ill. 1975). The rule is that rational planning prior to zoning change also requires such planning to precede the granting of a special exception or variance. *Kristenson* v. *City of Eugene Planning Comm.,* 544 P2d 591 (Oreg. 1976). Listening to the neighbors helps the authorities to make a rational decision.

> **EXAMPLE:**   There was a failure to give proper notice as required by the ordinance. The rezoning was held invalid. *Jarvis Acres, Inc.* v. *Zoning Comm.* 163 Conn. 44, 301 A2d 244 (Conn. 1972).

However, the great majority of the courts continue to treat rezoning as a legislative process. This means that there is no *judicial* requirement that neighbors be given notice and an opportunity to be heard before rezoning takes place. *State* v. *City of Rochester,* 268 NW2d 885 (Minn. 1978).

REFERENCES: 73 Mich. L. Rev. 1341; 75 Mich. L. Rev. 983 (1977); 12 Willamette L. J. 45 (1975).

In point of fact, the issue is not an earthshaking one. Almost all ordinances provide for notice to neighbors and hearing before an amendment is adopted. Indeed, if you want to see pure democracy at work, plan to attend such a zoning meeting. Tempers flare. Accusations are hurled. It's quite exciting.

At times, of course, the neighbors may choose to attack a rezoning in court on the ground that the required notice was not given. *Wheeling Bank* v. *Village of Mt. Prospect,* 64 Ill. App.3d 1038, 382 NE2d 128 (1978).

EXAMPLE: Notice to an apartment manager is not legal notice to the tenants. *Dupont Circle* v. *District of Columbia,* 403 A2d 314 (1979).

26.23 Nature of zoning

At this point it becomes possible to embark upon a discussion of the nature of zoning, namely, does a zoning use attach to the person who runs the land or to the land itself? Plainly, it attaches to the land. *Dexter* v. *Town Board,* 365 N.Y.S.2d 506.

EXAMPLE: After a zoning ordinance has been enacted zoning an area residential, John Smith buys a nonconforming store that had been erected prior to the enactment of the ordinance. Smith may legally continue to run the store. *Appeal of E. & G. Auto Parts,* 348 A2d 438 (Pa. 1975).

26.24 Variances

Even the best ordinance may cause unintentional hardship to particular tracts of land. Some elasticity is needed if these hardship cases are to be dealt with. Most ordinances create a board, usually called the *board of adjustment* or *board of appeals,* which is given the power to authorize individual property owners to deviate from the terms of the ordinances where literal compliance would cause *undue hardship or practical difficulties.* This authorization is called a *variance.* The courts have worked out a number of requirements that must be met if a variance is to be granted.

1. The hardship must be special and peculiar to the particular property.

EXAMPLE: A lot is so irregular in shape that if all the front, rear, and the side line restrictions were observed, no building at all could be built on the lot.

If the hardship complained of is a condition which affects all property in the district, the hardship is not special and peculiar to any lot in the area and no individual lot owner will be granted a variance.

EXAMPLE: Foul odors from a nearby industrial area exist in an area zoned as residential. No residential lot owner will be granted a variance to build a factory. A plea must be made to the authorities to amend the ordinance.

2. Hardship means that if the landowner complies with the provisions of the ordinance, he can secure no reasonable return from, or make no reasonable use of, his property. 29 N.C.L. Rev. 250. With respect to income property, a party seeking a variance must prove that the land in question, if devoted to its existing or any permitted use, will not yield a reasonable return. This involves a detailed showing of the price paid for the property, the taxes assessed, expenses of operation, annual income, and so on. Then if the net income earned is not a reasonable return on the amount invested, hardship is shown. *Crossroads Recreation* v. *Broz,* 4 N.Y.2d 39, 149 NE2d 65 (1958). The landowner should also show that reasonable return cannot be anticipated from other permitted uses. *Forrest* v. *Evershed,* 7 N.Y.2d 256, 164 NE2d 841 (1959). The fact that a man could make more money by devoting his property to another purpose is not legal hardship. Everyone knows that land is worth more for commercial or industrial purposes than it is for residential, and yet most of our land must necessarily be zoned residential.

3. The hardship must not be self-created.

EXAMPLE: *A* departs from the plans attached to his application for a building permit and builds his home five feet closer to the side lines of his lot than the ordinance allows. When the building inspector stops him, *A* applies for a variance. He will not get it.

EXAMPLE: The city in question has an ordinance specifying a minimum lot area. *A* owns a building on a legal size lot. He then sells the building and enough of the land so that the building still occupies a legal building site. However, the portion of the lot left to *A* is now less than legal size. He will not be given a variance to permit him to build. *Board of Zoning Appeals* v. *Waskelo,* 240 Ind. 594, 168 NE2d 72 (1960).

4. The proposed new use must not change the essential character of the neighborhood. It must be consistent with the general plan of the ordinance.

EXAMPLE: A variance will not be granted to permit introduction of a cemetery into an area zoned residential.

Some courts are so strict on this point that they will not allow a variance that changes the *use* permitted by the ordinance. In other words, they will allow deviation only from the area, height, and location regulations of the ordinance.

EXAMPLE: Some courts will not permit a variance for an apartment house in a single-family area because this would be a *use* variance. *Lee* v. *Board of Adjustment,* 226 N.C. 107, 37 SE2d 128 (1946); 168 ALR 1.

However, most courts will permit a use variance where the hardship is great.

EXAMPLE: *A* owns a vacant lot in a single-family dwelling zone, and noncon-forming apartment buildings are his neighbors on both sides, that is, these build-ings were built before the ordinance was passed and are allowed to continue in operation. He will be given a variance for the erection of an apartment building. The sound reason for this variance is that no one can be induced to build a single-family dwelling on such a building site.

In granting a variance, the zoning board may impose conditions. *Vlahos* v. *Little Boar's Head District,* 101 N.H. 460, 146 A2d 257 (1958); *Zweifel Mfg. Co.* v. *Peoria,* 11 Ill.2d 489, 144 NE2d 593 (1957); 49 ALR3d 492.

EXAMPLE: The board may put in a condition that the architecture of the per-mitted building conform to the architecture of neighboring structures, or that cer-tain areas be left open and landscaped.

A variance may be limited in time.

EXAMPLE: A variance given for five years is valid. *Bringle* v. *Board of Super-visors,* 4 Cal. Reptr. 493, 351 P2d 765 (1960).

Questions may arise as to who may apply for a variance. Clearly the land-owner may do so. A contract purchaser is also qualified. However, one who is merely negotiating for the purchase of the land cannot apply for a variance.

The larger the tract of land involved, the greater the likelihood a variance will be held invalid. *Topanga Assn.* v. *County of Los Angeles,* 113 Cal. Reptr. 836, 522 P2d 12 (1974). Large tracts should be dealt with by amendment.

26.25 Special exceptions

A common provision in zoning ordinances autho-rizes the board of appeals to issue special permits for special purposes, such as public utility structures, churches, hospitals, private schools, clubs, or cemeteries. Obviously, institutions of this character must be located somewhere, but some control must be exercised by the zoning authori-ties over their location so that adverse effects on the other property owners will be held to a minimum. Typically, the ordinance may list a number of different uses that may be licensed "where public convenience and welfare will be sub-stantially served." *Dunham* v. *Zoning Board,* 68 R.I. 88, 26 A2d 614 (1942). The distinction between special exceptions and variances is a technical one. In the case of variances, the board is given authority to authorize violations of the zon-ing ordinance in hardship cases. In the case of special exceptions, the ordinance itself lists certain cases in which certain special uses are to be permitted, and the board only determines whether facts exist to bring the particular case within the terms of the ordinance. *Stone* v. *Cray,* 89 N.H. 483, 200 Atl. 517 (1938). It is not necessary to show "practical difficulties or unnecessary hardship," as is true in variance cases. *Montgomery County* v. *Merlands Club,* 202 Md. 279, 96 A2d 261 (1953).

NEW DIRECTIONS: Looking toward the future, one might hazard the guess that increasing resort will be made to the special exception technique. In other words, variances will be hard to get, because by and large they will represent unwelcome deviations from the zoning ordinance. But the things the city really wants, such as garden apartments, shopping centers, and research laboratories will be readily procurable by means of an elastic special exceptions provision in the ordinances. *Cameo Park Homes, Inc.* v. *Planning Commission,* 150 Conn. 672, 192 A2d 886 (1963); *Ranney* v. *Istituto,* 20 N.J. 189, 119 A2d 142 (1955).

In some states, the special exception is referred to as a *special use. Tullo* v. *Township of Millburn,* 4 N.J.S. 509, 149 A2d 620 (1959). In others, it is called a *conditional use. Tustin Heights Assn.* v. *Board,* 170 Cal. App.2d 619, 339 P2d 914 (1959).

26.26   The floating zone   A *floating zone* is a special use district. No specific location is assigned to it in the zoning ordinance. When the need for such a zone arises, the same public body that enacts the zoning ordinance enacts an amendment to the ordinance carving a new zone out of some existing zone. It differs from the special exception in that, at least in the earlier ordinances, a zoning amendment passed by the city council or board of trustees was needed to create a floating zone.

Also in this unique type of zoning amendment, the usual rules applicable to zoning amendments are not applied. For example, in some states, for a valid zoning amendment one must show that a mistake was made in the original zoning ordinance or that the conditions have changed, requiring rezoning. This rule is inapplicable to floating zones. *Haldemann* v. *Board of Commrs.,* 253 Md. 298, 252 A2d 792 (1969).

EXAMPLE: Cluster housing in a planned unit development is often allowed to float to any part of the village.

There are a number of decisions sustaining the validity of the floating zone. *Rodgers* v. *Village of Tarrytown,* 302 N.Y. 115, 96 NE2d 731 (1951); *Huff* v. *Board of Appeals,* 214 Md. 48, 133 A2d 82 (1957); *Treme* v. *St. Louis County,* 609 SW2d 706 (Mo. 1980). *Cheney* v. *Village 2 at New Hope,* 429 Pa. 626, 241 A2d 81 (1968). There are a few cases to the contrary. *Rudderow* v. *Twp. Committee,* 114 N.J.S. 104, 274 A2d 854 (1971).

If one must hazard a guess as to the future of the floating zone, the conjecture must be that its prospects look bright. The initial hostility of planning officials has been converted to approbation. Mosher, *The Floating Zone: Legal Status and Application to Gasoline Stations,* 1 Tulsa L. J. 149, 156, 166, 167 (1964). The criticism that zoning amendments lend themselves to political influence is not well taken. It is a well-known fact that zoning ordinances traditionally zone large areas for single-family dwellings in the full knowledge that developers will come forward requesting apartment or other zoning, thus giving the authorities an opportunity to "take a look" at the developer and development.

This argument would invalidate all rezoning. Moreover, the antirezoning view can easily be circumvented under modern ordinances by allowing desired uses, such as research laboratories, to "float" into any zone on issuance of a special exception permit. *Summ* v. *Zoning Comm. of the Town of Ridgefield,* 150 Conn. 79, 186 A2d 160 (1962). Indeed, it has been frankly acknowledged that the special exception technique lends itself to the introduction of desirable uses into residential and other districts. *Lazarus* v. *Village of Northbrook,* 31 Ill.2d 146, 199 NE2d 797 (1964). Moreover, conditions may validly be attached to a special exception. *Houdaille Constr. Mats. Inc.* v. *Board of Adjustment,* 92 N.J. Super. 293, 223 A2d 210 (1967). In this manner the authorities can impose requirements that might be complied with prior to issuance of a building permit, such as greenbelt buffer areas. The proponents of floating zones, it appears, will surely carry the field.

26.27   Planned unit developments—cluster housing

The planned unit development (hereafter referred to as PUD) is one of the novel ideas in housing. Such developments consist of town houses, homes, apartments (both garden and high-rise), or combinations of such buildings, all with common open areas and some with private recreation facilities. The advantages offered are:

1. lower priced homes achieved by cost savings through more efficient land use and planning
2. small, private yards with a minimum of maintenance chores and a maximum of time and energy for recreational activities in the common areas
3. common areas of green open space providing an attractive setting
4. in some cases, shared facilities for swimming, golf, fishing, and so forth, and a recreation center for crafts, meetings, and other group activities
5. maintenance furnished by homeowners' association

The phrase *cluster housing* means that the individual homes, usually party-wall row houses, or apartment buildings are grouped together on relatively small plots of land with large surrounding areas of land left open for common recreational use. The cluster form of development is economical because the clustering of houses with party walls reduces the cost of supplying utilities and roads. Often a PUD is placed in a floating zone.

The old-fashioned zoning ordinance, with its rigid allocation of specific uses to specific zones, its building lines, and its minimum-area requirements, does not lend itself to the PUD type of development. Cluster development calls for smaller homesites, the land subtracted from homesites being added to common areas. However, the PUD can be listed as a special exception in the zoning ordinance. Alternatively, the zoning ordinance may include a special section devoted to the PUD, calling it variously a *Community Unit Plan, Dwelling Groups, Group Housing, Planned Residential Development,* or *Planned Building Groups.* Because approving a development of this sort involves a considerable exercise of discretion, it seems wise to provide that final approval of a special exception for a developer's proposal to create a PUD zone should rest with the city council, just as if an amendment to the zoning ordinance were being considered, and some ordinances so provide. *Rodgers* v. *Village of Tarrytown,* 302 N.Y. 115, 96 NE2d 731 (1951); *La Rue* v. *East Brunswick,* 68 N.J. Super. 435, 172 A2d 691 (1961); *DeMeo* v. *Zoning Comm.,* 148 Conn. 68, 167 A2d 454 (1961). The applicant for such zoning may, under many ordinances, be a government agency, since urban redevelopment plans sometimes call for a PUD.

Where cluster housing occurs in a residential zone that permits the type of housing planned for the PUD, it is simply a form of density zoning and offers no legal problems.

26.28   Contract zoning

An application by a landowner for rezoning often results in bargaining with the planning board or the city's governing body. At times a formal covenant is entered into by the landowner and the city contemporaneously with the rezoning.

> **EXAMPLE:** In granting rezoning of land from residential to shopping center use, the city exacted a recorded covenant from the landowner that he would maintain a buffer area of landscaped land between the center and adjoining residential land. This was held valid. *Buchholz* v. *City of Omaha,* 174 Neb. 862, 120 NW2d 270 (1963).

Some courts disapprove of contract zoning. The arguments against contract zoning are:

> 1. It is illegal to "bargain" for legislation. *Baylis* v. *City of Baltimore,* 219 Md. 164, 148 A2d 429 (1959). This argument is specious. Much of the legislation on our books was initiated and lobbied through by private interests. Moreover, the rezoning could have been enacted without any conditions. *Church* v. *Town of Islip,* 8 N.Y.2d 254, 168 NE2d 681 (1960). Why, then, would the imposition of beneficial conditions invalidate it? Also, since rezoning deals, as it often must, with particular parcels of land, it is difficult to legislate sensibly without taking cognizance of the special conditions relating to that particular parcel. *Ibid.*
>
> 2. The rezoning is not in accordance with the state zoning enabling act, which contemplates division of the city into zones plainly appearing on the zoning map. Contract zoning introduces a control of land use that appears in the recorder's office but does not appear on the city's legislative records. *Treadway* v. *City of Rockford,* 24 Ill.2d 188, 182 NE2d 219 (1962). Contra: *Goffinet* v. *Christian County,* 65 Ill.2d 40, 357 NE2d 442 (Ill. 1976); 63 Ill.B. J. 132.

It has been suggested that this sort of bargining is commonplace and stands a good chance of acceptance if it is accomplished by means of "private restrictions" voluntarily created and recorded by the landowner. Hagman, *Wisconsin Zoning Practice,* 11 (1962). At least one court has accepted this suggestion.

> **EXAMPLE:** The city of X suggests to D, a developer, that he record a declaration of restrictions restricting a specified area in his development for golf course purposes over a period of twenty-five years. He does this. In return the city rezones a part of the area from detached single-family dwellings to town houses. This arrangement is valid. *State ex rel Zupancic* v. *Schimenz,* 174 NW2d 533 (Wis. 1970).

At times a contract zoning ordinance provides that if the contract is breached, the zoning reverts back to the preexisting zoning. Such a provision is invalid in some states. *Stiriz* v. *Stout,* 210 N.Y.S.2d 325 (S.Ct. 1960). In other states, it is valid. *Goffinet* v. *Christian County,* 65 Ill.2d 40, 357 NE2d 442 (1976). Every legislative change of zoning requires a careful weighing of the need for such action in the light of the circumstances then prevailing. The automatic reverter provision is the antithesis of proper legislative consideration.

It remains impossible to make a definite statement of the law on this subject. Some courts reject contract zoning. Others permit it. Others permit a form of it. The trend is in favor of permitting contract zoning. *Goffinet* v. *Christian County,* 65 Ill.2d 40, 357 NE2d 442 (1976); 70 ALR3d 125.

> *REFERENCES:* 12 UCLA L. Rev. 897; 24 Maine L. Rev. 263; 1972 Urban L. Ann. 219; 67 Dick. L. Rev. 109; 23 Md. L. Rev. 121; 23 Hastings L. J. 825; 51 J. Urban L. 94; 1974 Planning, Zoning, and Em. Dom. Inst. (S.W. Legal Foundation) 121; 63 Ill. B. J. 132; 25 De Paul L. Rev. 616; 8 Loyola U. L. J. 642 (1977).

26.29 Density—in general

Density zoning deals with a number of related items all designed to reduce density of residential occupancy, for example: (1) minimum lot size or area; (2) minimum frontage; (3) front, back, and side yards; (4) maximum lot coverage (open space zoning); (5) minimum building size. The general purpose, to prevent overcrowding, is a valid one. *Town of Durham* v. *White Enterprises Inc.,* 348 A2d 70 (N.H. 1975).

In large-scale residential developments, sophisticated density concepts are applied.

> **EXAMPLE:** The ordinance may divide up the residential area of the city into districts of differing residential density. Thus, if our particular area permits single-family, duplexes, town houses, and apartments, the applicable zoning may permit a density of five dwelling units per acre. The developer, developing ten acres, let us say, can build fifty single-family units, or twenty-five duplexes, or five ten-unit buildings or one fifty-unit building. The usual lot size and building bulk restrictions apply unless combined with clustering.

As to zones other than residential, density is discussed under incentive zoning.

Front, back, and side yards require no discussion since they occasion no problems. Bulk variances deal adequately with the situation. For example, when sprawling ranch homes became popular after World War II, zoning boards handed out front and side line variances by the thousands.

**26.29(a) Density—
minimum lot area**

Many decisions sanction minimum area residential lot requirements. The theoretical legal basis for such zoning is that spacing buildings farther apart prevents the spread of fire and provides for ample light, air, and adequate sewage disposal. *Simon* v. *Town of Needham,* 311 Mass. 560, 42 NE2d 516 (1942); *Barnard* v. *Zoning Bd. of Town of Yarmouth,* 313 A2d 741 (Maine 1974). In a rural area, a minimum lot area of five acres has been sustained *as applied. Honeck* v. *County of Cook,* 12 Ill.2d 257, 146 NE2d 35 (1957). In connection with the validity of such zoning, courts consider the character of the area. A rural area *not in the path of development* is a favorable characteristic. Also favorable is the predominance of large tracts in single ownership; also the presence of historic sites. The presence of smaller lots in the neighborhood is unfavorable to the validity of the zoning. *Marquette Nat. Bank* v. *County of Cook,* 24 Ill.2d 497, 182 NE2d 147 (1962) (minimum area of 20,000 square feet held invalid where neighboring lots were 10,000 square feet in area); *Christine Bldg.* v. *City of Troy,* 367 Mich. 508, 116 NW2d 816 (1962) (requirement of 21,780 square feet held invalid where most lots were 15,000 square feet or less). Here the competitive disadvantage makes the larger lots virtually unsalable. Increase in minimum lot area is sometimes characterized as *upgrading.* Thus, an increase of minimum lot area from two acres to four acres has been sustained. *Senior* v. *Zoning Comm. of Town of New Canaan,* 153 A2d 415 (Conn. 1959). The courts have said that the maximum enrichment of developers is not a controlling purpose of zoning. *Ibid.*

In recent times environmental factors (water pollution, for example) have been cited in favor of such zoning. *Steel Hill Development Inc.* v. *Town of Sanborton,* 469 F2d 956 (1st Cir. 1973).

This type of zoning faces the problem of *substandard* lots, that is, smaller lots platted and sold before the *upgrading* by zoning amendment. In general, the courts have required the city to issue building permits or to have invalidated the zoning as to such substandard lots. *Harrington Glen Inc.* v. *Municipal Bd. of Adjustment,* 243 A2d 233 (N.J. 1968); *Fulling* v. *Palumbo,* 21 N.Y.2d 30, 286 N.Y.2d 249 (1967); *Grace Bldg. Co. Inc.* v. *Hatfield Twp.,* 329 A2d 925 (Pa. 1974) (holding that lot owner cannot be required to buy adjoining lot in order to come into compliance with the amendment). *Contra, Grobman* v. *City of Des Plaines,* 322 NE2d 443 (Ill. 1975) (denying relief to owners of substandard lot where they refused adjoining owner's offer to purchase).

An occasional decision refuses to protect the purchaser of a substandard lot on the ground that his purchase of the lot was a gamble. He bought the lot fully aware that it was substandard, probably at a bargain price. *Phoenix* v. *Beall*, 524 P2d 1314 (Ariz. 1974). This is akin to *self-created hardship*, which is a valid basis for refusing a variance.

26.29(b) Density— minimum frontage or lot size

Minimum frontage requirements have been sustained. *Clemons* v. *City of Los Angeles*, 36 Cal.2d 95, 222 P2d 439 (1950). With respect to such requirements, the problem of substandard lots has arisen quite frequently. Many ordinances exempt *previously platted lots* from this requirement. *Graves* v. *Bloomfield Planning Bd.*, 235 A2d 51 (N.J. 1967). In any case the courts have gone far in protecting substandard lots. *Milano* v. *Town of Patterson*, 93 N.Y.S.2d 419 (1947) (requirement of sixty-foot frontage inapplicable to previously platted twenty-three-foot lot). Courts have granted flexible relief. *Ziman* v. *Vill. of Glencoe*, 275 NE2d 168 (Ill. 1971) (court imposed three-foot side yard requirement). But a denial of a variance will be overthrown. A permit must be granted. *Jacquelin* v. *Horsham Twp.*, 312 A2d 124, 10 Pa. Comwlth 473 (Pa. 1973). As in the case of minimum area cases, occasionally relief is denied to a purchaser who buys *with knowledge* of the problem, *Klehr* v. *Zoning Bd.*, 320 NE2d 498 (1974 Ill. App.).

The owner of a substandard lot cannot be compelled to buy additional frontage. Nor can he be compelled to sell to a neighbor. *Smith* v. *Smith*, 53 N.J.S. 590, 140 A2d 58 (1958).

When an owner owns several contiguous substandard lots he must comply with the new frontage requirements. In effect, he must resubdivide the frontage into lots that comply with the new requirements. *Citizens Bank and Trust Co.* v. *City of Park Ridge*, 5 Ill. App.3d 77, 282 NE2d 751 (1972).

Checkerboarding is always struck down. This is a situation in which an owner of a number of contiguous platted lots conveys out alternate lots in order to qualify each substandard lot for a permit. Note, 16 Syracuse L. Rev. 612 (1965).

26.29(c) Density— minimum building area

Prescribing a minimum building area compatible with health requirements is within the police power. *Lionshead Lake, Inc.* v. *Twp. of Wayne*, 10 N.J. 165, 89 A2d 693, appeal dismissed, 344 U.S. 919, 73 S.Ct. 386, 97 L.Ed. 708 (1953) (requirement of 768 square feet for one-story building sustained). The only substantial issue in this area is whether such a requirement can occur on a *graduated basis*, with differing minimum building areas in differing residential zones. One court has rejected this approach. *Medinger Appeal*, 377 Pa. 217, 104 A2d 118 (1954). The logic of *Medinger* is superficially attractive. If a building area of 1,000 square feet suffices to protect public health, it is difficult to sustain a requirement of 1800 square feet in zone B. However, this approach overlooks the compatibility argument. Houses of differing value do indeed occur in the various areas of the city, and to keep new houses compatible with existing houses is a legitimate objective of zoning. *Garelick* v. *Board of Appeals*, 350 Mass.

289, 214 NE2d 60 (1966). The cases have been collected elsewhere. 9 ALR2d 1374, 1409. In line with the compatibility argument, a requirement of large houses in an area characterized by smaller homes could be invalid for that reason.

26.29(d) Density—minimum building area per dwelling unit

Zoning ordinances often prescribe a minimum lot area per dwelling unit. It is obvious that this is another version of the minimum lot area requirement, and still another version of the minimum building area requirement. The ordinances discussed here do not limit lot size but prescribe a minimum lot area per dwelling unit. *First National Bank of Skokie* v. *City of Chicago,* 25 Ill.2d 366, 185 NE2d 181 (1963) (2,500 square feet per dwelling unit sustained). Once again, the problem of graduated area requirements crops up.

> **EXAMPLE:** An ordinance specified various building areas in different zones. In an R-3 district the minimum lot area per dwelling unit was 2,500 square feet, while the minimum lot area in R-4 district was 9,000 square feet per dwelling unit. Such an ordinance was held valid. *Cosmopolitan National Bank* v. *City of Chicago,* 22 Ill.2d 367, 176 NE2d 367 (1961).

26.30 Exclusionary zoning—large lot zoning—apartments

One of the recent developments in zoning law is the appearance of the doctrine of *exclusionary zoning.* The attitude of the courts embracing this doctrine is, in large part, that the public welfare requirement of the police power does not stop at the city limits. Courts cannot think in terms of the welfare of the *municipality* and its present inhabitants in testing the zoning. In some states the *tight little island* concept of zoning is outmoded. Sager, *Tight Little Islands: Exclusionary Zoning, Equal Protection and the Indigent,* 21 Stanf. L. Rev. 767 (1969). The wants and needs of all the people living in the *region* must be considered. The poor people must not be zoned into the decaying central city and zoned out of suburbs. Some early decisions in this area struck down large lot zoning. *National Land and Investment Co.* v. *Kohn,* 215 A2d 597 (Pa. 1956); *Appeal of Kit-Mar Builders,* 439 Pa. 466, 268 A2d 765 (1970); *Board of County Supervisors of Fairfax County* v. *Carper,* 200 Va. 653, 107 SE2d 390 (1959). The inequitable aspect of such zoning, bearing heavily as it does on those who cannot afford to buy large lots, has long been the subject of discussion.

Now the battle is out in the open. The authorities, and they are numerous, are collected in *Township of Williston* v. *Chester Gale Farms, Inc.,* 300 A2d 107 (Pa. 1973). The *Williston* case also collects the authorities on exclusion of apartments from suburbia as a form of exclusionary zoning. Many poor people simply cannot afford to buy a house. However, the Supreme Court of Michigan has recently rejected the view that a village must provide for apartments. *Kropf* v. *City of Sterling Heights,* 391 Mich. 139, 215 NW2d 179 (1974).

The federal courts will shy away from this question. The "hot potato" will be tossed back to the state courts.

In the state courts the issue is left in doubt at this time.

26.30(a) Exclusionary zoning—town houses

342 A2d 821 (Pa. 1975).

Courts that compel a developing municipality to admit mobile homes will extend the same privilege to town houses. *Dublin Properties* v. *Bd. of Commrs.,*

26.30(b) Exclusionary zoning—Mount Laurel

The most important state court decision on zoning is *Southern Burlington County NAACP* v. *Twp. of Mount Laurel,* 67 N.J. 151, 336 A2d 713 (1975).

Very often other courts have followed in the footsteps of the highly respected New Jersey Supreme Court. Therefore its influence will be felt nationwide. Mount Laurel is a "developing municipality," that is, one with a good deal of vacant land left. Its zoning ordinance was a rather typical suburban ordinance. The residential zones permitted only single-family dwellings. Apartments and mobile homes were not permitted. Over 4,100 acres were zoned exclusively for industry, even though only 100 acres were occupied by industry. These aspects tended to keep out the poor and were obviously so intended. The court held that virtually the *entire ordinance* was void because its entire scheme and plan were designed to keep out low- and moderate-income housing. This alone makes the case important. It holds, in effect, that *the typical suburban zoning ordinance is invalid.* The case holds, moreover, that the public benefit idea that sustains the validity of zoning ordinances in the first place is the public benefit of the *region. The zoning must benefit those who live outside the municipality, not simply the residents of the municipality. Outsiders have a right to travel into the municipality and then remain there. The municipality must accept a "fair share" of the disadvantaged. Urban League* v. *Mayor & City Council* 442 N.J. Super 11, 359 A2d 526 (1976) (invalidating 11 ordinances); *Surrick* v. *Zoning Board,* 476 Pa. 182, 382 A2d 105 (1977); 51 Temple L. Q. 764 (1978). It must adopt a new zoning map with smaller lots that the poor can afford. Space must be allocated, the court said, for apartments and mobile homes. Justice Hall, the best-informed state judge in zoning matters, wrote the opinion for a unanimous court. It surely will be followed in Pennsylvania. *Kaiserman* v. *Springfield Twp.,* 348 A2d 467 (Pa.). New York will follow Mount Laurel. *Golden* v. *Planning Board of Town of Ramapo,* 30 N.Y.2d 359 285 NE2d 291 (1972). What other states will follow it is, of course, a matter for conjecture. To the extent that it is followed, it will render obsolete the various types of density provisions, such as large lot zoning in areas similar to Mount Laurel. The court found that the actions of the municipality were "deliberate." Hitherto the courts, in deference to the legislative bodies whose actions they were examining, had always entertained the view that the legislation was motivated by pure motives. Mount Laurel suggests that courts will no longer close their eyes to the obvious. After all, the court said, the poor must live somewhere.

A warning note must be struck. The court made it plain that its decision has no application to the fully built-up suburbs with only a few vacant lots left. Only municipalities with substantial open space that lie in the path of inevitable future, residential, commercial, and industrial demand and growth are affected.

The few vanguard decisions, like Mount Laurel, are "mere harbingers of what looms as the major, domestic, social and political battle of the decade ahead, a battle whose outcome will be of enormous importance in determining the structure of United States society for many years to come." *Twp. of Williston* v. *Chesterdale Farms, Inc.*, 300 A2d 107 (Pa.). No references are given because this last case contains a sufficient number. Moreover, the "law" will come out of battles still to be fought. Note that the decision makes no mention of race. It establishes the principle that discrimination against low-income groups is unlawful.

26.30(b)(1)   Exclusionary zoning—since Mount Laurel

There have been exclusionary zoning developments since Mount Laurel.

> **EXAMPLE:**   A New Hampshire town ordinance prohibited the issuance of more than four building permits per year to any one builder. It was held invalid. The court held that, as in Mount Laurel, "public benefit" means the benefit of the public of the entire state. The court criticized local governments that attempt to exclude outsiders by building a "moat around the city and pulling up the drawbridge." *Beck* v. *Town of Raymond,* 394 A2d 847 (N.H. 1978).

> **EXAMPLE:**   Massachusetts has held that the state has the power to compel local governments to provide for low- and moderate-income housing. *Board of Appeals* v. *Housing Appeals Committee,* 294 NE2d 393 (Mass. 1973).

> **EXAMPLE:**   New Jersey has held that ordinances in four suburbs requiring a minimum floor area were invalid as improper exclusionary zoning. *Home Builders League* v. *Twp. of Berlin,* 385 A2d 295 (N.J. 1978).

> **EXAMPLE:**   Pennsylvania has held that local governments must provide areas for town houses. *Dublin Ppties* v. *Bd. of Commrs.,* 342 A2d 821 (Pa. 1975).

> **EXAMPLE:**   A developer must be permitted to build a planned unit development with space for low-income residents. *Oakwood at Madison Inc.,* v. *Twp. of Madison,* 72 N.J. 481, 371 A2d 1192 (1977).

26.30(c)   Exclusionary Zoning—family zoning

Zoning ordinances that create zones exclusively for single-family homes have always been held valid. *Village of Belle Terre* v. *Boraas,* 416 U.S.1, 39 L. Ed.2d 797 (1974). However, in recent times these ordinances have come under attack where they limit occupancy to persons related by blood or marriage, or by a husband and wife and their children. See § 26.16.

EXAMPLE: A grandmother cannot be prohibited from living with her grand-son. *Moore* v. *City of Cleveland,* 52 L. Ed.2d 531 (1977); 71 ALR3d 693. Villages must recognize and admit the "extended family."

EXAMPLE: Such ordinances must not forbid unrelated widows—widowers, spinsters, or bachelors—from living together to share expenses. *State* v. *Baker,* 81 N.J. 99, 405 A2d 368 (1978).

The chief controversy relates to the idea that a group of retarded persons or children in a foster home can be regarded as a family.

EXAMPLE: Foster home for children cannot be barred from single-family zone. *Group House* v. *Board of Zoning,* 45 N.Y.2d 266, 380 NE2d 207 (1978).

EXAMPLE: Home for retarded adults properly excluded. *Oliver* v. *Zoning Comm.,* 31 Conn. Sup. 197, 326 A2d 841 (1974).

EXAMPLE: Group home with two surrogate parents and seven disturbed children must be permitted in one-family zone. *Group House* v. *Board of Zoning,* 408 N.Y.S.2d 377 (1979). Cases along this line are growing in number. Where are such homes to be placed? In a factory district?

26.30(d) Federal exclusionary zoning

Using federal legislation that forbids racial discrimination, the federal courts are evoking the idea of federal exclusionary zoning.

EXAMPLE: The City of Parma, Ohio, was found guilty of violating the federal racial legislation. The violations consisted of denying permits to low-income housing developers, requiring expensive on-site parking, placing height restrictions that would exclude high-rise apartments, etc. *U.S.* v. *City of Parma,* 661 F2d 562 (6th Circ. 1981) cert. den. Thus the federal law seems to forbid racial discrimination by cities as well as by private citizens. *U.S.* v. *City of Black Jack,* 508 F2d 1179 (8th Circ. 1974) cert. den. 422 US 1042. See 17 R.E.L.J. 72 (1982).

26.30(e) Exclusionary zoning—the integrated community

In some states that hold exclusionary zoning invalid, the courts feel that the municipality, as a whole, must be an integrated whole. This provides a balanced mix of single-family, apartment, and commercial uses and in doing so, the municipality must consider regional needs, keeping in mind the effect of the ordinance on neighboring communities. *Berenson* v. *Town of New Castle,* 38 N.Y.2d 102, 341 NE2d 236 (1975).

EXAMPLE: The municipality cannot totally exclude multifamily dwellings. This would deny access to persons who cannot afford to own homes. The ordinance failed to take into account regional needs. As can be seen, the court was forced to take over the planning function because the municipalities failed and refused to engage in sensible planning. This again presents the argument in recent cases that rational planning must precede rational zoning.

Modern courts want each municipality to house its fair share of the poor. *Urban League* v. *Mayor and City Council,* 359 A2d 526 (invalidating eleven different ordinances); *Surrick* v. *Zoning Board,* 476 Pa. 182, 382 A2d 105 (1977), 51 Temple L. Q. 764.

REFERENCES: 29 Rutgers L. Rev. 73 (1975); 30 *id.* 1237 (1977); 8 Seton Hall L. Rev. 460 (1977); 49 St. Johns L. Rev. 653 (1975); 45 U. Cinn. L. Rev. 115 (1976); 1976 U. Ill. L. For. 1; 37 U. Pitt. L. Rev. 442 (1975); 6 U. Mich. J. Law Ref. 290 (1973); 48 ALR3d 1210; 13 Wake Forest L. Rev. 13; 11 Suffolk U. L. Rev. 1; 52 Notre Dame Law. 48; 84 Harv. L. Rev. 1645; 6 Rutgers Camden L. J. 653; 86 Yale L. J. 385; 4 Fordham Urb. L. J. 147 (contrasting federal and state approaches); 8 Ind. L. Rev. 995; 7 Seton Hall L. Rev. 1.

26.31 Inclusionary ordinances

To insure that housing for lower income people will be built and widely dispersed, several communities (Fairfax County, Virginia; Montgomery County, Maryland; and Los Angeles, California) have adopted ordinances requiring developers to include a minimum amount of subsidized or low-cost housing in their projects. Kleven, *Inclusionary Ordinances—Policy and Legal Issues in Requiring Private Developers to Build Low Cost Housing,* 21 U.C.L.A. Rev. 1432 (1974). One such ordinance was held invalid. *Board of Supervisors* v. *Carper,* 214 Va. 635, 198 SE2d 600 (1973). But in California such ordinances are valid. 62 ALR3d 880.

REFERENCES: 33 Maine L. Rev. 29; 6 Urb. Law. 690.

26.32 Effect of zoning ordinance on restrictions

Restrictions contained in a deed, plat, or property owner's agreement are neither nullified nor superseded by the adoption of a zoning ordinance. *Chuba* v. *Glasgow,* 61 N.M. 302, 299 P2d 774 (1956); *Schwarzchild* v. *Wolborne,* 186 Va. 1052, 45 SE2d 152 (1947).

EXAMPLE: A deed provided that use of the land thereby conveyed was restricted to residence purposes. Thereafter, an ordinance was passed zoning this area for commercial purposes, and the owner attempted to construct a gasoline station thereon. It was held that the deed restriction would be enforced, and a court order was entered forbidding erection of the gasoline station. *Dolan* v. *Brown,* 338 Ill. 412, 170 NE 425 (1930).

However, a change of use in the zoning ordinance does help to show that a change in the neighborhood has taken place, and the court may well decline thereafter to enforce the building restrictions on the ground of change in neighborhood. *Goodwin Bros.* v. *Combs Lumber Co.,* 275 Ky. 114, 120 SW2d 1024 (1938); *Austin* v. *Van Horn,* 225 Mich. 117, 237 NW 550 (1931); 26 CJS *Deeds* § 171 (2).

> **NEW DIRECTIONS:** The older zoning ordinances permitted residences to be erected in any zone (cumulative zoning). The newer ordinances, by and large, forbid residential uses in commercial and industrial zones. Where the earlier building restriction calls for residential use and later zoning ordinance forbids residential use, the zoning ordinance supersedes the restriction. *1.77 Acres of Land* v. *State,* 241 A2d 513 (1968); *Grubel* v. *MacLaughlin,* 286 F.Supp.24 (1968); *Key* v. *McCabe,* 54 Cal.2d 736, 356 P2d 169 (1960); *Blakely* v. *Gorin,* 313 NE2d 903 (Mass. 1974); Hagman, *Urban Planning,* 308.

26.33 Mortgages

Zoning laws are binding on mortgagees. When a mortgagee loaned money for construction of a building that violated a zoning ordinance, the court refused to protect him although he was ignorant of the fact that the ordinance was being violated, since in dealing with real estate, all who are interested are required to take notice of zoning laws. *Siegemund* v. *Building Commissioner,* 263 Mass. 212, 160 NE 795 (1928). Accordingly, a mortgagee making a construction loan should satisfy himself that the contemplated improvement complies with existing ordinances. Otherwise he may find construction of the building halted by a court order after part of his mortgage money has been paid out.

26.34 Enforcement of zoning ordinance

It is usually provided in the zoning ordinance that any property owner wishing to erect a building must first apply to the commissioner of buildings or other proper official for a building permit. Every such application must be accompanied by plans and specifications of the contemplated structure. The official inspects the plans and declines to issue the permit if a violation of the zoning ordinance is disclosed. If, despite the fact that the contemplated structure would violate the zoning ordinance, the building permit is nevertheless issued, any other property owner whose property would suffer special damage by erection of the proposed structure, for example, a neighbor, may, if he acts promptly, obtain a court order prohibiting the erection of the building. *Garner* v. *County of DuPage,* 8 Ill.2d 155, 133 NE2d 303 (1956). Although it is advisable to do so, the complaining property owner need not first request the public authorities to take action. *Fitzgerald* v. *Merard Holding Co.,* 106 Conn. 475, 138 Atl. 483 (1927). If the complaining owner acts promptly in asserting his rights, but construction of the building is nevertheless begun, the offending property owner may be ordered by the court to demolish the illegal portion of the structure.

> **EXAMPLE:** Despite protests of an adjoining owner before the commissioner of buildings and the Zoning Board of Appeals, a permit was issued to a property

owner to construct an apartment building that violated the zoning ordinance in that it did not have a one-foot setback for every nine feet or rise above a height of seventy-two feet. While litigation was pending to declare the permit invalid, the apartment building corporation proceeded with construction of the building. Eventually, the courts declared the permit invalid, and the adjoining owner filed suit to compel the corporation to reconstruct the building to conform to the zoning ordinance. It developed that such reconstruction could be accomplished only at a cost of $343,837.07. Nevertheless, the court ordered the building corporation to reconstruct the building to comply with the ordinance. *Welton v. 40 East Oak St. Bldg. Corp.,* 70 F2d 377 (1934).

It is held in some states that if a permit is issued, and in reliance thereon erection of the building is begun, the city cannot thereafter enforce the zoning ordinance if it is discovered that the permit should not have been issued. *Shellburne Inc.* v. *Roberts,* 224 A2d 250 (Del. 1966). The law on this point is chaotic. 1971 Urban Law Annual 63.

EXAMPLE: The city allowed an apartment building to stand for over forty-three years although it violated the zoning ordinance. The city now seeks to fine the apartment owner. It can do so. The long delay does not bar city action. The philosophy here is that important public rights ought not be lost by inaction of public servants. *G & S Mtg. & Invest. Corp.* v. *City of Evanston,* 264 NE2d 740 (Ill. 1970).

As to the matter of a court finding that the village is barred (estopped) from enforcing its zoning laws against a particular tract of land, this usually arises from some action of the village that encourages the landowner to make substantial expenditures in the belief that he is acting legally. The village then seeks to invalidate a previously issued building permit, change the law, or otherwise pull the rug out from under the landowner. Courts at times protect the landowner, perceiving the injustice of allowing him to spend money in a mistaken belief encouraged by the city. At times courts permit the city to block construction, often in the unspoken belief that bribery was present. At all events, the decisions are in chaos. In Illinois alone, the decisions number half a hundred or more.

REFERENCES: 1971 Urb. Law Ann. 63; 29 Hastings L. J. 658 (1978); 49 N.C. L. Rev. 197 (1970); 6 ALR2d 960.

26.35 Planning

City and regional planning figures prominently in the life of many communities today. State laws authorize the adoption by planning commissions of master plans. Such a commission plans for the systematic and orderly development of the community, with particular regard for the location of future major street systems, transportation systems, parks, recreation areas, industrial and commercial undertakings, and residential areas, the creation and preservation of civic beauty, and other kindred matters, all looking not only to the present, but with a view to the orderly development of the unbuilt, as well as the built-up areas.

Generally, at present, the formulation of a master plan is not a precondition to the enactment of a zoning ordinance. True, the zoning ordinance must be rational and bear within itself some evidence of logical planning, but if that is present, it suffices. *Angermeier* v. *Sea Girt*, 27 N.J. 298, 142 A2d 624 (1958).

> **NEW DIRECTIONS:** Increasingly, the courts are looking for some comprehensive plan to guide them in their decision as to the validity of zoning. If there is a plan and the zoning or rezoning conforms to that plan, the courts are likely to sustain it. If the existing zoning is inappropriate when compared with an existing plan, the courts may strike it down. *Fasano* v. *Board of County Commrs.,* 264 Oreg. 574, 507 P2d 23 (1973).

> **EXAMPLE:** The plan showed the area was ideal for multifamily housing, but the ordinance zoned it as single-family. It must be rezoned multifamily. *City of Lousiville* v. *Kavanagh,* 495 SW2d 502 (Ky. 1973).

> **NEW DIRECTIONS:** If the municipality has no plan at all, the courts are likely to regard this as a good basis for striking down a zoning change. If the city has no plan, any change is, arguably, a planless change. *Forestville,* v. *County of Cook,* 18 Ill. App.3d 230, 309 NE2d 763 (1974). Planless change creates a hodgepodge of incompatible uses. If the court is to decide the validity of a proposed zoning change, it is entitled to know the city's long range plans for the general area. *801 Avenue C, Inc.* v. *City of Bayonne,* 127 N.J. Super. 128, 316 A2d 694 (1974); *Hall* v. *City and County of Honolulu,* 530 P2d 737 (Hawaii, 1975). This is one of the battlegrounds that will surely be fought on, hammer and tongs. The city fathers prefer to keep their plans secret, meanwhile zoning much land for single-family dwellings or industrial use, always intending to rezone the land when the "right" developer comes along and they have had a look at him. If they must come out into the open, and show on their plans that the area has a long-range future for multifamily dwellings, they will have a hard time rejecting rezoning for this purpose. At the same time the courts want to see "in public" what the long-range plans are so that they can make a rational decision on the score.

There are recent decisions dealing with planning.

> **EXAMPLE:** A zoning amendment that does not conform to the plan is invalid. *Barber* v. *Town of North Kingeslin,* 372 A2d 1269 (R.I. 1977).

> **EXAMPLE:** A variance must conform to the master plan. *Baker* v. *City of Milwaukee,* 533 P2d 772 (Oreg. 1975).

REFERENCES: 29 Fordham L. Rev. 635; 43 Geo. Wash. L. Rev. 120; 8 Natural Resources Law 455; 20 Law & Contemp. Problems 351; 74 Mich. L. Rev. 899 (1976); 73 *id.* 1341; 12 Syracuse L. Rev. 342; 116 U. Pa. L. Rev. 25; 35 Temple

L. Q. 59; 7 Univ. of Mich. J. L. Ref. 516 (1974); 9 Urb. Law. Ann. 69 (1975); 6 Urb. Law. 686; 7 *id.* 731; 1977 Planning, Zoning, & Em. Dom. Inst. 1 (1977); 1978 *id.* 205; 10 Willamette L. J. 358 (1974); 12 *id.* 45; 40 ALR3d 372.

26.36   Building codes   Most cities have adopted building codes specifying in great detail various requirements as to the construction of buildings, including requirements as to fireproof construction, load and stress, size and location of rooms, means of exit, windows and ventilation, sanitary equipment, electrical installation, chimneys, heating plant, mechanical refrigeration, illumination of exits, and standpipes. Often these are divided into separate codes, such as the electrical code or plumbing code. Innumerable special provisions will be encountered relating to special types of structures, such as theaters, schools, hospitals, garages, amusement parks, billboards, canopies, marquees, illuminated roof signs, and grandstands. Hazardous use units, such as drycleaning establishments, grain elevators, or paint-spraying rooms, are also subject to special regulations.

The fact that a building was erected while an older, more lenient law was in effect does not insulate it from newer, more rigid requirements. As long as the new standards are reasonable, the old buildings must conform to them.

> **EXAMPLE:** An ordinance required tenement houses to have a supply of water on each floor. All old buildings must comply with this ordinance. *Health Dept.* v. *Trinity Church,* 145 N.Y. 32, 39 NE 833 (1895).

A landowner who proposes to erect a building must establish not only that it will comply with the zoning ordinance, but that all requirements of the building code will be complied with. Hence an application for a building permit, with its accompanying plans and specifications, is examined not only for possible zoning ordinance violations, but also for possible violations of the building code. Thus the application may be handled by a number of different departments of the city, such as the fire department, board of health, or boiler inspection department, before the permit is finally issued.

Permits are required not only where new construction is contemplated, but also where enlargements, alterations, or substantial repairs of existing structures are to be made.

Many zoning and building ordinances provide that no newly constructed building may be occupied until inspected by a city official for violations of ordinances. If no violations exist, a *certificate of occupancy* is issued by the city. Obviously, it is dangerous to buy and pay for a newly constructed building without determining that a certificate of occupancy has been issued.

Local ordinances often provide that the commissioner of buildings or other proper official shall make an annual inspection of certain types of buildings. If any violation of the building code is disclosed, the owner or occupant is required to make the necessary alterations to make the building comply with the code. It is customary in some localities for an intending purchaser to cause a search to be made in the various departments charged with enforcing the building ordinances, such as the tenement house department, the building department, the fire department, or the health department. If any record of an existing violation is thereby disclosed, the seller is required to cure the violation. In order to avoid delay in closing the deal, the seller may permit the buyer to retain a portion of the purchase price as security to insure the seller's subsequent removal of the violation.

To achieve uniformity, states are beginning to adopt state building codes, as in New Jersey.

A building that is dangerously unsafe is a public nuisance and may be demolished by the city authorities without payment of compensation to the owner. *City of Honolulu* v. *Cavness*, 45 Hawaii 232, 364 P2d 646 (1961). Quite commonly laws and ordinances covering this situation go on to provide that the city has a lien, quite like a mortgage, on the vacant land for the expenses of demolition. This is called a *demolition lien.* In some states this lien is given priority over existing liens, such as mortgages.

There is some degree of uniformity throughout the country in building codes. Building Officials and Code Administrators, International, Inc. (BOCA), publish the BOCA Code, used primarily in the Midwest and East. The Southern Building Code Congress publishes a code used in the South. The International Congress of Building Officials publishes the Uniform Building Code, covering the West. Thus, to the lawyer, a court decision interpreting any of these codes can be used in any city that has adopted the code. The BOCA Code is amended every three years. The other codes are also amended at times as technology changes.

26.36(a) Building code violations—liability of landlord for injuries

The matter of a landlord's liability for personal injuries where he violates *state* laws is being discussed elsewhere. See Ch. 37. The new cases are beginning to apply this idea to *city* code violations. *Whetzel* v. *Jess Fisher Management Co.,* 282 F2d 943 (1960). Some of the older cases do not go this far. Today there are hundreds of "home-rule" municipalities in this country. Each one of these is similar to a little state legislature for that particular city. If *L* violates a home-rule ordinance, he is likely to be liable in a good many cities.

> **EXAMPLE:** The home-rule city of *X* passes an ordinance requiring all apartment stairways to be well lighted twenty-four hours a day. *L* turns off the lights at 11:00 P.M. despite the protests of tenants. *T* is injured on a dark stairway. He can sue *L*. It is the same as if a state law had been violated. Some prolandlord courts probably will continue to hold against the tenant.

27 LAND USE CONTROLS— LAND DEVELOPMENT, REGULATION, SUBDIVISIONS, AND DEDICATION

27.01 Dedication

Dedication involves the landowner's setting apart his land for some public use, followed by an acceptance of such donation by the public. Dedication is of two kinds—common law and statutory.

27.01(a) Common law dedication

No particular form is required for a common law dedication. It is not necessary that there be any written instrument. There must be an intention on the part of the landowner to dedicate his land to the public. He must, either by his words or acts, offer the land for some public use, and the public authorities must accept the offer. On acceptance of the offer, the city acquires an easement in the land dedicated.

> **EXAMPLE:** *A* owned a tract of land. He fenced off the tract, locating the fence approximately thirty-three feet north of the south line of his land. This thirty-three-foot strip was used by the public as a road and was later paved by the city. *A*'s acts showed an intention to offer the strip as a street, and the city's acts showed an acceptance of that offer. The city acquired an easement in the land for street purposes. Ownership of the street remained in *A*. 24 Baylor L. Rev. 592.

Once an offer of dedication has been accepted by the city it is irrevocable. 86 ALR2d 877. Whether it can be revoked *before* acceptance depends on the state law. 86 ALR2d 860.

If the intention to dedicate is lacking, there is no dedication.

> **EXAMPLE:** Suppose I own land abutting on a public street and have a store thereon located some five feet from the street line. To induce the public to look into my store windows, I pave the strip between the store and the street. This does not operate as a dedication of the strip as part of the street, for my intention

here is simply to make a more profitable utilization of my private property, not to give it to the public. *Nickel* v. *City* 239 SW2d 519 (Mo. App. 1951).

For the same reason, any sign placed on such a strip indicating that the same is private property will prevent the creation of a dedication, even though the public is permitted to use such strip. 18 CJS 91. Some owners of private streets or alleys periodically place chains across the street or alley or imbed markers in the pavement to show an absence of intention to dedicate.

It is often said that land can be dedicated only by the true owner thereof. *O'Rorke* v. *City of Homewood,* 237 So2d 487 (Ala. 1970). This is true. Nevertheless, dedications can be and are made by owners whose land is subject to easements or other rights. 69 ALR2d 1236.

> **EXAMPLE:** *R* owned land over which *X*, a neighbor, had a recorded driveway easement. *R* filed a plat in which he included the driveway in a public street dedicated by the plat. This is valid. The city acquires its rights subject to the rights of *X* to continue to exercise his rights under the easement. This is simply an application of the rule that one acquiring on easement does not acquire the exclusive right to its use. (See § 4.10.)

27.02 Subdivision plats

Successful subdivision planning involves far more than the mere drawing of street and lot lines on paper; it includes the planning of neighborhoods. This planning begins with the selection of the raw land, the economical planning of streets, lots, and utilities, and the control of house design. After a plan has been arrived at, the lots, parks, and streets into which the land is to be divided are staked out by a land surveyor, and permanent monuments are placed at the corners of the subdivision. After this has been done, the surveyor plots on paper the manner in which the land has been subdivided. This is called *platting the subdivision.*

The plat is signed and acknowledged by the owner. If the land is mortgaged, the mortgagee must join in the plat. 63 ALR2d 1160. Then it is necessary to obtain the written approval of various city and other authorities. This approval merely signifies that the plat conforms to local law. After all this has been done, the plat is recorded in the recorder's office. It then constitutes an offer of *ownership* of the public places shown on the plat.

27.02(a) Dedicated areas

Plats often contain donations or dedications of areas for parks or schools. One common trouble with these dedications is their ambiguity.

SUGGESTIONS

1. Do you want to create rights in the general public or only in the lot owners in the subdivision? For example, if you mark a tract of land on the plat as "beach" or "park," is it intended that the *general public* may use the area, or is it intended that only *lot*

owners shall use the area? The decisions are conflicting. 11 ALR2d 562. Make your intention clear. Place a legend on the plat as follows: "A perpetual easement appurtenant to each lot in this subdivision is hereby created for use of the area marked 'beach' as a private bathing beach only for owners of lots in this subdivision, members of their family, and guests. This must not be construed as a dedication to the general public. Ownership of the area is reserved to the subdivider and does not pass by any deed or mortgage of a lot."

2. To what *specific use* is the dedicated area to be put? For example, what is meant by such a general, ambiguous phrase as "public square"? Is it something like a park? Could a courthouse be built on it? A school? A church? A swimming pool? An athletic stadium? Spell out the specific use you want.

3. Who is to be the *legal owner* of the dedicated area? The city? The subdivider? The adjoining landowners? There is some advantage to putting ownership in the city. For example, it will usually rid the subdivider of the burden of paying taxes on the area and will relieve him of personal liability for accidents that may occur on the area. A plat of dedication may give only an easement. 11 ALR2d 549. Give the city a deed. Approval of a plat by a city is *not* an acceptance of ownership.

4. Is a *present gift* intended or merely some possible gift in the future? For example, what is meant by the phrase "reserved for park"? Or "proposed park"? *Anderson* v. *Tall Timbers Corp.,* 378 SW2d 16 (Tex. 1964). Does such a phrase create present rights in the lot owners or the city, so that the subdivider may not change his mind a year from now and build a house on the tract? Don't use ambiguous phrases.

5. Is the utility strip dedicated to the public? A plat often shows a strip across the rear of the lots marked *easement for public utilities.* Some courts feel that the use of the word *public* makes this a dedication to the public. *Nichol* v. *Village of Glen Ellyn,* 89 Ill. App.2d 467, 231 NE2d 462 (1967); but other courts disagree. *Island Homes* v. *City of Fairbanks,* 421 P2d 759 (Alaska 1966). This should not be left in doubt, for if the strip is not dedicated to the public, there is some control in the landowner over which companies come into that strip with their services.

SUGGESTION: Place a legend on the plat as follows: "A perpetual easement is hereby created in favor of all lot owners in this subdivision, over, under, and across the area marked *easement for public utilities* as an easement appurtenant to each lot in this subdivision for the installation, use, maintenance, repair, and replacement of public utilities, including sewer, water, gas, electricity, telephone and telegraph. Said areas are not dedicated to the public."

Even where the public authorities never accept a particular street, public park, or other public area so designated on a plat, any lot owner in the subdivision has a private right to have the area used as platted and may obtain a court order forbidding any other use. *Newton* v. *Batson,* 223 S.C. 545, 77 SE2d 212 (1953); *McCorquodale* v. *Keyton,* 63 So2d 906 (Fla. 1953).

Approval of the subdivision plat by the city or other public body is not an automatic *acceptance* of the streets, parks, and other public areas depicted on the plat. 26 CJS 479; 11 ALR2d 574. *Acceptance* is shown by the city's paving the streets, putting in sewers, and so on. 52 ALR2d 263. Therefore, if you want the city to assume *immediate responsibility* for these areas, you had best get the city council to pass an ordinance accepting this dedication. And if you want the city to have complete ownership of a park, for example, it is best to give the city a deed to the area and have the city council pass an ordinance accepting it, although in many states acceptance of a plat operates as a transfer of ownership to the city. Once an area has been dedicated, neither the subdivider nor the city can use the land for a purpose other than the dedicated purpose. *City of St. Louis* v. *Bedal,* 394 SW2d 391 (1965).

27.03 Conditional dedication—reservations by dedicator

A landowner making a dedication has the right to impose conditions. 26 CJS *Dedication* § 30.

> **EXAMPLE:** *R* dedicated land to *E City* as a highway subject to the condition that the city provide a frontage road giving him access to the highway. This the city failed to do. *R* can revoke the dedication. *People* v. *Lorenz,* 34 Ill.2d 445, 216 NE2d 123 (1966).

Likewise a dedicator may reserve a private easement over land he dedicates. 3 *Am. Law of Ppty.* § 12.132.

> **EXAMPLE:** *R* dedicates a park to *E City,* reserving an easement of ingress and egress over a specified portion of the park.

27.04 Subdivision regulation—plat approval

During the real estate boom of the 1920s countless subdivisions were laid out with no thought for potential need. Plats were recorded showing streets and parks that never materialized. Lots were sold to ignorant people who had no notion of their true value. When the crash of 1929 arrived, lot sales stopped. The market for vacant lots totally disappeared. Real estate taxes were not paid. These premature subdivisions became a disaster area. 36 Mo. L. Rev. 1; 3 Urb. Law. 126; 17 N.Y. L. Forum 1050. Hence laws were passed requiring a developer to submit his plat for approval before it is recorded. *Kligman* v. *Lautman,* 251 A2d 745 (N.J. 1969). In general, the legal philosophy is that if a landowner chooses to subdivide his land and to record a plat for that purpose, the public can legitimately impose reasonable restrictions on his use of the public records to accomplish his objectives. Even more important, the community has a stake in avoiding the problems of unpaid taxes and unusable streets that premature platting creates and an even greater stake in preserving the health of the community through proper sewer and water installations. Proper traffic control is also a legitimate objective. *Forest Const. Co.* v. *Planning Comm.,* 236 A2d 917 (Conn. 1967).

Today subdivision of land is subject to strict controls. 86 Yale L.J. 385 (1977). The governing body of the city or village or a planning board may retain in its own hands the power to approve or disapprove proposed subdivisions, or, where the state law permits, this power may be delegated to a planning commission. Control over land subdivision is exercised over the entire city and often a surrounding area of several miles. *Prudential Co-op Realty Co.* v. *City of Youngstown,* 118 Ohio St. 204, 160 NE 695 (1928); 11 ALR2d 524. However, this power to *approve* plats of land outside the city limits does not confer power to *zone* the area outside the city. *City of Carlsbad* v. *Caviness,* 66 N.M. 230, 346 P2d 310 (1959); *Village of Bensonville* v. *County of Du Page,* 30 Ill. App.2d 324, 174 NE2d 403 (1961). The city adopts regulations establishing standards of subdivision design, including regulations concerning utilities, streets, curbs, gutters, sidewalks, storm and sanitary sewers, fire hydrants, street lighting, street signs, and width, depth, and area of lots. No subdivision plat may be recorded unless it has been approved, and approval is withheld unless the plat complies with the regulations. In lieu of requiring installation of streets, utilities, and so on, before approval, the commission may accept a surety company bond guaranteeing that the installation will be made. It is impractical to install streets and then have them pounded to rubble as construction goes forward.

Like zoning, plat approval is a type of land use control. But it is different from zoning. There are two separate laws.

NEW DIRECTIONS: Zoning and plat approval combined. There is a trend toward combining the functions of rezoning and plat approval. The developer proposes a development that requires rezoning and submits a plat that conforms to the rezoning.

If a subdivider records his plat without the required approval, he runs the risk that the planning board or the city may procure a court order stopping all sales. *Wrongful Subdivision Approval by the Plan Commission: Remedies of the Buyer and City,* 29 Ind. L. J. 408 (1954). Moreover, in most states the law forbids the recording of a plat unless city approval is endorsed thereon. And in many states, selling land in an unapproved subdivision plat is subject to a fine. In some states, California, Michigan, and New Jersey, for example, the buyer of a lot in an unapproved subdivision may change his mind, abrogate the sale, and get his money back. *Platting, Planning & Protection—A Summary of Subdivision Statutes,* 36 N.Y.U. L. Rev. 1214 (1961). In other states—Idaho, Iowa, Massachusetts, Michigan, Nebraska, Rhode Island, and Wyoming, for example—the buyer of a lot in an unapproved subdivision may sue the seller for damages. Building permits are refused where the lots front on an unapproved street. Sometimes the subdivider divides up his area into building sites, but instead of recording a plat showing these building sites as lots on the plat, he sells off the sites by metes and bounds descriptions. No plat is recorded. Any such attempted evasion of the law is ineffective. Such conduct can be fined, and a court order can be issued forbidding such metes and bounds sales. In many states the recorder of deeds will refuse to accept for recording a deed in a metes and bounds subdivision. Also, building permits will be refused the lot owners. 77 ALR3d 1053.

Generally, it is required that the plat and subdivision conform to regulations or plans set forth in a statute or ordinance. The city, in other words, cannot arbitrarily withhold its approval. Its disapproval must be based on failure of the plat to conform to some general set of rules applicable to all developers. *Beach* v. *Planning Comm.*, 141 Conn. 79, 103 A2d 814; *People* v. *Massieon*, 279 Ill. 312, 116 NE 639.

Of course, the consequences of failure to comply with the plat law vary from state to state.

EXAMPLE: In Illinois a contract by the subdivider to convey land in an illegal subdivision is not void. *Bamberg* v. *Griffin,* 76 Ill. App.3d 138, 394, NE2d 910, (1979). Accord. *Edler* v. *Hale,* 13 Utah 2d 279, 373 P2d 383 (1962). See 77 ALR3d 1053.

27.05(a) Forced dedication

As the need for public control of platting gained acceptance, the pendulum began to swing steadily toward more rigorous controls. The cities, in addition to controlling the size and direction of streets, grading and paving, gutters and drainage, water and utility installation, etc., began to insist on dedication of land for schools and parks, and other contributions to the public. The requirements as to streets, sidewalks, sewer, and water have been upheld as valid. Yearwood, *Accepted Controls of Land Subdivision,* 45 J. of Urban Law 217 (1967). 36 Mo. L. Rev. 1. The other requirements have aroused controversy.

When it comes to city exactions of great magnitude, such as those requiring the developer to contribute parks, school areas, and sewage treatment plans, the problems become very difficult.

The city has two great powers, the police power and the power of eminent domain. The police power is the power to pass reasonable laws for the good of the public. The power of eminent domain is the power to acquire land for public purposes by paying for it. Where forced dedication is employed and sustained, the court is saying that this is an appropriate situation for exercising the police power. This does not require the payment of any compensation. The decisions are not entirely consistent from state to state. That is evident from a review of the following examples.

The following exactions were held valid under the police power without the necessity for the payment of compensation:

EXAMPLE: An ordinance requiring that the location, width, and alignment of platted streets conform to existing contiguous streets and to the city plan, and that abnormally steep grades, sharp curves, or dangerous intersections be avoided.

EXAMPLE: An ordinance requiring the subdivider to dedicate ample streets to the city. *Ayres* v. *City of Los Angeles,* 34 Cal.2d 31, 207 P2d 1 (1949).

EXAMPLE: An ordinance requiring the subdivider to pave streets and install utilities, gutters, and storm sewers. *Brous* v. *Smith,* 304 N.Y. 164, 106 NE2d 503 (1954); *Petterson* v. *Naperville,* 9 Ill.2d 233, 137 NE2d 371 (1956); *In re Spring*

Valley Development, 300 A2d 736 (Maine 1973); *Deerfield Estates Inc.* v. *Twp. of East Brunswick,* 286 A2d 498 (N.J. 1971).

EXAMPLE: The developer was required to contribute $120,000 toward drainage facilities. The court sustained this because the needs created by the development can be charged against the development. *Divan Builders, Inc.* v. *Planning Board,* 334 A2d 30 (N.J. 1975). The court gave consideration to the fact that improvement of drainage was made necessary by the development.

EXAMPLE: The city required 4 percent of the platted area to be set apart for parks and playgrounds. This was held valid because the need for parks and playgrounds was created by the subdivider's activity. *Aunt Hack Ridge Estates, Inc.* v. *Planning Comm.,* 160 Conn. 109, 230 A2d 45.

EXAMPLE: An ordinance requiring subdivider to dedicate land or pay a fee in lieu thereof for park purposes. *Assoc. Home Builders* v. *City of Walnut Creek,* 94 Cal. Reptr. 630, 484 P2d 606 (1971). This case contains a valuable review of the law on the subject.

EXAMPLE: A city may require that a developer donate land for recreation purposes because the need was "specifically and uniquely attributable" to the development. *Frank Ansuini Inc.* v. *City of Cranston,* 264 A2d 910 (R.I. 1970); *Dept. Pub. Works* v. *Exchange Nat. Bank,* 334 NE2d 810 (Ill. 1975).

EXAMPLE: A residential developer and school board entered into an agreement under which the developer agreed to contribute land and pay the board a sum of money for each home constructed. In return the developer received zoning special use permits. The court held the contract valid. *Board of Education* v. *Surety Dev. Inc.,* 321 NE2d 99 (Ill. 1975). The philosophy here is that the developer may be properly required to bear burdens which are "specifically and uniquely attributable" to his development activities. *Dept. of Pub. Works* v. *Exchange Nat. Bank,* 334 NE2d 810 (Ill. 1975).

EXAMPLE: A developer was required to dedicate land for a school site. *Krughoff* v. *City of Naperville,* 68 Ill 2d 352, 369 NE2d 892 (1977).

EXAMPLE: Substantial "tap in fees" (charges for connecting with the sewer system) have been sustained where the proceeds were to be used for improving the sewer system. *Home Builders Assn.* v. *Provo City,* 503 P2d 451 (Utah 1972).

Among regulations held invalid without payment of compensation are the following:

EXAMPLE: Ordinance increasing price of building permit, listing various charges, vastly in excess of the cost of processing the permit. *Merrelli* v. *St. Clair Shores,* 355 Mich. 575, 96 NW2d 144; *Daniels* v. *Point Pleasant,* 23 N.J. 357, 129 A2d 265.

EXAMPLE: Ordinance charging the subdivider $400 per acre to connect to city sewer system. *City of Los Angeles* v. *Offner,* 55 Cal.2d 103, 358 P2d 926 (1961).

EXAMPLE: Ordinances requiring subdivider to donate land for schools, parks, etc. *Pioneer Bank* v. *Mt. Prospect,* 22 Ill.2d 375, 176 NE2d 799; *Ridgemont Development Co.* v. *East Detroit,* 358 Mich. 387, 100 NW2d 301. Contrary decisions on this point are: *Jordan* v. *Menomonee Falls,* 28 Wis.2d 608, 137 NW2d 442; *Billings Properties Inc.* v. *Yellowstone County,* 144 Mont. 25, 394 P2d 182 (1964); *Jenad Inc.* v. *Scarsdale,* 18 N.Y.2d 78, 218 NE2d 673 (1966).

EXAMPLE: Ordinance requiring subdivider to contribute money for school or park. *West Park Ave. Inc.* v. *Ocean Twp.,* N.J., 244 A2d 1. *Berg Development Co.* v. *City of Missouri City,* 603 SW2d 273 (1980).

EXAMPLE: Ordinance limiting the number of permits a builder can receive at one time. *U.S. Home & Develop. Corp.* v. *LaMura,* 214 A2d 538 (N.J.).

EXAMPLE: Ordinance requiring subdivider to pay city 10 percent of the value of the subdivision where the plat showed no open public spaces. *Coronado Develop. Co.* v. *McPherson,* 189 Kans. 174, 368 P2d 51 (1962).

EXAMPLE: Refusal to approve plat because of the added burdens new housing would impose on public facilities. *Beach* v. *Planning Comm.,* 141 Conn. 79, 103 A2d 814.

EXAMPLE: Ordinance requiring dedication of land for street 700 feet distant from the subdivision. *McKain* v. *Toledo City Plan Comm.,* 270 NE2d 370.

EXAMPLE: However, the court held invalid a requirement by the County Planning Board that the developer dedicate a strip of land fronting on a county road where there was no perceivable connection between this requirement and the proposed development. *181 Inc.* v. *Salem County Planning Bd.,* 336 A2d 501 (N.J. 1975).

EXAMPLE: The requirement of a deposit by the developer without specifying its use was illegal. *Broward County* v. *James Development Corp.,* 311 So2d 371 (Fla. 1975).

NEW DIRECTIONS: As can be seen, there seems to be a strong current trend toward sustaining these exactions. In part, this new trend stems from the view that land developers buy land cheap because it is zoned agricultural or for single families. This is done deliberately by the municipality because it wishes to consider the desirability of the developer who comes in for rezoning to multifamily or commercial. Once rezoning is granted the land value shoots up astronomically. There is a feeling that the developer should share part of this increment or windfall with the municipality that conferred it.

The city's requirement that the developer give land for parks and schools must be reasonable. There is a very recent trend toward holding zoning ordinances invalid where they tend to keep the poor out of the suburbs. This idea has been applied to forced dedications.

EXAMPLE: The city of *X* adopts such extreme requirements for park and school dedications that the price of lots and homes is forced up, because the developer has less land to sell. The requirement may be held invalid. *Oakwood at Madison, Inc.* v. *Tp. of Madison,* 371 A2d 1192 (N.J. 1977).

REFERENCES: 8 Calif. W. L. Rev. 254; 52 Cornell L. Q. 871; 76 Dick. L. Rev. 651; 29 Okla. L. Rev. 155; 12 Syracuse L. Rev. 224; 26 U. Fla. L. Rev. 671; 27 U. Kans. L. Rev. 1; 9 U. Richmond L. Rev. 435; 2 Urb. Law 706; 43 ALR3d 862.

27.05(a) License tax on the business of developing

In lieu of, or in addition to, forced dedication contributions, some cities have imposed a license tax on the business of constructing dwellings.

EXAMPLE: Newark, California, imposed a license tax on the business of constructing dwellings. The courts sustained this. *Assoc. Home Builders* v. *City of Newark,* 95 Cal. Reptr. 648 (1971). Nevada has a law of this sort.

NEW LAWS: Vermont has enacted a capital gains tax on real estate sales. It has been held valid. *Andrews* v. *Lathrop,* 132 Vt. 256, 315 A2d 860 (1974).

These devices are schemes for capturing for the public, part of the increase in value created by public approval of this project.

27.06 Development rights

Professor John Costonis has pioneered the idea of transferring development rights.

NEW DIRECTIONS: A developer owns a landmark building, which he plans to demolish so that he can erect a modern office building. The city negotiates with him and he transfers to the city his "development rights" in the old building. The city in turn grants him additional development rights on other land he owns in the area, so that he can build a more extensive building than the law otherwise allows. This is a great oversimplification, but it conveys the idea. *Development Rights Transfer and Landmark Preservation,* 9 Urban L. Ann. 131 (1975).

27.07 Development rights—farm land

A special problem exists with respect to farm lands.

EXAMPLE: *X* owns a farm that has been in his family for many years. As the nearby suburbs expand, his land becomes valuable for a development, his real estate taxes soar. For example, his land might be worth $1,500 per acre for farming, but $10,000 to $25,000 per acre for development. Under state law, all land must be taxed uniformly at its full market value. X's taxes will go up.

One solution to this problem is for the county to buy the farmer's development rights. He is paid the excess value above the $1,500 per acre. He gives the county a release of his development rights. He and his successors may continue to farm the land. However, no one can use the land for development for housing or purposes other than farming. This reduces the land value back to $1,500 per acre. This situation is currently happening in Suffolk County, on Long Island, and elsewhere.

This technique of purchasing development rights was first used to preserve scenic areas. It is now being used to preserve landmarks and farm lands. 12 Urb. Law. 3 (1980).

Perhaps it will help you to understand this concept if you think of property ownership as a bundle of rights.

EXAMPLE: X owns land improved with a store building. X leases the building to Y for ten years. X has parted with his right to possession for ten years. In the same way X can sell to the county his right to develop the land.

27.08   Interstate Land Sales Act

The Interstate Land Sales Act, 15 USC § 1701 *et seq.*, and the regulations issued by the Office of Interstate Land Sales Registration (OILSR), 24 CFR § 1700 *et seq.*, have been amended in mid-1980. The act requires that lots not be sold or leased until a *statement of record* is filed with OILSR and a property report is given to the buyer. The statement of record is a comprehensive document detailing the information relating to the property and its developer. The property report is a condensed version of the statement of record and is written in a question-and-answer format.

The act requires that the property report be given to the buyer before the contract is signed. If not, the contract may be revoked at any time during the next two years after the contract is signed. A violation of the act may lead to criminal penalties and a buyer may sue the seller for damages.

The following transactions are exempt from the act:

1. The sale or lease of lots in a subdivision containing less than 25 lots.
2. The sale or lease of any lots on which there is a residential, commercial, condominium, or industrial building, or the sale or lease of land under a contract obligating the seller to build within two years. This is an important exemption because it benefits homebuilders and developers who contract in good faith to build a structure within two years.
3. The sale of evidences of indebtedness secured by a mortgage or deed of trust on real estate.
4. The sale of securities issued by a real estate investment trust.
5. The sale or lease of real estate by any government or government agency.

6. The sale or lease of cemetery lots.

7. The sale or lease of lots to any person who acquires such lots for the purpose of engaging in the business of constructing residential, commercial, or industrial buildings or for the purpose of resale or lease of such lots to persons engaged in such business.

8. The sale or lease of real estate that is zoned or restricted to commercial or industrial development. 15 USC § 1702(a).

The following transactions are exempt from the disclosure and registration sections of the act, but are subject to the act's antifraud provisions:

- The sale or lease of lots in a subdivision containing fewer than 100 lots.
- The sale or lease of less than 12 lots in a twelve-month period.
- The sale or lease of lots in separate unconnected parts of a subdivision, if the part of the subdivision contains less than 21 lots.
- The sale or lease of lots that are 20 acres or larger.
- The sale or lease of lots in a municipality or county that has set minimum development standards, if the subdivision meets local codes, each lot is limited by zoning or otherwise to single-family ownership, roads, water sewer, and other utilities are available to the lot, the seller must give a deed within 180 days, after the contract is signed, title evidence is available, the buyer has made an on-the-lot inspection of the property, and there are no high-pressure sales techniques used to sell the lot.
- The sale or lease of a mobile homesite if the lot is sold or leased by one party and the mobile home is sold or leased by another.
- The sale or lease by a developer who is operating on an intrastate as opposed to an interstate basis if the lot is free and clear of liens, the purchaser has made an on-the-lot inspection, the contract contains an estimate of when roads, utilities, and amenities will be completed and the buyer has a seven-day "cooling off" period to revoke the contract.
- The sale or lease of lots to buyers within the same "standard metropolitan statistical area" if the same sort of technical requirements set out in the above exemption are met. 15 USC § 1702(b).

The act also regulates installment contracts that are not subject to one of the exemptions by forbidding a damage clause that results in the forefeiture of amounts paid by the buyer in excess of 15 percent of the purchase price or the seller's actual damages. 15 USC § 1703(b)(3).

27.09 Local regulations

Regarding sales not covered by the Interstate Land Sales Act, most states have their local laws regulating lot sales. 21 Rutgers L. Rev. 720 (1967); Walter, *The Law of the Land: Development Legislation in Maine and Vermont,* 23 Maine L. Rev. 315 (1971).

27.10 Regulation of land sales—FTC

Because the Interstate Land Sales Act has not been very effective, the Federal Trade Commission now regulates interstate land sales also, and to a considerable extent its regulations overlap the Interstate Land Sales regulations. Both regulations forbid deceptive advertising, unfair sales techniques, and unfair provisions in land sale contracts. The FTC feels that its ability to harshly punish developers who violate its regulations will deter fraud in the sale of vacant lots.

27.11 Development regulation

An example of modern development regulation is the new law adopted in Vermont.

EXAMPLE: Vermont's new law provides for an Environmental Control Board and seven district environmental commissions. The latter agencies process permits which must be obtained for proposed developments of more than one acre in towns without duly adopted permanent zoning and subdivision regulations. In communities having these codes, permits are required for any development encompassing more than ten acres. Permits are awarded if the District Commission is satisfied that the proposed subdivision is found acceptable in four major aspects: that it will not unduly pollute air, land, or water; that it will pose no unreasonable burden on a community's capacity to deliver municipal services; that the application conforms to any duly adopted local, regional, and state plan, and that the project "will not have an undue adverse effect on the scenic or natural beauty of the area, aesthetics, historic sites, or rare and irreplacable natural areas."

Because of concern for the protection of the environment, scores of new laws and court decisions are appearing.

NEW DIRECTIONS: Because of concern for the environment, the land developer is or will be required to submit his plans to some public body that will grant him approval to go ahead only if no appreciable adverse effect on the environment will occur. *Friends of Mammoth* v. *Mono City Board,* 104 Cal. Reptr. 16. This will be especially true in offshore areas, swamplands, and wetlands.

EXAMPLE: *ABC Village* enacts a zoning ordinance barring all high-rise apartments. This ordinance is invalid. Developers cannot be singled out to bear all the financial burdens of pollution. *Westwood Forest Estates, Inc.* v. *Village of South Nyack,* 23 N.Y.2d 424, 297 N.Y.S.2d 129 (1969); 1 Urban Law, 228.

EXAMPLE: A developer bought a wilderness area. The county refused a building permit because it wanted the land kept in its natural state. This action was held invalid. If the public wants wilderness areas preserved, the court thought it must condemn them. *Harbor Farms Inc.* v. *Nassau County Planning Comm.,* 334 N.Y.S.2d 412 (1972).

NEW DIRECTIONS: Among the recent developments in this area are statutes providing for state regulation of land use. Keep in mind that traditionally *cities* and *counties* regulated land use. Now the *state* is stepping in.

EXAMPLE: Hawaii has created a State Land Use Commission, which has divided the state into *urban, rural, agricultural,* and *conservation* areas and land use in each area is limited to the uses permitted by state laws.

Some state laws are pretty drastic.

EXAMPLE: In Delaware, heavy industry is forbidden in a strip of coast land one to five miles wide.

EXAMPLE: Maine divides the state into *protection districts, management districts, holding districts,* and *development districts.* In protection districts, where presently development is negligible, the state will endeavor to preserve the present status.

The large-scale development is particularly vulnerable to state regulation. 56 Minn. L. Rev. 869.

EXAMPLE: In Maine and Vermont all large-scale developments are subject to state regulation. *In re Spring Valley,* 300 A2d 736 (1973).

NEW DIRECTIONS: Florida has enacted the Environmental Land and Water Management Act of 1972. Florida, of course, has vast expanses of marsh land, which developers can acquire cheaply. Such marsh land is essential to the health of the ecology. Florida divides the state into zones or areas. Thus, there are areas of "critical state concern."

EXAMPLE: The act sets forth principles for development of areas containing or having a significant impact upon environmental, historical, natural, or archaeological resources of *regional* or *statewide* importance, such as Big Cypress Swamp, the Florida Keys, or a jetport, or a new community. Municipalities must adopt development regulations that comply with these regulations or the state will impose regulations on the area.

Then there are areas involving development of regional impact (DRI).

EXAMPLE: A large hospital, a large shopping center, or a large housing development. These areas are not mapped by the state but are so designated when a developer proposes to build a project of the type listed in the state law as a DRI. The developer is required to fill out an enormously complex application, hundreds of pages in length. It is then considered by the municipality and a regional planning agency. As is evident, the Florida scheme focuses on relatively large developments.

NEW DIRECTIONS: By contrast, in Vermont state controls apply to residential developments with ten units or more, and in Maine the magic number is twenty acres. As can also be seen, regarding regulated projects, a developer must often obtain two approvals, one from the state or a regional commission and one from the municipality. This applies, for example, to California, Vermont, Maine, and the coastal zones of New Jersey and North Carolina. Also there is a third factor, environmental control, which brings in a third agency, such as the one established under the Federal Clean Air Act. This agency handles shopping centers and new towns, where the concentration of automobile traffic creates air pollution. At times the regulations will conflict with the Environmental Protection Agency (EPA) pushing for smaller parking areas (to restrict traffic) and the local agencies pushing for larger parking areas (to reduce traffic densities). Basically, this means that the expense of land development, including the cost of paying real estate taxes for as much as two years, goes up sharply.

Some developers now do not buy land. They simply buy an option or contingent contract, effective when all the legal hurdles have been surmounted. This also pushes up the cost of houses.

NEW DIRECTIONS: Some states (Colorado, for example) have taken over the regulation of prefabs. This is done because the villages have attempted to zone them out. Prefabs are largely constructed at a factory, and therefore regular mortgage financing is not available. Construction is financed under the Uniform Commercial Code, just as the sales of chattels are financed.

REFERENCE: A good discussion of the law relating to the new problems of land regulation will be found in Leahy, *Environmental Issues in Local Land Use Regulation,* 11 RPP & TJ 457 (1976).

27.12 Phase development—moratoria— "no growth"

Some municipalities have provided for phased development.

EXAMPLE: In 1966, the Town of Ramapo, New York, adopted a master plan that had been two years in the making for the future development of the town. It also adopted a comprehensive zoning ordinance. Nine-tenths of the town's unincorporated area was zoned residential. To implement the plan, the town enacted a capital budget for the construction of streets, parks, sewers, and so forth. This plan called for installation over an eighteen-year period, with specific phases to be completed at the end of the sixth and twelfth years. In 1969 an amendment to the zoning ordinance was adopted. This amendment required that a special permit would be necessary in order to construct a residence. When a permit was applied for, the zoning board would consider the area to be built upon, including availability of sewers, parks, schools, roads, firehouses. Each item was assigned a point value. A minimum of fifteen points was required to qualify for a permit. If public facilities were lacking, the developer was at liberty to construct the needed facilities at his own expense. In this fashion, he could proceed with his development as soon as he acquired the required points. The town considered only its own needs. The area outside the town was ignored. A residential developer applied for plat approval. His plan did not conform to the permit requirements. He was turned down. The ordinance was held valid. *Golden* v. *Town of Ramapo,* 30 N.Y.2d 359, 285 NE2d 291, 334 N.Y.S.2d 185, App. dsd. 409 U.S. 1003, commented on in 47 N.Y.U. L. Rev. 723 (1972). The scheme is called phased development.

A water-short municipality, after imposing a *moratorium on development,* must make a good faith effort to augment its water supply in order to permit the landowner, particularly the land developer, to proceed with erection of buildings. It is only after such efforts have proved fruitless that the hookup moratorium may be continued and, of course, development must stop because the water supply is unable to support added population. 27 Hastings L. J. 753 (1976). In short, a municipality can reasonably be expected to exert reasonable efforts. It cannot be expected to perform miracles.

NEW DIRECTIONS: "No growth" regulation. The Town of Petaluma adopted a housing and zoning plan that specified that only five hundred new home permits could be issued per year for five years. The federal courts sustained this. *Const. Ind. Assn. of Sonoma County* v. *City of Petaluma,* 522 F2d 897 (1975); 8 Urb. Law. 748, 776; 6 Seton Hall L. Rev. 207; 20 S.W. L. J. 794. The court held that the concept of public welfare is sufficiently broad to uphold Petaluma's desire to preserve its small town character, its open spaces, and low density of population, and to grow at an orderly and deliberate pace. Obviously, some state courts disagree violently with this point of view. *Harbor Farms Inc.* v. *Nassau Planning Comm.,* 40 App. Div. 2d 517, 334 N.Y.S.2d 412 (1972); 66 Ky. L. J. 99; 52 So. Calif. L. Rev. 1239. Stopping the growth of Petaluma does not stop the nation's population growth. It merely directs it somewhere else. It is disappointing to watch the federal courts dodging this issue. The *Petaluma* decision disregards the right of every citizen to travel everywhere and build a home when he finds a place he likes. *Constitutional Law—Rights to Travel—Phased Development Plan Unconstitutionally Burdens the Right to Travel of Persons Excluded,* 28 Vand. L. Rev. 987 (1975). As explained in the chapter on land use controls—zoning, federal court decisions get headlines, but the state courts are not bound to follow them.

EXAMPLE: In 1974 there came before the U.S. Supreme Court the question of the validity of an ordinance of the Village of Belle Terre on Long Island. The ordinance restricted land use to one-family dwellings, thus ensuring that the village would probably grow no larger than its population of 700 living in 220 residences. *Village of Belle Terre* v. *Boraas,* 416 U.S. 1536 (1974), 72 Mich. L. Rev. 508, 88 Harv. L. Rev. 41, 120. This decision totally ignores the enormous growth of population taking place in this country. It deals only with a claimed violation of the *federal Constitution.* Any state court is free to ignore it when determining whether a violation of the *state constitution* is involved.

EXAMPLE: Other courts have held no-growth ordinances illegal under state law. *Stoney-Brook Develop. Corp.* v. *Town of Penbroke,* 394 A2d 835 (N.H. 1978).

REFERENCES ON PHASED DEVELOPMENT: 4 Environ. Affairs 759; 9 Houston L. Rev. 189; 66 Ky. L. J. 99; 1 Pac. L. J. 461; 26 Stanf. L. Rev. 585; 63 ALR2d 1184.

27.13   Recapitulation   The decisions relating to moratoria are quite inconsistent. Where there is a genuine present dan-
ger to the public health, a *temporary* moratorium is valid.

> **EXAMPLE:** The existing sewage system could not handle any additional build-
> ings. Development may be halted *temporarily* while the system is expanded.
> *Lom-Ran Corp.* v. *Dept. of Environ. Prot.* 394 A2d 1233 (N.J. 1978). Accord:
> *Beck* v. *Town of Raymond,* 397 A2d 847 (N.H. 1978). See 6 Yale L. J. 489.

The key words here are (1) present danger, (2) *temporary moratorium,* and
(3) expansion of existing facilities. The reasoning is elementary. A landowner
has the constitutional right to put his land to use. A municipality cannot force a
landowner to leave his land vacant indefinitely. The federal Constitution protects a landowner's ownership of property. But ownership connotes a right to
put the land to use. In the exercise of its police power, a local government can
act to protect health. But somewhere along the line the landowner must be given
the right to use his land. Land developers frequently encounter questionable
conduct on the part of public officials, including delays in acting on applications
for building permits, the installing of sewer installations, and encouragement of
septic field construction that provides an excuse for large lot zoning that limits
newcomers to the well-to-do who can afford large lots, etc. See 32 Maine L. Rev.
29 (1980). The moratorium must be temporary and reasonably limited as to
time. *Smoke Rise Inc.,* v. *Washington Comm.,* 400 F.Supp. 1369 (1975); *Collura* v.
Town of Arlington, 329 NE2d 733 (Mass. 1975). *Grisor* v. *City of N.Y.,* 374 N.Y.S.2d
549. A moratorium is not the local government's only remedy.
    The opposition of existing communities to any growth is reflected in vari-
ous other measures. Counties around San Francisco have minimum requirements of 20, 40, and even 60 acres per home in agricultural areas. Local governments draw up boundaries beyond which they will not extend utility lines. Other
communities impose a substantial hookup charge of up to $5,000 per home on
furnishing of public services.
    All these steps together with those discussed in the zoning chapter are but
aspects of the great battle of the 1980s, the battle between existing communities
and those that would like to open them up to low-income persons. Up to the
present time, this cannot be regarded as an issue arising under the federal Constitution. The federal courts regard this as basically a state matter. In the states,
the results are apt to be spotty. California, Michigan, and New Jersey, for example, are on record as blocking the prohibition of mobile home construction. This
opens the door to low-income residents. Other states are likely to be less liberal.

REFERENCES ON "NO GROWTH" REGULATION: 3 Fordham Urb. L. J. 137
(1974); 26 Hastings L. J. 845 (1975); 6 Seton Hall L. Rev. 207; 30 S.W. L. J. 794;
19 Villanova L. Rev. 703 (1974); 26 U. of Fla. L. Rev. 750; 8 Urb. Law 748, 776;
62 Ky. L. J. 99 (1977–78); 52 So. Cal. L. Rev. 1239 (1979); 12 U. San. F. L. Rev.
357 (1979).

27.13(a) Moratoria—sewer and water problems

Some municipalities have resorted to the moratorium to stop unwanted construction.

> **EXAMPLE:** Cities that lack adequate sewer or other facilities have imposed a moratorium on issuance of building permits. If the time period is reasonable and the city has a definite plan for solving the problem, the moratorium has been sustained by some courts. *Smoke Rise Inc.* v. *Washington Suburban San. Comm.,* 400 F.Supp. 1369 (1975) (sustaining five-year moratorium); II Management & Control of Growth (Urban Land Institute, 1200 18th Street, N.W., Washington, D.C. 20036—very valuable collection of articles). Fairfax County, Virginia, tried a "no growth" moratorium approach, but lost. The Virginia Supreme Court held that permits *must* be issued to land developers. *City of Richmond* v. *Randall,* 205 Va. 506, 211 SE2d 56 (1975).

One writer takes the following position on moratoria; (1) the moratorium is valid if an actual emergency exists and a law or ordinance authorizes the moratorium; (2) the moratorium must be limited in time; (3) the city must have a program to end the emergency; (4) it is up to the court, not the village, to determine if these requirements exist. *The Thirst for Population Control,* 27 Hastings L. J. 753.

> **EXAMPLE:** In Colorado an interesting situation arose. The county in question required that the developer make arrangements for water and sewer service before receiving approval for his residential building plans. The city of Boulder was the only provider of sewer and water in the entire area, including land outside the city. The developer applied for such service and was refused, although it could readily be furnished. The court held that the city must furnish the sewer and water. The county and the city had contrived a situation between them under which the developer could not go ahead without sewer and water, but the city, the only provider, could refuse to furnish these services. Plainly, this indefinite ban on development violates the developer's rights under the state constitution. *Robinson* v. *Boulder,* 547 P2d 228 (Colo. 1976), commented on in 5 Real Estate L. J. 170.

However, a moratorium on building permits for a reasonable time, while the city attempts to cope with the problem, is valid. If during that time it is established that there simply is no water available for further building, the city can make the moratorium permanent. "You cannot get blood out of a turnip, and you cannot get water out of a dry well."

27.14 Estoppel—vested rights—development agreements

There has always been a reluctance to apply estoppel where a government body is involved. However, in land development matters, courts are increasingly resorting to this doctrine.

> **EXAMPLE:** In zoning cases where a city has issued a permit to a developer and he has, in reliance on a building permit, expended substantial sums (hiring architect, obtaining loan commitment, signing construction contract) but has not

as yet achieved nonconforming use status (see § 26.21) the courts will, at times, hold the city estopped to cancel the permit. See § 26.22(b). This is simply a legal way of stating that in the circumstances it would be unjust to permit a cancellation of the permit. Here the courts are balancing the obvious injustice to the developer against the public policy favoring an orderly development of land use that permits a city to alter its plans as circumstances indicate the desirability of doing so. Obviously, courts will differ in their approach to the problem. 29 Hastings L. J., 623, 651. The problem is enormously complicated where several different public bodies issue permits for different aspects of the development. 29 *id.* 657.

While the courts often approach this problem in terms of a question whether the developer's rights had "vested," it is hard to distinguish this view from the rule that protects nonconforming use status. If a final permit has issued, and substantial commitments were made in reliance on a final permit, the courts have to protect the developer.

> **EXAMPLE:** A developer expended $2,800,000 after the county had approved his plat. He had not obtained a final permit for the work. The court refused to protect the developer, since he had not obtained a final permit. *AVCO Community Developers Inc.* v. *South Coast Regional Commr.,* 17 Cal.3d 785, 553 P2d 546, 132 Cal. Reptr. 386 (1976), *cert. den.* 429 U.S. 1083 (1977).

The *Avco* decision led to dissatisfaction. Ultimately, California passed a law under which a developer can enter into an agreement with the local government. If the developer proceeds in good faith to comply with the agreement, his rights cannot be revoked. Holliman, *Development Agreements and Vested Rights in California,* 13 Urb. Law. 44 (1981); 54 Ore. L. Rev. 103. Perhaps similar laws will be enacted elsewhere. Especially where the developer has expended substantial sums with the encouragement of local government, the idea is gaining ground that "every citizen has the right to expect that he will be dealt with fairly by his government." *Hollywood Beach Hotel Co.* v. *City of Hollywood,* 329 So.2d 10 (Fla. 1976).

27.15   Failure to enforce drainage regulations

> **NEW DIRECTIONS:** A developer was given a permit on the condition that he provide proper drainage. He failed in this regard. An adjoining owner sued the city for failure to enforce its own drainage regulations. The city was held liable. *Breiner* v. *C. & P. Home Builders, Inc.,* 398 F.Supp. 250 (1975).

27.16   Resubdivision

A platted area is sometimes replatted *or resubdivided.* For example, if an ill-conceived subdivision, using the old-fashioned gridiron pattern, were to be acquired by a modern developer, he would go to the city and request that all streets and alleys be vacated, that is, officially abandoned by the city. Thereupon he would resubdivide the area into larger, irregular lots on curvilinear streets with utility easements over the rear substituted for outmoded alleys.

27.17 Sewer, water, and other utilities

When a land developer installs sewer, water, and other utilities in the streets or alleys of the development, the developer has no right to remove the utilities that he has installed. These utilities, as well as the street, are dedicated to the use of the lot owners. *Stegall* v. *Jackson,* 244 Miss. 169, 141 So2d 236 (1962); *City of Snyder* v. *Bass,* 360 SW2d 426 (Tex. 1962); *Oden* v. *Seattle,* 432 P2d 642 (Wash. 1967). Suppose, however, that he buys ninety-five lots in an existing subdivision of lots. No utilities have been installed. Under the state law in this particular state, the city, not the lot owners, owns the street. He makes a contract with the city under which he is to install sewer and water pipes in the street but is to retain ownership thereof. This contract is duly recorded. Thereafter, the owners of the other five lots seek to connect to his sewer and water pipes. They have no right to do so. They did not buy their lots in reliance on any representation made by him and cannot connect with his pipes. *Atchison* v. *De Roo,* 332 Ill. App. 251, 75 NE2d 46 (1947). Of course, the people who buy their lots from him and rely on his representations as to sewer and water are protected.

> **SUGGESTION:** A subdivider who wishes to retain ownership of his sewer and water mains, so that he can charge for their use, should make and record in the recorder's office a conveyance of such mains to his own water company before he makes any deed of lots to purchasers. Once a deed is made to a lot purchaser, it is arguable that the water main in the street in front of his lot belongs to the lot purchaser or is dedicated to his use, and therefore the subdivider cannot charge the lot purchaser for its use, where no deed to a water company has been recorded.

> **NEW DIRECTIONS:** Extension of utilities is a function of proper land development regulation. In the foregoing, the assumption was made that an abundance of water, sewer service, gas, and electricity exists and that all one needs is the legal right to tap into such service in order that development may proceed. In these times it has become evident that America suffers from an acute shortage of all of these heretofore abundant matters. Hence, extension of such a service has become a matter of proper land use and development regulation.

Subdividers often place dotted lines on their plats and mark the indicated areas "easement for public utilities." This phrase is too brief and general. What type of facilities are included in the phrase "public utilities"?

> **SUGGESTION:** Place a legend on the plat as follows: "A perpetual easement is hereby created over, in favor of all lot owners in this subdivision, under, and across the area marked *easement for public utilities* as an easement appurtenant

to each lot in this subdivision for the installation, use, maintenance, repair, and replacement of public utilities, including sewer, water, gas, electricity, telephone, and telegraph. Said areas are not dedicated to the public."

27.18 Environmental law— in general

Environmental laws and the trend those laws represent have created what is sometimes a hostile and expensive atmosphere for any developer to operate within. Often both local citizens and government agencies involved with a project have almost a programmed animosity toward the developer's motives and what he is attempting to accomplish. Laws, ordinances, regulations, and agencies have created a maze of red tape that causes the developer added expense and delay. Nonetheless, the goal of these enactments and programs is vital to the continuing well-being of the nation. Balance is crucial and emphasis shifts as priorities change. The energy crisis may temper the literal thrust of environmental laws and regulations. Federal budget restraint and fiscal reform may alter the vigor of government enforcement efforts.

27.18(a) NEPA

The National Environmental Policy Act (NEPA), 41 USCS § 4321 *et seq.*, among other things, requires that federal agencies prepare an environmental impact statement on major federal actions that significantly affect the quality of the human environment. These reports must detail: the environmental impact of the proposed action; adverse environmental effects, which cannot be avoided should the proposal be implemented; alternatives to the proposed action; the relationship between local short-term uses of man's environment and the maintenance and enhancement of long-term productivity; and any irreversible and irretrievable commitments of resources that would be involved in the proposed action should it be implemented. 42 USCS § 4332(c). Once the statement is prepared and comments from other concerned federal agencies are obtained, the agency review process may go forward giving due consideration to environmental factors. *Environmental Defense Fund Inc.* v. *Corps of Engineers,* 470 F2d 289 (1972).

Though the act places the ultimate burden of statement preparation upon the federal agency, the developer will be involved in providing data. Indeed, it is in the developer's best interest to assist in the quick and efficient preparation of the report as even preliminary work cannot go forward without the statement.

> **EXAMPLE:** Without the statement being prepared, the developer may be enjoined from cutting trees on wooded tract prior to the construction of housing project. *Silva* v. *Romney,* 473 F2d 287 (1973).

This assistance may be through the developer's in-house staff or through the efforts of a private concern that specializes in the preparation of these reports.

27.18(b) Environmental control—air

From a federal air pollution point of view (see 42 USCS 1857 *et seq.*), the developer must be concerned with whether or not the development is a stationary source of emission, produces hazardous materials, or creates an indirect source of pollution.

The federal law calls for the states to have authority and procedures to evaluate and prevent development where the emissions from the development itself, or those "mobile source activities" associated with it, interfere with the attainment or maintenance of air quality standards. 40 CFR § 51.18 (1975).

> **EXAMPLE:** The shopping center developer must not only be concerned with the exhaust systems and smokestacks of the structure; he must also design the facility so that traffic flow is such that exhaust fumes from cars attracted to the site do not foul the air.

As a point of interest, developers in areas where the air is relatively clean should not feel that, because the air is well within the relevant air quality standards, there is a margin for pollution. The concept of "nondegradation" is part of the Clean Air Act. *Sierra Club* v. *Ruckelshaus,* 344 F.Supp. 253 (1972) *aff'd.* 4 ERC 1815 (1972) *aff'd. sub. nom. Fri* v. *Sierra Club,* 412 U.S. 541 (1973). Congress, by stating that the purpose of the Clean Air Acts is "to protect and enhance" the quality of the nation's air resources, expresses its intent to improve the quality of the nation's air and to prevent deterioration of air quality. Thus, in areas where the air is pristine, the air quality standards adopted must provide, to the maximum extent practicable, for continued maintenance of air quality. This concept has special impact in the West, where the air is clean and the skies are clear.

27.18(c) Environmental control—water

Concern must also exist about any discharge of liquid effluent prohibited or regulated by the federal water pollution laws. 33 USCS § 1151 *et seq.* These laws require that a permit be obtained by every facility discharging effluent into the navigable waters or those water bodies that flow into navigable waters. This includes nearly all water bodies in the country.

27.18(d) State and local environmental legislation

What may loosely be called state environmental control laws are also significant factors to be reckoned with. Not only do they partially implement the federal laws but also they run the gamut from protecting the air and water to regulating wildlife and plant life. In some states, laws patterned after NEPA have been enacted that require the preparation of impact statements where major nonfederal actions have a significant effect upon the environment. See, for example, Cal. Pub. Res. Code § 21000 *et seq.* In their extreme form, state environmental laws require impact statements to be filed for the granting of zoning variances and even for the approval of minor land subdivision.

> **EXAMPLE:** A landowner applied to the local governing body for approval of a subdivision of a parcel of land. The governing body granted the approval without preparing an environmental impact report. This action was successfully challenged and the resolution approving the subdivision was rendered null and void. *Meyers* v. *Board of Supervisors,* 129 Cal. Reptr. 902 (1976).

Beyond state legislation, there has been a flurry of ordinances by counties and municipalities relating to control of the local environment.

27.18(e) Private actions

The various regulatory agencies are not the only sources of environmental law enforcement. Some statutes, 42 USCS § 1857 *et seq.* and constitutional provisions, give individuals who are not directly injured the power to enforce a right to a clean environment. *Parsons* v. *Walker,* 328 NE2d 920 (Ill. 1975).

> *REFERENCE:* Schwenke, *Environmental and Land Use Laws, Regulations and Permits: How They Affect Real Estate Transactions, Financing and Lawyers, and What to Do About It,* 14 R.P.P.&T.J. 851 (1979).

27.19 Energy crisis

The advent of the energy crisis has spawned a variety of federal and state laws and regulations. This area of the law is in a state of flux.

> *REFERENCES ON REGULATION OF LAND DEVELOPMENT:* 29 Hastings L. J. 623 (1978); 7 Real Est. L. J. 7 (1978); 86 Yale L. J. 385 (1977); 23 UCLA L. Rev. 904; 32 Wash. & Lee L. Rev. 989; 8 Urb. Law Ann. 3 (1974); 6 S.W.U. L. Rev. 607; 1 Hofstra L. Rev. 56; 56 Minn. L. Rev. 869; 10 Idaho L. Rev. 12; 19 Villanova L. Rev. 703; 54 Oreg. L. Rev. 103 (vested rights, 1978); 6 Ecology L. Q. 755 (vested rights, 1978); 33 St. Louis U. L. J. 219 (vested rights, 1979).
>
> *REFERENCES ON DEVELOPMENT MORATORIA OR "NO GROWTH":* 32 Maine L. Rev. 29 (1980); 52 So. Cal. L. Rev. 1239 (1979); 66 Ky. L. J. 99 (1977); 8 Urb. Law. 748; 6 Seton Hall L. Rev. 207; 30 S.W. L. J. 794; 26 Hastings L. J. 845; 3 Fordham Urb. L. J. 137; 19 Villanova L. Rev. 703; 26 U. Fla. L. Rev. 750.
>
> *REFERENCES ON PHASED DEVELOPMENT:* 11 Willamette L. J. 217 (1975); 8 Urb. Law. 512 (1976); 66 Ky. L. J. 99 (1977); 4 Environ. Affairs 758 (1975); 26 Stanf. L. Rev. 585 (1974); 1 Pac. L. J. 461 (1976).
>
> *REFERENCES ON STATE CONTROL:* 45 Fordham L. Rev. 1154 (1977); 9 Urb. Law. 629, 652 (1977); 25 Hastings L. J. 1165 (1974).
>
> *REFERENCES ON DEVELOPMENT AND THE RIGHT TO TRAVEL:* 31 Wash. L. Rev. 575 (1974); 6 Cumb. L. Rev. 541; 17 Ariz. L. Rev. 145; 6 Rutgers Camden L. J. 122; 28 Vand. L. Rev. 430; 10 Suffolk U. L. Rev. 623 (1976); 1 Hastings Constl. L. P. 153 (1974).

28 LAND USE CONTROLS— WETLANDS, THE PUBLIC TRUST, BEACHES, AND NAVIGABLE WATERS

28.01 Definition of the problem

There are two types of wetlands. *Inland wetlands* are marshes such as those found in every state of the union. *Coastal wetlands* are *estuarian* lands (salt marshes). An estuary occurs where an arm of the sea (salt water) extends inland to meet the mouth of a river (fresh water). The tides alternately flood and expose tidal marshes. Both types of wetlands are shallow. Land development is possible through "dredge and fill" operations. It is only recently that we have come to realize that our very national existence depends upon these wetlands and that these wetlands are disappearing as building construction goes forward. The reasons why these wetlands must be preserved are too numerous to mention, but a few will be listed:

1. Wetlands are nature's way of controlling floods. Wetlands act as giant sponges, absorbing vast amounts of water and releasing it gradually. If you pave the area, you have a flood problem. Estuarian lands, with their mixture of peat, bog, moss, and so forth, absorb incoming storms and are nature's way of preventing floods.

2. Inland wetlands maintain ground water at proper ground water levels. If you drain this ground water, a desert may result.

3. Estuarian lands are an important source of food supply. Carbohydrates and vitamins wash out to sea from the estuaries and greatly increase the number of fish and oysters that the ocean can produce. By far the greater quantity of ocean fish depends for survival on the estuaries. The deep sea, by and large, is empty of fish. A great many ocean fish can reproduce only in the estuaries. The classic illustration is that of the salmon that come back to the stream of their birth and go upstream to spawn. The fishermen, the fishing villages, and the tourist trade, therefore, depend upon the estuaries. Wild fowl, such as ducks and geese, cannot exist without the wetlands. They are necessary for reproduction, migration, and as winter feeding grounds. In these areas, hunters bring in substantial local revenue. Wild rice, turkey, deer, and so forth depend upon wetlands.

4. Wetlands absorb polluted air and water and make them clean and wholesome.

A recent court decision points up the legal problems that arise in the wetlands area.

EXAMPLE: Ronald and Kathryn Just, land developers, bought a large tract of land in Wisconsin. When their plans became public knowledge, Marinette County passed an ordinance making any reasonable use of wetlands land impossible. Cranberry picking and other low- or no-income activities were permitted. When the Justs went ahead in defiance of the law, they were stopped by the courts. The Wisconsin Supreme Court sustained the law. *Just* v. *Marinette County,* 56 Wis.2d 7, 201 NW2d 761 (1972), *cert. den.* U.S. S.Ct. The land was thus rendered worthless. The court, in a ruling contrary to hundreds of previous decisions, said that a landowner has no constitutional right to develop his land! The dilemma is plain. If all developers are allowed to develop wetlands, the landowners are protected from loss of their money, but in the meantime the surrounding country may perish.

The Marinette County case presents rather clearly a problem that exists in American constitutional law. Each government body has two powers that frequently come into conflict, the *police power* and the power of *eminent domain.*

EXAMPLE: *X* owns Blackacre. The city wants this land for a street. The city files a petition under its power of eminent domain. A jury fixes the value of the land, the city pays it, and the street is installed. This is an exercise of the power of eminent domain. No controversy exists.

Each public body also has *police power,* the power to govern. This is the great power of government, but it has its limits. The city, for example, can take *X*'s land in the preceding example for a street because *X* refuses to sell. But it must exercise the power of eminent domain to do so.

The situation is complex. The greater the need for preservation of the public safety in a given situation, or the closer the landowner's use approaches the nuisance level, or the greater the threatened harm, the closer the courts come to permitting the city to destroy the landowner's land value without paying him compensation.

EXAMPLE: In the city of Los Angeles, a residential section expanded until it closely approached a brick works that gave off a foul odor. The city passed an ordinance making brick-making illegal in the city. The courts upheld the decision because, in balancing the harm to the public against the gain to the public, it was clear that the gain to the public outweighed the benefit to the brick-maker, even though the land was reduced to zero value.

EXAMPLE: In the city of *X* a disastrous fire broke out. To save the balance of the city, the fire department dynamited a row of buildings to create a fire break. The city does this under the police power. It need not pay a penny of compensation. *Surrocco* v. *Geary,* 3 Cal. 70 (1853). The police power was properly exercised because of the great public danger.

Thus, the question arises: In the wetlands situation, is the danger to the public so great that filling in the wetlands would cause a calamity? If so, arguably the city can exercise its police power, its power to regulate and pay no compensation. If the danger does not reach these proportions, it must compensate the landowner.

This is a very great simplification of the problem over which the courts and scholars have fought bitter battles in the last few years. There is an almost total lack of agreement, and here we can merely draw attention to a few of the conflicting points of view.

28.01(a) The decisions

The decisions, of course, are conflicting:

28.01(a)(1) Prodeveloper decisions

Morris County Land and Imp. Co. v. *Twp. of Parsippany-Troy Hills,* 40 N.J. 539, 193 A2d 232 (1963). Here the township had amended its zoning ordinance to create a meadowlands zone designed to preserve the swampland for flood control purposes. Only minor uses were permitted, such as commercial greenhouses. The landowner wished to develop his land for intensive commercial development. The court held for the developer.

State v. *Johnson,* 265 A2d 711 (Maine 1970). The state of Maine passed a wetlands law. The state court held that the preservation of wetlands was a laudable purpose but that the cost must be publicly borne. The landowner must be paid by the state if his development rights are to be taken away.

Mac Gibbon v. *Board of Appeals,* 350 Mass. 635, 255 NE2d 347 (1970) is to the same effect as the above two cases.

28.01(a)(2) Antideveloper cases

Sibson v. *State,* 336 A2d 239 (N.H. 1975) and other cases follow the lead of *Just* v. *Marinette County. Sibson* involved a denial of a building permit that was to cover four acres of salt marshland that was part of a one-hundred-acre tidal wetland. The court sustained this denial because of the harm to the public. See also *Brecciaroli* v. *Connecticut Commr. of Environmental Protection,* 36 Conn. L. J. 42, p. 4 (S.Ct. Jan. Term 1975); *Potomac Sand and Gravel Co.* v. *Governor,* 293 A2d 241 (Md. 1972); *S. Volpe & Co., Inc.* v. *Board of Appeals,* 348 NE2d 807 (Mass. App. 1976); *State* v. *Reed,* 78 Miss. 2d 1004 (N.Y.).

28.02 Environmental factors

A final obstacle to land development in marshes is the emergence of the concept that environmental factors must be considered before a "dredge and fill" permit is issued. *Zabel* v. *Taub,* 430 F2d 199 (5th Circ. 1970), *cert. den.* 401 U.S. 910 (1971).

28.03 Conclusions on wetlands

It is difficult to extract rational rules out of all this, but certain things are plain with respect to *Just* v. *Marinette County.* The Wisconsin court's view that a landowner has no constitutional right to develop his land cannot possibly be correct. How would this country have reached its present state of development if this is the law? Who will buy vacant land if it can be taken from him without payment of a penny of compensation? Definitely, it should not be the law. There is a vast body of law on purchase and condemnation of development rights. Ironically, Wisconsin has pioneered in the purchase of development rights and is still doing so in acquiring scenic easements. "Development rights" exist. Also, the court failed to require evidence of the facts demonstrating the impact that the proposed development would have on the area in question. How can a rational decision be made if the facts are not known? Obviously, all these cases should be decided on their particular facts. Siegan, *Other People's Property,* 102 *et seq.* (1976). This last is the approach in zoning law, where each case is tested by looking at the ordinance *as applied* to the particular tract of land.

The choice is a difficult one, and the solution to the problem is nowhere in sight. State courts will differ. The United States Supreme Court is unpredictable. If unlimited development is permitted, the fishing and resort industries will be destroyed without compensation. That seems unfair, yet the danger to the public is very great. If the owners of marshlands and estuarian lands are not permitted to develop their properties, the loss to them is also very great. Here is a choice between two very great evils. Some courts will pick one side, other courts will pick the other.

28.04 Compensable regulations

One solution to the problem in which land developers are pitted against the public, and the evidence shows that proceeding with the development would cause great public harm, is to combine the two great powers of government, the police power and the power of eminent domain. Comment: *Compensable Regulations: Outline of a New Land Use Planning,* 10 Willamette L. J. 451 (1974). Rhode Island has already passed a law to compensate landowners for restrictions on the development of wetlands. *Ibid,* p. 454. Under this system the landowner receives *some* compensation for the restrictions placed on his right of development, but not the full market value of the land. Of course, developers are unhappy with this solution. The environmental enthusiasts are also unhappy. But the fact of the matter is that the landowner is entitled to some payment, and tax money is nowhere in sight to buy all these lands at market value. In legal effect, this is quite similar to the *scenic easement* or *development rights easement* discussed earlier. The landowner retains ownership of the land, is entitled to make some use of the land, but is not entitled to develop it. Anything less than this offends our sense of what is fair and just.

28.05   The public trust doctrine

Some states have used a different approach to avoid paying the landowner compensation.

EXAMPLE: In *International Paper Co.* v. *Mississippi State Highway Dept.*, 271 So2d 395 (Miss. 1973), a landowner claimed ownership of an island in the Pascagoula River because a prior owner, from whom he had purchased the island, had received a grant from the state. The state of Mississippi argued and its supreme court held that ownership of all tidelands, including the spaces between ordinary high- and low-water mark, the bed of a bay, and all bodies of land arising from the bay floor are forever held in a public trust by the state. Such land cannot be sold to private persons. Of course, since the state owns the land it can control whatever is built thereon. A number of states follow this public trust rule. Its application, currently, is hard to predict.

EXAMPLE: Marks, the owner of land abutting on the ocean, sought to fill and develop the tidelands abutting his property. The court held the power of the state to control its navigable waters and the land beneath them was held in a public trust and was within the absolute control of the state. *Marks* v. *Whitney*, 6 Cal.3d 251, 491 P2d 374, 98 Cal. Reptr. 790 (1971). This was true even though a prior owner had purchased the submerged land from the state.

28.06   Navigable waters

Another approach to the problem rests upon the claims of the federal and state government to control of navigable waters. It is, of course, elementary that both government bodies have and exercise control over navigable waters. What is surprising is the position they maintain, sustained by the courts, that "once navigable, always navigable." *U.S.* v. *Stoeco Homes*, 359 F.Supp. 672 (D.N.J. 1973). Thus, even though land under navigable water was filled and built as long as one hundred years ago, it is still navigable, and either public body can compel removal of the improvements. Navigable water is subject to federal and state *servitudes*. It is elementary that either government can halt construction if it can show that the construction is on "navigable waters." In this context, water is "navigable" if it is or once was navigable, or if it is or once was part of the tidelands and marshlands of the aquatic ecosystem surrounding the navigable water. *Potomac Sand and Gravel Co.* v. *Governor*, 266 Md. 358, 293 A2d 241 (1972).

EXAMPLE: Landowner wanted to dredge in the navigable waters of Boca Ciega Bay in order to create a trailer park. The permit was denied by the United States because construction would have a destructive effect on wildlife. *Zabel* v. *Taub*, 430 F2d 199 (5th Cir. 1970).

EXAMPLE: Where the builder erected mobile homes on coastal marshland without a permit, he was compelled to remove them. *U.S.* v. *Moretti*, 478 F2d 418 (1973).

EXAMPLE: The court blocked construction of a housing development in Ocean City, New Jersey, because it fell within the limits of "navigable waters." *U.S. v. Stoeco Homes, Inc.*, 359 F.Supp. 672 (D.N.J. 1973).

28.07   Beaches

Since the history of this country began, it has been assumed that one who buys lands abutting on waters, navigable or nonnavigable, has the right to enjoy the beach as his private domain. In lands abutting on tidal waters, this right generally stops at the high-water mark. Landward of that line the public has no right to picnic or stroll. *In re Opinion of Justices*, 313 NE2d 561 (Mass. 1974). In recent times the courts have suddenly discovered that the public should be allowed to use and enjoy these beaches and have evolved a variety of theories that would enable the public to enjoy such rights, much to the disgust of riparian landowners who paid vast sums of money for their riparian rights and the right to enjoy these beaches in privacy. Some remarkable legal decisions have been handed down in order to enable the public to enjoy the beaches.

EXAMPLE: In California it has been held that where a riparian landowner over a five-year period made no objection to the use of his beach by the public, there exists an *implied dedication* to the public, and the landowner must allow public use. The reference here is to the beach area above high-water mark, where ordinarily the public has no rights. *County of Orange* v. *Chandler-Sherman Corp.*, 126 Cal. Reptr. 765, 5 S.W.U. L. Rev. 48 (1973); 11 Santa Clara L. Rev. 327.

EXAMPLE: In Oregon the courts have held that the public has a *customary right* to the use of the dry sand area. *State ex rel Thornton* v. *Hay,* 462 P2d 671 (Oreg. 1969).

EXAMPLE: In New Jersey it has been held that land contiguous to a beach is unique and therefore subject to strict zoning. *Frankel* v. *Atlantic City,* 63 N.J. 333, 307 A2d 562 (1973). This makes sense. Any person buying beach property ought to recognize that the public will want it kept free from undesirable uses.

EXAMPLE: Under the "public trust" rule, Massachusetts holds that land *below* the high-water mark, even though sold by the state to a private landowner, remains subject to the public rights of fishing and navigation. *In re Opinion of the Justices,* 313 NE2d 561 (1974).

No doubt other states will reach out into the beaches under some theory or other to give the public rights therein. As can be seen, the California rule punishes the "nice guy." The Oregon rule, discovering a customary right after millions have been spent by purchasers of riparian land, seems unfair. The fact is, that private landowners are now being punished for years of public neglect.

REFERENCES: 4 Seton Hall L. Rev. 662 (1972); 1978 ABF Res. J. 397 (1978); and 86 Harv. L. Rev. 1582 (1972) discussing *Just* v. *Marinette County;* Large, *This*

Land is Whose Land? Changing Concepts of Land as Property, 1973 Wis. L. Rev. 1039 (especially valuable discussion); 58 Va. L. Rev. 876 (1972) (valuable); Hill, *Coastal Wetlands in New England,* 52 Boston U. L. Rev. 724 (1972); Binder, *Taking Versus Reasonable Regulation: A Reappraisal in Light of Regional Planning and Wetlands,* 25 U. of Fla. L. Rev. 1, (1972) (valuable); Kramon, *Section 10 of the Rivers and Harbors Act: The Emergence of a New Protection for Tidal Marshes,* 33 Md. L. Rev. 229 (1973) (valuable); Morris, *Federal Navigation Servitude; Impediment to the Development of the Waterfront,* 45 St. John's L. Rev. 189 (1970); 44 Notre Dame Law. 236 (1968); 4 Land & Water L. Rev. 521 (1969); Bartke, *The Navigational Servitude and Just Compensation—Struggle for a Doctrine,* 48 Oreg. L. Rev. 1 (1968); 52 Notre D. Law. 1015 (1977). See also 6 Fla. St. U. L. Rev. 983 (1978); 8 R.E.L. J. 166 (1979); 15 San Diego L. Rev. 1241 (1978); 29 S.C.L. Rev. 627 (1978).

29 LAND USE CONTROLS— HISTORIC AREAS AND LANDMARKS

29.01   In general   The literature on preservation of historic areas and landmarks through zoning is extensive. See e.g., *Bibliography of Periodical Literature Relating to a Law of Historic Preservation,* 36 Law and Contemp. Prob. 442 (1971); also, *Symposium of Historic Preservation,* 36 Law and Contemp. Prob. 309–444 (1971); *Martha's Vineyard: The Development of a Legislative Strategy for Preservation,* 3 Environmental Affairs, 396 (1974). Of recent interest is *Rebman* v. *City of Springfield,* 111 Ill. App.2d 430, 250 NE2d 282 (1969) (sustaining establishment of historical zone around the Abraham Lincoln home in Springfield and citing many cases holding that the preservation of historical areas is well within the concept of public welfare). To like effect are *M. and N. Enterprises Inc.* v. *City of Springfield,* 111 Ill. App. 2d 444, 250 NE2d 389 (1969), and *Fitzpatrick* v. *City of Springfield,* 10 Ill. App.3d 317, 293 NE2d 712 (1973). Where the economy of the area depends on tourism engendered by the historic quaintness of the area, the zoning is likely to be sustained. 63 Columb. L. Rev. 708, 720. Historic zoning prevents changes in the historic nature of the area.

Landmarks consisting of isolated buildings present a different problem. Note: *Landmark Preservation Laws: Compensation for Temporary Taking,* 35 U. of C. L. Rev. 362 (1965).

> **EXAMPLE:** In *Lutheran Church in America* v. *City of New York,* 345 N.Y.2d 121, 304 NE2d 371 (1974). An attempt to freeze an individual landmark that was located in a high economic development area failed.

The constitutional issue can be avoided, of course, by payment of compensation. It has been argued that the city could condemn a development easement by paying an award equal to the difference between the fair market value of the land before taking (when the landowner would have the right to demolish and construct to the highest and best use) and the fair market value immediately after taking the development easement. Note: *Landmark Preservation Law: Compensation for Temporary Taking*, 35 U. of Chicago L. Rev. 362 (1965). Such a device is virtually certain to stand up if attacked in the courts.

Predictably, *area zoning* will fare better than the freezing of individual *landmarks*. *Fred F. French Inv. Co.* v. *City of New York*, 39 N.Y.S.2d 587, 350 NE2d 381 (1976); *People* v. *Ramsey*, 28 Ill. App.2d 252, 171 NE2d 246 (1960).

The New York courts appear to have introduced a new idea on the subject of landmark preservation.

> **EXAMPLE:** The owners sought to construct an office building on the site of the Grand Central Terminal, a landmark building. The courts sustained the city's refusal to grant a permit. The court took the position that Penn Central, the landowner, owned other real estate in the vicinity of the terminal that would lose value if the terminal were not in operation. This is a new idea. You do not just look at the landmark property to see if it is operating at a loss. You look at the landowner's real estate in the vicinity to see how it would be affected by demolition of the landmark.

Part of the city scheme was to transfer the terminal's development rights to nearby Penn Central land.

The New York high court declared the scheme valid in *Penn Central* v. *City of New York*, 42 N.Y.2d 324, 366 NE2d 1271 (1977), affirmed, 438 U.S. 104. Thus we have here a state court's view of validity as measured under a state constitution, and the federal view as measured under the federal Constitution. A more detailed look at the facts is needed.

In 1967 the Landmark Preservation Commission declared Penn Central Terminal a landmark. Penn Central proposed a plan for erecting an office tower above the terminal. Permission was refused. The city proposed to transfer development rights to other Penn Central properties.

Both the New York court and the United States Supreme Court ruled in favor of the city. What is important here is what the courts did not dispose of. In the first place, Penn Central owns other properties in the vicinity of the terminal that derive their value from proximity to the terminal. In other words, the situation as it existed *before* the development scheme was initiated was a situation that was not harming Penn Central seriously. Penn was making money, and constitutional law does not guarantee any landowner more than a reasonable return. People enthusiastic about landmark preservation have hailed the decision. It is an important decision. But much more litigation will be needed before the law can be regarded as settled.

*REFERENCES ON **PENN CENTRAL** IN SUPREME COURT:* 8 Capitol U. L. Rev. 553; 11 Conn. L. Rev. 273; 1979 Detroit Coll. L. Rev. 143; 7 Ecology L. Q. 731; 92 Harv. L. Rev. 222; 25 Loyola L. Rev. 205; 14 New England L. Rev. 317; 5 Ohio North L. Rev. 719; 47 U. Cin. L. Rev. 654; 1978 U. Ill. L. F. 927; 18 Washburn L. J. 404.

*REFERENCES ON **PENN CENTRAL** IN NEW YORK COURTS:* 42 Albany L. Rev. 523; 57 B.U. L. Rev. 931; 27 Buffalo L. Rev. 157; 78 Columb. L. Rev. 134; 6 Fordham Urban L. J. 667; 91 Harv. L. Rev. 402.

30 HOMEOWNERS' ASSOCIATION

30.01 The homeowners' association

The homeowners' association (HOA) is an interesting legal creature. It derived its early utility in connection with enforcement of general plan building restrictions in the old-fashioned subdivision of single-family dwellings.

> **EXAMPLE:** Developer plats a subdivision of one hundred lots and in the accompanying declaration of restrictions creates a restriction that only single-family dwellings shall be erected and a fifteen-foot front building line shall be observed. The declaration also provides that *XYZ Corp.*, a nonprofit corporation whose members are the lot owners in the subdivision, shall be empowered to enforce the restrictions and shall collect an annual assessment from each lot owner. Ultimately, Developer sells out all the lots. He now has lost interest in protecting the lot owners. Lot Owner begins construction of a store that will come all the way to the street line. Any one homeowner might be disinclined to hire a lawyer and engage in litigation. However, *XYZ Corp.* warns Lot Owner to discontinue construction and to remove the foundations he has constructed. Lot Owner knows this is no empty threat. He complies.

30.02 Legal form of association

The home association has been called a *private government*. Gibson & Simms, *New Community Development*, 11 Washburn L. J. 227, 230 (1972). It is an incorporated, nonprofit corporation formed under the declaration of restrictions. *Merrionette Manor Homes Improvement Assn.* v. *Heda*, 136 NE2d 556 (Ill. 1956); *Garden Dist. Prop. Owners' Assn.* v. *New Orleans*, 98 So2d 922 (La. 1957); *Neponsit Property Owners' Assn.* v. *Emigrant Industrial Savings Bank*, 15 NE2d 793 (N.Y. 1938); *Rodruck* v. *Sand Point Maintenance Comm.*, 295 P2d 714 (Wash. 1956). Unincorporated associations must be avoided, for traditionally these have very little in the way of legal existence or status. *Moffat Tunnel League* v. *U.S.*, 289 U.S. 113 (1933); 40 Ind. L. J. 420 (1964). Moreover, in any unincorporated association, the members have the risk of unlimited liabilities, for example, for personal injuries. Likewise, an unincorporated association cannot hold ownership of land. *Delaware L. and Dev. Co.* v. *First Church,* 147 A 165 (Del. 1929); Ford, *Dispositions of Property to Unincorporated Non-Profit Associations,* 55 Mich. L. Rev. 67, 235 (1956).

There is something of a misnomer here. We constantly talk of the *home association.* But, in truth, often there is no true legal association. The body selected to act as the home association is often a nonprofit *corporation.* For convenience, we shall refer to the body as the *home association.*

The association is formed in accordance with the declaration. There are bylaws and a corporate charter. In the beginning the developer and his associates are the members of the corporation. A nonprofit corporation, be it noted, has no *shareholders.* It has *members.* As homes are sold, each homeowner automatically becomes a member of the corporation.

30.03 Membership

The membership in the HOA is automatic. Each unit purchaser automatically becomes a member and his membership passes automatically to his purchaser. *Paulinskill Lake Assn.* v. *Emmich,* 397 A2d 968 (N.J. 1978).

30.04 Association as a vehicle for enforcing restrictions, liens, and covenants

In any land development where both a home association and a declaration exist, the right of enforcement of restrictions, liens, and covenants is transferred by the declaration to the home association. *Merrionette Manor Homes Improvement Assn.* v. *Heda,* 136 NE2d 556 (Ill. 1956); *Garden Dist. Prop. Owners' Assn.* v. *New Orleans,* 98 So2d 922 (La. 1957); *Neponsit Property Owners' Assn. v. Emigrant Industrial Savings Bank,* 15 NE2d 793 (N.Y. 1938); *Rodruck* v. *Sand Point Maintenance Comm.,* 295 P2d 714 (Wash. 1956); 8 Urb. Law Annual 169. Subsequent owners of the land become burdened with the restrictions of these declarations and covenants and obtain the benefits of the association. *Lincolnshire Civic Association Inc.* v. *Beach,* 364 N.Y.S.2d 248 (1975).

At times, it is suggested that the association is acting as agent of the property owners. *Neponsit Ppty. Owners' Assn.* v. *Emigrant Ind. Sav. Bank,* 15 NE2d 793 (N.Y. 1938). At other times it is suggested that it is acting as a third-party beneficiary of the covenants in the declaration. *Anthony* v. *Brea Glenbrook Club,* 130 Cal. Reptr. 32 (1976). 40 Ind. L. J. 420, 430 (1964). Or it is acting as the assignee of the developer. *Ibid.* Occasionally, it is simply said that the association is a "convenient instrument by which the property owners may advance their common interests." *Neponsit Property Owners' Assn., Inc.* v. *Emigrant Ind. Sav. Bank,* 15 NE2d 293 (N.Y. 1938); Note, 24 Cornell L. Q. 133 (1939); *In re Public Beach, Borough of Queens,* 199 NE 5 (N.Y. 1935). It does no harm to combine all these thoughts into the declaration.

FORM: *XYZ Home Association,* as agent for the property owners under an irrevocable agency coupled with an interest, as beneficiary of all the covenants and provisions herein contained and as assignee of declarant, is vested with the right in its own behalf and in behalf of all owners and parties interested in the land described in this declaration to enforce all the covenants, liens, restrictions, and provisions herein contained.

30.05 Further uses and functions of the association

The home association–corporation was the logical vehicle to carry out its subdivision type activities when condominiums came along. Every condominium has a corporation of this type in which all the apartment owners automatically become members.

In some states, the condominium form of ownership may be utilized for horizontal and vertical developments. For example, town houses and cluster homes may be sold as condominiums, and the owners of those units become members of the condominium owners' association. In any case, the powers of the association are those established by the declaration, charter of incorporation, and bylaws. In many developments the powers and functions of the association are extensive and include the maintenance of the common elements such as stairwells, elevators, lobby, recreation building and green areas. The association in a PUD also maintains the parks, private streets, and other common areas. If a city is not providing such service, the association collects refuse, provides sewer and water and other services normally performed by a city. Commonly today, it performs exterior maintenance on the buildings and maintains the green areas around the buildings.

This last function relieves the unit owners of tasks regarded as burdensome today and enables the unit owner to devote his leisure time to recreation. The association levies and collects assessments for the services it performs. It enforces the building restrictions set forth in the declaration and deeds.

30.06 Master association

Many developments take place in stages. Often, the reason for this is a practical business judgment. If phase one sells out nicely, the developer moves on to phase two, and so on. It is a matter of convenience for each phase to have its own association, but to place a master association (or umbrella association) over the entire project. The master association employs a general manager and provides services needed for the entire project, such as bus transportation.

30.07 Right of first refusal

In condominiums, the documents often create a right of first refusal. This gives the HOA the right to buy at the sale price offered by a third party any unit that is put up for sale. *Barkus* v. *Smith,* 346 So2d 786 (Fla. 1978).

30.08   Mechanics of control

The mechanics by means of which the association exercises its control and powers are set forth in the declaration, the corporate charter, and the bylaws of the corporation.

30.09   Stages in transfer of control of common areas

One can think of the transfer of control over the development as taking place in phases. First comes the phase of land acquisition and assembly. Next comes the rezoning and plat approval stage. Next comes the preparation, execution, and recording of the declaration. Up to this moment the declaration lacks legal efficacy, for the developer owns all the land. Easements, covenants, and restrictions require divided ownership, with one property owner enforcing his rights against others. Finally comes the phase when the developer makes deeds to lot purchasers, subjecting the lots sold and the lots retained by him to the scheme of restrictions, covenants, and easements, and beginning the transfer of control to the homeowners.

Again, as the lot or homesite sales proceed, under the declaration and corporation documents, the developer's representation decreases, until ultimately the developer's rights are phased out. By establishing the association, the developer has absolute power in the beginning stages of growth of the development. By appointing the first board of directors he maintains effective control for the first several years of development. As development continues, however, the control of the board shifts to the owners through their ever increasing vote.

When the homeowners have gained control, they may adopt reasonable bylaws. *Hidden Harbor Estates* v. *Norene*, 309 So.2d 179 (Fla. 1972); *Breene* v. *Plaza Towers*, 310 NW2d 730 (N.D. 1981); *Ryan* v. *Baptiste*, 565 SW2d 196 (Mo. 1978); *Kenney* v. *Morgan*, 325 A2d 419 (Md. 1974); 72ALR3d 308. See § 32.03(c).

30.10   Standing to sue

At times the HOA files lawsuits, most often a suit against the developer or builder for defects in construction. The courts may hold that the HOA "lacks standing." This means that such a suit must be brought by the unit owners. *Friendly Village Comm. Assn.* v. *Silva E. Hill Const. Co.*, 31 Cal. App.3d 220, 107 Cal. Reptr. 123, 69 ALR3d 1142 (1973). The decisions are numerous and conflicting. In some states even an unincorporated association has been given the power to sue. *Tassan* v. *United Develop. Co.*, 410 NE2d 902 (Ill. App. 1980). See § 32.15.

30.11   Income tax

The problem of federal income tax on the HOA has been a thorny one. And, like all income tax problems, any solution is a temporary one, since income tax law changes constantly. However, for the year 1981 and until the law is changed, the HOA has the privilege of filing Form 1120-H for the given tax year and for each year thereafter. If this form is filed the HOA acquires a limited tax-exempt status. Its income from assessments will not be taxable. See, generally, Rev. Rul. 80-63, CCH Fed. Tax Rpts. § 6429 (3/12/80). However, almost every HOA will have income other than assessment income.

> **EXAMPLE:** The HOA places some of its funds in a Certificate of Deposit on which it receives an income of $1,000 for 1981. This income less a statutory $100 is taxable at 30 percent. Thus, $1,000 less $100, or $900, is taxable at the 30 percent rate.

30.12 Regulation

As with condominiums, there are various forms of disclosures required of developers of projects where homeowners' associations are involved. These regulations may be on the federal level, as required by the Interstate Land Sales Act, on the state level as required by state land sales acts or subdivision laws, or on the local level as required by county or municipal ordinance. In some instances there may even be regulation directed specifically at offerings of memberships in homeowners' associations. Parness, *Homeowners' Associations: Consideration for the Practicing Attorney*, 46 N.Y.S.B.J. 357, 360 (1974). The task for the developer and his attorney is to determine which regulations apply, and to comply with their requirements.

REFERENCES: *The Homes Association Handbook, Technical Bulletin* 50 (1964), and *Community Builders Handbook*, both published by Urban Land Institute, 1200 18th Street, N.W., Washington, D.C. 20036; 24 Emory L. J. 977; 9 San Diego L. Rev. 28; 8 Urb. Law Ann. 169 (1974); 123 U. Pa. L. Rev. 711 (1975); 48 St. Johns L. Rev. 736 (1975); 43 U. Chgo. L. Rev. 253 (1976).

---

31 THE DECLARATION OF RESTRICTIONS, EASEMENTS, LIENS, AND COVENANTS

31.01 In general

In today's land transactions property rights of considerable complexity are generated. This is true particularly of the condominium, the planned unit development (PUD), and the town house. Supplementing the local zoning ordinance in such development there will be found a scheme of private building covenants, easements, liens, and restrictions. The landowner in a condominium or PUD will covenant to do a number of things, for example, to pay maintenance assessments, which are foreclosable liens on the homesites or apartments. Each landowner in a condominium, PUD, or town house will enjoy a number of valuable easements over his neighbors' property, and his own property will be subject to easements in favor of his neighbors. There is general agreement among property lawyers that these detailed rights should be set forth in a *declaration of restrictions, easements, liens, and covenants,* and that only relatively brief reference should be made to them in the deeds of conveyance. *Leverton* v. *Laird,* 190 NW2d 427 (Iowa).

The legality of this device rests upon the rule that if a recorded document, such as a deed, makes reference to another document recorded in the same office, the two are read together. Thus the provisions of the declaration are treated legally as "set out" in the deed. 82 ALR 412, 416.

31.02 History of the declaration

We can now profitably look back at the historical development of this important declaration document. Originally, in creating general plan restrictions, the subdivider utilized deeds containing identical restrictions. This proved impractical.

> **EXAMPLE:** Subdivider records a plat dividing his land into 200 lots. He conveys 150 scattered lots by deeds containing identical restrictions. Subdivider dies. His heirs proceed to sell the remaining 50 lots to anyone who is willing to buy. No

restrictions appear in the deeds. Obviously, there is no general plan. The required uniformity is lacking.

Hence prudent developers began to place the restriction in the recorded plat of subdivision. This served two purposes. Since the plat covers *all* lots in the subdivision, a general plan of restrictions is revealed. And since a plat is a recordable document, its recording imparts constructive notice of the restrictions.

As time wore on, restriction plans became complex and lengthy. Physically, there was no room on the face of the plat for these complex restrictions. Hence the subdivider simply placed on the plat a legend stating: "All land in this subdivision is subject to the restrictions appearing in a Declaration of Restrictions recorded contemporaneously herewith." When the plat was handed to the recorder, it was accompanied by a separate typed document, called a *Declaration of Restrictions,* setting forth the restrictions and a statement that they were to be treated as part of the plat. This declaration was signed by the subdivider and duly notarized. This procedure is called *incorporation by reference.* It is quite valid.

When planned unit developments and condominiums came along, a need was perceived for legal machinery to enforce the assessments needed to operate the common areas. The declaration was again utilized, this time to create (1) the lien of the assessments and (2) the covenant by the unit owner to pay it. See Chapter 32. The declaration is now serving additional purposes.

Finally some legal body was needed to enforce restrictions, collect assessments, operate the condo and the PUD. So the homeowners' association was created and brought into the declaration.

As is evident, over a long period of time the declaration evolved into a very useful document.

31.03 Declaration and other document provisions

The home association declaration in a PUD is modeled in part after the condo declaration, which in turn is modeled after the declaration used to create building restrictions. Among other provisions, it will place some limit on a homeowner's right to make alterations in his unit.

In both the condo and the PUD, buyers like to see some limit on the increase in annual assessments, but there should be a provision that a stated percentage of unit owners can, at a regularly called meeting, authorize an expenditure that exceeds the maximum. If the roof leaks, for example, it must be fixed regardless of cost.

Many declarations contain a provision for fining a unit owner who violates building restrictions, altering his PUD unit without submitting plans to the plan committee, violating swimming pool rules, and so forth. Provision for such fines is included in the declaration, but details should be left to the bylaws. The bylaws should provide for notice to the offending unit owner and a hearing before the board. It is best that the findings and decision of the board be written up formally and placed in the association record book.

Every set of bylaws should state a percentage of the membership that will constitute a quorum. It is best to keep this percentage low. Members tend to shun these meetings. A member who monopolizes meeting time with irrelevant trivia can make meetings tiresome and boring.

The association should hold meetings in strict accordance with its bylaws and elect officers at the proper time. The elected secretary should keep careful custody of the association books and papers, insurance policies, and so forth. In a PUD the common area will be covered by title insurance in the name of the association. Of course, the association will take out liability insurance. It will take out hazard insurance on buildings owned by the association, for example, on recreation buildings. In a condo it will take out liability and hazard insurance.

If the local law requires the lien of an unpaid assessment to be recorded, the secretary attends to this and keeps the recorded notice of lien in his records. The bylaws will provide for interest on delinquent assessments.

Of course, assessments cannot be levied if the purpose is one not authorized by the documents. *Spitser* v. *Kentwood Home Guardians*, 24 Cal. App.3d 215 (1972).

Federal requirements exist as to FHA, VA, FNMA, and FHLMC loans.

31.04 Restrictions

Since all that is needed to create enforceable building restrictions or easements is a recorded document that gives public notice of such restrictions or easements, a recorded declaration will suffice for this purpose, when followed by deeds referring thereto. *Spencer* v. *Poole,* 207 Ga.155, 60 SE2d 371 (1972). *Davis* v. *Huguenor,* 408 Ill. 468, 97 NE2d 295; *Kosel* v. *Stone,* 146 Mont. 218, 404 P2d 894; *Lawrence* v. *Brockelman,* 155 N.Y.S.2d 604; 4 ALR2d 1364.

There will be restrictions as to the homesites or apartments and restrictions as to the common areas. For obvious reasons, the developer must not retain the right to modify the restrictions. This may destroy the general plan and render the restrictions unenforceable. 19 ALR 2d 1282. Also the declaration must be recorded before any deed or mortgage is recorded, for any deed recorded before the declaration will not be subject to the restrictions, easements, or other rights created by the declaration. All deeds are expressly made subject to the declaration.

For the protection of the developer in a PUD, a provision should be included making it clear that restrictions covering the present development do not "pour over" into his subsequent neighboring developments. *Craven County* v. *First-Citizens Bank and Trust Co.,* 237 N.C. 502, 75 SE2d 620; *Finucan* v. *Coronet Homes,* 191 SE2d 5 (S.C. 1972).

It is usual to provide that the restrictions will run till a stated date, and then continue for successive ten-year periods unless altered or abrogated by a vote of the lot or apartment owners. Care must be exercised in expressing the percentage vote. A *majority of the lot owners* is not the same as a vote of *the owners of a majority of the lots.* For example, a lot owner may die leaving fifteen heirs, and a question will arise whether they are entitled to one vote or fifteen votes. Probably one vote per homesite or per apartment is a workable rule, such vote to be cast only if a majority of the owners of that lot or apartment agree on their vote. The same observations are applicable to an amendment of the declaration in any other respect.

The fact that complex building restrictions can be created by a declaration of restrictions in no wise prevents the creation of restrictions by insertion thereof in the plat of subdivision. Indeed, that is the logical place for insertion of simple building restrictions. The declaration, as a means of creating building restrictions, is a modern innovation. It must be remembered that a plat of subdivision, although it is a physically large document, has the map of the subdivision thereon occupying about 90 percent of the space. Moreover, all the language on the face of the plat is hand-lettered by the surveyor. It is this factor that makes it convenient to use a separate typewritten declaration, often running ten pages or more where valuable homesites are involved.

REFERENCE FOR LAWYERS: Kratovil, *Building Restrictions—Contracts or Servitudes,* 11 John Marshall J. 465 (1978).

31.05 Easements

Since the law does not specify any particular form an easement must take, the creation of easements by means of a recorded declaration followed by a deed containing grants and reservations of the easements is universally recognized as a proper means of creating easments. The right to use the common areas must be accomplished by the creation of easements and covenants. It should not be done by *dedication.* A dedication is a giving of rights to the *public.* Hence, use of the word *dedication* is to be avoided for this word has no place in the creation of private, as distinguished from public, rights. *Drye* v. *Eagle Rock Ranch, Inc.,* 364 SW2d 196 (Tex. Civ. App.).

When a tall building is divided into office space (lower floors) and residential apartments (upper floors) the declaration of easements is quite complicated. It is accompanied by or incorporated into an operating agreement, which sets out the duties of the party who is to operate the elevators, repair water pipes and electrical systems, and so forth.

31.06 Phased development

It is quite possible to develop an area in several stages. This is a convenience to the developer. He can limit his investment to stage one, and, if it is not a success, he need not develop additional stages. The additional, undeveloped stages can be sold as raw land. It then becomes important to assure that the building restrictions on stage one do not "pour over" into the future undeveloped stages.

However, as to the common elements, for example, the swimming pool in stage one, the declaration should make clear whether or not the developer has the power to bring in several successive stages, all of which will share the use of the pool. Drafting can help.

> **CLAUSE:**   The developer reserves the right to add as an adjoining development a development no larger than the present development, containing a substantially identical number of substantially identical units, all of which will be subject to a declaration substantially identical with this declaration. In no event shall any land other than the present development be burdened by any restrictions, liens, covenants or easements affecting the present development in the absence of a provision to the contrary.

31.07   Party walls

Where party walls are involved, as in the town house, the declaration will contain a detailed provision regarding same, including a provision that the cost of reasonable repair and maintenance shall be shared by the owners who make use of the wall in proportion to such use.

31.08   Lien of assessments

Both in the condominimum and the PUD, the home association will want a provision in the declaration giving it the right to levy assessments on the homeowner for maintenance of the common areas. Again, this can be done in the declaration, since the law requires no great formality for the creation of equitable or contractual liens. *Prudential Ins. Co.* v. *Wetzel,* 212 Wis. 100, 248 NW791. Such assessment liens are enforceable by foreclosure, like a mortgage. *Rodruck* v. *Sand Point,* 48 Wash.2d 565, 295 P2d 714. The lien serves an important purpose. As the section on covenants shows, the declaration also gives the association the right to *sue* the homeowner for assessments, and to get a judgment against him. The covenants, in other words, create *personal liability.* But where the homeowner is financially irresponsible, or simply disappears, so that summons cannot be served upon him, the lien for his delinquent assessments can be foreclosed. Both methods of enforcement should be provided for. The declaration should state that any delinquent assessment bears interest at the highest legal rate and that attorneys' fees are collectible as part of the assessment.

31.09   Lien and assessment—priority with respect to mortgages

In both the condominium and the PUD there will usually be two liens, the lien of the mortgage on the home or apartment, and the lien of the assessments. Obviously, a question will arise as to whether foreclosure of a mortgage will wipe out delinquent assessment liens or vice versa. A mortgage recorded subsequent to the recording of the deed and declaration creating the lien is subject and subordinate to such lien, even as to assessments accruing subsequent to the recording of the mortgage. *Kell* v. *Della Vista,* 528 SW2d 651 (Ark. 1972); *Lessamer* v. *Gerston,* 381 So2d 1344 (Fla. 1980); *Prudential Ins. Co.* v. *Wetzel,* 212 Wis. 100, 248 NW 791. Foreclosure of the assessment lien wipes out the mortgage. Mortgages that antedate the effective date of the declaration or deeds will be prior and superior to the assessment liens (*Brosk v. Bank of St. Louis,* 533 SW2d 233 (Mo. 1979). *Kennilwood Owners' Assn. v. Kennilwood,* 28 N.Y.S.2d 239), so that foreclosure of the mortgage will cut out all unpaid assessments and the future liability of the lot to pay assessments. This creates a potential conflict. Mortgagees, especially those who are required by law to loan only on first mortgages, will insist that the lien of all assessments, even those created by an earlier declaration, be subordinated to the lien of their mortgages. The wishes of the mortgagee must prevail, since otherwise financing cannot be obtained. However, once the mortgage is foreclosed and the mortgagee has become the owner of the lot, the lien of future assessments should be binding on the mortgagee, as they would be on any other homeowner. This can be accomplished by a clause in the declaration as follows:

> **SUGGESTED FORM:**   The lien of the assessment provided for herein shall be subordinate to the lien of any mortgage or mortgages now or hereafter placed upon the properties subject to assessments and running to a bank, savings and loan association, insurance company, or other institutional lender; provided, however, such subordination shall apply only to the assessments which have become due and payable prior to a sale or transfer of such property pursuant to a decree of foreclosure, or any other proceeding in lieu of foreclosure. Such sale or transfer shall not relieve such property from liability for any assessments thereafter becoming due nor from the lien of any such subsequent assement. See § 32.04

31.10 Covenants

The creation of covenants that will impose *personal liability* on future landowners, for example, to pay maintenance assessments, is a technical matter. Hence in this instance it seems desirable to refer to the declaration for the text of the covenants, but to spell out *in the deed* the language by which the grantor and grantee, and their successors in ownership, agree to perform their covenants. Likewise, a covenant binding on the association to maintain the common areas, collect assessments impartially, and the like seems desirable. *Chimney Hill Owners Assn. v. Antignani,* 392 A2d 423 (Vt. 1978). Of course, where the plan is that the association will provide, at its expense, maintenance of the homesite and of the exterior of the home, that must be spelled out in detail in the declaration.

31.11 Association as a vehicle for enforcing restrictions, liens, and covenants

The enforcement of *restrictions, liens,* and *covenants* can legally be transferred through the declaration to an association or corporation formed by the home or apartment owners. *Merrionette Manor Homes v. Heda,* 11 Ill. App.2d 186, 136 NE2d 556; *Neponsit Property Owners' Assn. v. Emigrant Industrial Savings Bank,* 278 N.Y. 248, 15 NE2d 793; *Rodruck v. Sand Point Maintenance Comm.,* 40 Wash.2d 565, 295 P2d 714.

31.12 Deed clauses to implement the declaration

To fully implement the declaration, it is necessary to insert a clause in the deed to the homebuyer or apartment buyer. Such a clause might be:

SUGGESTED FORM: Subject to Declaration of Easements, Restrictions, Liens, and Covenants dated _____ and recorded in the Office of the Recorder of Deeds of _____ County, as Document No._____ which is incorporated herein by reference thereto. Grantor grants to the Grantee, his heirs and assigns, as easements appurtenant to the premises hereby conveyed, the easements created by said Declaration for the benefit of the owners of the parcel of realty herein described. Grantor reserves to himself, his heirs and assigns, as easements appurtenant to the remaining parcels described in said Declaration, the easements thereby created for the benefit of said remaining parcels described in said Declaration, and this conveyance is subject to said easements and the right of the Grantor to grant said easements in the conveyances of said remaining parcels or any of them, and the parties hereto, for themselves, their heirs, personal representatives, and assigns, covenant to be bound by the covenants, restrictions, and agreements in said document set forth. Said covenants and restrictions are covenants running with the land both as to burden and benefits, and this conveyance is subject to all said covenants and restrictions as though set forth in full herein. The land hereby conveyed is also subject to the liens created by said Declaration, and same are binding on the grantees, their heirs, personal representatives, and assigns. All of the provisions of said Declaration are hereby incorporated herein as though set forth in full herein.

In some decisions it has been held that the filing of the declaration would suffice to create restrictions even though they were not mentioned in the subdivider's deeds. *Kosel* v. *Stone,* 146 Mont. 218, 404 P2d 894; *Steuart Transp. Co.* v. *Ashe,* 304 A2d 788 (Md. 1973). But in California precisely the opposite has been held. There the declaration is totally ineffective unless the deeds refer to it. *Smith* v. *Rasqui,* 1 Cal. Reptr. 478. However, it suffices to state in the deeds that the land is "subject to covenants, conditions, restrictions, and easements of record," *Seaton* v. *Clifford,* 100 Cal. Reptr. 779; *Davis* v. *Huguenor,* 408 Ill. 468, 97 NE2d 295. Obviously, this is a poor practice. The full suggested form should be used.

A different rule is applied if all of the restrictions, liens, and covenants are included in a recorded plat of the subdivision. The usual rule is that a deed describing the land conveyed as a lot in a recorded subdivision automatically is treated as if the plat were attached to and formed part of the deed. After all, how can you possibly locate your lot without looking at the plat? And if you look at the plat you are bound to see the restrictions. The same rule applies if the plat states *on its face* that all lots are subject to restrictions set forth in a declaration "recorded contemporaneously herewith."

Where the owner of a condominium apartment, PUD unit, or town house is placing a mortgage on his property, a clause is inserted in the mortgage along the following lines:

CLAUSE: Subject to Declaration of Easements, Restrictions, Liens, and Covenants dated _____ and recorded in the Office of the Recorder of Deeds of _____ County in Book _____ page _____ as Document No. _____, which is incorporated herein by reference thereto. Mortgagor grants to the mortgagee, its successors, and assigns all rights of every description created by said Declaration for the benefit of the mortgaged premises, same to run with the mortgaged land. The provisions of said Declaration regarding liens of assessments are also incorporated herein by reference thereto.

31.13 Sale by homeowner

The declaration should provide that upon sale of a home or apartment, the seller shall not be liable for assessments levied or covenants or restrictions breached thereafter. Unless this clause is included there is a legal possibility of continuing liability.

31.14 Membership corporation

The declaration will set forth who the members are to be in the home association created for a PUD or for a condominium.

31.15 Marketable Title Acts

Under the Marketable Title Acts, rights in land—including covenants, restrictions, private assessment liens, and, in some instances, easements also—terminate after a stated period of time unless fresh recordings are made to keep these interests alive.

REFERENCE: For sample declaration of restrictions for detached single-family dwellings see FHA Land Planning Bulletin No. 3—Protective Covenants Data Sheet 40, also Sample Form Protective Covenants, both set forth in the Appendix to *Community Builders Handbook,* published by Urban Land Institute, 1200 18th Street, N.W., Washington, DC. 20036.

32 CONDOMINIUMS AND CO-OPS

32.01 In general   In the past two decades, the condominium has sprung from near obscurity to become a common form of property ownership. Some predict that it will become the dominant form of property ownership in the future. Interest rates and the cost of new housing may drastically curtail the ability of the American public to purchase detached housing. The town house, cluster homes, and apartments become obvious alternatives. If those living units are to be individually owned, the condominium form of ownership is an apt vehicle.

The condominium form of ownership may perhaps be best explained by comparing it to rental apartments. A typical apartment building consists of apartments, lobby, halls, stairways, roof, building walls, grounds, walks, and drives surrounding the building. The apartment is the private domain of the occupant. Its use is not shared with other occupants. But the other areas (lobby, halls, stairways, roof, walls, grounds, walks, drives), the *common elements,* are owned by the landlord and shared by the tenants. In the condo, the ownership follows this simple pattern. The apartment is purchased and becomes the exclusive domain of the owner, but *ownership* and use of the common elements is shared with all other apartment owners.

EXAMPLE: Developer acquires a tract of land and obtains a construction loan for the construction of a 50-unit condominium project. The building is built and Purchaser contracts to buy Unit #1. Purchaser really is buying Unit #1 plus a percentage interest in the common elements. Technically, the unit is bounded by the inner surface of the apartment walls and the common elements include everything in the project that is not part of a unit, i.e., the ground the project is built on, the air space above it, the outside walls of the project, walls between the units, its foundation and roof, the basement, stairs, elevators, foyers, swimming pool, janitor's apartment, water tanks, fire escapes, heating plant, air conditioning system, and so on.

The purchaser will own the unit just as if it were a separate house, and will become a tenant in common of the *common elements* with fellow unit owners. When the purchase closes, the construction mortgage will be released from Unit #1 and its undivided share of the common elements. If Purchaser finances the purchase of Unit #1, the lender will have a mortgage lien against Unit #1 and its share of the common elements.

Condominiums are not limited to apartments. Cluster homes, town houses, commercial structures of offices and other uses, campsites, parking spaces, hotels, and other projects have been submitted to the condominium form of ownership.

32.02 Common law condominiums

Every state has enacted laws establishing and regulating the condominium. When condominiums first became popular, some lawyers worried that a technical noncompliance with the law would put the project into limbo. Their fears were largely unfounded. If state law was not followed, a common law condominium was probably created. *Thisted* v. *County Club Tower Corp.*, 405 P2d 432 (Mont. 1965). This is similar to the situation where a subdivision plat that does not comply with the law is deemed to be a common law plat. *Sundstrom* v. *Village of Oak Park,* 30 NE2d 58 (Ill. 1940). The analogy seems persuasive except where the state law expressly states that all condominiums must conform to the statute.

Even if the condominium is created by common law concepts, several disadvantages befall the project that does not comply with the condominium statute. They include the following: (1) the assessor is not obliged to make a separate assessment on the unit and its common elements; (2) a mechanic's lien for work ordered by one tenant might attach to the whole building; (3) the restriction on partition of the common elements might be valid for only twenty-one years.

In short, the advantages of having a condominium conform to the condominium law are so great that it is essential that a unit buyer be assured that it does comply with the law. Title companies provide such insurance. Where title insurance is not available, check to see if the units are eligible for a FHA, VA, or FHLMC mortgage. These agencies insist that the condominium law be complied with. If they have approved the building, it complies.

32.03 Basic condominium documents

The creation of the condominium form of ownership and the regulation of the activities of the unit owners involve various basic or organic documents, many of which are not found in other forms of property ownership.

32.03(a) Basic documents—declaration

The condominium declaration is the basic organic document or constitution for the condominium. It spells out the extent of the interest that each purchaser acquires and the rights and liabilities of the unit owners. *Pepe* v. *Whispering*

Sands Condo. Assn., Inc. 351 So2d 755 (Fla. 1977). Once the declaration is recorded, the last act in creation of the condominium is accomplished and the condominium comes into existence. *State Sav. & L. Assn.* v. *Kauaian Dev. Co.,* 445 P2d 109 (Hawaii 1968).

State laws require the declaration to contain:

1. The name of the condominium.

2. A description of the property being submitted to the condominium form of ownership. A traditional legal description is used here.

3. A description of each unit. The condominium survey is a three-dimensional marvel of far greater sophistication than the two-dimensional version. It has to be. Condominium units are often cubes of air space, but it is necessary to describe these pieces of real estate with the same precision with which parcels of land are described.

There are three methods by which a unit of air space can be described:

1. *The subdivision plat method.* You record a plat of subdivision of air space and the air lots representing the individual units by means of a drawing. This will permit conveyance of a particular unit by its number, as shown on the plat.

2. *The land and apartment survey.* A survey is first made of the land, showing the location of the building. Space surveys of each unit on each floor are then made showing the elevation of the floor and ceiling surfaces, the dimensions of the inside surfaces of the walls of each unit, and their location with reference to the boundaries of the land projected vertically upward.

3. *Floor plan method.* In lieu of individual apartment surveys, make a survey of the land showing the location of the building and attach to it floor plans showing each unit's location, dimensions, and elevation from the ground floor surface, with a certification by the architect that the building was built substantially in accordance with the plans.

One difficulty with these methods is that the typical condominium unit is an apartment in a multilevel building.

PROBLEM: How does one describe the perimeters of an apartment located, let us say, on the twentieth floor of an apartment building? How does one describe with legal accuracy the exact height above ground level of the floor and ceiling of the apartment? Remember that a condo unit is basically a cube of space. Space is considered to be land that can be deeded and mortgaged. But it is harder to describe than a simple two-dimensional tract of land, such as a lot on which a house has been erected. As regards the house lot, the surveyor can go on the tract of land and place monuments or markers at the lot corners. But one cannot plant markers in the sky. Hence, the problem.

One part of the problem is simple. The surveyor can depict on the ground the proposed perimeters of the apartment unit and then state that such perimeters extended upward indefinitely. To grasp this idea, imagine a rectangular lot, with stakes at all four lot corners. Then imagine the lot line thus created as extending up to the sky. Now you have the perimeters of the lot, however high you can go, since surveyors, given the outlines of a tract of land at ground level, can, by use of instruments, extend the lot lines upward to the heavens.

The other problem is more difficult. Legally, one cannot measure the height of the floor and ceiling from "the ground." The ground is not a stable and definite legal marker. Indeed, in the process of erecting a building, the construction crew invariably levels and changes the grade of the ground. Many condo apartments are contracted for sale before construction begins.

Engineers have solved this problem.

> **EXAMPLE:**   In Chicago, for example, the city, by ordinance, has established an artificial horizontal plane beneath the surface of the entire city. This plane is uniform throughout the city. At many places throughout the city, concrete markers are placed extending about six feet downward from the sidewalk. The sidewalk is used because its grade is rarely altered. Each such monument contains a legend, stating, for example, "twenty feet above Chicago City Datum." The *Datum* is the artifical legal subsurface that extends at the same level throughout the entire city. The markers are called *Bench Marks.* There are hundreds scattered throughout the city, each identified by location and number. Now a surveyor, plotting a condominium unit on the twentieth floor, can show on his survey that the floor of the apartment is located ____ feet above Chicago City Datum as established by Bench Mark ____. The same is done with the ceiling. With this system, establishing vertical boundaries is a simple task for the surveyor.

The United Geodetic Survey has established its own *datum* and *bench marks.* Some surveyors prefer to use these because they are considered more accurate than city datum and city bench marks.

> 4. A description of the common elements. A common shortcut method of describing the common elements is to describe the entire parcel and add the language "except apartment parcels 1 to 100 inclusive."
>
> 5. A description of the limited common elements, areas that are common to only a few designated units, and the units to which the various limited common elements are assigned.
>
> 6. A statement of the share of each unit owner in the common elements. This share should be expressed as a percentage rather than a fraction. These shares are allocated upon several bases. In California each unit, irrespective of its size and value as compared to the other units, has one equal share with the other units. Cal. Civ. Code § 1353(b). In Illinois, the shares are computed on the basis of the value of the unit as compared to the value of the project as a whole. Ill. Rev. Stat. Ch. 30, § 304(e). Other states have more complex formulas for allocation. Va. Code Ann. § 55-79.55.
>
> 7. If the condominium is to be a phased or add-on condominium, see § 32.11, the declaration should give the option to add additional property to the condominium, state any limitations on the developer's ability to bring other land under the declaration, and set forth the manner of allocation of common elements, voting rights, and charges for common expenses, upon the joinder of the additional property. See Ill. Rev. Stat. Ch. 30, § 325.
>
> 8. If the condominium is a leasehold condominium, the declaration should identify the lease and state the unit owner's rights upon the termination of the lease.

There are other provisions that state law does not require the declaration to contain but they properly belong in the declaration because they affect the basic rights of the unit owners. They include:

1. A provision that ownership of an apartment and of the owner's share of the common elements shall not be severed or separated and that any conveyance or mortgage of the one without the other is prohibited. Also, that any partition suit with respect to the common elements is forbidden.

2. A provision giving the condominium association the right to levy assessments on the apartment owners for maintenance, and so forth, and creating personal liability on the unit owner plus a foreclosable lien on each apartment for any delinquency in paying the assessments applicable to each apartment unit, and stating the maximum assessment permitted.

Alternatives to foreclosure or eviction for nonpayment of assessments exist.

EXAMPLE: The association may post a list of delinquent owners in the recreation area or may deny the delinquent owner the use of the recreation facilities. To be safe, the declaration must provide for this latter remedy. Lowell, Prahl, Alessio, and Cazares, *Land Use and Operational Controls in the Planned Development*, 9 San Diego L. Rev. 38, 60 (1971).

Major buildings and projects present unforeseen engineering and legal problems that cause extraordinary expenses which the association must face.

EXAMPLE: Some cities have required installation of sprinkler systems in high-rise buildings. This can result in a big special assessment. Problems may also exist with elevator cables in high-rise buildings. Replacement could result in heavy assessments. These problems show the need to maintain adequate reserve levels to be built up over the expected useful life of the major replacement items such as roofs, carpeting in common areas, heating and cooling plant, and so forth.

3. Provision that in the event of total or substantial destruction of the building by fire or other hazard, or where the property reaches obsolescence, a stated percentage of co-owners' votes shall determine whether to rebuild or sell the property. A number of states have laws on this point.

4. A grant of easements to each apartment owner giving him rights of ingress and egress and other easement rights. As time goes by, buildings often settle. Thus, the condo unit sinks slightly into the common elements (the interior of walls that separate units), and common elements encroach into the units. To dispose of this problem, the condo declaration provides that as the building settles, the unit owner enjoys an easement to occupy the area not assigned to him by the surveys. Comment, 50 Calif. L. Rev. 299, 303 (1962). In tall buildings, the upper floors sway a good deal in a high wind. This is readily perceived when the water in the wash bowl sloshes around and chandeliers hung on chains sway perceptibly. Obviously, a unit in this area trespasses into the air space (common element)) surrounding the building. It is probably a good idea to include a "sway easement" in the declaration. Incidentally, people who suffer from giddiness should give this matter thought before purchasing a unit in an upper story.

NEW LAWS: Encroachment easements exist by virtue of statue in some states thereby allowing an easement for encroachment where the encroachment is the result of a deviation from the plat and plans of construction, repair, renovation, restoration, or settling or shifting. This statutory easement will not protect unit owners in the event of their wilful or intentional misconduct, or exculpate the contractor from liability for reason of failure to comply with the plans. Code Va. §§ 55-79.60.

5. A provision is needed stating that all easements, covenants, and agreements in the declaration run with the land. Some statement is also needed that the benefit and burden of these covenants run with each unit. A provision should be included that when any apartment owner sells, his personal liability for future breaches of these covenants ends with the sale.

6. The condominium owners want to have the ability to control occupancy to avoid the presence of incompatible neighbors. An outright restriction on the transfer of ownership without the association's consent would be invalid. *Rights of first refusal* are valid. These give the association the right to buy the unit at the same price a buyer from the unit owner is willing to pay. Practically speaking, these rights are rarely used because the association does not have the funds to make the purchase. Logistically, the unit owner's contract with a buyer must provide for this contingency, and the title company and buyer may require proof that the association was given notice of the sale and did not choose to exercise its right. Another valid declaration provision prohibits occupancy of the unit (not transfer of the unit) until the occupant is approved by the board. Ross, *Condominiums and Preemptive Options: The right of First Refusal,* 18 Hastings L. J. 585 (1967). Of course, these provisions cannot be used as a means of racial discrimination. 50 Calif. L. Rev. 299, 317 (1962). The right of first refusal should not apply to a sale made by a mortgagee who has acquired title through foreclosure. See generally *Backus* v. *Smith,* 364 So2d 786 (Fla. 1978); *Hoover & Morris Development Co.* v. *Mayfield,* 212 SE2d 778 (Ga. 1975); *Gale* v. *York Center Community Cooperative Inc.,* 171 NE2d 30 (Ill. 1961); *Lake Shore Club* v. *Lakefront Realty Corp.,* 398 NE2d 893 (Ill. App. 1979).

7. The unit owner's right to lease is a hotly debated issue. While estimates vary, somewhere between 25 percent and 33 percent of condo apartment units are owned by investors who rent their units to tenants. The inducements to do this include appreciation in value, income, and care-free management furnished by the HOA at the same monthly expense as is paid by owner–occupants.

Increasing opposition to this practice focuses on the alleged inattention of the investor to condo affairs. He attends no meetings and serves on no committees. He is indifferent, it is alleged, to tenant conduct that annoys owner–occupants and makes the building less desirable.

Restriction on the renting of units is valid, if done properly. *Seagate Condominium Assn., Inc.,* v. *Duffy,* 330 So2d 484 (Fla. 1976); *Kroop* v. *Caravelle Condominium, Inc.,* 323 So2d 307 (Fla. 1975). Probably a significant restraint of this character ought to be included in the declaration. Courts may refuse to apply the restriction in hardship cases, as where an owner dies and it is convenient to rent the unit while the estate is in probate. Indeed, it would be wise to except this and other hardship cases explicitly, so as to discourage courts from holding the entire restriction void for lack of reasonableness.

Unit owners who rent should not use printed tenant-type leases without amendatory language. Ordinary apartment leases contain provisions not suitable for condos, e.g., landlord will furnish heat, hot water, etc. The tenant's obligation to care for ordinary repairs, e.g., blocked drains, should be spelled out. Often, the association requires that all leases be on a prescribed form that causes the tenant to be aware of and agree to conform to the building rules.

Resort type condominiums present special problems. Suppose you put a clause in the declaration that rentals shall be for a minimum of two weeks. This type of restriction eliminates the danger of a motel type operation. But, if the restrictions on renting get too strict there is the danger that more and more units will be sold to permanent residents, who may amend the declaration to eliminate renting altogether. This, of course, is bad for those who bought the units basically for investment purposes, hoping to profit through renting the unit most of the year.

8. Most declarations have a clause obligating each unit owner to abide by all the rules or bylaws promulgated by the home association. Needed flexibility is obtained in this way since new and necessary rules can be enacted through the simple majority vote of a quorum, instead of a majority of the apartment owners. It is important that a method of enforcement exists for these rules. The declaration should allow the association to obtain injunctive relief. In this way the association may, in a serious case, have the court order the violation to cease.

9. The declaration should give the unit owners the right to amend the declaration and provide that the amendment will be binding upon all present and future owners. The declaration should state the procedure for amendment and the number of unit owners who must vote on the amendment for it to become effective. Until a body of condo law develops, courts will look for help in solving amendment problems to other sources, for example, the law developed in connection with amendments of general plan building restrictions.

EXAMPLE   An amendment conferring special privileges on one unit might well be considered illegal.

If the developer has the right to amend, he has broad power while he controls a majority of the units. The declaration should restrict the developer's activities in this regard to protect unit owners against unfair amendments.

32.03(b)   Basic condominium documents— deeds

The individual deed of a unit need not necessarily be a complex document insofar as its legal description is concerned. The basis for such description will already have been provided by: (1) recording of the subdivision plat; (2) recording of the declaration to which were appended the land and apartment surveys containing legal descriptions of the various apartments; or (3) recording of the declaration to which were appended the land survey and building floor plans, in which case the legal descriptions of the apartments will have been set forth in the declaration.

Thus, in the deed, the legal description of the individual apartment could be as follows:

PARCEL 1

The absolute and indefeasible fee simple title to the parcel of land, property, and space designated as Apartment Parcel 100 in the plat of subdivision recorded in the Recorder's Office of _____ County, _____ on November 1, 19 _____ as document No. 123456 (or: "in the Declaration recorded, etc." as the case may be).

The description of the common elements could be as follows:

PARCEL II

The absolute and indefeasible fee simple title to an undivided _____ percent interest in the land, property, and space known as Lot 1 in Block 1 in
Jones Subdivision, in Section _____, Township _____,
North, Range _____ East of the _____ Principal Merid-
ian, excepting from said Lot all the land, property, and space designated as
Apartment Parcels 1 to 100, both inclusive, in the plat of subdivision recorded in the Recorder's Office of _____ County,
_____ on November 1, 19_____ as Document No.
123456 (or: "in the Declaration recorded, etc." as the case may be).

The apartments excepted in Parcel II should, of course, consist of all the
family units in the building. Should there be any units that are intended to be
rented for commercial facilities, they should not be included among the apartments excepted, since they would be classed as part of the common elements.

An additional paragraph could be included in the developer's deed to the
first purchaser of an apartment, conveying all the rights, benefits, easements,
privileges, options, and covenants created by the declaration. It will do no harm
to repeat in this clause the statement that these run with the land, for it is this
document that gives life to the covenants.

Because of a dearth of modern cases touching on the specific question of
whether ownership of the space occupied by an apartment or upper floor in a
building would survive destruction of the building, it would be advisable to include in the deed a provision that it is the intention of the parties thereto that
the ownership rights thereby conveyed shall so survive.

32.03(c) Basic condominium documents— bylaws

The bylaws generally control the internal government of the associations. Bylaws will provide for:

1. the election of a board of managers, their term of
office, powers and duties, and the election of officers
of the board, i.e., president, secretary, treasurer;

2. notice to the unit owner of the proposed adoption of the annual budget;

3. a yearly accounting to unit owners;

4. notice to unit owners of board meetings;

5. quorum requirements for both board and unit owners' meetings;

6. number and method for calling unit owners' meetings;

7. the maintenance, repair, and replacement of the common elements;

8. the furnishing of a statement of account of any unit owner stating the amount of any
unpaid assessments or other charges;

9. the adoption of rules and regulations for the use of units and common areas.

As long as bylaws are reasonable they are binding. *Ryan* v. *Bapitiste,* 565
SW2d 196 (Mo. 1978); 48 St. Johns L. Rev. 1028. The problem, of course, re-

lates to the proper scope of bylaws. The greater the interference with rights considered rather basic, the greater the likelihood that courts will be disposed to hold that the provisions belong in the condo declaration. The declaration is the basic charter of fundamental rights. It is the proper place where limitations on such rights should be placed.

EXAMPLE: It would be best to include restrictions in rather fundamental rights (occupancy by children forbidden) in the declaration rather than in the bylaws. See § 32.03(a).

32.03(d)   Basic condominium documents— rules and regulations

Rules and regulations upon the use of the units and the common areas promote the communal nature of the condominium. 15A Am.Jur.2d *Condominiums and Cooperative Apartments* § 16. If they are reasonable, consistent with the law, and enacted in accordance with the bylaws, they will be enforced. Hickock, *Promulgation and Enforcement of House Rules,* 48 St. John's L. Rev. 1132, 1135 (1974); 94 Harv. L. Rev. 647 (1981). These are usually contained in a separate document.

Examples of common subjects of these rules include:

1. Reasonable restrictions against the occupancy of units by children under a specific age are probably valid. 100 ALR3d 241. *White Egret Condominium Inc., v. Franklin,* 379 So2d 346 (Fla. 1980). Some comment on this point must be made. The matter is one of state law. It does not follow that this rule will win acceptance in all states. States in the sun belt, retirement areas, are much more likely to sanction barring children than states like Massachusetts or Rhode Island. State laws forbidding all types of discrimination, including age discrimination, are being widely enacted. These laws may well prohibit restraints against occupancy by children. A social problem of major proportions is developing. Landlords are also barring children. The question is being asked, Where will the children live? 25 DePaul L. Rev. 64; 16 J. of Fam. L. 559; 67 Ky. L. J. 967; 40 Ohio St. L. J. 195; 19 Santa Clara L. Rev. 21. Childless two-income couples will find themselves in a legal battle against the family with children. Retirement condos are often limited to senior citizens. This argues for the validity of restrictions barring children. Retirement communities can also use indirect controls, like failing to provide schools, playgrounds, and other amenities for children.

The old racial restriction cases teach that restrictions against *occupancy* stand up better than restrictions against *sale. Doherty* v. *Rice,* 240 Wis. 389, 3 NW2d 734 (1942), *citing decisions from California and Michigan; Ritchey* v. *Villa Nueva Condo,* 81 Cal. App.3d 668, 146 Cal. Reptr. 695 (1978). Developers should prohibit *occupancy* by children rather than *sale* to families that have children, if they want to successfuly so limit the project. See § 25.04.

2. A rule prohibiting alcoholic beverages in the clubhouse area is valid. *Hidden Harbour Estates, Inc.,* v. *Norman,* 309 So2d 180 (Fla. 1975).

3. A rule prohibiting the use of washing machines in individual apartments is a valid means to prevent water damage to other apartments. *Forest Park Cooperative, Inc.,* v. *Hellman,* 152 N.Y.S.2d 685 (1956).

4. The installation of locks on the common areas is a valid reaction to vandalism problems. *Ryan* v. *Baptiste,* 565 SW2d 196 (Mo. 1978).

5. Restrictions against pets are valid. *Dulaney Towers Maint. Corp.* v. *O'Brey,* 418 A2d 1233 (Md. 1980). If the prohibition of pets on the property is adopted after pet owners have taken up occupancy, a lawsuit may develop. To avoid this problem, amendments often permit existing pets to remain.

6. It is also valid to require that each condominium owner is to keep his apartment in repair at his own expense but is not to interfere with the exterior of the building or any of the common elements.

7. A rule forbidding overnight parking in driveways was held reasonable. *Hollman* v. *Mission HOA,* 556 SW2d 632 (Tex. Civ. App. 1977).

32.03(e)   Procedure

Condominium procedure is governed, as has been said, by the condominium declaration, the corporate charter of the HOA, the local statute relating to such corporations, the corporate bylaws, and the rules adopted by the board. In addition, the local condominium statute may set forth procedural requirements for the annual meeting, enforcement of assessments, etc. 94 Harv. L. Rev. 647. And where court enforcement of the condominium documents is sought by the HOA or a unit owner, some courts treat this as a matter that is subject to constitutional requirements, such as notice and hearing. In this way the "private government" of the condo is subjected to judicial scrutiny in somewhat the same fashion as local government action. 94 Harv. L. Rev. 647.

32.04   Assessments

Every condominium and homeowners' association needs funds to maintain the common areas, staff the project, create reserves for the periodic replacement of major components, etc. Assessment against the unit owners provides these funds. In this way, the owners make monthly payments to fund the association budget, providing an orderly flow of funds to pay bills as they come due.

The declaration should establish the assessment process and a collection mechanism for past due payments. The declaration should allow the association to sue the delinquent unit owner and foreclose against the unit. In some jurisdictions, the delinquent assessment lien can be foreclosed by the power-of-sale foreclosure process, a quick remedy that does not require court proceedings. Cal. Civ. Code § 1356. To make the association whole, the declaration should provide that delinquent installments bear interest at the highest allowable legal rate and attorneys' fees and other costs incurred by the association in the collection process are added to the amount of the delinquent installment.

The possibility of foreclosure gives rise to a priority conflict between the association and unit mortgagees. In the typical situation, a condominium declaration is recorded to create the units and establish the lien against the units for assessments. Units are sold, and buyers finance their purchase with mortgages. If state law or the documents do not provide otherwise, the foreclosure of delinquent assessments will extinguish the mortgage, even if the delinquency occurs after the date of the mortgage. *Prudential Ins. Co.* v. *Wetzel,* 248 NW 791 (Wis. 1933); *Washington Fed. Sav. & L. Assn.* v. *Schneider,* 408 N.Y.S.2d 588 (1978); *Bessemer* v. *Gersten,* 381 So. 2d 344 (Fla. 1980). Though a contrary result has been reached under particular statutory language. *Brask* v. *Board of St. Louis,* 533

SW2d 223 (Mo. 1976). This is obviously a situation that chills unit sale financing and works against the long-term best interests of the condominium. A simple provision in the declaration subordinates the assessment lien to purchase money financing while requiring the foreclosing purchase money lender to pay assessments incurred after foreclosure. Kratovil and Werner, *Modern Mortgage Law and Practice* § 26.02 (2d ed., 1981).

> **EXAMPLE:** Lender financed Buyer's purchase of a condominium unit. If the suggested clause is in the declaration, Lender's lien will be prior to assessment liens against Buyer. If Buyer does not pay the mortgage as installments come due, the assessments will probably also go into default. Lender can foreclose and the purchaser at the foreclosure sale will take the title free of assessments due before the sale date. The buyer at the foreclosure sale, even if the lender is the buyer, will take the title subject only to the lien for those assessments that come due after the foreclosure sale date. See § 31.09.

In some states, a delinquent unit owner can be evicted just like a delinquent tenant. Ill. Rev. Stat. Ch. 30, § 309.2, & Ch. 57 § 13.1.

The assessment lien process is binding on the original and all subsequent buyers of the units, *Kell* v. *Bella Vista Village Property Owners Assn.*, 528 SW2d 651 (Ark. 1975), and the assessment percentages allocated to the various units cannot be changed without a unanimous vote unless the declaration clearly provides otherwise. *Thiese* v. *Leland House Assn.*, 311 So2d 142 (Fla. App. 1975).

The question of what may be a proper subject of an assessment expense is sure to generate interest and litigation. To date, the courts have given wide latitude to the association as long as it exercises its judgment in good faith for the benefit of the project. 77 ALR3d 1290.

> **EXAMPLE:** The association may purchase a unit for the resident manager of a large complex so he will be available at all hours. An assessment may be levied for this purpose.

As in all cases involving the validity of corporate action, every condo assessment levied by the board of directors is subject to scrutiny to determine if the power to levy the assessment for the particular purpose was one within the powers conferred on the condo HOA. In this instance it is necessary to examine the corporate charter of the HOA, the corporation statute under which it operates, and the condo declaration. The declaration, as the great bill of rights of the unit owners, may limit the powers the corporation might otherwise enjoy. 77 ALR3d 1290.

32.05 Condominium—termination due to destruction of building

The situation where the building is destroyed by fire or other casualty varies from state to state. Where rebuilding takes place with adequate insurance funds, the problems are not excessively complex. Where, however, a percentage of the owners have the right to vote to sell the property and divide the proceeds, problems exist unless the state law spells out a program. This has been done in some states, for example, New York, Hawaii, Mississippi, Nevada, Illinois, and Missouri.

32.06   Operational aspects—new condominiums

A number of steps must be taken to put a new condominium in operation. Among them are: (1) the election, in accordance with the bylaws, of a governing board by the unit owners; this usually takes place when about 75 percent of the units have been sold and occupied; (2) election of officers; (3) appointment of committees; (4) transfer of control from the developer to the newly elected board; (5) hiring of a new building manager, if it is desired to replace the developer's manager who has functioned from the date of first occupancy to the date the first board was organized; (6) review of insurance placed by developer; (7) review by the board of the completion of the building in accordance with plans and specifications; (8) adoption of rules governing swimming pools, pets, parking, and so forth. Hennessey, *Practical Problems of Residential Condominium Operation,* 2 Conn.L.Rev. 12 (1969).

Upon the transfer of control from the developer to the unit owners, many documents must be turned over to the new board, e.g., corporate record books, financial records, insurance policies, management contracts, etc.

After the completion of the building, normal operations include preparation of budgets by the Budget Committee, setting of assessments by the board, annual audits, approval of sales by unit owners, repair of building, etc. 2 Conn. L. Rev. 12. The common elements are operated and controlled by the board and the manager hired by the unit owners in accordance with the rules adopted by the unit owners. As a rule, no unit owner will be permitted to tinker with the common elements. *Sterling Village Condominium, Inc.* v. *Breitenbach,* 251 So2d 685 (Fla. 1971).

32.07   Board of directors

As in the case of any corporation, the board of directors controls the destiny of the building. It meets at least monthly. It appoints committees and hears committee reports. Often, its meetings are open to unit owners. Their complaints and suggestions are heard. The annual budget is a major concern. Fixing assessment rates and enforcing assessments against delinquent owners is another major concern. Dealing with repairs and replacement contracts in larger amounts than those entrusted to the manager is another concern. Hiring manager, auditor, and legal counsel will be a board matter, while hiring less important personnel, e.g., security guards, may be left to the manager. Procuring insurance is a board responsibility. Adopting rules (swimming pool hours, etc.) is a board matter. Bonding employees who handle money is also a board concern.

32.07(a)   Committees

A variety of committees will serve under the board of directors. There may be an Acceptance Committee. Its task is to review the building, possibly with the help of an architect, to establish what defects, if any, exist that require correction. The Maintenance Committee deals with maintenance problems after the building has been accepted. The Finance Committee reviews budget proposals with the help of the manager and condo auditor and proposes annual budgets.

32.08   Common elements

The common elements include every part of the condominium project that is not a unit.

> **EXAMPLE:**   A one-acre parcel of ground is developed as a condominium parcel. The building that houses the units covers one-half of the acre. The remainder of the land surface is devoted to the pool, driveway, green areas, and a clubhouse, all of which are common elements. So also are the lobby, elevators, stairways, roof, etc. of the building, every part of the building that is not a unit. The air space above the condominium is a common element, as is the ground below it.

These common areas are for the common use of all unit owners and are often subject to rules and regulations regulating their use for the mutual enjoyment of all owners.

32.08(a)   Common elements—limited common elements

Some state laws permit a class of common elements known as *limited common elements.* These are common elements shared by less than all unit owners, such as special corridors or stairways, common to certain apartments or a particular floor. These are collectively owned by the unit owners whose apartments they serve. Even though these areas are not for the use of all unit owners, they are subject to strict controls.

> **EXAMPLE:**   An owner of limited common elements that were originally built as screened enclosures remodeled the area by installing jalousie windows in lieu of the screens. The jalousies had to be removed or proper consents obtained. *Sterling Village Condominium, Inc.* v. *Breitenbach,* 251 So2d 685 (Fla. 1971).

32.08(b)   Common elements—invasion by unit owners

Since many town houses with their location at ground level are becoming condominiums, there is a temptation for a unit owner to invade the common elements.

> **EXAMPLE:**   The building in question was a one-story town house project with units separated by party walls. One unit owner decided to expand his unit, adding a story and excavating beneath the ground floor to add a workshop. The HOA stopped this. It was an invasion of the air space, a common element and the subsurface, also a common element. *Makeever* v. *Lyle,* 609 P2d 1084 (Ariz. 1980). But a small storage cabinet may not be deemed a violation. *Mission Hills Condo Assn.* v. *Penashio,* 97 Ill.App. 3d 305, 431 NE2d 221 (1981).

32.09 Real estate taxes

The real estate taxation issues relating to condominiums are simple but very important.

Before a particular condominium is created the real estate is taxed as a whole.

> **EXAMPLE:** A vacant piece of land has one tax bill; an apartment house has one tax bill.

When these properties are developed into condominiums, either through new construction or conversion, the tax bills must be split. Technically, the tax assessor *assesses* each condominium unit and its share of the common elements separately from every other unit and its share of the common elements. The laws of most states specifically require this separation of units for real estate taxation purposes. See, e.g., Ill. Rev. Stat. Ch. 30, § 310; Va. Code Ann. § 55-79.42.

The condominium owner must determine that this form of separate taxation is in place or, in the case of a new development, being processed. Otherwise, a delinquency in the payment of part of the taxes could result in delinquencies on the entire project. If the *tax division* is properly done, a unit owner need not be concerned with tax delinquencies affecting any other unit, because a tax sale affecting other parts of the development does not affect his ownership interest. *400 Condo. Assn.* v. *Tully,* 79 Ill. App.3d 686, 398 NE2d 945 (1979). See generally 71 ALR3d 952.

The problem of assessing for tax purposes a newly converted apartment building is complex.

> **EXAMPLE:** A rental apartment having 100 apartments, if sold as a rental apartment, has a market value of $1,000,000. If sold to a converter, it might sell for $1,500,000. Converters often pay a premium price. The converter, in turn, sells the 100 units at $30,000 each. As is evident, this gives the building a value of 100 times $30,000, or $3,000,000. Obviously, each unit owner is entitled to his own individual tax bill. But the aggregate of the tax bills will be higher than the old tax bill on the building when it was a rental. Meanwhile, the developer makes an estimate of what the tax bill will be. Often, this is a "low ball." It is deliberately understated. Any contract of sale made before the actual tax is fixed should provide for an escrow of a sum of money to cover a reprorating of taxes when the actual tax bill issues. But the buyer should be warned that as other conversions in the vicinity push the values up further, the tax bill is likely to increase.

32.10 Mortgages

The particular nature of a condominium causes the lender to be concerned with the questions that relate to any real property loan, plus:

> 1. The mortgage should provide: (a) that the unit owner's breach of a covenant of the declaration or the failure to pay assessments as they come due are defaults under the mortgage giving rise to the mortgagee's right to accelerate and foreclose; (b) that the

mortgagee may pay delinquent assessments and add those sums to the mortgage debt; and (c) that the mortgagor will not vote to amend the declaration without the mortgagee's consent. The FNMA and FHLMC have developed a Condominium Rider for attachment to their uniform instruments that adequately covers these points.

2. Any limitation on sale or rental of a condominium unit or any right of first refusal should be expressly inapplicable to a lender who buys the unit at his foreclosure sale or who takes a deed to a unit in lieu of foreclosure.

3. On a newly constructed or converted condominium, outsale lenders will likely insist on a presale requirement as a condition to funding any outsale loans. The percentage of required sales ranges from 25 percent to 50 percent. The presale requirement causes the sale contracts to be contingent upon the firming of financing for the outsales.

4. Because financing a condominium unit is really financing part of the building as a whole, the legal framework of the condominium must be examined. An endorsement to the lender's title insurance policy can be obtained to insure that the condominium has been legally created in conformity with state law.

5. The developer is dependent upon sales, and sales can only go forward if the outsale lenders find the loans acceptable. The lenders, in turn, look to see if the loans are acceptable on the secondary market and to the FHA. The FNMA, a major secondary market lender, requires:

a. the loans must be secured by units in one structure or in reasonably contiguous structures;

b. the common elements must be completed;

c. a 51 percent to 70 percent presale requirement;

d. that only one unit be owned by any one purchaser;

e. experienced, professional management;

f. the prior approval of all mortgagees to removing the property from condominium status, partition or subdivision of a unit or the common elements, and a change of the percentage interests in the common elements of the unit owners;

g. that assessment liens be junior to the first mortgage lien;

h. adequate reserves funded by monthly payments;

i. notice to the lender of a default by the owner under the condominium documents;

j. the right to examine the association books and records;

k. a reasonable method for dealing with condemnation;

l. encroachment easements;

m. no unreasonable restraint on alienation which would adversely affect the marketability of the unit or the ability of the mortgage holder to foreclose and thereafter sell or lease the unit;

n. fidelity bond coverage for those handling association funds;

o. a first mortgage lien;

p. title insurance that real taxes are assessed only against individual units together with their undivided interest in the common elements.

The FHLMC has similar requirements. See The Mortgage Corp., *Seller's Guide Conventional Mortgages* § 3.207.

6. If the mortgages are to have FHA insurance, any owner of five or more units cannot rent for a period of thirty days or less or provide customary hotel services to renters. 24 CFR § 234.15.

7. The mortgagee on a leasehold condominium will require:

a. that the unit owner's performance of a pro rata share of the leasehold obligation satisfies the obligation of that unit owner on the ground lease;

b. that the developer and unit owners be allowed to mortgage their interests;

c. that the lessor be obligated to notify unit owners and their mortgagees of defaults under the lease and give them the right to cure;

d. that the lease term run for an appropriate period beyond the end of the mortgage term. If FHA insurance is being sought, the lease term must run for at least fifty years from the date the mortgage is executed. 24 CFR § 234.65. See generally, Kratovil & Werner, *Modern Mortgage Law and Practice* § 26.07 (2d ed. 1981).

REFERENCES ON CONDOMINIUM FINANCING: Fegan, *Condominium Financing,* 48 St. John's L. Rev. 799 (1974); Jackson, *Lenders: What Your Attorney Should Check in Condominium and PUD Documentation,* 1#6 Lending Law Forum 2 (May 1976); Sakai & Reskin, *Leasehold Condominiums,* 2 Conn. L. Rev. 37 (1969); Vishney, *Financing the Condominium,* 1970 Law Forum 181; Whitman, *Financing Condominiums and Cooperatives,* 13 Tulsa L. J. 15 (1977); Zinman, *Condominium Investments and the Institutional Lender—a Review,* 48 St. John's L. Rev. 749 (1974).

32.11 Phased construction

Construction lenders and common sense require that large projects be constructed in stages rather than all at once. The later stages are built in and when sales volume justifies their construction.

Phasing also eliminates some problems with the legal logistics of setting up the condominium. Geis, *Representing the Condominium Developer: Tending the Paper Jungle,* 10 R.P.P.&T.J. 471 (1975). Many construction loan documents have presale requirements to be met before partial releases will be available to allow unit sales to close. For example, the lender may require 40 percent of the units to be sold before partial releases for the units will be given. If the total project is 200 units, 80 will have to be sold before closings can occur to give the developer the needed funds to pay down the construction loan and keep total interest costs at a minimum. If the project is built in phases, only 20 units need be sold before sales can close.

While phasing eliminates some problems, it creates other documentation problems which can be solved. Kratovil, *Modern Real Estate Documentation,* § 809 *et. seq.* (1975). Each phase will have its own condominium association. There will also be an *umbrella association* to manage the recreational and other facilities that serve the entire project. It is also important that the documentation set forth the complete plan for the phasing in of new units and the exact reallocation of each unit's common element percentage as new units are added. Fegan, *Condominium Financing,* 48 St. John's L. Rev. 799, 810 (1974).

32.12 Leasehold condominiums

Under the original condominium laws of most states, a condominium could not have been created on a leasehold estate. Statutory revisions have accommodated this gap in many but not all states. See, e.g., Fla. Stat. Ann. § 718.401; Va. Code Ann. § 55-79.54(e). Sakai & Reskin, *Leasehold Condominiums*, 2 Conn. L. Rev. 37 (1969).

Buyers purchasing units built upon a leasehold estate should take extra precautions. Proper care should be taken to insure that individual unit owners can protect their interests by making their separate payments of the lease rentals. This may be accomplished by a lease clause allowing a forfeiture to be lodged only against those unit owners in arrears in lease payments. State law may offer some protection in this regard. Va. Code Ann. § 55-79.54. The duration of the underlying ground lease must also be checked.

32.13 Developer control

When the condominium is first created by the recording of the declaration or master deed, the developer owns all of the units and all of the common areas and is the board of directors. Even as units are sold, the developer continues to own the unsold units and have the power within the association that is attributable to ownership of the unsold units.

> **EXAMPLE:** The developer has sold 25 units of a 100-unit condominium project. The developer retains 75 percent of the vote, an enormous power.

Some developers have used this period to their benefit at the expense of unit buyers. Expenses may be loaded toward unit buyers without the developer contributing his fair share. As the holder of the power to contract for the condominium project, some developers would, on behalf of the condominium, make a "sweetheart" contract with a corporation controlled by the developer.

> **EXAMPLE:** The developer, as president of the condominium board, would make a long-term contract with: the developer's management company to manage the complex; the developer's janitorial company to clean and maintain the common areas; the developer's landscaping company to manicure the lawns in the summer and plow snow in the winter.

Perhaps the most notorious of these practices was the recreational lease.

> **EXAMPLE:** The condominium documents would be drafted to exclude the recreational area: i.e., clubhouse, swimming pool, pool deck, stairway to beach, etc. These areas would not be common elements, but would be owned by the developer who in turn would enter into a long-term lease with the condominium board, with the developer signing as president of the board.

These arrangements generated a lot of litigation as the unit buyers tried, often without success, to break these agreements. 73 ALR3d 613.

At times these cases have been decided on narrow technical grounds that reveal an absence of imagination on the part of the courts.

> **EXAMPLE:** Before any units were sold, Developer entered into a management agreement with a wholly owned subsidiary. The agreement was highly unfavorable to the unit owners. The court sustained the agreement on the ground that no unit owner was injured when the agreement was signed. The court completely disregarded the modern development of the law of fraud, which allows recovery where injury to subsequently interested parties can reasonably be anticipated. *Lyons* v. *Christ Episcopal Church,* 71 Ill. App.3d 257, 389 NE2d 23 (1979).

The better rule forbids self-dealing by the developer and invalidates such contracts. *Avila South Condo. Assn.* v. *Kappa Corp.,* 347 So2d 599 (Fla. 1977).

The unit owners have, with mixed results, even attempted to use the antitrust laws to avoid these arrangements. *Spitz* v. *Buckwald,* 551 F2d 1051 (5th Cir. 1977); *Miller* v. *Prandos,* 529 F2d 393 (5th Circ. 1976). See, generally, Lewis & Jessell, *The Condominium Recreational Lease Controversy,* 9 RELJ 7 (1980).

The unit owners have found the real answer in both the market and the legislature. In several areas, units with recreation leases simply will not sell. Many states have amended their condominium laws in two ways. A specific time has been established for the developer to turn control of the property over to the buyers. See Ill. Rev. Stats. Ch. 30, § 318.2; Va. Code Ann. § 55-79.74. Contracts and leases made by the developer are cancelable by the owners when they take control. See Ill. Rev. Stats. Ch. 30, § 318.2; Va. Code Ann. § 55-79.74; 15 USC § 3607.

The courts have also begun to treat the developer as having special fiduciary duties toward the unit buyers. *Gov. Grove Condo Assn.* v. *Hill Dev. Co.,* 414 A2d 1177 (Conn. 1980).

32.14 Liability of developer for defects

As is the case with respect to any newly constructed residence, the developer–builder implicitly warrants to the first purchaser of a condominium unit that the building and the unit are fit for occupancy and free from obvious defects. *Tassan* v. *United Development Co.,* 410 NE2d 902 (Ill. 1980); 50 ALR3d 1071.

32.14(a) Fraud and nondisclosure

The law of fraud, including nondisclosure, is much the same with respect to sales of condominium units as it is with respect to any land sale.

> **EXAMPLE:** Condominium Developer held liable for failure to disclose known structural defects. *Cooper* v. *Jeone,* 128 Cal. Reptr. 724 (1976); *Gov. Grove Condo. Assn.* v. *Hill Dev. Corp.,* 414 A2d 1177 (Conn. 1980).

32.15 Association—suits

It frequently develops that the condominium unit owners, individually or collectively, participate in a lawsuit. These suits often involve the buyer's complaint against the developer for faulty construction or to avoid a "sweetheart" contract made by the developer with the association while he was in control of the project. Suits may also be generated by the business transactions of the association, i.e., service contracts such as trash removal, extermination, and the like, or the real property rights relating to the project as a whole, i.e., the encroachment of a neighboring project onto the common elements.

These suits are easier if the association can be the plaintiff rather than all members of the association. Generally, this is not allowed, but there are some exceptions to this rule. 72 ALR3d 314. The association can bring suits if:

> 1. The association owns the property that is the subject of the suit. *Raven's Cove Townhomes, Inc.* v. *Knuppe Development Co., Inc.,* 171 Cal. Reptr. 334 (1981);
>
> 2. A statute confers *standing to sue* upon the association, Ill. Rev. Stat. Ch. 30, § 318.3, as construed in *Tassan* v. *United Development Co.,* 88 Ill. App.3d 581, 410 NE2d 902 (1980), regarding condominium unit owners' association. See also Cal. Code Civ. Pro. § 374;
>
> 3. The suit is to rescind, reform, or seek recovery arising out of unconscionable provisions in recreation leases made while the developer was in control of the association. 15 USC § 3608.

This is a developing area of the law and local law must be thoroughly reviewed before any action is taken. See § 30.10.

32.16 Liability for injuries—liability insurance

The condo owners are owners and occupants of the common elements. As such owners and occupants, they become liable for injuries sustained by third parties to the same extent as any other owner. This liability corresponds to the liability of a landlord for proper maintenance of facilities enjoyed in common by the tenants, such as common stairways. It is this rule that makes it important for the condo to have adequate and comprehensive liability insurance. Workmen's compensation, elevator liability insurance, and the like are also needed. Knight, *Incorporation of Condominium Common Areas? An Alternative,* 50 N.C.L. Rev. 1, 6 (1971). A closer question relates to the possible liability of the apartment association to a condo owner.

> **EXAMPLE:** *A,* a condo owner, sustains injuries because of a negligently maintained common stairway. He sues the apartment association. By the modern rule, he will be allowed to recover his damages. *White* v. *Cox,* 95 Cal. Reptr. 265 (1971); Note, 25 Vand. L. Rev. 271 (1972). The theoretical legal problems are: (1) As a condo owner, *A* is, in effect, suing himself. (2) There are technical problems in suing an unincorporated association. In some states one or the other of these obstacles may prevent lawsuits of this nature.

32.17 Condominium insurance

Insurance of the condominium is a problem that can be solved through coordination of efforts.

Each unit owner can obtain fire and other hazard insurances on his apartment and its share of the common elements. Note the problem in insuring a condo unit, which is a cube of air space. Should a loss occur, the damage to the common elements must be repaired as a single enterprise for the benefit of all owners. The *master policy* covers the common elements. The laws of some states require that the condominium board obtain insurance on both the common elements and the units. See Ill. Rev. Stat. Ch. 30, § 312. It is extremely important that a dovetailing of coverage exist between the unit and master policies so that as far as any unit owners are concerned, the entire structure and range of risks are covered. This proper match of policies avoids a conflict or gap in coverage for such items as partitions, floor coverings, wall coverings, furniture, and fixtures. This problem can be avoided if the new standard form policies are used, and the association and unit owners purchase a package of coverage from the same broker who then tailors the unit owners' policies to meet individual needs.

The standardized master policies (MLB-29 through MLB-29D) provide coverage for the common elements, which, when properly used together with the unit owners' policy (HO-6), constitute the basis for a well-rounded insurance program. The HO-6 covers the amount of the interior of the unit not covered by the master policy, and personal liability coverage. Rohan, Reskin, & Sanchisico, *Recent Development in the Field of Insurance of Condominiums Project,* 48 St. John's L. Rev. 1084 (1974). These master policies waive the subrogation rights of the insurer as against any unit owner.

> **EXAMPLE:** *A,* the owner of Unit 12, falls asleep while smoking. The resultant fire causes smoke and water damage to the hallways. The master policy insurer could pay the loss to the association and by virtue of subrogation rights proceed to recover for the loss as against *A.* The waiver of the subrogation right prevents this from happening. The loss is paid by the insurance company and the matter is over.

Many lawyers feel that losses to the common elements should be paid to the insurance trustee named in the condominium declaration. The trustee is then authorized by the declaration to *adjust* the loss, that is, to agree with the insurance company as to the amount of loss and be exclusively entitled to hire contractors to rebuild the common elements.

The HO-6 policy provides coverage for $1,000 of unscheduled personal property, and $1,000 of unit owner's additions and alterations (fixtures, installations, or additions comprising the part of the building within the unfinished interior surfaces of the perimeter walls, floors, and ceilings of the units). The coverages may be increased by a special endorsement which can be tailored to meet the individual needs of the unit owners.

Some points to remember: (1) The unit owner may want an endorsement (Loss Assessment Coverage) to protect him against personal liability if the building's liability insurance is inadequate.

> **EXAMPLE:**   A brain surgeon visiting the building trips on loose flooring in the lobby and is permanently injured. He recovers a judgment of $1,500,000 against the HOA. The HOA carries only $1,000,000 liability insurance. It must levy an assessment of $500,000. Remember that each of the unit owners owns a percentage of the defective floor and is personally liable for such injuries. The endorsement in question covers this assessment.

(2) The HOA's liability insurance provides no coverage for injuries sustained in the unit itself. (3) The HOA's insurance does not cover a cabana, storage shed, etc. owned solely by the unit owner. (4) The HOA's insurance is probably an all-risk policy. Among the common exclusions in such policies are earthquakes, floods, water damage that occurs over a period of weeks (as from small roof leaks), termite damage, wear and tear, explosion of boilers. (5) The unit owner needs Additional Living Expense Coverage for the cost of hotel and meals while his unit is untenantable owing to fire or other damage. (6) The unit owner needs his own coverage for theft or damage to his personal effects, furniture, furs, stereo, cameras, etc. This should be the replacement value type. The other type covers value less depreciation. (7) The HOA should buy plate glass coverage if there are many large windows. (8) The HOA needs fidelity coverage on its treasurer and manager, all persons who handle money. (9) The HOA needs Workmen's Compensation and Employer's Liability coverage on its guards, maintenance men, manager, etc. (10) The unit owner's policy should be in the same company used by the HOA. There have been cases where two companies were involved and each pointed the finger at the other. (11) The unit owner may want a Medical Payments endorsement to cover injuries in his unit for which he is technically not liable, as where a baby sitter suffers burn injuries while fixing a snack. (12) Since many condos provide parking in garages controlled by the HOA, special Garagekeeper's Legal Liability coverage is needed, to protect the HOA on loss of cars by theft, fire, etc. (13) If the HOA operates a snack bar or vending machine it needs Products Liability Coverage to cover claims for illness due to contaminated food, etc. (14) If the HOA provides a car, uses a pickup truck, etc., the usual motor vehicle insurance is needed. (15) Officers and directors want Officers and Directors Liability Insurance, protecting them against various liabilities, e.g., failure to take out insurance and a loss occurs, or a unit owner sues for libel, slander, invasion of privacy, or what have you because his name has been posted in the lobby as delinquent in his assessments. Some directors feel that liability coverage is not needed where the HOA indemnifies them against liability, as is customary. This is a mistake. The insurance money will be needed by the HOA to pay the claim if the directors are found to be liable. (16) As in other insurance, the HOA can save money by purchasing an

insurance policy with a deductible. Liability coverage may carry a deductible as high as $2,500. The wisdom of such a purchase is debatable. One important benefit of liability coverage is the fact that the company is obligated to defend lawsuits at its expense. The expense and nuisance of defending a lawsuit for an amount less than the deductible is considerable. As to deductibles in the hazard insurance part of the policy, a different problem surfaces. If the damage is only to the unit, the deductible is borne by the unit owner. If the damage is to the building, the loss is borne by the HOA.

Of course, some cases present difficult problems.

EXAMPLE: A roof is damaged by storm and rain damage to several units results. Here the deductible must be spread among the HOA and unit owners involved.

It is important to remember that basically no lawyer can hide behind the insurance agent. He can listen to the agent's recommendations, but if there is a gap in coverage, the lawyer is liable.

32.18   Title insurance requirements

A prudent purchaser of a condo apartment will demand a title insurance policy. Preferably, it will contain specific coverage against mechanic's liens. It should also contain assurance that there are no delinquent condominium assessments, for such condominium assessments are, by law, a foreclosable lien on the apartment. In this connection, the management group furnishes the title company a certificate that all assessments have been paid, and the title company takes the risk of any inaccuracy in this certificate. The title company, in addition to making its usual search of the public records, also searches for assessment liens filed by the management group, for in some states these must be recorded. The title company also satisfies itself that the right of first refusal has been properly eliminated, and its policy insures the purchaser on this score. To supplement this coverage, the purchaser should demand a letter from the secretary of the condominium's board of directors that no unusual special assessments are in contemplation, for an apartment may go on the market because its owner wishes to avoid payment of a large assessment, for example, for automatic elevators.

In some areas it is commonly required by purchasers and mortgagees of condo units that the title company insure that the condominium complies with the local statute. By special request, this assurance is procurable everywhere.

32.19   Condominiums— regulation

There are various ways that condominiums are regulated. Building codes, zoning laws, and private building restrictions apply. Some laws are addressed solely to condominiums regulating their creation and sale. In some states, this is the same format used to regulate any other subdivision, requiring approval of public authorities. For example, in California, a "final public report" issued by the real estate commissioner must be given to a purchaser of a condominium or other subdivided land before a purchase contract is made. Cal. Bus. & Prof. Code § 11018.1. This report reveals all sorts of information about the project, including condition of title, soils condition, flood problem, nearby schools, and the like. Through these laws the state or local governments exercise their police powers to protect the health, safety, and well-being of local residents under the theory that disclosure of vital information to prospective purchasers allows them to make an informed decision. 123 U. Pa. L. Rev. 639 (1975).

32.20 Zoning

Some municipalities have tried to "zone out" condominiums. In this way a municipality might attempt to enforce a zoning ordinance to block a conversion of an apartment structure to condominiums. Any zoning ordinance that seeks to exclude condominiums while permitting similar tenant-occupied buildings is invalid. Zoning must deal with land use, not land ownership. *Claridge House One Inc.* v. *Borough of Verona*, 490 F.Supp. 706 (D.C. N.J. 1980); Cal. Civ. Code § 1390; Code Va. § 55-79.43; 71 ALR3d 866.

32.21 Conversion

The past several years have seen the conversion of hundreds of thousands of rental units into condominiums and cooperatives. Several factors have caused this wave of conversion activity. Increasing costs have tended to make apartment building construction and ownership an uneconomic business. It becomes especially unattractive when the value of a structure as an apartment building is compared to the total value of the apartment units in the structure. Indeed, the profits of successful conversion have caused developers to convert structure after structure in prime areas, i.e., Chicago's Lake Shore Drive area and the Gold Coast of Florida.

From the tenant–potential unit owner's point of view, the economic advantages and disadvantages are complex and difficult to analyze. It is almost universally true that the gross costs of unit ownership are more than the costs to a tenant of the same unit. These costs may be offset by the equity buildup caused by principal payments against the mortgage debt and appreciation in the value of the unit—a very substantial factor, in many cases. It is also probable that the cost to the purchaser of a unit in a converted building will be less than the cost to purchase a comparable unit if it had to be built today. The income tax advantages to the unit buyer must also be factored into the equation.

One other point of view must be considered. The municipality where the condominium is has a stake. Economically, real estate taxes will probably increase upon conversion. Politically, the city must determine whether the interests of renters and low-income tenants should be fostered or should ownership of a stake in the community be fostered. The debate rages on.

32.21(a) Conversion legislation

The wave of conversion activity has brought about a hue and cry of opposition. Tenants, especially senior citizens and handicapped persons, have excited the sympathies of the legislatures to enact statutes and local ordinances that in one way or another protect the preconversion occupants of the structure. Unit purchasers have also benefited from the flow of recent legislation.

Although the federal government has not specifically legislated in this area, Congress has suggested that states and local governments require that tenants be given adequate notice of the conversion and the first opportunity to purchase converted units. 15 USC § 3605.

In considering the resultant regulation, it must be remembered that the legislative bodies were reacting to and trying to serve several goals, including the preservation of the community's housing goals, i.e., fostering ownership or tenant rights; the protection of tenants from displacement without the adequate opportunity to find replacement housing; and the protection of unit purchasers.

While the outright prohibition of conversion is invalid, *Zussman* v. *Rent Control Board,* 326 NE2d 876 (Mass. 1975), regulation of the conversion process is allowed. *Grace* v. *Town of Brookline,* 399 NE2d 1038 (Mass. 1979). While the form of regulation varies from community to community and reference is directed to local laws and ordinances, the regulations often include: moratoria barring conversion for a period; tying government approval of the conversion to apartment vacancy rates; requiring the rent control board's approval of the conversion; requiring a notice to the tenants prior to the conversion of their units; requiring that tenants receive preemptive options to purchase their units, any unit in the building, or even the entire structure; requiring approval of the conversion by a percentage of the tenants; giving senior citizens and handicapped tenants the right to remain as tenants for extended periods of time after the conversion; requiring the converter to replace the rental units taken from the community by the conversion; giving displaced tenants relocation assistance; and disclosing the physical condition of major structural components of the structure and proposed budgets, past operating statements, and amounts recently spent for repairs to prospective purchasers. Ill. Rev. Stat. Ch. 30 § 330; Ann. Code Md. R.P. § 11-102; Va. Code § 55-79.94; Los Angeles, Cal., Mun. Code § 12.52; Oakland, Cal., Mun. Code § 7-7.01; Phila., Pa., Code § 9-1206; Santa Monica, Cal., Charter § 1803; Wash., D.C., Code § 5-1201; 1980 Duke L. J. 306; 8 Fordham Urb. L. J. 507 (1980); 78 Mich. L. Rev. 124 (1979).

32.21(b) Areas of concern for unit purchasers

The unit purchaser of a converted unit has some concerns in addition to those of the purchaser of a new unit.

The physical condition of the units and the structure as a whole is of grave concern. The report of a reputable engineer is essential as are pest control reports. Warranties will not generally be available for the structure and its components except for work recently done in connection with the conversion. Unless the appliances were replaced in the upgrading of the building for the conversion, they will not have warranties.

32.21(c)   Income tax considerations

If the owner of an apartment building is thinking in terms of a possible conversion, he must also consider the income tax consequences. The key questions are (1) is the property held by the taxpayer primarily for sale to customers, and (2) is the sale in the ordinary course of the trade or business of the taxpayer? If the answer is yes to either question, then capital gains treatment is not available.

The safest course is for the owner to sell to a stranger. He may bargain with the stranger on the theory that the building has added value because it is available for conversion. But the seller must not participate in the conversion activity or involve himself in any sales activities. All this must be left to the purchaser. The sale should be a cash sale. When the deal is closed, the seller must walk away with no interest in the project.

Any other type of deal, such as a sale to a controlled corporation, must be carefully analyzed by skilled tax counsel.

32.21(d)   Preconversion considerations

In addition to the ever present market analysis, the converter must analyze several other factors in deciding to purchase a project for conversion.

The impact of conversion and tenant's rights laws and ordinances must not be taken lightly. The tenants have awesome power under these laws. The marketing effort can be stopped dead by the legal and political acts of opponents to the conversion. If sales stop while expenses continue, the result is disaster for the converter.

Can the underlying mortgage against the property be paid and how can those payments be made?

> **EXAMPLE:**   *O*, an owner of an apartment building, wants to convert it to condominiums. The building is encumbered with an existing mortgage that permits no prepayment. Conversion is effectively blocked until the lender can be persuaded to accept a prepayment, for which he may well extract a substantial prepayment charge.

The existing mortgage may not be prepayable until a later date or the prepayment penalty may be reduced as the loan ages. Nonetheless, the converter wants to sell the units at an earlier date. Title insurance companies solve this problem by issuing policies that "insure over" the existing mortgage. To do this, the companies require a deposit of cash or triple-A securities that can be used to retire the old mortgage at its earliest due date. Of course, this underlying loan must not have a due-on-sale clause.

Any new financing must provide for partial payment. Often, lenders require that a minimum of 25 to 30 percent of the units be sold before the first of the partial releases are available.

EXAMPLE: In a 100-unit conversion, the lender may require that 30 units be sold and closed with a stated portion of the closing proceeds applied to the loan before the partial release clause becomes effective.

This necessitates a volume closing at a title company when the documents and funds for the 30 units are deposited, and, when all 30 units are ready to close, the appropriate partial releases of the underlying loan are recorded and the loan payment made by the escrowee. Thereafter, partial releases are available as individual units close.

The assumption of existing encumbrances may greatly assist the converter's payment of the building's purchase price, but additional financing is needed to pay the balance of the acquisition costs and the costs of conversion, i.e., attorneys' fees, title costs, engineering work, refurbishment, and marketing expenses.

During the time between the signing of the contract and the closing, the converter wants to be able to begin the preliminary work in anticipation of the conversion. For the developer, this is an important period of time; his interest meter is not yet running. The more preliminary items that can be cleared during this preclosing time, the less the cost of the conversion. To this end, the building's purchase contract should give the converter: (1) access to the property for the converter's own staff, his engineer and surveyor; (2) the ability to communicate with the tenants; (3) access to tenants' lease files; (4) control over leasing activity; and (5) access to operating information, i.e., service contracts, utility charges.

The physical condition of the property and its components, i.e., elevators, climate control system, roof, etc., must be carefully analyzed.

The tenant roster and rent roll should be examined. Here the goal is to determine the rights of the existing tenants. Any purchaser of the property will take subject to these rights. Second, an analysis of the tenant roster and rent levels may give some insight into the willingness of existing tenants to purchase units.

Operating statements for recent years will aid in determining the level of assessments to unit buyers, give evidence of repairs and maintenance, and perhaps reveal any special problems that the building may have, i.e., an unusual insect problem.

The condominium documents should comply with the requirements of GNMA, FNMA, FHLMC, etc. If not, the units will not be acceptable to permanent lenders because they will not be marketable in the secondary mortgage market. See Kratovil & Werner, *Modern Mortgage Law and Practice* § 26.09 (2d ed. 1981).

An interim loan will be necessary to finance conversion costs. The interim lender will require an end loan commitment to finance outsales. Outsales also necessitate a partial release clause in the interim loan.

The converter should require that the loan documents allow the rental of unsold units during the conversion process to generate funds to help the converter meet expenses.

32.22 Securities law problems

Many condominium developments are leisure-oriented projects in vacation areas. The unit purchaser intends to live in the unit for part of the year and hold the unit available for rent for the rest of the year. A managing agent is hired to rent out the various units. Taxpayers in high-income brackets are attracted by the tax deductions for taxes, mortgage interest, maintenance charges, insurance, and depreciation. This form of operation, however, raises the specter that the development may be subject to both federal and state securities laws.

The Securities Exchange Commission has taken the position that the offering of a condominium must be in compliance with the registration and prospectus delivery requirements of the securities laws if any one of the following are found:

1. The condominiums, with any rental arrangements or other similar service, are offered and sold with emphasis on the economic benefits to the purchaser to be derived from the managerial efforts of the promoter, or of a third party designated or arranged for by the promoter.

2. Participation in a rental pool arrangement is offered. In a rental pool, all rents are collected by the manager and divided equally among unit owners.

3. The offering of a rental or similar arrangement whereby the purchaser must hold his unit available for rental for any part of the year, must use an exclusive rental agent, or is otherwise materially restricted in his occupancy or rental of his unit. Securities Act Release No. 5347, CCH Fed. Sec. L. Rept., par. 79, 163 (1973).

Registration requirements may also be mandated by state securities or *Blue-Sky* laws.

EXAMPLE: An agreement for the sale of one of six units in a condominium project requires that the buyer enter into an exclusive management and rental agreement. Personal use of the unit was limited, in that the time for use had to be reserved far in advance; the owner had to maintain his unit in a rentable condition and had to pay a flat monthly fee for promotional activities to stimulate rentals. Promotional materials emphasized the investment rather than the residential aspects of ownership. The court found that state securities laws had been violated. *Lowery* v. *Ford Hill Investment Co.,* 556 P2d 1201 (Colo. 1976).

Not all rental arrangements fall under the securities laws such as when the units are not sold with an emphasis on the economic benefits befalling the purchaser from the managerial efforts of others. A unit buyer may enter into a *nonpool* rental arrangement with an agent who is not designated or required to be used as a condition of purchase whether or not the rental agent is affiliated with the developer.

EXAMPLE: *D,* a developer, offers condominium units in an ocean-front high-rise building. The sales emphasis is on the resort aspects of the development, and not on appreciation and return on investment caused by the developer's affiliate real estate management company's activity. In fact, no rental pool agreement is part of the package. *D* does, however, have a local real estate corporation which will, if asked, attempt to rent individual units for periods specified by the owners. No rental pool arrangement is available. No securities law registration is required. See generally, *Joyce* v. *Richie Tower Properties,* 417 F. Supp. 53 (1976).

REFERENCES: Burnman and Stone, *Federal Securities Law and the Sale of Condominiums, Homes and Homesites,* 30 Business Lawyer 411 (1975); Rohan and Reskin, *Condominium Law and Practice,* Ch. 18.

32.23 Timesharing condominiums

In the mid-1970s, a new form of condominium ownership, the timesharing condominium, was developed. Found in vacation areas where ownership of the unit for the entire year is unnecessary, expensive, and burdensome for many people, the timesharing concept allows the buyer to purchase a time slot of ownership. The original timeshare developments were in waterfront and recreational vacation areas. Today, we see the concept spreading into urban vacation areas such as New York, San Francisco, and New Orleans.

For the developer, the profit potential is large.

> **EXAMPLE:** A unit in a resort condominium may sell for $100,000. A two-week period of ownership of that same unit may sell for $10,000. Obviously, if all two-week periods can be sold for $10,000, the developer will sell the unit for $260,000. That is not always the case. Recreational and vacation areas are usually seasonal. Only the prime weeks can be sold for the top dollar. The remainder of the year usually sells for rather steep discounts. Marketing costs of timeshare condominiums are usually greater than for nontimesharing units. So are the risks.

For the unit buyer, the property, which would normally be used only occasionally, can be purchased at a much lower price; the lodging costs of vacations are somewhat stabilized; income tax deductions for real estate taxes and interest payments are available; and ownership burdens are generally reduced while the possibility of gain from appreciation continues. If the owner cannot use the occupancy period, it may be rented, often through the building manager, or, if the owner grows tired of vacationing in the same place every year, the use period can be swapped through nationwide exchange programs for periods in other timeshare condominiums all over the world.

Through the timesharing device, the buyer uses the unit for an agreed segment of the year with other buyers having the use of the unit for other segments. There are three basic formats used to allocate these ownership rights. First, in the *time-span* or *tenancy in common* format, the buyers are deeded an undivided interest in a particular unit as tenants in common with other buyers of the unit. At the same time, the buyers agree to limit their use of the unit to a designated time period.

Second, in the *interval ownership* format, purchasers are granted an estate for years for the agreed time period each year. This revolving estate for years lasts for the expected useful life of the project. At that point, all owners become tenants in common of the whole property.

Third, under a *vacation license,* the developer retains ownership and agrees to allow the buyers to use the premises for a stated period for a given number of years.

Some states have enacted legislation to specifically authorize and regulate timesharing condominiums. See, e.g., Fla. Stat. Ann. § 718.103 *et seq.,* 6 ALR4th 1289. Also, a Uniform Real Estate Time-share Act has been promulgated by the National Conference of Commissioners on Uniform State Laws. Burek, *Uniform Real Estate Time-Share Act,* 14 R.P.P.& T.J. 683 (1979).

Legislation of this type is necessary to resolve some of the legal problems that are unresolved in this relatively new form of ownership.

The management of a property of this kind is very important. The unit owners are truly absentee owners. They come to the property for two weeks every year only to return a year later. If a top-flight management company is not in control of the project, it may deteriorate rapidly, taking away many of the joys that the owner anticipated during his use period.

32.23(a) Timesharing condominiums—declaration

The declaration for the timesharing condominiums must address itself to the following special matters:

1. use and service periods with relevant undivided interests in the common elements;
2. exclusive right to use, and occupancy of each of the timesharing owners for their relevant periods;
3. collection and payment of costs such as telephone charges, firewood, repairs attributable to any owner's use, and common costs
4. waiver of right to partition.

This waiver goes beyond the waiver contained in the declaration of a non-timeshare condominium by waiving the right to partition between the various time segment owners of a particular unit.

REFERENCES ON TIMESHARING CONDOMINIUMS: Burek, *Timesharing: Pie in the Sky,* Chicago Title Ins. Co. Lawyer's Supplement to the Guarantor (July–Aug. 1979); Malleris, *Five Legal Hurdles in Time-Share Ownership,* 8 #2 Real Est. Rev. 97 (Summer 1978); Merritt & Cowan, *Time-Sharing Ownership of Vacation Residences,* 1 #4 ALI–ABA Course Mat. J. 89 (1977); *Resort Timesharing: A Consumers' Guide* (1981) by the American Land Development Association.

32.24 Commercial condominiums

The commercial condominium has existed for some time now, but has met with much more limited market acceptance than the residential condominium. It has its own unique set of advantages and disadvantages.

The advantages of owning a commercial condominium are: (1) rent increases are avoided, but increases generally occur in the assessments as costs generally increase; (2) an owner cannot be evicted to make room for more important tenants; and (3) well located and constructed units tend to increase in value. Commercial condominiums also have disadvantages which include: (1) the owner is locked into a particular location; (2) additional space is more difficult to obtain, if needed; (3) rent is totally tax deductible while commercial condominium owners are limited to tax deductions for mortgage interest, taxes, depreciation, and maintenance expenses; and (4) funds otherwise available for inventory and business expansion are tied up by the commercial condominium purchase.

32.25   Income taxes

The income tax treatment of a condominium is the same as the income tax treatment of a house. The two are treated the same both for ownership deductions purposes and gain on sale purposes. The special vacation home deduction rules apply equally to both.

32.26   Suggestions for the purchaser of a new condominium

1. Do the condominium documents conform to state law? If not, dangerous consequences may result. For example, the tax assessor may refuse to separately assess the unit. This problem can be solved by obtaining an endorsement to the unit buyer's title insurance policy insuring that a condominium has been created in accordance with state law.

2. Determine whether the purchase contract gives the developer the right to cancel if a stated percentage of the units are not sold. Check to see how many units are sold to determine whether such clause is likely to be invoked. The buyer may change position by selling existing property, subletting an apartment, etc. or incur expense by paying loan application fees only to be frustrated if the developer invokes this clause.

3. Check whether the burden of assessments for maintenance, and so forth, falls entirely on the apartments sold or is shared by the developer in proportion to the apartments remaining unsold and still owned by the development. In general, of course, the entire subject of assessments and the factors that make up the assessment level—maintenance costs, payroll expenses, cost of keeping up the recreational facilities, reserves, and so forth should be studied.

Obtain a copy of the proposed budget. Is it realistic? How many months of advance assessments must be paid by the buyer at the closing? In trying to "sweeten" a deal for a prospective buyer, a developer may price the unit to include a prepayment of assessments for a period, say six months. Unless the developer controls the association, and, on behalf of the association, credits the buyer's account, the developer's acts will not bind the association. When the developer passes control over the board to the unit owners, they may not share in the developer's attitude of largess and take action against the buyer for delinquent assessment payments.

4. Check whether the voting rights of the sold apartments give the apartment purchasers at least a minority representation in the homeowner's association. For example, if a

majority vote of the apartments in the building can elect a home association board of directors, the developer will have absolute control until a majority of the apartments are sold.

5. Check whether the documents require all purchasers to get their financing from a specified mortgage lender and, if so, what the lender's terms are likely to be.

6. Consider whether the prospective occupancy is such that the membership is likely to vote future assessments for maintenance and renovation in excess of your financial abilities as a purchaser.

7. The early contracts of sale for a condominium apartment will permit the developer to amend or modify the declaration but should not permit him to increase the buyer's assessments, or to increase the apartment cost, or to reduce the seller's obligation to pay the expenses on unsold apartments.

8. The contract of sale may state that the purchaser's rights are subordinate to the construction mortgage. This is necessary for the mortgagee's protection. *State Savings and Loan Association* v. *Kauaian Develop. Co.,* 445 P2d 108 (1968).

9. Determine what is done with your deposit or earnest money. The most conservative approach is to require that it be held in escrow. Many buyers who did not protect themselves had their deposits lost when the developer got into financial difficulty. Recent legislation in some states requires the deposit of these funds into a separate escrow account. See Fla. State. Ann. § 718.202; Va. Code Ann. § 55-79.95.

10. What is the reputation of the management firm? Determine the duration of the management contract, keeping in mind that long-term contracts may lock you into inefficient management. How much authority is delegated to the manager by the association? Too much delegation strips the unit owner of a voice in the running of the project. Who does the hiring and firing of employees? If the board interferes, favoritism can creep in and efficient management becomes difficult. Pay scales of employees should track with pay scales generally.

11. Has the board met regularly and have there been genuinely democratic elections so that no clique runs the operation? In this connection, check the bylaws for duration of the term of board members. Check the present composition of the board. Lawyers and accountants, for example, are likely to do a better job in running the building than nonprofessionals.

12. Look into the physical attributes of the unit. When the purchase is made in reliance upon a model apartment, drawing, or promotional material, there is an obvious need to compare the delivered product with the model. Do carpeting, draperies, furniture, and other furnishings in the model go with the unit? Where the unit is not completed, room dimensions, carpet grade, landscaping, finish hardware, appliance quality, etc. must be established. Before the contract is signed, the particulars of the finished product must be agreed upon and reduced to writing. What of the physical nature of the building and the unit? Is it well constructed, soundproof, etc.? Does the structure conform to local zoning ordinances and private restrictions? Is the unit located near the noisy parts of the building, lobby, elevators, trash chute, and so forth? What parking and storage space is allocated to the particular unit? Determine whether the common elements include the recreation areas (swimming pool, tennis courts, and so forth) or whether they are excluded from the condominium, retained by the developer, and then leased to the association on a long-term basis.

13. What is the developer's reputation? Go to other projects the developer has completed. Talk to the residents.

14. What type of insurance does the association buy for the building? What type of insurance does the unit owner have to buy?

15. Are children and pets allowed?

16. What are the rules about window coverings, balcony furnishings, physical changes of the units?

17. If the property is being bought as an investment, other factors must be considered. Are there restrictions on leases? Must a uniform lease form be used? Do you have the ability to check the credit of potential renters? Are you going to turn the property over to a management agent? Will rentals cover ownership costs, i.e., mortgage payments, taxes, insurance, assessments?

18. The tax assessment problem is complex.

EXAMPLE: A rental apartment having 100 apartments, if sold as a rental apartment, has a market value of $10,000,000. If sold to a converter, it might sell for $12,000,000. Converters often pay a premium price. The converter, in turn, sells the 100 units for $180,000 each. As is evident, this gives the building a value of 100 times $180,000 or $18,000,000. Obviously, each unit owner is entitled to his own individual tax bill. But the aggregate of the tax bills will be higher than the old tax bill on the building when it was a rental. Meanwhile, the developer makes an estimate of what the tax bill will be. Often this is a "low ball," deliberately understated. Any contract of sale made before the actual tax is fixed should provide for an escrow of a sum of money to cover a reprorating of taxes when the actual tax bill is issued. The buyer should be warned that as other conversions in the area push values up, the tax bill is likely to increase.

19. Review the basic condominium documentation, i.e., declaration, bylaws, and lease rules. Will you enjoy living under those rules? Will you enjoy group living generally?

32.27 Resales of condominium units

While many states require the developer to disclose certain information to prospective buyers, some states now require disclosures on resales of a unit by an ordinary unit owner. See Ill. Rev. Stat. Ch. 30, § 322.1; Va. Code Ann. § 55-79.97. The required disclosures include the basic condominium documents, a statement of anticipated capital expenditures, a statement of the status of the reserve fund, a statement of the fiscal condition of the association, a statement of the status of pending suits involving the association, a statement of insurance coverage, and a statement of the amount of unpaid assessments against the unit.

32.28 Condominium and cooperative ownership compared

The co-op type of apartment ownership is common in New York City. See § 32.28(a). There are significant legal and practical differences between the two types of apartment ownership.

1. The condominium owner holds title to the unit. In the cooperative, the owner buys shares in the cooperative apartment corporation that owns the building and enters into an occupancy agreement or proprietary lease for a particular apartment.

2. The mortgage on a condominium unit covers only the unit and its share of the common elements. In a co-op, the mortgage covers the entire property. If any substantial

number of tenants default, the foreclosure would wipe out all tenants. To avoid this result, the nondefaulting unit owners would have to carry the defaulting owners.

The advantage the condo enjoys with respect to mortgage financing should make the condo easier to sell or resell than a co-op, since it enlarges the number of potential buyers.

> **EXAMPLE:** *A* owns a condo apartment which he can sell to *B* for $30,000. *B* can obtain a mortgage loan of approximately $24,000, so that he needs only $6,000. *A's* existing mortgage, whatever its amount, would be paid off in the process, just as if *A* were selling a house. If *A* were selling a co-op in a comparable building on which the building mortgage had been paid down to 50 percent of the property value, *A* would be selling his apartment equity for $15,000 subject to the building mortgage, and he would have to find a buyer who has $15,000 in cash, for lenders do not lend on co-ops.

Some states now allow institutional lenders to make loans on the security of individual cooperative apartments, Ill. Rev. Stat. Ch. 32, § 780, and FHA insurance is available on these loans. 24 CFR § 203.437.

If a person desires a debt-free shelter, as many senior citizens do, a condo purchaser can pay cash for his apartment, as many purchasers do. A co-op purchaser has no choice but to accept his apartment subject to the mortgage on the building.

The condo, since it is owned by many people, not by a single corporation as in the case of the co-op, has no feasible way of putting a mortgage on the building in its later years when remodeling or repairs are needed.

> 3. Co-op leases provide that the lease may be terminated for failure to meet a monthly assessment or because the apartment owner has become bankrupt or been guilty of objectionable conduct. *Green* v. *Greenbelt Homes Inc.,* 232Md.496, 194 A2d 273. The condo owner is more secure in this regard.
>
> In a co-op, the apartment owner has the right to leave. If he has bad luck and cannot keep up his monthly payments, he can sublease his apartment, sell it, or at the worst, give it back to the landlord corporation. The modern co-op lease gives the lessee the right to cancel the lease after a specified number of years by surrendering his stock and his lease to the landlord corporation. In the condominium the owner, having signed a note and mortgage, has no right simply to "walk away." In case of default and foreclosure, there is always the possibility of a deficiency judgment.
>
> Another advantage that the co-op possesses is the ease with which one can control the type of neighbors one will have in the building. In the co-op, the lease provides that it cannot be assigned or subleased except with the written consent of the landlord corporation. The stock certificate provides that it can be transferred only in connection with an authorized transfer of the lease. This method has the advantage of simplicity and unquestioned legality. *68 Beacon St.* v. *Sohier,* 194 NE 303 (Mass. 1935); *Weisner* v. *791 Park Ave. Corp.,* 160 NE2d 720 (N.Y. 1959). Probably these restrictions must be exercised "reasonably." *Logan* v. *3750 North Lake Shore Dr.* 17Ill. App.3d 584, 308 NE 2d 278 (1974). For example, a refusal of consent based solely on racial grounds would not stand up in court. In the condominium method, the situation is more complicated. Typi-

cally, each owner of a condominium apartment holds his apartment subject to a right of first refusal should he desire to sell. Such a right of first refusal is probably valid. *Gale* v. *York Center Community Co-operative, Inc.,* 171 NE2d 30 (Ill. 1961). However, the method is clumsy. Also, since it calls for the apartment owners to buy the apartment at the price the selling apartment owner can obtain from an outsider, it requires a special assessment on the apartment owners.

Getting rid of a co-op owner who defaults in his monthly payments or fails to abide by the bylaws is easier in the co-op than in the condo. Just as an ordinary lease can be terminated for default in rent or breach of covenant, so also a co-op lease can be terminated for like grounds and the co-op lessee evicted by quick and inexpensive forcible detainer proceedings. *Green* v. *Greenbelt Homes, Inc.,* 194 A2d 273 (Md. 1963). In a condo, if a particular apartment owner fails to pay his monthly assessments, a lien on his apartment can be foreclosed, just as a mortgage is foreclosed, but the proceeding is costly and time-consuming. Making the condo owner behave, when his conduct becomes objectionable, is difficult.

4. In the condominium, the tax assessment is an individual assessment on the unit and its share of the common elements. As long as the tax on a particular unit is paid, failure of other unit owners to pay their taxes does not affect the nondelinquent unit. In the co-op, there is one tax bill on the entire building. If some owners do not pay their share, the others must carry the entire load or face tax foreclosure proceedings.

5. In a co-op, work and materials ordered by one tenant can result in a mechanic's lien against the entire building. In a condo, the lien is confined to the apartment where the work was done.

6. Where for one reason or another it becomes advisable to sell the building and the tenants wish to do so, this can be accomplished in co-ops by a vote of a percentage of the shareholders (who, of course, are the tenants). A two-thirds vote usually suffices. In the case of a condo, sale of the building is apt to require a unanimous vote, except in certain special situations, as where the building is destroyed by fire.

7. Both the condo owner and the co-op owner have the right to defer payment of income tax on a capital gain where the apartment is sold at a profit. Both have the same right to deduct from income for income tax purposes all payments made on mortgage interest and real estate taxes.

32.28(a) Mechanics and legal aspects of traditional co-op ownership

Cooperative apartments can be organized on either a trust or corporate basis, but the latter is by far the more popular. Under the corporate arrangement, a corporation is formed, and ownership of the land and building is acquired by the corporation. The corporation places a mortgage on the land for the purpose of buying, or, if the land is vacant, for the purpose of building. Since no mortgagee will lend up to the full value of the building, the balance of the necessary funds is raised by sales of stock to the prospective tenants. When he has purchased a specified number of shares, proportional to the value of the apartments, the prospective tenant receives a long-term lease of the apartment called a *proprietary lease,* from the corporation. The word *proprietary* means that it has the *attributes of ownership,* that it gives rights equivalent in *economic benefit* to outright ownership. Legally, however, a proprietary lease is a lease, and landlord and tenant law is applicable to it. This lease gives the tenant the right to possession of his apartment for the term specified in the lease, but requires the tenant to pay rent to the corporation, which rent payments consist of his pro rata share of the amounts needed to cover mortgage debt, taxes, and operating expenses. The annual cash requirements for the building are established by the board of directors of the corporation, and this sum is divided among the tenants in proportion to the number of shares allocated to each apartment, the bigger apartments having the larger shareholdings and assessments.

Restrictions are placed on the right of the lessee to assign or sublet. The common provision restricts the transfer of the stock and lease without the consent of the board of directors, thereby insuring some control over occupancy of the apartments. Of course, the consent cannot be arbitrarily withheld. *Sanders* v. *Tropicana,* 229 SE2d 304 (N.C. 1976). The lease provides that it is subject to any future mortgage placed on the building by the landlord corporation. A mortgage usually requires a two-thirds vote of the tenants. This clause facilitates refinancing of the existing mortgage.

It is significant that both a tenant's interest under a lease (his *leasehold*) and shares of stock are legally considered to be personal property. Thus, a sale of a co-op apartment is a sale of personalty.

> **EXAMPLE:** *R* entered into a contract to sell his co-op apartment to *E*. *E* made an earnest money deposit as is common in sales of land. *E* failed to go through with the deal. *R* declared the earnest money forfeited. *E* sued *R,* and the court held that since a sale of personalty was involved, damages must be determined under the Uniform Commercial Code, which confine the seller's damages to loss on resale to another party and incidental expenses. *Silverman* v. *Alcoa Plaza Associates,* 323 N.Y.S.2d 39 (1971); 21 Buff. L. Rev. 555 (1972); 29 Wash. & Lee L. Rev. 189 (1972).

There are, of course, many other legal consequences of this rule. For example, on the death of an apartment owner, his leasehold and shares pass to his administrator or executor, rather than to his heirs. As a result, a simple, informal sale by the executor or administrator is possible without the difficulties attendant upon sale of land owned by a deceased person. See *State Tax Comm* v. *Shor,* 371 NE2d 253 (N.Y. 1977).

32.28(b) Co-op on leasehold

Where a co-op is to be erected on a leasehold created by a ground lease, it will be necessary to include rather complex provisions in the ground lease for the protection of the leasehold mortgagee. For the protection of the tenants, a complex clause will be needed requiring the lessor (or any subsequent ground owner) to join in any necessary refinancing mortgage. This is needed because as the leasehold mortgage is reduced by payments, the apartment equity grows correspondingly in value. At some point, the apartment value will be such that a buyer who can pay cash for it may be hard to find. At that point it may be desirable to refinance with a larger mortgage, thus reducing the value of the apartment equities.

32.28(c) Co-ops— securities problem

In the cooperative apartment complex that is purchased for residential purposes, there appears to be no problem with entanglements caused by the Federal Securities law.

> **EXAMPLE:** In a large New York cooperative, prospective purchasers made a recoverable deposit on their apartments by buying shares of stock in the nonprofit housing corporation which held title to the property. The shares of stock were allocated to purchasers on the basis of the number of rooms in their apartment. When the tenant wanted to move out, he had to offer his stock back to the corporation at the initial selling price. The court found that the mere description of the certificates as "stock" did not render it a security subject to the Federal Securities Law. Noting that the purchasers intended merely to acquire a residential apartment for personal use rather than an investment for profit to be derived from the managerial efforts of others, the court found no security present. *United Housing Foundation, Inc.* v. *Forman,* 421 U.S. 837 (1975).

32.28(d) Cooperatives— conversion

In some areas, particularly New York, apartment buildings are being converted into cooperatives as well as condominiums. Because New York probably has more cooperative units than the remainder of the country, it has a very sophisticated cooperative conversion law. Because the cooperative development is both a mix of real estate and corporation concepts, the law has aspects of both bodies of law. *Richaras* v. *Kaskol,* 32 N.Y.S.2d 524, 300 NE2d 388 (1973).

> **EXAMPLE:** Purchasers must be given a cooperative prospectus or offering plan approved by the attorney general in much the same way that a stock offering is approved. N.Y. Gen. Bus. Law Act 23A.

32.28(e) Warranties of the building

The co-op unit owner sufficiently resembles an ordinary tenant so that he is entitled to the benefit of the warranties of the building that characterize an ordinary residential landlord and tenant relationship. *Suarez* v. *Rivercross Tenants, Corp.,* 438 N.Y.S.2d 164 (1981).

32.28(f) Sale of co-op apartment

The following suggestions may be appropriate for sellers and purchasers of existing co-op apartments:

> 1. You cannot afford to have the title to the entire building brought down to date. What you can do is have your lawyer check the existing title insurance policy, abstract, and opinion to see that the building corporation has good title to the property (subject only to the mortgage and the proprietary leases). This title evidence may be several years old.

Supplement this by getting an affidavit from the secretary of the corporation to the effect that the condition of title remains today as it was on the date of the title evidence which your lawyer examined and that no lawsuits are presently pending against the corporation. Some states, Illinois and New York, for example, have laws which allow the title companies to insure individual cooperative owners' interests.

2. Since you are buying the lease and stock of the present tenant, get the secretary of the building corporation to sign an affidavit stating: (a) that the stock is in fact owned by your seller and is fully paid for; (b) that the lease is owned by your seller, free of any subleases; (c) that the stock and lease are free from any assessments other than the current ones shown on the financial statement submitted to you by the corporation; (d) that the stock is free of restrictions on its transfer or those restrictions have been satisfied, 99 ALR2d 236; (e) that no defaults have occurred in the building's mortgage payments; (f) that none of the other tenants is currently behind in his payments; (g) that no proposal to remodel the building or increase assessments has come before the directors within the past year, for this may be why your seller is moving out; (h) how much space is rented to persons other than tenant–stockholders, for if this figure gets too high, you lose your income tax benefits; and (i) what insurance is carried presently. Get a certified copy of the co-op charter and bylaws and the directors' resolution authorizing your seller to sell you his lease and stock, for all co-ops restrict the right of the tenants to transfer their rights. Have your lawyer check the lease that you are about to buy and explain to you the restrictions (on remodeling of apartments, for example, or the right to sell, sublease, or operate a business in the apartment) and liabilities (special assessments, for example) that it creates. Have him explain what maintenance costs you must pay yourself, such as decorating.

3. It is quite important that an apartment seller who lists his apartment with a real estate broker for sale insert the *no deal, no commission clause* in the listing. This is important because if the co-op board turns down the purchaser, the seller does not want to be liable for a commission.

4. It is important that the contract of sale specify what appliances and other articles go with the sale of the apartment. The sale does not include these articles unless so specified, and normally they do not belong to the building corporation. The contract should also contain various warranties by the seller, such as a warranty that he owns the shares and lease and will so continue at closing, free of any liens or adverse interests, including mechanic's liens, that the shares are fully paid for, that no lease defaults will exist at closing, that the seller has no knowledge of building code violations, if any, or proposals to increase apartment assessments. For the seller's protection, the contract states that it is subject to approval by the co-op board, and that if the approval is refused, the buyer obtains return of his deposit. The contract clause as to closing costs requires some special attention. The seller normally agrees to pay the corporation's charges for transfer of the shares and lease.

If the buyers are husband and wife who wish to own the apartment in joint tenancy, the contract of sale should so state, and special language may be needed because of the personal property nature of the lease and shares.

EXAMPLE: In Illinois a deed of land to A and B "in joint tenancy" creates a joint tenancy. But to create a joint tenancy in shares and a leasehold probably requires the phrase "as joint tenants with the right of survivorship and not as tenants in common."

5. In states where a judgment against the owner of a leasehold creates a lien thereon, it probably will be necessary to have a title company make a search for such judgments.

6. If valuable furniture and appliances are being transferred, the buyer's lawyer may wish to make a search for Uniform Commercial Code financing statements against the seller.

ADDITIONAL REFERENCES ON COOPERATIVES: Clurman and Hebard, *Condominiums and Coops* (1970); Kehoe, *Cooperatives and Condominiums* (1974); Rohan and Reskin, *Co-op Housing Law and Practice* (1978); Fifkin, *Co-op Proprietary Leases,* 51 N.Y.S.B.J. 290 (1979); Hennessey, *Cooperative Apartments and Town Houses,* 1956 U. Ill. L. Forum 22; Isaacs, *To Buy or Not to Buy, That Is the Question: . . . What is a Cooperative Apartment?,* 13 Record of N.Y.C.B.A. 203 (1958); McCullough, *Cooperative Apartments in Illinois,* 26 Chi-Kent L. Rev. 303 (1948); Whitman, *Financing Condominiums and Cooperatives,* 13 Tulsa L. J. 15 (1977); 61 Harv. L. Rev. 1407 (1948); 111 U. Pa. L. Rev. 638 (1963); 68 Yale L. J. 542 (1959); 8 Fordham Urban L. J. 345 (1980) (maintenance and repairs); 46 St. Johns L. Rev. 632 (financing symposium); 38 Geo. Wash. L. Rev. 958 (low income co-ops); 12 U. of Miami L. Rev. 13; 16 *id* 305. 2 U. of Conn. L. Rev. 30; 50 Calif. L. Rev. 299; 19 Stanf. L. Rev. 978; 18 *id* 1323; 21 Buffalo L. Rev. 555 (sale 1973); 40 U. of Cin. L. Rev. 40 (1971); 29 Wash. & Lee L. Rev. 189 (1972); 49 Harv. L. Rev. 158.

---

33 PLANNED UNIT DEVELOPMENTS

33.01 The planned unit idea

The *planned unit development* (PUD) consists of detached homes, town houses, both garden and high-rise apartments, or combinations of such buildings, all with common open areas and sometimes with private recreation facilities. The developer is permitted a higher density, allowing him to construct more units per acre than is allowed under a standard lot and block subdivision. This more efficient land use results in lower prices for buyers. The purchaser is free of the work and worry of outside maintenance which is often transferred to the homeowners' association. Small private yards and shared recreation facilities reduce the chores associated with any particular unit and give the owners a place for relaxation and enjoyment. The municipality benefits in that the streets and utilities which are generally the municipality's responsibility to repair, replace, and maintain, are often privately owned and maintained by the property owners. 32 Maine L. Rev. 29 (1980).

The PUD is created by recording a plat of subdivision which delineates the building lots and common areas and the recording of a declaration of covenants, conditions, and restrictions which sets forth the rules governing the property, creates an association which may hold title to the common areas, provide that membership in the association is automatic upon the purchase of a unit, establish voting rights and the rights of the owners to use the common areas, set out the obligation of unit owners to pay assessments to defray expenses for the maintenance of the common areas and that such assessments are a lien on the unit until paid.

33.02 Cluster housing

The phrase *cluster housing* means that the individual homes, row houses, or apartment buildings are grouped together on relatively small plots of land with large surrounding areas of land left open for common recreational and park developments. The cluster form of development is economical because the clustering of houses reduces the cost of supplying utilities and roads.

33.03 Town houses

Housing costs have risen sharply, and row houses—now called town houses—have penetrated many areas of our country. Commonly, town houses are built as individual units in a series of five to ten houses with party walls between the units and a side yard on the end units only. In former times, row houses were most often erected facing the street, so that as one passed by a block of row houses, all that was seen was a solid wall of house fronts. Nowadays, town houses are often erected at right angles to the street line or in clusters. It is obvious that innovative layouts will result in more units being erected than under the older layout schemes.

The town house is, historically, the first of the modern housing developments to make extensive use of the concept of shared common ground, though on a very small scale.

Like the more modern subdivisions of single-family dwellings it is invariably set up with a declaration of restrictions, to which is added a declaration of necessary easements. The walls, of course, are party walls, and easements must exist for this purpose. Also, all houses except those closest to the street need easements of ingress and egress over a central walk. Easements are also needed for common gutters and downspouts, common sewer and water lines, common electric light and telephone wires, and so forth. In many cases, builders of these projects have proceeded with complete indifference to the legal requirements of such a situation and have sold off such units without any mention of the easements required. Probably implied easements exist for all these necessary common uses. *Gilbert* v. *Chicago T. & T. Co.,* 7 Ill.2d 496, 131 NE2d 1 (1956). A better way of handling this is by use of a declaration of easements.

With increasing frequency town house developments are organized under the condominium form of ownership and are therefore subject to the local condominium law.

In some states the town house development with its dwelling units and common areas is depicted on a recorded plat. In other instances the boundaries of the units and common areas are depicted on a map attached to the declaration.

33.03(a) Future of town houses

As is evident, town house construction deals economically with the use of land. In old-fashioned one-family home construction, one home would have been erected on each lot. Town house construction gives several dwelling units per lot. Town house construction is economical. Walls are shared. Plumbing and electrical wiring in the common walls are shared. Energy saving is great, especially as respects inner units. They expose only small front and back walls to the elements. The future will see a great deal more town house construction. The energy crisis and the inflation crisis have made the traditional one-family home a luxury few can afford.

REFERENCES: 40 Ind. L. J. 419; Krasnowiecki, *Condominiums Compared to Conventional, Subdivisions with Homes,* 1 RELJ 323 (1972); Krasnowiecki, *Townhouses with Home Associations: A New Perspective,* 123 Pa. L. Rev. 711 (1975).

33.04   Home association

An important feature of most planned unit developments is the home association, which is vested with control of the common areas. See Ch. 30.

33.05   Outline of legal steps to take in creating a PUD

Before the first lot is sold, the developer obtains zoning and subdivision approval, incorporates the nonprofit home association, and records the land subdivision plat and declaration of covenants and easements for all of the land in the planned unit. His plat identifies (1) property to be transferred to public agencies, such as any proposed public streets, (2) the individual homesites, (3) the common areas to be transferred by the developer to the home association, and (4) any other parcels, such as a church site or shopping center, to be kept by the developer or transferred to others.

Recorded contemporaneously with the plat is a *declaration of easements, covenants, restrictions, and liens.* It is hereafter referred to as the *declaration.*

The PUD documents should:

1. legally create an automatic membership, nonprofit corporation with voting rights in each family unit;
2. include a contract by the developer to convey ownership of the common areas to the home association within a reasonable, definite time;
3. appropriately restrict the uses of the home lots and common areas by means of the declaration;
4. grant each lot owner easements for the use and enjoyment of the common property, using the declaration;
5. create a lien on each home lot for assessments which will (a) assure sufficient funds for maintenance of the common areas but (b) provide adequate safeguards for the lot owners against undesirably high charges, again using the declaration;
6. include covenants by the home association to operate and maintain the common areas in the declaration.

33.06(a)   Common areas— plat provisions

Since it is imperative that the common areas be kept in the ownership of the home association and not dedicated to the public, the recorded plat must bear on its face a legend relative to all the common areas indicating that the area is *not* dedicated to the public and that its ownership is reserved to the developer (who later will deed it to the association). If such a legend is lacking, courts may hold that any area having the appearance of common grounds is, by implication, dedicated to the public. However, since the homebuyers will want the developer to deed the land to the home association, an agreement to do so should be contained in the plat or in the accompanying declaration or in a separate contract. Also, appropriate language must be incorporated in the text of the plat to indicate that the individual homeowners take easements in the common properties but no ownership therein. This means that the legend on the plat should be quite comprehensive as:

> Full ownership of the tracts marked *park, playground, private lake, golf course* (describe all other such areas) is retained in *ABC* (the developer) for ultimate conveyance to *XYZ*, a nonprofit corporation whose membership will be composed of homeowners in this development, all according to the provisions of the declaration of restrictions, easements, liens, and covenants filed contemporaneously herewith, and made a part of this plat. Conveyances of lots in this subdivision shall not be deemed to convey title to any part of the retained areas. Said areas are not dedicated to the public. With respect to the total area embraced in this plat, and all parts thereof, easements, covenants, liens, and restrictions are created in and by the declaration aforesaid.

33.06(b) Common areas—agreement of developer to convey to home association

The declaration will contain an agreement that not later than a set date the developer will convey the common areas to the home association. The declaration should be signed as *accepted* by the home association so that it can enforce this agreement.

33.06(c) Common areas—easements—paramount rights of home association

The declaration should create easements in favor of all of the homeowners in the development for access over the private walks and streets, for utilities, water, sewers, and other services, and for use of the common areas, etc., but it should make such easement grant expressly subject and inferior to certain rights of the home association. These rights should include the right of the association to exercise, free and clear of all private rights created in the homeowners, the following rights: (1) the right of the association to suspend the enjoyment of the common areas by any homeowner and the furnishing of services by home association (garbage removal, furnishing water, and so forth) to the delinquent homeowner while his maintenance assessments remain unpaid; (2) the right to manage, maintain, and control the common areas for the benefit of the homeowners, and to promulgate reasonable rules toward this end; (3) the right to dedicate part or all of the common properties to the public for public use; (4) the right of the home association to charge reasonable admission and other fees for the use of the common areas.

33.06(d)   Common areas— public or private ownership—right to dedicate

The right to dedicate part or all of the common properties to the public is also important. Since many planned unit developments seek out less expensive land beyond the boundaries of existing villages or cities, the home association, on occasion, is set up initially to furnish urban services to the community. As soon as a village is formed and is prepared to furnish urban services (streets, sewer, water, and the like), the home association may choose to transfer these systems to the village. Provision for such ultimate transfer must be made in the declaration. It is true that public ownership of the other common areas (swimming pools, etc.) would eliminate the burden of paying real estate taxes thereon and the cost of maintaining the common areas, but such public ownership, especially of recreational common areas, would encourage public use, which would adversely affect the residents of the subdivision; hence it is to be avoided. An alternative is the creation of a public district with the same boundaries as the development. This public body can levy assessments for maintenance but is responsive to the wishes of the voters who are homeowners in the development.

33.06(e)   Common areas— artificial lakes

In some planned developments, an artificially created lake is one of the attractive common facilities. It is quite clear that neither the public nor any public body has any rights whatever in lakes so created. The developer has the legal right to reserve to himself the right to dictate who may use the lake, or he may grant this right to the homeowners. *Mayer* v. *Grueber,* 138 NW2d 197 (Wis. 1965); *Thompson* v. *Enz,* 154 NW2d 473 (Mich. 1967).

33.07(a)   The declaration— building restrictions

The declaration will establish a comprehensive general plan of restrictions governing minutely the structures and uses permitted in the development, both on the homesites and on the common areas. The plat or declaration should also vest in the home association the right to pass upon the plans of any structure to be erected by any home buyer or any alterations to the exterior of any building. 40 ALR3d 864.

33.07(b)   The declaration— covenants

The declaration will contain covenants binding on each homeowner to pay the assessments levied on his lot for maintenance charges, which covenants create a *personal liability* on which a personal judgment can be obtained by the association against a defaulting homeowner. It will also contain covenants by the home association to (1) maintain and operate the common property; (2) administer architectural controls; (3) enforce other covenants; and in some cases (4) maintain all or part of the exterior of individual homes. The covenants provide for amendments, but any amendment requires a vote of the homeowners.

33.07(c)   The declaration— lien for maintenance

The declaration provides for the imposition of a maintenance assessment on each lot in the development. Home associations tend to operate somewhat informally. The danger here is that if procedures grow too lax (meetings held on days other than those set in bylaws, notice of meeting lacking or defective, etc.), the assessments made by the association may be declared invalid. *Noremac, Inc.* v. *Centre Hill Court, Inc.,* 178 SE 877 (Va. 1935).

33.07(d)   The declaration— restraints on sales

Any provision in the declaration or deeds that a homeowner cannot sell his lot except by consent of a majority vote of the association is invalid. Such a clause is an illegal restraint on alienation (sale). *Mountain Springs Assn.* v. *Wilson,* 196 A2d 270 (N.J. 1963). Also invalid is any clause where only a member of the home association can purchase a homesite. *Ibid.* Nor can the declaration or by-laws of the association provide that sales by a homeowner to a future purchaser can only be made to a purchaser approved by the association. *Tuckerton Beach Club* v. *Bender,* 219 A2d 528 (N.J. 1966). No refusal to sell can be racially motivated. *Sullivan* v. *Little Huntington Park,* 396 U.S. 229 (1969). It is safe to provide that any homesite purchaser automatically acquires membership in the home association as a normal incident of home ownership. Other acceptable provisions are discussed in the condominium chapter.

33.08   Mortgage problems

A mortgage on a PUD homesite should contain a covenant of the mortgagor to pay all assessments and a covenant not to vote to amend the declaration without the mortgagee's written consent.

Under FHA and VA rules it is necessary that all common areas be owned by the home association free of any mortgage. Thus, if the seller to the developer takes back a purchase money mortgage, it should contain a provision for release of the common areas from the mortgage on payment of a nominal sum.

33.09   Taxes on common areas

The common areas have no sales value to a third party. They are encumbered with easements that render them valueless to any purchaser. The value of the common areas is reflected in the increased value they contribute to the residential areas. Hence, the tax assessor should not assess the common areas at the value they would have if unencumbered by easements. *People* v. *O'Donnel,* 139 App. Div. 83, 124 N.Y.S. 36 (1910); *Matter of Crane-Berkely Corp.* v. *Lavis,* 238 App. Div. 124, 263 N.Y.S. 556 (1935).

There is no guarantee of this result until the matter has been worked out with the local assessor. Assessors tend to be rather independent individuals. Basically, the problem is one of persuasion.

33.10   Regulation

Just as in the condominium situation, state and local goverments have reacted to developer abuses by enacting consumer legislation relating to assessments, management contracts, recreation area leases, and so on.

33.11   Condominium compared

Although there is nothing in the concept of the condominium which would prevent its use as a PUD, basically there is no need to create a condominium. A PUD home has its own mortgage as does a condominium. Furthermore, it is not necessary to distribute the ownership of the common properties among the lot owners as in condominiums. The PUD makes a different but satisfactory provision for the common areas.

33.12   Zoning

The old-fashioned zoning ordinance, with its rigid allocation of specific uses to specific zones, its building lines, and its minimum area requirements, does not lend itself to the PUD type of development. Cluster development calls for smaller homesites, the land subtracted from homesites being added to common areas. However, the PUD can, it seems, be listed as a special exception in the zoning ordinances. Goldston & Schever, *Zoning of Planned Residential Developments,* 73 Harv. L. Rev. 241, 251 (1959). Alternatively, the zoning ordinance may include a special section devoted to the PUD, calling it variously a Community Unit Plan, Dwelling Groups, Group Housing Planned Residential Development, or Planned Building Groups. Because approving a development of this sort involves a considerable exercise of discretion, it is wise to provide that final approval of a developer's proposal to create a PUD zone should rest with the city council, just as if an amendment to the zoning ordinance were being considered, and some ordinances so provide. *Rodgers* v. *Village of Tarrytown,* 96 NE2d 731 (N.Y. 1951); *LaRue* v. *East Brunswick,* 172 A2d 691 (N.J. 1961); *DeMeo* v. *Zoning Comm.,* 167 A2d 454 (Conn. 1961); Goldston & Schever, *Zoning of Planned Residential Developments*, 73 Harv. L. Rev. 241, 255 (1959). The applicant for such zoning may, under many ordinances, be a government agency, since urban development plans sometimes call for a PUD.

The village cannot thrust PUD zoning on the landowner if the land is not suited to that purpose.

As can be seen, the PUD zone is a sort of floating zone. (See § 26.26) And the modern courts that sustain floating zones will sustain PUD zoning.

EXAMPLE: *X* owned a 187-acre tract located in an area zoned for single-family residences. He sought to have it rezoned to planned unit development with cluster residential areas. This was done and upheld. *Orinda Homeowners Committee* v. *Board of Supervisors,* 90 Cal. Reptr. 88 (1970).

On the whole, the modern decisions are likely to sustain the validity of PUD zoning even though it is a far cry from "cooky-cutter" single-family dwelling zoning, 43 ALR3d 888, and even though the density requirements are different from those applicable to conventional subdivisions. *Peabody* v. *Phoenix,* 485 P2d 565 (Ariz. 1971).

> **EXAMPLE:** PUD zoning was sustained against attack on the ground that PUD zoning departed from the uniformity one finds in old-fashioned zoning. The court pointed out that in a PUD zone true uniformity is achieved in that the cluster housing, typical of the PUD, is found in each PUD zone. *Orinda Homeowners Committee* v. *Board of Supervisors,* 90 Cal. Reptr. 88 (1970); *Prince George's County* v. *M & B Const. Corp.,* 297 A2d 683 (Md. 1972); *Continental Homes* v. *County of Lake* 346 NE2d 226 (Ill.1972); *Gray* v. *Trustees,* 313 NE2d 366 (Ohio, 1973); 81 Dick. L. Rev. 153; 49 Conn. B. J. 503 (1975).

Zoning law does not require that each zone have only one permitted use. *Cheney* v. *Village 2 at New Hope,* 241 A2d 81 (Pa. 1968).

Obviously, the PUD brings into play the concept of exclusionary zoning which is discussed in the chapter on zoning.

33.12(a) Plat approval and zoning combined

It is evident that where a local government is called upon to assign a floating zone area to a PUD, it is almost impossible to separate the plat approval process from the rezoning process. Hence, many local governments have adopted a unitary approval process that combines the two operations. 29 Hastings L. J. 647.

REFERENCES: 81 Dick. L. Rev. 153; 73 Harv. L. Rev. 24; 35 Mo. L. Rev. 27; 22 Okla. L. Rev. 108; 1 Real Est. L. J. 245; 114 U. Pa. L. Rev. 3; 10 Willamette L. J. 422; 43 ALR3d 885 (all dealing with PUD zoning).

---

34 BUILDING CONSTRUCTION AND BUILDING WARRANTIES

34.01 In general

This chapter deals mainly with new home construction, with occasional mention of significant aspects of large-scale construction.

34.02 Construction contracts

There are different types of construction contracts:

1. I own a lot and hire you to build a house according to certain plans and specifications prepared by my architect. This is a construction contract only.

2. You are a subdivider and builder. I pick out a site in your subdivision, and you contract to build a house (like one of your model homes, perhaps) and deliver the house and lot at a specified price. This is a contract for the sale of land and for the construction of a house. Both the law of sale contracts and the law of construction contracts are applicable to this situation.

3. You are a subdivider and builder, and I decide to buy a house that I find under construction in your subdivision. This is essentially the same as (2) above.

In situations 2 and 3 above you have the sell-and-build type of contract. The contract is one for the *sale of land* and also for the *construction of a home. Dieckman* v. *Walser,* 144 N.J.Eq. 382, 168 Atl. 582 (1933). It must comply with the requirements of law as to both types of contracts.

EXAMPLE: *R* contracted to sell *E* a lot and build a home thereon. The contract of sale portion was complete, but there were no plans or specifications giving the details of the building. The contract was invalid. *Griesenhauer* v. *Bellea Lake Development Co.,* 421 SW2d 785 (1967).

EXAMPLE: The contract called for sale of a lot and construction of a home, payment when home was ready for occupancy. The seller could not obtain a certificate of occupancy. Since the seller could not perform the building part of the contract, he could not enforce the sale part. *Sloan* v. *Pinafore Homes, Inc.,* 310 N.Y.S.2d 731 (1970).

34.03   Types of sell-and-build contracts

There are several types of sell-and-build contracts.

EXAMPLE: Seller contracts to sell a lot to Buyer. The contract requires that Buyer apply for a mortgage loan of $15,000, and is contingent on the procuring of this loan. When the loan is obtained, the deal is to be closed, deed and mortgage recorded, and thereafter Seller is to construct the building, using the mortgage money for this purpose. After the closing of the deal, the contract between the parties is simply a construction contract.

EXAMPLE: Seller contracts to sell a lot to Buyer, to erect a house thereon, and when the house has been completed, to deed the completed house and lot to Buyer. Here Seller will get his own construction loan, build the building with his own construction loan proceeds, and deliver the completed package to Buyer. This has some advantages to Seller. The handling of the construction disbursements does not involve Buyer, whereas in the previous example Seller must go to Buyer for documents every time a construction disbursement is to be made. After all, in the previous example, it is Buyer's money, loaned to him by the mortgagee, that is being used for construction.

EXAMPLE: Builder contracts to build a home for Buyer and to deed the completed house and lot to Buyer. Builder applies to *XYZ Savings and Loan Association* for a mortgage loan. A long-term mortgage in the sum of $20,000 is placed on the property by Builder, but *XYZ* loans only $18,000 to Builder. When the building is completed, Builder deeds to Buyer, who assumes the mortgage and receives the additional $2,000 to enable him to pay Builder.

SUGGESTION TO HOME BUYER: When you buy from a professional subdivider and builder, you are often dealing with a man who does not yet own the land that he is selling you. He may have only an option or contract to buy the land. If the builder runs into financial difficulties, he may never be able to pay up his option or contract or be able to transfer ownership to you. Moreover, as financial troubles develop, mechanics' liens are filed and mortgage foreclosures instituted. In such case, you will find that the possibility of obtaining ownership or getting your money back is nil. Therefore, it is best for you to get a deed to the property as early as possible, before you have put too much money into the house.

34.03(a)   Sell-and-build contracts—signatures

Some sell-and-build contracts contain a clause that the seller is not bound unless an officer of the seller corporation signs for the corporation. Obviously, the buyer should not accept a contract signed only by a salesman. Indeed, it is always advisable to insist on an officer's signature.

34.03(b)   Sell-and-build contracts—mortgage clauses

Every sell-and-build contract has a clause requiring the buyer to apply for a mortgage loan. The deal will go one of two ways.

> **EXAMPLE:**   Builder will convey the land to Buyer who puts on a mortgage, and Builder uses the proceeds of the loan to build the home.

> **EXAMPLE:**   Builder has Buyer apply for a mortgage loan. As soon as the lender has approved Buyer for the loan, Builder puts a construction mortgage on the lot and uses the proceeds of this loan to build the home. When the home is completed, Buyer signs the permanent mortgage, the proceeds of which are used to pay off both Builder and the construction loan.

But in either case the buyer must qualify for a mortgage loan, so the contract calls for him to apply for a mortgage loan; the deal is off if he fails to qualify.

34.03(c)   Delay in completion

A prospective buyer should read the contract before signing it. The time set for completion is an important matter to a buyer who is planning to sell his present home. Carefully read the clause that gives the builder additional time to complete. It may be so broad that the completion date is virtually meaningless.

34.03(d)   Sell-and-build contracts—subordination of contract to construction loan

Many sell-and-build contracts contain a clause subordinating the contract to any construction mortgage put on the property by the builder.

> **EXAMPLE:**   Builder sells a lot to Buyer under a contract by which Builder will build a home for Buyer like a model home he has displayed to Buyer. Builder will now put a construction loan mortgage on the lot to Lender. Probably Lender will want to see the contract to make certain that the land is under contract and also to see the sale price. Having actual notice of the contract, Lender's rights would be subordinate to Buyer's rights, and a deed from Builder to Buyer could wipe out Lender's mortgage. Therefore the contract will state that Buyer's rights are subordinate to Lender's lien.

34.03(e)   Sell-and-build contracts—builder liability

Obviously, the seller–builder in a sell-and-build contract has all the liabilities of a building contractor set forth in this chapter. *Jones* v. *Galewood*, 381 P2d 158 (Okla. 1963).

34.04   Mechanic's liens

Mechanics and materialmen are persons who furnish labor or materials in the construction of improvements on land. A mechanic or materialman who has furnished such labor or material on the landowner's order can, by complying with certain formalities, acquire a lien on the land and improvements in question if the landowner fails to pay him. The lien is called a *mechanic's lien,* and the person furnishing the work or material is the *mechanic's lien claimant.* These liens resemble mortgages and in many states are foreclosed in the same manner as mortgages.

Certain kinds of labor and materials are not *lienable.* For example, if labor or materials are furnished to a tenant and the articles thereby produced are, in legal contemplation, *trade fixtures* and thus removable by him at the termination of his tenancy, a lien will not attach to the landlord's title.

> **EXAMPLE:** *A* leases a store to *B* as a barber shop. *C* installs barber chairs at *B*'s order. *C* has no lien on the land for any unpaid balance due on the chairs. The chairs are trade fixtures.

Generally, lienable work and materials must be such as become a permanent part of the building structure. Thus, medical care furnished an employee of the contractor, even if the injury was suffered on the building site, is not lienable. Printing, stationery, and telephone service furnished the contractor are not lienable. Nor is the furnishing of tools, machinery, cranes, hoists, and so forth, lienable, for those do not become a permanent part of the building. 57 CJS 536; 36 Am.Jur. 57. In a number of states the law has been amended recently to give a mechanic's lien for the rental of machinery needed in construction.

34.04(a)   Contract or consent of owner

Mechanic's lien laws differ from state to state in dealing with the problem of work ordered by one other than the landowner. In some states, a lien claimant must show that he was hired by the landowner *or his agent* to furnish the labor or materials for which a lien is claimed. Laws of this kind are known as *contract statutes.* In other states, it is sufficient if the lien claimant can show that the owner had knowledge of and consented to the doing of the work, even though the work was ordered by some person other than the owner, such as the tenant. These laws are known as *consent statutes.*

Consent usually involves more than a mere failure to object to the doing of the work. Often the landowner is powerless to prevent the third person, such as a tenant, from ordering the construction or improvements. Some *affirmative consent* by the landowner is required, as when a lease requires the tenant to erect a building. At times, however, the same result is reached regardless of which statute is applied.

> **EXAMPLE:** Landowner leases an obsolete movie theater to Tenant, the lease providing that Tenant will use the premises only as a savings and loan association and that Tenant will make the necessary alterations at his own expense. Here, if Tenant fails to pay for the work and materials, those furnishing the same will have mechanic's liens on Landowner's land. In a consent state, the lease is treated as giving consent for the doing of the work, and in a contract state the lease is re-

garded as making Tenant the agent of Landowner for the ordering of the work. Thus the result is at times the same whether the state is a contract or a consent state. 79 ALR 962.

Knowledge and consent also figure in the situation where the landowner has entered into an installment contract to sell the land to a purchaser and the purchaser has ordered work done on the building. If the seller has no knowledge of the work and it is not provided for in the installment contract, the seller's title does not become subject to the mechanic's lien, and the lien attaches only to the buyer's equity. As in the case of leases, however, where the contract of sale expressly requires the doing of certain specific work, the resulting mechanic's lien claim is binding on the seller. 57 CJS 573.

Whether work ordered by one spouse will ripen into a lien binding on the other spouse is a subject on which the laws differ from state to state. 57 CJS 552, 592.

A number of states, including California, Colorado, Minnesota, Nevada, New Mexico, Oregon, South Dakota, and Washington, have a special type of consent statute. In these states, the landowner is deemed to have authorized and consented to improvements ordered by others (tenants, contract purchasers, and so on) unless within a specified time of learning of the work (usually three to ten days) the landowner posts a notice of nonresponsibility in some conspicuous place on the premises. 123 ALR 7, 85 ALR2d 949. In Nevada, the notice of non-responsibility must also be recorded.

As far as co-owners are concerned, no lien will attach to the interests of those co-owners who do not consent to the work.

> **EXAMPLE:** A father and his minor children owned the property as tenants in common. The father ordered certain labor and materials. The mechanic's lien attached only to the father's interest in the property. *Patrick* v. *Bonthius,* 124 P2d 550 (Wash. 1942). One co-owner cannot put a lien on the shares of his nonconsenting co-owners.

34.04(b) Contractors and subcontractors

Mechanic's lien laws distinguish between contractors and subcontractors. A *contractor* is one who was hired by the landowner to construct the improvement. A *subcontractor* has not dealt directly with the landowner, but has a contract with, or was hired by, the contractor.

> **EXAMPLE:** Owner hires *GC,* a general contractor, to build a house. *GC* hires *SC,* a subcontractor to do the electrical work. *SC* buys his electrical supplies from Supplier. *GC* is a contractor. *SC* is a subcontractor. Supplier is called a subsubcontractor, treated differently from a subcontractor in some states.

Since the legal rights of general contractors differ from those of subcontractors, and since the procedures that they must follow to establish their liens are also quite different, the distinction between general contractors and subcontractors is important. Laymen may sometimes mistake a general contractor for a subcontractor.

> **EXAMPLE:** Owner retains Architect to supervise construction and to let the various contracts for plumbing, electrical work, and so on. All the individual contractors are *general contractors,* for they are dealing with the landowner through his agent.

In some states the law places on the landowner and on the construction lender the burden of seeing to it that the subcontractors are paid for their work and materials. This is something of an oddity. If I hire you to build a building for me, very likely the construction contract will call for me to pay the contract price to you. Nevertheless, the law steps in and says that, despite the contract, my mortgage lender and I must hold back part of the contract price and pay it to the subcontractors. In order that the landowner may know those whom it is his duty to protect and also to enable him to hold back adequate funds to pay them, the law usually requires subcontractors to give the landowner personal notice of their liens within a set time, and failure to do so invalidates their liens. *Gray* v. *McKinley,* 43 So2d 421 (Ala. 1949). This notice must be given to all landowners.

> **EXAMPLE:** *A* and *B* own land in joint tenancy. They hire *GC* to erect a building. *GC* hires *SC* to do the plumbing. *SC* is a subcontractor. If he serves notice of his subcontractor's lien only on *A, SC* has a lien only on *A's* half interest in the land. He has no lien on *B's* share. *Liese* v. *Hentze,* 158 NE 428 (Ill. 1927).

34.04(c) Performance by contractor

In general, where the general contractor seeks to assert a lien, he must show that the contract was *substantially performed* by him. 57 CJS 605. Likewise, any subcontractor seeking to assert a lien would have to show that his job was substantially performed by him. Where the contract specifies that no payment will be made without production of an architect's certificate, a general contractor claiming a lien must be able to produce the certificate. 57 CJS 606.

34.04(d) Inception and priority of lien

The law as to the particular time when a mechanic's lien attaches to the land varies from state to state. There are definite groupings or classifications of states in this regard:

> 1. In a few states (Washington, for example), the lien of any particular mechanic attaches when he commences *his* particular work. In such states, the mechanic's lien is not prior to any mortgage that was recorded prior to the commencement of the very work for which the lien is filed.

> **EXAMPLE:** *A* and *B* commence work on a building, and afterward the owner mortgages the land to Lender. Thereafter, *D* and *E* begin work on the same con-

struction job. *A* and *B* have priority over Lender, and Lender has priority over *D* and *E*.

2. In many states (Arkansas, California, District of Columbia, Georgia, Louisiana, Michigan, Minnesota, Nevada, New Mexico, Ohio, Oklahoma, Tennessee, Utah, and Wisconsin, for example), all mechanic's liens growing out of a particular construction job date back to the beginning of the job.

EXAMPLE: Owner hires *GC* to erect a building, and *GC* hires *SC* to dig the foundation. *SC* begins work in January 1968. In February 1968, Owner records a mortgage to Lender which mortgage is intended to provide funds for construction. The carpenter, mason, electrician, and so on come on the job in March 1968. All mechanic's liens date back to January, and all liens therefore have priority over Lender's mortgage.

3. In a few states (Illinois and Maine, for example), a mechanic's lien attaches to the land as of the date of the contract for the improvement; that is, as of the date on which the owner ordered the work done.

EXAMPLE: Owner hires *GC* on January 8, 1968, to build a building in Chicago. As is true of most contracts for construction, the contract is not recorded. On January 10, 1968, Owner records a mortgage to Lender, which mortgage is intended to provide funds for construction. Work on the construction site begins on January 17, 1968. *GC*'s mechanic's lien dates back to January 8, 1968, and therefore enjoys priority over Lender's mortgage.

4. In a few states (New York and South Carolina, for example), a mechanic's lien does not arise as against the mortgagee until notice thereof is filed in the proper public office.

EXAMPLE: Owner, on January 8, 1968, hires *GC* to erect a building. *GC* commences work on January 12. On January 19, 1968, Owner records a construction mortgage to Lender, and Lender disburses funds under this mortgage for such construction until February 28, when a mechanic's lien claim is filed by a subcontractor. Lender discontinues disbursement and files a foreclosure suit. Lender has complete priority over the mechanic's liens, because all his disbursements were made prior to the filing of any mechanic's liens.

5. In some states (Colorado, Illinois, Missouri, North Dakota, Oregon, South Dakota, Virginia, and Wyoming, for example), the law declares that a mechanic's lien for work or materials furnished after a mortgage lien has attached to the land shall have priority over the mortgage *as to the building but not as to the land.* In a number of these states the matter of priority of lien as between the construction mortgage and the mechanic's lien claimants is decided in a way that is quite disadvantageous to the mortgagee.

EXAMPLE: Owner of vacant land procures a construction loan mortgage from Lender which is recorded on January 10, 1968. On January 17, Owner hires *GC* to build the building. Construction begins on January 24. Mechanic's liens were filed. Both Lender and the mechanic's lien claimants file suits to foreclose. The court will hold that the mechanic's liens are a prior and superior lien as to the buildings, so that, in practical effect, the mechanic's liens will be a prior lien as to most of the value of the property, and the mortgagee will have no choice but to pay off the mechanic's lien claimants. 107 ALR 1012.

6. In Indiana the mechanic's liens enjoy equality of lien with the construction mortgage. *Ward* v. *Yarnelle,* 91 NE 7 (Ind. 1910); 80 ALR2d 187.

7. In Missouri a curious rule is followed. The construction lender is considered, from the very fact that he has made a construction loan, to have subordinated his mortgage to the mechanic's liens. *H. B. Deal Const. Co.* v. *Labour Discount Center,* 418 SW2d 940 (Mo. 1967).

Of course, no great harm comes to the mortgagee if the landowner remains solvent and is able to pay off all mechanic's lien claimants. Unfortunately for mortgage lenders, many construction projects do not get completed and sold as planned, so that the construction mortgage and the mechanic's lien claimants are plunged into a contest as to their respective rights in the land and buildings.

34.04(e)   Notice of lien   In many states, laws require a mechanic's lien claimant to file a notice of his lien in some public office within some specified time, usually within some period after completion of the work. Usually it is required that this notice state the amount claimed to be due, the name and address of the claimant, the type of improvement, a description of the land, and the name of the landowner or landowners. 57 CJS 693; 52 ALR2d 12; 27 ALR2d 1169. The requirement that lien claims be filed within a specified time of the completion of the work often leads to controversies.

> **EXAMPLE:** In Illinois, the law provides that lien claims must be filed within four months after completion of the work. *X* completes his work satisfactorily, but more than four months elapses before *X* realizes that he has failed to file his lien claim. *X* sends a workman back to perform some trifling task, like repairing a defective lock. This does no good. The job was really finished more than four months ago, and *X* cannot prolong this period by subterfuge. 57 CJS 661.

34.04(f)   Waiver and release of lien   As construction or repair work goes forward, liens of the general contractor and subcontractors attach to the land. Both the landowner and any mortgagee involved naturally want to get rid of these liens, which can be accomplished by procuring waivers of their liens from the parties furnishing labor or material. There are *partial waivers* and *final waivers.* Suppose that a subcontractor, such as a plumbing, electrical, or plastering subcontractor, has finished half his job and wants to be paid for that half. When the homebuilder pays him, he demands from the subcontractor a waiver of his lien for the work and materials furnished. This waiver recites that it waives all liens for *work and materials furnished.* This means, of course, for work and materials furnished *up to the date of the* *waiver.* No lien is waived as to the work still to be done. When final payment is made to that particular party, the homebuilder demands from him a final waiver, which waives all lien *for work and materials furnished or to be furnished* meaning that he has no lien at all on the land or buildings. Even if he must come back to repair or replace defective work or material, he can claim no lien on the property, which is important, because the objective is always to get the building built at the price and at the bids submitted by the various mechanics. There is trouble ahead if any of the mechanics is legally able to assert a lien for a sum greater than the amount he agreed to work for.

When a mechanic has filed a lien claim in some public office as required by law, it becomes necessary, when his claim has been paid or settled, to release his lien from the public records. As a rule, the waiver form is not appropriate for this purpose. Instead, a form called *release of mechanic's lien* is used. It is very similar to a release of mortgage and is filed in the same office where the lien claim has been filed.

34.04(g)   Time limit on enforcement of lien

It is usually provided that a mechanic's lien ceases to exist unless steps are taken to enforce or foreclose it within a specified time, usually one or two years, after the filing of the lien claim.

34.05   Extras

Extras are probably the largest factor creating disputes between owners and contractors. There is a propensity on the part of some contractors to bid low in order to get the job and then try to bail their way out of a losing job by claiming extras. Also, an owner is frequently "inspired" during the course of construction and orders changes or extra work and materials indiscriminately without a definite understanding as to the cost. A contractor who is providing extras does not have to make a competitive bid in order to obtain the work. There is therefore a tendency on the part of some contractors to charge more money for extras than the ordinary markup used in bidding for work. The contract should therefore specifically require that all extra charges must be reduced to a written instrument, signed by the owner, describing the work to be performed and the amount to be paid. Such a provision is valid. 2 ALR3d 631. In the interest of both the contractor and the owner, this procedure should be religiously followed. The owner's architect has no power to waive this provision of the contract. He cannot order extras verbally. 2 ALR3d 686. However, if the owner himself verbally orders the extra work, he is liable. 2 ALR3d 658. By ordering the extras verbally, the owner has waived the provision requiring a change order to be in writing. Also, the contract should require the owner to deposit additional funds with the mortgage lender in order to assure the contractor and the mortgage lender that there will be adequate funds to complete the building when extra work or materials are ordered.

In addition to disputes with respect to the cost of extras, disputes often arise as to whether or not a given item is an extra or is included under the original contract. If the plans and specifications made a part of the contract are sufficiently detailed, the possibility of a dispute over whether a particular item is an extra can be minimized.

34.06   Progress payments   If I hire you to erect a building on my land, the contract will almost certainly fix a total price for the entire job. However, your subcontractors will not wait for their money until the building is finished. Therefore, the contract will call for *progress payments* to the general contractor and the subcontractors as the building goes up. A widely used formula provides for a payment of 35 percent of the proceeds to the contractor when the house is under roof, 30 percent of the contract price when the house is plastered, and the balance of 35 percent when the building is completed and accepted by the owner. However, the contract often provides that only 85 percent of the full amount of a progress payment due the *general contractor* is payable when the progress payment falls due. The owner holds back 15 percent of each payment due the general contractor (often called a *retention*) until the building has been completed and accepted by the owner with all lien waivers produced. On big jobs, the contract will call for retention on work done by the bigger subcontractors. After all, you cannot tell whether heating or air conditioning will work until you try it, and if it doesn't, the retention is an effective inducement to get the necessary repairs done.

As a progress payment is demanded, the contract often calls for an inspection to be made by the owner's architect, who certifies that the work and material for which payment is claimed are in place and in accordance with the contract. If the owner has no architect, this inspection should be made by the mortgage lending institution. On FHA loans, an inspection will also be made by the FHA.

A question often arising is whether a contract that calls for progress payments is a total contract for a total job at a total price or can be broken up into as many parts as there are progress payments. In other words, is the contract divisible?

EXAMPLE: A contract to build a schoolhouse for a price of $2,610 provided that $300 was to be paid when first floor joists were in, $300 when second floor joists were in, $1,000 when the building was enclosed, $400 when the plastering was done, and the balance when the building was completed. After the plastering was completed and all payments made up to and including the payment due at that time, a windstorm destroyed the building. The court held: (1) A builder is not excused from completing the building by the fact that the building, while under construction, is destroyed or damaged by fire, storms, or sinking of the soil; he must rebuild and complete the job without a penny of additional compensation. (2) A building contract is entire; it is not divisible. A contractor who abandons the job, as this contractor did when the windstorm destroyed the building, has not earned a penny. Therefore, he must refund to the owner all progress payments already made. *Superintendent of Schools* v. *Bennett,* 27 N.J.L. 513. On both points, the court was correct. 22 ALR2d 1345.

However, if the contract is not to *build,* but to *repair* or remodel an existing building, the contractor is relieved of liability for further performance if the building is destroyed by fire or other casualty and the destruction is not due to the contractor's negligence. *Matthews Const. Co.* v. *Brady,* 104 N.J.L. 438, 140 A 433 (1928). Moreover, the contractor can recover for the value of labor and materials furnished up to the time of the destruction.

Failure of the landowner to make a progress payment is a material breach of the contract. It entitles the contractor to suspend work until payment has been made. *Watson* v. *Auburn Iron Works, Inc.,* 318 NE2d 508 (Ill. 1974).

34.07 Mortgage money

Any builder who builds on contract for a landowner should insist that the landowner have a definite commitment for a satisfactory construction mortgage loan before construction begins, and the construction contract should be made subject to this condition.

> **SUGGESTION TO BUILDER:** Require the landowner to furnish you a photostatic copy of the lender's commitment to make the mortgage loan.

34.08 Cash down payments from homebuyers

Builders usually insist that the homebuyer make a cash down payment. What to do with it is the question. Homebuyers are often reluctant to pay a builder a large sum of money before construction has begun. And builders are often reluctant to start construction when they have no assurance that the homebuyer will be able to come up with the money. One solution is to have the homebuyer deposit his money with the mortgage house that is financing construction. This is acceptable to the mortgage house, for under the typical construction loan agreement, this deposit is used for the initial stages of construction, and the mortgagee's loan money is not used until later stages of construction have been reached. Another idea is to deposit the buyer's money with some bank as escrowee, with directions to turn the money over to the builder as specified stages of construction are reached.

> **NEW LAWS:** In some states (New York, for example), new laws require the builder to keep the buyer's deposit in an escrow. In other states a builder who diverts the deposit to another job is guilty of a crime. *State of Washington* v. *Thomas William McDonald,* 463 P2d 174 (Wash. 1969). In still other states, laws making a builder criminally liable for diverting deposits to other jobs are invalid on the ground that imprisonment for debt is no longer legal. *State v. Janing,* 182 Neb. 539, 156 NW2d 9 (1968). Obviously, this is a problem without a solution.

34.09 Substantial performance

If a building contractor finishes the building in strict accordance with the plans and specifications and in a good and workmanlike manner, he is, of course, entitled to collect the full contract price. However, it is virtually impossible to complete a building contract in strict compliance with every tiny requirement of the plans and specifications. If the builder performs substantially according to the contract, he is entitled to collect the contract price, less a deduction that will compensate the owner for the builder's deviations from the contract. Substantial performance is hard to define. If the owner gets substantially the building that he contracted for, and the deviations are trifling and unintentional, there is substantial performance. For example, if I hire you to build a house according to my plans at a price of $12,000, and you fulfill your contract except that two rooms have the wrong wallpaper, which it would cost $100 to remedy, clearly there substantial performance, and you are entitled to collect $11,900. The following are illustrations of cases where substantial performance was found lacking.

EXAMPLES: (1) The footings were inadequate for wet ground, so that the foundations sank and the floors sagged. *White* v. *Mitchell,* 123 Wash. 630, 213 Pac. 10 (1923); (2) the contract called for a six-room house, and the builder erected a five-room house; (3) the foundations and walls of the house cracked immediately after completion of construction due to a soil condition that the builder did not properly correct. *Newcomb* v. *Schaeffler,* 131 Colo. 56, 279 P2d 409 (1955); (4) in New York, it is generally held that if the deviations amount to more than 10 percent of the contract price, substantial performance is lacking. *Rochkind* v. *Jacobson,* 110 N.Y.S. 583.

If you contract to erect a building for me, and your performance is less than substantial, one of several consequences is possible:

1. If I am in a generous frame of mind, then even though the building is not the kind that you agreed to build, I may accept the building as a complete and satisfactory substitute for the building contracted for. Here I must pay the full contract price. No deductions are allowed because of the defects. *Zambakian* v. *Leson,* 77 Colo. 183, 234 Pac. 1065 (1925).

EXAMPLE: As the building went up, the owner inspected it and noticed the deviations from the contract. But he moved in, telling the builder that the building was satisfactory and that the contract price would be paid. This is full acceptance. All deviations were waived. *Hooper* v. *Cuneo,* 227 Mass. 37, 116 NE 237 (1917).

Often in these cases, you will find that the owner has with full knowledge of the defects paid the entire contract price. Since this is full acceptance, he cannot therefore sue the builder for damages because of defects he knew about when he paid his money. *Houlette & Miller* v. *Arntz,* 148 La. 407, 126 NW 796 (1910). And there are always words, acts, or both on the landowner's part indicating full acceptance of the building. *Aarnes* v. *Windham,* 137 Ala. 513, 34 So 816 (1903). Often the builder has a printed form that he asks the landowner to sign. This form recites that the building has been constructed in complete conformity with the contract.

2. I may accept the building as substantial performance but reserve the right to deductions because of the deviations.

EXAMPLE: The owner discovers defects as the building goes up, protests the defects, but continues to proceed with the builder on the basis and assumption that their contract is still in force. *Otto Misch Co.* v. *E. E. Davis Co.,* 241 Mich. 285, 217 NW 38 (1928). The builder gets the contract price, less a deduction to compensate for the deviations. *Gray* v. *Wood,* 220 Ala. 587, 127 So 148 (1930); 17 CJS 1101, 1105.

3. I simply move into the building because it is on my land and I cannot avoid it. My attitude at all times after discovering the defects is that the builder has breached his contract and ought not to be paid anything. Most courts will nevertheless award the builder the value of the building, on the theory that it must be worth something to the landowner and that to give the builder nothing would be unduly harsh. Other courts, however, are less merciful with the builder. They say that I have a right to use my own land and the buildings on it, and since the builder's performance fell short of substantial performance, he is entitled to nothing. 5 Corbin, *Contracts* 551; 107 ALR 1411.

4. If I demolish the structure, or refuse to make any use of it, in most states the builder will be unable to collect a penny. 3 Corbin, *Contracts* 790.

34.10   Liability of seller–builder for defects in land or building

The subject of liability of the seller–builder for defects in land or building has grown tremendously in recent years.

In reading this material, one must be constantly aware of the fact that much of this material is new law, made *by the courts,* in very recent times. Some courts currently lag behind the times.

Also, one must be aware of the *remedies* that the courts afford. A court that is quite content to give a buyer his money back if the house that he buys turns out to be a lemon might not permit him to sue the seller–builder for damages. Or, a court that is quite content to allow the *first purchaser* to sue a seller–builder for defects in the house might not allow a second purchaser of the now used house to sue the seller–builder.

The obligations of the seller of a *new* house under the old law differ from those of the seller of an *old* house. The obligations of the seller of a *completed* house differ from those of the seller of a house yet to be constructed. One who sells a house *to be constructed* has builder liability. One who sells a *completed* house does not, at least under some older cases. Suppose you, as a builder, have a house in the process of construction. *X* sees it and signs a contract to buy it. You have *builder liability* to *X.* As long as the seller has workmen on the job, the house is not fully completed, and therefore when the house is sold, the contract is treated as though it were a contract (1) to sell the land and (2) to finish the house. In short, it is a sell-and-build contract. Builder liability means that the courts hold the builder on two counts: (1) *he must build in a good and workmanlike manner;* (2) *the structure when completed must be reasonably fit for its intended purpose.*

Markman v. *Hoefer,* 252 Iowa 118, 106 NW2d 59 (1960); *Jones* v. *Gatewood,* 381 P2d 158 (Okla. 1963); *Fain* v. *Nelson,* 56 Wash.2d 217, 356 P2d 302 (1960). These are called *implied warranties.*

> **EXAMPLE:** Exterior stucco peeled off soon after the house was completed. The builder is liable. He has failed to build in a good and workmanlike manner. The same would be true if the concrete footings were faulty and the building settled, causing cracked plaster and ill-fitting doors. 4 Western Reserve L. Rev. 361.

> **EXAMPLE:** Builder builds a barn for Farmer, but the hayloft collapses when filled with hay. Builder is liable. The structure is not fit for its intended purpose.

In addition to liability on the two implied warranties, a builder is liable for failure to use ordinary care and skill. This is called *negligence liability.* For example, a builder must use ordinary care in the selecting of building materials, and if he should carelessly select beams of inadequate strength, he would be liable for injuries resulting from collapse of the house. However, if a builder uses ordinary care in the selection of building material, he is not liable for injuries caused by hidden defects in the materials.

> **EXAMPLE:** You, as a builder, buy steel rods for roof trusses from a reputable dealer and, owing to hidden defects in the steel, the roof collapses. You are not liable, because you were not negligent.

There was an obvious defect in the law, as stated above. Under the old law, the seller of a completed house had no builder liability.

> **EXAMPLE:** A builder has fully completed a house at the time he sells it to you, and thereafter defects in construction come to light, such as inadequate waterproofing of basement walls, leaky roofs, faulty foundation, and so forth. The builder had no liability, because the implied warranties existed only where some construction remains to be done at the time the house is sold. Newer decisions reject this view.

The buyer of a newly completed house is at a disadvantage, because in an older house time brings to light the defects in construction and the buyer can see the defects for himself. To cure this situation, efforts are being made to get builders to give express warranties. If I buy a newly completed house from you, I could insist that you sign a document requiring you to make good any defects in construction that come to light within a year of the date of your deed conveying the property to me.

There is a historical reason for the distinction between sales of completed houses and houses not yet completed. The old law, which is today undergoing much change, but which still holds true in a few states, tells us that *when we buy a thing,* the rule is *caveat emptor.* We buy at our own risk unless we specifically demand and receive warranties of quality. This is the old law applied to sales of completed houses. The old law states that when you hire a man *to do a job,* he has a legal obligation to do the work correctly, which is the law that we apply to sales of houses to be constructed or completed.

> **NEW DIRECTIONS:** Beginning in 1964, the courts began to throw the old rules overboard. They began to hold that in every sale of a completed residence by a builder–seller there is an implied warranty that the home was built in a workmanlike manner and is fit for habitation. *Carpenter* v. *Donohoe,* 154 Colo. 78, 388 P2d 399, 402 (1964); *Bethlahmy* v. *Bechtel,* 415 P2d 698 (Idaho 1966); *Waggoner* v. *Midwestern Develop., Inc.,* 154 NW2d 803 (S.D. 1967); *Moore* v. *Werner,* 418 SW2d 918 (Tex. Civ. App. 1967); *Humber* v. *Morton,* 426 SW2d 554 (Tex. 1968); *Theis* v. *Heuer,* 280 NE2d 300 (Ind. 1972) citing many articles; also *Tavaros* v. *Horstman,* 542 P2d 1275 (1976). The philosophy here is that the average buyer of a new home is ill equipped to detect the defects and shortcomings of jerry-built construction. It is likely that all states will come to this point of view in time. 25 ALR3d 383. At this writing the new rule has been adopted in more than half the states.

Thus, it is now the rule that a builder–seller of a residence, completed or in the process of construction, implicitly warrants to his *first purchaser* that the house was, in its major structural features, constructed in a good and workmanlike manner. That is, the structure is of reasonable quality, is reasonably fit for its intended purpose, and is free of building code violations. The theories behind this rule are that the buyer of a new house relies on the skill of a seller-builder, that the buyer is incapable of detecting defects in construction, and that most defects in construction are hidden from view.

Also it has been said that this rule would tend to discourage much of the sloppy work and jerry-building that has become perceptible over the years. *Cochran* v. *Keeton,* 252 So2d 307 (Ala. 1971) (citing 7 Williston, *Contracts,* [3d ed. 1963] § 926).

It has also been said that the idea of *caveat emptor* ("let the buyer beware") is out of harmony with modern homebuying practices. *Humber* v. *Morton,* 426 SW2d 554, 562 (Tex. 1968).

One court, in applying the rule, stated that it found indefensible the difference in protection accorded the purchaser of a kitchen mop (money back if defective) and a $50,000 home (no remedy under the old law if building collapsed). *Wawak* v. *Stewart,* 449 SW2d 922 (Ark. 1970), noted 24 Ark. L. Rev. 245.

34.10(a) Liability of seller–builder—remedies

Among the remedies available against a seller-builder who has breached his implied warranty are the following:

> 1. The buyer may rescind (terminate the transaction) and obtain *restitution of the money he paid the seller–builder. Bethamy* v. *Bechtel,* 91 Idaho 55, 415 P2d 698 (1966);

Tavaris v. *Horstman,* 542 P2d 1275 (Wyo. 1975). This is a risky business. To back out of the deal, the buyer must move out. There is danger of vandalism and then the ultimate danger, the possibility that he will not win his lawsuit.

2. The buyer may sue the builder–seller for *damages for personal injuries* suffered as a result of the defective condition. *Tavaris* . *Horstman,* 542 P2d 1275 (Wyo. 1975); *Calvera* v. *Green Springs Inc.,* 220 So2d 414 (Fla. 1960).

3. The buyer may sue the seller–builder for damages *equal to the difference between the sale price and the actual value of the defective building.* This is the normal recourse of the buyer. *Hanavan* v. *Dye,* 4 Ill. App.3d 576, 281 NE2d 398 (1972); *Crowley* v. *Terhune,* 437 SW2d 743 (Ky. 1969).

34.10(b) Limitations of liability

Builder–sellers may, at times, attempt to disclaim liability. The documents may state that the home is sold "as is." Or there may be a clause specifically disclaiming any liability for defects. Such limitations are not favored. In general, the courts feel that unsophisticated buyers are unaware of the true meaning of the fine print. If the builder–seller truly wishes to disclaim liability for defects, he had best put this in a separate document, in big print, and have the buyer sign a receipt acknowledging that he has read the document and agrees to it.

As soon as a new rule creating liability is adopted, lawyers get to work to try to limit it. Thus, according to some courts, the new rule of builder–seller liability extends only to the first purchaser, the party who bought from the builder–seller.

> **EXAMPLE:**   Builder built a house. After completion of construction he sold it to Buyer #1 who later sold it to Buyer #2. The house developed cracks because of defective foundations. Buyer #2 repaired the cracks. He cannot sue Builder. Implied warranty liability, so far, has been applied only to sales of new houses. *Gallegos* v. *Graff,* 508 P2d 798 (Colo. 1973).

It is doubtful that this exception will survive. It is bad law. The whole idea behind the new rule was to do justice, to place the loss where it belongs. This means placing the loss on the builder–seller because it was his faulty work that caused the loss. In the above example, there is no reason why Builder should not be liable. Some courts are beginning to so hold.

REFERENCES: 8 RELJ 303 (lists decisions in 38 states as recognizing implied warranty on part of builder–seller, and 10 states as not having addressed the issue). On sales "as is" see *Century Display Co.* v. *D. R. Wagner Const. Co.,* 376 NE2d 993 (Ill. 1978); that rule does not apply to commercial buildings, see *Dawson Industries* v. *Godley Const. Co.,* 29 N.C.App. 270, 224 SE2d 266 (1976); that rule applies to sale of condo unit, *see Tassan* v. *United Dev. Co.,* 88 Ill. App. 3d 581, 410 NE2d 902 (1980) and to sale of co-op; *Suarez* v. *Rivercross Tenants Corp.,* 438 N.Y.S.2d 164 (1981), and to sale of leasehold, *Lemlee* v. *Breedon,* 462 P2d 470 (Hawaii 1969); as to effect of disclaimer of liability see *Herbly* v. *Dunbar Bldg. Corp.,* 415 NE2d 1224 (Ill. App. 1980); that it extends to a second purchaser for a reasonable time, see *Terlinde* v. *Neely,* 271 SE2d 768 (S.C. 1980) and *Moxley* v. *Laramie Builders,* 600 P2d 733 (Wyo. 1979); *Elden* v. *Sommers,* 631

P2d 739 (Okla. 1981); *Hermes* v. *Staino,* 437 A2d 925 (NJ 1981); *Blagg* v. *Fred Hunt Co.* 612 SW2d 321 (Ark 1981); *Park* v. *Sohn,* 89 Ill.2d 453 (1982); 10 ALR 4th 385.

34.11 Products liability

The idea of *products liability* arose in the sale of chattels.

> **EXAMPLE:** Buick Motor Company manufactured a defective automobile. This was sold to its dealer, who sold it to *X. X* suffered injuries owing to the defects and recovered damages from Buick. *MacPherson* v. *Buick Motor Co.,* 217 N.Y. 382, 111 NE 1050 (1916).

Prior to this time, a person could sue only the person who sold him a defective product, for example, the car dealer. Now it is possible to sue the manufacturer. In its modern version as expressed in some decisions, products liability does not require the injured party to prove carelessness in manufacture. All that is needed is to show that the product was defective and that *bodily injury* resulted. The philosophy is that the manufacturer is better able to stand the loss than the injured party. He can raise his prices or take out insurance against such risks. *Greenman* v. *Yuba Power Products Inc.,* 59 Cal. 2d 57, 377 P2d 897 (1963); 76 Yale L. J. 887.

This view is beginning to appear in real estate law.

> **EXAMPLE:** Builder erected a home that had a defective hot water system. The home was sold to Buyer, who rented it to Tenant. Tenant's son was scalded. Builder was held liable. *Schipper* v. *Levitt & Sons, Inc.,* 44 N.J. 70, 207 A2d 314 (1965), noted in 51 Cornell L. Q. 389; 19 Okla. L. Rev. 417; 41 Wash. L. Rev. 166.

This liability extends only to those "in the business" of building. It would not apply to a homeowner selling his own home. 21 Hastings L. J. 483.

One important aspect of this products liability is that it extends beyond the *first purchaser* of the house. *Cooper* v. *Cordova Sand & Gravel Co., Inc.,* 485 SW2d 261 (Tenn. 1972).

> **EXAMPLE:** Builder built a house and sold it to Buyer #1 who later sold it to Buyer #2 whose infant son was injured because of defective construction. Builder is liable. *Wright* v. *Creative Corp.,* 498 P2d 1179 (Colo. 1972).

34.12 FHA and VA warranties

There are laws allowing FHA and VA to compensate buyers if their new homes develop certain structural defects. These agencies may correct the defect, pay the homeowner to have it corrected, or acquire the building by buying it from the owner. FHA and VA require the buyer to file his claim within eighteen months of purchase. See sections 518(a) and 509(c) of the National

Housing Act of 1949 as amended in 1964 and 1977, also § 1827, Title 28 USCA (as to VA). For some unexplained reason, there is little publicity about and little use of these programs.

Where new residential construction is approved for HUD mortgage insurance prior to the beginning of construction, the builder is required to deliver to the purchaser a warranty that construction was carried out in accordance with the plans and specifications. 12 USC 1701j-1. While technically this is not the same as the responsibility the courts have placed upon builder–sellers, many defects occur because of the builder's noncompliance with the plans and specifications.

> **EXAMPLE:** A foundation may crack because it was installed over ground that did not meet the compaction requirements of the specifications or because concrete of a lesser grade than required in the specifications was used. Furthermore, specifications usually require that work be done in a workmanlike manner.

VA has an almost identical warranty.

Both warranties are good for one year from date of completion.

34.13 Warranties of used homes

The National Association of Realtors has a nationwide program of warranties issued in connection with the sale of used homes. Other organizations also offer warranties. Cost of the coverage, usually borne by the seller, ranges from $65 to $450. Most plans call for an inspection by the warrantor. Items covered usually include central heating and cooling systems, interior plumbing, electrical systems, roof, walls, ceilings, water heaters and softeners, and built-in appliances. Obviously, a buyer who wants such a warranty should require the contract of sale to specify it.

34.14 VA warranties

The VA has requirements for warranties of good construction if it is to insure the mortgage loan. These requirements are:

1. An insurance-backed warranty for one year against defects caused by poor materials or workmanship.
2. A similar warranty for the first two years against faulty electrical, plumbing, and heating and cooling systems.
3. Direct insurance coverage for years three through ten against structural defects.
4. A system for handling disputes with builders and, if necessary, arbitration arranged by the American Arbitration Association or a similar group.

34.15 Seller's warranties

Of course, one frequently encounters warranties by the seller of a used home. Often they relate to the heating, air conditioning, electrical, water, and drainage systems. Often they are placed in the contract of sale. If so, they survive the closing of the deal. They are not *merged* into the deed. *Rouse* v. *Brooks,* 66 Ill. App.3d 107, 383 NE2d 666 (1979). The better practice is to repeat them in the deed.

34.16 Broker's warranties of used homes

Some big brokerage firms (Century 21 Real Estate Corporation, for example) provide warranties where a home is sold by one of their brokers.

34.17 Consumer product warranties

Typically, a builder incorporates into his structure various items that fall under "consumer products" as defined by the Magnuson–Moss Warranty Act. 15 USC § 2301 *et seq.* Because of this new law, he must, prior to the sale of any consumer product that is covered by a warranty, fully, conspicuously, and understandably disclose the terms of the warranty and whether it is "full" or "limited" in terms of its duration. 15 USC §§ 2302, 2303. The Federal Trade Commission has taken the position that the act applies to separate items of equipment attached to real property whether or not they are fixtures under state law. The key to understanding the separateness test lies in the distinction between the physical separateness of an item and the separate function of that item.

> **EXAMPLE:** A furnace has a mechanical, thermal, or electrical function apart from the realty, whereas roofing shingles have no function apart from the realty. When sold by a builder to a home buyer as part of the home, the furnace is covered by the act and the shingles are not.

Using this test the FTC has decided that the following consumer products are covered by the act when they are sold as part of a home: boiler, heat pump, electronic air cleaner, exhaust fan, thermostat, space heater, furnace, air conditioning system, humidifier, central vacuum system, smoke detector, fire alarms, fire extinguisher, garage door opener, chimes, water pump, intercom, burglar alarm, electric meter, water meter, gas meter, gas or electric barbecue grill, whirlpool bath, garbage disposal, water heater, water softener, sump pump, refrigerator, freezer, trash compactor, range, oven, dishwasher, oven hood, clothes washer, clothes dryer, ice maker.

Using the same test, the FTC has found that the following are not consumer products when sold as part of a home: radiator, convector, register, duct, cabinet, door, shelving, windows, floor covering, walls or wall covering, ceiling, vanity, gutter, shingles, chimney and fireplace, fencing, garage door, electrical switch and outlet, light fixture, electric panel box, fuse, circuit breaker, wiring, sprinkler head, water closet, bidet, lavatory, bathtub, laundry tray, sink, shower stall, plumbing fittings, medicine cabinet.

A last category or group contains separate items or equipment, which are consumer products under the act when sold as part of a condominium, cooperative, or multiple family dwelling because they are not normally used for personal family or household purposes within the meaning of the act: fusible fire door closer, TV security monitor, emergency backup generator, master TV antenna, elevator, institutional trash compactor. FTC advisory opinion 12/17/76, *CCH Trade Regulation Reports,* par. 21245.

Even though the builder does not make these pieces of equipment himself, he is nonetheless bound by the disclosure sections of the act because he is a "supplier" under the terms of the act. 15 USC § 2301(4).

The builder can comply with the terms of the law by clearly and conspicuously displaying the text or a quote of the text of the written warranty covering the consumer product in close conjunction to each warranted product; or by maintaining in each of the seller's locations an indexed binder containing copies of all warranties on consumer products; or, if the warranty text is printed on the product box, by displaying the package.

> **EXAMPLE:** When the builder incorporates into his structure dishwashers, disposals, ranges, refrigerators, and range hoods he should either display next to, or taped onto, the appliances, copies of the warranties given by the manufacturer of those applicances or keep in his model office a binder which contains those warranties. This binder should be displayed in a conspicuous place and potential buyers should be afforded the opportunity to review its contents prior to the sale. The builder should make similar disclosure of his own warranty if that warranty covers the consumer products.

> *REFERENCE:* Peters, *How the Magnuson–Moss Warranty Act Affects the Builders/Seller of New Housing,* 5 R.E.L.J. 338 (1977).

34.18 Code violations   In every contract to build, it is implied that the building will be constructed in conformity with all laws and ordinances. It is rather universally required that a building permit be issued by the city before construction is begun, and before such a permit is issued, the plans and specifications will be examined by the city to see if the building planned complies with all ordinances. However, after the permit is issued, the builder may nevertheless (either willfully in order to cut costs, or through ignorance or negligence) violate ordinances in the process of erecting the building. If the building as constructed violates laws or ordinances, the builder will be compelled to allow his buyer as an abatement or deduction from the contract price a sum adequate to remedy the defects. *Schiro* v. *W. E. Gould & Co.,* 18 Ill.2d 538, 165 NE2d 286, 49 Ill. B.J. 209 (1960). Or if the buyer discovers the ordinance violations after he has paid the entire contract price, he may sue the builder for damages. *Gutowski* v. *Crystal Homes, Inc.,* 26 Ill. App.2d 269, 167 NE2d 422 (1960); *Brunke* v. *Pharo,* 3 Wis.2d 628, 89 NW2d 221 (1958). Ordinance violations may also render title unmarketable. Advertising for sale a building that contains ordinance violations may constitute a fraud upon the buyer.

All of these legal remedies may be rather poor comfort to the landowner. If the building contains serious violations of ordinances, the city may refuse to permit the owner to occupy his building. It may compel demolition of the building. It may fine the landowner, and the fine may be very substantial.

34.19   Suggestions

1. Before starting construction, the builder should give thought to the mechanic's lien problem. Before he can collect any money on his contract, he will often be called upon to furnish a sworn statement showing all subcontractors and their contract prices. As he hires his subcontractors, he should make memoranda from which this affidavit can later be prepared.

2. The builder should also make arrangements to prove what work and materials are going into the building. If the builder is not paid and must establish a mechanic's lien claim against the premises, he must be able to prove in court (perhaps a year or so later) by truck drivers' tickets or other direct evidence of some witness present at the time, what materials were delivered to the building site and incorporated in the building.

3. Before starting construction, the builder should provide himself with all necessary insurance as to fire, casualty, and liability.

4. Before starting, the builder should also take whatever steps are necessary to shore up his neighbor's building or to notify the neighbor to attend to this. My neighbor has the right to have my land support his *land* in its natural condition, so that if both tracts are vacant, if I excavate near the line, and his soil falls into the excavation, I become liable to him for damages. However, if he erects buildings on his land, he has no right to have my soil support his *buildings.* But if I propose to excavate, I should notify my neighbor of my plans in good time, so that *he* may shore up and take other precautions to protect *his building.* Then if I proceed to excavate with due care, I will not be liable if his building tilts or collapses into my excavation if such fall is due to the weight and pressure of the building. Although I am not obligated, in the absence of a city ordinance, to support my neighbor's building, I may be liable to him for damage caused to his building by my excavation if the excavating is done without proper care. Failure to exercise proper care exists in the following situations: (a) where I fail to notify my neighbor of my intention to excavate, thus giving him no opportunity to protect his property; (b) where I notify my neighbor of my intention to excavate, but my excavation is deeper than, or different from, the excavation described in my notice; (c) where I leave my excavation open for a long period of time; (d) where I open the entire excavation at one time when it would have been possible and safer to dig in sections, as where the soil consists of sand, gravel, or loam; (e) where I allow water to collect in my excavation, and seepage of the water causes my neighbor's building to fall (*Horowitz* v. *Blay,* 193 Mich. 493, 160 NW 438); (f) where I allow water and silt from my neighbor's land to collect in my excavation, thereby withdrawing support from his buildings, which then fall (*New York Central* v. *Marinucci Bros.,* 337 Mass. 469, 149 NE2d 680; 50 ALR 486). In many cities, ordinances have been passed that impose on an excavator a qualified duty to support adjoining buildings. A specified notice (ten days is common) of any intended excavation must be given the adjoining owner, and he is given a right of access to the excavation for the purpose of protecting his building. If the excavation is less than a specified depth (nine, ten, and twelve feet are common) and it becomes necessary for the adjoining owner to extend his foundation downward, he must do so at his own expense. But the cost of extending the foundation below the specified depth is borne by the excavator. Ordinances of this type are common throughout the South and on the Pacific Coast. All code requirements for the construction of protective coverings over sidewalks, for fences surrounding the excavation, for shoring up sidewalks and streets, and so on should be complied with.

5. Before starting on construction, the builder should procure a survey showing the ex-

act boundaries of the premises with the corners plainly marked. He should thereupon recheck the applicable setback ordinances and the provisions of all plot and deed restrictions. The building must comply with both public and private restrictions. He should especially watch for building line violations.

A building contract may contain the following provisions designed to protect the landowner against mechanic's liens:

1. A requirement that the building be completed free and clear of all mechanic's and materialmen's liens.

2. A clause waiving all mechanic's and materialmen's liens, both of the general contractor and all subcontractors and materialmen. If the state law requires a contract such as this to be recorded, the contract should be duly acknowledged (in order to qualify it for recording) and recorded.

3. A requirement that the contractor hold the landowner harmless against all mechanic's liens and mechanic's lien litigation.

4. A requirement that the landowner, his architect, and mortgage lender be furnished all contractors' statements, subcontractors' statements, partial waivers, and waivers of lien as construction goes forward according to the progress payments schedule.

5. A provision that subcontractors will be paid directly by the landowner or his mortgage lender, not by the general contractor.

6. A provision for a holdback of a percentage of all payments to the general contractor until a specified period of time has elapsed after completion of the building. This gives the landowner leverage to compel the general contractor to correct defective work without asserting any lien claim.

7. A provision that progress payments will be made only as a specified architect certifies that the work is in place and is satisfactory. The timing of the progress payments should coincide with the timing in the construction loan agreement.

With respect to the construction contract the following observations are pertinent:

1. Let the construction contract specifically provide at what stages payments are to be made, in what amounts, and how much is to be held back from each payment by the owner to insure correction of faulty work.

2. For the protection of all parties, let the construction contract provide what supervision the architect will provide, which should dovetail into the architect's contract with the owner; what drawings the architect will provide the builder; what authority the architect has to give orders to the builder; how such orders are to be given (whether verbally or in writing), and so on.

3. Where there is a supervising architect, be sure that the construction contract provides that no payments will be made except on the production of architect's certificates that the builder is entitled to receive payment and that the work done qualifies for payment both as to quality and quantity.

4. The contract should specify that the supervising architect has authority to order the contractor to correct work that was not performed in a proper manner according to the plans.

5. To prevent controversy, let the construction contract provide that final payment and acceptance by the owner will not bar any claims for latent defects.

6. Many construction contracts provide that the building is to be completed in a specified time and that the builder shall pay specified sums for delay beyond the specified completion time, except where such delays are caused by strikes, bad weather, and so forth.

7. Building contracts should provide that the builder be obligated to protect the landowner against liability to adjoining owners, members of the public, and employees and subcontractors, and also to take out insurance policies to protect against such liabilities.

REFERENCES: 23 St. Louis U. L. J. 205 (1979) (symposium on construction contracts); 8 Forum 210 (1972) (construction management); 6 U. of Mich. J. L. Reform 447 (construction management); 90 ALR3d 507 (design defects); 58 Iowa L. Rev. 1221 (design defects); 45 U.M. K.C.L. Rev. 75 (design defects); 62 ALR3d 208 (subcontractor's recovery against landowner).

REFERENCES ON SUBCONTRACTORS' BIDS: 18 Maine L. Rev. 297; 43 Marq. L. Rev. 384; 18 UCLA Rev. 389; 37 U. Cin. L. Rev. 798; 19 U. Chgo. L. Rev. 237; 10 Wm. & Mary L. Rev. 212; 9 Rutgers Camden L. J. 387; 48 Miss. L. J. 883; 13 John Marsh. L. Rev. 565 (1980)

---

35 REHAB

35.01 In general
There is a national enthusiasm for buying old buildings and restoring them to their former glory, but with modern plumbing, heating, and electricity. Rehabilitation of older buildings is occurring both to residential and commercial structures. These buildings are typically closer to the core of the city where cultural and business activity is centered. The aesthetic and economic advantages are a powerful draw to this form of real estate.

If the structure has a strong shell, as is typical with older brick or stone structures, i.e., Georgetown row houses, the costs of acquisition and rehabilitation may be considerably less than the cost of new construction. When the income tax treatment of rehab expenses and favorable loan terms is considered, the economics of rehabilitation are even more attractive.

35.02 Appraisals
Increasingly, as home values skyrocket, professional appraisals are required by lending institutions. Appraisers have a number of professional organizations. One is the American Institute of Real Estate Appraisers, affiliated with the National Association of Realtors. It confers the prestigious title Member Appraisal Institute (MAI). There is also the American Society of Appraisers and the Society of Real Estate Appraisers.

The role of the appraiser in large construction is well understood. But a great expansion in the use of appraising is taking place as the rehab process continues to assume increasing importance in home renovation. Among other things, the appraiser will consider: an economic analysis of the neighborhood; street patterns and the width of streets; convenience to public transportation; the availability of stores and service establishments; community or neighborhood organizations; density of population; degree of home ownership; rent and income levels; and zoning, building codes, and other regulations restricting design or use.

35.03 Architect's role

The architect has an indispensable role in the rehab process. His first step is to conduct a feasibility study and provide a realistic estimate of the cost of the rehab, including the cost of bringing the structure into compliance with current building codes. These estimates are based upon actual costs of the same or similar work performed on similar structures and can only be made after a complete detail of exactly what construction work is to be done has been made.

The architect will also help you find a reliable contractor. They are scarce. Then loan funds will be disbursed by the lender to the contractor on his production of the architect's approval of the work done and waivers of mechanic's liens by trades involved in the work.

35.04 Building codes

Although building codes are intended primarily for new construction, they are also applied to rehabilitation projects through two widely used regulatory "trigger mechanisms"— the "25/50 percent rule" and change of occupancy requirements. These are called trigger mechanisms because they "trigger" new construction code requirements onto a rehabilitation project.

The 25/50 percent rule, usually one of the administrative requirements of a typical building code, requires that when the cost of the rehabilitation work to be done exceeds a stated percentage (usually 50 percent) of the value of the building (which, for many urban buildings, may be very low), the entire building must then be brought up to new construction code requirements.

Since most U.S. buildings no longer meet new construction oriented codes (because the requirements in those building codes generally have been increased over time) the imposition of the 25/50 percent rule can and does add costs to the rehabilitation project.

The change of occupancy requirement, also usually one of the administrative requirements contained in a typical building code, states that when the occupancy of a building is changed, then the entire building must be brought up to the new construction requirements contained in the building code. An occupancy change, for example, could involve the conversion of a large, old single-family residence into a multifamily residence, a care facility, or a retail store.

NEW DIRECTIONS: Several cities have enacted revised building ordinances that have taken some of the rigidity out of the old codes that were primarily enacted to control new construction. These new rehab codes are often written in simplified language understandable to the layman and provide for the creation of a board to grant exceptions from code requirements if the rehabber's proposal will be equal to or better than the code requires.

35.05 The contractor Getting a reliable contractor is a must on any substantial rehab job. The National Home Improvement Council, 11 E. 44th Street, New York, N.Y. 10017, will give you a list of their members. There are local branches, like the Professional Remodelers Assn., 20 E. Delaware, Chicago, Ill., who can give an up-to-date list of local members. Membership provides a measure of assurance of honesty and competence. Checking with the local Better Business Bureau also helps. Checking with customers who have had recent work done is a must. Your bank or thrift institution that will finance the work is a good source of names. Your lawyer will check to see that your contractor is licensed, if local law requires. Some states have good regulations.

> **EXAMPLE:** The California licensing law requires a home improvement contractor to pass an exam and pay a license fee of $2,000. If two complaints are lodged against a contractor he loses his license. Nevada, Arizona, Oklahoma, Florida, Virginia, Michigan, and other states have licensing laws.

Of course, if you are hiring an architect he is sure to know the reliable contractors.

35.06 Contractor's bonds Bonding companies write bonds insuring that the contractor will complete the job. However, most small contractors are not bondable. Incidentally, if you ask the contractor if he can get a bond, and he answers affirmatively, get the bond even if you must pay for it yourself. As discussed elsewhere, you really get two bonds for the price of one.

35.07 The job contract When you are ordering a job done, it is best to put as much detail as you can into the contract. Of course, architects do this routinely. But many jobs will be ordered by you alone. It is customary to state the number of inches of crushed stone, the name and model of the faucet, the catalogue number of the chandelier, etc. State that all work must conform to the building code and will be redone at contractor's expense if the city inspector orders it redone, as occasionally happens. State that before commencement, the contractor will furnish you satisfactory proof that he has workmen's compensation and public liability insurance and is a licensed contractor. Manufacturers and dealers often furnish product warranties. Ask the contractor to list all warranties he expects to receive and list these as items to be delivered at completion of job.

35.08 Payment Many contractors ask for a down payment. If you have checked the contractor's references and they are satisfactory, you can agree to pay him a small amount down, say 15 percent. He gets credit from suppliers but will need to pay wages to his workmen. On bigger jobs a final payment on the order of 15 percent will be made after completion of the job. The difference is often paid as the job goes forward.

35.09 Lien waivers

As work is done, the trades expect to be paid. An architect or other job supervisor checks the job first. He determines that the work has been done properly and in accordance with the contract and specifications, also how much money each trade is entitled to. Normally, the contract calls for holdbacks or retentions. *Holiday Develop. Co., & J. A. Tobin Const. Co.,* 549 P2d 1376 (Kans. 1976); 107 ALR 960; 54 ALR3d 848. A common retention is 10 percent of the amount due. As each trade is paid, a mechanic's lien waiver is demanded for the work done. When a trade completes its work, a final mechanic's lien waiver is demanded.

35.10 Bid and specification analysis

The building inspector may undertake to review the bids if you have no architect. This is important. A subcontractor is not required to do anything other than what his bid, including the specifications, requires him to do. Analyzing specifications for completeness is important.

35.11 Permits

Some fly-by-night contractors never obtain building permits. This may lead to heavy fines if this is discovered by the Building Department. An architect will not permit work to begin until he has verified that proper permits were obtained.

35.12 Rehab supervision

If you do not plan to have the rehab work supervised by an architect, you may be able to hire a building inspector to do the job. Some inspectors will even give estimates of job cost, which can be used to check the general contractor's bid. Of course, a general contractor undertakes in his contract to supervise the work of the subcontractors.

35.13 Insurance

On a substantial job, talk to an insurance agent. He may recommend that the job be covered by special insurance ("builder's risk"). At completion, your home insurance should be increased to cover the value added by the job.

35.14 Loans

Many lenders advance the funds only after the rehab job has been completed. FHA insurance may be obtained for rehab loans before the job begins. Long-term low-interest loans may also be available under various government programs.

Bear in mind that the rehab lender who finances the job has several risks to weigh, namely: (1) The value of the building as is. (2) The value to be added by the rehab job. (3) The ability of the contractor to do the job properly.

It may be possible to get a loan commitment that will become effective when and if the rehab job has been completed. Then obtain a short-term loan from a rehab lender, who will rely on the other loan commitment for ultimate payment. The rehab lender will then make periodic inspections so that he is satisfied with the progress and get proper mechanic's lien waivers at each stage of the job.

The giant purchasers of mortgages, FNMA, and FHLMC, have announced a program and prepared a required mortgage form for rehab loans. Randolph, *The FNMA/FHLMC Uniform Home Improvement Loan Instruments: A Commentary and Critique*, 16 A.B.A. Real Ppty., Prob. & Tr. J. 546 (1981). This informative article explains all the legal and practical ramifications of these instruments. It is must reading, since all mortgage lenders will wish to tailor their loans so that they are available for sale in the secondary market.

35.15 Income tax considerations

As with most areas of real estate practice, income tax considerations play a role in the investment decision. Rehabilitation is no exception. The tax benefits here are especially attractive because they result in an income tax credit or a deduction from the taxes due to the government as opposed to a deduction from income.

The Economic Recovery Tax Act of 1981 broadened the benefits available with the rehabilitation tax credit. This credit now comes in three levels. A credit is given for 15 percent of the cost of rehabbing a structure that is thirty to thirty-nine-years-old. The credit increases to 20 percent of the rehab expenses for buildings forty-years-old or older and to 25 percent for *certified historic structures*. The credit is not available for the rehab expenses of single family or multifamily residential structures unless they are certified historic structures.

Another requirement to qualify a rehab job for income tax purposes is that twenty years must have elapsed between the present rehab work and the last rehab job. If an income tax credit was allowed on a rehab job within the last twenty years, it will not be allowed on a current rehab job. Obviously, you must check to see if rehab expenditures were made within the last twenty years.

REFERENCES: *Rehab Know-How Is: More than Hammer and Nails* (free pamphlet issued by American Institute of Real Estate Appraisers, 430 No. Michigan Avenue, Chicago, Ill. 60611).

---

36 MOBILE HOMES

36.01 The mobile home contrasted with the stick-built home

Massachusetts Institute of Technology has called the mobile home industry "the most efficient building industry in the world." Bernhardt, *Building Tomorrow* (1978). The industry has the capacity to produce low-cost high-quality shelter that complies with strict federal standards. Most mobile homes are sold fully equipped with major appliances, furniture, draperies, lamps, and carpeting all included in the purchase price. Optional features include air conditioning, dishwasher, disposals, and other items typically found in a modern home. Warranties on components are available.

By federal law, the "mobile home" is now referred to as a "manufactured home."

36.02 Chattel aspects

A manufactured home resting on land owned by one other than the homeowner has often been, for that reason, deemed to remain a chattel. *Farmers Union Mut. Ins. Co.* v. *Denniston*, 376 SW2d 252 (Ark. 1964); *In re Estate of Horton*, 606 SW2d 792 (Mo. App. 1980). This is in keeping with rule-of-fixture law generally that a chattel placed on land owned by a third person remains a chattel, since it would be unrealistic to attribute to the homeowner an intention to make the home the property of the landowner.

36.03 Fixture aspects

On the other hand, a home owned by *A* and placed by him on land owned by him is a fixture and is part of the land. Normally, the intention to make the home a fixture is revealed by the removal of wheels, the attachment of the home to a permanent foundation, and the use of permanent utility connections. *George* v. *Commercial Credit Corp.*, 440 F2d 551 (7th Cir. 1971); *Bell* v. *City of Corbin City*, 395 A2d 546 (N.J. 1978); *State* v. *Work*, 449 P2d 806 (Wash. 1969).

36.04 Federal controls The construction of manufactured homes is now controlled by the federal government under the National Mobile Home Construction and Safety Standards Act, 42 USC §§ 5401, *et seq.* 24 CFR Part 280 *et seq.* This code is promulgated by HUD, but it varies throughout the country to meet geographic conditions. Elaborate federal safety factors are set forth. Inconsistent state laws and ordinances are ineffective. Each home is inspected at the factory where a plate is installed showing that the home complies with federal law.

36.05 Mortgage sources In 1981 Candlewick Glen, a 42-unit manufactured housing subdivision in the Tacoma, Washington, area was approved by FNMA. These homes will be sold as a package, land and building, in the same way homes are sold in a stick-built development. Financing was with twenty-nine-year mortgages, 5 percent down payment. In the Phoenix area, Sun Lakes, a $75,000,000 planned community of manufactured homes, has an identical format. This is the wave of the future. Inflation, the slump in building construction, and the population increase combine to push home prices up each year. Move the manufactured home into a typical land development and you have a salable commodity at reasonable prices.

On the home-and-land type of deal, traditional mortgage financing is also available, for example, from a savings and loan association, which will loan up to 90 percent of the total cost of land, home, setup charges, sales tax, etc. FHA and VA loans are available. The mortgages are sold in the secondary market to GNMA and FNMA. These loans, in turn, are pooled, securities issued against the pool, and sold to investors.

36.06 Furniture Traditionally, mobile homes were sold complete with furniture, carpeting, draperies, etc. Furniture, of course, is personal property. Where this practice is followed, and the home and lot are sold and financed as real estate, a chattel filing under the UCC will accompany the mortgage. The practice is less prevalent today than formerly.

36.07 Warranties A warranty is now obtainable on the purchase of a mobile home in much the same manner that the HOW warranty operates. The corporation issuing the warranty is Housing Warranty Corporation (HWC). HWC enrolls manufacturers, in contrast to HOW, which signs up builders.

36.08 Building restrictions The areas of manufactured housing law that have given rise to much litigation involve building restrictions and zoning. Initially, it should be noted that many of these cases involve an isolated home placed on a lot in a community of stick-built homes. This is a situation calculated to provoke litigation. It is improbable that the new manufactured housing developments will trigger any great volume of litigation.

Many older restrictions prohibit "trailers." Often the litigated case lacks an adequate description of the type of structure involved. It cannot be determined, for example, if the modern double-wide home was involved.

At any rate, there are decisions to the effect that a manufactured home of one kind or another cannot be erected where the restrictions prohibit *trailers.*

The more modern, better-reasoned decisions hold that a typical manufactured home constructed on the owner's land does not violate a restriction forbidding trailers. *Hussey* v. *Ray,* 462 SW2d 45 (Tex. 1970); *In re Willey,* 120 Vt. 359, 140 A2d 11 (1958); *Manley* v. *Draper,* 44 Misc. 2d 613, 254 N.Y.S.2d 739 (1963); *North Cherokee Village* v. *Murphy,* 248 NW2d 629 (Mich. App. 1977); *Morin* v. *Zoning Board,* 102 R.I. 457, 232 A2d 393 (1967); *Douglas Twp.* v. *Badman,* 206 Pa. Super. 390, 213 A2d 88 (1965); *Heath* v. *Parker,* 93 N.M. 680, 604 P2d 818 (1980). The last case is significant. It is recent. The home involved a structure containing three bedrooms, two full baths, 1,440 square feet of floor space, a patio, a 200-square-foot porch, a 672-square-foot two-car garage. The court commented on the fact that this structure was more handsome and more livable than many stick-built homes. This is obviously the way court decisions will tend. The restrictions using the word "trailer" were framed in an older time, when the double-wide was unknown. The federal government now by law refers to these structures as manufactured housing.

36.09   Zoning

The zoning decisions are numerous and conflicting.

First of all, there are decisions holding that it is a violation of constitutional law to attempt, directly or indirectly, to bar a poor person's access to the suburbs by excluding manufactured housing. *Meyers* v. *Board of Supervisors,* 394 A2d 669 (Pa. 1978). The great leading case on this point is *Robinson Twp.* v. *Knoll,* 410 Mich. 293, 302 NW2d 146 (1980). In that case a township zoning ordinance attempted to exclude mobile homes except in mobile home parks. The court held this aspect of the ordinance was invalid. The court pointed out that manufactured housing has undergone drastic change and improvement since the days of "trailers"; that many mobile homes compare favorably in appearance with stick-built homes; that so far as plumbing and other health factors are concerned, mobile homes compare favorably with stick-built homes; that Vermont by statute forbids discrimination against mobile homes. There was a dissenting opinion that cited cases from Alabama, California, Colorado, Connecticut, Florida, Illinois, Kansas, Maine, Massachusetts, Minnesota, Missouri, New Hampshire, New Jersey, North Carolina, Ohio, Pennsylvania, Tennessee, Washington, and Wisconsin, all, the dissent stated, sustaining ordinances that excluded mobile homes.

Some comment is appropriate. (1) Michigan is considered a conservative state. Nevertheless, it came down on the side of manufactured housing even though this required the court to overrule prior Michigan law and to deal with a strong dissent. (2) The decisions cited by the dissent are not particularly persuasive. Many were decided before the current housing shortgage. The dissent was surely making a frightful mistake in citing California, New Jersey, and Pennsylvania, which have come down hard in favor of manufactured housing. (3) Studies show that the only detached home 90 percent of American families can afford is a mobile home. (4) The federal government with its building codes virtually guarantees a minimum standard of quality in mobile home construction whereas the figures on HOW warranties and the litigated cases on defective homes reveal that there is still a great deal of poor stick-built construction going on.

The federal government's views strongly affect state decisions. 55 N. C. L. Rev. 1289, 1305.

The authors feel that within the next decade the Michigan view will be the prevailing view in this country. At least one authority feels that states will step in with *state laws,* as has taken place in California, to invalidate *city ordinances* that exclude manufactured housing. 55 Cornell L. Rev. 491, 514. The subject is discussed in 54 Am.Jur.2d *Mobile Homes* §13.

Second, the particular tract of land may be such that a zoning ordinance barring manufactured housing would be invalid as applied. Such homes might provide the only reasonable use for the land. *Czech* v. *City of Blaine,* 253 NW2d 272 (Minn. 1977).

36.10   Exclusionary laws and ordinances

The suburbs are quite generally hostile to the introduction of manufactured housing. Most of their exclusionary ordinances are illegal.

EXAMPLE: An ordinance limiting manufactured housing developments to four new units per year was discriminatory and void where stick-built homes were not so limited. *Begin* v. *Inhabitants of Sabaltus,* 409 A2d 1269 (Maine 1980).

36.11   Antitrust

Park owners have, at times, enacted rules barring homeowners where the home was not purchased from the park owner. This is called a *closed park.* Probably this is a *tie-in sale,* illegal under the antitrust law.

36.12   Taxes

In past times, manufactured homes were taxed as motor vehicles or personal property. 71 Yale L. J. 71, 705. Nine states place a use tax on mobile homes. 21 DePaul L. Rev. 1008, 1011. Some states levy a license fee. *Ibid.* Where the landowner owns the home, it is often taxed as real estate. 21 DePaul L. Rev., 1008, 1012. Any discussion of this problem seems pointless at this time. If manufactured housing goes into land developments where land and home are sold as a unit, these must be taxed as real estate. See 7 ALR 4th 1016.

36.13 Future of mobile homes

One can discuss the future of this industry only if old prejudices can be put aside. Certain facts are so clearly evident that to dispute them would be foolhardy. Inflation is here to stay. This is an unwelcome but obvious fact. Factory built homes are much less expensive than stick-built homes. Stick-built homes vary in quality of construction. The home builders, with their warranty program, will unquestionably improve the quality of the stick-built home. But the mobile home already has a substantial degree of quality control imposed by federal regulation. The hazard insurance program is at least equal in quality to that offered on stick-built homes. The Federal Trade Commission, at present, seems determined to prove that the mobile home warranty program needs improvement. The evidence does not appear to support this contention. The industry "can produce the full range of housing types available in conventional markets, equalling or exceeding them in design quality, function and cost performance." Bernhardt, *Building Tomorrow* (1980).

At all events, mobile homes are substantially more affordable than stick-built homes. The energy crisis will continue indefinitely. It will compel production of more energy-efficient homes. The federal code makes it possible to accomplish this at a national level simply and efficiently. The present patchwork of federal and state tax incentives for stick-built energy-efficient homes is so inefficient that income tax returns show few people are taking advantage of the incentives. Energy-saving techniques have proved visionary, inefficient, or even dangerous as regards the stick-built home. All this seems to assure the future of the mobile home. To be sure, the well-to-do will always enjoy luxury, stick-built homes. But even for the middle class, the typical home will shrink in size.

37 LANDLORD AND TENANT

37.01 In general   In the centuries following the Battle of Hastings (1066), when William the Conqueror crushed the English armies and became king of England, the feudal system of real estate law that prevailed in a large part of continental Europe became part of the English way of life. Its intricacies are a twice-told tale and need not be repeated here. We must, however, look at the bottom rung of the social and economic ladder. Here we find the landlord renting a small farm to a tenant. Rent was often paid in the form of a share of the crops. Indeed, sharecropping still exists, though on a small scale. The house in which the tenant lived was a primitive structure. The tenant worked with primitive tools. He was a jack-of-all-trades and could repair almost any defect in house or tools. In 1588 England defeated the Spanish Armada; its ships began their long rule of the oceans of the world, and England became a trading nation. The formation of modern trading law (contract law) began. But in the meantime, the law of landlord and tenant had been formed. Basically, it was prolandlord law. The tenant took the premises as he found them, and the landlord had no obligation of repair.

Then, as time moved on, the Industrial Revolution changed the face of England. Many men worked in factories. Such a worker was not a jack-of-all-trades. Tenement buildings, the predecessor of the modern apartment, began to appear as cities grew up around the factories. Still, the courts applied the old agricultural landlord and tenant law to the new state of affairs. Beginning about 1970 the courts began to reexamine their thinking. *Javins* v. *First National Realty Corp.,* 428 F2d 1071, *cert. den.* 400 U.S. 925 (1970). Several things became evident. The tenant, since he was not a jack-of-all-trades, lacked the skill to make repairs. Repairs, by and large, were beyond the means of the low-income tenant. Obviously, no bank would loan the low-income tenant money to make repairs. The defect might spring up in an area of the apartment to which the tenant had no access.

Modern courts made a 180-degree turn in their thinking on the law applicable to residential renting. They began to regard the renting of an apartment basically as a contract for the furnishing of services, including the service of maintaining the structure in a habitable condition, free from building code violations. This development made all of the flexibility that is characteristic of modern contract law available to the courts. This change of thought is surely the law of most states even though some state courts have not had the opportunity to so hold.

Meanwhile, the law relating to stores, industrial plants, and commercial leasing remained as it had been. Tenants of these structures had the sophistication to protect themselves. Much of the noncontroversial law relating to residential leasing also remained unchanged.

37.02 Leases and periodic tenancies

The relationship of landlord and tenant may exist by virtue of a formal, written *lease* or of a periodic tenancy, such as a *tenancy from month to month*.

EXAMPLE: Tenant sees an "apartment for rent" sign on a building, goes in, makes a verbal arrangement with the owner for the rental of an apartment, pays his first month's rent, and later moves in. He is a *tenant from month to month.*

EXAMPLE: Facts as above, but the landlord and tenant, instead of agreeing verbally, sign a lease for one year. Tenant is a tenant under a lease.

One important difference between leases and periodic tenancies relates to the rights and liabilities of the parties during the existence of the landlord–tenant relation. When the relation of landlord and tenant exists without a written lease, the law implies certain rights and liabilities on the part of both. In a *month-to-month tenancy,* for example, the tenant is entitled to the exclusive possession of the rented premises, and the landlord has no right to enter thereon for the purpose of making repairs. But in many leases, the parties expressly agree that the landlord shall have this right. In other words, a lease is a contract, and most of the rights and duties of the parties are governed by the provisions of the contract, whereas in a month-to-month tenancy the rights of the parties are governed by rules of law.

Another difference between a lease and a periodic tenancy relates to the termination of the tenant's right of occupancy. In the case of a lease, at the expiration date fixed in the lease, the tenant need not give notice to the landlord before moving out, nor is any notice needed by the landlord to the tenant. In the case of periodic tenancies, certain notices must be given in order to terminate the tenancy.

37.03 Tenancy from month to month

The tenancy from month to month is generally created when no definite term of letting is specified by the parties and the rent is payable monthly. This kind of tenancy is very common. A tenant who pays rent monthly and has no lease is a tenant from month to month.

A tenancy from month to month cannot be terminated except by giving notice. That is, the landlord cannot evict the tenant unless he first gives the tenant the notice required by law, and the tenant continues liable for rent unless he gives the landlord the required notice. In many states, a month's or thirty days' notice is required, but the period varies from state to state.

The notice to terminate a month-to-month tenancy must state a proper termination date, and must give the tenant the full number of days' notice to which he is entitled.

EXAMPLE: Landlord rents an apartment to Tenant on a month-to-month tenancy beginning as of the first of the next month. In the state in question a landlord must serve a thirty days' notice to terminate such a tenancy. After some months, Landlord serves a notice on November 1 terminating Tenant's tenancy as of November 30. The notice is void. It gives Tenant less than thirty days' notice. Landlord will lose the eviction suit and must serve a new and proper notice.

37.04 Tenancy from year to year

A *tenancy from year to year* is one that continues for a year and then is automatically renewed for another year and from year to year thereafter unless due notice of termination of the tenancy is given at the time and in the manner required by law for the termination of the tenancy.

While a year-to-year tenancy can be created in other ways, it most commonly is created when a lease for a year or more has expired and the tenant continues in possession paying rent, which the landlord accepts, and the parties have made no other agreement as to the character of the tenant's occupancy.

When a tenant has a lease for a year or longer, and after the lease has expired the tenant remains in possession of the premises, it is said that the tenant *holds over*. The landlord may, if he wishes, hold the tenant as a tenant from year to year. Observe that it is the landlord who may hold the tenant. The tenant cannot, by holding over, compel the landlord to extend the tenancy. The landlord may evict the tenant if he wishes to do so. But if the tenant holds over, even for one day, he becomes liable for another year's rent should the landlord wish to hold him. *Clinton Wire Cloth Co.* v. *Gardner,* 99 Ill. 151. Once the landlord accepts the rent, he also is bound to the tenancy. And once the tenancy is established neither party can terminate it in the middle of the year. And if either party wishes to end the tenancy *at the end of a yearly period,* proper notice must be served for this purpose.

In certain situations, a tenant who holds over after his lease has expired will not become a tenant from year to year.

1. Before the lease expires, the landlord notifies the tenant that if he remains in possession he will do so as a tenant from month to month. Or the landlord and tenant may specifically agree that the tenant remains as a month-to-month tenant. In either case, the new tenancy is a month-to-month tenancy.

2. The lease contains a clause that if the tenant holds over without any new agreement being reached, he does so as a month-to-month tenant. Other leases say that the lease is renewed for one year. The clause is valid.

3. Before the lease ends, the landlord and tenant negotiate for a new lease, and the negotiations are in progress when the lease ends. After the lease ends, the tenant remains in possession, paying a monthly rent. He is a month-to-month tenant. Be careful, however, for if negotiations have ceased before the lease ends, a tenant holding over will be held as a tenant from year to year.

4. Suppose that when the lease ends the tenant is so ill that his doctor forbids him to move. In some states, this will nevertheless result in the creation of a year-to-year tenancy; in other states, a year-to-year will not be created.

The rule that if a tenant holds over even one day after the expiration of his lease he becomes liable for another year's rent as a tenant from year to year is harsh, and many states have abolished or restricted it.

37.05   Tenancy at will

A tenancy at will may be terminated by either party whenever he wishes to do so.

EXAMPLE: A tenancy at will arises under an agreement that the tenant may occupy until the premises are sold or rented to a third person, until the landlord is ready to construct new buildings, until the land is required by the landlord for his own use, or whenever the letting is for an indefinite term.

37.06   Lease defined

A lease is both a contract and a conveyance. It is a conveyance by the landlord to the tenant of the right to occupy the land for the term specified in the lease. It contains a contract by the tenant to pay rent to the landlord and usually contains numerous other promises and undertakings by both landlord and tenant. The legal interest of the tenant in the land is called a *leasehold estate* or *a term for years.* It is legally considered to be personal property.

37.06(a)   Necessity of writing

In all but a few states, a lease for less than one year may be verbal, but a lease for a period longer than one year must be in writing.

37.06(b)   Requirements of lease—in general

Many states have laws that require a written lease to comply with requirements applicable to deeds.

37.06(c)   The lessor

The landowner and his or her spouse should be designated as lessors. The same reasons that make it necessary for the wife or husband of a landowner to join in a deed requires the spouse to join in a lease. *Fargo* v. *Bennett,* 35 Idaho 359, 206 Pac. 692; *Benson* v. *Dritch,* 244 SW2d 339 (Tex. 1951). As a matter of business practice, short leases such as one-year apartment leases are often made by the owner without his wife's signature, for in such situations, trouble is extremely improbable. A lessor should be of age and of sound mind. When the lease is executed by an executor or trustee, the will or other trust instrument must be examined to determine if he has power to make the lease in question. If the lessor is a corporation, the lease must be authorized by the directors or stockholders, as required by the local law.

37.06(d)   The lessee

The lessee should be of age and of sound mind. If the lessee is a trustee or executor, the will or other trust instrument must authorize him to enter into leases such as the one in question.

37.06(e)   Description of the premises

The lease must describe the leased premises with certainty. There is a tendency in short-term leases to designate the leased premises inadequately. Of course, if it is an entire building that is being rented, it is sufficient to describe it by street number, city, and state.

37.06(f)   Duration or term lease

Leases are sometimes classified as *short-term* or *long-term* leases. This has no great legal significance. With the exception of the rule that leases for more than one year must be in writing, the rules governing short-term and long-term leases are generally the same. Long-term leases often run for ninety-nine years. In some states laws have been passed limiting the duration of leases. The lease should fix the date on which the term of the lease begins and the duration of the lease. In fixing the term of the lease, it is better to avoid a description of the term as running *from* a particular day *to* another day, since a question may arise as to whether or not a lease from or to a particular day includes or excludes such day. It is better to describe the term as *commencing on* a certain day and *ending on* a certain other day.

37.06(f)(1)   Condominium statutes and ordinances

Various laws and ordinances extend the duration of a residential lease when the building is converted to a condominium.

37.06(g)   Signature of lessor and lessee

The signature of the lessor is necessary to give effect to a lease. It is the universal practice to obtain the lessee's signature also, though it is not essential that the lease be signed by the lessee if the lessee accepts the lease and takes possession of the leased premises. *Bakker* v. *Fellows*, 153 Mich. 428, 117 NW 52 (1908). It is customary to execute leases in duplicate. If the lessor signs one duplicate and hands this to the lessee, and the lessee signs the other duplicate and hands this to the lessor, the effect is the same as if both signatures had been placed on each duplicate. *Fields* v. *Brown,* 188 Ill. 111, 64 NE 1033.

37.06(h)   Seal   In a number of states, written leases must be executed with the same formality as deeds. In these states, a lease should be under seal.

37.06(i)   Witnesses   A few states require a lease that exceeds a certain specified duration to be witnessed.

37.06(j)   Acknowledgment   Some states require leases that exceed a specified term to be acknowledged. In any case, if the lease is to be recorded, it should be acknowledged.

37.06(k)   Recording   Even though a lease is not recorded, the tenant's possession will normally give the whole world constructive notice of his rights. However, this rule has been abolished in a number of states as to leases exceeding a specified duration—namely, one year in California, Florida, Georgia, Hawaii, Idaho, Mississippi, Montana, Oklahoma, Rhode Island and three years in Indiana, Minnesota, New Mexico, North Carolina, Ohio, Tennessee, Wisconsin, Wyoming. A few states specify longer durations.

In some states (New York, Pennsylvania, and Ohio, for example) the law permits the recording of a brief *memorandum of lease* instead of the original lease. This enables the parties to keep secret the rent specified in the lease.

37.07   Rent   Unless there is an agreement providing otherwise, rent is not due until the end of the rental period.

> **EXAMPLE:** *A* agreed to rent certain premises to *B* as a tenant from month to month. Rent was fixed at $80 per month, but nothing was said as time for payment of rent. The rent is not due until the end of each month.

Most leases, however, provide that rental is payable in advance on the first of each month.

Because of the embarrassment caused a landlord by his inability to put a new tenant in possession, and because of the difficulty attendant upon renting premises out of the normal season, a number of states require a tenant who remains in possession after the termination of his lease to pay double rent for the period intervening between the expiration of the lease and his eviction. And many leases provide that a holdover tenant shall pay double rent if he remains in possession after the lease has expired. The lease may provide for additional amounts other than double rent.

37.07(a)   Rent—net lease and gross lease

There are various types of *net leases,* but, in general, such a lease requires the tenant to pay real estate taxes, special assessments, insurance premiums, and other charges normally borne by the landowner. The tenant assumes the risk that taxes may increase, special assessments may be levied, and that the building may be destroyed by fire. In a fully net lease the tenant must rebuild a destroyed building, paying rent meanwhile. In a gross lease the tenant pays only his rent, and the landlord bears taxes and other burdens normally borne by a landowner.

37.07(b)   Rent—percentage leases

Leases of retail locations often provide for a *percentage rent.* Such a lease usually provides a minimum fixed rent. Over and above this minimum, the rental is fixed at a percentage of the tenant's gross sales. The percentage of gross income that is to be charged usually presents no great problem, for commonly accepted percentages for each type of retail establishment are published periodically by the National Association of Realtors. However, it is obvious that if such a lease is prepared for a department store in a shopping center, it will be necessary to fix different percentages for different departments within the single store. Deductions from gross sales are usually allowed for sales and luxury taxes and merchandise returned by the shopper. Care should be exercised to include in gross sales all income from vending machines, telephone booths, pay toilets, lockers, weighing machines, stamp machines, and so on; and also services rendered on the premises, hairdressing and the like. Services rendered at cost, clothing alterations and employees' cafeteria, for example, are usually excluded. Income from subtenants and concessionaires is included. The lease should state whether *gross income* includes sales made by mail and sales to employees. The lease should require the tenant to conduct business throughout the year, for obviously, if the store is closed, the percentage rent stops or drops. Further, the lease should fix the hours and days on which the store is to be open. A provision should also be included forbidding the establishment of a competing store within a specified radius. Since the landlord is depending on the particular tenant's ability to run a profitable business, the lease should forbid any assignment or sublease or even the occupancy of the premises by anyone other than the tenant, unless the landlord consents. The lease should require "continuous operation" by the tenant and define what hours and days are meant by this phrase.

37.07(c)   Rent—office leases

In office leases, rent is often charged by the square foot. Hence it is important to know how many *usable* square feet the tenant is getting. The lease may define the square footage as including space occupied by pillars and so forth, which may be useless to the tenant.

37.07(d)   Rent—escalation

Because of the push of inflation, most commercial or industrial leases today contain a rent escalation clause. It must be carefully drafted. Of course, increase in taxes is a sound basis for escalation. 48 ALR3d 287. The trick in a new building is to find some three- or four-year period that will average out as the basis on which the step-up in rent will be predicated. This is necessary because the tax assessor sometimes gives the building assessment a "tax break" in the early years. *Rodolitz* v. *Neptune Paper Products Co.,* 22 N.Y.2d 383, 283 NE2d 682 (1976). Increases in building maintenance wages are one valid source of escalation. *Simons* v. *Federal Bar Bldg. Corp.,* 275 A2d 545 (D.C. 1971). Energy costs are sometimes included as a separate escalator. The newer leases permit the landlord to estimate the escalation and charge each month or quarter the amount of his estimated escalation. Thus, he is using the tenant's money to meet escalations. At the end of the year he settles up.

Another type of escalator ties the increase to increased real estate taxes and *operating costs.* This last poses some problems. Obviously, it requires the landlord to furnish audited statements of increased operating costs and taxes. Also, some language is needed to limit the landlord's right to polish the brass doorknobs twice a week, so to speak, or to hire his brother at a fancy salary.

Leases that step up rent to compensate for increased operating costs leave another problem in the landlord's lap, namely, the declining value of the dollar collected as rent. The landlord copes with this by selecting an appropriate Consumer Price Index and providing that base rent shall step up quarterly or annually as the Consumer Price Index registers increases in inflation. If the landlord has a mortgage with a variable interest rate, he should try to insert an interest rate escalator provision into the lease so interest adjustments can be matched by rental adjustments.

REFERENCE: Shinkel, *Net Leases: A Critical Review,* 46 J. of Ppty. Management 146 (1981).

37.08   Ground leases and commercial leases distinguished—legal and financial aspects— mortgages of the leasehold

There is no legal distinction between commercial leases and ground leases. Nevertheless, there are economic differences between them that have legal implications. A *commercial lease* is a lease of a building or part of a building such as a store to a tenant. If the tenant agrees in his lease to make improvements, as a rule they are limited in scope. In a *ground lease,* the landowner leases the vacant ground to a tenant who covenants in the lease to erect a building on the premises. The true ground lease is a *net lease* under which the tenant pays all expenses including taxes, insurance, and repairs. The landlord in a commercial lease and his mortgagee are concerned with the tenant's credit standing, since this is their assurance that the rent will be paid. This is the reason, for example, why you will find a shopping center promoter looking for national chain stores as tenants. And because the landlord and his mortgagee depend on the cash flow from triple-A tenants, the lease will forbid any assignment or sublease without the landlord's consent. In a ground lease, on the other hand, (1) the landlord looks for his security to the fact that the tenant will erect a valuable building on the property and will have to keep up his rent in order to prevent loss of his investment in the building by the landlord's forfeiting the lease for nonpayment of rent; and (2) the tenant expects to borrow money to erect the building. This makes it necessary to draft the lease in such a fashion that the lessee's rights under the lease (the "leasehold estate") can be mortgaged without the landlord's permission and the lease should so state. And since the mortgagee who forecloses will want the unhampered right to sell to anyone, the ground lease should not limit the lessee's right to assign without the landlord's consent. Also, the term of the lease should be long enough to make the mortgage on the leasehold a legal investment for banks, insurance companies, and other institutional investors. For example, a state law may provide that a mortgage on a leasehold is not a legal investment for banks or insurance companies unless the unexpired term of the lease exceeds twenty-one years. Some states have a fifty-year minimum.

To better enable the lessee to borrow money for the erection of the building, a ground lease may provide that the landlord will join in the mortgage without, however, incurring any personal liability by signing the mortgage note. Or the lease may provide that the landlord's title will become subordinate to the mortgage on the leasehold. The landlord who signs such a lease must understand that this weakens his legal position, since foreclosure of the mortgage will extinguish his ownership. On the other hand, if the construction mortgage is only on the leasehold estate, foreclosure of the mortgage simply results in transfer of the leasehold to the mortgage lender, who then becomes the tenant paying rent to the landlord.

When the construction mortgage mortgages only the leasehold, provision should be included in the lease for special notice to the mortgagee of the leasehold in case of default in payment of rent, so that the mortgage lender can step in and cure the defaults, thereby preventing a forfeiture of the lease, which would cancel his mortgage.

37.09   Use of the premises   Unless the terms of the lease prevent it, the tenant may use the premises in lawful ways that were not discussed during the lease negotiations. This use by the tenant is often a point of controversy. Many leases state that the premises are leased *for the business of selling cigars,* or *to be used as a real estate office.* Oddly enough, courts seem to feel that such language does not limit the tenant to the stated use. Unless the lease states that the property is to be used *only* for a particular purpose, he may make any use of the property he wants to, so long as such use is not materially different from that to which the rented premises were customarily put. *Lyon v. Bethlehem Engineering Corp.,* 253 N.Y. 111, 170 NE 512 (1930); 51 CJS 1017.

> **SUGGESTION TO LANDLORD:**   Include a clause under which the tenant covenants to use the property only for a specific purpose. Include at the end of the tenant's covenants a clause giving the landlord the right to terminate the lease if the tenant violates any of his covenants. Be sure you state clearly what the permitted use includes. For example, if you specify that the tenant is to operate a drugstore, does this permit a lunch counter?

When the lease definitely restricts the use that the tenant may make of the premises and the tenant branches out into some unauthorized business, the landlord need not terminate the lease, even if the lease gives him power to do so. He may, instead, procure a court order forbidding the tenant to engage in the unauthorized business. This is desirable when the tenant is a highly solvent one, such as a chain store, and the rent is favorable to the landlord. It also protects the landlord in those cases where he has agreed with other tenants not to allow competing businesses in the same building.

A lease of business property automatically gives the tenant the right to advertise his business on the leased property if the lease does not forbid this use.

> **EXAMPLE:**   In the case of a lease of an entire building, it would give the tenant the exclusive right to place advertising signs on the walls and roofs of the building, for example, to maintain window signs and to have his name on a lobby directory board. In the case of a lease of a portion of a building, the lessee, not the landlord, would have the right to place advertising signs on the exterior walls of the portion leased to the tenant. 6 De Paul L. Rev. 63; 51 CJS 1020; 20 ALR2d 941.

Usually, however, where various floors are leased to different tenants, the landlord is considered as retaining exclusive possession of the roof. And obviously, if *L* leases the second floor to *A* and the third floor to *B*, *A*'s signs must not extend above the dividing line between the second and third floors.

37.10   Incidental rights of lessee or tenant—services and easements

Among the incidental rights a tenant enjoys, though not mentioned in his lease, are:

1. The right of tenant, his guests, business visitors, deliverymen, etc., to use the means of access the building provides, namely, front and rear entrances, arcade entrances, lobbies, corridors, stairs, escalators, and elevators, suite entrances from reception rooms or private offices (though the landlord, through reasonable regulations, may require delivery to be made at a trademan's entrance, require freight to use freight elevators, etc.), also the right to use common toilets, common laundry facilities, etc., and the right to have electric wires and conduits, also water and steam and gas pipes, cross the landlord's part of the property to service tenant's quarters. This is an aspect of the law of implied easements, 24 ALR2d 123.

The landlord should try to get a provision giving him the right to make reasonable changes in these facilities. To accommodate a new tenant, for example, the landlord may wish to move the washroom to another floor.

2. The right to have heat, hot water, etc. furnished where the only means of obtaining them consists of facilities controlled by the landlord for the benefit of all tenants.

37.11   Liability of landlord

Until recent times the rule of *caveat emptor* (let the buyer beware) applied to the landlord and tenant relationship. Unless the lease provided otherwise, the landlord had no duty to the tenant to put the rented premises in a habitable condition or to make any repairs whatever. Even if the building at the time it was rented was in a dangerous or ruinous condition or even wholly unfit for occupancy or use, or if it became so after it had been rented, the tenant had to pay the stipulated rent for the entire term of the lease. This, of course, placed the burden on a prospective tenant of making a careful inspection of the premises before signing a lease and of insisting that the lease contain covenants to keep the premises in repair if that was the tenant's wish and the landlord was willing to agree.

Since the landlord had no duty as to the condition of the premises, he was not liable to the tenant or his family for injuries or property damage suffered because of defects in the premises at the time of renting or occurring thereafter.

EXAMPLE: Landlord rented an apartment to Tenant. The flooring was obviously decayed and dangerous. It collapsed and Tenant was injured. He had no right to sue Landlord.

There were and are some exceptions to these rules:

1. When the landlord lets for a short term of a few days, weeks, or months a fully furnished house supposedly equipped for immediate occupancy as a dwelling, the landlord implicitly represents, in many states, that the premises are safe and habitable. If the premises are not habitable, as when they are infested with vermin, the tenant has the right to move out, and his liability for rent ceases. *Young* v. *Povich,* 121 Maine 141, 116 Atl. 26 (1922); 28 ALR 48. Also, the landlord is liable to the tenant and his family for injuries sustained from defects in the rented premises or the furnishings thereof. *Hacker* v. *Netschke,* 310 Mass. 754, 39 NE2d 644 (1942); *Mease* v. *Fox,* 200 NW2d 791 (Iowa 1972).

2. Where there are concealed defects that would make the premises dangerous to a tenant and that the tenant could not discover on an inspection of the premises, but that are known to the landlord, the landlord must inform the tenant of the existence of such defects. If he fails to do so, and as a consequence an injury is suffered by the tenant, his family, or his customers or guests, the landlord is liable for such injuries. *Mease* v. *Fox,* 200 NW2d 791 (Iowa 1972). Lawyers call this *fraud* liability.

EXAMPLE: Premises were leased as a barber shop and residence. Sewer gas often escaped into the premises which fact was known to the landlord. He did not disclose this fact to the tenant, and the tenant and his family became seriously ill from sewer gas. The landlord was liable for the injuries.

3. The landlord normally retains control over parts of the building used in common by the tenants, such as halls, stairs, elevators, and sidewalks leading from the building to the public street or sidewalk. With respect to such common facilities, the landlord must exercise due care to correct any dangerous conditions that develop. If he fails to do so,

he is liable for injuries suffered by the tenant, his family, his customers or other persons lawfully on the premises, such as delivery men.

EXAMPLE: Landlord leased a flat in his apartment building to Tenant. The stairways were used in common by the tenants. A stair became defective, and this condition was brought to the attention of Landlord, but he failed to correct it. Tenant slipped on the stair and was injured. Landlord was liable.

The duty of the landlord to use care to keep facilities used in common by the tenants in repair extends to appliances furnished by the landlord for the tenants' common use, such as laundry appliances, common toilets, playground equipment, and dumbwaiters. It also extends to the roof, chimneys, eaves, flues, outside walls, and swimming pools. 39 ALR3d 824. This duty extends also to the malls, walks, parking areas, etc., of a shopping center. 95 ALR2d 1344.

This liability of the landlord rests upon the fact that he is in exclusive control of these common areas. With control goes liability. This is a form of *occupier liability.* Prosser, *Torts,* 405.

4. Where the landlord, even though not legally obligated to do so, makes repairs, but is negligent in so doing, he is liable for any resulting injuries.

EXAMPLE: Landlord, though not obligated to do so, repaired a floor in an apartment that he rented to Tenant. The work was carelessly done, and Tenant was injured. Landlord is liable. 78 ALR2d 1258.

In recent times court decisions and state law have in some states completely transformed the law of the liability of landlord to his tenant where residential premises are involved. *Jack Spring, Inc.* v. *Little,* 50 Ill.2d 531, 280 NE2d 208 (1972); *Mease* v. *Fox,* 200 NW2d 791 (Iowa 1972). Thus, the rules stated in this section and in the following four sections are still applicable to renting of commercial and industrial buildings and to the extent that they give rights to residential tenants are also still applicable, but the rights of the tenant as to residential premises have been greatly expanded in a number of states. This parallels the amazing spread of the new rules creating an implied warranty of habitability in the sale of new homes by professional builders.

NEW DIRECTIONS: It seems inevitable that the new rules in landlord and tenant law will spread as rapidly as those relating to sales of new homes. It is equally clear that these new rules will be resisted in some states, so that the law will run an uneven course.

37.12 Liability of landlord for injuries to third person

As a rule, whenever a landlord would be liable to a tenant, as, for example, when the landlord is careless with respect to care of common stairways, he will be liable to others who stand in the tenant's shoes, such as members of his family, guests, employees, and business visitors and delivery boys.

There are other situations where a landlord is liable to a third person.

1. When the landlord rents the premises for a purpose that involves the admission of large groups of the public as patrons of the tenant (amusement park, theater, etc.) and at the time the lease, or any renewal lease, is signed, the premises are in a dangerous condition (dangerous doorways, steps, floors), the landlord is liable to the tenant's patrons for any injuries that they may suffer. *Webel* v. *Yale University,* 125 Conn. 515, 7 A2d 215 (1939); 17 ALR3rd 422, 873.

EXAMPLE: Landlord leased premises to Tenant as a tavern, dance hall, and restaurant and a patron was injured while dancing when her heel caught in a floor register. Landlord is liable. *Torwick* v. *Lisle,* 268 Minn. 197, 128 NW2d 330 (1964).

2. With respect to pedestrians on public walks or streets adjoining the rented premises, there is an additional rule imposing liability on the landlord, namely: When the premises at the time of the renting are in a dangerous and defective condition, the landlord is liable to strangers for injuries resulting therefrom. 52 CJS 105; 31 ALR2d 1334.

EXAMPLE: At the time the premises were leased to the tenant, a hole in the sidewalk leading to a coal bin was in a defective condition, and a pedestrian was thereafter injured as a result. The landlord was held liable. *Great Atlantic & Pacific Tea Co.* v. *Traylor,* 239 Ala. 497, 195 So 724 (1940). The reason for this rule is that a dangerous condition of premises constitutes a *nuisance,* and the liability of the landlord results from his leasing premises on which a *nuisance* exists. *Morgan* v. *Sheppard,* 156 Ala. 403, 47 So 147. The liability exists even though the defect is not concealed. And if the premises were safe when originally leased but are defective when the lease is renewed, the landlord is liable for injuries sustained by strangers after the date of the renewal. Of course, the tenant would also be liable for such injuries.

NEW LAWS: There are a number of state laws making landowners liable for deaths or injuries in private swimming pools. *Raponotti* v. *Burnt-Mil Arms, Inc.,* 273 A2d 372 (N.J. 1971).

3. Where the lease involves a use of the premises that is inherently dangerous, the landlord will be liable to third persons injured by the tenant's negligence if the landlord failed to exercise due care in selecting a responsible tenant.

EXAMPLE: The landlord leased a filling station to a tenant who had no experience in this line of work. An explosion occurred and the plaintiff was injured. The landlord was held liable. *Benlehr* v. *Shell Oil Co.,* 402 NE2d 1203 (Ohio 1978).

REFERENCES on landlord liability; Restatement Torts (2d) § 361 (Common stairways rule); Restatement, Property (2d) §17.1 *et seq.;* 66 ALR3d 202; *Jones* v. *Houston Apartments,* 572 SW2d 1 (Tex. 1978) (common stairways rule); *Pagelsdorf* v. *Safeco Ins. Co.,* 284 NW2d 55 (Wis. 1979); 68 ALR3d 382; 67*id.* 490, 587.

37.13 Lease obligating landlord to repair

If the lease requires the landlord to make repairs, and the landlord violates this obligation, the tenant may pursue one of the following courses:

1. He may abandon the premises if they become untenantable.

2. He may make the repairs himself and deduct the reasonable expense or cost thereof from the rent.

3. He may occupy the premises without repair and deduct from the rent the decrease in rental value occasioned by the landlord's failure to repair. Here, however, the tenant runs the risk of having his lease forfeited for nonpayment of rent if he appraises the situation incorrectly.

4. He may pay full rent and sue the landlord for the decrease in rental value occasioned by the landlord's failure to repair.

When the lease obligates the landlord to repair, and he fails to do so, and the tenant suffers an injury as a result, some courts hold the landlord liable; others do not. The view that the landlord should be held liable is growing in favor. 78 ALR2d 1252. Accompanying every contract is an unspoken duty to perform with skill and care and to be liable for negligent performance. 17A CJS *Contracts* § 494(1). In any event, the landlord has no duty to inspect the rented premises he has agreed to keep in repair, for normally the landlord has no right to enter on the rented premises without the tenant's consent. It is the tenant's duty to notify the landlord of any condition requiring repair, and no liability on the landlord's part arises until this has been done and the landlord has failed to make repairs as agreed. 163 ALR 314.

37.14 Statutes imposing duty to repair

The old rules relieving the landlord of the duty to keep rented premises in repair were evolved before the emergence of large cities, with the attendant problems of urban life. Obviously, workers of low income living in tenements in large urban centers cannot afford to keep their premises in repair. If the landlord fails to make needed repairs, they simply are not made. In many states laws have been passed imposing on landlords the duty to keep rented housing accommodations in repair. 45 Ill. L. Rev. 205; 93 ALR 778; 17 ALR2d 704. In California, Montana, North Dakota, and Oklahoma, the tenant is given the right to move out if needed repairs are not made, but if the tenant is injured because of the landlord's failure to make repairs, the landlord is not liable. In some states, Michigan, New Jersey, and New York, for example, the landlord is liable if the tenant suffers injuries as a result of the landlord's negligent failure to make repairs. *Altz* v. *Lieberson*, 233 N.Y. 16, 134 NE 703 (1922); 17 ALR2d 708.

> **EXAMPLES:** In states following the New York rule, landlords were held liable for the following injuries: tenant injured by fall of ceiling; tenant injured as result

of landlord's failure to repair hole in bathroom floor; and tenant's child injured when defective radiator valves blew off.

Many of the statutes and ordinances do not even mention the tenant. The ordinance may simply impose a fine of $100 on the landlord if, for example, he fails to keep a light burning in a stairway for twenty-four hours a day. However, in some states resourceful lawyers for tenants have persuaded the courts that such ordinances create an implied right in a tenant to sue the landlord for personal injuries sustained from an accident that would not have occurred but for the landlord's failure to comply with the ordinance. Prosser, *Torts*, 191.

In many cities, especially home-rule cities, ordinances exist making the landlord liable for failure to repair or for violation of building codes. *Bell* v. *Willoughby Tower*, 46 Ill. App.2d 45, 196 NE2d 487 (1965).

37.15 State laws permitting tenant to make repairs

A few states have laws permitting the tenant to make minor repairs where the landlord refuses to do so, typically limited to an amount not exceeding one month's rent, and to deduct this amount from the rent. 37 Brooklyn L. Rev. 396.

37.16 Repairs—office leases

Most office leases require the tenant to surrender the premises at the end of the lease in their original condition, *ordinary wear and tear excepted.* This last clause is given its normal meaning.

> **EXAMPLE:** When Tenant surrendered the premises there were patches in the carpeting, a damaged air conditioner that ran all night because Landlord had installed no thermostat, and scratches in office panels. This is ordinary wear and tear. *Urban Management Corp.* v. *Ford Motor Credit Co.,* 263 So2d 404 (La. App. 1972).

37.17 Repairs—recapitulation

The problem of repairs is one of great complexity. Among the numerous problems are the following:

> 1. Effect of laws or ordinances authorizing Tenant to pay rent into an escrow of some sort while Landlord is in breach of his obligation to repair. 40 ALR3d 821.
>
> 2. Right of Tenant to make deductions from rent payments because of Landlord's failure to repair. 40 ALR3d 1369.
>
> 3. Landlord's failure to repair as amounting to a constructive eviction, permitting Tenant to move without liability for further rent. 86 ALR3d 351.
>
> 4. Landlord's breach of covenant to repair as giving rise to Tenant's action for damages for mental anguish. *Cherberg* v. *Peoples Nat. Bank,* 544 P2d 1137 (Wash. 1955). (Landlord was using situation to pressure Tenant to move.)

5. Landlord may be liable for lost profits of Tenant if lease permits Landlord to terminate lease in case of fire damage and he unduly delays repairs. *Flame* v. *Oak Lane Shopping Center,* 369 A2d 1220 (Pa. 1977).

6. In an ordinary office lease situation, Landlord must make repairs at his expense where ordered by public authority. *Buckley* v. *Ligget,* 218 A2d 515 (D.C. 1966); 22 ALR3d 521.

7. If lease requires Tenant to carry insurance, Tenant is liable for repairs up to amount of any deductible in the insurance policy. *Burger Chef. Systems, Inc.* v. *Melford Co.,* 547 F2d 786 (4th Cir. 1976).

8. Where Landlord covenants to repair and carry insurance, Tenant may maintain specific performance to compel Landlord to repair. *Evco Corp.* v. *Ross,* 528 SW2d 20 (Tenn. 1975).

9. General covenant by Tenant to *repair* may compel Tenant to *rebuild* in case of destruction of building. 38 ALR2d 782, 703 (older cases). This rule may well disappear as the doctrine of unconscionability develops further.

10. Measure of damages where Landlord breaches his covenant to repair. 80 ALR2d 983.

11. Landlord's duties under covenant to repair and rebuild where building is damaged or destroyed by fire. 38 ALR2d 682.

12. Rights and remedies of Tenant on breach of Landlord's covenant to repair. 28 ALR2d 446.

37.18 Lease of building to be constructed by landlord

Where a building or part thereof is leased to a tenant while it is in the process of construction, there is an implied warranty that the building is suitable for the tenant's purposes.

> **EXAMPLE:** Landlord leased a building under construction to Tenant as a furniture store. The roof leaked and furniture was damaged. Landlord is liable. *J. D. Young Corp.* v. *McClintic,* 26 SW2d 460 (Tex. 1930); 11 B.U.L. L. Rev. 119.

37.19 Eviction by title paramount

If the tenant is evicted from the premises by a stranger having a paramount or better title than his landlord, the tenant is not liable to his landlord for rent accruing after such eviction.

> **EXAMPLE:** Landlord mortgaged his land to Lender. Thereafter, Landlord leased the mortgaged land to Tenant. Landlord defaulted in his payments on the mortgage, and Lender took possession of the premises, as he had the right to do under his mortgage, evicting Tenant. Tenant is not liable for rents accruing after the eviction, since Lender is coming in under a paramount title.

37.20 Liability of tenant for injuries to third person

When a stranger is injured by reason of a defective condition of the premises, it is often difficult to determine whether the landlord or tenant is liable. If the landlord has made no agreement to repair and the premises were in a safe condition when rented, and if the defective portion is in the exclusive possession of the tenant, the tenant is liable but the landlord is not, since the landlord has no control over such premises and is in no position to prevent the dangerous condition.

> **EXAMPLE:**   A stranger slipped and fell into a coal hole that was defectively covered but was in a safe condition when the premises were rented. The basement into which the hole opened was used by the first-floor tenant. He alone had a key to this basement, and the landlord had no access thereto. The tenant alone was liable. *West Chicago Masonic Assn.* v. *Cohn,* 192 Ill. 210, 61 NE 439 (1901).

Or suppose the tenant of an upper floor goes out, leaving the water running, and the water runs over and drips through the ceiling and ruins plaster and rugs in the apartment beneath. The landlord is not liable since the tenant is in exclusive possession of his apartment, but the tenant is liable both to his landlord and to the tenant below, because the damage resulted from his carelessness.

37.21   Insurance   The prudent property owner should protect himself against liability claims by taking out Owners', Landlords', and Tenants' Public Liability Insurance, commonly referred to as O.L.&T. insurance, which provides coverage against legal liability for accidents resulting in bodily injuries or death arising out of ownership, occupation, or use of the premises. Liability for injuries sustained by employees is not covered by this policy, but they should be covered by workmen's compensation or employer's liability insurance. Insurance should be obtained protecting the landlord against liability for property damage. If there is an elevator on the premises, insurance will be needed to protect against injuries arising through operation of the elevator. Special "dram shop" insurance should be purchased if alcoholic beverages are sold on the premises.

37.22   Repairs and alterations by tenants— liability of tenant to landlord   When the lease does not provide otherwise, the tenant has no duty to the landlord to make any substantial, extraordinary, or general repairs, such as the replacing of a worn-out furnace or water heater. But it is the tenant's duty to repair broken windows or leaking roofs and to take such other steps as needed to prevent damage from the elements. If he fails to do so, he is liable to landlord for any resulting damage. *Suydam* v. *Jackson,* 54 N.Y. 450.

The tenant must not make any material change in the nature and character of the building leased, as by removing walls, cutting new doorways, and the like, even though such alterations increase the value of the property. The theory is that when the tenant vacates the building, the landlord should find it in much the same condition as it was when the tenant took possession. *F. W. Woolworth Co.* v. *Nelson*, 204 Ala. 172, 85 So 449 (1920).

When the lease obligates the tenant to make repairs or to keep the premises in repair, some courts say that the tenant must repair or rebuild if the building is damaged or destroyed by fire, flood, lightning, rain, accident, or other causes beyond the tenant's control. 45 ALR 12, 106 ALR 1358. Other courts today refuse to impose such a heavy burden on the tenant. *Seevers* v. *Gabel*, 94 Iowa 75, 62 NW 669. Under the modern law of unconscionability, it is unlikely that any court would force the tenant to rebuild. It is not a risk he consciously assumed. A lease provision for repairs may require the tenant to replace rotten floors, a worn-out furnace, and the like. The tenant is liable to his landlord for damage occasioned by carelessness, as where damage results from the tenant's negligence in permitting a bathtub to overflow. 10 ALR2d 1012.

37.23 Damage to or destruction of the leased premises

Unless the lease provides otherwise, the rule is that when *land and building* are rented, the tenant is not excused from paying rent if *building* is destroyed by fire, flood, or wind.

> **EXAMPLE:** A lease was made of the premises at 143 and 145 Lake Street, Chicago, Illinois. The buildings were destroyed by fire, but the liability for rent continued. A lease containing a description by street number leases the land as well as the building.

Quite a number of states—Alaska, Arizona, California, Connecticut, Kentucky, Maryland, Michigan, Minnesota, Mississippi, Montana, New Jersey, New York, North Carolina, North Dakota, Ohio, South Carolina, West Virginia, and Wisconsin, for example—have abolished this harsh rule. In these states, it is the rule that if a building is destroyed or rendered untenantable, the tenant is relieved of further liability for rent. 35 B. Y. U.L. Rev. 1284. Many lease forms provide that if the building is destroyed by fire, the lease ends automatically. Predictably, many more modern courts will take this approach even where the lease is silent.

The rule that liability for rent continues when the building is destroyed does not apply to a lease of an apartment, flat, office, or floor of a building. Such a lease is not a lease of land.

When the building is not destroyed, but the apartment is rendered *untenantable* by fire, leases usually provide that the landlord has a certain time in which to make the necessary repairs, and in the meantime, the tenant is not liable for rent. Under this clause, if the landlord fails to make repairs during the specified period, the lease ends automatically.

The "untenantability" clause is poorly drawn at times. A fire may leave an office suite untouched but may destroy the elevators. Greater detail is needed than is found in many leases.

If the lease requires the landlord to *repair* the building, this may be interpreted as requiring him to *rebuild* it if it is destroyed by fire or other casualty. 38 ALR2d 685.

NEW DIRECTIONS: The Restatement of Property 2d § 5.4 takes the position predicted in the last edition of this book, namely, that when the building is destroyed (by fire, windstorm, etc.) without fault on the tenant's part, the tenant may terminate the lease and end his liability for rent. This is a sound rule. No doubt most courts will follow this view.

REFERENCES: Teodori v. *Werner,* 415 A2d 31 (Pa. 1981) (tenant's liability for rent ends when building destroyed); 99 ALR3d 738; 34 Mo. L. Rev. 132; 7 Real Est. L. Rev. 187.

37.24   Damage or destruction of the leased premises *before* tenant takes possession

If the rented premises are damaged by fire or other cause or otherwise rendered unsuitable for the use contemplated by the parties and this occurs *before* Tenant takes possession, Tenant may terminate the lease without liability to Landlord.

EXAMPLE: The building was destroyed by fire before Tenant took possession. He could cancel the lease. Restatement, Property 2d § 5.2 (Tentative Draft). The theory is that Tenant has no way of protecting the property before the possession date.

37.25   Repairs and services by landlord

Many state laws place on the landlord the burden of repairing residential premises where defects are discovered during the lease term. Restatement of Property 2d Ch. 5, statutory note 3(a). And some of these laws give the tenant the right to sue for damages if the landlord fails to repair. *Ibid.*, statutory note 3(b). Some of these statutes permit the tenant to pay less than the stipulated rent. This is called an abatement of rent. *Ibid.*, statutory notes 3(c) and 3(d). Some of these statutes deal with the landlord's failure to provide services such as water, gas, electricity, etc. Some of these laws allow the tenant to suspend payment of rent. *Ibid.*, statutory note 3(e) and 3(f). Rent withholding as described in this text is permitted by many statutes. *Ibid.*, statutory note 3(g).

Because courts today are beginning to build their local law on the basis of statutes widely enacted in other states, it seems quite likely that rules embodied in statutes of this sort will find wide expression in court decisions everywhere.

37.26   Taxes

In the absence of a provision in the lease to that effect, the tenant is not obliged to pay real estate taxes on the leased land.

37.27   Fixtures

The respective rights of landlord and tenant in and to fixtures installed by the tenant are discussed in Chapter 3.

Trade fixtures not removed by the tenant before he moves out become the property of the landlord. The fact that such items are attached to the landlord's building seems to make this result natural and acceptable to the courts. However, as to the tenant's ordinary personal property that is not in any way attached to the building, for example, furniture or stock in trade, this does not become the landlord's property simply because the tenant has moved out or been evicted. The landlord must keep or store these articles for the tenant. Some state laws cover this point.

37.28   Cancellation clause

Leases may contain a clause conferring on the landlord the privilege of canceling the lease in the event of a sale of the property and upon giving a certain specified notice to the tenant. This clause is of value when the landlord sells the premises to a buyer who desires more or less immediate occupancy. Great care must be exercised in serving the notice of cancellation. For example, if the lease says that the *landlord* may cancel the lease in case of a sale, a notice served by his *purchaser* may be void. 163 ALR 1019. Notice of cancellation should be served personally unless the lease specifically allows notice by mail. Each tenant is entitled to his own copy of the notice.

37.29   Assignments and subleases

Unless the lease provides otherwise, a lessee may assign his lease or sublet the premises. Whether a particular instrument is an assignment or sublease does not depend upon the name given the instrument by the parties. An assignment simply transfers the leasehold estate to a new owner, the assignee. A sublease creates a new and distinct leasehold estate in the sublesee. If the lessee transfers the *entire unexpired remainder* of the term created by the lease, the instrument is an assignment. If the lessee retains *part of the term, however small the part may be,* or transfers only part of the leased premises, the instrument is a sublease.

> **EXAMPLE:** Landlord leases certain premises to Tenant for a term beginning on May 1, 1950, and expiring on April 30, 1952, at a rent of $100 per month. On July 1, 1950, Tenant executes to *X* a "sublease" for a term beginning on July 1, 1950, and expiring April 30, 1952, at a rent of $150 per month. The instrument is an assignment.

> **EXAMPLE:** Landlord leases to Tenant certain premises for a term beginning on May 1, 1950, and expiring on April 30, 1952. On July 1, 1950, Tenant executes to *X* an "assignment" of said lease except the last day of the term. The instrument is a sublease.

The difference between assignment and sublease is important, since an assignee becomes liable to the original lessor for rent, whereas a sublessee is liable only to the sublessor, who, of course, is the lessee under the original lease. Of course the lessee in the original lease continues liable for rent to the original lessor, notwithstanding the assignment or sublease.

If the lease forbids an assignment without the lessor's consent, it does not necessarily prevent a sublease. If the lease forbids a sublease, it does not necessarily prohibit an assignment. As a rule, a commercial lease prohibits both assignments and subleases without the lessor's consent.

Suppose Landlord makes a lease to Tenant Corp. and Shareholder, the holder of all the stock in Tenant Corp., sells all his stock to Buyer. This is not a violation of covenant not to make an assignment or sublease without the landlord's consent. The lease remains in Tenant Corp. Only the stock has been transferred. *Alabama Vermiculite Corp.* v. *Patterson,* 124 F.Supp. 441. Many leases forbid such a transfer of stock.

An assignment or sublease made without the lessor's consent, in defiance of the provisions of the lease, is not wholly void. If, after learning of the assignment or sublease, the lessor accepts rent from the assignee or sublessee, he waives his right to object to that particular assignment or sublease.

The spouse of the assignor need not joint in assignment of the lease. A leasehold estate is personal property and there are no dower rights in personal property.

37.30 Mortgages of the leasehold

If the lease contains no provision that would prohibit a mortgage of the leasehold, the tenant may place a mortgage on the leasehold estate created by the lease. In such a mortgage, the description of the mortgaged premises should read somewhat as follows:

> Leasehold estate created by lease dated May 1, 19_____ and recorded in the Recorder's Office of _____ County, _____, on May 2, 19_____, as Document 1,000,000, from John Smith, as Lessor, to Henry Brown, as Lessee, demising for a term of years commencing on May 1, 19_____, and ending on April 30, 19_____, the premises described as follows, to wit: (here insert description of leased premises).

One difficulty with such a mortgage is the fact that the tenant may default in his rent payments, and if he does, the landlord may declare the lease forfeited. Of course if default and forfeiture occur, the mortgage is thereby extinguished. A side agreement between the landlord and mortgagee may provide that before forfeiting the lease the landlord will give notice of the default to the mortgagee and a stated time to make good the defaults. It may also provide that if the lease is terminated, the mortgagee will be entitled to receive a new lease for the balance of the term on the same rent and terms as the old lease.

Another question that arises is with respect to the liability of the mortgagee for payment of rent. In title and intermediate states, which regard a leasehold mortgage as an assignment of the leasehold, the mortgagee becomes personally liable to the landlord for rent, under the rule stated in the preceding section that an assignee becomes liable to the original lessor for rent. *Williams* v. *Safe Deposit Co.,* 167 Md. 499, 175 Atl. 331 (1934). For this reason, it is a common practice in leasehold mortgages to omit the last day of the term, so that the mortgage mortgages the leasehold *except the last day thereof.* By excepting the last day of the term, the mortgage becomes a sublease rather than an assignment, and the mortgagee does not become personally liable to the landlord for rent due under the lease. Mortgages are treated as assignments or subleases depending on whether they cover all or less than all the unexpired term of the lease. In states that follow the lien theory of mortgages, a mere mortgage of the leasehold does not make the mortgagee liable for rent. Kratovil and Werner, *Modern Mortgage Law and Practice,* § 22.09 (1981).

37.31 Deed of rented premises

A landlord may, of course, sell his real estate, and the buyer will take it subject to existing leases and periodic tenancies. The deed alone confers on the buyer the right to collect rent falling due after the sale and the right to declare leases forfeited for nonpayment of rent if that right is reserved in the lease. *Lipschultz* v. *Robertson,* 407 Ill. 470, 95 NE2d 357 (1950). So far as the collection of future rent is concerned, it is unnecessary that the lessor execute to his purchaser an assignment of his rights under existing leases.

A tenant has the right to continue making rent payments to his original landlord until he is notified of a sale of the property. Therefore, one who buys rented property should promptly notify all tenants that all future rent must be paid to him.

A serious question arises when the tenant prepays the rent called for by the lease and the property is thereafter sold. The buyer of the property no doubt assumes that he will be entitled to collect the future rents called for by the lease and is then confronted by a tenant armed with rent receipts for such rent. In some states, the tenant must pay such rent over again to his new landlord, whereas in other states, the rent payments are good as against the new landlord. 49 Am.Jur.2d § 554.

37.32 Abandonment of the premises

Leases usually provide that if the lessee abandons the premises before the expiration of the lease, he shall nevertheless continue liable for rent until the expiration of the lease, and any reletting by the landlord shall not relieve the tenant of further liability.

However, upon abandonment of the premises by the lessee, it is the duty of the landlord in most states to mitigate damages, that is, to take charge of the property, and, if possible, relet or rerent it and thus reduce the amount for which the lessee remains liable. 40 ALR 190, 126 ALR 1219. The lessor may deduct the expenses of such reletting, including commissions and decorating, from the rent collected on such reletting, and he may apply the balance on the original tenant's liability.

> **EXAMPLE:**   Landlord leased premises to Tenant #1 for one year at $50 per month. After six months, Tenant #1 abandoned the premises. The premises were vacant one month and were then relet to Tenant #2 for $40 per month, the expenses of reletting, including commissions and decorating, being $50. The landlord thus realized on the reletting $200 minus $50, or $150. Tenant #1's liability is $300 minus $150, or $150.

The courts are not in agreement as to the extent of Landlord's duty where Tenant abandons the premises. Some courts put the landlord under an obligation to seek another tenant so that the damages caused by Tenant's abandonment can be reduced. *Scheinfeld* v. *Muntz TV, Inc.,* 67 Ill. App.2d 28, 214 NE2d 506 (1966). Other courts require no affirmative action by Landlord. But they do compel him to accept a suitable subtenant found by the abandoning tenant. *Reget* v. *Dempsey-Tegeler Co.,* 96 Ill. App.2d 278, 238 NE2d 418 (1968). 48 Ill. B. J. 546. Often the lease spells out the landlord's duties.

It is usual to insert a provision in the lease to the effect that the lessor shall not be under any obligation to relet and that he may permit the premises to remain vacant and sue the lessee for the full amount of the rent. This was the law in most states even in the absence of such a provision in the lease. 40 ALR 190, 126 ALR 1219. Under today's law there is a serious question whether the courts will compel the landlord to relet no matter what the lease says. Ordinarily the landlord will relet the premises rather than permit them to remain vacant, for rent collections from an existing tenant are money in the landlord's hands, whereas the liability of the previous tenant is at best a doubtful asset.

If the landlord relets after abandonment of the premises by the tenant, there is danger that this may amount to a surrender or termination of the lease, thus releasing the tenant from further liability for rent. In some states, a reletting automatically releases the liability of the tenant who has abandoned the premises, whereas in other states, the tenant is released *unless* the landlord gives him notice of his intention to hold him liable despite the reletting. 110 ALR 368. In the great majority of states, the question is regarded as one of intention. If the landlord's acts indicate an acceptance of the tenant's abandonment and an intention to regard the lease as terminated, the tenant's liability for future rent is terminated. 110 ALR 368. In effect, there is a *surrender.* As above suggested, the notice given by the landlord is employed to show that he does not intend to treat the lease as terminated by the abandonment. Suppose, however, that the landlord relets to a new tenant for a new term longer than the term of the original lease. In some states, this is viewed as being inconsistent with the continued existence of the earlier lease, and the earlier lease is thereby terminated. *Ralph* v.

Deiley, 293 Pa. 90, 141 Atl. 640 (1928); 61 ALR 773. Therefore, the lease provisions covering this point *(the abandonment clause)* should include clauses giving the landlord the right to relet for a term longer than the original lease without in any way releasing the tenant's liability.

37.33 Surrender

A *surrender* is an agreement by landlord and tenant to terminate the tenant's lease or tenancy, followed by a delivery of possession of the premises to the landlord. A surrender releases the tenant from liability for rent thereafter accruing.

> **EXAMPLE:** Premises were leased by Landlord to Tenant for the term from April 1, 1903, to April 1, 1906. On March 31, 1904, Tenant #1 told Landlord that he wished to give up his lease, and Landlord accepted this offer, telling Tenant #1 to allow a new tenant, Tenant #2 to move in and to turn the keys over to him, Tenant #2. This procedure was a surrender, and Tenant #1 was not liable for rent accruing thereafter.

Observe that it is the agreement between landlord and tenant that distinguishes a surrender from an abandonment by the tenant.

If the landlord, with the tenant's consent, gives a new lease to a stranger during the existence of the tenant's lease, this is a surrender.

> **EXAMPLE:** Landlord leased a store to Tenant, who sold the business to Buyer. Landlord then gave Buyer a new lease. This is a surrender of the old lease.

The making of a new lease between landlord and tenant operates as a surrender of a prior inconsistent lease. If the tenant merely abandons the premises, the fact that the landlord accepts the keys does not constitute a surrender.

37.34 Home-rule ordinances

In this period of an acute shortage of housing many local governments, especially those having home-rule powers, have enacted ordinances for the protection of tenants.

> **EXAMPLE:** The city of Evanston, Illinois, has enacted a comprehensive ordinance protecting tenants. Among its provisions is one requiring the landlord to attempt to relet the apartment where the tenant abandons it. *City of Evanston* v. *Create Inc.,* 85 Ill. 2d 101, 421 NE2d 196 (1981).

37.35 Termination of tenancy for nonpayment of rent

Virtually all leases provide that the lease may be forfeited and the tenant evicted for nonpayment of rent or for violation of the terms of the lease. Although the lease contains a clause permitting the landlord to declare the lease forfeited for nonpayment of rent, the landlord must not suddenly declare a forfeiture if he has been in the habit of accepting tardy rent payments. He must first notify the tenant to pay his rent by a specified reasonable time, and if the tenant fails to pay within the time specified, then and only then may the landlord declare a forfeiture. *Cottrell* v. *Gerson,* 371 Ill. 174, 20 NE2d 74 (1939).

Year-to-year and month-to-month tenancies likewise may be terminated on the giving of a short notice specified by law if the tenant defaults in his rent payments.

When the landlord evicts the tenant because of the tenant's defaults, the tenant's liability for future rent is ended unless the lease contains a clause, called the *survival clause,* to the effect that the tenant's liability shall survive such eviction. Such lease clauses are now commonplace.

37.36 Warranty of habitability

Perhaps the most meaningful new rule that has gained the widest acceptance is the rule that rented residential multifamily premises must be habitable and kept this way during the rental period. *Old Town Development Co.* v. *Langford,* 349 NE2d 744 (Ind. App. 1976), citing many cases and articles. This is an "implied warranty."

What, precisely, is included in this warranty is something which the courts have not yet decided. At a minimum, the landlord warrants that the premises are free from substantial building code violations and will remain so during the rental period. Other courts go further, and it seems probable that most courts will expand the warranty beyond freedom from building code violations. Most courts, it is plain, will hold the landlord liable if the premises become unsafe or unsanitary, and thus unfit to live in. *Kline* v. *Burns,* 276 A2d 248 (N.H. 1971); *Boston Housing Authy.* v. *Hemingway,* 293 NE2d 831 (Mass. 1973); 40 ALR3d 73.

Many reasons have been marshalled for finding that the landlord warrants the habitability of rented apartments. Tenants do not have the skills to keep apartments in repair and do not even have access to many plumbing, heating, and electrical facilities that fall into disrepair. *Javins* v. *First Nat. Realty Corp.,* 428 F2d 1071; *DePaul* v. *Kauffman,* 272 A2d 500 (Pa. 1971); *Mease* v. *Fox,* 200 NW2d 791 (Iowa 1972); 40 ALR3d 646.

REFERENCES: 56 B.U.L. Rev. 1; 62 Cal. L. Rev. 1444; 25 Case Western L. Rev. 371; 56 Cornell L. Rev. 489; 77 Dick. L. Rev. 77; 1975 Duke L. J. 999; 40 Fordham L. Rev. 123; 58 Iowa L. Rev. 656; 39 Mo. L. Rev. 56; 16 Vill. L. Rev. 395; 22 Case Western Reserve L. Rev. 739; 47 Chicago–Kent L. Rev. 1; 20 Cleve. St. L. Rev. 169; 2 Conn. L. J. 61; 56 Cornell L. Rev. 489; 20 DePaul L. Rev. 955; 1970 Duke L. J. 1040; 40 Fordham L. Rev. 123; 2 Rurgers–Camden L. J. 120; 23 U. Fla. L. Rev. 785; 31 U. Pitt. L. Rev. 138; 6 U. of San Francisco L. Rev. 147; 16 Vill. L. Rev. 383, 395.

37.36(a) Knowledge of tenant

The tenant's knowledge of building code violations when he rents the premises does not deprive him of his remedies. In all rundown buildings the code violations are clearly visible. *Foisy* v. *Wyman,* 111 Cal. Reptr. 7, 515 P2d 160

(1974). The implied warranty is to the effect that the premises will be *maintained* in habitable condition.

37.36(b)   Two flats

The warranties rule applies to two flats. *South Austin Realty Assn.* v. *Sombright*, 361 NE2d 795 (1977).

37.36(c)   Business properties

Presently, the courts have not applied the warranty of habitability to business properties. *Yuan Kane, Inc.* v. *Wm. Levy*, 26 Ill. App.3d 889, 326 NE2d 51 (1975); *Service Oil Co., Inc.* v. *White*, 542 P2d 652 (Kans. 1976); *Van Ness Indust., Inc.* v. *Claremont Paint Co.*, 324 A2d 102 (N.J. 1976); *Coulston* v. *Telescope Prod. Ltd.*, 378 N.Y.S.2d 553.

37.36(d)   Homes

It has been held that the warranty applies to rental of a home. *Pole Realty Co.*, v. *Sorrells*, 84 Ill. 2d 178, 417 NE2d 1297 (1981); *Fair* v. *Negley*, 390 A2d 240 (Pa. 1978); *Lemle* v. *Breiden*, 462 P2d 470 (Hawaii 1969).

37.36(e)   Disclaimer of warranty

It has been held that a clause in the lease whereby the tenant waives or disclaims the benefit of any warranty of habitability is against public policy and void. *Teller* v. *McCoy*, 153 SE2d 114 (W. Va. 1979); *Boston Housing Authy.* v. *Hemingway*, 293 NE2d 831 (Mass. 1973).

37.37   Reduction of rent

Some courts have awarded *T* a reduction in rent proportionate to the loss of habitability. *McKenna* v. *Begin*, 325 NE2d 587 (Mass. 1975); *Javins* v. *First Nat. Realty Corp.*, 428 F2d 1071 (1970); *Hinson* v. *Deli*, 26 Cal. App.3d 62; 102 Cal. Reptr. 66 (1972); *Academy Spires, Inc.* v. *Brown*, 111 N.J.S. 477, 268 A2d 556 (1970). They have even extended this remedy to public housing. *Housing Authority of City of Newark* v. *Scott*, 348 A2d 195 (N.J. 1976).

NEW LAWS: Some states (Hawaii, Louisiana, Maine, Massachusetts, Virginia, Washington, West Virginia, and Wisconsin) have passed laws providing for rent reduction.

NEW DIRECTIONS: Where the building is in violation of the implied warranty of habitability but the tenant pays full rent, the new decisions say that the landlord is liable to repay the excess rent to the tenant. It has been held that he can sue the landlord to get back part of the rent paid. *Berzito* v. *Gambino*, 114 N.J.S. 124, 274 A2d 865 (1970). He can also sue the landlord for damages. *Marini* v. *Ireland*, 56 N.J. 130, 265 A2d 526 (1970); *Winn* v. *Sampson Co.*, 398 P2d 272 (1965).

NEW LAWS: Maine has a new law to this effect.

NOTE FOR LAWYERS: The subject of building and housing code violations has attracted much attention. 21 Baylor L. Rev. 372 (1969); 56 B.U.L. Rev. 1 (1976); 53 Cal. L. Rev. 304; 5 Duquesne L. Rev. 413; 56 Iowa L. Rev. 460; 56 Geo. L. J. 920; 39 Geo. Wash. L. Rev. 152; 55 Minn. L. Rev. 82; 66 Mich. L. Rev. 1753; 12 Villanova L. Rev. 631; 32 U. Pitt. L. Rev. 626; 30 *id.* 148; 39 U. Cinn. L. Rev. 600; 25 Wash. & Lee L. Rev. 335.

37.38   Void lease because of building code violations

The presence of building code violations when the lease is signed may affect the validity of the lease.

NEW DIRECTIONS: Courts have held that the presence of building code violations when a lease of the apartment was signed rendered the lease void. *Glyco v. Schultz*, 289 NE2d 919 (Ohio 1972); *King v. Moorhead*, 495 SW2d 65 (Mo. 1973); 66 Mich. L. Rev. 1953. This rule deprives the landlord of the benefit of all "fine print" in the lease. *Saunders v. First Nat. Realty Corp.*, 245 A2d 836 (1968); *Longnecker v. Hardin*, 130 Ill. App.2d 468, 264 NE2d 878 (1970); 21 Vand. L. Rev. 1117; *Robinson v. Diamond Housing Corp.*, 463 F2d 853 (1972). Or the tenant may choose to declare the lease void. *Mease v. Fox*, 200 NW2d 791 (Iowa 1972). If the code violations were not in existence when the lease was made it is not void. *Hinson v. Deli*, 2 Cal. Reptr. 661.

37.39   Rent withholding

Up to present time, if a tenant failed to pay rent, the landlord could have him evicted. Today the courts that recognize an implied warranty of habitability and freedom from building code violations have begun to devise additional remedies for the tenant if the premises are in disrepair. One of these is rent withholding, under which the tenant keeps the rent or part of it if the building or apartment becomes untenantable or substantial building code violations occur. The other is the rent escrow, under which the tenant pays the rent to the court or to a third party. Some cities and states have enacted laws along this line. *Clore v. Fredman*, 59 Ill.2d 20, 319 NE2d 18 (1975); *Mease v. Fox*, 200 NW2d 791 (Ia. 1972), 40 ALR3d 821. As a rule, when the building code violations have been corrected, the rent deposited in the escrow (or a part thereof) is released to the landlord. *Klein v. Allegheny County*, 269 A2d 647 (1972); *Bell v. Tsintolas Realty Co.*, 430 F2d 474 (1970); 29 Md. L. Rev. 202; 40 ALR3d 821; 46 L.A.B. Bull. 161. Of course, eviction is postponed as long as the rent is being paid into the escrow. *Kipsborough Realty Corp. v. Goldbetter*, 367 N.Y.S.2d 916 (1975); *Sabul v. Lipscomb*, 310 A2d 890 (Del.1973).

NEW DIRECTIONS: Courts have begun to evolve additional new remedies for tenants where building code violations exist. First, the court finds that there is an implied covenant or obligation on the landlord's part to keep the premises free from major building code violations. Then, if the landlord fails to perform this duty, the court finds the tenant is entitled to a rent reduction. *Jack Spring Inc. v. Little*, 50 Ill.2d 351, 266 NE2d 338 (1972). Or the tenant can make the repairs and deduct the cost from future rents. *Marini* v. *Ireland,* 56 N.J. 130, 265 A2d 526 (1970); *Mease* v. *Fox,* 200 NW2d 791 (Iowa 1972).

REFERENCES on rent withholding because of implied warranty of habitability or presence of building code violations: 21 Baylor L. Rev. 372; 53 Cal. L. Rev. 304; 5 Duquesne L. Rev. 413; 56 Geo. L. J. 920; 39 Geo. Wash. L. Rev. 152; 57 Ill. B. J. 920; 2 Loyola U. L. Rev. (La.) 105; 55 Minn. L. Rev. 82; 66 Mich. L. Rev. 1753; 30 U. Pitt. L. Rev. 148; 66 N.W.U. L. Rev. 790.

37.40 Retaliatory evictions

As the renters have grown more militant in reporting building code violations to the city authorities, landlords have retaliated by refusing to renew the leases of the militants. Up to recent times, the landlord would have been within his rights.

NEW DIRECTIONS: Today many courts would not permit the landlord to evict a tenant where his sole reason for doing so is a desire to retaliate for the reporting of building code violations. 40 ALR3d 753; 18 Will. L. Rev. 1119 (1973).

EXAMPLE: *T,* a tenant in an apartment, complained repeatedly to the landlord about building code violations. Receiving no satisfaction, *T* complained to the building department, which ordered *L* to cure the defects. When *T*'s lease expired, *L* filed an eviction suit. The court refused to evict *T,* because *L* was retaliating against *T.* The court allowed *T* to remain in possession until the code violations were eliminated and *T* could find another place to live. *Markese* v. *Cooper,* 333 N.Y.S.2d 63.

There are a number of cases holding that the entire doctrine of retaliatory eviction is inapplicable where the landlord simply seeks to oust the tenant so that he can remove a crumbling building from the housing market altogether. *Robinson* v. *Diamond Housing Corp.,* 463 F2d 853 (1972). This appears to make sense. If the landlord simply cannot keep the building in good shape, he should be permitted to demolish it. 51 N.C. L. Rev. 162 (1972).

But if the landlord raises the rent outrageously to get rid of a tenant who complains about building code violations, the tenant can move out and sue the landlord for damages, including damages for mental distress and punitive damages, that is, damages in an amount sufficient to constitute a punishment for the landlord's wrongdoing. *Aweeka* v. *Bonds,* 97 Cal. Reptr. 650 (1971).

So far the doctrine of retaliatory evictions has been applied only to residential properties. *Commercial Area Development* v. *Goodie Brand Packing,* 372 N.Y.S.2d 324 (1975).

NEW LAWS: Many states have enacted laws forbidding retaliatory eviction, for example, Massachusetts and New Hampshire. However, most of the law is judge-made law.

37.40(a) Retaliatory eviction—motive

To retaliate is to "get even" with someone for something he has done. This requires an *intention* to get even. As to landlord's motives, see Player, *Motive and Retaliatory Eviction of Tenants,* 1974 U. of Ill. L. F. 610.

> **EXAMPLE (1):** *T* complains to the city about building code violations in the building. Immediately, *L* serves notice on *T* that his month-to-month tenancy is terminated. There is an intention to retaliate.

> **EXAMPLE (2):** Facts as in the example given above, but *L* does not act until three years after *T*'s complaint.

Establishing intention to get even is simple in Example (1). It is next to impossible in Example (2).

37.40(b) Retaliatory eviction—the time factor

Many states have passed laws that fix a time that determines motivation.

> **EXAMPLE:** In California, if Landlord acts against Tenant within sixty days after Tenant has complained, it is assumed he is trying to "get even." Other states have other limits. Player, *supra,* p. 615.

37.40(c) Retaliatory eviction—landlord's protected activities

The landlord is not trying to "get even" if Tenant complains, and landlord raises rents generally and evenly so that he can pay for repairs. Landlord must spread the cost over the anticipated life of the repairs. Player, *supra,* p. 623.

A landlord may take the entire building off the rental market if he feels the cost of needed repairs would be beyond his means, but he must not single out the tenant who complained and evict only him.

37.40(d) Retaliatory eviction—the philosophy underpinning the new rule

The philosophy that sustains and supports the new rule was expounded in *Edwards* v. *Habib,* 397 F2d 687 (D.C. Cir. 1968). The court reasoned: (1) building codes cannot be enforced unless tenants can report violations without fear of Landlord's vengeance; (2) use of the state courts to evict complaining tenants would be action by the state taken to punish Tenant for exercising his constitutional right of *free speech.* Player, *Motive and Retaliatory Eviction,* 1974 U. of Ill. Law Forum 610 (excellent reference).

37.40(e) Retaliatory eviction—protected activities

Tenant activities against which Landlord must not retaliate include: (1) tenants' meetings; (2) complaints to the building code department; (3) forming a tenants' union; and (4) lawful rent withholding. Player, *supra,* p. 614.

37.40(f) Laws and ordinances

Various laws and ordinances give specific protection to the residential tenant against unfair conduct of the landlord.

EXAMPLE: Illinois has a statute and Illinois cities have ordinances on the subject of retaliatory eviction and rent withholding. *Clore* v. *Fredman,* 59 Ill. 2d 20, 319 NE2d 18 (1974).

37.41 Limitations on the landlord's right to select tenants, renew leases and tenancies, and to evict tenants

Under the old law, which is still true except regarding residential units, the landlord could rent to whomever he pleased, refuse to rent, refuse to renew leases, and evict any tenant whose lease or tenancy has been terminated. Now the court decisions and statutes are beginning to impose limits in all these regards:

NEW DIRECTIONS: Public housing. Where any public body is the landlord, the tenant's tenancy cannot be terminated without a hearing and inquiry into the reasonableness of the termination. *Thorpe* v. *Housing Authority,* 393 U.S. 268 (1968). Thus, in the case of such a landlord there are strict limits on the landlord's right to evict. *CHA* v. *Harris,* 275 NE2d 353 (Ill. 1976).

37.41(a) The quasi-public landlord

It certainly seems logical to hold that where a public body, such as a city or a housing authority, is the landlord, the tenant will have constitutional rights that tenants of private landlord do not have. But in recent times the notion has gained currency that private landlords who receive government assistance in some form are *quasi-public landlords,* and their tenants have at least some of the rights of tenants in public projects.

EXAMPLE: *L,* a landlord whose building was erected by FHA financing and who received a real estate tax exemption, could not refuse to accept *T* as a tenant because *T* was a welfare recipient. *Colon* v. *Tompkins Square Neighbors,* 294 F. Supp. 134 (1968). *L* cannot accept benefits from the government and turn his back on the wards of the government.

EXAMPLE: *L,* a landlord, in the identical situation of the landlord in the preceding example, refused to renew *T*'s lease. *T* had been an outspoken advocate of tenants' rights and had organized demonstrations against *L*. The court held that *L* could not evict *T* without giving him notice and a hearing to show that *L* was acting with good cause. *McQueen* v. *Drucker,* 317 F.Supp. 1122 (1970). *T* had the right to free speech.

EXAMPLE: Some courts require such landlords to give the tenants notice and to hold a hearing when the former wants to increase rents. 28 ALR Fed. 839.

This court-made law has now been formalized in HUD rules. 8 Urb. Law. 605 (1976).

37.42 Deposits in court

Where a dispute exists between *L* and *T*, the eviction court has power to order the rent deposited in court until the dispute is resolved. *McNeal* v. *Habib*, 346 A2d 508 (D.C. 1975).

37.43 Landlord's duty to protect against criminal acts

Traditionally, the landlord has been regarded as having no duty to protect his tenants against criminal acts of third parties. 59 Georgetown L. J. 1163.

NEW DIRECTIONS: However, under the new notion that the lease is a contract for services, the courts are beginning to place upon the landlord the duty to protect the tenant against criminal acts of third persons which he should have foreseen might occur. *Kline* v. *1500 Mass. Ave. Apt. Corp.,* 439 F2d 477. This would be especially true if the landlord's advertisements make mention of security protection or where the building is in a high-crime area or where the building has a record of criminal activity. 59 Georgetown L. J. 1185. There will be a tendency toward the application of a ''higher-the-amount-of-rent, the-greater-the-duty-of-care'' principle applied in the case of hotel guests. 59 Georgetown L. J. 1189.

EXAMPLE: *T,* an elderly tenant, was assaulted and robbed as he entered his apartment. The apartment was in a high-crime area. *T* sued his landlord, *L,* contending *L* was negligent in failing to provide adequate lighting and door locks. The Michigan Supreme Court held *L* was liable. *Johnston* v. *Harris,* 198 NW2d 409 (Mich. 1972); 43 ALR3d 331.

EXAMPLE: *L* held liable to *T* because *L* failed to furnish adequate locks. *Braitman* v. *Erie Inv. Co.,* 350 A2d 268 (N.J. 1976).

EXAMPLE: *L* held liable where an intruder set fire to the building, causing damage to *T*'s property. *Warner* v. *Arnold,* 210 SE2d 350 (1974).

EXAMPLE: If a second burglary occurs, *L* is clearly liable. The facts show that burglary was foreseeable. *Stribling* v. *CHA.* 34 Ill. App.3d 551; 346 NE2d 47 (1975).

REFERENCES: Pippin v. *CHA,* 78 Ill. 2d 204, 399 NE2d 596 (1979); *Loesser* v. *Nathan Hale Gardens,* 425 N.Y.S.2d 104 (1980); *Secretary of Housing* v. *Layfeld,* 152 Cal. Reptr. 342 (1978); *Smith* v. *General Apartment Co.,* 312 SE2d 74 (Ga. 1977); *Bratman* v. *Overlook Terrace,* 68 N.J. 368, 346 A2d 76 (1975); *Knapp* v. *Wilson,* 535 SW2d 371 (Tex. 1976); 1970 Duke L. J. 543; 74 Dick. L. Rev. 543; 5 U. of San Francisco L. Rev. 378; 62 Va. L. Rev. 383 (1976); 9 R.E.L.J. 311 (1980); 43 ALR3d 331; 44 U. Conn. L. Rev. 405 (1975); 70 Dick. L. Rev. 236 (1966); 63 Mass. L. Rev. 61 (1978); 8 R.E.L.J. 61 (1978); 9 Urb. L. Ann. 259

(1975); 30 Stanf. L. Rev. 725 (1978); 8 Suffolk L. Rev. 1305; 5 U. of Richmond L. Rev. 148; 1975 Wis. L. Rev. 160; 67 ALR3d 490, 587; 66 *id.* 202.

37.44   Tenant unions

Because one tenant has little bargaining power as against a landlord, tenant unions have been formed. 59 Ill. B. J. 732; 23 U. Fla. L. Rev. 79. These unions engage in collective bargaining with landlords. Tenant organizations which have recognized the need for more tenant control have developed a variety of goals. The most frequently sought goals include:(1) negotiation of a new lease for use between individual tenants and the landlord; (2) development of a grievance procedure and/or plan for arbitration of disputes; (3) recognition of the tenant organization as the exclusive representative of the landlord's tenants; (4) formulation of a satisfactory way to handle tenant needs and to bring the buildings into compliance with the building code; (5) participation of the tenant organization in decisions about rent increases; and (6) provision of adequate security for the dwelling units. 46 L.A.B. Bull. 163. Some tenant unions have engaged in rent strikes. 3 Columbia J. Law & Social Problems 1 (1967). By legal maneuvers some unions have been able to stall evictions for as long as nine months. 46 L.A.B. Bull. 162.

A landlord must not refuse to renew a tenant's lease simply because the tenant has been active in a tenants' union. *Engler* v. *Capital Management Corp.,* 271 A2d 615 (N.J. 1970).

37.45   Residential tenants

As is evident, the law of landlord and tenant is progressing steadily toward a compartmentalization. The law for residential tenants is developing safeguards that do not exist, for example, with respect to business tenants. 54 Cal. L. Rev. 670 (1966); 41 U. Colo. L. Rev. 541 (1969); 54 Georgetown L. J. 519 (1966); 5 Suffolk L. Rev. 213; 46 Yale L. J. 508; 6 Wake Forest L. Rev. 119; 1968 Wash. U. L. Q. 461 (1968).

37.46   Rent control

A number of local governments have adopted residential rent control ordinances. Such ordinances have been held valid. *Inganamort* v. *Borough of Ft.Lee,* 62 N.J. 521, 303 A2d 298 (1973); *Birkenfeld* v. *City of Berkeley,* 550 P2d 1001 (Cal. 1976); *Marshall House* v. *Rent Control Bd.,* 266 NE2d 876 (Mass. 1971); 30 Rutgers L. Rev. 1025.

NEW DIRECTIONS: There is a law that has been drafted to protect tenants. It is called the Uniform Residential Landlord and Tenant Act (URLTA). It places obligations on the landlord, like complying with building codes and keeping common areas in a clean and safe condition. It gives the tenant the right to withhold rent if the landlord fails to perform. It forbids harassment or retaliation by the landlord. A version of this law has been enacted in Alaska, Arizona, Delaware, Florida, Hawaii, Kentucky, Nebraska, New Mexico, Oregon, and Washington. Other tenant protection laws have been enacted in Massachusetts, New Jersey, Texas, and New York. More such legislation is on the way.

37.47 Eviction—partial eviction—constructive eviction—partial constructive eviction

A landlord who evicts his tenant wrongfully obviously can no longer collect rent. Indeed, even if the eviction is only from part of the premises, the same result follows.

EXAMPLE: Landlord leased Lot 1 to Tenant. The lot was improved with a house and garage. Landlord wrongfully took possession of the garage. Tenant is not liable for rent, even though he continues to occupy the house. *Tuchin* v. *Chambers,* 439 SW2d 849 (Tex. 1969).

If the landlord's conduct makes the premises untenantable, or if the stairways, walks, or elevators become unusable, a *constructive eviction* occurs, and if the tenant moves out as a result, he is no longer liable for rent. *Mease* v. *Fox,* 200 NW2d 791 (Iowa 1972).

EXAMPLE: Landlord fails to supply heat in the wintertime to an apartment rented to Tenant. Tenant moves out. He is no longer liable for rent.

EXAMPLE: Infestation of apartment with vermin is a constructive eviction. This is a matter under control of landlord. 27 ALR3d 924.

EXAMPLE: Foregoing is especially true where caused by landlord's acts, as by his failure to pick up garbage. 27 ALR3d 935.

EXAMPLE: Infestation of a house presents a harder problem because the tenant has some measure of control here. Nevertheless, infestation of a house with rats is a constructive eviction, since this may be beyond tenant's control. *Lemle* v. *Breeden,* 51 Hawaii 426, 462 P2d 470 (1969). Of course, this would be a constructive eviction in an apartment.

EXAMPLE: Water leaking through a roof or into a basement is a constructive eviction. 33 ALR3d 1356.

Matters wholly beyond the control of the landlord are not a constructive eviction.

EXAMPLE: An adjoining tenant had noisy machinery that prevented tenant from holding seminars. There is no constructive eviction. *Finkelstien* v. *Levinson,* 343 N.Y.S.2d 849 (1973).

NEW DIRECTIONS: Changes are taking place in the old law of constructive eviction. The right to move out is worthless when there is an acute shortage of rental apartments. Thus, the line between actual eviction and constructive eviction has become blurred, and the courts are introducing new ideas that are designed to achieve justice and to place little emphasis on labels.

EXAMPLE: Landlord leased a restaurant to Tenant who took possession, not knowing that part of the leased premises was not available for occupancy. The court held this was "actual partial eviction" and that Tenant could occupy the occupiable part without paying rent. *Metzenbaum* v. *Crepes D'Asic,* 367 N.Y.S.2d 645.

EXAMPLE: Landlord leased Tenant an apartment. Tenant was forced to discontinue use of the terrace because of water dripping from the building's air conditioner. The court permitted Tenant to remain in occupancy and to discontinue paying rent. The court held this was "partial constructive eviction." *East Haven Assoc., Inc.* v. *Gurian,* 313 N.Y.S.2d 927 (1970).

EXAMPLE: Tenant, an orthodontist, resisted eviction because Landlord was not furnishing proper heating and air conditioning. The court held that because of this breach on Landlord's part, Tenant was not required to pay the rent and could not be evicted. *Demirci* v. *Burns* 124 N.J.S. 274, 306 A2d 468 (1973).

EXAMPLE: Landlord leased a store building to Tenant, with a covenant to repair. Part of the building was destroyed by fire. The court allowed Tenant to occupy the remainder of the building with a reduction of rent. *Coppola* v. *Tidewater Oil Co.,* 244 N.Y.S.2d 898 (1963).

NEW LAWS: Statutes are being enacted on the subject of rent withholding and the other new rules. *De Paul* v. *Kauffman,* 441 Pa. 386, 272 A2d 500 (1971). The New Jersey statute even includes mobile homes in its retaliatory eviction statute. In Maryland Tenant may repudiate the lease within thirty days of occupancy if the warranty of habitability has been breached.

37.47(a)   Prior law

Up to the present time the law has been that a tenant who claims that his landlord's conduct amounts to a constructive eviction must vacate the premises within a reasonable time after the landlord has failed to correct the condition. 75 ALR 1114. Some courts will continue to adhere to this view. However, the newer view recognizes the dilemma that confronts the tenant and permits him to use this defense while retaining occupancy of the rented premises. 1 ALR4th 849.

REFERENCE: Restatement of Property 2d § 6.1, Comment h, adopts the view of the recent decisions that the tenant need not abandon the premises where the landlord is guilty of conduct amounting to a constructive eviction. Instead, he may sue for damages or claim an abatement of rent.

37.48   Unconscionability

The notion that the court can strike down an unconscionable lease or any unconscionable provision thereof has become part of the law of landlord and tenant. Restatement of Property 2d § 5.5; Berger, *Hard Leases Make Bad Law,* 74 Columb. L. Rev. 791; 24 Baylor L. Rev. 443, 498.

EXAMPLE: An apartment lease obligated Tenant to pay Landlord as additional rent in attorneys' fees upon commencement of any proceeding by Landlord as a result of Tenant's default. The clause was held void. *Weidmen* v. *Tomaselli,* 365 N.Y.S.2d 681.

EXAMPLE: Landlord, an oil company, leased a filling station to Tenant under a lease with a clause stating that Landlord would not be liable for loss or damage resulting from the negligence of Landlord's employees and that Tenant would pay for any such loss. One of Landlord's employees sprayed gasoline over Tenant, and severe burns resulted. The court held the clause void and awarded damages to Tenant. *Weaver* v. *American Oil Co.,* 276 NE2d 144 (Ind. 1971).

The courts have even held that Landlord must renew a lease if refusal to do so would be unconscionable.

EXAMPLE: Landlord, an oil company, had leased the filling station to Tenant for many years. Tenant had spent a great deal of money in improving the station and building up a business. The court compelled Landlord to renew the lease. *Shell Oil Co.* v. *Marinello,* 294 A2d 253 (N.J.)

37.49   Fair dealing

Some courts will strike down any provision of a lease if enforcement would not be considered "fair dealing." Berger, *Hard Leases Make Bad Law,* 74 Columb. L. Rev. 791, 805.

EXAMPLE: Landlord leased commercial premises to Tenant with an option to renew. Tenant failed to exercise the option within the time allowed, but Landlord, after such expiration, notified Tenant that his lease would soon end. Tenant then tendered to Landlord the money needed to renew the lease, but Landlord refused. The court held that Landlord was not injured by the technical defect and compelled Landlord to renew the lease. *George W. Miller & Co.* v. *Wolf Sales & Service Co.,* 318 N.Y.S.2d 24 (1971); 74 Columb. L. Rev. 791, 805. It will probably be a long time before other courts decide to be as liberal as this.

38 RACIAL DISCRIMINATION IN REAL ESTATE

38.01 History

The history of slavery and race relations up to the time of World War I is thoroughly documented. The modern history begins with World War I and much of it occurred in Chicago.

During World War I the Chicago meat packers recruited black workers in the southern states. Up to that time the black areas of Chicago had been relatively stable. But with the vast demand for meat for our allies and ourselves created by the war and the dwindling pool of white manpower, the meat packers saw fit to bring blacks into Chicago, and the black areas began to expand into adjoining white areas. Tension resulted. Rioting broke out and many deaths occurred.

This was followed by another period of violence, during which new black churches were bombed.

Finally, the police brought the situation under control.

In lieu of violence, white neighborhoods created the restrictive covenant. This document was an agreement designed to cover an entire neighborhood. The property owners in the areas bordering black areas agreed that their properties would never be occupied by blacks. The theory was that agreements not to *sell* to blacks were invalid under the old English rules forbidding restraints on sales of land. But a restriction dealing only with *occupancy* was thought to be valid. *Doherty* v. *Rice,* 240 Wis. 389, 3 NW2d 734 (1942).

However, in time these covenants were attacked on the ground that they could only be enforced by court proceedings. Court proceedings are *state action.* State action that produces racial discrimination is forbidden by the Constitution. The Supreme Court ultimately so held. *Shelley* v. *Kraemer,* 334 U.S. 1, 3 ALR2d 441 (1948). *Shelley* v. *Kraemer* has been the subject of much learned comment, e.g., 110 U. Pa. L. Rev. 473; 108 *id.* 1; 60 Columb. L. Rev. 1083; 84 Harv. L. Rev. 59.

611

38.02 Racial discrimination—federal laws—history

The Thirteenth Amendment to the federal Constitution abolished slavery. It took effect on December 18, 1865. Many southern legislatures adopted the "Black Codes," which, in effect, placed severe restrictions on the newly won rights of Negroes. Congress therefore passed a civil rights bill effective on April 9, 1866. Thereafter the Fourteenth Amendment was ratified on July 28, 1868, and the Fifteenth Amendment on March 30, 1870. On May 31, 1870, a new Civil Rights Act was passed. And on April 20, 1871, Congress enacted another statute, and still another statute on March 1, 1875. 42 USCA § 1981 *et seq.* These laws are hereafter referred to as the Civil War laws. The history is set forth in detail in 50 Mich. L. Rev. 1323 (1952). Paralleling the new laws creating new rights were new laws giving the federal courts power to enforce these rights. 90 Harv. L. Rev. 1133, 1147 (1977).

The Civil War laws were neglected for a long period of time. When they were revived in 1961, there was still no inkling that they would be used by Negroes to enforce their rights in real estate. 90 Harv. L. Rev. 1133.

Then came the decision in *Jones* v. *Alfred H. Mayer Co.,* 392 U.S. 409, 20 L.Ed.2d 1189 (1968), decided under the Civil War laws. Please note that this case was pending in the lower courts while Congress was deliberating on the Open Occupancy Law of 1968.

> **EXAMPLE:** In 1965 *A,* a black, sought to purchase a home from *B,* a professional builder, in a subdivision owned by *B. B* rejected *A,* his rejection being racially motivated. *A* filed an injunction suit against *B* to prohibit *B* from so discriminating. In 1968 the court entered a judgment ordering *B* to sell to *A* at the price prevailing at the time of the wrongful refusal in 1965, which was substantially less than the current market of such a home. *B* must absorb this loss. *Jones* v. *Alfred H. Mayer Co.,* 392 U.S. 409 (1968). The court held that the Civil War laws were still alive.

38.03 Federal legislation—the 1968 law

A federal "open occupancy" law was enacted in 1968. 42 USCA § 3601 (Title VIII).

The law covers dwellings, including homes and multifamily residences (two-flats, duplexes, apartments), and also vacant land acquired for construction for such purposes. No doubt acquisition of vacant land zoned for residential purposes will be regarded as subject to the law. Condominiums and co-ops also come under the law. The law applies to sales, leases, and all types of rental agreements. It does not include properties used *exclusively* for commercial or industrial purposes. But if *part* of the building is used for residential purposes, the building is subject to the law.

The law creates new and important rights. Some are spelled out fairly clearly. Others will come into sharper focus only after the Supreme Court has interpreted the law. Some observations can be made. Where *bias* against a person is based on race, color, religion, or national origin, the following are unlawful:

1. To refuse to sell or lease or negotiate for sale or lease because of such bias, or to discriminate in the furnishing of services or facilities.

EXAMPLE: A landlord cannot furnish maid service to white tenants and refuse this service to blacks.

2. To discriminate in exacting terms of the sale or lease, for example, by asking a higher price because of the race of the buyer.
3. To advertise in the newspapers or post notices on the building that particular races will not be welcomed as buyers or tenants.
4. To state that a dwelling is not available, where such statement is made because of the race of the party seeking to buy or rent.
5. For a lender to refuse a party a loan or to insist on higher interest rates or harsher loan terms because of racial reasons.
6. For real estate brokers to refuse membership in their organizations or multiple-listing services because of racial reasons.
7. To induce a person to sell by creating fears of racial change in the neighborhood.

Enforcement of the law is complex. In general, the Secretary of the Department of Housing and Urban Development (HUD) is entrusted with some of the machinery of enforcement. The following procedures are available:

1. If there is a substantially equivalent remedy under a state law or ordinance, HUD notifies the appropriate state officials to enforce the law.
2. The party discriminated against may file a suit for damages. *U.S.* v. *Peltzer,* 377 F.Supp. 121 (N.D. Ala. 1974).
3. The court may issue injunctions restraining violation of the law, and set aside deeds or leases, except that no deed or lease shall be set aside if entered into before a court order has issued and the grantee or lessee had no actual knowledge of the proceedings. One is left with the inference that a court that sets aside a deed to a white person can order a sale thereof to a black who made an earlier comparable offer and was rejected because of racial bias.
4. The United States attorney general may obtain injunctions restraining violations of the law, if a "pattern or practice" is evident. *U.S.* v. *Mintzes,* 304 F.Supp. 1305 (D.Md 1969).
5. In certain instances the law provides for fines against, or imprisonment of, persons using force or threat of force to bring about racial discrimination in housing.

As is evident, Congress should have repealed the Civil War laws when it enacted the Open Housing Law. It failed to do so. This was an oversight. Thus, we have two overlapping laws. But the result is that racial discrimination not forbidden by one law is forbidden by the other. For example, Congress meant to allow a homeowner to sell his home as he pleased so long as he used no broker and did not advertise. But this is forbidden by the old law. It is a confusing situation.

38.04   Federal legislation— the Civil War laws

In the Civil War laws it is provided that American citizens of every race and color shall have the *same right* throughout the country to purchase, lease, sell, hold, and convey real and personal property as is enjoyed by white persons. Laying stress on the phrase "the same right," the Supreme Court has held that this law prohibits all racial discrimination, *private and public,* in the sale and rental of property. Thus, every "racially motivated refusal to sell or rent" is prohibited. *Jones* v. *Alfred H. Mayer Co.,* 392 U.S. 409 (1968). This law to some extent overlaps the Open Housing Act of 1968, to some extent goes beyond it, and to some extent omits protection afforded by the 1968 law. 42 USCA § 1981 *et seq.*

> **EXAMPLE:**   *A* owns his home which he occupies with his family. This is the only land he owns. He offers it for sale without employing a broker, but declines to sell to *B,* a black. His refusal is motivated by *B*'s race. This refusal is wrongful under the Civil War law. Such a situation is expressly omitted from the coverage of the 1968 law under which a person owning only one home and selling it without a broker is not forbidden to discriminate.

> **EXAMPLE:**   In the example given above, *B* seeks the aid of the attorney general of the United States. He will not succeed. The Civil War law makes no provision for furnishing such aid.

> **EXAMPLE:**   *A* refuses to sell his store to *B,* a black, his refusal being racially motivated. This refusal is prohibited by the Civil War law, but does not come under the 1968 law.

> **EXAMPLE:**   *A* owns a large apartment building. For racial reasons he refuses to rent an apartment to *B,* a black. Both laws forbid this type of discrimination.

As the Supreme Court has pointed out, the Civil War law does *not* do the following:

> 1. It does not forbid discrimination on grounds of religion or national origin:

> **EXAMPLE:**   *A,* a member of *XYZ Church,* owns only one home. He offers his home for sale without the aid of a real estate broker. As purchasers appear, he states verbally that he will sell only to members of *XYZ Church.* The 1866 law does not forbid such action.

> 2. It does not deal specifically with discrimination in the provision of services or facilities in connection with the sale or rental of a dwelling, for example, furnishing maid service to apartment tenants.
> 3. It does not prohibit advertising or other representations that indicate discriminatory preferences.

4. It does not refer explicitly to discrimination in financing arrangements or in the provision of real estate brokerage services.

5. It does not enable a rejected purchaser or tenant to call upon the attorney general or any other federal officer for aid.

6. It makes no express provision for the bringing of damage suits by rejected purchasers or tenants, but the court has indicated it has kept an open mind on the question of whether a right to damages could be implied or inferred from the language and purpose of the law.

Racial covenants are totally invalid now. *Mayers* v. *Ridley,* 465 F2d 630.

Other federal court decisions make it clear that the courts mean to enforce the federal laws.

EXAMPLE: The courts have held that the recorder of deeds cannot record a racial covenant. *Mayers* v. *Ridley,* 465 F2d 630.

EXAMPLE: A landlord was forbidden to state that no Jews or Blacks had ever lived on the premises.

EXAMPLE: A newspaper can be enjoined from publishing discriminatory advertising. *U.S.* v. *Hunter,* 324 F.Supp 529.

38.05   Remedies for racial discrimination

In considering the remedies available for racial discrimination, one must remember that today's courts do not hesitate to improvise remedies where the statute is silent. These are called *implied remedies.* 61 L. Ed.2d 910. Damages have been allowed. 85 ALR3d 351.

REFERENCES: 7 Boston Coll. Ind. & Comm. L. Rev. 495 (1966); 5 Columb. Human Rts. Rev. 335 (1973); 1970 Duke L. J. 819; 82 Harv. L. Rev. 834 (1969); 18 West. Res. L. Rev. 278 (1966).

EXAMPLE: Landlord refused to rent to Tenant because she was black. She recovered damages of $10,000 for emotional distress and $10,000 punitive damages (to punish Landlord). *Parker* v. *Shonfeld,* 409 F.Supp. 876 (1976).

EXAMPLE: A white plaintiff can sue a landlord who refuses to rent to her because she has a black husband. *Hodge* v. *Seiler,* 558 F2d 284 (CA 5th 1977).

And, as has been mentioned, there are laws giving the federal courts power to entertain suits charging racial bias. 90 Harv. L. Rev. 1133.

38.06   Fair housing developments—zoning

In the area of racial litigation, some aspects are beginning to crystallize: (1) In instances of isolated individual discrimination, the court decisions appear to give adequate implementation to state and federal legislation. The damage awards for individual acts of racial discrimination are growing in size. They are calculated to offer deterrence to individuals and to groups, like real estate boards, that might otherwise be tempted to perpetuate discriminatory practices. (2) With respect to villages that seek to perpetuate geographic racial discrimination, the litigation has been largely ineffective.

The litigation has been protracted and indescribably expensive. Case after case has gone up and down from trial courts to reviewing courts like a yo-yo, running up astronomic attorneys' fees and court costs.

The Department of Justice, in consequence, has made a frontal attack on suburban segregation policies, hoping to open up white villages to minorities. The philosophy here, in addition to the strictly legal notion of achieving the racial equality mandated by the Constitution, is that of providing homes for minorities close to the places of employment offered by prospering suburbs.

> **EXAMPLE:**   Parma is a working- and middle-class suburb of Cleveland. Its population is more than 100,000, virtually solid white. The United States filed suit against the city alleging racial exclusion as evidenced by: (1) Its refusal to enact a fair housing ordinance. (2) Its opposition to all public and low-income housing. (3) Its rejection of a developer's plan for low-income housing. (4) Its refusal to apply for federal grants that would require racial integration. (5) Its enactment of ordinances requiring a referendum on zoning changes. The city sought a dismissal of the suit. The court refused to dismiss. *U.S.* v. *City of Parma* 661 F2d 562 (N.D. Ohio 1979).

> **EXAMPLE:**   Black Jack was an unincorporated area in St. Louis County. Developers announced a plan for low-income, multiracial housing. The community incorporated as a city and passed a zoning ordinance that excluded multifamily dwellings. A federal court struck down the ordinance as palpably discriminatory. The plaintiff developers then sought a court order compelling the village to admit multiracial housing. The court of appeals ordered the city to come up with a plan that would provide low-income housing. *Park View Heights Corp.* v. *City of Black Jack,* 605 F2d 1033 (8th Cir. 1979) *cert. den.* 48 U.S.L.W. 3552, 1980.

These decisions are indicative of the assumption by the Justice Department of an activist role in this area.

In general, where the public authorities are taking action that will concentrate location of low-income housing in racially segregated areas, most courts will endeavor to block this move. 52 J. of Urb. L. 897.

> **EXAMPLE:**   A developer wanted to build a multifamily residential housing project and sought rezoning for that purchase. It was refused. However, the courts found that the refusal to rezone was due to the opposition of the white residents. The court ordered rezoning. *Dailey* v. *City of Lawton,* 425 F2d 1037 (1970), 5 J. of Law Reform 357 (1972).

> **NEW DEVELOPMENTS:**   Bills are pending in Congress on this subject. A steady stream of legislation, both state and federal, can be expected.

38.07   Permitted discriminations

The federal law does not prohibit an owner from considering any factors other than race which he feels are relevant in determining whether to rent to one individual or another. Such factors, which an owner might consider, include the *credit standing of the applicant, his assets, his financial stability, his reputation in the community, his age, the size of his family, the ages of his children, his past experience as a lessee or tenant, the length of time he plans to occupy the premises, and whether he is or is not a transient.*

The owner may also consider more subjective factors in determining whether he will rent to one individual or another. Thus, he may consider the applicant's appearance, his demeanor, the owner's estimate of his trustworthiness or truthfulness, or other subjective factors. Indeed, businessmen utilize such conclusions and opinions in their daily affairs.

Although such factors are subjective, they may be considered. Nonetheless, the owner may later be called upon to demonstrate in court that these and not racial motivations were responsible for his decision in refusing to rent or sell to a black. Subjective factors are by their nature difficult to prove and often have little more than the credibility of the individual witness behind them.

An owner may even refuse to rent to an individual simply because he does not like him. No one is required to rent or sell to an individual he doesn't like. As in other cases, however, the owner may later be called upon to demonstrate in court that his personal dislike of an individual, rather than the individual's race, was responsible for his decision to refuse him as a tenant.

The owner may consider such factors as those set out above in determining whether to rent or sell to any individual. He is not precluded by any federal statute from considering such factors. Indeed, *any* factor, other than race, which is relevant to a decision whether to rent or sell to an individual may be considered, and the list of factors set forth above is not intended to be, and could not constitute, an exclusive list. *Bush* v. *Kaim,* 297 F.Supp. 151 (1969); 7 Seton Hall L. Rev. 168 (1975).

> **EXAMPLE:** *L* refused to rent to *B* (a black) because *B* did not meet *L*'s requirement that a tenant have an income equal to 90 percent of the rent. This was not discriminatory. *Boyd* v. *Lefrak Org.,* 509 F2d 1110 (1975); 89 Harv. L. Rev. 1631; 7 Seton Hall L. Rev. 168 (1975).

38.08   State constitutions, state laws, court decisions, ordinances, commission rulings and orders

An increasing number of states and cities have enacted laws and ordinances forbidding racial discrimination in housing. Such laws set up commissions to hear complaints of racial discrimination. The following are illustrations of state commission orders and court decisions enforcing local open housing laws.

> **EXAMPLE:** An apartment owner discriminated against a Black by refusing to rent him an apartment. The Black filed a complaint with the state commission. An

order was entered requiring the owner to rent an apartment to the Black at the regular prevailing rental and to desist from acts of discrimination in rental practices against the Black or any other persons because of race, religion, or national origin. *In re Ruth,* 12 Race Relations Rep. 1703 (Cal).

EXAMPLE: A commission ordered the landlord to rent to a Black who had been refused occupancy for racial reasons. White tenants who later moved in with knowledge of the problem were required to vacate. *City of N.Y.* v. *Camp Const. Co.,* 11 Race Relations Rep. 1949 (N.Y.).

EXAMPLE: The court sustained a commission order ousting a white tenant because he was not a bona fide tenant ignorant of the landlord's earlier attempt to discriminate against a Black seeking to rent the same apartment. *Feigenblum* v. *Comm.,* 278 N.Y.S.2d 652.

EXAMPLE: A white subdivision was subject to a recorded declaration giving the homeowners' association a preemptive option, that is, the right to buy any homesite at the same price another party would offer. A homeowner entered into a contract to sell to a black. The contract was specifically made subject to the recorded declaration. The association then gave notice of exercise of its preemptive privilege. The court held that exercise of such a privilege would be illegal under the state fair housing law if done solely because of racial bias. *Vaught* v. *Village Creek,* 7 Race Relations Rep. 849.

38.09   Landlord and tenant

Quite a number of cases arising either under federal or state law have held the landlord guilty of racial discrimination. See 11 U. of Fla. L. Rev. 344.

EXAMPLE: The landlord accepted a Black tenant and then resorted to incredibly evasive tactics to discourage the tenant. He was held liable for damages. *Jackson* v. *Concord Co.,* 253 A2d 793.

EXAMPLE: The landlord refused to rent a house to a black, and a relative of the landlord agreed to cover up for the landlord by buying the house. Both were held liable. *Rody* v. *Hollis,* 500 P2d 97 (Wash. 1972). The damages awarded can be great ($20,000). *Parker* v. *Shonfeld,* 409 F.Supp. 896 (1976).

EXAMPLE: Midland, the owner of an apartment complex, restricted blacks to buildings 65 and 66, and there were only two black families in the remainder of the complex. Racial discrimination is established. *Midland Homes* v. *Penn. Hum. Rel. Comm.,* 333 A2d 516 (Pa. 1975).

EXAMPLE: The commission found the landlord guilty of discrimination in rejecting a Black tenant but refused to oust a white tenant to whom the landlord later rented the apartment. The white tenant was an innocent party unaware of the discrimination. The court sustained this ruling. *Comm.* v. *City Builders, Inc.,* 277 N.Y.S.2d 434.

EXAMPLE: Exclusive rental agents found to have refused to rent to plaintiffs on the basis of their race are liable under the law for their unlawful conduct even where the management agreement stated that leases and tenants shall be approved by owner and where their actions are at behest of their principal. *Jeanty* v. *McKey & Pogue, Inc.,* 496 F2d 1119 (7th Cir. 1974).

EXAMPLE: A landlord had no right to evict a tenant because the tenant married a Black. *Prendergast* v. *Synder,* 50 Cal. Reptr. 903, 413 P2d 847.

But at times the court finds that discrimination is not present.

EXAMPLE: *L* refused to rent to a black lawyer, claiming that *L* disliked all lawyers and regarded them as troublemakers. No discrimination was shown. *Kramarsky* v. *Stahl Management,* N.Y. S.Ct. 11/3/77.

38.10   Brokers

A broker may lose his license under state law if he is guilty of racial discrimination.

EXAMPLE: *B,* a broker, represented to a black person that a home was not available for sale. In fact, it was so available. *B* was suspended. *Strickland* v. *Dept. of Registration,* 376 NE2d 255 (Ill. 1978).

EXAMPLE: *B,* a broker, engaged in blockbusting, i.e., he represented that the area was changing, values were declining, and women were unsafe. *B* was disciplined. *In the Matter of Butterfly & Green Inc.* v. *Lorenzo,* 30 N.Y.2d 250, 326 NE2d 799 (1975).

Quite a number of city ordinances forbidding discrimination—for example, by real estate brokers—have been upheld as valid. *Chicago Real Estate Board* v. *Chicago,* 36 Ill.2d 530, 224 NE2d 793.

Federal and state legislation forbidding "blockbusting" by real estate brokers is valid. 34 ALR3d 1432; *U.S.* v. *Hunter,* 459 F2d 205 (4th Cir. 1972).

EXAMPLE: A broker is forbidden to tell property owners that the neighborhood is "going colored." This is true even if the prospective buyer asks this question. *Brown* v. *State Realty Co.,* 304 F.Supp. 1236.

EXAMPLE: The rule against blockbusting applies even to statements like "This is a changing neighborhood." *U.S.* v. *Mintzes,* 304 F.Supp. 1305.

Of course, a broker who violates either law is liable for damages.

38.11   Seller and buyer

Racial discrimination by a seller is illegal.

EXAMPLE: A black bought a vacant lot adjoining the seller's home, using a white nominee to accomplish the purchase. When the seller discovered the identity of the real purchaser he brought suit. The court refused to set aside the transaction. *Hirsch* v. *Silberstein,* 227 A2d 638 (Pa.).

38.12 Options

Options must not be used as a discrimination tool.

EXAMPLE: A white subdivision was subject to a recorded declaration giving the homeowners' association a preemptive option, that is, the right to buy any homesite at the same price another party would offer. A homeowner entered into a contract to sell to a black. The contract was specifically made subject to the recorded declaration. The association then gave notice of exercise of its preemptive privilege. The court held that exercise of such a privilege would be illegal under the state fair housing law if done solely because of racial bias. *Vaught* v. *Village Creek,* 7 Race Relations Rep. 849.

38.13 Mortgages—redlining

It is illegal for mortgage houses to "redline" black areas. The word "redlining" comes from the practice of marking black areas in red on a map, thus indicating the areas where loans will not be made. 8 Pac. L. J. 719.

38.14 Mortgages—foreclosure

A mortgage house must not discriminate against black persons in its foreclosure practices. *Harper* v. *Union Sav. Assn.,* 459 F.Supp. 1254 (1977).

EXAMPLE: If a mortgage house routinely grants a sixty-day grace period to whites it must do likewise regarding blacks.

38.15 Builder–seller discrimination

A builder–seller must not discriminate among his customers.

EXAMPLE: A *Corp.* had *X, Y,* and *Z* as its shareholders. It engaged in the building and selling of homes in a black area of Chicago. *X, Y,* and *Z* also had other corporations engaged in building identical homes in white areas of the Chicago metropolitan area. In the black area, *A Corp.* sold only on installment contracts, even where the buyers could make large cash payments and obtain mortgages. It sold at prices higher than it charged for identical homes in white areas. The corporation and *X, Y,* and *Z* were held guilty of racial discrimination. *Clark* v. *Universal Builders,* 501 F2d 324 (CA 7th 1973), 88 Harv. L. Rev. 1610, 1975 Duke L. J. 781, 12 Houston L. Rev. 476, 28 Rutgers L. Rev. 1009.

EXAMPLE: In 1965 *A,* a black, sought to purchase a home from *B,* a professional builder, in a subdivision owned by *B. B* rejected *A,* his rejection being racially motivated. *A* filed an injunction suit against *B* to sell to *A* at the price prevailing at the time of the wrongful refusal in 1965, which is substantially less than the current market of such a home. *B* must absorb this loss. This example is the precise, factual situation in *Jones* v. *Alfred H. Mayer Co.,* 392 U.S. 409.

38.16 Housing projects   Many local housing authorities and HUD have been instructed by the courts to develop housing projects in predominantly white areas. They must not be confined to the ghetto areas of the inner city. *Hills* v. *Grautreaux,* 425 U.S. 284, 96 S.Ct. 1538, 47 L. Ed.2d 792 (1976); Ackerman, *Integration for Subsidizing Housing,* 26 Stanf. L. Rev. 245 (1974); 47 Chi-Kent L. Rev. 253 (1970); 22 Syracuse L. Rev. 1139; 5 Ga. L. Rev. 603 (1971); 83 Harv. L. Rev. 1441; 64 N.W.U. L. Rev. 720.

A housing authority cannot discriminate in favor of a minority.

> **EXAMPLE:** A housing authority gave preference to members of the Jewish faith because of the proximity of a synagogue to the housing project. This violated federal law. *Otero* v. *N.Y. City Housing Authority,* 314 F.Supp. 737 (1972).

38.17 City services   The city must not discriminate racially in its provisions of municipal services.

> **EXAMPLE:** In one town in question, 97 percent of the homes that fronted on unpaved streets and were not served by sewers were occupied by blacks; all street lights were installed in white sections; surface water drainage, traffic control signs, and so forth were all in white sections. This was invalid. *Hawkins* v. *Town of Shaw,* 437 F2d 1286 (5th Cir. 1971).

38.18 Oral contracts   Oral contracts to sell land to blacks come under the federal law.

> **EXAMPLE:** *V,* a vendor, entered into an oral contract to sell to *P,* a black. *V,* thereafter, tried to back out of the deal. The court held that it would enforce an oral contract where *V* was motivated by a desire to avoid selling to a black. *State* v. *Bergeron,* 187 NW2d 680 (Minn. 1971).

38.19 Private parks   Even private parks are subject to the federal laws against racial discrimination.

> **EXAMPLE:** Little Huntington Park is a private park owned by a nonprofit corporation. *A,* who owned an adjacent house and stock in the corporation, leased his house to *B,* a black, and assigned his membership stock to *B.* The club canceled *A*'s membership. The club's membership was open to every white person. The court thought this was comparable to a racially restrictive covenant. It held that *A* and *B* could recover damages against the corporation. *Sullivan* v. *Little Huntington Park, Inc.,* 396 U.S. 229 (1969).

38.20 Charitable trusts   In former times quite a number of charitable trusts were set up for white persons only. These trusts can no longer be operated for the sole benefit of whites. 25 ALR3d 736.

EXAMPLE: A trust was established for "poor white male orphan children." The court held that exclusion of blacks violated the law, removed the old trustees, and appointed new trustees with directions to admit blacks. *Pennsylvania* v. *Brown,* 392 F2d 120 (3d Cir. 1968). A similar result was reached in *Dunbar* v. *Board of Trustees,* 461 P2d 28 (Colo. 1969), and *Bank of Delaware* v. *Buckson,* 255 A2d 710 (Del. 1969).

38.21 Proof of discrimination

Basically, what current legislation forbids is discrimination. *Discrimination* is not merely a state of mind. *Prejudice* is a state of mind, but *discrimination* is prejudice coupled with action or inaction motivated by that prejudice.

Discrimination can be shown by *express* proof of *intention. Hawkins* v. *Town of Shaw,* 461 F2d 1171 (5th Cir. 1972).

EXAMPLE: A builder stated that "no one is going to force me to sell a house in this development to a black." This proves discrimination if followed by sales only to white persons. *Jones* v. *The Haridor Realty Corp.,* 37 N.J. 384, 181 A2d 481.

Or it may be established by circumstantial evidence.

EXAMPLE: *A* offered a house for sale for $35,000 on terms set forth in a broker's listing. Promptly *B,* a black, tendered an offer at the price and terms stated. *A*'s refusal of *B*'s offer would be evidence of discrimination, especially if *A* sold later to a white person at the same price, thereby showing that his refusal of *B* was not motivated by a desire to withdraw the house from sale.

EXAMPLE: The fact that there are no black tenants in an apartment building will weigh against the owner, and the refusal of even one financially qualified black applicant for an apartment may be sufficient proof of discrimination. *U.S.* v. *Real Estate Development Corp.,* 347 F.Supp. 776.

EXAMPLE: A homeowner stated before witnesses that he would not sell to Jews. He therefore refused to sell to the complaining party, a Jewish person, and later entered into a contract to sell to a Gentile. The commission ordered the owner to sell to the Jew at the same price the Gentile offered. Observe the quandary of the seller here, who may find he has a legal liability to the Gentile. *Tisman* v. *Burda,* 12 Race Relations Rep. 1966 (N.Y.).

38.22 Impact or intent

A deeply troubling question relates to the necessity of establishing the presence of discriminatory intent where racial discrimination is charged.

If the lawsuit charges a violation of the federal Constitution, one frequently cited decision holds that it is necessary to prove an intention to discriminate.

EXAMPLE: The village of Arlington Heights (a suburb of Chicago) had a traditional zoning ordinance, establishing some single-family zones. A developer sought a rezoning of land in such a zone so that he could construct low-income housing, which, of course, would accommodate black persons. The village population was white. The village refused the rezoning. The Supreme Court held that no violation of the federal *Constitution* was shown. There was no *intention* to discriminate, *Village of Arlington Heights* v. *Metrop. Housing Develop. Corp.,* 429 U.S. 252, 50 L. Ed.2d 450 (1971), 91 Harv. L. Rev. 1427.

In a later phase of this case, the issue was whether the Open Housing Act of 1968 had been violated.

> **EXAMPLE:** In this lawsuit the court pointed out that the construction of the apartments would give the village its first subsidized low-cost housing. This would enable blacks to move into a village that had theretofore been exclusively white. Thus the village's refusal to rezone had a discriminatory *impact* in that it perpetuated segregation in Arlington Heights. A violation of the statute had been established. *Metrop. Housing Develop. Corp.* v. *Village of Arlington Heights,* 558 F2d 1283 (CA 7th 1977).

This is by no means the end of the story. A bitter controversy is raging over these very issues. 57 U. of Detroit J. of Urb. Law 707 (1980); 1977 Duke L. J. 1267; 125 U. Pa. L. Rev. 540 (1977); 46 U. of Cin. L. Rev. 611 (1977); 6 San Diego L. Rev. 207 (1977).

38.23 Testers and steering   A group of blacks visited real estate brokers in the village of Bellwood, Illinois, asking to be shown homes. In point of fact, they were not genuine purchasers. They were "testing" the brokers. The brokers attempted to "steer" these "purchasers" to black areas of the village. The court held that *steering* was illegal and that *testers* could sue to have a court prohibit this steering. *Gladstone Realtors* v. *Village of Bellwood,* 99 S.Ct. 1601 (1979).

38.24 Miscellaneous rulings   The Department of Justice has made some strong rulings in this area.

> **EXAMPLE:** The department has ruled that an appraisal report must not refer to population changes as affecting the value of the property.

> **EXAMPLE:** The department has ruled that title insurance policies must not show recorded racial restrictions.

> **EXAMPLE:** The department has ruled that an abstract of title must now show a recorded racial restriction unless it also states that same is invalid.

39 TAXES, SPECIAL ASSESSMENTS, AND FEDERAL INCOME TAX

39.01 In general

General taxes are levied by various taxing bodies, such as states, cities, villages, counties, or school districts, to raise revenue needed for the performance of various public functions, such as maintaining roads, schools, parks, police departments, fire departments, county hospitals, and mental institutions. One of the most important sources of revenue is the tax on real estate. Although this tax is encountered in most, if not all, states, laws regarding levy, assessment, and collection of the tax vary considerably, so that few general statements can be made that will be universally true.

39.02 Constitutional aspects

One aspect of taxation has recently attracted much attention. Since schools are typically financed through local property taxes, the "property-rich" areas provide more funds for education than the "property-poor" areas. The mathematics of this method of taxation results in better educational opportunities for some because more money is spent on facilities, while others from the property-poor areas receive what is thought to be an inferior education. The United States Supreme Court has determined that this is a matter for the states to regulate. *San Antonio Independent School District* v. *Rodiguez,* 411 U.S. 1 (1973). Some states have addressed this issue and found that this method for financing education violates constitutional principles. *Serrano* v. *Priest,* 487 P2d 1241 (Cal. 1971).

39.03 Steps in taxation

The nine principal steps in real estate taxation are: budgeting, appropriation, levy, assessment, review of the assessment, equalization, computation, collection of the tax through voluntary payment by the taxpayer, and collection of the tax through compulsory methods, such as tax sale.

624

39.03(a)   Budgeting

Budgeting involves an annual determination of how much money is to be spent by each taxing body and for what purposes. Keep in mind that in each state there are numerous bodies—cities, villages, counties, school boards, and sanitary districts—that have the power to levy taxes, and each body must prepare its annual budget and make its annual appropriation and tax levy.

39.03(b)   Appropriation

Appropriation is the step where the taxing body formally enacts into law its decision to spend the money, with a specification of the particular purpose for which the money is to be spent, the amount to be spent for each purpose, and the source from which the funds are to be derived.

39.03(c)   Levy

The appropriation usually provides that part of the money to be spent is to be raised by property taxation. It thereupon becomes necessary to levy a tax for this purpose. When the legislative body of some taxing unit, such as the village board of a village or the school board of a school district, votes to impose a tax of a specified amount on persons or property, this action is known as the levy of a tax. The levy is an indispensable step in arriving at a valid tax.

It is the levy that provides a field day for tax lawyers. Various technical defects will invalidate part or all of the tax levy, and attorneys for railroads and other big taxpayers are most astute in discovering these technical defects. As a rule, only those taxpayers who file proper objections may take advantage of these technical defects. Taxpayers who pay their money without formal objection cannot get their money back if the tax is later held invalid.

39.03(d)   Tax rate limitations

In levying taxes, taxing bodies must see to it that they do not spend more than the law allows. Tax rate limitations will be found both in state constitutions and state laws.

39.03(e)   Assessment

Assessment of real estate for taxation involves determining the value of each parcel of land to be taxed. In assessing real estate, a book or list is first prepared by the proper officer, containing a description of all the taxable real estate in his town, county, or district and the names of the owners thereof. This book is turned over to the tax assessor, who proceeds to place a valuation on each parcel of land and enters such valuation in the book. This book is called the *tax list* or *assessment roll*.

In assessing land, the assessor should consider various factors, such as market price of similar land, income, depreciation, obsolescence, and reproduction cost of buildings. Actual methods vary widely. Farmland is still usually taxed at its market value, but urban land is often assessed differently. In assessing urban land, assessors often place a value on the land as though it were vacant and then value the building at what it would cost to build today, deducting from this figure an allowance for depreciation. The two valuations are then added together to fix the total assessment. Assessors may employ experts and use experts' scientific procedures as a basis for their valuations. But any wholesale turning over of valuation to experts would be illegal, for it is the assessor's judgment, based perhaps on expert advice, that the law requires.

In some states, it is the practice to assess property at a certain percentage of its true value. This is not objectionable as long as the assessor assesses all property at the same proportion of its true value. Likewise, if all the property is uniformly overvalued, the courts will not intervene. The main thing is uniformity. If a taxpayer can show that his property is assessed at its full value, whereas the rest of the property in the district is uniformly assessed at less than its full value, the court will lower the assessment complained of to the general level.

39.03(e)(1)   Uniformity

Under various constitutional provisions it is required that the taxation of property be equal and uniform, so that taxpayers owning tracts of substantially equal value will pay substantially the same amount of taxes. This is an ideal difficult, if not impossible, to attain, and courts are aware of that fact. Hence if the assessor has made an honest mistake in assessing a particular tract of land, the courts as a rule will not intervene. Courts do not sit to correct mere errors in an assessment. The error can be corrected only by an appeal to the board of review or other body designated to review and correct the assessor's valuations.

39.03(e)(2)   Exemptions

Each state grants various exemptions from taxation. The nature and form of these exemptions vary from state to state. Common exemptions are those extended to public property, charitable organizations, schools, religious institutions, and cemeteries. There are also some states that extend partial exemptions to senior citizens.

39.03(e)(3)   Review of assessment

All states provide some method by which the taxpayer can have the assessor's valuation reviewed and corrected by some higher authority. The procedures vary widely. In New England, the reviewing board is often a town tribunal, such as the selectmen. In other areas, the reviewing officials may be called a *board of equalization* or a *board of review*. In some states, a further appeal is provided to a higher board of review. In other states, the decision of the first board of review can be appealed directly to some court. Culp, *Administrative Remedies in the Assessment and Enforcement of State Taxes* 17 N.C. L. Rev 118 (1939). As a rule, the taxpayer cannot appeal to the courts unless he has first appeared before the board of review or other initial reviewing body. *First Nat. Bank* v. *Weld County,* 264 U.S. 450 (1924).

39.03(e)(4)   Equalization   Equalization is the raising or lowering of assessed values in a particular county or taxing district in order to equalize them with the total assessments in other counties or taxing districts.

> **EXAMPLE:**   The board of equalization deducts a certain percentage from all assessments made in a certain township because the township assessor valued the property on a higher level than did the assessors of other townships.

This function is usually performed by a board known as the *board of equalization.* The board of equalization does not handle complaints of individual taxpayers, but raises or lowers the assessment of each county or taxing district as a whole in order to bring the assessment into line with assessments in other counties or taxing districts.

39.03(f)   Computation of tax   The amount of the tax that a particular tract of land must pay is computed by multiplying the assessed value of the tract by the tax rate applicable to the land in that particular taxing district. The tax is then entered on the tax books.

39.03(g)   Lien   Tax laws usually provide that real estate taxes are a lien on the land. Often it is provided that such a lien is prior and superior to all other liens, both those that antedate and those that come after the date on which the tax lien attaches to the land.

39.03(h)   Payment   Payment to the proper official at the proper time discharges the lien of the tax.

When the *tax records* show a tax is paid, a purchaser or mortgagee who relies on such records is protected against enforcement of the tax should it later develop that the tax actually remains unpaid. *Jackson Park Hospital* v. *Courtney,* 4 NE2d 864 (Ill. 1936). A number of states make provision for the issuance of a certificate by some tax official showing all unpaid taxes on the property. Purchasers who rely on such certificates are generally protected against errors in the certificate. *Burton* v. *City of Denver,* 61 P2d 856 (Colo. 1936); *Amerada Petroleum Corp.* v. *1010.61 Acres of Land,* 146 F2d 99 (1944); 21 ALR2d 1273. When a landowner redeems from a tax sale and the certificate of redemption shows that all delinquent taxes have been thereby redeemed, a purchaser or mortgagee who relies on such a certificate will be protected if it later develops that some delinquent taxes in fact remain. *Jones* v. *Sturzenberg,* 210 Pac. 835 (Cal. 1922).

A purchaser or mortgagee is not ordinarily protected in relying on a *tax receipt* showing full payment of the taxes. Despite issuance of the receipt, the tax collector is allowed to show that a part of the tax remains unpaid. However,

South Dakota has a law making a tax receipt conclusive evidence that all prior taxes have been paid.

39.03(i)   Proceedings to enforce payment of taxes

Various special remedies are provided by local law for the collection of unpaid real estate taxes.

Tax sale is a common method. It is usually preceded by the giving of notice, often by publication, to the delinquent taxpayer. Unless the taxpayer appears and defends, which he may do if the tax is illegal or if he has some other defense, a judgment will be rendered for the amount of the tax and penalty due. This judgment orders the land to be sold. Thereafter, notice of the coming sale is published, and on the date fixed for sale the land is sold at public sale. Usually a certificate of sale is issued to the purchaser, stating that he will be entitled to a deed at the expiration of the redemption period if no redemption is made. In some states, the state, county, or city is permitted to bid at the tax sale.

The landowner or other persons interested, such as mortgagees, may redeem the land from the tax within the period specified by the local law. If redemption is not made, a tax deed is issued to the purchaser.

Although state laws vary as to the validity of tax titles, a tax title acquired through normal tax sale usually constitutes the flimsiest sort of title, since deviation from the technical requirements of the law will invalidate the title. In some states, however, a tax deed is regarded as a conveyance of good title to the land. *Thomas* v. *Kolker,* 73 A2d 886 (Md. 1950); *Shapiro* v. *Hruby,* 172 NE2d 775 (Ill. 1961).

An alternative method of enforcement of the tax lien is by foreclosure, the procedure being similar to that employed in mortgage foreclosure. In some states, a good title can be acquired through tax foreclosure.

39.03(i)(1)   Effect of tax sale on junior interests

When real estate taxes obtain priority over junior interests either because they become a lien prior to the creation of the junior interests or by force of law, the law of many states results in a purchaser at a tax sale taking a title that is free of encumbrances such as mortgages, liens, and so forth.

> **EXAMPLE:** *O* purchased property giving a purchase money mortgage to *M. O* failed to pay the real estate taxes levied against the property. The land was sold to *P* at a tax sale. *P* took the land free of *M*'s mortgage. Most lenders handle this problem by adopting some means, such as a mortgage escrow account, to insure that the taxes are paid.

Of course, the owner cannot, for his own benefit, use this theory to rid his property of liens to which it would otherwise be subject.

> **EXAMPLE:** *O* owns property subject to a purchase money mortgage that he placed against the property. *O* allows the taxes to go into default and be sold. *O* then purchases at the tax sale. *O* holds the property subject to the mortgage. 134 ALR 289. The result would be opposite if *T*, a bona fide disinterested third-party purchaser, bought at the tax sale.

39.03(i)(2) Termination of easement by tax sale

An almost insoluble problem exists with respect to the effect of a tax sale of the servient tenement. The owner of the easement, of course, receives his tax bill on the dominant tenement. He does not even receive the tax bill on the servient tenement.

> **EXAMPLE:** *A* owns Lot 1 and *B* owns Lot 2. *A* grants to *B* an easement for ingress and egrees for driveway purposes over the southern twenty feet of Lot 1. *A* fails to pay his taxes and all of Lot 1 is sold to *X* at a tax sale. Under the law in this state, a tax sale wipes out all prior easements. Obviously *B* must arrange to keep a check on the taxes on *A*'s Lot 1 and pay them, if necessary, to prevent loss of his easement. He can include a provision in the easement grant requiring *A* annually to furnish *B* a paid tax bill, and also a provision that any taxes advanced by *B*, or his successors, will be a foreclosable lien on Lot 1.

The law on this subject has been in some confusion. In some states a tax sale does *not* destroy easements. *Northwestern Imp. Co.* v. *Lowry*, 66 P2d 792 (Mont. 1937); *Ariz. R.C.I.A. Lands, Inc.* v. *Ainsworth*, 515 P2d 335 (Ariz. 1973); *Clippinger* v. *Birge*, 547 P2d 871 (Wash. 1975); Restatement, Property § 509(2)(e). One basis of this rule is the thought that the land was assessed based upon its *value*. That value was determined by taking the easement into consideration.

> **EXAMPLE:** Tract A is valued at $10,000 without being encumbered by an easement. Assessment is based upon this value. If the property were encumbered by an easement, its value would be $9,000. The assessment in the later case would be based upon $9,000.

By this same theory, the holder of the dominant estate is protected in that the easement will continue for the benefit of his land irrespective of the failure of the owner of the servient estate to pay taxes. The result is justified by the theory that the easement enhances the value of the dominant estate, and assessment is based upon this enhanced value. 20 U. Chi. L. Rev. 262, 264 (1953). In almost all states, laws have been passed to conform to the above. Ill. Rev. Stat. Ch. 120 § 7476. The minority view is discussed elsewhere. Note, 51 Harv. L. Rev. 361 (1937); see *Powell on Real Property*, par. 686.

In a similar view, a tax sale will generally not extinguish a restrictive covenant to which the land is subject. 168 ALR 529, 536.

39.04 Special assessments   There is a distinction between public improvements, which benefit the entire community, and local improvements, which benefit particular real estate or limited areas of land. The latter improvements are usually financed by means of special, or local, assessments. These assessments are, in a certain sense, taxes. But an assessment differs from a general tax in that an assessment is levied only on property in the immediate vicinity of some local public improvement and is valid only where the property assessed receives some special benefit differing from the benefit that the general public enjoys. *Production Tool Supply Co.* v. *City of Roseville*, 253 NW2d 350 (Mich. 1977). In fact if the primary purpose of an improvement is to benefit the public generally, as with, for example, the erection of a county courthouse, it cannot be financed by special assessments even though it may incidentally benefit property in the particular locality.

Special assessments are often imposed for opening, paving, grading, and guttering streets, construction of sidewalks and sewers, installation of street lighting, and so on.

39.05 Federal income tax   While the law of federal income taxation is vast and complex, no one dealing with real estate should ignore the tax implications of his transactions. A slight alteration in the structure of the transaction can result in large tax savings. Ignorance of the tax consequences of a deal can cause large, unexpected tax liabilities.

We begin our discussion of income taxes with a basic example and build upon it as we proceed.

> **EXAMPLE:** Mr. and Mrs. Homebuyer purchased a home for $92,000. They paid $22,500 down and took a mortgage for $70,000. The lender required 2½ percent to be paid as points. The closing occurred on April 1, 1979. The Homebuyers paid $400 in attorney's fees, $150 for title insurance, $20 in recording fees, and a surveyor's fee of $100. The real estate taxes on the house were $1,200 per year payable December 31 of each year. Shortly after purchasing the house, The Homebuyers added a family room at a cost of $20,000.

The first thing we must do is establish the Homebuyers' basis. *Basis* in tax language is the cost of the house for purposes of calculating gain or loss on its sale. The tax law allows the Homebuyers to add various items to basis to decrease the taxable gain. The sum of the basis and allowable additions is the *adjusted basis*.

The taxpayer's basis includes acquisition costs such as attorney's fees, title insurance premiums, recording charges, etc.

Adjusted basis is determined by adding the following to the basis:

> 1. the cost of improvements which add to the value of property, but not repairs that merely maintain the property in good condition,
> 2. assessments to pay for local improvements such as streets and sidewalks.

Adjusted basis is reduced by:

1. the amount of any residential energy credit if the cost of the items for which the credit was taken was added to the basis of the property,
2. the amount received for granting an easement;
3. the amount of any depreciation claimed;
4. losses from fire or other casualty.

Turning to our example, the Homebuyers' basis and adjusted basis would be calculated as follows:

Purchase price	$ 92,500
Surveyor's fee	100
Attorney's fee	400
Title insurance	150
Recording fee	20
Basis	$ 93,170
Family room addition	20,000
Adjusted basis	$113,170

39.05(a) Annual income tax deductions relating to real estate

Now that the Homebuyers have purchased their home, its ownership generates tax deductions that will be available if they elect to itemize their deductions. These include:

1. yearly mortgage interest, including points paid upon the origination of the mortgage;
2. real estate taxes (note that amounts paid into a mortgage escrow account for the payment of taxes are not deductible, only the taxes actually paid to the tax collector are deductible);
3. casualty losses.

If the property is income producing property, the taxable income from the property's operation would be determined by subtracting the following additional items from the revenue:

1. depreciation;
2. insurance, utility charges, and expenses related to the operation of the property.

If the property is sold, the taxpayer is only entitled to deduct the real property taxes allocable to the portion of the year that the taxpayer owned the property.

EXAMPLE: Homebuyers sold the house on June 31, 1982. Real estate taxes for 1982 in the amount of $1,200 are payable on or before December 31, 1982. Homebuyers would be allowed to deduct $600, even though the taxes were actually paid by their purchaser. The adjustment or proration between buyer and seller would take place as a credit to the buyer on the closing statement. The purchaser, even though he actually pays the tax, would only be entitled to a deduction of $600, the tax allocable to his period of ownership.

Similarly, only part of the year's mortgage interest would be allowed as a deduction for the Homebuyers. They will also have the additional deduction of any prepayment penalty that is assessed by their lender upon the early payment of the mortgage upon the sale of the home.

39.05(a)(1) Depreciation

A depreciation deduction is allowed for the annual loss of usefulness and value that occurs to business and income producing property. This deduction, which does not reflect any out-of-pocket expenditure by the taxpayer, allows the taxpayer to reduce taxable income. The taxpayer may elect the *straight line* method of depreciation, the 175 percent of the *declining balance* method, or, if the property is low-income housing, the 200 percent of the declining balance method. The depreciation period may be a fifteen-year *accelerated period* or a thirty-five- or forty-five-year *optional extended period*, but if either of the optional extended periods are used, the straight line method and not an accelerated method of computation must be used.

> **EXAMPLE:** If a business property costs $1,000,000, *straight line* depreciation over fifteen years would generate an annual depreciation expense of $66,667, or one-fifteenth of $1,000,000, to result in fifteen equal depreciation expenses over fifteen years, fully depreciating the asset. Straight line depreciation over the extended thirty-five-year period would generate an annual depreciation expense of $28,571.

The declining balance method is a bit more complicated. It produces a higher depreciation deduction during the earlier years of the depreciation period by applying a higher percentage to the value of the asset after accumulated depreciation for prior years is subtracted from the value of the asset.

> **EXAMPLE:** If the property costs $1,000,000 and the 175 percent declining balance method is used over a fifteen-year period the calculation is:

Year 1

Cost	$1,000,000
Straight line depreciation over 15 years	$ 66,667
times	175%
Depreciation for the first year	$ 116,667

Year 2

Cost	$1,000,000
Minus first year depreciation	116,667
Book value at end of first year	$ 883,333
Straight line depreciation over 15 years on the book value at end of first year	$ 58,889
times	175%
Depreciation for the second year	$ 103,056

The depreciation expense shields or shelters income from the property, reducing ordinary income by what is essentially a bookkeeping device. It also reduces the adjusted basis of the property. When the property is sold, the gain is calculated and perhaps given capital gains treatment. The application of the depreciation expense deduction then effectively transforms ordinary income, taxable at full value, into long-term capital gains income, 60 percent of which is excluded from taxation.

EXAMPLE: In the above example, $219,723 in income was expensed out as depreciation. This saved the taxpayer $109,862 in taxes that a 50 percent bracket taxpayer would have had to pay if the depreciation expense was not available. If the property is then sold for $1,000,000, its original purchase price, the tax on the gain would be calculated as follows:

Basis	$1,000,000
Less depreciation for 2 years	219,723
Adjusted basis	$ 780,277
Selling price	$1,000,000
Less adjusted basis	780,277
Gain on sale	$ 219,723
Long-term capital gains factor	40%
	$ 87,889
Tax rate	50%
Tax	$ 43,945

In this way the taxpayer paid only $43,945 of taxes instead of $109,862 on $219,723 of income, a tax savings of $65,917.

The IRS, recognizing this tax leakage, has adopted *recapture* rules that recapture some depreciation for treatment as ordinary income. These rules are:

1. If straight line depreciation is used, no recapture will occur.

2. If a depreciation method that exceeds the straight line method is used on residential property, the depreciation that exceeds straight line depreciation is recaptured.

3. If the declining balance method of depreciation is used for nonresidential property, *all* depreciation is recaptured.

39.05(a)(2)   Home office expenses

A homeowner may be allowed to subtract from his income, expenses relating to an office maintained at home. The rules covering this expense and its deductibility are very strict.

1. The deduction is only allowed if a portion of the residence is used *exclusively* and on a *regular basis* either as the taxpayer's principal place of business or as a place of business used by patients, clients, or customers in meeting or dealing with the taxpayer in the normal course of his trade or business. The exclusive use test is strict. Any dual personal and business use will disallow the deduction.

2. The deduction may not exceed the gross income derived from the use of the home office during the taxable year.

3. Only the portion of household expenses attributable to the "home office" are deductible and no "home office" deduction is allowed when the taxpayer has a primary place of business elsewhere and uses his "home office" only incidentally.

Even though a taxpayer has a principal office outside of the home, a deduction may be taken for the expenses of a home office used as the principal place of a secondary business.

EXAMPLE: A doctor who worked at a hospital may deduct expenses for property rental activities conducted out of a bedroom office in his home. *Edwin R. Curphey,* 73 TC 766 (1980).

Obviously, the IRS will challenge large home office expenses in respect to minor business activities.

39.05(b)   Tax aspects of the sale of property

In addition to the impact of annual deductions explained above, the sale of any property may bring about taxable consequences. The taxpayers' gain on the sale of their old home would be calculated as follows:

EXAMPLE: Homebuyers sold their home on March 31, 1982, for $130,000. They spent $500 to paint some areas readying the house for sale, $7,800 for real estate broker's commission, $400 for legal fees, and $400 for title and escrow fees.

Selling price		$130,000
Minus selling expenses		
Broker's comm.	$7,800	
Legal fees	400	
Title & escrow	400	
		8,600
Amount realized		$121,400
Minus fix-up expenses		500
Adjusted sale price		$120,900
Minus adjusted basis		113,170
Gain on sale		$ 7,730

The fixing-up expenses that are spent within ninety days of signing the contract that results in the completed sale of the house are subtracted from the amount realized to calculate the gain on which the tax is postponed.

If the Homebuyers buy a new home for a purchase price higher than the *adjusted sale price* of the old house, they must postpone any of the gain on the sale of the old home for income tax purposes. To qualify for this postponement of gain, both homes must be the Homebuyers' principal residence and the new home must be purchased within twenty-four months before or after the sale of the old home. Remember, the tax on the gain is *postponed*, not forgiven. Gain that is postponed in this manner is merely subtracted from the adjusted basis of the new home.

> **EXAMPLE:** Within the prescribed twenty-four-month period, the Homebuyers purchased a replacement home for $160,000, paying $500 in legal fees, a $100 surveyor's fee and $500 in title, escrow, and recording fees. Since the purchase price of the new home, $160,000, was more than the adjusted sale price of the old home, $120,900, gain on the sale of the old home would be postponed.

Purchase price	$160,000
Surveyor's fee	100
Attorney's fee	500
Title, escrow, & recording	500
Basis	$161,100
Minus gain postponed	7,730
Adjusted basis of new home	$153,370

If the Homebuyers did not buy a new home, or if the purchase price of the new home was less than the adjusted sale price of the old home, the Homebuyers will be subject to tax on some or all of the gain unless they qualify for an exclusion.

39.05(b)(1) Exclusion of gain on the sale of a residence by persons over 55 years of age

Taxpayers may exclude from their gross income $125,000 of gain on the sale or exchange of their principal residence if they were 55 or older before the date of the sale or exchange and lived in the property as their principal home for three of the five years preceding the sale. If the taxpayers are 65 or older, they qualify for the exclusion if they lived in the property for five of the eight years preceding the sale.

While this exclusion is available only once during any taxpayer's life, it is useful to exclude profits deferred from the sale of previous homes owned by the taxpayer.

39.05(b)(2) Capital gains treatment

When property is sold for a gain, that gain is subject to taxation. If the seller is a *dealer* in that kind of property, the gain is taxed as ordinary income.

EXAMPLE: A homebuilder sells houses for a living; his profits are ordinary income from an income tax point of view. The houses are held primarily for sale to customers in the ordinary course of the homebuilder's trade or business.

But, if the taxpayer is not a dealer, the sale of investments made over the course of years, including the taxpayer's home, will be given *capital gains treatment.* This is generally more favorable to the taxpayer. Only 40 percent of the long-term capital gains (gains on property held for more than one year) is taxed. A simple application of these formulas to the Homebuyers' situation is revealing.

EXAMPLE: If we assume that the Homebuyers are in the 50 percent tax bracket and for some reason the $7,730 gain on the sale of their old house was not to be postponed or excluded and was not eligible for long-term capital gains treatment, their tax would be calculated as follows:

Gain on sale	$7,730
Tax rate	50%
Tax	$3,865

If long-term capital gains treatment is available, their tax would be calculated as follows:

Gain on sale	$7,730
Long-term capital gain factor	40%
Amount of gain subject to tax	$3,092
Tax rate	50%
Tax	$1,546

Long-term capital gains treatment saves the Homebuyers $2,319 in income taxes.

39.05(b)(3) Tax-free exchanges

Exchanges of property have received a lot of attention recently. If properly structured, the exchange will not be taxable, i.e., even though a gain or loss is realized, it will not be recognized for tax purposes. The new property is treated as if it were the same property that the taxpayer had before the exchange. Exchanges are nontaxable if they meet the following requirements:

1. The exchange is of business or investment property.

2. The exchange is of like kind property, i.e., real estate for real estate—not real estate for personal property.

3. The exchange is of tangible property, not stocks, bonds, beneficial interests in trusts, etc.

4. The exchange is not of property held for sale, i.e., a merchant's inventory. Internal Revenue Code § 1031(a).

The tax-free exchange is generally a desirable transaction if the taxpayer intends to reinvest the proceeds of the sale of the property in other property. By using the tax-free exchange, the taxpayer has more dollars to reinvest because the IRS will not take its cut out of the gain that would have been realized upon the sale.

Since the taxpayer is more apt to find a buyer who will pay for the property than a buyer who has acceptable exchange property, the transaction is often set up as a three-party exchange.

> **EXAMPLE:** Taxpayer with property #1 worth $1,000,000 finds Buyer willing to pay the price but without acceptable exchange property. The Taxpayer finds property #2 also worth $1,000,000 and owned by Owner. Taxpayer transfers property #1 to Buyer, Buyer pays $1,000,000 to Owner for property #2, and Buyer transfers property #2 to Taxpayer. There are variations on the format, but the result is the same.

Frequently, the replacement property cannot be located immediately, but the buyer needs the taxpayer's property immediately. A *deferred exchange* may be worked out in this circumstance.

> **EXAMPLE:** Taxpayer transfers property to Buyer and receives some form of contractual right to receive a stated dollar value of suitable real property in exchange, when that property is found. The value of the property to be exchanged to the Taxpayer increases over time at an agreed rate until the replacement property is found.

This type of transaction may be given tax-free exchange status, *Starker* v. *U.S.*, 602 F2d 1371 (9th Cir. 1979), but the law in this area is not entirely clear.

REFERENCES ON FEDERAL INCOME TAXES AFFECTING REAL ESTATE: Levine, *Real Estate Transactions, Tax Planning;* Sandison et al., *Federal Taxes Affecting Real Estate.*

INDEX*

Abstract of title 11.02
  abstractor 11.02(a)
  abstractor's liability 11.02(a) (1)
Acknowledgment 6.03(n) et seq.
  certificate 6.03(n) (1)
  date 6.03(n) (8)
    expiration of commission 6.03(n) (11)
  foreign 6.03(n) (7)
  invalid—effect 6.03(n) (6)
  liability of notary 6.03(n) (12)
  necessity 6.03(n) (3)
  seal 6.03(n) (10)
  signature of officer 6.03(n) (9)
  venue 6.03(n) (5)
  who may take 6.03(n) (4)
Adverse possession 2.11(b)
Air rights 2.04
  trespass 2.05
Beaches 28.07
Bill of sale 2.06
Brokers 8.01 et seq.
  antitrust 8.11(a)
  authority 8.26
  commission
    amount 8.15
    flat fee 8.06(f)
    lien 8.15(a)
    procuring cause of sale 8.13
      seller's ignorance that buyer was
        procurred by broker 8.13(a)
    provision in sale contract 8.06(g)
    splitting
      with other broker 8.17
      with buyer 8.03

duties
  conflict of interest 8.19
  disclosure 8.20
  double agency 8.18
  liabilities for breach 8.23
  loyalty 8.18
  misrepresentations 8.21
  purchaser 8.24
  skill and care 8.22
earnest money 8.16
  risk of loss 8.16(a)
employment
  contract 8.06
    exclusive agency 8.09
    exclusive right to sell 8.10
    form 8.06(c)
    open listing 8.08
    unconscionability 8.06(d)
    written 8.06(b)
  duration 8.14 et seq.
    contract provision 8.14(b), 8.14(j)
    revocation 8.14(c) et seq.
      after broker's performance 8.14(d)
      bad faith 8.14(e)
      before broker's performance
        8.14(c)
      by sale 8.14(f), 8.14(h)
      damages 8.14(i)
      notice 8.14(g)
who may employ 8.06(a)
ethics 8.07
franchising 8.28
functions 8.04
license 8.02

*References are to section numbers.

Brokers (*cont.*)
  multiple listing 8.11
    antitrust 8.11(a)
  performance 8.12
    after expiration of listing period 8.12(b)
    Ellsworth Dobbs 8.12(d)
    no deal, no commission clause 8.12(e)
    price differing from listing 8.12(c)
    procuring cause of sale 8.13
    terms differing from listing 8.12(c)
  racial discrimination 8.27
  salesmen 8.05
  unauthorized practice of law 8.25
Building codes 26.36, 34.18
  violations 26.36(a)
Building construction 34.01 *et seq*
  building codes 26.36, 34.18
  contracts 34.02
    delays 34.03(c)
    mortgages 34.03(b)
      subordination to construction loan
        34.03(d)
    signatures 34.03(a)
    types 34.03
  delays 34.03(c)
  downpayment 34.08
  extras 34.05
  FHA 34.12
  liability of builder 34.03(e), 34.10
    limitations 34.10(b)
    products liability 34.11
    remedies 34.10(a)
  mechanics' liens 34.04
    contract or consent of owner 34.04(a)
    contractors 34.04(b)
    enforcement of lien 34.04(g)
    inception of lien 34.04(d)
    notice of lien 34.04(e)
    performance 34.04(c)
    priority of lien 34.04(d)
    subcontractors 34.04(b)
    waiver of lien 34.04(f)
  mortgage money 34.07
  performance 34.09
  product liability 34.11
  progress payments 34.06
  suggestions 34.19
  VA 34.12
  warranties
    brokers' 34.16
    consumer products 34.17
    FHA 34.12
    Magnuson-Moss Warranty Act 34.17
    sellers' 34.15
    used homes 34.12
    VA 34.12
Building erected on wrong lot 3.08
Cemetary lots 2.10
Certificate of title 11.04

Closings 10.01 *et seq.*
  bulk sales affidavits 10.04
  chattel lien search 10.03(d)
  closing agent 10.03(i)
  closing date 10.05
  closing documents 10.03(b), 10.06(b)
  closing letter 10.08(a)
  closing statement 10.07
    credits due buyer 10.07(b)
    credits due seller 10.07(a)
    other items 10.07(c)
  deed into seller 10.06(e)
  escrows (*see* Escrows)
  evidence of title 10.03(a)
  inspection of the property 10.03(f)
  insurance premiums 10.06(d)
  lawyer's role 10.02
    conflict of interest 10.02(a)
  liability of closer 10.11
  maintenance of property prior to closing
    10.03(g)
  mortgage closing 10.09
    borrower's concerns 10.09(a)
    building code violations 10.09(e)
    documents of loan file 10.09(g)
    loan closing statement 10.09(d)
    RESPA 10.09(b)
    title defects 10.09(c)
    zoning violations 10.09(e)
  ordinance violations search 10.03(e)
  pre-closing considerations 10.03(a)
  prior approvals 10.03(h)
  prorations 10.07
  sale closing 10.01
  survey 10.03(c)
  title 10.06(a)
  utility bills 10.06(c)
  water bills 10.06(c)
Community property 14.13 *et seq.*
  curtesy 14.13(e)
  deeds 14.13(c)
  descent 14.13(d)
  divorce 14.13(f)
  dower 14.13(e)
  mortgages 14.13(c)
  property acquired during marriage 14.13(b)
  separation 14.13(f)
  theory 14.13(a)
  wills 14.13(d)
Condemnation 2.11(a)
Conditions 25.12 *et seq.*
  enforcement 25.12(a) *et seq.*
  nominal 25.12(b) (2)
  reverter acts 25.12(b) (1)
  running with the land 25.13
  violations 25.12(b) (3)
Condominiums 32.01 *et seq.*
  assessments 32.04
  association—suits by 32.15

board of directors 32.07
  committees 32.07(a)
bylaws 32.03(c)
commercial 32.24
common elements 32.08
  invasion 32.08(b)
  limited 32.08(a)
common law 32.02
conversion 32.21
  buyer's concerns 32.21(b)
  income taxes 32.21(c)
  legislation 32.21(a)
  preconversion considerations 32.21(d)
cooperative compared 32.28(a)
declaration 32.03(a)
deeds 32.03(b)
destruction of building 32.05
developer control 32.13
developer liability 32.14 *et seq.*
  fraud 32.14(a)
  nondisclosure 32.14(a)
income taxes 32.25
insurance 32.17
  liability 32.16
leasehold 32.12
liability 32.16
mortgages 32.10
operation 32.06
phased construction 32.11
procedure 32.03(e)
real estate taxes 32.09
regulation 32.19
resales 32.27
rules and regulations 32.03(d)
securities laws 32.22
suggestions to buyer 32.26
termination 32.05
timesharing 32.23(b)
  declaration 32.23(b)
title insurance 32.18
zoning 32.20
Constructive notice 7.02
Contracts of sale 9.01 *et seq.*
  abandonment 9.32
  acknowledgment 9.23
  apportionment 9.17
  assignment 9.28
  buyer 9.06
  certainty 9.09(a)
  completeness 9.09
  contingent contracts 9.13
    approvals 9.13(c)
    financing 9.13(a)
    sale of house 9.13(b)
  date 9.18
  deed 9.10(a)
    deed to stranger 9.29
    effect 9.27
  delivery 9.22

drafting suggestions 9.43
earnest money 9.11
effect of contract 9.26
fairness 9.34
financing 9.12
fraud 9.36
good faith 9.04(a)
hardship 9.33, 9.39
informal 9.03
installment (*see* Installment contracts)
insurance 9.16
liability for injuries 9.40
  builder liability 9.42
  installment contract 9.41
marketable title 9.10(b)
  building code violations 9.10(b) (4)
  chattels 9.10(b) (7)
  easements 9.10(b) (2)
  encroachments 9.10(b) (6)
  leases 9.10(b) (5)
  liens 9.10(b) (1)
  Marketable Title Law 9.10(b) (10)
  miscellaneous 9.10(b) (8)
  mortgages 9.10(b) (1)
  restrictions 9.10(b) (3)
  title insurance 9.10(b) (9)
  zoning violations 9.10(b) (4)
misrepresentation 9.36
  building ordinances 9.36(b)
  buyer's fraud 9.36(d)
  opinion 9.36(a)
  right to reply 9.36(c)
  zoning 9.36(b)
mistake 9.35
mortgages 9.12
nondisclosure 9.36(e)
  building ordinances 9.36(e) (1)
  half-truths 9.36(e) (2)
  zoning 9.36(e) (1)
performance
  time 9.30
possession 9.14
pre-contract consideration 9.02
property sold 9.08
  description 9.08(a)
prorating 9.17
ratification 9.38
recording 9.25
remedies
  buyer 9.31(a)
  election 9.31(c)
  exclusive remedies 9.31(d)
  promissory estoppel 9.31(b)
  restitution 9.31(b)
  seller 9.31
rents 9.14
risk of loss 9.16
sale price 9.06
seal 9.21

Contracts of sale (*cont.*)
  seller 9.05
    spouse 9.05(a)
  signature 9.19
    agents 9.20
  taxes 9.15
  title to be conveyed 9.10(b)
    curing defects 9.10(d) (1)
    evidence of title 9.10(d)
      time for furnishing 9.10(d) (1)
    time of existence of good title 9.10(c)
  unconscionable 9.04
  witnesses 9.25
  written contract 9.01(a)
Cooperatives 32.28 *et seq.*
  condominiums compared 32.28(a)
  conversion 32.28(d)
  leasehold 32.28(b)
  sale 32.28(f)
  securities problems 32.28(c)
  warranties 32.28(e)
Co-ownership 14.01 *et seq.*
  bankruptcy of co-tenant 14.11
  federal tax liens 14.12
  grants by one co-tenant 14.10
  rights and obligations of co-owners 14.09
Co-tenants 14.01 *et seq.*
  (*see also* Co-ownership)
Courts—Opinions 1.02
Covenants, declaration 31.01 *et seq.* (*see also*
      Declaration of restrictions, easements,
      liens, and covenants)
Curtesy 14.14(j)
  divorce 14.14(k)
Declaration of restrictions, easements, liens,
     and covenants 31.01 *et seq.*
  assessments, lien 31.08
    priority 31.09
  covenants 31.10
  declaration 31.03
  deeds 31.12
  easements 31.05
  enforcement 31.11
  history 31.02
  Marketable Title Acts 31.16
  membership 31.14
  party walls 31.07
  phased development 31.06
  restrictions 31.04
  sales 31.13
Dedication 27.01 *et seq.*
  common law 27.01(a)
  conditional 27.03
  forced 27.05
  plats 27.02
    approval 27.04
    dedicated areas 27.02(a)
  reservations by dedication 27.03

deeds 6.01 *et seq.*
  acceptance 6.03(m)
  acknowledgment 6.03(n) *et seq.*
  after acquired title 6.06
  bargain and sale deed 6.02(c)
  blank 6.03(b) (1)
  coercion 6.03(a) (1) (i)
  consideration 6.03(c)
    support deed 6.03(c) (1)
  delivery 6.03(l)
    acceptance 6.03(m)
    family transaction 6.03(l) (4)
    lifetime of grantor 6.03(l) (2)
    several grantors 6.03(l) (1)
    third persons 6.03(l) (3)
  dower—waiver 6.03(f)
  draftsmanship 6.10
  exceptions 6.08
  fraud 6.03(a) (1) (i)
  grantee 6.03(b)
  grantor 6.03(a)
    competency 6.03(a) (1)
    corporations 6.03(a) (3)
    infants 6.03(a) (2)
    seal 6.03(i)
    signature 6.03(h)
      witnesses 6.03(j)
    spouse 6.03(a) (4)
  homestead—waiver 6.03(f)
  mistake 6.03(a) (1) (i)
  official conveyances 6.05
  quitclaim deed 6.02(a)
  reservations 6.08
  support deeds 6.03(c) (1)
  title conveyed 6.07
    fee or easement 6.07(a)
  transfer taxes 6.03(k)
  warranty deed 6.02(b)
    special warranty deed 6.02(b) (1)
Development rights 27.06
  farm land 27.07
Discrimination 38.01 *et seq.*
  brokers 8.27, 38.10
  charitable trusts 38.20
  city services 38.17
  federal laws 38.02
    Civil War laws 38.04
    1968 law 38.03
  history 38.01
  housing projects 38.16
  impact or intent 38.22
  landlord and tenant 38.09
  mortgages (*see* Mortgages, application and
    commitment, discrimination)
  options 38.12
  oral contracts 38.18
  permitted discriminations 38.07
  private parks 38.19

proof 38.21
remedies 38.05
sale of real estate 38.11, 38.15
state laws 38.08
steering 38.23
testers 38.23
zoning 38.06
Dominant tenement 4.02
Dower 14.14 *et seq.*
  assignment 14.14(b)
  consummate 14.14(a)
  contracts 14.14(f)
  curtesy 14.14(j)
  divorce 14.14(k)
  election 14.14(h)
  fee title in lieu 14.14(i)
  inchoate 14.14(a)
  joint tenancy 14.14(c)
  leaseholds 14.14(e)
  mortgages 14.14(d)
  release 14.14(g)
Earnout 23.02
Easements 4.01 *et seq.*
  appurtenant 4.02
  conservation 4.13(d)
  creation 4.05 *et seq.*
    agreement 4.05(c)
      party walls 4.05(c) (1)
    declaration 4.05(k)
    estoppel 4.05(j)
    grant 4.05(a)
    implied 4.05(e)
      common scheme or plan 4.05(e) (3)
      requirements 4.05(e) (1)
    mortgage 4.05(d)
    prescription 4.05(g)
      party driveway 4.05(g) (1)
      public highway 4.05(g) (3)
      state laws 4.05(g) (2)
    reservation 4.05(b)
    sale by reference to plat 4.05(i)
  declaration 31.01 *et seq.* (*see also*
      Declaration of restrictions, easements,
      liens, and covenants)
  dominant tenement 4.02
  in gross 4.04
    cable television 4.04(a)
  license distinguished 4.02
  location 4.06
  maintenance 4.11
  mortgage 4.05(d)
  necessity 4.05(f)
  party driveways 4.05(g) (1)
  pipeline 4.06(a)
  profits of the soil 4.09
  repair 4.11
  scenic 4.13(b)
    -income taxes 4.13(b) (1)

servient tenement 4.02
solar 4.13(c)
streets 4.13(a)
structure 4.08
termination 4.12
  tax sale 4.12(a)
unlocated 4.06
use of easement premises 4.10
Economic impact upon the law 1.03
Eminent domain 2.11(a)
Energy crisis 27.19
Environmental Law 27.18 *et seq.*
  air 27.18(b)
  local ordinances 27.18(d)
  National Environmental Policy Act 27.18(a)
  private actions 27.18(c)
  state laws 27.18(d)
  water 27.18(c)
Escrows 10.10 *et seq.*
  agreement 10.10(c)
  conflict between contract and escrow 10.10(e)
  land assemblies 13.05
  long-term escrows 10.10(i)
  mortgages 10.10(h)
  nature 10.10(a)
  operation 10.10(a)
  purpose 10.10(a)
  requirements 10.10(b)
  revocation 10.10(d)
  title passage 10.10(f)
    relation back 10.10(g)
Estates in land 2.08
Evidence of title 11.01 *et seq.*
Fixtures 3.01 *et seq.*
  agreements 3.06
  agricultural 3.04
  annexation 3.02
    constructive 3.03
  domestic 3.04
  removal 3.04
  secured financing and fixtures 3.05
  severances 3.07
  tenant's fixtures 3.04
  test to determine whether article is a fixture
    3.03
  trade fixtures 3.04
Foreclosure 24.01 *et seq.*
  bankruptcy 24.08
    stay 24.09
  conscionable conduct 24.07
  deficiency 24.04
  development 15.04
  discrimination 37.14
  mortgagee as owner 24.11
  power of sale 24.05
  sale
    mortgagee as purchaser 24.10
  types 24.02

Gaps and gores 13.03
Ground rents 23.01 *et seq.*
  improved property 23.01(b)
  Maryland system 23.01(a)
  modern developments 23.01(e)
  Pennsylvania system 23.01(d)
  redemption 23.01(c)
Hazardous waste sites 6.09
Historic areas and landmarks 29.01
Holding agreements 13.08
Homeowners' Association 30.01 *et seq.*
  control 30.08
    transfer 30.09
  enforcement of restrictions, liens, and
        covenants 30.04
  functions 30.05
  income tax 30.11
  legal form 30.02
  master association 30.06
  membership 30.03
  regulation 30.12
  right of first refusal 30.07
  standing to sue 30.10
  uses 30.05
Homestead 14.15
Income taxes (*see also* various subheads, i.e.,
        Condominiums, income taxes)
  alternative mortgages 16.18
    reverse annuity mortgage 16.05
  condominiums 32.25
    conversion 32.21(c)
  deductions 39.05(a)
    depreciation 39.05(a) (1)
    home office 39.05(a) (2)
  easements, scenic 4.13(b) (1)
  Homeowner's Association 30.11
  installment contracts 22.15
  purchase money mortgage 19.03
  rehabilitation 35.15
  sale of property 39.05(b)
    gain
      capital 39.05(b) (2)
      exclusion 39.05(b) (1)
    tax free exchanges 39.05(b) (3)
Installment contracts 22.01 *et seq.*
  acceleration 22.13
  assignment 22.07
  balloons 22.05
  bankruptcy of seller 22.19
  broker's commission 22.02
  building code violations 22.20
  due-on-sale clause 17.10
  equitable conversion 22.16
  escrows 22.18
  forfeiture 22.21
    damages 22.21(e)
    procedure 22.21(b) *et seq.*
      acceleration 22.21(b)
      declaration 22.21(c)

  recovery of buyer's money 22.21(d)
      seller's remedies 22.21(f)
      trifling defaults 22.21(a)
  impounds 22.12
  income taxes 22.15
  insurance 22.14
  interest rate 22.09
  joint tenant purchasers 22.04
  judgment against seller 22.16
  liability for injuries 9.41
  mortgages 22.17
  prepayment 22.11
  prorations 22.10
  recording 22.08
  spouse's joinder 22.03
  title search 22.06
Insurance 12.01 *et seq.*
  acts of insured 12.08
  amount recoverable 12.12
  assignment 12.16
  builder's risk insurance 12.18
  business interruption insurance 12.19
  coinsurance clause 12.13
  contracts for the sale of land 12.15
  description of property insured 12.05
  double insurance 12.11
  homeowners policies 12.03(b)
    liability coverage 12.03(b) (1)
    medical payments 12.03(b) (2)
    personal property coverage 12.03(b)
  increase of hazard 12.10
  insurable interests 12.06
  interest covered by policy 12.07
  liability insurance 12.17
    contractors 12.17(a)
    homeowners 12.03(b) (1)
  mortgage interests 12.14
    mortgage clause 12.14(a)
      foreclosure 12.14(a) (1)
  public insurance adjuster 12.21
  rent loss insurance 12.20
  standard fire policy 12.02
    hazards covered 12.03
      business interruption 12.03(d)
      extended coverage
          endorsement 12.03(a)
      hostile and friendly fire 12.03(c)
      rent loss 12.03(d)
  unoccupancy clause 12.09
  when protection attaches 12.04
Interstate Land Sales Act 27.08
Joint tenancy 14.02 *et seq.*
  contracts of sale 14.05
  creation 14.02(b) (1)
    four unities 14.02(b) (1)
  creditors' rights 14.02(e)
  disadvantages 14.02(d)
  dower 14.14(c)
  estate tax 14.06

inheritance tax 14.06
murder 14.04
severance 14,02(c)
survivorship
    abolition 14.02(a)
tenancy in common distinguished 14.02
Land—defined 2.01
Land development regulation 27.01 *et seq.*
    agreements 27.14
    dedication (*see* Dedication)
    development rights 27.06
        farm land 27.07
    estoppel 27.14
    Federal Trade Commission 27.10
    Interstate Land Sales Act 27.08
    licenses 27.05(b)
    local regulations 27.09
    moratoria 27.12
        sewer problems 27.13(b)
        water problems 27.13(b)
    "no growth" 27.12 *et seq.*
    phased development 27.12
    private right of action 27.15
    resubdivision 27.16
    sewer 27.17
    utilities 27.17
    vested rights 27.14
    water 27.17
Landlord and tenant 37.01 *et seq.*
    abandonment 37.32
    assignments 37.29
    building code violations 37.38
    criminal acts of third persons 37.43
    damage to leased premises 37.23
        before tenant takes possession 37.24
    deed 37.31
    discrimination 38.09
    due process
        eviction 37.41
        quasi-public landlord 37.41(a)
        renewal of leases 37.41
        selection of tenants 37.41
    eviction
        constructive 37.47
        deposits in court 37.42
        due process 37.41
        partial 37.47
        retaliatory 37.40
            motive 37.40(a)
            philosophy 37.40(d)
            protected activities
                landlord 37.40(c)
                tenant 37.40(e), 37.40(f)
                time factor 37.40(b)
    fair dealing 37.49
    fixtures 37.27
    ground leases 37.08
    home rule 37.34
    incidental rights of tenant 37.10

insurance 37.21
leases 37.02
    acknowledgment 37.06(j)
    building to be constructed by landlord
        37.18
    cancellation clause 37.28
    defined 37.06
    description of premises 37.06(e)
    duration 37.06(f)
        condominiums 37.06(f) (1)
    lessor 37.06(c)
    recording 37.06(k)
    requirements 37.06(b)
    seal 37.06(h)
    signature 37.06(g)
    term 37.06(f)
    witnesses 37.06(i)
    writing 37.06(a)
liability
    criminal acts of third persons 37.43
    landlord 37.11
        injuries to third person 37.12
    tenant 37.20
mortgages 37.30
municipal ordinances 37.34
periodic tenancies 37.02
        month to month 37.03
        year to year 37.04
rent 37.07
    control 37.46
    deposits in court 37.42
    escalation 37.07(d)
    gross lease 37.07(a)
    net lease 37.07(a)
    nonpayment 37.35
    office leases 37.07(c)
    percentage 37.07(b)
    reduction 37.37
    withholding 37.39
repairs 37.13 *et seq.*
    landlord's duty 37.13, 37.25
    office leases 37.16
    statutes 37.14
    tenant's liability to landlord 37.22
    tenant's right to repair 37.15
residential tenants 37.45
subleases 37.29
surrender 37.33
taxes 37.26
tenancy at will 37.05
title paramount 37.19
unconscionability 37.48
use of premises 37.09
warranty of habitibility 37.36
    business properties 37.36(d)
    disclaimer 37.36(f)
    homes 37.36(e)
    knowledge of tenant 37.36(b)
    two flats 37.36(c)

Landmarks 29.01
Land trusts 13.07, 23.03
Land use controls—building restrictions (*see* Restrictions)
Legal descriptions 5.01 *et seq.*
  adjoining owners 5.09
  area 5.08
  buildings 5.17
  gaps and gores 13.03
  general description 5.06
  highway as boundary 5.14
  indefinite 5.11
  metes and bounds description 5.02
  "Mother Hubbard" 5.06
  omissions 5.12
  correction 5.13
  parts of lots 5.16
  plats 5.04
  popular name 5.05
  street address 5.07
  streets as boundaries 5.14
  surveys 5.01(a)
    government survey 5.03
  tax bills 5.18
  waters as boundaries 5.15
Liens, declaration 31.01 *et seq.* (*see also* Declaration of restrictions, easements, liens, and covenants)
Life Estates 2.08(b)
Minerals 2.02
Mobile homes 36.01 *et seq.*
  antitrust 36.11
  building restrictions 36.08
  chattel aspects 36.02
  exclusionary laws 36.10
  federal controls 36.04
  fixture aspects 36.03
  furniture 36.06
  future 36.13
  mortgages 36.05
  National Mobile Home Construction and Safety Standards Act 36.04
  taxes 36.12
  warranties 36.07
  zoning 36.09
Mortgages 15.01 *et seq.*
  acceleration 15.31
    owner occupancy clause 15.31(a)
  alternative mortgage instruments 16.01 *et seq.*
    adjustable mortgage loans 16.03(d)
    balloons 16.11
    call provisions 16.12
    convertible mortgages 16.07
    deferred interest mortgage 16.09
    direction of interest rate movement 16.03(h)
    due-on-sale clause—ARM 16.03(k)
      GPM 16.04(e)
    federal preemption 16.12
      Parity 16.17(a)
    frequency of interest rate adjustment 16.03(g)
    graduated payment mortgage 16.04(a)
      due-on-sale clause 16.04(e)
      form 16.04(d)
      truth-in-lending 16.04(f)
      usury 16.04(g)
    implementing interest rate adjustments 16.03(i)
    income taxes 16.18
    index 16.03(e)
    interest on interest 16.13
    interest rate adjustable loans 16.03
      risks 16.03(a)
    intervening liens 16.14
      exceeding the face amount of the loan 16.14(a)
    limits on interest rate movement 16.03(f)
    mortgage tax 16.19
    negative amortization 16.02
    negotiability 16.16
    pledged account loans 16.04(c)
    reverse annuity mortgages 16.05
      discrimination 16.05(a)
      due-on-sale clause 16.05(c)
      income taxes 16.05(e)
      negotiability 16.05(d)
      secondary market 16.05(d)
      truth-in-lending 16.05(b)
    rollover mortgages 16.03(c)
    secondarily liable parties and interest rate adjustments 16.03(j)
    secondary mortgage market—ARM 16.03(l)
    shared appreciation mortgage 16.06
      clogging the equity 16.06(c)
      ownership consideration 16.06(b)
      refinance provisions 16.06(a)
    usury 16.15
    variable rate mortgages 16.03(b)
  application and commitment 15.13
    commitment fees 15.13(a)
    damages 15.13(b)
    denial 15.13(f)
    discrimination 15.13(d)
    false applications 15.13(h)
    flood insurance 15.13(c)
    redlining 15.13(e)
    truth-in-lending 15.13(g)
  assignment 15.34
    notice 15.34(a)
  assumption 15.33
  convertible mortgages 16.07
  debt 15.22

Anaconda clause 15.22(h)
description of debt 15.22(d)
future advances 15.22(e)
    obligatory advances 15.22(e)
    open-ended advances 15.22(g)
    optional advances 15.22(f)
guarantees 15.22(i)
personal liability 15.22(b)
priority of lien 15.22(c)
deed absolute given as security
    15.09(d)
deed in lieu of foreclosure 15.40
deed of mortgaged premises 15.32 (see also
    Mortgages, sale subject to existing
    mortgage)
deed of trust 15.09(b)
deferred interest mortgage 16.09
description of mortgaged property
    15.24
due-on-sale clause 17.01 et seq.
    ARM 16.03(k)
    economic duress 17.08
    estoppel 17.09
    events that trigger 17.03
    federal lenders 17.02
    FNMA 17.05
    form 17.06
    GPM 16.04(e)
    installment contracts 17.10
    owner occupancy 17.04
    purchase money mortgage 19.09
    RAM 16.05(c)
    statutes 17.07
    tax free bonds 17.11
equitable mortgages 15.09(c)
equity finance outs 19.14
equity investments 16.08
equity of redemption 15.03
    (see also Redemption)
escrows 15.26
execution 15.20
extension agreements 15.37
federalization 15.06
federal forms 15.41
foreclosure (see Foreclosure)
graduated payment adjustable mortgage loan
    16.04(b) (see also Mortgages, alternative
    mortgage instruments)
graduated payment mortgage 16.04(a) (see also
    Mortgages, alternative mortgage
    instruments)
history of mortgage law 15.02
impounds 15.26
institutionalization 15.05
interest 15.25
    buydowns 23.05
    usury 15.25(a)
interest-only mortgage 16.10

junior mortgages 21.01
    condominium assessments 21.14
    first mortgage provisions 21.07
    FNMA 21.03
    foreclosure agreement with senior
        mortgage 21.05
    form 21.02
    interest 21.11
    open-end senior mortgage 21.13
    prepayment 21.10
    rents 21.12
    right to pay senior mortgage 21.04
    second mortgage companies 21.09
    statutes 21.08
    subordination 21.06
        institutional mortgages 21.06(a)
leases
    advance payments 15.30(b)
    antedating mortgage 15.28
    assignments 15.30(c)
        active assignment 15.30(d)
    lease cancellations 15.30(b)
    rent reductions 15.30(b)
    subsequent to mortgage 15.29
lien theory 15.08
limitations 15.36
marshalling of assets 15.39
master mortgage 15.21(a)
mortgage backed securities 16.20
    FHLMC 16.20(b)
    GNMA 16.20(a)
    municipals 16.20(d)
note 15.16
    negotiability 15.16(a)
participations 15.23
parties 15.17
payment 15.35
    balloon 15.35(e), 16.11
    final payment 15.35(f)
    joint mortgagees 15.35(b)
    late charges 15.35(d)
    payment to agent 15.35(a)
    prepayment 15.35(c)
possession 15.30
private mortgage insurance 15.15
purchase money mortgage 19.01 et seq.
    balloon note 19.10
    call provisions 19.11
    contract provisions 19.19
    co-ownership 19.17
    deficiency judgments 19.12
    discounting 19.06
    due-on-sale clause 19.09
    FNMA 19.07
    form 19.13
    income tax 19.03
    insurance 19.08
    legal advantages 19.02

Mortgages (*cont.*)
  payment 19.18
  recitals 19.16
  truth-in-lending 19.15
  usury 19.04
  real estate taxes 15.27
  recording 15.21
    master mortgage 15.21(a)
  release 15.38
    partial 15.38(a)
  rents 15.30
  reverse annuity mortgages 16.05 (*see also*
    Mortgages, alternative mortgage
    instruments, reverse annuity
    mortgages)
  sale subject to existing mortgage 18.01 *et seq.*
    assumptions 15.33, 18.04
    buyer's liability 18.03
    protection of seller 18.02
  secondary mortgage market 15.07
  shared appreciation mortgage 16.06 *et seq.* (*see
    also* Mortgages, alternative mortgage
    instruments, shared appreciation
    mortgage)
  title theory 15.08
  variable rate mortgages 16.03(b) (*see also*
    Mortgages, alternative mortgage
    instruments, variable rate mortgages)
  wrap-around mortgages 20.01 *et seq.*
    documents 20.03
    usury 20.02
Navigable waters 28.06 *et seq.*
Nominees 13.04
  authority 13.04(a)
  trust declaration 13.04(b)
Oil and gas 2.03
  leases 2.03
    unless lease 2.03
    drill or pay lease 2.03
    rentals 2.03
      delay rentals 2.03
    royalties 2.03
      overriding royalty 2.03
    working interest 2.03
Opinion of title 11.03
Options 13.10
Partition 14.08
  party walls 4.05(c) (1)
  personal property 2.06
Planned unit developments 33.01 *et seq.*
  declaration 33.07 *et seq.*
    covenants 33.07(b)
    liens 33.07(c)
    restraints on sales 33.07(d)
    restrictions 33.07(a)
  cluster housing 33.02
  common areas 33.06(a) *et seq.*
    artificial lakes 33.06(e)
    conveyance to HOA 33.06(b)

    dedication 33.06(d)
    easements 33.06(c)
    plats 33.06(a)
    public ownership 33.06(d)
    taxes 33.09
  condominium compared 33.11
  creation 33.05
  home association 33.04
  mortgages 33.08
  plat approval 33.12(a)
  regulation 33.10
  taxes 33.09
  townhouses 33.03
    future 33.03(a)
  zoning 33.12
    plat approval 33.12(a)
Plats (*see* Dedication, plats)
Real estate brokers (*see* Brokers)
Real Estate Settlement Procedures Act 10.09(b)
Real estate taxes 39.01 *et seq.*
  appropriation 39.03(b)
  assessment 39.03(e) (1)
    equalization 39.03(e) (4)
    exemptions 39.03(e) (2)
    review 39.03(e) (3)
    uniformity 39.03(e) (1)
  budgeting 39.03(a)
  computation 39.03(f)
  constitutionality 39.02
  enforcement 39.03(i)
    tax sale 39.03(i) *et seq.*
      effect 39.03(i) (1), 39.03(i) (2)
  levy 39.03(c)
  lien 39.03(g)
  payment 39.03(h)
  rates 39.03(d)
  steps 39.03
Realtors (*see* Brokers)
Recording and constructive notice 7.01 *et seq.*
  actual knowledge 7.05
  bona fide purchasers 7.04
  chain of title 7.07
  constructive notice 7.02
  contents of recorded document 7.09
  defective instruments 7.06(b)
    legal descriptions 7.06(b) (1)
  foreign language 7.10
  instruments entitled to be recorded 7.03
  leases 7.12
  liens 7.11
  persons protected 7.04
  possession as notice 7.05(a)
  recorder's office 7.02(a)
  tract index 7.08
  what constitutes recording 7.03
Record title 11.05
Redemption
  clogging 15.03(b)
  equity of redemption 15.03

statutory 24.03
waiver 15.03(a)
Rehabilitation 35.01 *et seq.*
  appraisals 35.02
  architect's role 35.03
  bid analysis 35.10
  building codes 35.04
  contract 35.07
  contractor 35.05
    bonds 35.06
  income tax 35.15
  insurance 35.13
  loans 35.14
  mechanics' lien waivers 35.09
  payment 35.08
  permits 35.11
  specifications 35.10
  supervision 35.12
Restrictions 25.01 *et seq.*
  apartments 25.03(c) (4)
  building plans 25.06
  business purposes 25.03(c) (11)
  condominium 25.03(c) (7)
  declaration 31.01 *et seq. (see also* Declaration of
    restrictions, easements, liens, and
    covenants)
  duplex 25.03(c) (10)
  dwelling 25.03(c) (6)
  enforcement 25.11 *et seq.*
    abandonment 25.11(d)
    change in neighborhood 25.11(b)
    delay 25.11(f)
    general plan 25.03(b)
    lapse of time 25.11(g)
    numerous violations 25.11(c)
    state laws 25.11(i)
    statutes of limitations 25.11(h)
    violations by enforcer 25.11(e)
  extension 25.08
  family 25.03(c) (9)
  general plan 25.03 *et seq.*
    creation 25.03
    enforcement 25.03(b)
    interpretation 25.03(c)
    notice 25.03(a)
  incidental uses 25.03(c) (2)
  ingress and egress for prohibited use 25.07
  location 25.03(c) (1)
  modification 25.08
  mortgage foreclosure 25.09
  private controls distinguished from public
    controls 25.01
  racial 25.14
  release 25.08
  residence 25.03(c) (3)
    form 25.03(c) (8)
  senior citizens 25.04
  tandem house 25.03(c) (5)
  violations—minor 25.10

Sale and leaseback 15.10
  setting aside transaction 15.10(a)
Sale and manageback 23.02
Servient tenement 4.02
Settlements (*See* Closings)
Social impact upon the law 1.03
Sources of real estate law 1.02
Special assessments 39.04
Subdivision trusts 13.06
Surveys 5.01(a)
  government survey 5.03
Tandem houses 14.16(a)
Taxes (*See* Real estate taxes)
Tenancy by the entireties 14.03 *et seq.*
  brokers' listings 14.03(d)
  contracts of sale 14.05
  creation 14.03(a)
    defective 14.03(b)
  creditors' rights 14.03(e)
  deeds 14.03(d)
  deeds between spouses 14.03(c)
  divorce 14.03(f)
  estate tax 14.06
  inheritance tax 14.06
  leases 14.03(d)
  mortgages 14.03(d)
  murder 14.04
  tenancy in common 14.07
    joint tenancy distinguished 14.02
Title insurance 11.06
  commitments 11.06(f)
  title insurance policy 11.06(a)
    easement policies 11.06(e)
    endorsements 11.06(c)
    leasehold policy 11.06(d)
    residential policy 11.06(b)
Torrens system 11.07
Trees and crops 2.07
Trends in real estate law 1.02
Trespass 2.05
Trusts 2.09
Unmarried cohabitants 14.16
  homosexuals 14.16(b)
  tandem houses 14.16(a)
Validity 26.06
  factors 26.05(a)
  federal court 26.05(c)
  invalidity 26.05(d)
  reasonableness 26.05(b)
Variances 26.24
Vendor's liens 15.11, 23.04
Wetlands 28.01 *et seq.*
  environmental factors 28.02
  regulations 28.04
    public trust 28.05
Zoning 26.01 *et seq.*
  accessory uses 26.18
  amendments 26.22 *et seq.*
    after permit 26.22(b)

Zoning (*cont.*)
    conditional 26.22(c)
    procedure 26.22(d)
    reliance rule 26.22(a)
  apartments 26.17
  bulk zoning 26.15
  change of neighborhood 26.20
  children 26.09
  cluster housing 26.27
  contract zoning 26.28
  density 26.29 *et seq.*
    minimum building area 26.29(c)
      minimum building area per dwelling unit
        26.29(d)
    minimum frontage 26.29(b)
    minimum lot area 26.29(a)
  development control 26.13
  downzoning 26.14
  effect on restrictions 26.32
  enforcement 26.34
  exactions 26.07
  exclusionary
    apartments 26.30

    family zoning 26.30(c)
    integration 26.30(e)
    large lot 26.30
    Mount Laurel 26.30(b)
    townhouses 26.30(a)
  family 26.30(c)
  floating 26.26
  future 26.03
  history 26.02
  incentive 26.19
  inclusionary 26.31
  mortgages 26.33
  nonconforming uses 26.21
  noncumulative 26.04
  planned unit developments 26.27
  planning 26.35
  prohibitory 26.12
  referendum 26.06
  rezoning 26.22
  senior citizens 26.08
  single-family 26.16
  special exceptions 26.25
  spot zoning 26.22